INDUSTRIAL ECONOMICS

For
Elizabeth
and
Susie

ERRATA
The text on pages viii & ix should be reversed.
P. 17. For line 36 read:
'the importance, not of monopoly, but of the monopoly *model*,'
P. 106. for fn. 34 1.8 read

$$\therefore n(\alpha) = e^{-\sum\limits_i s_i \log s_i}$$

P. 143. Last equation should read:

$$pX - \sum_i c_i x_i - pX\left(-\frac{X}{p} \cdot \frac{dp}{dX}\right) \sum_i \left(\frac{x_i}{X}\right)^2 = 0$$

P. 187. For line 11 of text read:
'brium price. Assuming this to be a constant elasticity we may write'
P. 308. For 2nd equation read:

$$p > \delta > g$$

P. 331. For 2nd line of text read:

'If the valuation ratio is unity
$$M = K - D \text{ and } \Pi' = \Pi - iD'$$

P. 388. For 4th equation read:
$$'I_t = \beta[\alpha(1-\lambda)Q_t + \lambda K_{t-1} - K_{t-1}]'$$

P. 389. For 1st equation read:
$$'I_t = \beta(K_t^* - K_{t-1}) + \delta K_{t-1}'$$

P. 389. For 2nd equation read:
$$I_t = \beta[K_t^* + (\delta - 1)K_{t-1}]'$$

P. 399. For 2nd equation read

$$'C = q\left(\delta + r - \frac{\dot{q}}{q}\right)'$$

P. 411. Fig. 11.3 is upside down.

INDUSTRIAL ECONOMICS

Theory and Evidence

DONALD A. HAY
and
DEREK J. MORRIS

OXFORD UNIVERSITY PRESS
1979

Oxford University Press, Walton Street, Oxford OX2 6DP

OXFORD LONDON GLASGOW
NEW YORK TORONTO MELBOURNE WELLINGTON
KUALA LUMPUR SINGAPORE JAKARTA HONG KONG TOKYO
DELHI BOMBAY CALCUTTA MADRAS KARACHI
IBADAN NAIROBI DAR ES SALAAM CAPE TOWN

CASEBOUND ISBN O 19 877112 6
PAPERBACK ISBN O 19 877113 4

Set by Hope Services, Abingdon
and printed in Great Britain by
Richard Clay (The Chaucer Press) Ltd.,
Bungay, Suffolk.

PREFACE

In recent years Industrial Economics has emerged as a major area of economic analysis both in terms of theoretical and empirical research and in terms of the number of courses at undergraduate and graduate level. This book, stemming originally from lecture and seminar series at both levels, is designed for those pursuing such courses. It presupposes only a standard course in the Theory of the Firm and the ability to read a regression equation. It takes the reader through several stages of theoretical developments and empirical testing to an understanding of the major issues now facing the subject and the lines of research currently being pursued. Chapter 1 provides an overall perspective of the subject, our views as to the important issues and themes to be covered, and an overall outline of what follows. We hope that the book provides a comprehensive text for those on a third-year undergraduate course in Industrial Economics, and a thorough grounding for those embarking on graduate study.

Responsibility for drafts of chapters 1, 4, 6 and 8 to 11 was allotted to Derek Morris, and for chapters 2, 3, 5, 7 and 12 to 17 to Donald Hay. We have however cooperated closely in the preparation of the book, have read and criticised each others' material several times, and have incorporated comments and criticisms in subsequent revisions. Editing has also entailed movement of sections between chapters so we both take full and equal responsibility for all contained herein.

The debts we have accumulated in the preparation of this book are numerous. Several colleagues and students have read some or all of the manuscript, and provided invaluable advice and criticism with regard to content, style and presentation. Our thanks go to John Wright, Jim Mirrlees, Colin Mayer, Bruce Trotter, David Rhind-Tutt, Alan Richeimer and Jeremy Edwards.

In addition two anonymous publisher's reviewers provided helpful comments for which we are most grateful. Responsibility for all remaining errors remains entirely and unreservedly with us.

Our thanks go to Elizabeth Hay and Joe Wilkins for between them typing at least two drafts of the whole book. We congratulate them on deciphering our particularly unreadable handwriting. Christine Budgen and Jennifer Stone provided invaluable assistance in the P.P.E. Reading Room of the Bodleian Library, particularly in connection with a vast amount of xeroxing of articles. The library staff of the Oxford Insitute of Economics and Statistics were also invariably helpful.

We also wish to record our thanks to all those who have given us permission to reproduce tables, diagrams and equations. Finally we would like to thank very much Richard Bennett for preparing a detailed subject index and an author index. We view this as being indispensable in a long textbook and we are immensely grateful to him for relieving us of this very time-consuming task.

Oriel College   DEREK MORRIS
Jesus College   DONALD HAY

May 12th 1978

CONTENTS

PART 1

Introduction

1

A PERSPECTIVE OF INDUSTRIAL ECONOMICS

1 INTRODUCTION

The main purpose of this book is to present the theory and evidence which goes under the general heading of Industrial Economics. Such a task immediately raises two problems. First, as in several areas of economics, there is often disagreement on both the theoretical and empirical issues involved. No attempt will be made to skate over such controversies, but the possibility of explaining the differences and making productive reconciliations will be explored. Second, and more serious, there is both confusion and conflict over the three main elements of this (or any) discipline—its scope or purpose, its concepts, and its methodology. This situation gives rise to our subsidiary aim, namely to provide a framework within which such differences can be reconciled. This introductory chapter attempts to identify those differences, analyse their causes, and out of this generate a new perspective of industrial economics around which the theory and evidence in the rest of the book can be built.

The basic problem underlying the current state of industrial economics lies in the nature and multiplicity of its origins. People have been interested in the economic behaviour and performance of industries since the beginning of the industrial revolution, but the delineation of a specific area of economics under the title of Industrial Economics is a phenomenon of the last forty years only. The period in between was characterized by several different approaches to the topic, each with its own objectives and practitioners, with its own methods and terminology. Industrial economics, in absorbing and developing strands of thought from several of them, has gained much in its power and usefulness, but has also inherited some of the divisions which existed between its parent disciplines.

Most economists would regard industrial economics as being primarily an elaboration of, and development from, one major element in the mainstream of economic thought—the Theory of the Firm. This comprises the analysis of different market structures, and their implications for economic welfare. It was generally developed on the basis of a profit maximization assumption and the tools of marginalism, though, as more recent work has shown, neither of these is essential. To view industrial economics as a development of this is understandable. Both are concerned with the economic aspects of firms' behaviour, seeking to analyse such behaviour and draw normative implications from the analysis. Both have been concerned with market structures, costs, and competition. In addition, all those who study industrial economics as a specialism after a formal training in general economics will have had a thorough grounding in the theory of the firm because it is a major component of microeconomics. They will therefore immediately perceive the intellectual and historical links between the theory of the firm and industrial economics. Whilst not wishing to quarrel with this notion, three points which we will examine must be stressed. First there is an important sense in which the traditional theory of the firm represents a long detour in the history of the study of firms' economic behaviour. Second, the development of industrial economics can partly be seen as a consequence of several important inadequacies and faults of analysis in the theory of the firm. Third, while the latter provides a main foundation for the study of industrial economics, several important influences from outside have given a totally different character to industrial economics. We first, therefore, examine briefly the development of the theory of the firm, and identify the problems inherent in it. Both tasks throw useful light on the present state of industrial economics, and the perspective we shall adopt below. We will then contrast that with other contributory approaches, describing the numerous difficulties that have arisen in the process of integration. This prepares the way for the presentation of the framework which we will subsequently adopt.

2 THE EARLY THEORY OF THE FIRM

The development of the theory of the firm can easily be traced back to Adam Smith, and the *Wealth of Nations*.[1] He regarded a product as having two prices; its market price at which it changed hands, and its 'natural' price or 'value'. The latter he regarded as primarily dependent on the labour necessary to make the product, though he conceded that this was only easily applicable in an undeveloped economy, and that the existence of other factors of production complicated (although it did not destroy) this labour theory of value.

Much of his work concentrated on this 'natural' price, and later writers criticized him for ignoring demand considerations. In fact, however, he did not ignore them. Rather he did not dwell on them long because he presumed that except for rare and generally tempo-

[1] A. Smith, *An Inquiry into the Nature and Causes of the Wealth of Nations* (London, 1776).

rary exceptions the forces of competition would drive the market price into equality with the natural price. Deviations between the two were essentially temporary disturbances. Barring this, he could conclude that if one product commanded a higher market price than another it was because of the higher costs of the factors of production required to produce it. High profit was not normally seen as the difference between natural and market price, for competition prevented this, but as a sign that there was some particular difficulty or cost involved in providing capital, resulting in a higher natural price than otherwise.

Subsequent writers, particularly Jevons, developed the analysis of demand which was missing in terms of the now familiar utility theory.[2] In addition there was much elaboration on the nature of costs and the factors of production, but Smith's assumption that competition generally kept prices in line with costs was not challenged for nearly a century. More important still, the work of Alfred Marshall, which probably represented the single most important contribution to economics from Smith to Keynes, and certainly the most important in English, embodied this view.[3] Marshall's work dispensed with the idea that value was independent of market price. Instead it absorbed Jevons' view that prices depended on marginal utility (with supply only important in as far as it affected output and hence utility at the margin) into a unified picture of price as determined by both supply and demand equally. But it nevertheless retained the view that competition generally ensured the equality of price with unit costs of production. Escape by a firm from such pressure into a position of monopoly was recognized as possible, but the latter was again viewed, at least in the private sector, as generally temporary. This was largely due to the inevitable rise and fall of firms (despite the possibility of scale economies) as changes in the composition of the firm's management caused fluctuations in business vitality, as new firms brought new enthusiasm and spirit into competition with established firms, and most of all because of the great difficulties of avoiding competition if a product were ever to have a market of significant size.

Two points are particularly important here. First Marshall, like Smith, was concerned to identify general principles lying behind observed economic behaviour. He combined theory with the practical aspects of business life, preferring to place more weight on the latter if they conflicted. Second, he did not formally analyse his concept

[2] S. Jevons, *Theory of Political Economy* (London, 1871).
[3] A. Marshall, *Principles of Economics* (London, 1890), *idem, Industry and Trade* (London, 1919).

of competition. Clearly it was presumed to be intense, and a number of its characteristics—independence of action by a large number of buyers and sellers, information about transactions—were commented upon, but there was no systematic analysis of it. The only reference to 'perfect competition' in the first edition was in fact in a rather pejorative context.

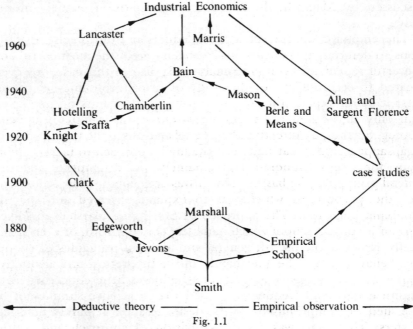

Fig. 1.1

Starting from about this time, two quite separate developments can be identified, and are shown graphically in Figure 1.1. One development pursued the practical and empirical aspect, observing the historical development and actual behaviour of particular firms and industries. More will be said about this later. The other attempted to analyse market competition, and in particular tried to *establish the specific conditions under which competition would result in the equalization of prices and costs*, which had been so ubiquitously presumed hitherto. This was not only a very different objective from that of Marshall, who as we have seen carried out no such analysis, but also created a quite separate path from those concerned with purely empirical researches. In the work of Jevons and Edgeworth[4] the emphasis is placed on establishing the conditions from which the equating of price and average cost and the absence of monopoly profits would follow. The utilization of differential calculus both

[4] See S. Jevons, op. cit., and F. Y. Edgeworth, *Mathematical Physics* (London, 1881).

encouraged and facilitated this pursuit. This approach was further developed by Clark in America,[5] but culminated in the work of Knight, who refined the Perfect Competition model into its current form and identified the now familiar long list of necessary conditions for the elimination of supernormal profits at minimum average cost.[6] In addition the marginal analysis was applied to the other case discussed by Marshall, the absence of competition, namely monopoly.

The emphasis on correct logical deduction from precise assumptions to determinate conclusions has been one of the most useful and powerful aspects of economic analysis. It also in this case, however, created three problems for the study of firms' economic behaviour. First it could explain the size of a firm and the limits on its expansion only if the long-run average cost curve was eventually upward sloping. Second, by directing theoretical analysis in the way described, a gap appeared in what had been the main approach to market behaviour for over a hundred years, namely the attempt to identify general principles, the basis of which was actual industrial phenomena and the purpose of which was to explain observed and specific economic behaviour. The approach of Smith and Marshall dissolved into an empirical school which had little concern with, or even specifically rejected the use of, general and abstract principles of economic behaviour, on the one hand, and a theoretical and deductive school of great elegance and rigour which was little concerned with empirical data and frequently argued that a science should not be tarnished or compromised by the desire to look at purely practical matters. The result was a serious division of approach and almost complete separation of developments on the theoretical/deductive and empirical/practical fronts.

Third, and not surprisingly, this led to conflict not only over the proper methodology to adopt in studying firms' economic behaviour but also over even the basic concepts used in such study. In particular the 'firm' of perfect competition, which was a cornerstone of general equilibrium theory, became a dimensionless and indivisible decision-taking unit quite unrecognizable to even the most superficial observer of actual firms operating in an ordinary industrial context.

Thus by the early 1920s there was a very deep division. On the one side was the empirical school which, at its most descriptive level, included the histories and development of individual firms and industries, and studies of the current structure and behaviour of one or more industries. Any aspect of industrial organization might be

[5] J. Clark, *The Distribution of Wealth* (New York, 1899).
[6] F. Knight, *Risk, Uncertainty and Profit* (New York, 1921).

covered, including the lives of the dominant personalities, the organizational structure of the business involved, the history of firms' product development, their merger and takeover activity, investment, employment, research and advertising policy, and their financing etc. The impact on profits and efficiency was frequently covered, but not the wider impact on resource allocation and welfare. The approach was entirely empirical, and the many differences between real-world firms recognized as important factors in determining the course of industrial competition. Indeed emphasis was frequently laid on the uniqueness of the firms, products, and competitive situations which were described, and on the factors influencing them. There was little rigour in these studies and relatively few generalizable conclusions. Only much later, particularly in the work of Sargent Florence[7] and Allen,[8] did this approach systematically review the characteristics, development, and behaviour of the main sectors of industry with a view to providing a more comprehensive picture.

On the other side was the so-called Theory of the Firm concerned almost exclusively with price and output decisions and their impact on efficiency, resource allocation, and economic welfare. It employed a deductive approach, had little regard for empirical support, and generally ignored historical and institutional aspects. The 'Firm' was indivisible, and being representative did not embrace differences between actual firms. Above all the theory comprised, first, a perfect competition model which in its picture of firms' activities seemed quite exceptionally far from reality, and a monopoly model which was little more realistic and which, by its assumption of no direct competition, seemed inappropriate for nearly all then existing private sector industries. It is no exaggeration to say that by the early inter-war period the discrepancy between standard economic analysis and empirical observation was no less great in the study of firms' behaviour than it was in what we now refer to as the macroeconomic field.

The first step in an attempt to bridge this gap was a seminal paper in 1926 by Sraffa.[9] He noted that real firms generally refrained from further expansion not because it would cause costs to rise above a given market price, but because it would require an unacceptable fall in price to achieve it. While Arrow has subsequently demonstrated that downward sloping demand curves will occur even in perfect

[7] P. Sargent Florence, *Logic of Industrial Organisation* (London, 1933).
[8] G. C. Allen, *British Industries and their Organisation* (London, 1933).
[9] P. Sraffa, 'The Laws of Returns under Competitive Conditions', *E.J.* 36 (1926), 535–50.

competition while the market is in disequilibrium,[10] it was none the less a valid conclusion that, because of product differentiation, competing firms could face downward sloping rather than horizontal demand curves and this could then explain a limit to the size of a firm even with a downward sloping long-run average cost curve. This of course paved the way for Chamberlin's theory of Monopolistic Competition, with its focus of attention on product differentiation and a downward sloping demand curve.[11] (see page 10.)

The effect of this was to allow firms other than monopolists some discretion over price and the ability to pursue a policy at least somewhat different from their competitors. Thus attention began to switch towards the individual firm rather than the industry as the basic object of study. The previous analysis had centred round the equilibrium of an industry, the firm only being included in as far as it *was* the industry (monopoly) or had to be in its own equilibrium in order for the industry to be so (perfect competition). Now the emphasis was to shift more to the firm, with the concept of the industry first weakened and finally rejected (see below).

The main motivation behind Chamberlin's work was the belief that neither the perfect competition nor the monopoly model appeared to be related to the real world in which firms competed, but produced different prodcts. Not only did the assumptions appear to clash with reality but, as we have seen, the predictions also: e.g. that firms cannot choose their price but can sell as much as they want to at the going price. Thus, although the theoretical framework he used was in some ways the same, in particular the use of marginal analysis, the development was a major attempt to move back into the middle ground between deductive theory and empiricism which represented the true successor of Marshall's work.

So glaring had the gap between theory and evidence become that the monopolistic competition model was absorbed into the mainstream of microeconomic theory extraordinarily quickly. As Triffin pointed out, whilst many important developments have been recognized as such only many years, decades, or even in some cases a century after their inception, monopolistic competition was a part of nearly all microeconomic texts within five years.[12]

[10] K. T. Arrow, 'Towards a Theory of Price Adjustment', in M. Abramovitz (ed.), *The Allocation of Economic Resources* (Stamford University Press, 1959).

[11] E. H. Chamberlin, *The Theory of Monopolistic Competition* (Harvard University Press, 1933).

[12] R. Triffin, *Monopolistic Competition and General Equilibrium Theory* (Harvard University Press, 1941), p. 17.

3   MONOPOLISTIC COMPETITION

The model of monopolistic competition was probably the single most important antecedent of what we now term Industrial Economics. Yet, despite its almost instant success in the 1930s, it generated, and continues to generate, much criticism and controversy, most of which is generally ignored in introductory texts. As many of the problems in industrial economics which we will have to tackle first arise in this model we will briefly examine the nature of the arguments involved.

The model itself is summarized in Figure 1.2, which shows the cost and revenue curves for a representative firm. *APC* shows long-run average production costs and *LRAC* shows long-run average costs

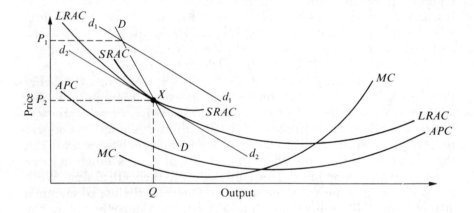

Fig. 1.2

including a given amount of selling costs, i.e. advertising expenditure, promotional costs, packaging, etc. Marginal Cost, *MC*, passes through the minimum point of both. Initially the price is P_1. The line $d_1 d_1$ shows the demand curve facing the firm if no other competing firm changes price. It is downward sloping becuase of product differentiation. *DD* shows the demand curve facing the firm if all competing firms changed price in step. It is in fact a 'share-of-the-market' demand curve.

Because there are a large number of firms it is assumed that each can ignore the repercussions of its own price change on others. This Chamberlin referred to as his 'Symmetry' assumption. Thus each acts as if it faces $d_1 d_1$, and, because the marginal revenue curve associated with $d_1 d_1$ (not shown) is above marginal cost, it will lower price. But because this diagram shows the representative firm, i.e.

because all firms reason in this way, all firms lower price and so all in fact move down DD. Had MC been above MR, all would have moved up DD. As the price falls so the line d_1d_1, which was only appropriate given that other firms charged price P, also falls. The price–output locus is therefore constrained to be DD. With free entry and therefore only normal profit in equilibrium, price ends up at P_2 where Average Revenue equals Average Cost. The 'particular' demand curve associated with P_2 is d_2d_2 and this must be tangential to the average cost curve. If it were not it would cross it, meaning that supernormal profits would be made at another output level and that P_2 was not an equilibrium price.

The equilibrium point X gives rise to the familiar excess capacity theorem. As d_2d_2 is downward sloping it must be a tangent to AC before its minimum point. To achieve point X requires a plant with its $SRAC$ tangent to point X, which is then operated at a sub-optimal output level. Both short- and long-run average cost are above their minimum.

The attacks on this model were numerous:

(1) To deal with competition between differentiated products, Chamberlin introduced the concept of the 'competing group' of firms. These produced products which might be physically very dissimilar, e.g. hot water bottles and electric blankets, or physically very similar ones, e.g. different brands of matches, but which in all cases were close substitutes for each other.

A number of economists have attacked the concept of the competing group, and Chamberlin himself recognized major deficiencies in it. Despite the essential features of product heterogeneity, all firms were assumed in the analysis (initially at least) to have identical cost and demand curves (Chamberlin's 'uniformity' assumption), and it is not clear that this has any meaning if the units of output are physically dissimilar. If the outputs of two firms genuinely are different, then the costs per unit output are logically not comparable. Only if we reduce the analysis to cost (or price) per unit of service supplied by both can the comparison be made, but then we are dealing with an identical service and the notion of product heterogeneity has gone. In other words we can, for example, compare price per wash, but not the price of a washing machine with the price of launderette services.

This is important for two reasons. First, there is a logical inconsistency in combining downward sloping demand curves derived from product heterogeneity with equal cost curves derived from the uniformity assumption. Second, even if this is overlooked the tangency solution of monopolistic competition does not follow. If products really are different then there is *no* particular reason why the producers of any one should be forced to a position where only normal profit is being made, by either an existing or potential competitor. The profits that come from providing something unique can only be competed away by another producer selling the *same* product. If the products are heterogeneous then each producer is a monopolist, albeit facing a rather elastic demand curve, and supernormal profits may be made (and perhaps excess capacity avoided). The monopolistic competition conclusions only follow from the inadmissible combination of products which are 'uniform', allowing the use of the whole apparatus of perfect competition, but heterogeneous to ensure a negatively sloped demand curve. Thus product differentiation alone can raise price above average cost even where there is free entry and many buyers and sellers, and this holds even if the products, though different, are very similar.

Chamberlin later dropped the assumption of uniformity, but no new analytic framework appeared. The results were simply the conclusion that firms may or may not make supernormal profits, and an inability to identify the conditions of equilibrium. This logical flaw thus prevented the monopolistic competition model from generating conclusions different from either the monopoly model or the perfect competition model. It should also be added that if the 'symmetry' assumption is dropped then the problems get worse. We run into all the difficulties of indeterminacy that arose when the attempt was made to analyse oligopoly within the same framework.

(2) The second difficulty arising from the introduction of product heterogeneity was the disappearance of any criterion by which to define an industry or 'competing group'. Under both perfect competition and monopoly it was the limits of product homogeneity which defined the industry. Once this had gone it was an arbitrary matter where one drew the limits in a continuous chain of substitutability between products in order to specify an industry. There might sometimes be larger gaps in the chain at certain points which could be used to delineate industries, but the concept of an industry lost all theoretical underpinning and frequently was empirically ambiguous. For example, are record-players and hi-fi in the same industry; are record-players and tape-recorders; are tape-recorders and cassette-recorders? Do take-away restaurants compete with ordinary restaurants or with domestic cooking appliances, or both, or neither? Are tea, coffee, and soft drinks in the same competing group or not, and either way do we include beer in it or with spirits etc? In the most detailed examination of this issue, Triffin concluded that one could analyse general equilibrium of all firms, and the

equilibrium of each individual firm within that, but faced an intractable problem in analysing the partial equilibrium of a group of firms.[13] Worse still, as Kaldor suggested, close examination of the chain of substitution might well show a string not of arbitrarily delineated overlapping monopolistic competitors but a string of overlapping oligopolies in which the impact of price changes on two or three near competitors was sufficient to render the symmetry assumption invalid and oligopolistic interdependence and indeterminacy the normal state of affairs.[14]

(3) Problems are no less evident when we turn to the more empirical side and in particular the predictive power of the model. The standard approach in recent years to a programme of model testing has been that presented by Samuelson in his *Foundations of Economic Analysis*.[15] This involves making qualitative predictions, i.e. of direction of change in a variable but not the magnitude of change, from qualitative models, i.e. those in which the slopes of functions are known, and the direction of shift in parameters, but again no magnitudes. Thus the prediction of a decrease in output as a result of an increase in an *ad valorem* tax under certain assumptions about the slope of demand and supply functions (and motivation) is a simple and typical case.

Now, as Archibald has shown, virtually no such predictions emerge from the monopolistic competition model.[16] The reason for this is primarily that the relation between the 'share-of-the-market demand curve' and the 'particular' demand curve is not specified, i.e. if the former shifts to the left as a result of contraction of demand in the market, the latter may end up more or less elastic, depending on whether few or many firms leave the industry, yet the final result for firms' price, output, and capacity utilization invariably depends on which occurs. Even if either the number of firms or the level of total demand is assumed fixed when the other changes Archibald argued that no useful prediction emerges. He concluded that the model's complexity demonstrated that the Samuelson approach is only really useful for very simple cases, and that quantitative information is required in order to get useful predictions.

Added to this is the fact that an important element in both the monopolistic competition approach and in the real world where product heterogeneity exists is the existence of selling costs and

[13] R. Triffin, op. cit.
[14] N. Kaldor, 'Market Imperfection and Excess Capacity', *Economica*, N.S. 2 (1935), 33–50.
[15] P. Samuelson, *Foundations of Economic Analysis* (Cambridge, Mass., 1947).
[16] G. C. Archibald, 'Chamberlin versus Chicago', *R. Econ. Studs.* 29 (Oct. 1961), 2–28.

product quality as important decision variables. The introduction of these make it even more difficult to obtain any useful predictions, particularly as the analysis of product quality has to face the problem of an appropriate measure of it which can be related to other variables in the analysis. The existence of advertising alone makes it impossible to make useful predictions, even if price is regarded as a parameter in the model.[17] Over all, Archibald concludes that little can be learned unless we start to place restrictions on the way in which variables affect each other.[18]

(4) If we concentrate on the few predictions that the model *does* provide we run into still more problems. Two are considered, the first being the prediction that all monpolistic competitors will make only normal profits. Unfortunately we cannot infer from the absence of supernormal profits in an industry with product differentiation that the model is correct. It might be that entry is free and this has squeezed profits down to normal as predicted. On the other hand it might be that a firm has monpoly control of a factor of production or of a segment of the market. The supernormal profits this permitted would in the long run lead to the revaluation of the factor or factors of production, or, if suppliers could act together to raise the price, to an actual rise in costs. In either case profits over and above all costs and rents would tend to zero. In short, reported profits above normal are either a sign of incorrect valuation of factors or the inclusion of rents not part of 'true profit'.

The prediction however that has attracted most attention is that of long-run excess capacity and permanently unexploited economies of scale. The most obvious difficulty is that there is very little, if any, evidence of either and so the most important prediction of the model appears to be quite false. Two sorts of criticism have been made of the model in relation to the excess capacity theorem. The first, by Friedman, echoes the criticism above.[19] The dependence of accounting costs on profits, and hence on demand, means that the average cost curve normally used is inadmissible in defining full capacity. If, for example, demand increased but the physical production function and factor prices remain

---

[17] See G. C. Archibald, 'Profit-Maximising and Non-Price Competition', *Economica*, N.S. 31 (Feb. 1964), 13–22.

[18] Results can nevertheless be obtained by introducing quite plausible and reasonable general restrictions. See J. Hadar, 'On the Predictive Content of Models of Monopolistic Competition', *S. Econ. Journal*, 36, no. 1 (July 1969), 67–73.

[19] M. Friedman, 'More on Archibald versus Chicago', *R. Econ. Studs.* 30 (Feb. 1963), 65–7. This and a number of other articles on the Monopolistic Competition debate by Stigler and Archibald are reproduced in C. K. Rowley (ed.), *Readings in Industrial Economics* (London 1972), vol. 1, part 2.

unchanged, then the rents carried by the firm's specialized factors would increase, and the minimum point of the average cost curve would shift to the right. But this would not mean capacity had changed. The proper concept of capacity, he argues, is the output at which short-run and long-run marginal costs are equal, for then the firm has no incentive to change the size of the plant. On this basis the monopolistic competition solution is a full-capacity one no less than the Perfect Competition one, or indeed the Monopoly one provided the firm has minimized costs for the output level chosen.[20] All that can be saved from the model is the fact that, nevertheless, competition with product differentiation may drive firms to the point where all economies of scale cannot be fully achieved.

The other approach is due to Demsetz and shows up some faulty analysis in Chamberlin's model.[21] All the curves in Figure 1.2 are drawn on the assumption of a *given* level of selling costs, namely the amount considered optimal at point X. But in fact selling costs like price and output are completely variable. With a different price and output there would be a different optimal level of selling costs, so that the curves $LRAC$, $SRAC$, and d_2d_2, being drawn on the assumption of *fixed* selling costs, are quite irrelevant. Instead it is necessary to construct the price/output and average cost/output points that result when selling costs are optimal for *each* level of output. A number of possible relationships between price, selling costs, and output can be hypothesized, but at least one plausible set is:

(a) At low levels of output it is profitable to increase output *and* price by raising selling expenditure.

(b) At higher levels of output the cost of expansion at constant price by increasing selling costs is too high to permit increased profit and expansion is more profitably achieved partly by increasing selling costs but partly by lowering price.[22] The result is that in Figure 1.2

---

[20]
$$SRMC = \frac{dSRTC}{dQ} = \frac{d(SRAC.Q)}{dQ} = \frac{QdSRAC}{dQ} + SRAC$$

$$LRMC = \frac{dLRTC}{dQ} = \frac{d(LRAC.Q)}{dQ} = \frac{QdLRAC}{dQ} + LRAC$$

But at X in Figure 1.2 $SRAC = LRAC$ and $\dfrac{dSRAC}{dQ} = \dfrac{dLRAC}{dQ}$

Therefore $SRMC = LRMC$.

[21] H. Demsetz, 'The Welfare and Empirical Implications of Monopolistic Competition', *E.J.* 74 (1964), 623–41.

[22] This requires that selling costs lower the price elasticity of demand at low output levels and raise it or leave it constant at higher levels. See W. Perkins, 'A Note on the Nature of Equilibrium in Monopolistic Competition', *J.P.E.* 80 (1972), 394–402.

the *LRAC* curve rises progressively further above the *APC* curve, and, much more importantly, the price/output locus available to the firm is an inverted 'U', termed by Demsetz the '*mutatis mutandis* average revenue curve' (*MAR*). Tangency between *LRAC* and *MAR may* therefore be achieved at any point on the *LRAC*, showing that the Chamberlin excess capacity solution is far from necessary. Furthermore, evidence that firms frequently prefer to change output by altering selling costs at existing prices at least suggests that they are at the peak of the *MAR* curve and would therefore be at the minimum point of the *LRAC*.

Demsetz goes on to show that on this basis the model regains some predictive power but loses nearly all the features that originally distinguished it from perfect competition.[23] It should be remembered however that the objection to the necessity of normal profit resulting from monopolistic competition in (1) above applies equally well in this newer version.

We are now in a position to indicate the significance of the monopolistic competition debate. Judged in terms of the theory of the firm, we find that in between perfect competition and monopoly, all we have are lots more monopolies. Monopolistic competitors differ in exactly the same way as monopolists, i.e. they have different downward sloping demand curves for different products, the position of which depends on consumers' preferences and income and is indeterminate within the analysis. At one level we end up with the useful but hardly revolutionary conclusion that the monopoly analysis is perhaps somewhat more important than had hitherto been thought. For some this has meant continued adherence to the perfect competition model. In some cases, notably the work of Triffin, it has led to the conclusion that there is an irreconcilable division between abstract general equilibrium theory and real-world industrial phenomena. Study of the latter would then be back to what Stigler referred to as '*ad hoc* empiricism'. In historical terms this would suggest that even the first steps to reintegrate the two aspects of Marshall's work failed, and that general theory and empirical research are as distant as ever.

Nor might this conclusion be altered if we were to adopt the perspective of the empirical school. This emphasized a whole range of real-world phenomena which were considered important in firms'

[23] For discussion of Demsetz's model see G. C. Archibald, 'Monopolistic Competition and Returns to Scale', *E.J.* 77 (1967), 405–12, and H. Demsetz's reply in the same volume, 412–20. For elaboration of the parallel between Monopolistic and Perfect Competition see H. Demsetz, 'Do Competition and Monopolistic Competition Differ?', *J.P.E.* 76, no. 1 (1968), 146–8, and Y. Barzel, 'Excess Capacity in Monopolistic Competition', *J.P.E.* 78 (1970), 1142–9.

and industries' behaviour, but which were not included in monopolistic competition (see later). Even advertising and product quality had made only a halting and largely unsuccessful entry. Thus, the monopolistic competition model probably did little if anything to alter this school's view that the theory of the firm had little to do with firms' behaviour. In short it is not difficult to show that as a model monopolistic competition failed both theoretically and empirically.

Yet this conclusion misses the great significance both in general and specific terms which the development has had for Industrial Economics and for the issues with which we will be concerned in this book. It will be useful to ennumerate these implications.

(I) First and foremost, Chamberlin provided a sophisticated classification of main and subsidiary forms of market structure and examined the theoretical relationships between, on the one hand, the different industrial structures and, on the other, the performance in terms of prices, profits, advertising, and efficiency that each generated. Whatever the drawbacks of his models, there is no doubt that Chamberlin in this way provided the basis upon which economists, in particular Mason[24] and Bain,[25] could generate empirically testable hypotheses about the structure–performance relationship which are at the heart of much current industrial economics. In addition the monopolistic competition model, by introducing such realistic aspects as product differentiation, product change, and selling costs, allowed subsequent researchers to integrate theoretical models with the institutional approaches, trust problems, marketing studies, and descriptive price and profit studies etc. then existing, and which economists such as Berle and Means[26] were surveying and explaining (see Figure 1.1). In this way it is no exaggeration to say that Chamberlin's work was the catalyst that generated industrial economics as currently practised.

(II) Hardly less important, Triffin's conclusion that general theory and empirical research must inevitably be separate could be overcome and the two aspects combined very productively once one major conclusion of the above discussion was incorporated, namely the importance, not of the monopoly, but of the monopoly *model* as a starting point for all cases apart from Perfect Competition.

The monopoly model did not suffer from the logical difficulties

[24] E. S. Mason, 'Price and Production Policies of Large Scale Enterprise', *A.E.R. Supplement*, 29 (Mar. 1939), 61–74.

[25] J. S. Bain, *Industrial Organisation* (New York, 1959) is his later and most comprehensive work.

[26] A. A. Berle and G. Means, *The Modern Corporation and Private Property* (New York, 1932).

of monopolistic competition, removal of which difficulties, as
seen, led back to monopoly. Nor did it contain many assumptions
which seemed grossly at odds with the real world. It did not necessarily predict either excess capacity or normal profits in equilibrium.
Its difficulty was that it excluded all competition and therefore contained *no explanation of the relative position of the revenue and cost
curves*. Thus it had only one conclusion—that supernormal profits
could be made. It said nothing about the determinants of the level of
supernormal profits. Finally, it said nothing about new entry, because
that had to be impossible if the firm were to remain a monopoly.

The way forward for industrial economics was to recognize that
(i) perfect competition is inappropriate because of product differentiation, (ii) this means nearly all firms are partly 'monopolistic',
(iii) their performance depends on the relationship between their
demand and cost curves, (iv) this depends, among other things, on
the competition faced, i.e. the price and specification of all other
goods, but on some more than others, (v) what is therefore needed is
a general analysis backed up by empirical evidence of the factors that
determine the demand/cost relation and the implications of it. Thus
emphasis moved right away from assumptions of common cost and
revenue curves, and from deducing whether only normal profits are
possible in the long run. Instead it was placed on the diversity of
cost curves, on the extent to which substitutes are close or distant,
on the ease with which close substitutes can be produced, on the
efforts by firms to strengthen their monopolistic element by preventing this, on the role of pricing in determining the relationship,
and, most of all, on the systematic variations in profits from negative
to low to high that these factors cause. The fourfold classification of
market structure—Perfect Competition, Monopolistic Competition,
Oligopoly, and Monopoly—was replaced by a continuous spectrum
running from low (in the limit zero) substitutability to high (in the
limit infinite) substitutability in which anything less than infinite
substitutability could permit supernormal profits depending on the
numerous links between the degree of substitutability and the
demand/cost curve relationship.

In other words, while the theory of the firm presented the representative firm's cost and demand curve and attempted to answer the
question, 'What will the long-term relationship between them be?',
industrial economics presents them and attempts to answer the
question, 'What determines the relationship between costs and
demand and how is the relationship connected to its determinants?'
This is less demanding in that it requires few predictions from the
model alone and no purely deductive delineation of the concepts

used, especially that of the competing group.

(III) At the theoretical level only one clear distinction remains within this spectrum, namely between cases where competitive reactions to, for example, a price change are assumed to be taken into account (oligopoly), and those where they are not. It is again Chamberlin's work which, though itself dealing with oligopoly much more briefly and ending up totally indeterminate, nevertheless reintroduced the issue into the mainstream of economic thought a century after Cournot and others had started to grapple with the problem.[27] In addition, the view of firms as being part of a chain of substitutability led as we saw to the view that 'local' oligopoly might be a very typical structure. In fact oligopoly theory is now an important and rapidly developing area, and has a chapter to itself as a result (Chapter 5).

(IV) However the subject developed from Chamberlin's work, it was clear that product differentiation and downward sloping demand curves would be central. This is indeed the case, but at first sight is a rather difficult problem. How for example do we compare products which are different, and how do we measure product differentiation? Can we give rigorous meaning to products being 'less' and 'more' differentiated, and how does it relate to the demand curve for a product? Fortunately these problems have proved to be tractable utilizing a model of spatial competition first developed by Hotelling.[28] Characteristics space analysis, as it is called, which analyses products as different combinations of particular qualities or characteristics has, in particular through Lancaster's work,[29] become an important part of consumer theory and has, like oligopoly theory, become a central area in Industrial Economics. It is in fact generating surprising but useful and empirically validated conclusions, and Chapter 3 looks at this in detail.

(V) All these developments helped to deal with another difficulty which monopolistic competition had thrown up, namely the delineation of an industry. Two stages are involved. First, empirically an industry could now be any section of the chain of substitutability such that the firms in it had 'significant' effects on each other but firms outside it did not. The determination of what effects were empirically significant was of course arbitrary, but this did not undermine any aspect of the theory, as had been the case in monopolistic competition, nor of course did it undermine the validity

---

[27] A. Cournot, *Researches into the Mathematical Principles of the Theory of Wealth* (Paris, 1838). English Translation by N. Barron (New York, 1897).

[28] H. Hotelling, 'Stability in Competition', *E.J.* 39 (1929), 41–57.

[29] See K. Lancaster, *Consumer Demand: A New Approach* (New York, 1971).

of the empirical evidence. Second, and more recently, it has been demonstrated that it is possible to give a rigorous theoretical definition of an industry, under certain conditions, using characteristics space analysis.[30] This again is examined in Chapter 3. Thus we have a theoretically tenable and empirically testable view of firms competing within an industry but facing downward sloping demand curves, which is a main element in industrial economics and the true successor to Chamberlin's monopolistic competition model.

(VI) The next factor of importance which Chamberlin's work brought out and subsequent analysis emphasized was the role of new entry into an industry and the barriers facing potential entrants. Chamberlin's original market structure classification illustrated that a fundamental determinant of the relation between cost and revenue curves for a firm was the ease or otherwise of entry, and later work, particularly that of Bain, demonstrated how central this was.[31] The new analysis of product differentiation and the view of firms as strung out in a chain of overlapping oligopolies naturally caused the concept of new entry to undergo further investigation, and is another issue resulting from Chamberlin's work which will occupy an important place in what follows (see Chapter 6).

Thus far we have painted a picture of the new and constructive developments that fairly rapidly emerged from the monopolistic competition model and the criticism and controversy it generated. But, in sharp distinction to the points above, which were the more immediate and relatively uncontroversial consequences, the model also at least unlocked the door to the empirical side on a number of other issues the pursuit of which has had profound and controversial effects on the study of industrial economics. It is to these that we next turn.

4   PROBLEMS IN INDUSTRIAL ECONOMICS

An important and in many ways perhaps crucial aspect of the gap between the theoretical and empirical approaches which existed by the 1920s was that of *discretion*. Descriptive studies of firms, particularly the giant ones, and the more normative disciplines of business economics, management science, operational research, finance, accounting, etc. all illustrated the considerable amount of discretion—over prices, output, size, advertising, and so on—which business managers typically have. There was very little evidence of the automatic, mechanistic, and necessary response to given cost and demand

[30] K. Lancaster, *Consumer Demand: A New Approach* (New York, 1971).
[31] See J. Bain, *Barriers to New Competition* (Harvard University Press, 1956).

conditions posited in the then existing theory of the firm, still less of firms being tied to a given market price. For the empirical school this led to further focus of attention on actual business decision-taking, resulting in even more scepticism about the theory of the firm and even doubt as to whether a firm could usefully be regarded as a single decision-taking unit at all.

The monopolistic competition model, while introducing short-run price discretion along a downward sloping demand curve, did not itself introduce long-run discretion. Ultimately free entry drove all firms to the intersection of the long-run average cost and share-of-the-market demand curves. But the subsequent 'monopolistic' interpretation described above did permit such discretion even in the long run, and this has had four very important ramifications.

(I) First it served to keep attention focused at least partly where Chamberlin had directed it, namely, on individual firms, not least because supernormal profits could be used to enable firms to maintain or improve monopolistic positions. Despite continued concern with industry as a whole, the wealth of empirical evidence on power and discretion of firms understandably found a more direct response at a theoretical level in the concept of a firm as an entity with some market power and to some extent independent over over-all industry performance. Even the examination of such basic issues as long-run average cost curves reveals how important inter-firm differences may be in the study of industrial economics (see Chapter 2). It therefore became a very real question whether to place emphasis on (i) the economic behaviour of an industry or market, in particular the prediction of a market's responses to changes that could influence it, with the firm then being construed as a representative unit within it and used in effect as a mental construct in what is essentially a theory of market resource allocation, or (ii) the firm itself, with the concept of the firm determined by observation of actual firms and with the implications for the behaviour of the market as a whole being of secondary importance. One must, of course, be careful not to exaggerate this difference. Clearly the first approach does not deny that real-world firms are very heterogeneous and that their managers have considerable discretion in decisions, nor does the second approach deny the significance of market competition for a firm's behaviour. In addition, behind the distinction lies a difference of purpose, with the former more directly concerned with the effects of different market structures, the latter with individual firm characteristics such as size, growth, and market strategy. Nevertheless, there is heavy overlap in their concern with profitability, efficiency, and the nature of the competitive process, and there is a very clear difference between (i) an approach which emphasizes the primacy of market characteristics and implies the impossibility of individual discretion being used for long in a way other than that dictated by the market, and (ii) one which sees the firm as having considerable power and discretion, as able to at least partly escape purely external market pressures and as therefore being the more central concept in the analysis of such economic phenomena.

Behind this issue lies an even more fundamental one. The 'firm' in general equilibrium theory, like the consumer, is a single decision-taking unit. Co-ordination between individual producers and consumers is carried out entirely by the operations of the market. Actual firms on the other hand carry out many activities, mass production, distribution, selling, etc., and co-ordinate them by internal direction and planning. They are in fact islands of planning in a sea of otherwise market co-ordinated transactions. In principle transactions internal to a firm could generally be co-ordinated via the market, and the emphasis on the firm which seems natural to the empirically oriented misses the question which inevitably arises for the general equilibrium theorist, namely why do firms exist at all. This question, which has received spasmodic but increasing attention, has as it turns out rather less than intuitively obvious answers (see Chapter 2) and raises some interesting issues in industrial economics.

(II) The second issue which discretion raises is that of firms' objectives, for the possibility of supernormal profits implied that firms might choose to forgo some profit in return for more of alternatives, for example leisure, size, inefficiency, etc.

The mainstream approach has continued to assume that profit maximization—sometimes short-run, but more usually long-run nowadays—is the only significant motivation of the firm. This has been justified in numerous ways—its inherent plausibility, its supposed rationality, countless statements by businessmen to that effect, even uncertainty as to what to replace it by—but increasingly because of the power of the model using this assumption to generate empirically validated conclusions. More recent approaches on the other hand have been prepared to explore other possible motivations in the light of the observed behaviour of real-world firms. This in turn has introduced the idea of multiple goals, of conflicting goals, and of the possible inappropriateness therefore of regarding the firm as a single unit with a single goal. Again differences of purpose are involved, with much of the latter approach concerned with more detailed short-term responses to changes in the economic environment and the former approach concerned with longer-term trends, but different motivational assumptions nevertheless frequently provide different explanations for observed behaviour, and conflicting predictions over the effect of environmental change. So far, unfortunately, problems of testing, interpretation of results, and inconsistency of different conclusions have all played a part in preventing any clear-cut resolution of the disagreement over what assumptions to make about motivation. This has not however prevented the development primarily by Marris of what amounts to a new theory of the firm, based on observation of modern corporations, but with a broader and in many ways more rigorous theoretical base, as far as motivational assumptions are concerned, than had previously been the case (see Chapter 9).

(III) Once the firm was recognized as a primary concept in the theory of the firm and real-world firms a legitimate source of evidence on firms' behaviour, it began to become clearer just how many factors involved in business behaviour there were which were largely ignored in the theory of the firm. The latter was generally not well equipped to deal with issues such as firms' financial structure, the growth of firms, some aspects of collusive behaviour, objectives other than profit maximization, research and development, conglomerate firms, and many other issues. In particular it was no longer clear that the best way to deal with uncertainty was to assume it away, as had hitherto been the case, even with respect to something as central to the theory of the firm as pricing (see Chapter 4). Thus, although the monopolistic competition model itself made relatively few and generally unsuccessful steps towards being empirically supportable, it formed a bridge, even one might say a lightning-conductor, to the wealth of empirical information on firms' behaviour which in the next thirty years was to generate models of the firm altogether different from, indeed not even comparable with, the monopolistic competition model which triggered the development.

(IV) The final and culminating consequence of introducing discretion was the recognition that, as a result, the structure–performance relationship, though valid and useful, was only one aspect of the picture. For supernormal profits permitted discretion not only over price but over a range of decisions, investment, research and development, mergers, etc., which between them could significantly alter the cost and industry structures in which a firm found itself. In other words there was a performance–structure relationships also, which unless incorporated might seriously diminish the scope and validity of theory and evidence based on the reverse relationship.

It is against this background that the present framework and some of the conceptual problems of industrial economics can be explained.

It is not concerned with simply adding further descriptive material, nor with elaborating largely deductive *a priori* theories, but with developing theories which recognize and can incorporate the complexities of the real world, and with using the information available to test which theory provides the best explanation of the evidence. It thus retains a deductive approach, but places considerable emphasis on checking both its assumptions and predictions and on providing a coherent analytical framework into which different pieces of evidence can be fitted and through which they can be explained. But given what has been said it is not surprising to find significantly different approaches which it is hard to reconcile and compare.

In practice there has been a tendency towards two related but separate lines of development. The first is more directly in the tradition of monopolistic competition developments. It is reasonably unified and continues to focus primarily on the Industry as the main factor both theoretically and empirically; generally presumes profit maximization; continues to focus on a relatively small number of important variables—primarily price, output, and profits, though expanding the context in which they are examined to include advergising, price discrimination, product quality, and of course competitive interdependence. Finally it adheres to the structure-conduct-performance framework which arose after Chamberlin's work.

The second has appeared more recently; owes more to the infusion of empirically based theorizing noted above; and is therefore much more diffuse. It focuses on the Firm as the central concept; assumes considerable discretionary power; generally rejects profit maximization as the assumed motivation; tends to incorporate selected variables out of an almost limitless range as and when they seem useful; and recognizes that much business behaviour is concerned with changing the structure faced by firms to their advantage.

Having described this distinction three points must be made immediately. First it is a distinction quite separate from the theoretical/ empirical one that existed before. It is true that many studies are easily identified as being one rather than the other, but this for the most part appears a sensible division of labour, rather than a divisive element. Recognition that theory and evidence must complement each other is one of the strengths of industrial economics, and the problems arise from attempts to deal properly with their integration rather than in any return to the old division. Second, the distinction to some extent reflects division of opinion over whether in addition to predictive power the 'realism' of assumptions should be used as a test of a theory. Friedman's famous argument[32] that it should not has generated much discussion, examined in Chapter 8. But while dissatisfaction with the realism of the theory of the firm's assumptions was a major force in the move to monopolistic competition and beyond, and has therefore caused much division and argument within the field of industrial economics, it has not in practice hindered its development. Rather it has spurred the subject on in the search for theories which were acceptably realistic for their authors but also could stand the test of predictive power in comparison to others.

Third, it must be stressed that both approaches are valid and have proved very useful. The difference lies not in one being superior but in the fact that one or other is more appropriate for different sorts of investigation, a point considered further below. Much of the challenge in industrial economics is in determining in a particular area which is the more suitable basis.

Finally, although we have talked of two approaches, there is of course a whole spectrum, running from studies which seek to elaborate on or test the market implications of the traditional approach, at one end, to those which assume a variety of maximizing and non-maximising goals, introduce many new variables, are based closely on empirical observation of actual firms, and presume the market to be considerably less important than the firm, at the other. The result unfortunately is a vast proliferation not only of theories and evidence, but also of concepts, terminology, and analytical method. This provides a fertile background for controversy, but also frequently makes it very difficult to relate or compare different studies, and thereby resolve the controversy. Thus, in moving from the familiar ground of the theory of the firm, as covered in microeconomic theory, to industrial economics, the student is moving into an important and rapidly growing area, different in approach, but one which requires an over-all framework that emphasizes the unifying features of the subject rather than the divisive ones and which enables the student to relate constructively the many different strands of thought.

5 A FRAMEWORK OF INDUSTRIAL ECONOMICS

Although about industrial economics, this book is more specifically about the general determinants of the market economic behaviour of private manufacturing firms. This excludes a number of other important aspects of industrial economics, including non-manufacturing,

[32] M. Friedman, 'The Methodology of Positive Economics', in M. Friedman, *Essays in Positive Economics* (Chicago Unviersity Press, 1953).

nationalized industries, and firms' economic behaviour in other areas, particularly the labour market. A number of topics of great importance at present are touched upon only slightly, if at all, including the efficiency of management, the role of incentives, determinants of industrial productivity and international comparisons of profits, efficiency, and industrial growth. Nor is there much examination of the workings of various government agencies set up to intervene in the industrial sector. This is partly because some are better examined in a more macroeconomic context, partly the lack of adequate evidence on several of them, and partly a question of space. Mainly, however, it is because the emphasis on generality in industrial economics has been accompanied by an emphasis on the role of industrial structure in the competitive process and the analysis of the main decision variables within firms' control. Both reflect the historical emphasis on firms' behaviour in markets as opposed to wider questions concerning the performance of the industrial sector as a whole. It is, none the less, regrettable that industrial economists cannot offer more in the way of microeconomic theory, research, or evidence to explain some broader issues, in particular the very different levels of productivity in the industrial sectors of different countries.

The framework for our purpose can be illustrated diagrammatically. First we represent the more traditional approach, as in Figure 1.3. In the top left-hand corner are shown the central issues stemming from the theory of the firm, namely the determination of

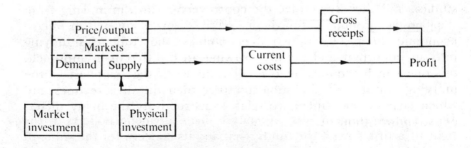

Fig. 1.3 Market Model

price and output in markets by demand and supply. Price and output determine gross receipts out of which current costs are paid, leaving profit. Current costs depend on the actual output level, and the cost conditions facing the firm. The latter depend on the capital stock of the firm, built up by successive investment expenditures. The history of this approach is the study of price/output decisions in the light of market supply and demand conditions, their consequences for profit and cost levels, and (usually quite separately) the level of investment in the light of its marginal efficiency and interest rates. As we have seen, Chamberlin's model of monopolistic competition brought in the possibility of market investment (advertising, etc.) as a means of influencing the demand conditions faced, and there have been subsequent attempts to integrate these more fully into the monopolistic competition model, so this may be added to the diagram.

Almost entirely separate from this, and until recently generally part of the empirical school, was work concerned with the financial decisions and behaviour of individual firms and the systematic aspects of these across firms. This can be shown as in Figure 1.4.

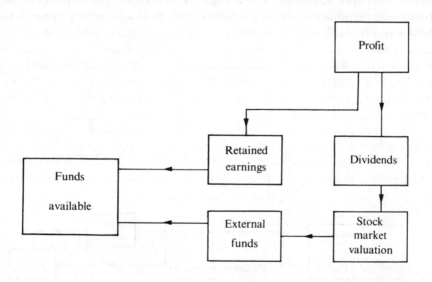

Fig. 1.4 Financial Model

Here a main concern was to analyse firms' dividend policies in the light of a firm's need for funds itself and its concern for the value of its shares. (For simplicity, taxation and interest payments are ignored. See Chapter 10 for the full model.) The dividends paid out of profits are an important determinant of the firm's stock market valuation, though the relationship naturally requires an examination of the behaviour of financial markets. High stock market valuation might represent an aim in itself, but is also necessary in order to attract new funds from new or existing shareholders. Both the supply of internal funds from retentions and of external funds will therefore depend on the financial policy adopted by the firm.

Besides the market model and the financial model, there is an expenditure model. Although there has been some examination of marketing and advertising expenditure in the theory of the firm and an analysis of capital expenditure on plant and equipment which could apply at both macro- and microeconomic levels, the more recent emphasis on empirical research has generated a large new literature in both areas. Their determinants have been explored in considerably greater detail, in the process of which new models of greater complexity but greater analytical power have been established. In addition, increasing attention has been paid to another important form of expenditure, namely that on research and development. All this is shown in Figure 1.5, which shows the different types of expenditure, and illustrates the largely ignored aspect of firms' decisions that they are alternative and competing uses of a firm's funds.

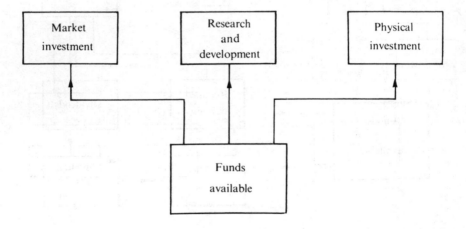

Fig. 1.5 Expenditure Model

The first step in establishing a comprehensive framework is to recognize that these are complementary models, focusing on different aspects of firms' behaviour, and that we can provide an over-all picture of firms' economic behaviour by putting the three together as in Figure 1.6. The market model explains the profits generated, the financial model analyses the division of profit, and the expenditure model examines the use of the total funds made available to provide (i) market investment and product research and development, both of which influence the demand conditions facing the firm, and

(ii) plant expenditure and process research and development, both of which influence the cost and supply conditions facing the firm. In addition, it is expectations of market conditions which determine the expenditures made and the finance which will be made available both internally and externally. The clockwise relation is the chronological one, the anti-clockwise relation the forward-looking or expectational one. In total we have a summary picture of all the major economic activities of firms with which we will be concerned.

Figure 1.6 is a picture of a representative firm, but unlike that in the theory of the firm it has many interlocking facets. Although it will generally be useful to continue to look at parts of it separately, some recent work attempts to analyse the circularity of the picture

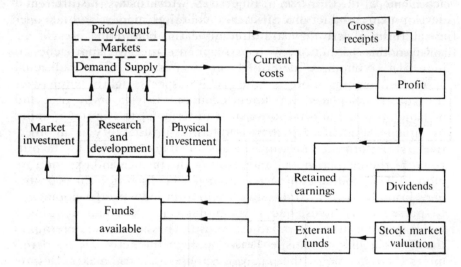

Fig. 1.6 Complete Model

as a whole. This circularity leads us to draw a distinction which arises directly from the discussion in the previous section and which we believe is a useful guide in understanding in the context of Figure 1.6 how the diverse elements in current industrial economics can be interpreted and reconciled. This is the distinction between the concepts of the *Passive* firm and the *Active* firm.

6   PASSIVE AND ACTIVE BEHAVIOUR OF FIRMS

At any point in time, firms will be pursuing one or more objectives in the face of several constraints. Passive behaviour consists of attempting to maximize the achievement of the objective(s) within given constraints. The prime example of the passive context is seen in the original theory of the firm. The firm was faced with a given set of possible short-run cost conditions, one of which applied in the short run and any of which may apply in the long run. Market structure was given, and with it the shape and position of the demand curve. The firm then pursued its objective (usually profit maximization) passively, setting price to obtain the highest profit the constraints would allow. A totally passive policy would then involve acceptance of the consequences of this situation, which could include stable or deteriorating profit and departure from the industry.

In contrast, active behaviour involves the attempt over time to modify and/or remove the constraints, thus permitting the better achievement of the firm's objectives. Advertising, research and development, product diversification, collusion, merger, and takeover are all forms of active constraint-manipulating behaviour.

Given this distinction, we can reappraise the two approaches to industrial economics described in section 4. The traditional approach, focusing more on the passive aspects, rightly emphasizes the constraints placed on firms' economic behaviour by cost and demand structure and response to it in terms of the limited number of variables available. It rightly emphasizes profitability as an objective and performance measure because of its central role as the outcome of the market model and input to the finance and expenditure models. The modern approach recognizes the discretion those profits may bring for a firm to distance itself from industry developments, to pursue other goals, and to manipulate its environment using a wider range of decision variables. Thus the passive aspect determines the firm's ability to pursue 'active' policy; the active aspect determines the outcome of the passive responses the firm makes. Despite the differences to which attention has been drawn the two approaches are complementary, ultimately being different facets of firms' over-all behaviour. While we shall examine each part of Figure 1.6 in different chapters it must be stressed that many issues, from the achievement of economies of scale and trends in industrial concentration to firms' investment, growth, and takeover policy, all of which are vital for an understanding of industrial efficiency and economic welfare, can only be adequately examined if this two-way interrelationship is recognized. In addition, policy implications in the context of government intervention may well be inappropriate or even entirely inapplicable if they are drawn from only partial consideration of the whole picture, or if they ignore the ways in which a firm modifies, but is also modified by, the industrial structure it faces.

Many of the debates in industrial economics can be regarded as stemming from a difference of view about the relative importance of passive and active behaviour. Scepticism about the impact of active decisions will tend to be associated with belief in the efficiency of competititve markets, while those who believe the reverse will tend to downgrade the importance of industrial structure, focusing more on the economic power that resides in the company sector and the lack of external constraints on it. Whether advertising and acquisition are seen as part of the competitive process or attempts to thwart it, with emotive overtones in each case, will depend on whether the active or passive perspective is adopted. The priorities thought proper to attach to research in industrial economics will also depend on it.

Ultimately, however, it seems reasonable to conclude only that different circumstances may make one more appropriate than the other. For example, it seems likely that in recessionary periods, competitive pressures will increase, profits will be greatly reduced, and the possibility of a significant active policy being employed will be reduced along with them, leaving firms' skill in optimizing under tight constraints as the main factor. Active expenditure policies and mergers typically decline, the threat of new products or new firms appearing is much diminished, and consumer emphasis on low prices may well be increased. Cyclical upswings would, however, see the reverse of all of these. Again, if we are concerned with the longer-term regularities of firms' economic behaviour, then *a priori* both aspects must be included.

A more problematical case is the question of whether the passive aspect is appropriate where small firms are concerned, and the active one where large firms are concerned. This seems quite plausible and undoubtedly has some truth in it. Much evidence, however, points the other way. Small firms generally employ many if not all of the active policies mentioned and frequently face or deliberately create monopolistic or oligopolistic segments in a market based on geographical or product specification. Large firms no less than small ones find themselves having constantly to monitor and revise price and product policies in a number of different markets, in each of which they are typically constrained by existing and potential competition and the interdependence which results. Thus we have to tread cautiously in making broad statements about the role of each approach.

Much of this chapter has been concerned with the antecedents of
industrial economics, the history of their development, and their
significance for the present state of play in industrial economics.
From this it appears that, from the standpoint of the analysis of real-
world economic behaviour, the theory of the firm was almost
impossible to apply and was geneally silent on a number of issues
important in the industrial world. In many ways it was a long detour
away from the main thrust of Marshall's work. It created a large gulf
between itself and empirical analysis and led to controversy, indeterminacy, error, and partial demise when attempts were made to reintegrate it. Out of this however has come a stronger-based discipline
in direct descent from Marshall which transcends the theoretical/
empirical distinction and which can embrace the different
approaches which its early development generated. The rest of this
book examines the topics that go to make up the integrated framework that has emerged in this chapter.

    In Part II we focus on the passive aspects. Chapter 2 looks at the
theory and evidence on firms' cost structure and Chapter 3 at industrial concentration and the problems raised by product differentiation in this context. Following the market model of Figure 1.3,
Chapter 4 examines price behaviour in the light of cost and demand
conditions. Price behaviour where oligopolistic interdependence is
involved is sufficiently important that examination of it is grouped
together separately in Chapter 5. Chapter 6 then introduces the
structural problem of latent competition from potential new
entrants. Concluding Part II, Chapter 7 pulls these aspects together,
looking at the structure–performance relations that result and, in
particular, the vexed problem of the relative importance of concentration and new entry in the determination via price behaviour of
profitability. Part III adopts the active view of firms. As we have
seen, this focuses attetion on the nature of the firm itself and the
objectives it pursues, and these are the subject of Chapter 8. Then
Chapter 9, incorporating the results of the preceding chapter,
presents a model of the active firm as a whole. This paves the way for
examination of the financial model in Chapter 10 and of the
expenditure model in Chapters 11 to 13. (Investment in Plant and
Equipment, Marketing, and Research and Development respectively.)
Chapter 14 examines the direct manipulation of structure by merger
and takeover and Chapter 15 concludes Part III with a review of the
structure–performance relationships that emerge when both are seen
as variables and causally dependent on the other.

It would have been possible to conclude the book at that point, but two factors argued against it. First, behind the analysis, the theorizing, and testing of industrial economics lies the belief that it can tell us something about the welfare implications of firms' behaviour. Second, an important result of the integrated framework adopted is exposure of the huge gap between standard static welfare analysis and the real-world industrial problems with which policy has to grapple. It therefore becomes important to see if a rigorous and coherent welfare analysis can be developed which will be of use to public bodies charged with making prescriptions about industrial structure and acceptable conduct and performance. Chapters 16 and 17 review developments in this field, the former in the passive mould, the latter in the active.

Finally it must be emphasized that the use of the active/passive distinction to explain our framework and group the issues does not conflict with the structure/goals/conduct/performance classification that has been referred to at different points in the chapter. The full range of topics under each is covered as follows:

Structure — Costs, Concentration, Product Differentiation, and Entry Barriers.

Goals — Profit maximization, alternatives to Profit and Non-Maximizing.

Conduct — Pricing, Marketing, Financing, Plant Investment, Research and Development, and Merger.

Performance — Profitability, Efficiency, Growth, and Welfare.

The investigation of passive and active behaviour is none the less a new and, we believe, equally useful theme in dealing with the diffuse area of industrial economics.

PART II

The Analysis of Markets

2

COSTS AND SUPPLY CONDITIONS

There are two reasons why an economist is preoccupied with cost. The first arises from the economist's traditional concern for the efficiency of allocation of resources. The concept of cost here is 'opportunity cost', the observation that the use of a resource in the production of a good precludes its use in the production of an alternative good. The cost to society of the resources is its value in the best alternative use. The second reason for interest in costs is more pragmatic, and is centred on the firm rather than on the allocation of resources in the economy as a whole. This is the idea that costs to some extent determine prices, that prices determine market share, and that all these together determine the profitability of the firm. The theory has traditionally emphasized scale of operations as the main determinant of costs.

The analysis which follows is motivated by the latter reason.[1] In the next section we ask two questions in the context of the traditional analysis of economies of scale. What are the limits to attainable plant cost at different scales of output? What evidence is there that plants are in fact operated at the minimum cost for their output? In section 2 we move from the plant to the firm, and assess the effects of multiplant operations and vertical integration, as well as the costs and effectiveness of management. Section 3 discusses the difficulties inherent in the use of firm data for empirical analysis of costs. The survivor technique is explained in the following section: this method involves a wider concept of efficiency, including size-related advantages in advertising, R and D, and the capital market, which receive more detailed consideration later in the book.

1 PRODUCTION, COSTS, AND ECONOMIES OF SCALE AT PLANT LEVEL

(a) The production function, costs of inputs, and cost minimization

The textbook theory of costs examines the solution to the following problem facing the single-plant firm. The firm wishes to produce a certain level of output in a given time period. There are a variety of methods of production currently available. The firm has to pay for the use of productive resources. What method of production should

---

[1] The allocation of resources, and the opportunity cost concept, are examined in Part IV.

the firm adopt? The solution given is that the firm will seek that method or technique which minimizes its expenditures on resources: the firm will minimize cost.

The problem can be simply formalized.[2] Technically efficient methods are deduced by eliminating all those techniques of production that use absolutely more of all inputs than another available technique. Suppose that the firm is seeking to make Q_1 per unit time with inputs X_1 and X_2 in the same time period (Figure 2.1). Then a

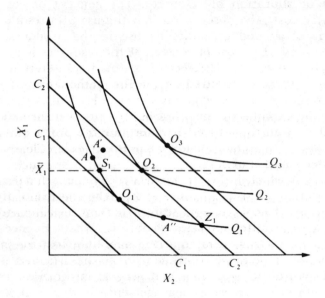

Fig. 2.1

point such as A' represents an inefficient combination of inputs since it uses more of both X_1 and X_2 than the technique A. However we cannot compare A and A'' on technical grounds alone, since A'' uses more of X_2, but less of X_1, than A. Points such as A and A'' represent the technically efficient combinations of X_1 and X_2 in the production of Q_1 per unit time. The whole mapping of technically efficient input combinations in output space is called the production function and is written $Q = F(X_1, X_2)$. This may be plotted, for varying levels of Q, as an isoquant diagram. Thus, in the diagram, Q_1 and Q_2 are isoquants, and trace the locus of combinations of X_1 and X_2 that produce Q_1 and Q_2 respectively.

[2] See M. J. Farrell, 'The Measurement of Productive Efficiency', *J.R.S.S.* 120 (1957), Series A, Part 3, 11–28, on the distinction between 'technical-efficiency', represented by the isoquant, and 'price-efficiency', the choice of least-cost production point on the chosen isoquant.

The choice of the least-cost technique from the technically efficient set for a given output per unit time depends on the price of productive resources. The problem is to minimize total cost of inputs, subject to the required output constraint. Thus if the unit prices of inputs X_1 and X_2 are P_1 and P_2 respectively, then the firm seeks to minimize cost

$$C_1 = P_1 X_1 + P_2 X_2$$

subject to

$$Q_1 = F(X_1, X_2)$$

where Q_1 is the required output.

The graphical solution to this problem is to consider the various combinations of input quantities that are available for a given outlay. This is a linear function such as $C_1 C_1$ in the diagram. Clearly the firm will only be satisfied with producing at a point where such a cost line is tangential to the isoquant. If the firm is producing at a point where the cost line cuts the isoquant, e.g. Z_1, then the firm can produce more output for the same expenditure at O_2 or can reduce its costs for the same output by moving to O_1.[3]

Optimal points such as O_1 and O_2 can be derived for each level of output. Each of these corresponds to a given level of output and a given level of cost. So that we may deduce a cost function

$$C = f(Q)$$

[3] The mathematical technique is the Lagrange multiplier. We seek the minimum of the augmented function

$$L = P_1 X_1 + P_2 X_2 - \lambda[F(X_1 X_2) - Q_1]$$

So $\dfrac{\partial L}{\partial X_1} = P_1 - \lambda\dfrac{\partial F}{\partial X_1}$ and $\dfrac{\partial L}{\partial X_1} = P_2 - \lambda\dfrac{\partial F}{\partial X_2}$

Putting these equal to zero for a minimum yields the conditions,

$$\frac{P_1}{P_2} = \frac{\partial F/\partial X_1}{\partial F/\partial X_2} = \frac{dX_2}{dX_1}$$

i.e. the ratio of the prices should equal the slope of the isoquant. The condition can be generalized for many inputs.

and hence an average cost curve.

$$\frac{C}{Q} = \frac{f(Q)}{Q}$$

This is the long-run average cost curve of traditional cost theory. It relates the average cost of production to the level of output per unit time, assuming that the firm minimizes costs. The firm chooses at each output the 'best techniques' given the prices of inputs: there are no restrictions on its choice. If its choice is restricted, by one of the inputs not being variable, then different levels of output can still be obtained by varying inputs of the other resources. But in such cases the input proportions will certainly be non-optimal and costs will be higher than under complete freedom of choice of inputs. If, for example, the input of X_1 is fixed at $\bar{X}_1$, in Figure 2.1, then the plant is constrained to produce output Q_1 with the more expensive factor combination at S_1 rather than the optimal combination at O_1. Only for output O_2 are input combinations optimal, and hence costs as low as they could be. These points also determine a level of total costs for each level of output, from which the short-run average costs can be derived. The textbook short-run average cost curve is traditionally drawn with a U-shape, for reasons that are not implausible. If a resource is fixed, the application of a less than optimal amount of the co-operating factors will mean that the fixed factor is not fully utilized, and so unit costs will be greater. Amounts of co-operating factors greater than the optimal level, given the fixed factor, will encounter diminishing returns and hence higher unit costs. In both the long run and the short run the shape of the average cost function depends on the properties of the underlying efficient technology (the production function), and the relative prices of inputs. The particular point of interest is whether the long-run function shows any systematic tendency to increase or decrease with the scale of operations. This has been the objective of most investigations of firm costs by economists, and dominates the theoretical and empirical work we discuss below.

(b) The costs of capital services

The simple analysis has to be complicated somewhat if one of the inputs to production is in the form of services from capital equipment. By capital equipment is meant any productive resources which once purchased furnish services over a number of production periods. The problem is to ascertain the cost of those services in a single time period. This is usually thought to comprise three elements. The first is simply the depreciation or depletion of the resource over time. If the resource has a fixed life regardless of how much use is made of it the depreciation will be simply a given proportion of the initial cost of the resource (assuming that prices do not change). However some machinery will deteriorate at a rate dependent on use, in which case it is right to charge depreciation in any period depending on how much it has been used. The second element is the money interest forgone by the entrepreneur in investing in capital goods or equipment rather than leaving his money in a riskless asset. The third element is a risk premium over and above the riskless rate of interest to compensate the entrepreneur for putting his money into a risky productive enterprise. The sum of these three elements is sometimes called 'normal profits'. If gross profits do not equal or exceed this level the entrepreneur will not be induced to undertake the investment again, but will deploy his funds elsewhere once the resource has been fully depreciated. The measurement of 'normal profits' cannot be other than highly subjective. Most resources do not have ascertainable lives, especially since their demise may be for economic reasons, for example replacement by a lower cost technique, rather than technological. And there can be no objective measure of the necessary price of risk.

The matter is further complicated by a world where the prices of inputs and productive assets is continually changing. If all prices move together this can be accommodated by an adjustment in the nominal rate of interest in the calculation of 'normal profits', assuming that the firm knows what the rate of inflation is going to be, and its expectations are fulfilled. But if the relative prices of assets and other resources change over time we need to impute a new value to capital assets based on what they could earn in alternative uses. But such an imputation may not be at all easy in the absence of markets for second-hand capital assets.

(c) Sources of scale economies

Reasons for expecting economies of scale in production are many. Specialization and division of labour in production, the existence of indivisibilities, the economies of increased physical dimensions of some plant, and economies of manual resources are often quoted. One method of giving empirical substance to these effects is the engineering approach to estimating cost functions. This involves the costing of engineering blueprints for different levels of output, using given costs of inputs. At each level of output the lowest cost estimate is accepted as the relevant point on the long-run average cost curve.

The advantage of this method is that it is reasonably easy to approximate the rather strict theoretical requirements for average costs, including homogeneity of output, homogeneous inputs at constant costs, and static technology.

In the following we shall pursue the analysis of Haldi and Whitcomb.[4] They present estimates under three heads:

(i) *The cost of individual units of industrial equipment.* These fall under two headings. The first is that of indivisibilities. At a given point in time, certain basic items of industrial equipment may be available in only a limited number of capacities. For each size of equipment we shall find increasing returns, due to the spreading of fixed costs, up to the capacity of operation of the equipment. We expect the costs to demonstrate an irregular pattern with discontinuities. If, however, there is no objection on technical grounds to the construction of the equipment at all sizes (and in general there will not be), economies of scale due to indivisibilities need not exist (in the very long run). Such a situation might imply diseconomies in the capital goods sector, where long production runs of standardized equipment will have lower costs than a one-off production to meet the precise specifications of each buyer of the equipment. In practice then we would expect indivisibilities to be important.

The second source of economies in equipment derives from the well-known geometric properties of containers and pipes of all kinds. Put simply, the cost of construction of any container increases with its surface area, whereas the capacity increases with volume (i.e. cost increases with r^2, volume with r^3, where r is one dimension of the container). In engineering design work this is the origin of the so called '0·6' rule of thumb, whereby it is assumed that on average a 100% increase in capacity will lead to only 60% increase in cost.[5]

Haldi and Whitcomb estimated scale coefficients for 687 types of basic equipment, fitting the logarithmic function,

$$C = aX^b$$

where C is cost, X is capacity and a and b are constants. They found that 618 (90%) showed increasing returns (defined as $b < 0.90$ to exclude those b which did not in their view differ significantly from one, given the quality of data). (See Table 2.1).

[4] J. Haldi, D. Whitcomb, 'Economies of Scale in Industrial Plants', *J.P.E.* 75 (1967), 373–85.

[5] H. Chenery, 'Engineering Production Function', *Q.J.E.* 63 (1949), 63, 507–31, provides a precise derivation of the relationship of cost to capacity in the case of transportation of gas by pipeline.

TABLE 2.1

Values of scale coefficient, b†	Basic industrial equipment		Plant investment costs		Total operating cost	
	Number of estimates	%	Number of estimates	%	Number of estimates	%
Under 0·40	74	10·7	9	4·1	4	12·5
0·40–0·49	102	14·9	12	5·4	1	3·1
0 50–0 59	143	20·8	22	10·0	5	15·6
0 60–0 69	147	21·4	45	20·4	3	9·4
0 70–0 79	92	13·4	61	27·6	10	31·3
0 80–0 89	60	8·7	37	16·7	9	28·1
0 90–0 99	30	4·4	20	9·0	0	0·
1 00–1 09	20	2·9	6	2·7	0	0
Over 1·10	19	2·8	9	4·1	0	0
Totals	687	100·0	221	100·0	32	100·0

Source: Tables 1, 2 and 3 of J. Haldi and D. Whitcomb, 'Economies of scale in industrial plants', *J.P.E.* 75 (1967), pp. 373–85. © 1967 by the University of Chicago. All rights reserved.

†Estimate of b in $C = aX^b$.

(ii) *Cost of plants and process areas.* Under this heading they investigated the costs of operating equipment grouped to form a complete plant or process. At this level we incorporate the effects given under (*a*) above. If there are indivisibilities in the individual items of capital equipment then a plant comprising those items will experience economies of scale up to the point where each item of equipment is at the optimal size. At lower outputs, at least part of the equipment will be underutilized. Larger scale may also permit some specialization and division of labour between parts of the plant. The point closely parallels the division of labour, to which we will return in the next section.

Haldi and Whitcomb investigated 221 engineering estimates of costs for complete plants. Using the same criteria as before, 186 showed scale economies, with a median b of 0·73. (See Table 2.1.)

(iii) *Operating cost.* The major item under this head is specialization, which may parallel the specialization in equipment noted above. As the level of output increases, labour can be assigned to special tasks. The gain is that in the repetition of single operations workers may be more efficient than in performing a wider range of tasks. This is particularly true if the worker can be associated with a single piece of capital equipment designed specifically for his task, and which he uses all the time. Haldi and Whitcomb point out that for many process plants large increases in capacity may require relatively few extra workers ($b < 0.40$), since the main tasks are to regulate and monitor performance, and expansion of the plant need not increase the work required.

Size may also lead to economies in maintenance staff. The law of large numbers makes the number of breakdowns more predictable in a plant using a large number of machines, so that the number of stand-by maintenance staff need not be increased in proportion to size. A simple illustration can demonstrate this point: suppose the probability that a machine will break down in a given production period is p. Assume that each breakdown occupies one maintenance man in each period. If n is quite large, the expected number of breakdowns in n machines in a given period can be described by the binomial distribution with mean np and variance $np(1 - p)$. For large n ($\geqslant 30$) this distribution is approximately normal. Suppose the firm wishes to provide a maintenance staff large enough to cope immediately with a breakdown, excluding the rather rare occurrences when a large number of machines break down simultaneously. It might accept a 5% chance of not being able to do this. Then the maximum amount of labour required is given by L

$$L = np + 1.96\sqrt{np(1-p)}$$

so maintenance labour per machine is given by

$$\frac{L}{n} = p + 1.96\sqrt{\frac{p(1-p)}{n}}$$

which is a diminishing function of n.

A more practical example would involve the firm in calculating the acceptable probability of a breakdown without a maintenance man immediately available; not arbitrarily, but by weighing the costs of an extra man against the expected losses from not being able to cope with a breakdown immediately. But the substantive point still holds: stand-by labour costs per machine will fall with the number of machines operating. (We note that a similar calculation applies to stocks of spare parts which are subject to a similar stochastic pattern of replacement.)

According to Haldi and Whitcomb there are few scale economies in the use of materials, but economies may be substantial in the use of energy, as larger motors perform more efficiently than small ones. These economies refer to value added; a firm may also realize substantial pecuniary economies if it is able to contract for supply of materials in large orders:

A final category of operating cost is the cost of working capital, particularly capital tied up in stocks of materials. Large scale may be an advantage, since optimal stock requirements only increase as the square root of input per unit period, as the following example from Baumol[6] illustrates:

Let the carrying cost, including interest payments and storage be k per unit of inventory. Let the total requirement of the input per year be Q. Assume that it is acquired in quantities D, on Q/D occasions through the year. Then the average inventory is $D/2$. Let the cost of each shipment be $a + bD$, where a is a fixed cost (telephone, correspondence, billing) and b is a standard delivery charge per unit.

Then the total cost per inventory is ordering plus holding costs:

$$C = \frac{kD}{2} + a\frac{Q}{D} + bQ$$

We now wish to find that level of D which minimizes C. Differentiating the expression with respect to D and putting the derivative equal to zero we have

$$D^2 = \frac{2aQ}{k}, \text{ so } D = \sqrt{\frac{2aQ}{k}}$$

Substituting back into the cost equation gives average cost of inventory

$$\frac{C}{Q} = b + \sqrt{\frac{2ak}{Q}}$$

i.e. the average cost is a diminishing function of level of throughput, Q. This economy is in addition to those arising from stochastic sources.

---

[6] W. J. Baumol, *Economic Theory and Operations Analysis*, 3rd edn. (Englewood Cliffs, 1972), Chapter 1.

(d) Minimum efficient scale of plant

The evidence presented by Haldi and Whitcomb gives the various elements of scale economies according to source. The alternative method of presention pioneered by Bain,[7] is to estimate the scale at which costs become constant, further economies of scale being negligible. The minimum efficient scale (MES) so derived can be expressed either in units of output, or more usefully as a percentage of the total relevant market—national, regional, or product market. Bain supplemented this with information on the extent to which sub-optimal plants suffered cost disadvantages compared to MES plants. Two recent studies have provided new estimates for a number of industries, in the U.K. and the U.S., based on interviews with firms and on technical literature associated with each sector. The conclusions of Pratten[8] for the U.K. are presented in Table 2.2. A number of sectors have a MES which approaches 100% of the market, and in many sectors a few optimal plants could serve the whole market. However in the majority of sectors the cost disadvantages of smaller plants are relatively small, reaching 10% in only a quarter of the cases. An alternative presentation is that of Silberston,[9] who used the data of Pratten's study to fit the scale curve

$$C = aX^b$$

where C = average cost, X = output, and a and b are constants. b is then a measure of scale economies. He found b to be substantially less than unity in all 24 sectors for which he had data. The mean value of b was 0·73, the median 0·74. The estimates are given in Table 2.2, column (4).

The second study is that of Scherer et al.[10] for twelve sectors. The results are summarized in Table 2.3, giving MES as percentage of the U.S. and U.K. markets, and the percentage cost disadvantage at one-third of the MES. For obvious reasons the MES plant is a higher proportion of required capacity in the U.K. than in the U.S. Once again the cost disadvantages of sub-optimal scale seem to be slight, except for glass bottles, cement, and integrated steel.

[7] J. S. Bain, 'Economies of Scale, Concentration and the Conditions of Entry in Twenty Manufacturing Industries', *A.E.R.* 64 (1954), 15–39.

[8] C. F. Pratten, *Economies of Scale in Manufacturing Industry*, D.A.E. Occasional Paper 28 (Cambridge, 1971).

[9] Z. A. Silberston, 'Economies of Scale in Theory and Practice', *E.J.* 82 (1972), 369–91.

[10] F. M. Scherer, A. Beckenstein, E. Kaufer, R. D. Murphy, *The Economics of Multi-plant Operations* (Harvard University Press, 1975).

TABLE 2.2

Industry etc.	(1) MES as % of U.K. market	(2) MES as % of regional market	(3) % increase in cost at 50% MES	(4) Scale factors calculated by Silberston
Oil refining	10	40	5	0·66
Ethylene	25	100	9	0·62
Sulphuric acid	30	100	1	0·75
Dyes	>100	—	22	0·47
Polymer manufacture	35	66	5	0·70
Filament yarn	16	33	7	0·85
Beer	3	6	9	0·37
Bread	1	33	15	0·62
Detergent powder	20	—	2·5	0·74
Cement	10	40	9	0·77
Bricks	0·5	5	25	0·62
Steel production	33	—	5-10	0·80
Rolled steel products	80	—	8	0·82
Iron castings: cylinder blocks	1	—	10	0·80
" " small engineering castings	0·2	—	5	0·86
Cars: one model	25	—	6	—
range of models	50	—	6	0·82
Aircraft: one type	>100	—	20	0·68
Machine tools: models	>100	—	5	0·86
Diesel engines: models	10	—	4	0·86
Turbo generators	100	—	approx. 5	0·86
Electric motors	60	—	15	0·74
Domestic electric appliances: range of 10 models	20	50	8	0·84
Electronic capital goods	100	—	8	—
Footwear (factory)	0·2	—	2	0·93
Newspapers	30	100	20	0·51
Plastic (single product)	100	—	substantial	—

Sources:
    Columns (1), (2), (3) from C. F. Pratten, *Economies of Scale in Manufacturing Industry*, University of Cambridge, Department of Applied Economics, Occasional Papers, no. 28 (Cambridge University Press, 1971).
    Column (4) from Z. A. Silberston, 'Economies of Scale in Theory and Practice', *E.J.* 82 (special issue, 1972), pp. 369–91.

(e) The length of production runs

A further dimension of scale at the plant level which does not enter explicitly into the usual treatment of economies of scale is the total planned output of the product.[11] This is important in all cases where

[11] A. Alchian, 'Costs and Outputs', in M. Abramovitz *et al.*, *Allocation of Economic Resources: Essays in Honor of B. F. Haley* (Stanford, 1959), 23–40, has incorporated both learning effects (see next section) and the length of production runs in a formal analysis of costs.

TABLE 2.3

Industry	MES as % of U.S. market	MES as % of U.K. market	% increase in costs at 1/3 MES
Brewing	3·5	9·2	5·0
Cigarettes	6·5	30·3	2·2
Fabrics	0·2	1·8	7·6
Paints	1·4	10·2	4·4
Petroleum refining	1·9	11·6	4·8
Shoes	0·2	0·6	1·5
Glass bottles	1·5	9·0	11·0
Cement	1·7	6·1	26·0
Steel	2·6	15·4	11·0
Bearings	1·4	4·4	8·0
Refrigerators	14·1	83·3	6·5
Storage batteries	1·9	13·0	4·6

From F. M. Scherer *et al., The Economics of Multiplant Operation* (Harvard University Press, 1975), Table 3.11, p. 80 and Table 3.15, p. 94.

a major part of costs is a fixed initial cost which can be spread across all subsequent output. A longer production run means lower cost. This may enter the normal average cost curve if higher output per time period is associated with greater *total* production. But it need not, and so merits separate consideration, not least because the effect is well understood by businessmen and affects their pricing of various product lines. Examples include book publishing, where the major cost is type-setting, so that unit costs depend critically on the number of copies made. A similar situation prevails in the car industry and engineering sectors, where design and tooling-up costs are substantial, and long production runs help to keep unit costs down. An extension to the basic idea is that long production runs may permit a change of technique. Small production runs may be produced on a job-lot basis, involving relatively unspecialized plant and a good deal of labour. Larger runs may permit the use of specialized tools and altogether greater automation in a production line. And there will be associated gains from learning by doing.

In some cases the gains from longer production runs have to be set against the costs of maintaining larger average inventories. The inventory analysis set out above for stocks of materials can be interpreted to fit the case. Let Q be the demand for the output in question, and let $a + bD$ be the cost of production for a run of length D (i.e. a is the fixed cost and b the unit cost). Then the optimal run length is given by

$$D^* = \sqrt{\frac{2aQ}{k}}$$

We note that the optimal run length increases as the square root of the fixed costs, and inversely with the cost of holding inventories, k.

Scherer *et al.*[12] found length of production run to be a significant source of economies in four of the twelve industries they studied: fabric weaving, shoes, antifriction bearings, and refrigerators.

(f) Learning effects

Cost engineers have long been aware that the efficiency of a plant increases over time, as the work force becomes more skilled by repetition in performing the same manual tasks. This phenomenon of the 'learning curve' was first quantified for the aircraft industry.[13] The level of labour produtivity in manufacture of airframes at a point in time is a function of the cumulative number of airframes of a given model that have been made previously. The relationship could be approximated by,

$$\log m = a + b \log N$$

where m is labour input, N is the cumulative number of airframes made in the plant. a and b are constants with $b < o$.

Subsequent studies have shown that a similar improvement in productivity occurs in a large number of situations.[14] Baloff[15] has emphasized that the 'learning' phenomenon is not confined to increases in labour productivity. It occurs in such capital intensive sectors as steel, basic paper products, glass containers, and the *automated* manufacture of electrical conductor and electrical switching components. He stresses the improvement of cognitive skills by the engineers who run the place, rather than manual skills: every new plant has a 'start-up' period when the engineers are learning to oper-

---

[12] Scherer *et al.* op. cit.

[13] A. Alchian, 'Reliability of Progress Curves in Airframe Production', *Econometrica*, 31 (1963), 679–93.

[14] See, for examples, L. Rapping, 'Learning and World War II Production Functions', *R. Econ. Stats.*, 47 (1965), 81–6, on shipbuilding; L. E. Preston, E. C. Keachie, 'Cost Functions and Progress Functions: an Integration', *A.E.R.* 54 (1964), 100–7, on radar equipment; and L. Dudley, 'Learning and Productivity Change in Metal Products', *A.E.R.* 62 (1972), 662–9, on metal products.

[15] H. Baloff, 'The Learning Curve: Some Controversial Issues', *J.I.E.* 14 (1965–6), 275–82.

ate it. He also shows that learning effects are not continuous, as the above model would suggest: learning effects diminish and die out after a certain cumulative output is reached. Finally he notes that the value of b varies between products and processes, even in the same industry. Alchian,[16] for example, shows that the learning process is far from uniform for airframes; there is a different b value in each case.

2 ECONOMIES OF SCALE AND THE FIRM

Examination of economies of scale at the plant level omits many attributes of real firms. Common to all firms, of whatever size and complexity, is management; and most larger firms will involve multiplant operations and vertical integration of plants. It was Bain[17] who first drew attention to the existence of multiplant operations in many manufacturing sectors, and inquired whether this phenomenon was attributable to further scale economies, not available to a single plant firm. The costs of management were introduced into the theory of long-run costs by Kaldor,[18] and provided a rationalization for the assumption of U-shaped long-run average cost curves so necessary for the perfect competition model. We must now look at these matters in more detail.

(a) Multiplant operations

The economics of multiplant operations has been greatly illuminated by the work of F. M. Scherer *et al.*[19] They present evidence on the existence of multiplant operations in 155 U.S. manufacturing sectors in 1963. This is reproduced in Table 2.4. It is notable that single plant operations are exceptional, and that in more than half the sectors the average leading firm has more than four plants. Scherer *et al.* give a number of reasons for the existence of multiplant operations, arising from the cost side of a firm's operation.

The first arises from the existence of dispersed geographical markets and significant transport costs in delivering the product to those markets, and has been the subject of detailed analysis by location theorists.[20] Here we present a very simple illustration. In Figure 2.2 we separate unit production costs and unit transportation costs, on the assumption that the firm pays the latter. Production

[16] Alchian, op. cit. (1963).   [17] Bain, op. cit.
[18] N. Kaldor, 'The Nature of the Firm', *E.J.* 44 (1934), 60–76.
[19] Scherer *et al.*, op. cit.
[20] M. Beckmann, *Location Theory* (New York, 1968), Chap. 3.

TABLE 2.4

Total number of plants operated by 4 leading firms	Number of industries with indicated level of multiplant operations
4	2
5–8	26
9–16	46
17–32	47
33–80	25
over 80	9
Mean	28·3
Median	18·4

From Scherer *et al.*, *The Economics of Multiplant Operations* (Harvard University Press, 1975), Table 5.1, p. 176.

costs of a single plant in the long run are shown by *LRPC*, which slopes downwards reflecting the economies of scale at plant level discussed in the previous section. Unit transport costs (*UTC*) are shown as rising with output. As more is produced so more distant markets are served and hence unit transport costs rise.

Following Scherer *et al.*, this can be demonstrated for the case of a plant with market share S, serving a circular market area of radius R with uniform demand density D per square mile, and freight rate of T. Consider the market at radius r. The demand arising at this radius is $2\pi r.D.S.dr$. The transport cost per unit is Tr. So

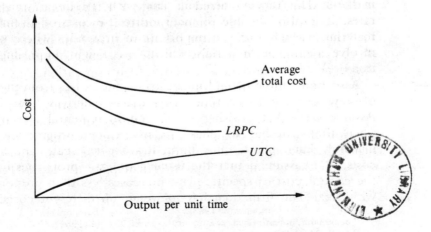

Fig. 2.2

transportation cost is given by $2\pi D.S.Tr^2.dr$. Over a circular market of radius R, transport costs are given by

$$\tau(R) = \int_0^R 2\pi DS\,Tr^2 dr = \tfrac{2}{3}\pi DS\,TR^3$$

Total sales of the good, Q, are given by

$$Q = SD\pi R^2$$

(i.e. the demand density times the market area). Substituting for R in the transport cost equation, gives transport cost per unit as

$$UTC = \frac{\tau(Q)}{Q} = \frac{2T\sqrt{Q}}{3\sqrt{SD\pi}}$$

This is clearly an increasing function of output Q, though less than proportionately so. Combining the production and transport costs gives an average total cost curve that is U-shaped. Clearly a firm will minimize costs by locating an optimal plant in each of the regional markets with sufficient demands to warrant it. The number of such plants will be larger (for a given demand), the less the plant economies of scale and the higher the transport costs. This simple model can be extended (with difficulty) to the optimal location and outputs of a number of plants owned by one firm, in geographical markets with varying demands and with non-linear transportation rates. It is also possible to incorporate the costs of assembling raw materials, which may be important in industries where processing involves heavy raw materials, which 'lose weight' in production (e.g. iron ore).[21]

A second source of multiplant economies arises from the addition of new capacity over time. The analysis derives from Manne.[22] Assume a market growing at a given incremental rate over time. Then the firm has to phase its investment programme to meet demand. Each plant, once built, has a given scale, and associated costs. It is assumed that the usual geometric properties imply that the capital cost of specific plant increases less than proportionately with size. The firm then has to weigh up different costs. Assume

[21] Beckmann, op. cit., Chap. 2.
[22] A. S. Manne, *Investments for Capacity Expansion* (London, 1967 and Cambridge, Mass., 1967).

initially that the firm must always meet demand. Then it can choose between frequent additions to capacity at small scale, or less frequent additions at large scale. The former reduces the degree of excess capacity that is borne on average by the firm, but this is offset by higher per unit capital costs. Less frequent additions imply that much capacity will lie idle, having been constructed in advance of demand. Scherer *et al.* formulate the problem as follows. Let the demand increase in absolute amounts of G per annum. The firm is deciding what size plant to install now, to last for T years, i.e. with capacity GT. At the end of T years, $2T$ years, $3T$ years . . . similar additions to capacity will be made. The firm chooses T so as to minimize the present value of the capital costs. The cost of a plant is a function, $f(GT)$, of installed capacity, GT. Let $C(G,T)$ be the present value of capital costs. Then at time T the firm is faced with precisely the same pattern of costs from subsequent investments. So we may write

$$C(G,T) = f(G,T) + C(G,T)e^{-rT}$$

where r is the discount rate, applied continuously.

$$\therefore C(G,T) = \frac{f(GT)}{1 - e^{-rT}}$$

Further analysis requires a specific function for $f(GT)$. Using the evidence of Haldi and Whitcomb noted above, Scherer *et al.* substitute:

$$f(GT) = \alpha(GT)^{\beta}$$

where $\beta \leqslant 1$ is the scale parameter. Differentiating $C(G,T)$ with respect to T we derive an expression for minimizing investment cost:

$$\beta = \frac{\hat{T}re^{-r\hat{T}}}{1 - e^{-r\hat{T}}}$$

where $\hat{T}$ is the optimum investment cycle time. Numerical methods give values of $\hat{T}$ for varying scale economy parameters, β and discount rates, r (see Figure 2.3). In general, increasing values of r and β lead to shorter investment cycle periods and hence smaller plants.

A similar methodology can be applied to more complex and

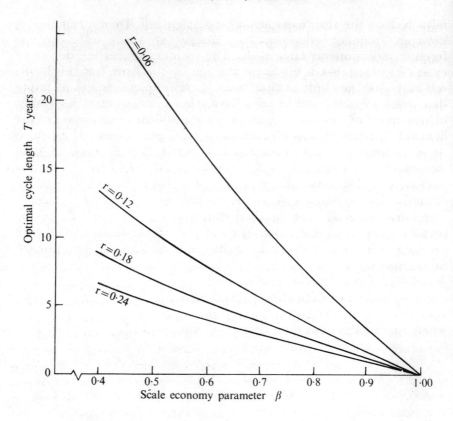

Fig. 2.3 Source: F. M. Scherer *et al., The Economics of Multiplant Operations*
(Harvard University Press, 1975), p. 39.

realistic cases (Manne). For example, scale economies in production
costs as well as capital costs can be incorporated; the growth of the
market can be exponential rather than in absolute increments: and
the possibility of capacity deficits can be allowed, with a penalty
cost for failure to supply. This penalty cost is presumably to be
interpreted either as consumer dissatisfaction, or as the cost of obtaining supplies from other producers. If it is low there is an incentive to extend the length of the cycle. However such an analysis
assumes that there is some sort of agreement on investment phasing
between firms in the sector, together with agreements to trade
excess supplies to meet other firms' capacity deficits. Finally the
analysis may introduce location as an additional variable. Deficits
in one region can be made up by supplies from an excess capacity
plant in another region, incurring the cost penalty of the freight

rate. Manne has shown that complex investment phasing with inter-regional product flows can bring substantial cost savings over the 'naive' approach of treating each region separately.

A third reason for multiplant operation is to achieve product specialization in different plants. The advantages of so doing are fully described in sections 1(e) and 1(f) above, and may be sufficient to offset the cost disadvantage of smaller plants. The reasons for product diversification itself must be sought in the markets rather than on the cost side of a firm's operations. For example a benefit may be derived from operating in markets in which the pattern of returns is not correlated, or inversely correlated. The effect of this is to reduce the variance of the firm's total returns, and so reduce risks. This argument is examined in detail in the context of conglomerate mergers in Chapter 14.

Finally, it is argued that multiplant firms have more flexibility in their operations. This can contribute to lower costs (compared to single plant firms) in a number of ways. First, fluctuations in output between plants can be offsetting (unless transport costs are very large), so that a breakdown in one plant can be met by the supplies from the others. This reduces the level of inventories that is necessary to avoid supply shortages. Second, as Patinkin showed,[23] the multiplant firm can respond to reductions in demand by closing down high cost plants, and running the remainder at full capacity. Independent producers with the same plants would tend to keep all of them open, operating at less than capacity. The force of this argument depends critically on the shape of the *SRAC* function. If it is 'tightly' U-shaped, then the gains can be substantial.

Scherer *et al.* made an intensive study of multiplant operations in twelve sectors in six nations. The results they present are based both on quantitative analysis, and on interview data from 125 companies in the 12 sectors. They carry out a further regression analysis on 155 U.S. census industries with published data only. The latter suggests three variables explain much of the multiplant operations in the top four firms in each sector: economies of scale, transportation costs for the finished product, and the size of the market. While the first two of these can be related directly to the theory, the size of the market has no obvious interpretation, other than the fact that larger markets (in terms of the number of plants of *MES* that could serve the market) mean that large firms will have more plants. But this says nothing about the cost (or market) advantages of large multiplant firms in these cases. The analysis is confirmed by cross-section

[23] Don Patinkin, 'Multiple-Plant Firms, Cartels and Imperfect Competition', *Q.J.E.* 61 (1947), 173–205.

analysis of the twelve sectors in six countries. A typical regression result is:

$$MPO_3 = 4 \cdot 35 - 0 \cdot 312 * COST + 0 \cdot 342 * TRANS + 0 \cdot 0533 ** SIZE$$
$$ (2 \cdot 31) \qquad\qquad (4.17) \qquad\qquad (11 \cdot 59)$$
$$R^2 = 0 \cdot 698$$

*significant at 0·05 level, **at 0·01 level: t-statistics in parentheses. (See Scherer *et al.*, pp. 226–7.)

MPO_3 is average number of plants operated per firm in 1970 by the three leading firms in a sector in a given country, COST is the percentage increase in costs at one third of MES, TRANS is the transportation cost per dollar of f.o.b. mill product value on a haul of 350 miles, and SIZE is the number of MES plants that could have provided for domestic consumption in a given country in 1967.

Perhaps the most interesting contribution of the book is the summary of the interview evidence from firms. On the basis of this the authors present the very tentative estimates of multiplant economies in the twelve sectors reproduced in Table 2.5.

We should note that these estimates include a number of advantages of size that are not connected with *multiplant* operations

TABLE 2.5

	Number of MES plants needed to have not more than a slight* handicap	Share of U.S. market in 1967: %	Average market share of leading 3 U.S. firms in 1970
Beer	3–4	10–14	13
Cigarettes	1–2	6–12	23
Fabric weaving	3–6	1	10
Paints	1	1·4	9
Petroleum	2–3	4–6	8
Shoes	3–6	1	6
Glass bottles	3–4	4–6	22
Cement	1	2	7
Ordinary steel	1	3	14
Bearings	3–5	4–7	14
Refrigerators	4–8	14–20	21
Batteries	1	2	18

Source: F. M. Scherer *et al.*, *The Economics of Multiplant Operations* (Harvard University Press, 1975), p. 336.
*'Slight' is defined as a 2% cost disadvantage.

specifically. Advantages such as advertising, access to distribution channels, larger R and D departments, favour large size, and large size then *implies* multiplant operation.

(b) Vertical integration

Vertical relations between firms can take a number of forms, of which complete integration is only one. Stigler[24] suggested that the degree of integration was determined by the size of the industry. When the industry is small many production services are provided on a small-scale basis within each firm. However as the scale of the industry expands, it may be possible for these services to be provided by independent firms with consequent economies of scale and specialization. The end of such a process would be a large number of relatively small firms each performing a separate role in the production process. Efficiency here is related to the size of the industry, not the size of the firm. Stigler suggests that such relations between firms will require a common location (to keep transport costs low) and he thus explains the phenomenon of regional 'swarming', such as is observed in the automobile industry. Stigler never suggested that relationships of the kind described were anything other than normal market relations. However, Richardson[25] and Blois[26] have drawn attention to the existence of relationships that go beyond the usual market transaction, yet stop short of full integration. All the examples imply some long-term commitment on the part of buyer and seller: they include long-term supply contracts, the co-ordination of supplies by major retailers, and co-operation on technology and product design. Some of these commitments are so closely defined and monitored, that they amount to vertical integration in all but legal form. The distinction is presumably that at some stage the contracts will run out, and at that point either buyer or seller could find another partner. Explanations of vertical integration fall into two categories. The more traditional explanations centre on the supply conditions for essential inputs. More recent work has emphasized the cost of transacting, rather than the price of the inputs themselves.

We distinguish a number of facets of the traditional arguments. The first is those cases where vertical integration leads directly to reductions in operating costs (e.g. the saving of fuel for reheating metal where the various stages of manufacture in iron and steel products are concerned), or the saving of transport costs by locating

[24] G. J. Stigler, 'The Division of Labour is Limited by the Extent of the Market', *J.P.E.* 59 (1951), 185-93.

[25] G. B. Richardson, 'The Organization of Industry', *E.J.* 82 (1972), 883-96.

[26] K. J. Blois, 'Vertical Quasi-Integration', *J.I.E.* 20 (1971-2), 253-72.

two vertically integrated processes in the same plant. A second set of cost advantages has been described by Oi and Hurter.[27] They see 'backwards' integration into input sectors as a method to secure the price, where the input supply is monopolized with a monopoly price set. It is then in the interests of the firm to produce its own input, so long as it can do so for less than the monopoly price. The oddity about this possibility is the lack of competition in the supplying sector. If the firm itself can enter the input-supplying sector with its own relatively small demand, what is the barrier to another firm entering to supply a number of such firms, and thus obtain scale economies? Adelman[28] suggests that this situation may arise through lags in the growth of supply of input, when output demand is growing strongly. The firm in the output sector can see demand growing and is afraid of input supply bottlenecks, which firms in that sector will exploit by raising price. In the absence of futures markets for the inputs, vertical integration or co-ordinated planning may be the solution. The securing of quality of supply by vertical integration meets a similar objection: why can it be achieved only by this means? The firm will also wish to ensure a steady flow of essential inputs. If the fluctuations in the price of inputs are due to real changes in the supply position (e.g. climatic effects on supply of an agricultural raw material), vertical integration will not protect the firm. But if price fluctuations arise from inelastic supplies and demand variability, leading to elements of monopoly in the supply price, the vertically integrated firm need not take any account of the variable rent element in its own costings. Vertical integration may also be motivated by the desire to avoid 'foreclosure' by a rival, who obtains control of the supply position and then refuses to supply. In the long run an alternative supplier would emerge, but the damage to other firms may be substantial in the interim. So each firm vertically integrates to secure its own supply position against its rivals. In each of these cases, then, there is a failure of markets to supply profitable outputs. The reason for vertical integration is not market failure of the monopoly kind, but rather that the firms supplying the output are the most likely to see the profit opportunities in the input sector, and thus respond to them. There are no *cost* savings which could not be obtained by a strictly 'market' solution, without vertical integration. Indeed agreements and co-ordination between

[27] W. Y. Oi, A. P. Hurter Jnr., *Economics of Private Truck Transportation* (New York, 1965), Chapter 2, 31–67. Reprinted in B. S. Yamey (ed.), *The Economics of Industrial Structure* (Harmondsworth, 1973).

[28] M. A. Adelman, 'Concept and Statistical Measurement of Vertical Integration', in N.B.E.R., *Business Concentration and Price Policy* (Princeton, 1955).

firms at the two stages could eliminate the need for integration altogether. A third cost advantage from vertical integration can arise in the case of 'forward integration' by a monopolist supplier (A) of an input into a competitive output sector (X). The analysis has been developed by Vernon and Graham[29] and by Schmalensee.[30] If X uses fixed coefficients in production, then there are no gains from vertical integration. The demand for A is a derived demand from that for X. All monopoly elements in the situation are already exploited by A. Suppose, however, that there is substitution in production of X between the input A and all other inputs. Then we can follow the analysis presented by Vernon and Graham, in Figure 2.4. The output

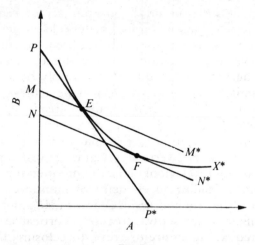

Fig. 2.4

of X is X^*, shown by the appropriate isoquant. Before vertical integration, with a monopoly price for A, the price line is PP^* and production is at E. The actual marginal cost of A gives the price line MM^*, so PM is the profit accruing to the supplier of A (in terms of B). After integration, the single firm produces at F, basing its decision on the marginal cost of A. It has substituted more A for B in production, and its costs are correspondingly lower (shown by NN^*). Assuming that output remains at X^*, there will be an additional profit equivalent to MN (in terms of B). While this analysis is technically correct, there is some doubt as to its empirical relevance. Scherer *et al.*[31] reported that fixed coefficients in production tend

[29] J. M. Vernon, D. A. Graham, 'Profitability of Monopolization by Vertical Integration', *J.P.E.* 79 (1971), 924–5.
[30] R. Schmalensee, 'A Note on the Theory of Vertical Integration', *J.P.E.* 81 (1973), 442–9.
[31] F. M. Scherer *et al.*, op. cit., 130.

to be dictated by the available capital equipment.

A fourth case where integration *may* affect costs arises in bilateral monopoly, when a monopoly supplier of an input A faces a monopsonist buyer who is engaged in the manufacture of X. In Figure 2.5, MC is the marginal cost curve of the supplier of A, and MR is

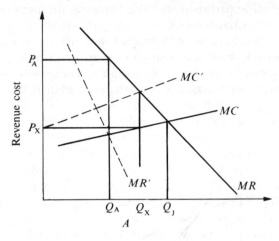

Fig. 2.5

the marginal revenue product of A in the manufacture of X. To the buyer of A, MC is the *average* cost curve, and hence MC' is the marginal supply price. He equates MC' to his MR, and seeks to purchase the quantity Q_X at supply price P_X. The seller of A, on the other hand, views MR as his *average* revenue curve, so that MR' is his marginal revenue. As a monopolist he seeks to equate MR' to MC, implying an offer of Q_A at price P_A. The actual outcome *if they bargain myopically* will lie in between these, depending on their relative bargaining strengths. If, however, they were integrated as a single firm, the relevant behaviour curves would be MR and MC, leading to joint output Q_J where $MC = MR$, hence greatly enhanced profits. Unless A is produced under constant costs, the actual costs of production will change with integration. However, as Machlup and Taber have indicated, if the two separate firms bargain about price *and* quantity, they should reach the joint profit maximizing position without integration being necessary. The only indeterminacy arises in the division of profits between them: perhaps this would be most easily resolved by integration! But we can safely dismiss the myopic case as a curiosity.

We note in passing that traditional arguments for vertical integration *only* hold up when there is an element of cost saving involved.

All the arguments based on the idea that integration will permit the capture of monopoly profits can be shown to falter (Bork,[32] Comanor[33]), as we have suggested. Hence our treatment of vertical integration from the viewpoint of costs. This does not exclude the possibility that vertical integration will be important as a means of expansion and diversification by the growing or merging firm (see Part III, especially Chapter 14).

More recent explanations of vertical integration have concentrated on the comparison of relationships between firms mediated entirely by markets with relationships involving some sort of co-ordination. The basic query concerning the nature of the firm was raised in a seminal article by Coase.[34] If the price mechanism is the co-ordinator of economic activity *par excellence*, why do firms exist as centres of organization by management? Coase argued that there are costs of using the price mechanism, notably information and contract costs. Forming a firm and giving the entrepreneur power to act, within defined limits, as co-ordinator of production, can save some of these costs. The limit to the size of firms is then the efficiency of the entrepreneur: as the number of transactions increases, so the efficiency of the manager in allocation and co-ordination of tasks decreases.

Williamson[35] has developed this argument in more detail, by specifying the precise transactions that are involved. He distinguishes between static analysis, and dynamic analysis with uncertainty introduced. The first case is that of vertical relationships between two stages of production in basically static markets, as envisaged in the traditional models of vertical integration described above. There are some transactions costs involved in arranging contracts between the parties, but once this is done no further costs are involved. In this case there is little saving in transaction costs from vertical integration.

In the second case we introduce dynamic uncertainties. In the absence of futures markets for all relevant goods, contracts are inevitably incomplete. A once-for-all contract would have to specify all future contingencies, and would be impossible to negotiate. The

---

[32] R. H. Bork, 'Vertical Integration and Monopoly', in B. S. Yamey (ed.), op. cit., Reading 17, 263–9.
[33] W. S. Comanor, 'Vertical Mergers, Market Power and the Anti-Trust Laws', *A.E.R.* 57 (1967), 254–65.
[34] R. H. Coase, 'The Nature of the Firm', in A.E.A., *Readings in Price Theory* (London, 1953).
[35] O. E. Williamson, 'The Vertical Integration of Production: Market Failure Considerations', *A.E.R. Papers and Proceedings*, 51 (1971), 112–23; 'Markets and Hierarchies: Some Elementary Considerations', *A.E.R. Papers and Proceedings*, 53 (1973), 316–25.

alternative is a series of short-term contracts. But these would not enable the supplier to be sure about his long-run investment plans. And the first supplier might obtain advantages due to experience which would make renegotiation difficult. Vertical integration would reduce transactions costs by eliminating the need to make contracts of this kind. A further difficulty with market transactions in this situation is 'strategic misrepresentation risk'. One firm may not be able to decide whether another has fulfilled its terms of the contract, *after* the event, because information is not available to it. A particular case is that of a contract for an input the final cost or performance of which is subject to technological uncertainty. In so far as the supplier can shift the risk to the buyer, for example by means of a cost-plus contract, he has then lost the incentive to minimize cost or otherwise maintain performance. Vertical integration can reduce this risk of 'moral hazard', by providing for detailed supervision of the project.

Unfortunately there is very little evidence on the cost savings arising from integration. The phenomenon has received little systematic attention empirically. Adelman[36] suggested two ways in which the degree of vertical integration could be measured. The first is the ratio of income to sales, where income reflects the value added in processing. For the firm this ratio depends on how 'close' it is to primary production. Consider an industry with three firms in primary production, manufacturing, and distribution, each stage contributing one-third of value added. Then the index would have values 1·0, 0·5, and 0·33 for the three firms. The index for an industry is similarly biased by 'nearness' to primary production, but also reflects the number of stages in production undertaken in separate firms. A vertically disintegrated industry will have high sales figures (reflecting inter-firm sales) compared to an integrated industry with the same value added. Hence the integrated sector will have a higher index. A second index proposed by Adelman is the ratio of inventory to sales. The reasoning is that the longer the production line, the greater the stocks of work in progress (between production processes) within the vertically integrated firm. This index is not 'distorted' by nearness to primary production. Adelman presented values of the index for sectors of the U.S. economy in 1939 and 1947, but without a systematic analysis. The topic has been neglected since, except for *ad hoc* analyses of particular sectors where vertical integration is a feature of the market structure.

---

[36] Adelman, op. cit. (1955).

(c) Management costs

Alchian and Demsetz[37] have emphasized that the essential feature of co-ordination within firms is not 'fiat' management, but rather the 'team' use of inputs. The essence of team production is that several types of resources are used, the product is not the sum of the separable outputs of each competing resource, and not all resources are contributed by one person. The jointness of resources in production immediately leads to a problem. There is always an incentive for one member of the team to shirk, or to take non-pecuniary benefits, since the reduction in output will be a loss which will fall on all members of the team and not just on himself. Williamson[38] links this particuarly to the problems of information, and moral hazard. A new member of a team may misrepresent his abilities and hence ask for a higher reward than his productivity would really warrant, and then account for a poor performance in terms of some difficulty of the work rather than his own qualities. Hence there is a need for someone within the organization to monitor performance by each member of the team, and make sure that each one is rewarded according to his productivity. In the classical firm, the monitor is the entrepreneur himself. He makes contracts with the team members, and has the right to terminate them. He is the residual claimant on the surplus of the firm after all team members have been paid, and hence is self-disciplining. In Kaldor's analysis[39] of the firm it is the limits to the capacity of the entrepreneur which lead to increasing costs in the long run. However two features of modern firms undermine this conclusion. The first is that the entrepreneur is replaced by the manager in the typical firm. He is responsible to the shareholders, and hence his performance is monitored by them: the threat is that he will lose his position if his performance is unsatisfactory. The second is that there is no reason why such an organization should not employ many managers. This leads directly to the idea of a hierarchy in the organizational structure of the firm. Each set of managers is in turn monitored by a manager at the next level in the hierarchy. The question is then whether such a hierarchical pattern of control by management will lead to increasing costs.

Williamson's model[40] assumes a strict hierarchy of management in the firm, with a constant 'span of control', S at each level. Thus the top manager has S immediate subordinates, who in their turn have

---

[37] A. Alchian, H. Demsetz, 'Production, Information Costs and Economic Organization', *A.E.R.* 62 (1972), 777–95.

[38] O. E. Williamson, 'Hierarchical Control and Optimum Firm Size', *J.P.E.* 75 (1967), 123–38.

[39] Kaldor, op. cit.   [40] Williamson, op. cit.

s subordinates reporting to them, and so on. Starbuck[41] observes that such a strict hierarchy is probably too formalized, but he accepts it as a reasonable first approximation. The task of the hierarchy is to transmit orders down to the lowest level (and to receive information back),[42] but we assume that only the proportion α of such orders are actually transmitted at each stage in the hierarchy. Such a cumulative information loss has been observed in psychological experiments on the transmission of messages along a chain of command. The only 'productive' workers are those at the lowest level, and output is in direct proportion to their effective number (there are no economies of scale or other inputs). The qualification, 'effective', refers to the loss in control down the hierarchy, which reduces the amount of useful work that they do. Thus if there are n levels in the firm, there will be S^{n-1} workers. But they will only receive α^{n-1} of the instructions from the top management level, so that their *effective* work is only $(\alpha S)^{n-1}$, and output is $(\alpha S)^{n-1}$ assuming a one-to-one relation of effective input to output.

The workers are paid a basic wage w_o. At successively higher levels in the hierarchy the wage increases by a proportion β. Thus the top manager receives $w_o \beta^{n-1}$. Total cost is given by summing wage costs at each level of the hierarchy.

Consider an n-level hierarchy firm: then total output Q is given by

$$Q = (\alpha S)^{n-1}$$

The wage costs for this output is given by C

$$C = \sum_{i=1}^{n} w_o \beta^{n-i} S^{i-1}$$

i.e. at each level, i, we multiply the wage (salary) appropriate to that level, $w_o \beta^{n-i}$, by the number of managers at that level in the hierarchy, S^{i-1}. Observe that the levels are numbered from the top down-

[41] W. H. Starbuck, 'Organizational Growth and Development', in J. G. March (ed.), *Handbook of Organizations* (Chicago, 1964).

[42] M. J. Beckmann, 'Management Production Functions and the Theory of the Firm', *J. Econ. Th.* 14 (1977), 1–18, has analysed a model in which each level of the hierarchy is characterized by a production function. Supervision from the next higher level combines with management at a given level to 'produce' supervision of the level below. Given the salary structure, the span of control is determined endogenously rather than given as in Williamson's model and in Beckmann's earlier contribution ('Some Aspects of Returns to Scale in Business Administration', *Q.J.E.* 74 (1960), 464–71).

wards, so that the top manager is level 1 and the workers are level n. By appropriate summation of terms we obtain

$$C = w_o \frac{S^n - \beta^n}{S - \beta}$$

So average cost:[43]

$$\frac{C}{Q} = \frac{w_o}{S - \beta} \cdot \frac{S^n - \beta^n}{\alpha^{n-1} S^{n-1}} = \frac{w_o}{1 - \beta/S} \cdot \frac{1}{\alpha^{n-1}} \left[1 - (\beta/S)^n \right]$$

We may now examine the behaviour of average cost as the scale of the enterprise increases, and hence the number of levels in the hierarchy. The first term is a constant. The second term describes the effect on average cost of control loss. Even if α is only slightly less than one, indicating some loss of effective operation, costs rise quite sharply as the size of the firm increases. Only if $\alpha = 1$, i.e. all instructions are perfectly passed down the hierarchy, does this effect not exist. The size of this effect on costs leads one to doubt the validity of the formulation. It is, for example, unlikely that a large corporation would accept a cumulative control loss of this kind without using alternative methods to ensure compliance. Techniques of control are more effective than the analysis would suggest.

The third term implies that average costs increase with size, as $(\beta/S)^n$ diminishes with n. However, empirical work suggests that this effect is unlikely to be very important. Williamson reports that the largest 500 corporations in the U.S. have a normal span in the range 5–10, while the average value of β is 1·3 to 1·6. Hence the value of $(\beta/S)^n$ rapidly diminishes with n. (Suppose $\beta/S = \frac{1}{5}$. Then for $n = 2$ average costs are 4% below the asymptotic value. For $n = 4$, the difference is less than $\frac{1}{5}$%).

Unfortunately only parts of this model can be regarded as established. There is good evidence on the span of control in companies. Starbuck[44] suggests that the model should include a separate span at

---

[43] This expression is similar to that obtained by Beckmann, though his analysis ignores control loss, so that in effect $\alpha = 1$. Williamson obtains the above expressions for output and cost in his analysis, but chooses to approximate cost by

$$w_o \frac{S^n}{S - \beta}$$

omitting the power function of β. He does not justify this procedure.
[44] Starbuck, op. cit.

the lowest level of operations: the span of control for operatives usually exceeds that for the managerial hierarchy above them. He also cites evidence to suggest that S increases with total employment. Larger corporations have a rather flatter hierarchy than small ones. Williamson presents evidence on β gathered from the salary structure of General Motors in a number of years, and shows that it is stable over time and that the wage hypothesis is supported by the data. Direct evidence on average costs is not easily available, but Starbuck reports a number of studies on the proportion of administrative workers to production workers. Suppose a $(n + 1)$ hierarchy firm with span of control S. Then the number of production workers (P) is S^n. The number of administration workers (A) is given by

$$A = 1 + S + S^2 + \ldots\ldots + S^{n-1}$$

$$= \frac{S^n - 1}{S - 1}$$

$$\text{So } \frac{A}{P} = \frac{1}{S-1}(1 - 1/S^n)$$

As n increases, A/P tends to the value $1/S-1$: and the approach to the limiting value is likely to be rapid for the normal span of control. This is confirmed by empirical studies reported by Starbuck, where A/P is shown to be constant for firm size greater than 100 (i.e. $n = 2$ or 3). One defect with the analysis remains the lack of strict empirical justification for the formulation of control loss and any direct empirical evidence as to how great it might be. Williamson infers, from the size of companies, that a value of about 0·9 for α could be about right. But this lacks independent confirmation. Nor does the analysis take into account Williamson's important work on organizational structures, which is discussed in Chapter 8. Two features of that analysis can be noted here. The efficiency of the organization can be affected both by the way in which functions are allocated within the firm, and by the method of monitoring performance. There is more to efficiency of organizations than the simple notions of control loss and hierarchy.

(d) X-efficiency

The discussion of management in the previous section leads naturally to a discussion of the degree to which managers can actually achieve efficiency in production. The assumption of production analysis is that the firm will operate on the frontier of efficient techniques, at a technique determined by least cost. This assumption was challenged in a seminal article by Leibenstein.[45] Collating evidence from diverse sources he concluded that many plants could operate more productively without any change in inputs. For example, a summary of I.L.O. productivity missions, mainly in developing countries, showed reductions, from simple reorganization of production without capital investment or technical progress, of more than 25% of costs. Similarly, Johnston[46] had reported on the very great improvements in output or reductions in cost resulting from the implementation of the recommendations of management consultants. Rostas,[47] in a comparison of productivity in the U.S. and U.K., had found identical technologies in use, but much higher output in the U.S. It is not easy to disentangle causal factors from this collection of evidence. 'Learning curves', and different qualities of management, could account for at least some of it. However, Leibenstein also postulated a further contributory cause, for which he coined the term 'X-efficiency', which depends on the internal and external motivation to the efficiency of the firm.

The analysis of internal motivation to efficiency begins with the fact that contracts for labour supply within the firm are incomplete. They do not include a specification of the job, so the effectiveness of the labour depends on the motivation to effort, within the plant. Leibenstein has made a number of further contributions[48] in an attempt to model this phenomenon. A simple example is shown in Figure 2.6. Assume that the worker is paid on a time basis, T_1, T_2, and T_3 reflecting three possible working periods. Within the plant the worker can undertake two activities, α and β. The firm would prefer the time to be allocated along the locus OV, which maximizes output (shown by isoquants Q_1, Q_2, Q_3). But the individual maximizes *his* utility by operating on the locus OU, since he has a preference for activity β (shown by the indifference curves I_1, I_2, I_3). Indeed, unless the firm can monitor the activities of the worker, it is along OU that he will operate.[49]

In fact, the individual's choice extends over a wider range of attributes, which Leibenstein summarizes as choice of activity,

[45] H. Leibenstein, 'Allocative Efficiency v. X-Efficiency', *A.E.R.* 56 (1966), 392–415.

[46] J. Johnston, 'The Productivity of Management Consultants', *J.R.S.S.* 126 (1963), Series A, Part 2, 237–49.

[47] L. Rostas, *Comparative Productivity in British and American Industry*, N.I.E.S.R. Research Paper 13 (Cambridge, 1964).

[48] H. Leibenstein, 'Organizational or Frictional Equilibria, X-Efficiency and the Rate of Innovation', *Q.J.E.* 83 (1969), 600–23.

[49] Leibenstein ('Aspects of the X-Efficiency Theory of the Firm', *Bell Journal*, 6 (1975), 580–606) has abandoned this analysis in later work, and has a much more complex set of behavioural/psychological postulates to explain the individual's action.

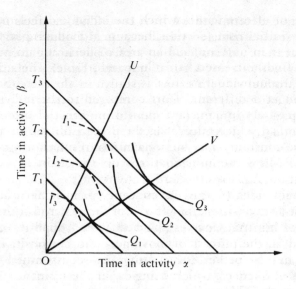

Fig. 2.6

pace, quality, and time spent, which together define an effort position. Associated with each effort position there is an associated productivity value and utility value. For exposition we reduce all the attributes to a single index of 'effort'. The utility of the individual is shown as a flat-topped curve in Figure 2.7, representing a

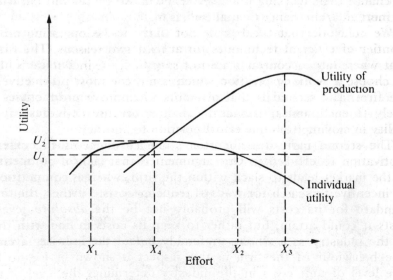

Fig. 2.7

wide range of efforts within which the individual feels comfortable. There is an initial rising section, because individuals like to do something rather than nothing, and an area of declining utility where the individual finds increased effort uncomfortable. The utility of the firm from the individual's effort is shown in the same diagram, with a maximum at a different effort compared to the individual utility curve. Hence only by constant monitoring can the firm induce that supply of effort which maximizes the firm's utility from production. It has to be constant, since any relaxation of monitoring when effort is at X_3 will allow the individual to relax his effort towards his preferred position, X_4.

Leibenstein adds to this his concept of 'inert areas'. Associated with each effort position is a set of work routines that the individual develops for himself. Once established at such a position, there will be disutility in the process of moving to another position, since the individual has to be dislodged from his accustomed routines. We represent the fixed cost of moving by the amount of utility U_2U_1 in the diagram. This defines for the individual a range of efforts X_1X_2, within which he will not wish to incur the disutility of moving to the maximum at X_4. This range is his 'inert area': even if he knows there is a better way of working he will not be bothered to make the move. We may now visualize a hierarchical structure within the firm, each level with its own 'inert area'. Every instruction passed down the hierarchy may require various levels to take some sort of action to change their working practices. The chance that it will fall within an inert area, and hence be nullified, is high.

We conclude that the firm is not likely to be operating on the frontier of efficient techniques for at least two reasons. The first is that where labour contracts are not specified, the individual is likely to choose a working position which is not the most productive for the firm. The second is that attempts to improve productivity are likely to encounter resistance to change, because of individual disutility in moving from one effort position to another.

The second part of Leibenstein's theory concerns the external motivation to efficiency. One argument is that lack of competition in the market leads to slack within the firm, whereas competition is an incentive to search for ways of reducing costs. Further, the firm's standard for its costs will probably not be the *absolute* level of costs it could attain, but rather to keep its costs in line with those of the industry as a whole, preferably *below* the industry average. The behaviour of the firm in this respect is shown in Figure 2.8. The level of unit costs in the industry determines the level of unit costs that the firm will seek in the current period. We may now sum

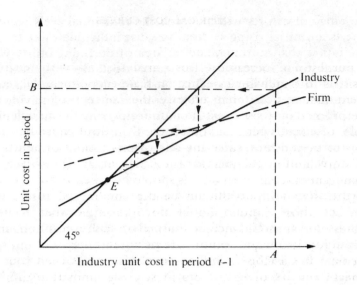

Fig. 2.8

the reaction curves of each firm, weighted by its output share, to obtain an industry curve. Suppose the industry starts with unit costs *OA*. Then at least some firms will have costs greater than this, and will reduce their costs, and hence the industry average, to *OB*. There will follow a number of subsequent cost reducing moves, including possibly the elimination of high cost firms, until the industry reaches equilibrium at *E*, when search for cost reduction will cease. That equilibrium level may represent a minimum cost point, but there is no reason to suppose that it must. If the sector is not particularly competitive, the pressure on firms will be less, and the cost reaction curve for each firm would be steeper, with a higher equilibrium cost level.

Unfortunately, none of these theoretical issues has received empirical confirmation. Leibenstein's constructs are plausible but not yet substantiated. Williamson[50] has proposed an alternative theory to explain the level of costs in non-competitive environments. He sees the managers of firms as deliberately creating costs to absorb profits in monopolistic environments. The nature of this expenditure is determined by the preferences of the managers. This idea receives further consideration in Chapter 8.

[50] O. E. Williamson, *The Economics of Discretionary Behaviour* (Chicago, 1967).

3 EMPIRICAL COST CURVES

(a) Costs in the long run

The purpose of empirical cost analysis, as with engineering analysis, is to search for evidence on scale economies. We recall the stringent assumptions that underly the concept of a cost curve, before proceeding to the question of measurement. The independent variable is output per unit time period: output must be constant during the period, otherwise the outcome is a trace of points on the *SRAC* curve and not a point on the *LRAC* at all. The output should be homogeneous. All observations should be taken from a given technology. Costs of inputs should be the same to all firms, and the quality of those inputs should not differ between them. The estimates of cost should include 'normal profits' on capital, including correct depreciation and appropriate risk premia.

Friedman[51] developed a theoretical critique of approaches to the measurements of economies of scale, demonstrating that even were accurate data available, the *LRAC* curve would be *in principle* non-observable. We start with a competitive industry. All firms are price takers and there is freedom of entry to the industry, ensuring that all costs represent the opportunity costs of factors and not monopoly rents, which would be difficult to identify. In a deterministic competitive model every firm in long-run equilibrium will be producing at the minimum point of its *LRAC*. By definition the cost curve will be identical for all firms, and thus all we can observe is a single output/cost combination. Every firm will have the same size and the same costs. Nor does it help if we allow factors to differ between firms. If one firm has a rather better factor, for example management, theory requires competitive bidding between firms for the use of that resource. The price of the resource will be bid up until its rent brings the costs of the firm up to the same level as the others. By definition there cannot be excess profits over 'normal'. Thus the competitive case saves us the trouble of distinguishing 'normal' or 'contractual' cost from monopoly profit, but leaves us with no information. Alternatively we may accept that the *LRAC* is L-shaped with a horizontal section beyond a minimum output. But then we obtain no more information than a scatter of points along the horizontal stretch of the curve.

Another possibility would be to retain the competitive model, but to assume that firms make errors in planning the scale of their

[51] M. Friedman, 'Comment', N.B.E.R. Business Concentration and Price Policy (Princeton, 1955), 230–7.

output. Suppose that a firm was below optimum size for this reason. Then the firm is making less than normal profits. However, in terms of accounting cost the firm will simply be earning a smaller gross profit. The assets of the firm will be automatically revalued at a lower asset value to reflect the lower gross profit. Total reported costs will just absorb revenue. Such cases could be identified in principle by deviations of the historical costs of assets (properly depreciated and allowing for inflation) from the current valuation. But this returns us to the problem of assessing 'normal' cost, which we hoped to avoid by examining the competitive case.

The third possibility is that the production function of the firm is not determinate, but stochastic, in that a given level of inputs (and hence constant level of total cost) gives a variable quantity of output. In production engineering such random fluctuations in output are regarded as normal. The outcome of observing such a situation would be that a given level of cost would be divided by varying amounts of output. The result would be a hyperbolic cost function with average cost falling with output. To describe this as economies of scale would be misleading.

The conclusion of Friedman's analysis is that to measure economies of scale we require a situation with a fragmented market and firms of different sizes (see Figure 2.9). But then we immediately introduce the possibility of monopoly profits and the difficulty

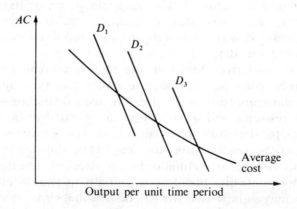

Fig. 2.9

of distinguishing those costs which are 'normal'. The problem is particularly acute where the firm revalues its assets on the basis of its monopoly position. Again a proper assessment of capital cost involves knowledge of the second-hand value of the assets.

With these difficulties in mind we turn to the problem of interpreting empirical cost data. The typical situation is shown in Figure
2.10. The analyst fits a regression line through a scatter of points.
The temptation is to identify this with the *LRAC* curve of the
firm. However it is a rule of interpretation that the deviations from
the regression line should be consistent with the hypotheses concerning the generation of the points.

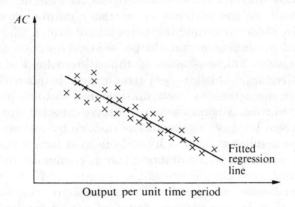

Output per unit time period

Fig. 2.10

The first interpretation is simply that we have made errors in
collecting the data. This simply reopens the whole question of
'normal' cost. Johnston[52] and Walters[53] emphasize the following
difficulties with the data:

(i) It is difficult to distinguish the element of 'monopoly' profit
in a reported profit figure. Even the theoretical exercise of arguing
towards 'normal' profit on the basis of historical cost minus depreciation is not possible where there have been price changes. A more
serious problem with historical cost data is that older firms may have
paid less than the new firms for their capital equipment (even if there
has been no change in technique in the interim) simply because of
inflation. A serious bias could be introduced if large firms happened
to be on average the older firms, and smaller firms the new ones.
The use of historical costs could give an entirely false impression of
scale economies.

(ii) Further pitfalls in firm cost data arise from the conventions
adopted in depreciating equipment. These may, for example, be

[52] J. Johnson, *Statistical Cost Analysis* (New York, 1960).
[53] A. A. Walters, 'Production and Cost Functions', *Econometrica*, 31 (1963), 1–66.

arranged to reap the advantages of tax allowances, and not reflect the economic life of the asset at all.

(iii) The firm may assign fixed cost on an output basis, so that all reported costs are calculated as variable costs.

(iv) Input costs may vary substantially between firms, leading to different cost structures.

(v) The firm may have specific factors whose rents are not fully imputed. It is common sense that differences in the efficiency of firms may arise from differences in the qualities of factors that they employ. And in pure theory we could still retrieve the situation by insisting that rents should be imputed to the more efficient factors. However, outside pure competition, the whole question becomes extremely arbitrary, since there may be no basis on which to do the imputation. Let us suppose that the efficient factor is a manager with more skill or more information than others. There is unlikely to be any · market valuation that can be put on his services. Even more difficult is the situation where a production advantage cannot be attributable to one particular factor, but is a feature of a complete bundle of resources. An example could be a factory with a good history of industrial relations. Again, full imputation is possible in theory, but extremely unlikely in practice. There are two reasons for this. The first is simply ignorance concerning the sources of efficiency. The second is that firms may deliberately decide not to pay rents for managerial efficiency. They may prefer to translate their efficiency into lower prices, thus giving themselves a competitive edge in the markets in which they operate.

If imputation does not occur, then we can expect systematic cost differences which are worth investigating for their own sakes. For example, if we are examining costs in coal mining, we must examine the environmental factors that give different real costs of production, such as depth of shaft and thickness of coal seams.[54]

The second interpretation of deviations from the regression line is derived from our awareness of the market situations in which firms operate. To get observations at all we must be observing a fragmented market. One possibility is that the firms absorb some monopoly profit potential by operating with a degree of slack on the cost side. Not being under any pressure, they are not forced to minimize costs. This may reflect 'X-efficiency', described earlier in the chapter, or the phenomenon of expense preference on the part of managers. Managers gain utility from expanding their staff, since

[54] C. B. Winsten, M. Hall, 'The Ambiguous Notion of Efficiency', *E.J.* 69 (1959), 71–86.

it enhances their personal prestige, and may increase their salary (indeed will do so if the hierarchy model of managers' remuneration is correct). So we may expect costs to be higher in monopoly situations because of the deliberate expense preference of managers.

If this interpretation of the deviations from the regression line is correct, we are clearly wrong in interpreting the line as the *LRAC* curve. Instead we should look for the lowest costs in each size class, assuming that all rents have been properly attributed to costs and that the data is accurate. It is the lower boundary of the scatter of points that will give us the minimum costs for each level of output.[55]

The third interpretation of the data is even more discouraging.[56] The implication of a *LRAC* curve is that if a small firm with high costs succeeds in expanding its capacity it will be able to emulate the cost performance of its larger rivals. This is based on the presumption that all factors are freely available and in elastic supply, so that every firm has the same cost opportunities. The alternative view is that every firm is a unique bundle of resources, with its own cost curve. Then the scatter of points could be interpreted as in Figure 2.11.

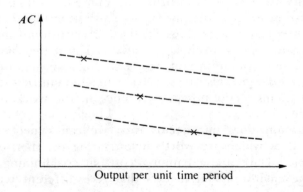

Fig. 2.11

The significance of this alternative hypothesis is not that large firms are more efficient, but that more efficient firms tend to get larger markets.

[55] See, for example, the work of C. B. Winsten, M. Hall, 'The Measurement of Economies of Scale', *J.I.E.* 9 (1961), 255–64, on scale and productivity in retailing. Average productivity increases with scale but the productivity of the most productive small shops exceeds that of the largest retailers.

[56] P. J. D. Wiles, *Price, Cost and Output*, 2nd edn. (Oxford, 1961), Chapter 12.

Finally, the plants in the industry may not be using a single vintage of technology, as the theory requires. There will always be lags in adjustment to new technology, which may themselves have an economic rationale: as Salter[57] emphasized, old vintages will continue to be operated so long as they earn some quasi-rents. The discussion cannot be complete without an investigation of the diffusion of process innovations in the sector over time.

Apart from the issue of interpretation of the data, we note that the attempt at measurement raises the question of scale. We are seldom able to observe costs in a plant making a homogeneous output at a constant rate over a unit time period. Where outputs are heterogeneous, output must be valued in value terms, not in physical terms. This raises all the usual problems of valuation. We have noted that a 'monopolistic' situation is essential to obtain a spread of output observations. But then similar physical outputs may have different values dependent on whether they are sold in more or less competititve markets. If one is to adjust cost to exclude abnormal profits one must adjust prices too. All outputs should be given a common value.

In practice the scale of the firm may vary not in final output but in the degree of vertical integration, or depth in production. This can be incorporated by using value added as the measure of output (subject once again to the problem of valuation). But the danger of this procedure is that one may not be comparing like with like. Similar value added may indicate either deeper production or expansion of scale at one level of the production process. One would not expect these to have the same cost structure. Finally, an increase in scale for a firm may reflect an increase of a number of plants of a given size or one larger plant. A good example is retailing, where expansion may be via a chain of shops or by increasing the size of a large store. Clearly these represent alternative aspects of scale, and comparisons between the two will be of little value.

The main results of cost curve analysis were summarized by Johnston[58] and Walters[59] and there has been little work on them since (perhaps because of the difficulties adumbrated above). It is notable that the majority of the studies reported were for nationalized sectors or public utilities. Rather few studies of private sector manufacturing costs are available. The evidence suggests falling or constant *LRAC* over the ranges of output at which firms operate in the sectors for which estimates are available.

[57] W. E. G. Salter, *Productivity and Technical Change*, 2nd edn., with addendum by W. B. Reddaway (Cambridge, 1966).

[58] Johnston, op. cit.   [59] Walters, op. cit.

(b) Costs in the short run

Costs in the short run have attracted much less attention in the literature, possibly because it is thought that they have few implications for behaviour in oligopolistic industries. We consider the behaviour of *SRAC* when demand (and hence output) fluctuates about the design capacity of the plant. Evidence is obtainable from examination of firms' costs and additionally from direct questioning of businessmen. The cost data suggest a pattern where direct cost is more or less constant up to full capacity (Walters[60]). This is interpreted as evidence of fixed coefficients in production. We have no need to estimate fixed costs to assert that they will decline hyperbolically with output. So the typical *SRAC* curve will slope down continuously to full capacity. This conclusion is reinforced by the survey of 350 firms by Eiteman and Guthrie.[61] They asked businessmen what they *thought* was the shape of their *SRAC*. The response supported the idea of *SRAC* declining up to capacity, though some firms suggested that the minimum cost point was in fact at slightly less than full capacity. The more impressionistic evidence of Andrews[62] comes to a similar conclusion. The traditional textbook curve has *SRAC* rising gently as planned capacity output is exceeded. The evidence here is much less satisfactory. But it seems that for many processes capacity really defines a limit to output, so that *SRAC* rises very sharply at that point. This does however exclude the possibility of running the same machinery for longer hours in overtime periods. Such a pattern would lead to a discontinuity in *SRAC* since direct labour cost would presumably rise sharply.

4   THE SURVIVOR TECHNIQUE

The survivor technique for estimating the relative efficiency of different sizes of firms was advocated by Stigler.[63] In part it represented an attempt to make a fresh approach to the problem of economies of scale that would not founder on the problems of valuation (as in the case of empirical cost curves), or for lack of information (in the case of engineering cost curves). The idea behind the technique can be simply stated: if there are economies or diseconomies of scale in a particular industry, and if the industry is reasonably competitive, one would expect firms in the lowest cost size range to increase their share of the market over time. So the

[60] Walters, op. cit.
[61] W. J. Eiteman, G. E. Guthrie, 'The Average Cost Curve', *A.E.R.* 42 (1952), 832–8.
[62] P. W. S. Andrews, *Manufacturing Business* (Oxford 1949).
[63] G. J. Stigler, 'The Economies of Scale', *J. Law Econ.* 1 (1958), 54–71.

application of the technique is straightforward. Firms in an industry are classified according to size class. The share of industry output coming from each size class is then calculated over time. A fall in share over time then indicates an inefficient size: and increase in share indicates efficient size. Stigler used this method to examine the steel and automobile industries in the United States. For example he deduced that in the steel industry average cost was falling up to a size of about 5% of industry capacity, then remained constant up to about 30% of industry capacity where the curve rose again.

The technique has come in for a great deal of criticism on both theoretical and empirical grounds. The theoretical criticism is that the efficiency of the firms that is being tested is not merely a matter of size and costs. It is rather a complete evaluation of the survivability of different-sized firms over time. As we shall see in later chapters,[64] there may be systematic size advantages in raising capital, in R and D expenditure, in advertising, and in diversification. There may also be disadvantages if large plants have poorer labour relations than small ones, as the limited evidence for the United Kingdom would suggest.[65] All these matters are neglected in the textbook analysis of long-run average costs with fixed input costs, given technology and a common stable environment. Stigler acknowledges this, and in fact stresses in his original article that he is looking for a broader concept of efficiency. The difficulty with empirical cost studies is that we are not certain that costs reported are for an identical level of service in each case. For example, a firm may have low costs *because* it gives poor service (e.g. delivery system, reliability, after-sales service). It would be very difficult to adjust cost data for

[64] Cost of capital, Chapter 10; R and D expenditure, Chapter 13; Advertising, Chapter 12; and Diversification, Chapter 14.

[65] Shorey (J. Shorey 'The Size of Work Unit and Strike Incidence' *J.I.E.* 23 (1974–5) pp. 54–71) found some slight evidence for a positive effect of the size of *plant* on strike incidence, but suggested that large *firms* benefited from the development of specialized personnel and labour relations functions within the firm. The data of the U.K. Department of Employment is particularly notable.

Incidence of stoppages by size of plant, 1971–3

Plant Size	Annual average no. of stoppages per 100,000 employees	Annual average no. of working days lost per 1,000 employees
11–24	8·0	14·8
25–99	19·2	72·4
100–199	23·0	155·0
200–499	25·4	329·1
500–999	29·7	719·4
1,000+	28·7	2,046·1

Source: *Department of Employment Gazette* (Feb. 1976), 116.

such differences. But they will show up in the degree of customer acceptance. A high cost firm may grow because of its service, a low cost one may decline. It is precisely this kind of efficiency in markets that the survivor technique is supposed to measure (though one may doubt whether it is obvious that such differences are *size* related, as the technique proposes).

However in a later reflection on the debate[66] Stigler persists in the view that one can draw inferences about scale economies. This must be based on the assumption that differences in costs are a major element in the competitive struggle between firms, and that the other possibilities are subordinate. Suppose we start with the textbook conditions, assuming a *LRAC* curve which has a range of constant minimum costs. In long-run equilibrium we will expect all firms to be in this size range: differences in growth rates should be random, and changes in the size distribution of firms will also be random. If firms are not in the optimum range we expect them either to be eliminated or to grow to the optimal size. Thus the experience of firm sizes in the non-optimal range will be non-random. The two objections to this are the existence of heterogeneous resources, and the existence of fragmented markets. The first Stigler circumvents by resorting to the familiar proposition that in the very long run all resources will enter markets and earn rents, according to their value in alternative uses. Suppose a firm of sub-optimal size survives by virtue of an especially good location or especially good management. Eventually the firm will receive an irresistible offer for its location, and managers will be lured away by other firms: or the firm will itself grow to optimal size. The existence of fragmented markets is a more serious obstacle to the use of the technique. Here the argument must rely on the proposition that in the very long run no high price market is entirely safe from entry, though inefficient firm sizes may take longer to be eliminated. Sadly, it seems as though the technique is most applicable in competitive sectors: but those are precisely those sectors where it is easiest to interpret actual cost data. Since the survivor technique gives at best only the approximate shape of the cost curve, one might conclude that the benefit of the technique is small. Besides, the modern work on the growth of the firm makes it abundantly clear that relative costs are only one of a very large number of determinants of firm growth, thus vitiating the direct inference of scale economies from the survivor technique.[67]

The empirical criticism of the survivor technique is that it fails

[66] Stigler, op. cit. (1958).   [67] See Part III, especially Chapter 9.

to produce the required results. Shepherd[68] examined work by Saving[69] and Weiss,[70] and added his own survivor estimates for 117 sectors in the U.S. in 1947, 1954, 1958. The results were most discouraging. In over 60% of the cases even an optimistic assessment of the data failed to produce any clear pattern of an optimal size range. One could infer from this that these sectors were in long-run equilibrium with all plants at optimal size ranges. But it is perhaps more realistic to suggest that in these cases the growth experience of firms is related to more than simple cost differences. If cost differences do occur, their effect on growth of firms is swamped by the other elements in the growth process already hinted at.

More recently, Rees[71] has used the survivor technique to derive estimates of optimal *plant* sizes in U.K. manufacturing. He argues that this avoids some of the criticism of applications to firm sizes, because plants reflect preferred technologies alone. Hence we are nearer to the *LRAC* concept. He derived consistent estimates for only 30 out of the 71 sectors that he examined. This is scarcely an impressive result and must cast further doubt on the usefulness of the technique.

Hymer and Pashigian[72] have used firm growth rates in a different way to deduce some evidence about cost conditions. They concentrate on the empirical result that whereas the mean rate of growth of firms does not seem to vary with size, the variance of growth rates diminishes. They interpret this as evidence that small firms have higher costs than large ones. As a result small firms face two possibilities in the long run. Either they will be eliminated from the industry (accounting for large negative deviations in growth rates) or they must try to grow fast to reach a larger and thus more competitive size (large positive deviations). The alternative hypothesis is that costs are constant above a certain minimum size. The difference in variance would then arise from the diversification of larger firms. Large firms are simply groupings of small firms. Thus if the variance of growth rate for a small firm is unity, the variance of an amalgamation of small firms (constituting a large firm) is $1/\sqrt{n}$ where n is the number of small firms amalgamated in a larger firm. However the

[68] W. G. Shepherd, 'What does the Survivor Technique Show about Economies of Scale?' *S. Econ. Journal*, 33 (1967), 113-22.

[69] T. R. Saving, 'Estimation of Optimum Size of Plant by the Survivor Technique', *Q.J.E.* 75 (1961), 569-607.

[70] L. Weiss, 'The Survival Technique and the Extent of Sub-Otpimal Capacity', *J.P.E.* 72 (1964), 246-61.

[71] R. D. Rees, 'Optimum Plant Size in UK Industries: Some Survivor Estimates', *Economica*, 40 (1973), 394-401.

[72] S. Hymer, P. Pashigian, 'Firms' Size and Rate of Growth', *J.P.E.* 70 (1962), 556-69.

evidence for a number of 2-digit sectors is that the ratio of variances for large firms to that of small firms is too great. The hypothesis of constant costs is not therefore supportable. However these conclusions are open to the same theoretical critique as the survivor technique. Inferences about scale economies are only acceptable if it is assumed that differences in costs are the sole explanation of differences in firms' growth rates.

5 CONCLUSIONS

The chapter began by examining the traditional theory of economies of scale at the plant level and the attempts to quantify them. The method of engineering estimates of costs was seen to provide reasonable evidence on minimum attainable production cost in the form required by the theory. Extension of the analysis to the firm, to include the cost and effectiveness of management, and the effect of structural features such as multiplant operation and vertical integration, is more difficult, and there are important gaps in the evidence. This analysis is the basis for estimates of the minimum efficient scale of plant or firm, which is usually expressed as a percentage of total market output. This is an important element of market structure in the barriers-to-entry theory of price which we will examine in Chapter 6. It is also one determinant of the size and number of firms in a sector, and hence is related to concentration (see Chapter 15).

Examination of the costs of real firms reveals serious weaknesses in the traditional theory. The first is that the concept of 'normal costs', incorporated in the long-run average cost curve, cannot be deduced directly from the actual cost data of firms. The difficulties concern the imputation of rents to specialized, more efficient factors, and the problem of distinguishing 'normal profit' from other surpluses. Indeed such a procedure would only be valid where one was comparing a number of firms making a competitively fixed homogeneous product. This is scarcely likely to be the normal case. A second weakness is that in practice the costs of firms are affected by features particular to themselves, like their business history, their degree of diversification and vertical integration, and even the nature of competition in their product markets. *How much* they are affected is an unanswered empirical question, but such evidence as there is suggests that it is likely to be substantial. So there can be no excuse for regarding scale as the sole significant or systematic determinant of firm costs. This leads to the view that each firm is, to a greater or less extent, a unique bundle of resources. Questions about the efficiency of such bundles—both as to the ultimate determinants of their costs, and as to their actual efficiency—are clearly very important. The survivor method is one attempt to test this rather broader view of efficiency, though the emphasis is still on scale. The lack of success of the method suggests that we need to probe more systematically into other determinants of efficiency besides scale. The idea of the firm as a unique bundle of resources has much more in common with the approach we will be taking in Part III of the book, where the emphasis shifts from markets to the firm itself, and the efforts which the firm makes to grow and develop.

PRODUCT DIFFERENTIATION AND MARKET CONCENTRATION

At any given time a firm is operating in one or more markets, and the outcomes in these markets determine its current profits. Traditional analysis, as we saw in Chapter 1, has placed great emphasis on the structure of markets as the determinant of behaviour and performance. Structure is thought to have two aspects. The first is the degree of product differentiation. This describes the extent to which basically similar products vary in quality or other attributes. The second is market concentration, which includes not only the numbers of firms in the market, but also their relative sizes. The purpose of this chapter is to set out rather more precisely what is the nature and significance of these market attributes, and in the case of concentration to describe methods of measurement. We will also note the theoretical problems raised by the definition of industries, and see how some of these difficulties are reflected in empirical work.

1   PRODUCT DIFFERENTIATION AND DIFFERENT PRODUCTS

The period following the publication of Chamberlin's *Theory of Monopolistic Competition* was marked by intense discussion within the economics profession as to the definition of an industry or market. The problem can be succinctly summarized. Chamberlin's theory required the definition of groups of closely substitutable products which would form an industry or market. This was a departure from perfect competition where the product was assumed to be homogeneous. But as soon as some differences are allowed, it was argued, then the whole formulation of an industry becomes arbitrary. since all goods are substitutes to some degree. At what point does one draw a line round a group of products and refer to it as an industry? The conclusion to the debate is that this does indeed involve some arbitrary classifications of products, but that the concept of the industry is so useful analytically that the exercise is worthwhile.[1]

This section of the chapter will not be able to provide any new conclusion to the debate. However we will examine two alternative

[1] M. Olson, D. McFarland, 'The Restoration of Pure Monopoly and the Concept of the Industry', *Q.J.E.* 76 (1962), 613–31.

though related frameworks within which the difficulties may be clearly illustrated, and which enable us to discuss the nature of the demand curve for a differentiated product. One framework goes back to the work of Chamberlin,[2] who illustrated his argument by an analogy drawn from spatial economics. The other framework, more favoured in recent work, derives from the 'goods character-istics' theory of demand developed by Lancaster.[3] Both frameworks start from the premise that a good is a bundle of characteristics desired by the consumer, which constitute the qualities incorporated in the good. These qualities vary from one good to another. We ex-pound the Chamberlin theory first.

Analysis of demand in terms of characteristics requires that the utility function of the individual be defined in terms of character-istics rather than goods. In Figure 3.1 we show a simple example of

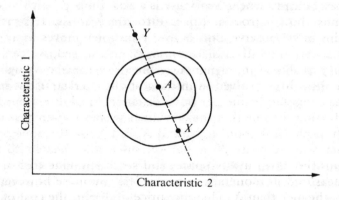

Fig. 3.1

the characteristics 'space' generated by two characteristics. The in-difference map superimposed on the space refers to one consumer's preferences between different characteristics embodied in a good. We shall note that this indifference map does not have the same prin-ciples as the normal indifference map used in consumer theory. The characteristics represent neither 'goods' nor 'bads', they are simply the objective characteristics of the goods, evaluated differ-ently by different consumers. Hence there is no reason why the in-difference map should not be 'closed' as in the diagram. In this case the preferred mix of characteristics is given by the point A, which

[2] E. H. Chamberlin, 'Monopolistic Competition Revisited', *Economica*, N.S. 18 (1951), 343–62.
[3] K. J. Lancaster, 'A New Approach to Demand Theory', *J.P.E.* 74 (1966), 132–57.

is the 'peak' of the indifference contours. Let us now suppose that no good with those characteristics exists, but that goods represented by points X and Y do. Then although X is not precisely what the consumer wants, clearly Y is even less so. So with a choice between X and Y only, X will be chosen. It might be thought that the consumer could achieve his desired position at A by consuming an appropriate mixture of goods X and Y, since a linear combination of their characteristics can give the point A. This is analytically convenient, but unrealistic. If Minis are made in light blue and dark blue, and my preference is somewhere in between, I cannot get what I want by somehow mixing the two. Nor is it simply a matter of indivisibilities. Even if a Mini were somehow infinitely divisible I would still end up with a mixture of the two, and not my preferred medium-blue. To avoid such apparent nonsense, it seems better to argue that *in general* the consumer must accept either X or Y, though there may be cases where a mixture is a possibility.[4]

We must now introduce prices into the analysis. The method of doing this is to observe that as the consumer moves away from A he incurs disutility: if this disutility can be priced, we can convert the utility analysis into a monetary one. To simplify we will assume that the disutility involved in moving about characteristics space has the same monetary value per unit 'distance' in all directions from A. Let us further assume that the consumer wishes to purchase one unit of the hypothetical good A. Now if X and Y are the same price, the consumer will purchase X as before, since it is 'nearer' to the preferred position A in utility space, and so the psychic cost of moving to it (measured in monetary terms) is less. Suppose however that Y is much cheaper than X. Then the price of Y plus the cost of moving from A may be less than the equivalent cost of X. In that case Y will be purchased. This is the point at which Chamberlin used the analogy from spatial economics. Assume that the consumer is located at A in a geographical plane and there are two sources of supply of a good, Y and X, Y being further away than X. Assume further that the consumer pays the transport costs of obtaining the good. Then if X and Y have the same price the consumer will go to X to purchase the good because of its proximity. But, if the price of Y falls, at some point the *total cost* of obtaining supplies there will be less and the consumer will transfer his custom. The analogy holds precisely for characteristics space, as we have seen. The major complication in that case is that the cost of movement in characteristics space need not by any means be constant in different directions. Consumers may be more prepared to compromise on one of the desired

[4] For example, in portfolio analysis: see Chapter 14, pp. 474–82.

specifications than on others. This will be expressed by the shape of
the indifference contours in characteristics space.

Finally we need to consider the consumer's level of income. For
example, it may be objected that every student's preferred product
characteristic mix is an E-type Jaguar or similar high-performance
sports car, but most will settle for a Mini. However this is simply explained by the introduction of an income constraint which will
delimit the range of products that the consumer can choose between
(in just the same way as the budget line constrains choice in the
normal analysis of indifference curves).

This analysis can now be used to illustrate the question of substitutability. We can imagine a number of similar products located
close together in characteristics space. In the same space a large number of consumers will have preferences. Subject to his income constraint, each consumer will buy that product for which the sum of its
price and the psychic cost ('transport' cost) is to him least, given his
most preferred point. If the price of one product falls, then some
consumers who were previously marginal purchasers of another good
will switch, but many consumers will prefer to stay with their existing purchases despite the relatively higher price. The rate at which
consumers transfer their custom depends on the psychic cost which
they attach to deviations from their preferred characteristics mix.
Where preferences are weak, the indifference surface will be
relatively flat and a change in price will precipitate large shifts in
consumer purchases. Where preferences are strong, psychic costs
will be large and few consumers will shift in response to changes in
price. This is the typical situation of product differentiation. The
goods have closely similar characteristics, but certain differences in
quality that make choice a matter of importance for at least some
consumers. We are not even particularly concerned here whether the
quality differences are real or not: clearly there are *real* quality differences between say a Mini and a Rolls-Royce. Not so clear are the
differences between some brands of soap-powder. But so long as at
least some consumers believe they exist and attach a value to them,
then for our purposes (and from the point of view of the firm) they
are significant.

The question of the 'creation' of such differences by persuasive
advertising, operating on the consumers' preferences, is left to
Chapter 12. Here we summarize the main conclusion of that analysis.
First, advertising and marketing expenditures have two effects that
are conceptually distinct. One is that consumers' preferences are
shifted in characteristics space: the other is that those preferences
are 'strengthened', so that the psychic disutility of moving from a

preferred position is increased. Second, advertising and marketing should be viewed as investment expenditures which generate a stock of 'goodwill' or 'brand loyalty' over time. Together with product differentiation, these then determine market shares.

Implications for the demand curve of a differentiated product follow from this analysis. In characteristics space, a price reduction on one differentiated product will have an immediate effect on 'near neighbours', i.e. the firms located nearest to it.[5] If there are few of these, their market share is substantially squeezed, and they are likely to retaliate by reducing their own price, which in turn will lead to retaliation from their 'near neighbours'. So the effect of the price cut can be spread across the market, with shares remaining as before, but with lower profits. If the firm is aware of this possibility it will avoid initiating price cuts. The analysis of the 'kinked demand curve' (see Chapter 5) will hold. If there are many near neighbours, the effect on any one may be negligible. Hence we can expect the firm to be able to adjust the price on a single product without necessarily provoking reactions from rivals.

Can we use the same characteristics framework to distinguish different products? Figure 3.2 shows the preference map for a typical consumer in characteristics space. We assume that most consumers

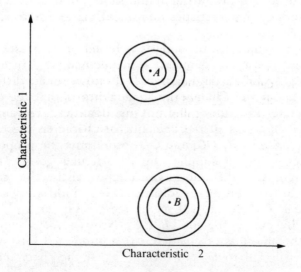

Fig. 3.2

[5] The question of how many 'near neighbours' a product may have has been discussed by G. C. Archibald, G. Rosenbluth, 'The "New" Theory of Consumer Demand and Monopolistic Competition', *Q.J.E.* 89 (1975), 569–90.

have a similar contour map, and that the goods *A* and *B* are available. Then it is clear that major relative price changes between *A* and *B* are not likely to lead to much substitution of one good for the other. Only those consumers whose preference map 'peaks' between *A* and *B* are likely to transfer their custom, and by assumption in this case there are few of them. In this case, then, there is likely to be little interdependence between the demands for *A* and the demands for *B*. Such elasticity of demand as exists will not be due to the cross-elasticity of *A* and *B*. This is a clear case of separate products. This situation will be most common where goods have totally different characteristics, and are thus 'located' in totally different dimensions of characteristics space. Indeed, our definition of substitutability is based on proximity in that space, where proximity does, of course, depend on the strength of preferences (i.e. 'transport cost') as well as the objective characteristics themselves. In practice it may be impossible to make this precise distinction between different goods and differentiated goods. However the matter is unlikely to pose major empirical problems. We probably can distinguish satisfactorily between a group of products 'located' in the vicinity of *B*, and forming a 'market', and the very different relation illustrated between *A* and *B*. Finally we note that in the case of a homogeneous product all firms are producing at the same point in characteristics space. So product characteristics do not influence the division of the market between firms.

The second framework of analysis is based on Lancaster's 'goods characteristics' theory of demand, as developed by Lancaster himself[6] and by Archibald and Rosenbluth.[7] The main difference in assumptions from the Chamberlinian analysis is that the characteristics are themselves 'goods', and not just qualities.[8] The analysis can be conducted in terms of the demand for characteristics. In Figure 3.3, each ray, *OA*, *OB*, *OC*, and *OD*, represents the proportions of characteristics 1 and 2 supplied in a particular good. The points a, b_1, c, d, represent the amounts of characteristics that can be obtained initially for a unit expenditure. *IC* is an indifference curve for one individual. Clearly he will maximize his satisfaction, given his preferences, by purchasing good *B* at b_1. Now we vary the price of *B*. As it rises, the amounts of characteristics purchased for one unit of expenditure will fall to b_2 and then to b_3. If the characteristics are

[6] Lancaster, op. cit.   [7] Archibald and Rosenbluth, op. cit.

[8] Differing proportions of two characteristics embodied in a good can be plotted along a single dimension in Chamberlin's quality space. For example, the ratio in which Lancaster's characteristics 1 and 2 can be combined runs from zero to infinity, so all possible combinations can be represented along a single line.

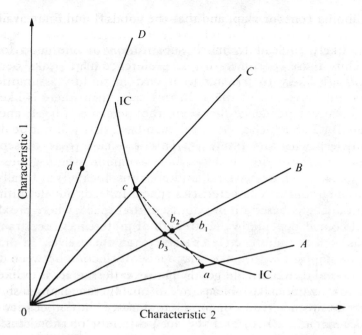

Fig. 3.3

separable, the demand for *B* will fall to zero, when the price rises beyond the point represented by b_2. At that point, it becomes cheaper to obtain the desired combination of characteristics in the form of a mixture of *A* and *C*, along the dotted line *ac*. If the characteristics are *not* separable from the good, then the point b_3 becomes the critical point for the consumer whose indifference curve is shown in the diagram. He will then prefer to purchase *C*. Finally we should note that a fall in price of *B*, say to b_1, will have adverse effects on the demand for *A* and *C*, depending on consumers' preferences. The conclusion for demand curves of differentiated products which follows is precisely the same as that derived from Chamberlin's analysis. The variation in the price of *B* has a direct effect on the demands for *A* and *C*. Hence a reaction in those prices is to be expected. However, Archibald and Rosenbluth show that when the number of characteristics is four or more,[9] the number of near neighbours is on average $n/2$, where *n* is the number of firms. The interdependence of near neighbours is thus weakened when *n* is large, and each product may have its own differentiated demand curve.

[9] Four characteristics in Lancaster's analysis is the equivalent of the 2-dimensional quality space of Chamberlin's analysis.

Within this framework there is also a natural definition of an industry. Suppose that z is a $m \times l$ vector of characteristics, and that x is a $n \times l$ vector of goods. Then we can define a consumption technology by a $m \times n$ matrix, B, of coefficients, which defines the relationship of characteristics to goods:

$$z = Bx$$

If on inspection we find the B matrix to be block triangular, e.g. of the form

$$\begin{bmatrix} B_1 & O & O \\ O & B_2 & O \\ O & O & B_3 \end{bmatrix}$$

then it seems natural to define an industry by the $m_1 \times n_1$ block of coefficients which make up B_1 and so on. These are products that have certain characteristics in common, shared by no other products. This does not of course, exclude the possibility of substitution in consumption between one group of products and another. That could only be excluded on the assumption of weakly separable utility functions, i.e. that the marginal rates of substitution between the characteristics of one group is independent of the quantity consumed of any characteristic outside the group. Whether the consumption matrix is block diagonal is a matter of empirical analysis.

The characteristics framework has been extensively used in econometric work on the pricing of differentiated products, relating the price of a differentiated good to the bundle of characteristics that it represents.[10] For example, Cowling and Cubbin,[11] in their work in the U.K. car market, included the following indicators of quality: horsepower, passenger area, fuel consumption, length, power-assisted brakes (or not), four forward gears (or not), and quality of trim. These were the explanatory variables in a regression analysis of car prices, as follows:

---

[10] See, for examples, K. Cowling, J. Cubbin, 'Price, Quality and Advertising Competition', *Economica*, 38 (1971), 378-94; K. Cowling, A. J. Rayner, 'Price, Quality and Market Share', *J.P.E.* 78 (1970), 1292-1309; M. Ohta, Z. Griliches, 'Automobile Prices Revisited: Extensions of the Hedonic Hypothesis', in N. Terleckyi (ed.), *Household Production and Consumption*, N.B.E.R. Studies in Income and Wealth, No. 40 (New York 1975), 325-90; and references in J. E. Triplett, 'Consumer Demand and Characteristics of Consumption Goods', in Terleckyi (ed.), op. cit.

[11] Cowling and Cubbin, op. cit.

$$\log P_i = \alpha_0 + \sum_j \alpha_j \cdot V_{ji} + u_i$$

Explanatory variable: V_j	Coefficient: α_j	t statistic
Constant	2·3554	9·79
b.h.p.	0·00075643	1·91
Passenger area	0·00002242	0·97
Fuel consumption	−0·0037334	−1·67
Length	0·0019591	1·40
Power-assisted brakes	0·10640	3·14
Four forward gears	0·058276	3·92
Quality of trim	0·04239	2·43
	$\bar{R}^2 = 0·94$	

Triplett[12] has raised a number of questions about the interpretation of these 'hedonic' functions. The regression coefficients are interpreted as the marginal implicit prices of the characteristics. In a competitive framework, these marginal prices would reflect both the marginal cost of supplying a unit of characteristic *and* the marginal valuation of the same. However, if the differentiation of the product gives the firm its own demand curve, then the price may include some 'monopoly' element, exceeding marginal cost. It must then reflect the consumers' marginal valuation. (It is not however possible to deduce the demand *curve* for a single characteristic, or for a bundle of characteristics, from the hedonic function.) The actual functional forms used in hedonic analysis are also puzzling. The forms usually used are linear (with a constant intercept), semilog or loglog. In the first case, the presence of the constant is not explained: if the good is a parcel of characteristics, the price of the good should be equal to the sum of the valuation of the characteristics it contains. Semilog and loglog forms imply a budget constraint with diminishing marginal cost in the supply of characteristics, which seems implausible. We also note that the hedonic function assumes that packaging of characteristics is continuous, when in fact only a limited number of goods is on offer. Finally, we can never be sure that the hedonic function is complete: there may always be some important characteristic we have failed to include.

The advantage of the goods–characteristics approach is that it gives some prospect of empirical applications. However it seems that it is only applicable to goods like consumer durables where the

[12] Triplett, op. cit.

specification in terms of desirable characteristics is reasonably obvious. But it will not be satisfactory for goods where the 'quality' is not monotonically related to the *quantity* of characteristics in the eyes of all consumers.

We may summarize our conclusions on product differentiation as follows. We are basically interested in it as an element of market structure. First, it provides insights into the question of how to define markets. There is still a general sense in which everything is a substitute for everything else, but there is some possibility that we can define groups by their proximity in characteristics space. This becomes the criterion in use for empirical definitions of markets. Second, the nature of the demand curve for a differentiated product has been clarified. If there are less than four characteristics, then 'near neighbour' effects predominate. However many products there are in the market, the firm cannot expect any freedom to set its own price without provoking reactions from near neighbours. The firm does not therefore have an independent demand curve. With four or more characteristics the 'near neighbour' effect disappears, and the number of products in the market is the critical feature. Two further features affect the degree of interaction between competing products. One is the distribution of consumer preferences in characteristics space. The other is the strength with which these preferences are held, or, in Chamberlinian analysis, the disutility to the consumer of moving from his preferred position. The effect of advertising on these features of differentiated markets is discussed in Chapter 12. But in so far as the cumulated effect of advertising over time concentrates consumer preferences in the vicinity of the products on offer, *and* increases the disutility to consumers of moving from their preferred position in quality space, it clearly reduces the substitutability between competing products in the group. This is the phenomenon of 'brand loyalty'. Third, product differentiation and 'brand loyalty' affect the conditions of entry. Because of economies of scale there will be a limited number of products in characteristics space, each with its own market area (on the spatial analogy). A new entrant can only succeed if he can place his product in characteristics space so as to attract a sufficient market for minimum economic scale of production. A characteristics space that is already crowded with products will be hard to enter, especially if advertising has had the effect on consumer preferences that we have just noted. Product differentiation as a barrier to entry is further discussed in Chapter 6.

2 CONCENTRATION: THE THEORETICAL IMPLICATIONS[13]

In this section we make some tentative suggestions as to how concentration in a particular market is likely to influence the behaviour of firms in that market. By concentration is implied the extent to which an economic activity is dominated by a few large firms. There are two dimensions of measurement. The first is the number of firms. The second is the relative sizes of these firms, measured for example by their market shares. We consider in the next section how it may be possible to capture these dimensions in a single descriptive statistic.

The first implication of the number of firms is for the consumers of the good in question. Let us suppose that there is some price variation among firms, so that the average price is m, but the dispersion of prices can be approximated by the standard deviation σ (where $\sigma > 0$). Given variability between firms, it will be advantageous to the consumer to initiate a search for a low-priced supplier. Such a search will be costly: it will involve time and even money to obtain a number of quotations. Fortunately, we can characterize the outcome of the search process in terms of the minimum price P that he can hope to find after inquiring at n firms: it is given by[14]

$$P = m - \sigma\sqrt{2 \log n}.$$

The implication is that more search is expected to lead to lower price quotations. However as n increases, so the expected marginal reduction in price declines. The rational consumer will stop searching as soon as search costs exceed the prospective reduction in price quotation, i.e. exceeds $q(\partial P/\partial n)$, where q is the quantity required. If the market is occupied by only a few firms it is possible that it will be worthwhile for the consumer to inquire of every firm. If there are many firms, and particularly if search is costly, the consumer may only canvass a few firms. For example, it is common for the prices of essential foodstuffs to vary between supermarkets in the same shopping area. So long as price differentials are not persistent over a long period of time, it is unlikely that shoppers will compare prices between all supermarkets before making purchases. The time and energy involved is just not worth it when the price deviations (σ) may

---

[13] The debt of this section to L. Hannah, J. Kay, *Concentration in Modern Industry* (London, 1977), Chapter 2, is acknowledged.

[14] See A. Alchian, in E. S. Phelps (ed.), *Microeconomic Foundations of Inflation and Employment Theory* (New York, 1970); G. J. Stigler, 'The Economics of Information', *J.P.E.* 69 (1961), 213–35. A derivation is provided by M. G. Kendall, A. Stuart, *The Advanced Theory of Statistics*: Vol. 1, *Distribution Theory*, 3rd edn. (London, 1969), 333–6.

be small anyway. The argument is strongest where the good is purchased only infrequently. Then the buyer does not build up an 'experience' of purchasing the article—i.e. a cumulative process of search. Finally, the returns to search are likely to be greatest where expenditure on the good is relatively important in the consumer budget (Pq is large relative to income).

As Stigler[15] points out, the costs of search will also be determined by other institutional elements in the market. One possibility is the existence of localized markets for particular commodities, e.g. fruit and vegetable markets, which can reduce search costs. Alternatively informative advertising may reduce the search costs to the consumer, especially where prices are published in a trade journal in which all firms advertise. In general, Stigler argues, we would expect more search and more information to lead to a more 'competitive' situation in which price differentials would tend to disappear.

A second implication concerns the interdependence of firms in the market. We distinguish two situations. In the first there are few firms selling a homogeneous product, at a single price. Then variations in supply by one firm may have a significant effect on the market supply, involving a change in the equilibrium market price, thus affecting the revenues of all other firms. In the second, firms are selling a differentiated product, with non-uniform prices. Variations in price and quantity supplied by one firm have their primary impact on the market shares of other firms, though the market enlarging effect noted in the first situation may also occur. In both cases the number of firms and their relative sizes are important, as an examination of the appropriate elasticity formulae will show.[16]

In the case of a homogeneous product, the quantity elasticity is the relevant measure, since there is a uniform industry price. We are interested in the effect on that price of an increase in quantity supplied.

Let the market demand function be $p = f(X) = f(x_1 + \ldots + x_i + \ldots + x_n)$ where x_i is the output of one firm and $\Sigma x_i = X$ is market output. The revenue for firm i is given by

$$R_i = p \cdot x_i$$

[15] Stigler, op. cit.

[16] The seminal work is that of R. L. Bishop, 'Elasticities, Cross Elasticities and Market Relationships', *A.E.R.* 42 (1952), 779–803, which was extended by A. C. Johnson, P. Helmberger, 'Price Elasticity of Demand as an Element of Market Structure', *A.E.R.* 57 (1967), 1218–21, and J. R. McKean, R. D. Peterson, 'Demand Elasticity, Product Differentiation and Market Structure', *J. Econ. Th.* 6 (1973), 205–9. We also draw in part on the analysis of Hannah and Kay, op. cit., Chapter 2, and K. Cowling, M. Waterson, 'Price-Cost Margins and Market Structure', *Economica*, 43 (1976), 267–74.

So marginal revenue $= \dfrac{\partial R_i}{\partial X_i} = p + x_i \dfrac{\partial p}{\partial X} \cdot \dfrac{\partial X}{\partial x_i}$ where $\dfrac{\partial X}{\partial x_i} = 1$

$$= p\left(1 + \frac{x_i}{X} \cdot \frac{X}{p} \cdot \frac{dp}{dX}\right)$$

Clearly the magnitude of this depends on the market share of the firm X_i/X. Where firms are of different sizes, we can use a weighted average of *all* the firms in the market to derive an 'average' marginal revenue, MR.

$$MR = \frac{1}{X}\left[\sum_i px_i + \sum_i x_i^2 \frac{dp}{dX} \right]$$

$$= p + p \sum_i \left(\frac{x_i}{X}\right)^2 \cdot \frac{X}{p} \cdot \frac{dp}{dX}$$

Following Bishop, we define $e = (X/p) \cdot (dp/dX)$ as the market 'quantity elasticity of demand', i.e. the percentage change in price with a marginal percentage change in quantity supplied. $\Sigma_i (x_i/x)^2 = H$ is the Herfindahl index of concentration which we will discuss in the next section. It has the property that it diminishes with concentration. For example, if there are n equal-sized firms in the industry, $H = 1/n$. Hence we can write:

$$MR = p(1 + He)$$

Low concentration (many small firms) implies that average marginal revenue does not differ significantly from p. No firm is likely to be able to exercise any influence on the market price. But high concentration (H high, due to fewness of firms and/or the large relative size of some firms), implies that the average marginal revenue is significantly different from p for at least some firms with a large share in the market. Hence they have some 'monopoly power' over price.

The second situation is more difficult to model, since it involves differentiated products with non-uniform prices. In principle at least the firm has some freedom to set its own price, within the limits described in the previous section. So price elasticity is the relevant measure for analysis.

The argument is cast in the familiar form of elasticities of demand by Bishop.[17] He defines the usual own price and cross elasticities of demand, with respect to a change in i's price, all other prices remaining constant, but all quantities variable. Each formula is the ratio of the relevant percentage changes in variables.

So *own* elasticity is given by,

$$E_{ii} = \frac{\partial q_i}{\partial p_i} \cdot \frac{p_i}{q_i}$$

And *cross* elasticity is given by

$$E_{ji} = \frac{\partial q_j}{\partial p_i} \cdot \frac{p_i}{q_j}$$

i.e. the latter formula gives the ratio of the percentage change in j's sales arising from a change in i's price (j's price remaining constant) to the percentage change in i's price.

The formulae may be illustrated with a numerical example, following Bishop. Suppose there are 101 firms in the industry, producing closely related products. Let E_{ii} for any one firm be −5: i.e. as any one firm shades its price it increases the quantity sold (in percentage terms) by five times the percentage fall in price. The increase in q_i must come from the 100 other firms in roughly equal amounts. Hence E_{ji} is 5/100 or 0·05. In general then,

$$E_{ji} = -\frac{E_{ii}}{n-1} \text{ where } n \text{ is the number of firms.}$$

As n increases, so E_{ji} tends to zero: the impact upon other firms becomes negligible.

We may also note the relationship

$$n - 1 = -\frac{E_{ii}}{E_{ji}}$$

i.e. the number of firms is related to the ratio of the own elasticity to the cross elasticity. We have derived this formula from a situation with equal-sized firms. But Bishop suggests that $-E_{ii}/E_{ji}$ may be used

[17] Bishop, op. cit.

as a 'numbers-equivalent' in cases of unequal-sized firms, where E_{ji} is a suitable weighted average of the cross elasticities for the j firms.

Similar considerations apply in the case of inequality in the size of firms. Fluctuations in the output of large firms will significantly affect industry output and hence price. Those of small firms will not. Further, the behaviour of a small firm is likely to have a negligible effect on the market share of the other firms, while a large firm trying to expand can only do so by significantly affecting the others. In general, inequality of firm sizes leads to a more important role for the large firms, which must take 'industry' considerations into account, while a small firm can afford to act more or less independently. Again Bishop illustrates this with a numerical example. Consider a 101-firm industry, producing closely related products. Let firm i have 50 per cent of the market, the other firms 0·5 per cent each. Let $E_{ii} = E_{jj} = -5$, i.e. the own price elasticity is the same for every firm. However the firm i will view the industry situation very differently from the other firms: any action that it takes will have considerable impact on all the other firms, both individually and as a group. For firm i it is as if the industry were a duopoly, since the 'numbers equivalent' ratio of elasticities would give

$$-\frac{E_{ii}}{E_{ji}} = 1.$$

For the firm j, however, the situation is as if they were one of 200 firms, since the elasticities ratio will be

$$-\frac{E_{jj}}{E_{ij}} = 199.\text{[18]}$$

So the large firm will accept the discipline of interdependence, while a small firm can afford to ignore this. We conclude that the size distribution will have important effects, independent of the number of firms.

However, Bishop's argument does not make full use of the 'market area' analysis of differentiated products described in the previous

[18] Because firm i has half the market, a 5 per cent increase in its market can only be at the expense of a 5 per cent loss in market for *each* of the other firms. But a 5 per cent increase in market for one of the j firms has to be drawn from the market share of the remaining firms, i.e. 99·5 per cent of the market. This is *as if* there were 199 firms of the same size.

section, and so may be quite misleading. In characteristics space, interdependence between firms is reflected in the fact that a price cut on one product expands its market area at the expense of other products in the neighbourhood. Thus if the ith product has a market 'area' v_i, and price p_i, the change in market area with respect to price is dv_i/dp_i. (The change in *demand* then depends on the price-elasticity of demand for the product from individual consumers located within the market area, and on the number and incomes of those consumers. If we assume that consumers are evenly distributed by preferences in characteristics space, and that their uniform incomes and tastes imply an inelastic demand for the good in question, then changes in market area are equivalent to changes in demand.) The value of dv_i/dp_i depends on two variables. The first is the disutility of movement in characteristics space: if this is high, the market boundary will shift out very little. The second is the extent of the market boundary: big markets will have 'long' boundaries and hence will gain more market share in absolute terms than a small market. Now this change in market area is at the expense of all other products, j, which are near neighbours of i. The number of products, j, will, as we have seen, depend on the number of characteristics defining the space: however we assume four or more for purposes of the present analysis, so the average number of neighbours is $n/2$, where n is the number of products. The degree to which any one j will be affected is determined by the 'length' of the market boundary that it shares with product i.[19] We conjecture that it will *on average* be related to the relative size of j's market among all the near neighbours of i. The relationship is *less* than proportionate however.[20] So in reaching an average effect, larger market shares should be

---

[19] Hannah and Kay, op. cit. 12–15 can ignore this problem, since they deal with products located in a single quality dimension along a line. The 'market boundary' between products is always the 'width' of the line.

[20] Consider a market of radius r in n characteristic space. Market volume is given by the formula

$$V_i = c(n)\pi r_i^{\,n} \quad \text{(where } c(n) \text{ is a constant whose value depends on } n\text{)}$$

The market boundary is given by the first derivative of this:

$$b_i = nc\pi r_i^{\,n-1}$$

$$\therefore \frac{db_i}{dV_i} = (n-1)(c\cdot\pi)^{\frac{2n-1}{n-1}} V_i^{-1/n}$$

which is positive, but diminishing with V_i.

i.e. a given small increase in market value can be achieved with a smaller increase in market boundary the larger is the initial volume.

weighted less. We conclude that the extent of interaction among product markets in characteristics space is a function of the degree of concentration in the market, and the cost of movement in utility space.

The third implication of concentration concerns the ability of each firm to keep a check on other firms' activities. In any market situation some management effort will be involved in the task of gathering information about other firms, not only price, but also product investment and merger plans. Clearly the magnitude of the task increases directly with the number of firms in the industry. But an increase in the number of firms of equal size will lead to a lessening interdependence between firms, and hence presumably to a lower value for information about the activities of other firms. In a situation where firms are of unequal size it will be sufficient for firms to watch only the large firms in the industry: at least they will warrant more observation than smaller firms. But the information most easily available to a firm is the behaviour of its own sales. A firm will have some idea of what market share it expects, and a fluctuation which is unlikely in the light of past experience will alert the wise manager to investigate more closely. A typical case could be the market for a homogeneous good with an established price set by a price leader and accepted by other firms. One firm may then try to increase its market share by offering secret discounts to some customers of its rivals. What is the likelihood that secret discounts will be discovered? And what is the probability that fluctuations in market shares will provoke firms to take 'retaliatory' action by cutting price (and thus upsetting the equilibrium in the market) in the mistaken belief that someone else is secretly cutting price? The first query was answered by Stigler,[21] and the second by Hannah and Kay:[22] both answers point to the Herfindahl measure of concentration as an important determinant of the probabilities involved.

The critical question posed by Stigler was whether a secret price cutter will be able to escape detection by other members of the group, given that they will lose customers to him. The point is that firms will expect some random fluctuation in sales over time, and their problem is to distinguish a random loss of market from one which is due to a secret price cutter. Stigler shows that the expected variance of a firm's sales due to random switching by customers will be least where the Herfindahl index is large. So a firm that persistently does well will be more quickly suspected of cheating by its rivals. It may be objected that this is an overelaborate model. One

[21] G. J. Stigler, 'A Theory of Oligopoly', *J.P.E.* 72 (1964), 44–61.
[22] Hannah and Kay, op. cit.

can scarcely imagine managers calculating the probabilities of some fluctuation in demand occurring. But all the theory requires is that they should have some idea of normal fluctuations in market share, which are likely to be smaller when concentration, as measured by the Herfindahl index, is high.

Hannah and Kay[23] use a similar framework to analyse the possibility that the price discipline of the oligopolistic group will be broken because a random fluctuation in market share is taken for evidence of secret price cutting.

Suppose there are n customers in all, each buying the same amount. Each has the probability s_i of buying from firm i. Hence the expected market share of i is s_i, with standard deviation $\sqrt{s_i(1-s_i)/n}$. Variability of market share is expressed as the ratio of the standard deviation to the mean, and is greater for small shares than for large ones. However small firms will probably accept this on the basis of past experience. Even if they do not, their contribution to output would be small, and they alone are not likely to upset the market equilibrium and price. We suppose that the market situation is stable, unless firms with an aggregate market share of at least s believe that there is secret price cutting. Each firm sets a level of minimum expected sales, such that the probability of selling less is p. Should it sell less than this, it will join the group of disappointed firms. So its contribution to that group is s_i with probability p, and zero with probability $(1 - p)$. This distribution has mean ps_i and variance $p(1 - p)s_i^2$. Summing over all firms, the fraction of output arising from disappointed firms is p, and the variance of that fraction is $p(1 - p)\Sigma s_i^2$. Hence for a reasonable number of firms in the industry, the probability of the critical level s being exceeded is dependent on the variance, which is proportional to Σs_i^2, the Herfindahl index of concentration.

We note that the very elements of concentration that make firms more interdependent—fewness of firms and inequality of firm size— are also aids to the positive development of co-operation between frims. The essence of co-operation between firms is the maintenance of information flow between them. Unless a formal cartel agreement is set up (of which more in Chapter 5), co-operation depends on two-way links between firms. For N firms this involves no less than $(N(N - 1))/2$ channels of communciation.[24] Clearly this grows very rapidly as N increases (e.g. 45 for $N = 10$). The breakdown of even

---

[23] Hannah and Kay, op. cit.

[24] There are N firms. Each has links with $(N - 1)$ others, making $N(N - 1)$ in all. But each pairwise connection has been counted twice, once from each end as it were. So the total is $(N(N - 1))/2$.

one link may lead to a breakdown in the process of co-operation. Exactly the same argument applies to an industry with unequal sizes of firms: the more unequal they are the more likely that a substantial proportion of industry output will be controlled by a few firms which can then co-ordinate their activities as outlined above. Thus the two dimensions of concentration which we have outlined not only emphasize the interdependence of oligopolistic firms, they also provide the conditions under which a co-operative solution to the oligopoly problem is possible.

In our discussion of concentration we have discussed the effect on the behaviour of firms *within* the market already. The possibility of new entry has been ignored. Yet there can be no doubt that (i) existing firms will have an eye to potential entrants, (ii) that potential entrants are likely to be deterred by evidence of a tight oligopolistic group that is prepared to act together to deter entry. This means that existing levels of concentration are only a part of the explanation of firm behaviour.

3 MEASURES OF CONCENTRATION

The previous section has suggested that concentration, the degree in which activity in a market is dominated by a few large firms, will have important effects on the behaviour of firms, in both differentiated and homogeneous markets. It would of course, be possible to set out the salient features of industrial structure in a descriptive fashion. But it is difficult to compare the characteristics of one industry as against another, just by looking at the data. This is particularly true in the case of econometric work, where one is looking at concentration as a determinant of market performance. It is highly inconvenient not to have some summary measure or index of concentration. In fact a number of such indices have been proposed,[25] and widely used (as we will see in Chapter 7). However, it is important to remember that concentration measures are statistical artefacts: they only take on meaning from the *theoretical* justification for constructing them in a particular way. Hannah and Kay[26] have suggested a number of general criteria that such measures should meet.[27]

[25] See G. Rosenbluth, 'Measures of Concentration', in G. J. Stigler (ed.), *Business Concentration and Price Policy*, N.B.E.R. (Priceton, 1955), and P. E. Hart's survey, 'Entropy and other measures of concentration', *J.R.S.S.* 134 (1971), Series A, 73-85.

[26] Hannah and Kay, op. cit.

[27] See also discussion in Hall and N. Tideman, 'Measures of Concentration', *J.A.S.A.* 62 (1967), 162-8.

(i) If one concentration curve lies entirely above another it represents a higher level of concentration. The concentration curve is constructed by plotting cumulative shares of market output attributable to the largest 1, 2, 3 . . . in firms in the market, as shown in Figure 3.4. On this criterion A is more concentrated since a given number of firms accounts for a higher proportion of output in A than in either B or C. But the comparison of B and C is ambiguous.

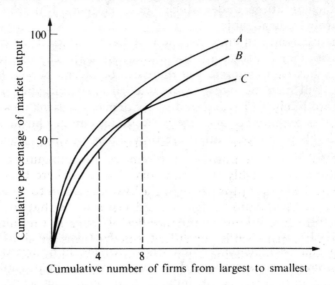

Fig. 3.4

(ii) The sales transfer principle must hold (i.e. if sales are transferred from a small firm to a large one, concentration has increased).

(iii) Merger increases concentration.

(iv) There is some s, $0 < s < 1$ such that if a new firm enters and gains market share $s_j < s$, while the relative shares of all existing firms are unchanged, concentration is reduced. The intuition behind this criterion is that new entry increases the number of firms, and in that sense therefore decreases concentration: but if the new entrant has a sufficiently large market share he could displace the concentration curve vertically over a substantial part of its length, hence increasing concentration by criterion (i).

Armed with these criteria, we may now look at the actual measures themselves.

(a) Concentration ratios

The most popular measures of concentration in empirical work are those derived directly from the concentration curve. Two are commonly used, each relating to a single point on the line. The first is the proportion of output attributable to the top n firms in the industry: the concentration ratio, CR_n. Often industrial census gives this type of data almost directly. Census disclosure rules ensure that any breakdown in the data is only given in aggregates of 3 or more firms. A second measure, used rather less since it requires interpolation from the published statistics, is the number of firms that comprise a given percentage of industry output (e.g. 70 per cent).

These measures come in for two criticisms. The first is that both measure only one point on the curve, so the rankings of industries depends critically on the point chosen. In Figure 3.4, on the basis of eight firm concentration ratios, industries B and C are identical. For measures of more than eight firms, B is more concentrated than C. As the whole purpose is to remove the ambiguity of descriptions, this is thoroughly unsatisfactory. Nor can there be said to be any theoretical reason for preferring a four firm ratio to an eight firm or a twenty firm ratio.[28] The second criticism is that the measure takes no direct account of the *number* of firms in the industry. In one sense this criticism is unjustified, since if firms are all of an equal size and one is considering a ten firm ratio, the ratio will be 100 per cent for 10 firms and 10 per cent for 100 firms. The main point at issue seems to be that two industries could both have ten firm ratios of 50 per cent, but one with 20 smaller firms and the other with 200 smaller firms, and they would not be distinguished. However we may doubt, from our earlier theoretical discussion, whether this difference between the industries is particularly important.

The concentration ratio meets Hannah and Kay's criteria at least

[28] T. R. Saving, 'Concentration Ratios and the Degree of Monopoly', *I.E.R.* 11 (1970), 139–46, has provided a rationale for the use of concentration ratios, albeit on rather strong assumptions about firm behaviour. He considers a homogeneous good market of n firms that is characterized by a price leadership cartel or dominant firm and a price-taking fringe of competitive firms outside the cartel. The cartel sets a profit maximizing price, taking into account the supply of the competitive fringe at various price levels. Given the elasticity of supply of the competitive fringe, we know from the previous section that the effect of restriction of output on the market price will be greater, the larger the share of the cartel in the market. Thus, if the competitive fringe is small relative to the cartel, their increased supply when the cartel restricts output will be insufficient to prevent a substantial price increase (given the market elasticity of demand). Hence the cartel's monopoly power will be greater, and the average price–cost margin higher, the greater is the concentration ratio. The problem with this is that we do not usually have an explicit cartel situation, and the measures of the concentration ratio are based on an arbitrary number of firms, and not on a cartel group alone.

in those cases where a change in industry structure affects the largest firms (i.e. firms 1 to n for CR_n). Thus a transfer of sales to one of these firms, or a merger involving one of them, will increase the measure. So will large-scale entry, which displaces a smaller firm from the top n firms. But any change outside firms 1 to n will have no effect on the index. (Hart[29] sees this as an advantage of the measure, since in his view small-scale entry will have little effect.)

(b) Herfindahl index and related measures

Hannah and Kay[30] have sought a measure that will take into account all the firms in the market, and at the same time will meet their conditions. The measure they propose is a symmetric strictly concave function, of which the simplest form is:

$$R = \sum_i s_i^{\alpha}$$

where s_i is the market share of the ith firm, and α is an elasticity parameter, the value of which determines the weight given to large firms relative to small ones. For example, as α tends to zero, so the index is simply the number of firms: as α gets large so the weight given to small firms becomes negligible. The index is best known with the value $\alpha = 2$, which is the popular Herfindahl[31] index

$$H = \sum_i s_i^2$$

The properties of the H-index have been explored by Adelman.[32] He relates the measure directly to the concentration curve. Our intuition suggests that the steeper is any segment of the curve, *ceteris paribus*, the greater should be the concentration index. Now the slope of any segment of the curve is given by

$$\frac{a_i}{A} \cdot \frac{1}{m_i}$$

where a_i is the total size (measured say in assets or sales) of any group of consecutively ranked firms m_i and A is the total size of the industry. Now to get a concentration index for the whole industry

---

[29] Hart, op. cit.   [30] Hannah and Kay, op. cit.
[31] A. O. Hirschman, 'The Paternity of an Index', *A.E.R.* 54 (1964), 761.
[32] M. A. Adelman, 'Comment on the "H" Concentration Measure as a Numbers-Equivalent', *R. Econ. Stats.* 51 (1969), 99–101.

we need to sum the slopes of all segments in the curve, with an appropriate weight. If the weight adopted is the share of each group of firms in total industry size the sum becomes,

$$\sum_i \left(\frac{a_i}{A} \cdot \frac{1}{m_i} \cdot \frac{a_i}{A} \right)$$

and if the summation is done for *each* firm individually, $m_i = 1$, and the index is the Herfindahl index.

The index reflects both the numbers of firms and their relative sizes. For example, n firms of equal size give an H value of $1/n$, which diminishes with n. The effect of inequality in relative sizes is best illustrated by an example. A duopoly with equal sized firms has $H = \frac{1}{2}$. Shares of $\frac{1}{4}$ and $\frac{3}{4}$ give $H = \frac{5}{8}$, and of $\frac{1}{10}$ and $\frac{9}{10}$, $H = \frac{82}{100}$.[33] Adelman also points out that the H-index can be used as a numbers-equivalent index. That is, a given H-index can be translated into the number of equal-sized firms that would give the same value of the index. This may help us to grasp the implications of different H values obtained for two industries with different firm size distributions. Hannah and Kay derive a similar 'numbers-equivalent' from the more general index, R. We know that n equal-sized firms have an R-index $n^{(1-\alpha)}$. Hence we can write the numbers-equivalent as

$$n(\alpha) = \left(\sum_i s_i^{\alpha} \right)^{1/(1-\alpha)}$$

[33] Alternatively we may consider the variance of firm sizes in an industry.

$$\sigma^2 = \frac{1}{n} \sum_i \left(\frac{1}{n} - \frac{a_i}{A} \right)^2$$

where σ^2 is the variance and n is the number of firms. This expression may be rearranged to give

$$n\sigma^2 = \sum_i \left(\frac{1}{n^2} - \frac{2a_i}{An} + \frac{a_i^2}{A^2} \right) = H - \frac{1}{n}$$

so

$$H = n\sigma^2 + \frac{1}{n}.$$

In this form we can easily discern the separate contribution of numbers of firms and inequality in firm sizes. Clearly, if all firms are the same size, $\sigma^2 = 0$ and the index becomes the reciprocal of the number of firms. A monopoly has an H value of 1, and H diminishes as the number of firms increases. Similarly, for a *given* number of firms, H increases with inequality in firm sizes, i.e. as σ^2 increases.

The interpretation of the numbers-equivalent is that it enables us to think of the size distribution of firms in a market as if it were n firms of equal size, which makes comparisons of different markets intuitive. The justification of the index is that it meets the criteria set out by Hannah and Kay, and that the theoretical implications of concentration examined above suggest that the R-index (and more specifically the Herfindahl) may be the appropriate measure.

Two empirical questions remain: what are the appropriate values of α to use, and how easy is the index to calculate? Hannah and Kay work with the range of values from 0·6 to 2·5,[34] reflecting their uncertainty as to the appropriate value for α. They make 256 pair-wise comparisons between actual populations of firms in different markets. In 101 cases the concentration curves intersected, but 38 of these occurred either for the largest firm, or for the smallest firms accounting for the last 2 per cent of 3 per cent of output, and were otherwise unambiguous. The range of values 0·6 to 2·5 gave a clear ranking of two sectors, which coincided with their intuition on the basis of the concentration curves.

Adelman[35] points out that it is not necessary to have information on *all* firms to obtain a reasonable approximation to the H-index in a particular case. Suppose we have information on firms ranked 1 to n, which have a total of s per cent of the market and assume that the market of the nth firm is s_n. Then the remaining firms in the

---

[34] When $\alpha = 1$ it appears that $n(\alpha)$ is undefined. Instead we look at the limit of n as $\alpha \to 1$ (Hannah and Kay. op. cit., 56–7). Let $\alpha = 1 + h$. Then as $h \to 0$, $s_i^\alpha \to s_i + h s_i \log s_i$, by Taylor's expansion.

Hence
$$\sum_i s_i^\alpha \to 1 + h \sum_i s_i \log s_i$$

and log
$$\log \sum_i s_i^\alpha \to h \sum_i s_i \log s_i$$

From the definition of $n(\alpha)$, $\log n(\alpha) = \dfrac{1}{1-\alpha}\log \sum_i s_i = -\dfrac{1}{h}\log \sum_i s_i$

Hence as $\alpha \to 1$,
$$\lim \log n(\alpha) = -\sum_i s_i \log s_i$$

$$\therefore n(\alpha) = e - \sum_i s_i \log s_i$$

$\sum_i s_i \log s_i$ is the H. Theil (*Economics and Information Theory*, Amsterdam, 1967) entropy index, which is sometimes proposed as a suitable measure of concentration.

[35] Adelman, op. cit.

industry must have $(1 - s)$ per cent of the market between them (and they obviously cannot exceed size s_n). Their maximum contribution to the H-index will be when they are of equal size. So we may estimate the *maximum* value of H for the industry. In practice we may need no more information than is needed for an eight firm concentration ratio.[36]

The frequency distribution of numbers-equivalent Herfindahl indices in 125 U.K. manufacturing sectors is presented in Table 3.1.

TABLE 3.1

*Numbers-equivalent Herfindahl indices for 125 U.K.
3-digit manufacturing sectors in 1968*

Equivalent number of firms	Number of sectors	%
0–5	7	5·6
5–10	18	14·4
10–20	25	20·0
20–50	43	34·4
50–100	18	14·4
>100	14	11·2
	125	100·0

Source: M. Waterson (unpublished): University of Newcastle, U.K. Calculated from 1968 Census material on enterprise size distribution by employment. The calculation makes the (erroneous, but unavoidable) assumption that there is no size variation *within* each size category. Hence the reported numbers-equivalents are *maximum* values.

These tend to underestimate the degree of concentration in each sector, partly because of how they are calculated, but also because no account is taken of the existence of sub-markets (by product or location) within each industry sector. We conclude that fewness of firms (in the numbers-equivalent sense) is a feature of many U.K. markets. It is therefore right to emphasize oligopoly behaviour in subsequent chapters.

(c) Measures of inequality in firm sizes

One measure is derived from the Lorenz curve. The Lorenz curve plots cumulative percentages of industry size against cumulative percentages of firms, starting with the smallest firm, as in Figure 3.5.

[36] R. Schmalensee, 'Using the H-Index of Concentration with Published Data', *R. Econ. Stats.* 59 (1977), 186–93, has examined in detail the practical problem of deriving estimates of H from published data (notably published concentration ratios).

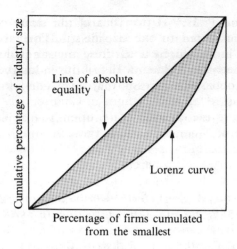

Fig. 3.5

A point on the line gives the percentage of firms that account for a given percentage of industry output. If one started with the largest firm this could give a measure analogous to that of the concentration ratio. However it is not often used in this form. More commonly the Gini coefficient is calculated as a summary statistic. This gives the stippled area in the diagram as a proportion of the area of the triangle *ABC*. The coefficient has a maximum of 1 and a minimum of 0. The properties of the coefficient, and its defects, can best be illustrated by examples. The first point is that the index is only a measure of relative size; it takes no account of numbers of firms. For example if all firms are of equal size the Lorenz curve will follow the diagonal (the line of absolute size equality) however many firms there may be. Even more striking is the case where there is a monopoly, when the Gini coefficient is equal to zero: as it would be for 10,000 equal sized firms! An advantage of the index is that it takes account of all firms in the industry, and does not suffer, like the concentration ratio, from the defect of only accounting for one point on the curve. (On the other hand, the need to know the complete size distribution may be a distinct disadvantage from the point of view of the availability of statistics.) It is often suggested that the Gini coefficient should be supplemented by the number of firms or some other measure of absolute concentration.

Alternative measures of inequality in firm sizes which have been extensively used in the analysis of *aggregate* industrial concentration over time are the variance of the logarithms of firm size (see, for example, Hart and Prais,[37] Utton[38]) and the slope coefficient of a Pareto distribution fitted ·to the size distribution (see for example, Ijiri and Simon[39]). The interest in these measures derives from the fact that the underlying frequency distributions can be viewed as the outcome of a stochastic process over time. This derivation of the measures is discussed at some length in Chapter 15.[40] However we should note that these measures are open to serious question as adequate measures of concentration. Hannah and Kay[41] point out that it is possible to find cases when merger reduces the number of firms in an industry, and where the concentration ratio rises substantially, and yet the variance of logarithms will decline. This counter-intuitive result (as far as measuring concentration is concerned) is due to the fact that the logarithmic transformation greatly understates the significance of the growth of large firms. A second objection[42] is that the theoretical distribution may be a poor fit for the data at the market level: so the value of the parameters of the fitted distribution reflect only a small part of the true state of affairs. For this reason Hart[43] prefers the measures based on the concentration curve at the market level.

The sharpest attack on inequality measures has been made by Hannah and Kay. Not only do all such measures fall on at least two of their criteria, but Hannah and Kay also argue that inequality *per se* is not interesting, from the point of view of firm behaviour. They imagine a market dominated by large firms, without any small firms at all. Inequality will be low. Then a number of very small firms start operations. Inequality measures will register a large increase. Yet no one would suppose that market conditions *or* market behaviour will change as a result.

4   PROBLEMS OF INDUSTRIAL CLASSIFICATION

In practice, empirical work operates with the Standard Industrial Classification.[44] This is a numerical classification scheme, with a larger number of digits indicating a more disaggregated classification.

[37] P. E. Hart, S. J. Prais, 'The Analysis of Business Concentration', *J.R.S.S.* 119 (1956), Part 2, 150–91.

[38] M. A. Utton, 'The Effect of Mergers on Concentration', *J.I.E.* 20 (1971), 42–58.

[39] Y. Ijiri, H. Simon, 'Effects of Mergers and Acquisitions on Business Firm Concentration', *J.P.E.* 79 (1971), 314–22.

[40] See below, pp. 501–508.   [41] Hannah and Kay, op. cit.

[42] R. E. Quandt, I. H. Silberman, 'On the Size Distribution of Firms', *A.E.R.* 56 (1966), 416–32.

[43] Hart, op. cit.

[44] See F. M. Scherer, *Industrial Market Structure and Economic Performance* (Chicago, 1971), 53–7.

Thus the single-digit classification distinguishes broad sectors of the economy like Agriculture and Forestry, Manufacturing Industry, Trade. Two-digit classification distinguishes industrial sectors within the 1-digit sectors, for example Chemicals or Textiles within manufacturing. Three and four digits subdivide even further, until the five-digit classification covers individual product classes. In the United States, a further subdivision into products at the 7-digit level is available. The basis for this classification is similarity on the production side and not any substitutability on the demand side. To quote an often-used example, under this system plastic buckets are classified as Plastics, metal ones as Metal Working, and wooden ones under Wood Products. But clearly these all enter the same market and compete with each other. The only way around this problem is to work with as detailed a breakdown of the S.I.C. as is possible (3- or 4-digit classifications), and to reclassify where necessary.

A further difficulty is that establishments are allocated to census classes on the basis of the principal products that they make. Their minor product lines may well fall in another census class, but the whole of their output and employment is attributed to the class of the firm's principal product. This could lead to substantial deviations of actual concentration from the measures computed with census data. Sargent Florence[45] suggested two further indices that should be computed to assess the scale of this problem in a particular census class. The first is the degree of specialization, which is the proportion of gross output of a census class accounted for by its principal products. The second is the degree of exclusiveness, or the extent to which the establishments in a particular census class are responsible for the total national output of the appropriate principal products. The further these indices deviate from 100 per cent, the less weight can be attached to concentration measures based on data for the census class.

There has been some discussion of the appropriate measure of firm size. The use of gross output or sales has the difficulty that it includes inter-firm sales which do not enter final markets. This is particularly the case where a sector has successive stages in production carried out in part by different firms and in part by vertically integrated firms. The extent of vertical integration of production will have a substantial effect on total reported sales. One way round this difficulty is to use value added as the measure rather than sales. But this brings its own problem of interpretation: if we are interested in market behaviour, the interest focuses on sales by each firm in 'final'

[45] P. S. Florence, *Investment, Location and Size of Plant*, N.I.E.S.R. (Cambridge, 1949).

markets. If there are various stages in production the correct procedure is to identify a 'market' for the semi-processed product at each stage. Transfers of semi-processed goods within vertically integrated firms should be included as part of the 'market' for these semi-processed goods, despite the fact that no price is paid for them in practice. The segmentation of the market by transfers within firms is an important market feature. However the prospect of obtaining such information is negligible. Employment or assets are sometimes used in place of sales or output measures. The defects of such measures are the same as those described above for value added, with the additional defect that there may be systematic biases. For example, if large firms in a sector are generally more capital intensive than small ones, asset measures will tend to emphasize the importance of large firms, employment measures to diminish them.

4

PRICING BEHAVIOUR

1   INTRODUCTION

Having in the last two chapters examined two major structural characteristics which firms face we are now in a position to start considering firms' conduct and its relation to those characteristics. The previous chapter brought in the issue of product heterogeneity and Chapter 11 will look at advertising and other selling costs in the broader context of the Active firm. In Chapters 4–6 we will be concerned with pricing, and will only bring in other forms of competitive conduct if germane to the issue of price behaviour. While this chapter looks at the basic theory and evidence arising from the monopoly model, Chapter 5 brings in the problem of oligopolistic interdependence and Chapter 6 the influence of potential competition.

The role of pricing has of course been central in the economic analysis of resource allocation problems for over a century. Despite this there are still many unresolved issues in the study of pricing and it is as well to start by pointing out the difficulties that have been inherent in relating theory and evidence on pricing.

1. There is no generally accepted view on how firms actually take their price decisions, even though there have been a large number of empirical studies of the matter, in one form or another. There are four reasons for this state of affairs.

(*a*) Different studies have generated conflicting observations.

(*b*) There are considerable pitfalls in inferring what businessmen are doing in a given situation from what either they say they are doing, or what they appear to be doing. (Such difficulties are amplified later.)

(*c*) There are a large number of ways in which a price decision may be made, and it is very likely that different situations require and involve very different pricing procedures. Alfred, for example has categorized types of situation as follows:[1]

(i) Type of Product:	Consumer	
	Industrial	
(ii) Type of Competition:	Competitive	
	Oligopolistic	
	Monopolistic	

---

[1] A. M. Alfred, 'Company Pricing Policy', *J.I.E.* 21, no. 1 (Nov. 1972), 1–16.

  (iv) Age of Product: Existing Product
                               New Product
  (v) Nature of Production: Single Product
                               Joint Products
                               Multi (Interchangeable) Products
                               Vertically Integrated Products
  (vi) Variations in Capacity: Utilizing existing capacity
                               Anticipating new capacity

Other categorizations could be added, but this list is enough to illustrate the great variety of possible pricing situations. Nearly all of the classifications can be combined with each other, and each combination may well result in its own peculiar pricing methods. It may well be, therefore, that for some purposes at least it is not necessarily useful to generalize about pricing procedures.

(*d*) In addition, firms differ in their management expertise, application, and effort. This may result in different degrees of importance being attached to pricing and different degrees of sophistication being exhibited in the pricing decision process.

2. Second, there is disagreement over the importance to be attached to pricing in the competitive process. Some, following traditional developments, have seen it as central, and much work has been done on price theory which excludes any other competitive vehicle. Increasingly, however, economists have begun to adopt a perspective familiar to businessmen, in which price is but one, and sometimes a relatively minor, competitive instrument, along with advertising, product differentiation, market dominance, etc. The relatively low level in the managerial hierarchy at which prices are frequently determined may add weight to the view that a firm's prices are often not regarded as necessarily central to its competitive strategy.

3. Third, as Silberston has emphasized, it is often not at all clear what is meant by 'the price' of a product.[2] Published or catalogued prices are frequently different from actual transactions prices as a result of discounts, special offers, methods of (and delay in) payment, trade-in values, amounts bought and transport charges. Manufacturers' prices not only differ from wholesalers' and retailers' prices but may well be subject to different influences. Many industrial transactions prices are determined by negotiation, by tendering, or after secret reductions from published prices. As a result, both micro- and macroeconomic investigations of pricing are likely to suffer from inadequate information on actual transactions prices.

4. Fourth, and often overlooked, is the fact that the factors determining the *level* at which a price is set, and the factors determining

[2] Z. A. Silberston, 'Price Behaviour of Firms', *E.J.* 80, no. 319 (Sept. 1970), 511–82.

whether and by how much it will be *altered*, may be very different, thus requiring different types of analysis and generating different pictures of how prices are determined. Instances will be noted where this distinction is of importance.

5. Until very recently price theory comprised a series of models all of which assumed either explicitly or by implication a world of certainty, in which the position and shape of cost and revenue curves were known to the firm. It seems plausible to imagine that price behaviour under uncertainty might be significantly different, and recent theorizing suggests that this is in fact the case.

6. Not unrelated to this, firms typically hold stocks of finished products. This breaks any direct link between production and sales and thereby creates more price discretion for firms. This again introduces new factors which limit the applicability of earlier price models to observed price behaviour. In addition the introduction of stock changes into the picture serves to remind us that firms will frequently be carrying out disequilibrium price adjustments which are not themselves normally encompassed in models designed to explain the equilibrium price level and its determinants.

In the light of all these factors it is not perhaps surprising that difficulties appear in interpreting price behaviour. To make the subject manageable we adopt the following approach. Section 2 briefly reviews the price behaviour predicted by the standard monopoly model which Chapter 1 argued was the proper starting-point. Uncertainty is then introduced to see how this changes the predictions made. Sections 3 and 4 then review and comment on the micro- and macroeconomic evidence available on how firms appear to make pricing decisions in practice, and relate it to the theory. Section 5 examines the role of inventories and order books in price behaviour.

In keeping with the over-all approach of the book, we will be almost exclusively concerned with the passive aspects of firms' behaviour, i.e. their pricing decisions in the light of given costs and market structure conditions. Brief reference to more active, constraint-manipulating objectives will be made, but by and large this is more appropriately left to the latter part of the book.

2 MONOPOLISTIC PRICE THEORY

In its most general form, the theory of monopolistic pricing is characterized by only three elements — the assumption of profit maximization, a downward sloping demand curve for a single differentiated product, and an average cost curve that may have any slope and which can be drawn as U-shaped to cover all possibilities. Writing marginal revenue (MR) as the first derivative of total revenue and similarly for marginal cost (MC), we obtain (with P = price, Q = output, AC = average cost)

$$(a)\ MR = \frac{d(P \cdot Q)}{dQ} = \frac{QdP}{dQ} + P \qquad (b)\ MC = \frac{d(AC \cdot Q)}{dQ} = \frac{QdAC}{dQ} + AC$$

Setting $MR = MC$ for profit maximization we obtain

$$P = AC + Q\left(\frac{dAC}{dQ} - \frac{dP}{dQ}\right)$$

The values of AC and dAC/dQ at the equilibrium price depend on the cost structure of the firm, and the values of Q and dP/dQ depend on the demand conditions it faces. The simplest comparative static theorems examine the consequences for the profit maximizing price of altering these. Suppose first that there is a shift in the cost structure. Using δ to denote changes in equilibrium values when functions *shift* (as opposed to d which gives derivatives of *given* curves), we obtain

$$(c)\ \frac{\delta P}{\delta AC} = 1 + \left(\frac{dAC}{dQ} - \frac{dP}{dQ}\right)\frac{\delta Q}{\delta AC} + Q\frac{\left(\delta\dfrac{dAC}{dQ} - \delta\dfrac{dP}{dQ}\right)}{\delta AC}$$

In theory the expression may have any positive or negative value, but if the demand curve is linear and we assume that the change in cost structure is a given change in marginal cost for all levels of output, then it is constrained[3] to be between 0 and 1. We therefore have the conclusion that prices will rise when variable costs rise but the profit margin will fall both absolutely and as a percentage of the price. If on the other hand the change is in fixed costs alone, then the expression has the value 0, giving the familiar result that fixed costs do not affect profit maximizing prices.

The reaction to changes in demand can also be disaggregated. Given that $MR = Q(dP/dQ) + P$ we can first consider changes in dP/dQ, with P and Q unchanged (a pivoting of the demand curve), and second a change in P and Q with no change in dP/dQ (a lateral shift of the demand curve). In the first case marginal revenue un-

[3] See Appendix for formal proof of this and other statements in this section.

ambiguously falls as the demand curve becomes steeper leading to decreased output and higher price. The absolute profit margin rises, but the percentage margin on price may rise or fall dependent on the shape of the average cost curve. If this is horizontal, the margin unambiguously rises. In the second case, marginal revenue unambiguously rises as the demand curve shifts to the right, raising output but leading to either a higher or lower price dependent on the relative gradients of the demand and marginal cost curves. In fact, however, it requires the gradient of the *MC* curve to be negative and within a particular range to generate a price reduction, and we shall ignore this possibility. The profit margin may rise or fall both in absolute and percentage terms depending on the shape of the average cost curve. Again, they rise if *AC* is constant. These results are summarized in Table 4.1, where the values in parentheses hold if average costs are constant.

TABLE 4.1

	Price	Profit Margin $P-AC$	Percentage Margin	$\dfrac{P-AC}{P}$
Rise in Fixed Costs	0	—		—
Rise in Variable Costs	+	—		—
Rightward shift of Demand Curve	+	?(+)		?(+)
Steepening of Demand Curve	+	+		?(+)

Either type of demand change will lower the elasticity of demand and we shall equate this in interpreting empirical evidence as an 'increase' in demand. It would of course be possible, however, for one to occur while the reverse of the other was occurring. It is clear from the table that the impact of demand on profit margins is very ambiguous in general terms. If, however, we assume average costs are constant, then the margin always rises in response.[4]

Once it is recognized that firms, even if they know their cost structure with certainty, very rarely if ever know the demand conditions they face, the picture changes. Very little at all can be said unless assumptions are made about the relationship between uncertainty and the other variables, and about how decision-takers view the uncertainty. The most useful approach has been first to adopt the Principle of Increasing Uncertainty, which states that the dispersion of possible total revenue resulting from a firm's price or output

---

[4] For a fuller derivation of optimal prices see W. Nordhaus, 'Recent Developments in Price Dynamics', in O. Eckstein (ed.), *The Econometrics of Price Determination* (S.S.R.C./ Federal Reserve System, 1972), 16–49.

decision increases with the Expected Value of total revenue.[5] Second we presume decision-takers are risk averse; they require ever larger increases in Expected Profit to compensate for constant increases in risk as measured by the dispersion of profits. Third, unlike the case of certainty, we now have to distinguish between firms which set price and sell the (as yet unknown) amount demanded and those which set output and sell it at the (as yet unknown) price which results. This is because in the latter case total revenue is unknown but not total cost. In the former *both* are unknown even if the cost curve is known. This makes the quantity-setting firm easier to analyse.

Taking this case first, the above assumptions imply that output will be set below the monopoly output, for although there is a loss of expected profit there is a gain from the reduction of risk consequent upon lower expected total revenue which did not exist in the case of certainty.

Turning to output responses to structural change, these also differ somewhat. A rise in fixed costs reduces expected profit. The existing risk, previously acceptable, is no longer so and output will be reduced in order to reduce risk. Output will still fall in response to an increase in variable costs but generally by less than is the case under certainty. This is because the lower dispersion of total revenue associated with the lower expected total revenue reduces the extent to which maximum profit will be forgone to reduce risk.

An upward shift of the (expected) demand curve will make risk avoidance more 'expensive' in terms of profit forgone and lead by itself to a rise in output. In addition the higher expected return will permit more risk to be borne by the risk averse firm. It is at least conceivable however, that a firm might be a risk *lover* to such an extent that this now *negative* effect could more than offset the 'substitution' effect above and actually reduce output. The final case of a pivoting of the (expected) demand curve is indeterminate because more or less risk may be borne dependent on whether expected return falls or rises.

The indeterminacy increases, however, once we explicitly consider price, as opposed to quantity setting. Now, because of uncertainty about cost, the dispersion of profit cannot be inferred purely from the dispersion of total revenue. While it seems likely that price will rise if any type of cost increases, if the demand curve shifts upwards, or if the latter pivots clockwise none of these are logically necessary even given our initial assumptions. In addition it is not possible to say

[5] See H. E. Leland, 'Theory of the Firm Facing Uncertain Demand', *A.E.R.* 62 (1972), 278-91.

unambiguously whether price will be set above or below the level it would be at under certainty; for example, a higher price might *increase* profit uncertainty if higher cost uncertainty offset lower revenue uncertainty. Further assumptions are necessary if this possibility is to be excluded.[6] As price setting is far more prevalent than quantity setting, recognition of uncertainty seriously undermines the predictive content of the monopolistic price model, unless restrictions on the magnitudes involved are introduced.

The other difficulty raised by uncertainty is as follows. Under certainty the price of a homogeneous product would have to be the same for all firms. Uncertainty permits a variety of prices and so it is rational for consumers to search for lower prices up to the point where the expected gain from searching further is cancelled out by the cost of search. But, as Rothschild has argued, firms would then face the same downward sloping demand curves, and if they are profit maximizers and have the same costs they will set the same price.[7] Hence the variability of prices would disappear. Models by Fisher, Diamond, and Rothschild[8] all give a single price, whereas a *spread* of prices is often observed and unless this is just a reflection of product heterogeneity it is likely to be explained in some way by uncertainty.

Two ways forward are:

(i) To presume constant shocks to the system which prevent full convergence.

(ii) To introduce the idea that firms vary price partly to get information about demand. A model by Rothschild and Yaari indicates that generally it does not pay to get much information this way and that prices may differ through 'error' therefore.[9]

In what follows it is sufficient to bear in mind the results of the certainty model, noting that uncertainty may modify the results and, in particular, cause prices to respond to fixed costs.

---

[6] If the uncertainty is multiplicative, i.e. $q = f(p) \cdot U$, then the ratio of risk to expected return is the same at all prices and nothing is gained by departing from the price level under certainty. But if some element of demand is independent of price then a higher price, by reducing the ratio of uncertain to certain demand, does reduce risk and leads to a higher price under uncertainty.

If the uncertain demand curve is additively separable, i.e. $d(dq/dp)/du = 0$, then it can be shown that an increase in uncertainty, U, will increase $d\pi/dp$ while leaving dq/dp unchanged. The result is a price lower than under certainty. See H. E. Leland, op. cit.

[7] M. Rothschild, 'Models of Market Organisation with Imperfect Information: A Survey', *J.P.E.* 81, no. 6 (Nov. 1973), 1283–1308.

[8] F. M. Fisher, 'Quasi-Competitive Price Adjustment by Individual Firms. A Preliminary Paper', *J.Econ. Th.* 2 (June 1970), 195–206; P. Diamond, 'A Model of Price Adjustment', *J. Econ. Th.* 3 (June 1971), 156–68; M. Rothschild, op. cit., 1298–9.

[9] See M. Rothschild, op. cit., 1299–1300 and appendices.

3 EMPIRICAL EVIDENCE ON PRICING: DIRECT OBSERVATION

Empirical evidence on firms' pricing decisions first entered the mainstream of economic thought in 1939 in the shape of Hall and Hitch's now famous article, based on their interviews with 38 businessmen.[10] Of these, 30 stated that their basic approach was to calculate or estimate unit costs and arrive at a price by adding a desired, 'normal' or conventional margin to it, to allow for profit. Both this and other studies cited below have revealed a number of variants of this practice, the differences between which are important in evaluating price behaviour and empirical studies of it.

(i) Typically firms only include the more easily identifiable costs, e.g. labour, raw materials, fuel, and transport, in estimating 'unit costs', other costs generally referred to as overheads[11] being allowed for by addition of a conventional margin prior to or in conjunction with the addition of one for profit. The delineation between these costs is largely arbitrary and varies from firm to firm.[12]

(ii) In a multi-product firm where various costs, in particular overheads, are joint costs, firms may differ in their allocation of these across products.

(iii) Firms may employ one or more of a number of methods for obtaining unit cost figures.

(a) Current actual unit costs.

(b) Average unit costs over a period.

(c) Expected unit costs.[13]

(d) 'Standard' unit costs, i.e. unit costs at some normal or planned rate of capacity utilization.[14]

Subsequent studies indicate that average cost pricing is very prevalent. Andrews, in a much longer study and on the basis of various investigations, supported the principle as valid and incorporated it into a theory of competition.[15] Hague also found it to be typical,[16]

---

[10] R. Hall, C. Hitch, 'Price Theory and Business Behaviour', *Oxford Economic Papers*, no. 2 (May 1939), 12–45.

[11] These will sometimes include the 'fixed' costs referred to in introductory economic texts, e.g. plant and machinery, but (a) these can be included in the basic calculation on a unit basis, and (b) variable costs, e.g. administrative staff, may be included in overheads.

[12] 'Full Cost' pricing is only an appropriate term if either (a) *all* costs are included in the unit cost calculation, or (b) the percentage added for overheads is accurately based on the actual output levels obtaining when the output being priced was produced.

[13] See M. A. Adelman, 'The A & P Case', *Q.J.E.* 63, no. 2 (May 1949), 238–57, for an interesting example of this case.

[14] In all cases these costs are 'accounting costs', i.e. expenditure or liability incurred by the firm. They do not include the opportunity costs referred to in Chapter 2, and to this extent accounting profit will be higher than firms' true profit.

[15] P. W. S. Andrews, *Manufacturing Business* (London, 1949).

[16] D. Hague, 'Economic Theory & Business Behaviour', *R. Econ. Stud.* 3 (1949), 144–57.

and a series of studies of specific industries appearing in the 1950s contained evidence on industrial pricing policies which further confirmed the very widespread use of average (or occasionally full) cost pricing.[17]

In the 1960s and 1970s further evidence has come from more diverse sources to underline its importance. Fog examined 139 firms in Denmark and found average cost pricing to be by far the most dominant form.[18] Fitzpatrick added to a growing number of studies in the United States which had the same general conclusions.[19] The behavioural approach to the theory of the firm stimulated further interest in detailed empirical work, most notably in this context that of Cyert, March, and Moore, who were able to predict retail prices very accurately on the basis of wholesale costs and a percentage mark-up rule.[20] Most recently, from a large number of other studies which have supported the Hall and Hitch[21] findings, we may mention that of Skinner in which approximately three-quarters of 166 firms on Merseyside used one form or another of average cost pricing.[22] It is interesting to note that this is almost exactly the same percentage of respondents as in the Hall and Hitch study thirty-one years earlier.

There of course remains the not insignificant number of firms who did not appear to use this approach. A number of investigations, including several already mentioned, have identified several other pricing procedures. Smyth found evidence that in some cases firms derived a target acceptable cost level by deducting a desired profit margin from a market determined price.[23] Alfred quotes the case of the International Harvester Company, which adopted a similar

---

[17] See for example: I. F. Pearce, 'A study in price policy', *Economica*, N.S. 23 (May 1956), 114–27; R. Robson, *The Cotton Industry in Britain* (London, 1957); D. Hague, *The Economics of Man-made Fibres* (London, 1957); A. Pool, C. Llewellyn, *The British Hosiery Industry: A Study in Competition* (Leicester University Press, 1958).

[18] B. Fog, *Industrial Pricing Policies* (Amsterdam, 1960).

[19] A. Fitzpatrick, *Pricing Methods of Industry* (Colorado, 1964).

[20] R. M. Cyert, J. G. March, C. G. Moore, 'A Model of Retail Ordering and Pricing by a Department Store', in R. E. Frank, A. A. Kuehn, W. F. Massey (ed.), *Quantative Techniques in Marketing Analysis* (London, 1962), 502–22.

[21] See for example: R. Barback, *The Pricing of Manufactures* (London, 1964); N. Balkin, 'Prices in the Clothing Industry', *J.I.E.* 5 (Nov. 1956), 1–15; J. Sizer, 'The Accountant's Contribution to the Pricing Decision', *Journal of Management Studies*, 3 (May 1966) 129–49; H. Edwards, *Competition and Monopoly in the Soap Industry* (Oxford, 1962); G. F. Rainnie (ed.), *The Woollen & Worsted Industry* (Oxford, 1965). The work of the Monopolies Commission and the National Board for Prices and Incomes has also revealed further examples.

[22] R. C. Skinner, 'The Determination of Selling Prices', *J.I.E.* 18 (July 1970), 201–17.

[23] R. Smyth, 'A Price-minus theory of cost', *Scottish Journal of Political Economy*, 14 (1967), 110–17.

approach for new products;[24] Many examples of 'price-lining' exist;[25] and Fog even found cases where the allocation of costs was determined by the desire to make a conventional margin and a desired price consistent.[26] Selection of a price equal to (or in some constant relation to) that set by a dominant firm (or group of firms) has been frequently reported, and conditions of very intensive competition may mean that prices are dictated entirely by the market, independent of the cost conditions facing the firm.[27]

Other approaches mentioned in the literature which can effectively exclude consideration of costs include various types of discriminatory pricing, penetration pricing (i.e. setting price at a level which ensures a very rapid increase in either market share, or in the demand for a new product, in order to obtain considerable economies of scale), and the use of price to indicate (genuinely or spuriously) a particular degree of product quality. The implications of such procedures are discussed later.

None the less, the dominant method of pricing is that based on average cost, with the apparent implication that only supply side considerations are important in determining prices. By itself however it throws no light on either pricing objectives or the validity of the monopolistic pricing model, for the selection of any price is equivalent to the selection of the margin which together with average cost gives that price. This can be simply illustrated by considering the profit maximizing price when average costs are constant.[28] In equation (c) on page 115, dAC/dQ is zero. Subtracting AC from both sides and dividing by P we obtain

$$\frac{P - AC}{P} = -\frac{QdP}{PdQ} = \frac{1}{E_D}$$

[24] A. M. Alfred, op. cit.

[25] i.e. selling a range of heterogeneous products all at the same price, e.g. fashion clothing.

[26] B. Fog, op. cit.

[27] In fact it has been found that even considerable product differentiation may not permit much flexibility for firms to pursue average cost pricing. See G. Maxey, Z. A. Silberston, *The Motor Industry* (London, 1964). Note however that this view is based on the uniformity of prices (but not margins), rather than on an investigation of the pricing process itself, which was not included in the study.

[28] The fact that firms can estimate a unit cost figure for normal ranges of production independent of actual output indicates that for pricing purposes firms often think of their average variable (or average total) cost curves as horizontal. This may well be because of the use of average or standard unit costs and avoids the difficulty of having to estimate demand (in order to estimate output and average costs) before the price resulting from average cost pricing can be calculated.

where E_D is the price-elasticity of demand. So if the margin expressed as a fraction of price equals the reciprocal of the price elasticity of demand, the price is profit maximizing however the price was determined. The crucial questions therefore concern whether the margin responds to demand in the way predicted and how simple pricing rules of thumb might generate such margins.

To examine these it is useful to distinguish three groups. (*a*) Those firms which never vary the margin (though even here reallocation of costs as mentioned above may preserve some discretion over price for the firm). (*b*) Those which adopt a margin which is applied in all normal situations, but varied in the light of unexpected or exceptional conditions including demand ones. (*c*) Those which systematically determine prices in the light of demand considerations and for whom the margin is simply the result of this price on the one hand and their unit costs on the other.

In Hall and Hitch's original work, 40 per cent of those using average cost stated that they added a fixed margin, its size being predominantly determined by what they regarded as in some sense 'justified' and/or conventionally acceptable within the industry. The other 60 per cent, while also stressing these two factors, admitted that in certain circumstances some variation in the margin would be permitted,[29] including changed demand. Nearly all of the other studies so far referred to also found examples of this second category, notably Fog. Now such behaviour could quite well be the heuristic process by which firms attempt to maximize profits. The need for this arises because the choice of a profit maximizing price is potentially very complex. The best price depends on a range of complex cost and demand data, on estimates of elasticities, of effectiveness of various sales strategies, on likely reactions from existing or potential competitors, etc. and the computational problems arising are generally very great. More important, under uncertainty, firms never know what price will maximize profits, nor whether they have been maximizing profits. Even maximization of expected value of profits is generally ruled out by the absence of information on probabilities, the number of variables involved, and the asymmetric effects of a large unexpected gain, and a large unexpected loss. Quite often the only possible response is a process of trial and error, which has three components: (*a*) use of a simple rule of thumb to establish a price; (*b*) repetition of acceptable decisions and avoidance of unacceptable ones; (*c*) adjustment upwards of the acceptable level of profit if the existing level is repeatedly achieved, and

---

[29] In fact in nearly all cases this involved cutting the margin if demand was depressed. Only two claimed that they might raise it in periods of high demand.

downwards if repeatedly missed. Clearly average cost pricing with adjustable margins can be seen as such a reaction to complexity and uncertainty about demand conditions. It represents a 'best first move' which massively reduces information gathering costs, but does not prevent sequential adjustment towards profit maximization if this is the objective of the firm.

A number of studies have directly supported this. Baumol and Quandt generated by computer a series of cost/output and demand/price points and calculated the profit that would be earned by using the average cost pricing principle.[30] They then also calculated, on the basis of different possible cost and demand functions which fitted the original data, the maximum possible profit. For several very plausible cost and demand functions they found that the average cost principle generated approximately 80 per cent of the maximum possible. Bearing in mind the heavy reduction in the cost of market research, and the impossibility of removing all uncertainties, a rule with this degree of success might well effectively be a profit maximizing approach.[31] In support, Day was able to show in a simple computer experiment that very simple decision rules based on repeating changes that increased profit and reversing ones that reduced them could lead a firm to profit levels little less than maximum.[32] The two conditions necessary for this were a reasonably stable environment and the interpretation of very small improvements as indicating that further change would produce only insignificant further gains.

Such simulations have a certain amount of direct empirical support—e.g., Skinner's study referred to above implied much the same behaviour. He found that nearly three-quarters of his interviewees used 'variable (or direct or marginal) costing' despite, it will be remembered, three-quarters of the total actually setting prices by the addition of a margin to full cost.[33] The implication would appear to be that between 50 per cent and 75 per cent of his sample firms determine the margin to be added on the basis of marginalist principles. Skinner contrasts this with the findings of Sizer, who, on

[30] W. Baumol, R. Quandt, 'Rules of Thumb and Optimally Imperfect Decisions', *A.E.R.* 54 (Mar. 1964), 23–46.

[31] Various limitations of the study suggest tha the figure may be somewhat on the high side, but the approach and implications are none the less instructive.

[32] R. H. Day, S. Morley, K. R. Smith, 'Myopic Optimising and Rules of Thumb in a Micro Model of Industrial Growth', *A.E.R.* 64, no. 1 (Mar. 1974), 11–23. In another study he and others show that a combination of profit maximization with a 'safety first' approach to demand uncertainty can generate price policies of essentially the average cost pricing form. See R. H. Day, D. J. Aigner, K. R. Smith, 'Safety Margins and Profit Maximisation in the Theory of the Firm', *J.P.E.* 79, no. 6 (1971), 1293–1301.

[33] R. C. Skinner, op. cit.

the basis of his own and others' work, recognized some modification, especially 'shaving' of margins in particular circumstances, but rejected the notion of widespread and systematic determination of the margin by marginalist principles.[34] Sizer in reply suggested that Skinner's evidence on 'variable (direct or marginal) costing' should not be equated with marginalism as embodied in theoretical models but simply the division of costs into fixed and variable elements and the use of the latter in pricing, in other words just average cost pricing.[35] Thus there are considerable problems of terminology and interpretation in identifying how margins are determined on the basis of accounts of it from price setters themselves.[36]

Finally there are a number of studies which suggest price behaviour in the third category of price formation, namely systematic incorporation of demand factors on price. Eiteman argued that sales directors were frequently asked for information on whether the volume response to a change of margin would make the latter justified in terms of higher profit, and that this was simply the real-world counterpart of essentially marginalist pricing.[37] Earley examined 110 very successful American firms and found a variety of pricing methods which, despite their dependence on cost data, were basically attempts to improve profits by marginalist techniques.[38] In addition Hague identified a number of firms which he regarded as attempting to select a margin so as to maximize profits.[39]

It might be thought that the easiest way to test whether average cost pricing is used to maximize profit is to estimate whether the price–cost margin is in fact equal to the reciprocal of the Elasticity of Demand. This, however, is extremely difficult because

[34] J. Sizer, op. cit. The three other studies referred to by him are: J. Goodlad, 'Industrial Management', *Management Accounting*, 43 (May 1965); M. Howe, 'Marginal Analysis in Accounting', *Yorkshire Bulletin of Economic & Social Research*, 14 (Nov. 1962); H. Hart, D. F. Prussman, *A Report of a Survey of Management Accounting Techniques in the S.E. Hants Coastal Region* (University of Southampton, 1963).

[35] J. Sizer, 'Note on "The Determination of Selling Prices" ', *J.I.E.* 20 (Nov. 1971), 85–9. He also rejected Skinner's argument that perhaps Sizer had failed to discover a marginalist approach, because those questioned were non-accountants who did not understand the terminology, on the grounds that most of those interviewed were in fact accountants.

[36] This harks back to 1946 when Machlup first attacked Hall and Hitch for not realizing that they had simply observed the rules of thumb which businessmen used to approximately achieve the results precisely described by the marginalist analysis. He likened it to a car driver who can drive 'optimally' without knowing the engineering principles or calculating the forces involved, nor even knowing the engineering terminology. See F. Machlup, 'Marginal Analysis & Empirical Research', *A.E.R.* 36 (Sept. 1946), 519–54.

[37] W. J. Eiteman, 'Price Determination in Oligopolistic & Monopolistic Situations', *Michigan Business Reports*, no. 33 (University of Michigan, 1960).

[38] J. S. Earley, 'Marginal Policies of Excellently Managed Companies', *A.E.R.* 46, no. 1 (Mar. 1946), 44–70.

[39] D. Hague, *Pricing in Business* (London, 1971).

(i) information on elasticities is hard to find (indeed that is one rationale for using average cost pricing), (ii) there is little information on firms' margins over marginal cost even if we assume this to equal average variable cost, (iii) short- and long-run elasticities will normally be different and so a knowledge of the firm's time horizon is required to make the test. Cowling and Rayner[40] found short-run elasticities[41] from 2·81 to 5·58, implying mark-ups of between 18 per cent and 35 per cent, which make it difficult to reject out of hand the hypothesis that firms attempt to maximize short-run profit. None the less, the general conclusion is that firms very rarely attempt this.

The very thorough study by Kaplan, Dirlam, and Lanzillotti identified five major pricing objectives—to stabilize price and/or margin; to maintain or improve market share; to achieve a target return on investment; to meet competition; and to allow for the characteristics of each particular product market.[42] The last two may well be consistent with profit maximization in the short run, but the first three would not be in general. Skinner found a considerable number of managers who thought profits in the short run could be increased by altering their prices.[43] In addition a price rise of at least approximately 5 per cent of average was thought necessary to have any impact on demand. As, *ceteris paribus*, this would increase profits at least 50 per cent in the average firm, it further undermines belief in a short-run profit maximization.[44] It follows from this that pricing must be viewed in a longer-term perspective. This however raises a number of difficulties. If, as is usual, we assume long-run profit maximization in the form of the present value of all future profits, then it is essential to know all the repercussions thought likely to occur as a result of the price set, including competitors' reactions, structural changes (new products, new firms, mergers, etc.). These issues are examined in Chapters 5 and 6, where longer-term demand conditions and the structural characteristics on which they depend are introduced and related to price behaviour.

An impressionistic summary of the microeconomic evidence reviewed is given in Table 4.2, which indicates the three different

[40] K. Cowling, A. Rayner, 'Price, Quality & Market Share', *J.P.E.* 78, no. 6 (Nov. 1970), 1292–1309.

[41] The prices were adjusted to allow for quality differences between competing products.

[42] A. Kaplan, J. Dirlam, R. Lanzillotti, *Pricing in Big Business* (Washington, 1958).

[43] R. Skinner, op. cit.

[44] The apparent belief in relatively low demand elasticity, which applies for downward price movements as well, does not fit well with Cowling and Rayner's evidence of higher elasticities. The difference may partly be explained by a very short term perspective on the part of Skinner's interviewees, and possibly by heavy non-linearity of elasticity, i.e. small price changes have little effect, but larger ones have proportionately much larger effects.

TABLE 4.2

Classification of Pricing Procedures

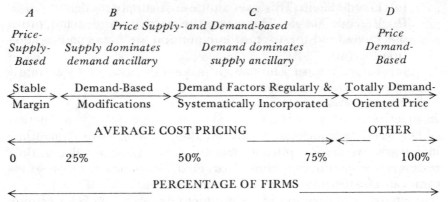

A	B	C	D
	Price Supply- and Demand-based		
Price- Supply- Based	*Supply dominates demand ancillary*	*Demand dominates supply ancillary*	*Price Demand- Based*

Stable Margin ⟷ Demand-Based Modifications ⟷ Demand Factors Regularly & Systematically Incorporated ⟷ Totally Demand- Oriented Price

AVERAGE COST PRICING ⟶ ⟵ OTHER ⟶

0   25%   50%   75%   100%

PERCENTAGE OF FIRMS

categories of average cost pricing plus the case where it is not applied. (Category *C* includes those cases where acceptable cost figures are derived from desired prices and margins, and cases of reallocation of accounting costs for the same purpose.) The size of the divisions is at best a vague indication only. The proportions will undoubtedly vary with the sophistication of a firm's management, possibly also with the size of the firm, and have probably changed over thirty-five years, with more firms moving from *A* to *B* and from *B* to *C*. In addition *A* and *B* may be rather more important in the initial determination of the price of a new product, with *C* and *D* being much more important when subsequent price changes are being considered. Failure to distinguish these may be partly responsible for the widespread examples of partially contradicting results. The main conclusion is that increases in demand do appear to have the impact on margins predicted (if the former is interpreted as a fall in the elasticity of demand), but the sensitivity of margins (as opposed to prices) to cost changes is not so clear. Finally, this summary supports the initial point made that it is dangerous to generalize about firms' pricing procedures.

4   EMPIRICAL EVIDENCE ON PRICING: ECONOMETRIC ANALYSIS

These microeconomic studies have been increasingly supplemented by econometric analysis of industry-based or even economy-wide quantitative data, some of it based on a microeconomic pricing decision model, and some explicitly directed at explaining variations in the relevant economic variables at the macroeconomic level. Here again conflicting evidence exists. In principle all models should fall into one or other of four types.[45]

1. Price = Cost + Margin
   (a) Fixed Margin. This gives a pure cost/supply model
   (b) Variable Margin. This means the elasticity of demand, profit objectives, and the form of competition are important in addition to costs.
   (c) Target return. The margin is then determined by setting a price to achieve the target.
2. Price is a function purely of excess demand.

In practice many models are hybrid of the form; price is a function of costs and excess demand. In what follows we first examine some major and auxiliary studies relating price to cost and demand, then review some conflicting studies of price behaviour over the trade cycle, and finally look at critical assessments of the latter.

A major investigation of U.S. prices by Eckstein and Fromm allowed for cost and demand influences, short- and long-term aspects, different pricing goals, and the role of inventories and order books (see later), and concluded that of the price variations explained, roughly 50 per cent could be attributed to cost changes, and 50 per cent to demand.[46] A typical eclectic equation from their study is

$$WPI = 0{\cdot}030 + 0{\cdot}491 \ ULC_t^N + 0{\cdot}543 \ ULC_{t-1}^N + 0{\cdot}267 \, (ULC - ULC_t^N)$$
$$\qquad\qquad\quad (3{\cdot}62) \qquad\qquad (4{\cdot}29) \qquad\qquad\quad (2{\cdot}73)$$

$$+ \ 0{\cdot}186 \ Pm + 0{\cdot}001 \ \frac{x}{x_k} + 0{\cdot}326 \ \Delta \left(\frac{Ou}{S}\right)_{t-1} \quad \bar{R}^2 = 0{\cdot}982$$
$$\quad (5{\cdot}82) \qquad (2{\cdot}91) \qquad (2{\cdot}46)$$

where *WPI* is the wholesale price index
       ULC is unit labour costs
       ULC^N is normal or standard unit labour costs
       Pm is an index of material input prices
       x/x_k is the industrial operating rate
       Ou/S is the ratio of unfilled orders (at period end) to average sales volume during the period.

This equation shows both normal unit labour costs *and* deviations of

[45] See P. H. Earl, *Inflation and the Structure of Industrial Prices* (Lexington, 1973).

[46] O. Eckstein, G. Fromm, 'The Price Equation', *A.E.R.* 58, no. 5 (Dec. 1968), 1158-83. They also found a tendency for prices to rise whenever the level of capacity utilization was above approximately 80 per cent.

actual from normal to be important[47] as well as material costs and two separate demand variables. Quarterly change equations, apart from predictably lower correlation coefficients, give much the same pattern of results, which are amongst the strongest discovered.

A number of other studies have been based on trying to correlate price movements with different variables representing the impact of demand changes. Brownlie regressed profit margins on the ratio of output to horse power of installed machinery (in effect a capacity utilization measure) as a demand variable, and obtained equations which in both cross-sectional and time-series form indicated a signifiant demand effect.[48] If, however, firms calculate price by adding conventional margins to average *variable* cost, then increases in demand, by reducing average *fixed* costs will tend to increase the realized profit margin despite no change in the conventional margin. It is not clear therefore that these results confirm the variability of prices as a function of demand changes.

The results do however fit with McFetridge's investigation of the Canadian Cotton Textile Industry, in which, having incorporated the effect of standard unit costs,[49] approximately 50 per cent of the remaining price variation was explained by demand.[50] Here the demand variables used were the deviation between the actual and desired ratio of unfilled orders to sales, and the deviation between the actual and desired ratio of finished inventory to sales.[51] The main supply–demand regression was

$$P = -0.567 + 0.115 \frac{\Delta ULC^N}{ULC^N} + 0.14 \frac{\Delta MC}{MC}$$
$$\quad (1.47) \quad (1.89) \qquad\qquad (3.56)$$

$$+ 3.46 \frac{U}{S} - 2.81 \frac{I}{S} \qquad \bar{R}^2 = 0.44$$
$$\quad (5.0) \qquad (3.8)$$

where MC is material cost
       U/S is the unfilled orders variable
       I/S is the inventory variable.

[47] The course of *actual* labour costs may well of course reflect demand changes over the cycle.

[48] A. Brownlie, 'Some Econometrics of Price Determination', *J.I.E.* 13, no. 2 (Mar. 1965), 116–21.

[49] Actual average costs were found to have little significance.

[50] D. McFetridge, 'The Determinants of Price Behaviour: A Study of the Canadian Cotton Textile Industry', *J.I.E.* 22, no. 2 (Dec. 1973), 141–52.

[51] Based on the assumption in both cases that the desired level was (*a*) constant, and (*b*) equal to the average actual level over the period examined.

A lagged formulation made little difference. It is noteworthy that while normal unit labour costs were just significant, actual unit labour costs were not, but the demand variables were highly significant.

Ripley and Segal took data from 395 different industries at the S.I.C. 4-digit level as a basis for a cross-sectional analysis of the effect of costs on price variation.[52] Their basic equation was:

$$\Delta P = \begin{array}{c} 1\cdot22 \\ (12\cdot0) \end{array} + \begin{array}{c} 0\cdot36\,\Delta ULC \\ (9\cdot9) \end{array} + \begin{array}{c} 0\cdot17\,\Delta MC \\ (7\cdot3) \end{array} - \begin{array}{c} 0\cdot20\,\Delta X \\ (8\cdot0) \end{array} \quad \bar{R}^2 = 0\cdot57$$

X is real output.

The negative real output term was taken to indicate the effect of rapid growth in lowering unit costs independent of labour and material costs because of technological advance. The coefficients demonstrate that cost increases will result in lower margins as the initial theory predicted. The $\bar{R}^2$ is consistent with Eckstein and Fromm's results on the effect of costs on prices.

It may be added that Shinkai came up with not dissimilar results for Japanese industry.[53] He, like Lund and Rushdy for Britain (see below), and Eckstein and Fromm for the U.S., found that costs explain roughly half (46 per cent) of price variation. On the other hand, although dummy variables for demand were very significant, they explained only between 10 per cent and 14 per cent of price variation on their own, added virtually nothing to the equations containing cost variables, and made the labour cost variables insignificant. For example,

$$\frac{P_{it}}{P_{it-1}} = 0\cdot5051 + 0\cdot4949\frac{PI_{it}}{PI_{it-1}} + \underset{(0\cdot87)}{0\cdot130\,ULC} - \underset{(0\cdot63)}{0\cdot110\,UFC}$$
$$\underset{(4\cdot37)}{-\,0\cdot0092\,INV} \quad \bar{R}^2 = 0\cdot49$$

P_{it} is the price index of industry i at time t.
PI is input price.
UFC is unit financial cost.
INV is an inventory (demand) dummy.

[52] F. C. Ripley, L. Segal, 'Price Determination in 395 Manufacturing Industries', *R. Econ. Stats.* 55, no. 3 (Aug. 1973), 263–71.
[53] Y. Shinkai, 'Business Pricing Policies in Japanese Manufacturing Industries', *J.I.E.* 22, no. 4 (June 1974), 255–64.

This is not necessarily a different result from other studies, however, because actual as opposed to normal unit labour costs were used. Consistent results, but using a somewhat different procedure, were also found for Benelux countries and France by Phlips.[54]

Another way of attempting to discover the impact of demand on prices is to examine whether fluctuations in demand over the trade cycle are associated with fluctuations in prices and/or profit margins. In the first of a series of such studies Neild found that the introduction of a demand variable (based on unemployment in relation to unfilled vacancies) added virtually nothing to the explanatory power of the best price equation based on input costs, productivity, and lagged prices.[55] He concluded that there was considerable short-term stability in the price–cost relationship at the aggregate level and that the pressure of demand had no significant impact.

Similar implications with regard to the impact of demand were found by Godley and Nordhaus.[56] They first removed all cyclical variations from quarterly data covering all unit cost components (labour, materials, fuel, services, and indirect taxes) in order to derive figures for 'normal' unit costs, i.e. the value of unit costs if output were exactly on its long-term trend path. They next assumed that prices were derived solely by adding a constant percentage[57] to 'normal historical unit cost', with the figure for each category of cost based on the normal unit cost of that input at the time of its purchase.[58] Thirdly, the price series so generated was compared with the actual movement of prices between 1955 and 1970, and found to give what they considered a good fit, except for the fact that the actual margin exhibited a long-term decline from 1961 to 1970.[59] The main correlation in log form was:

---

[54] L. Phlips, 'Business Pricing Policies and Inflation—Some Evidence from EEC Contries', *J.I.E.* 18 (Nov. 1969), 1-14.

[55] R. R. Neild, 'Pricing and Employment in the Trade Cycle', N.I.E.S.R. Occasional Paper 21 (1963). Input costs and productivity together determine unit costs.

[56] W. A. H. Godley, W. D. Nordhaus, 'Pricing in the Trade Cycle', *E.J.* 82 (Sept. 1972), 853-82.

[57] The margin existing in 1963

[58] This involves deriving the lag between purchase of inputs and sales embodying them from the stock/sales figures and assumption concerning (i) the fraction of bought-in materials entering at the beginning of the productive process, and (ii) the rate at which the other inputs enter the process.

[59] This might be the result, according to Godley and Nordhaus, of (i) a rise in non-included costs, e.g. Selective Employment Tax, Regional Employment Premium and Profits Tax, (ii) control of steel prices, (iii) Incomes Policy and/or (iv) increasing competitive pressures, perhaps resulting from an overvalued currency.

$$\Delta\ln P_t = 0\cdot001399 + 0\cdot000238\,\Delta\ln(X/XN)_t$$
$$(1\cdot42) \qquad\quad (0\cdot66)$$

$$+\ 0\cdot6248\,\Delta\ln \hat{P}_t \qquad \bar{R}^2 = 0\cdot36$$
$$(5\cdot36)$$

where P_t is actual price
  $\hat{P}_t$ is predicted price
  X/XN is a capacity based demand variable.

The minute and insignificant coefficient of the demand variable is striking.

In addition a series of 100 tests were carried out (10 different demand variables with each of 10 different equation specifications) to see if any demand influence could be identified. Of these 96 generated insignificant parameter values (50 positive, 46 negative) and of the 4 significant ones, three were negative in sign. It is just possible that the one significant positive value could be more important in theory than all the other 99 values if the latter included inadequate specifications and inappropriate demand variables, but even this is undermined by their estimate that in this one case the movement of demand from trough to peak of the cycle would itself only raise prices 0·002 per cent.

The implications of these two studies, which do much to disturb the eclectic position revealed in the previous references, have themselves been challenged. Neild's work was criticized by Lund and Rushdy.[60] They argued first that two of Neild's three main equations implicitly contained a demand element. All three in measuring the costs to which the given margin was to be added calculated unit labour costs as w/k where w is the wage rate and k is labour productivity, but in two versions a productivity *trend* figure was used rather than actual productivity to allow for price being based on 'normal' rather than actual cost. In this case a cyclical upswing in demand which tends to be associated with an above-trend level of productivity will give lower *actual* unit labour costs than Neild's measure of it. A good correlation between prices and Neild's measure therefore implies that *actual* margins are rising rather than constant in time of rising demand.

The significance of this point is twofold. First it illustrates that a

---

[60] F. Rushdy, P. Lund, 'The Effect of Demand on Prices in British Manufacturing Industry', *R.Econ. Studs.* 34 (1967), 361–74. For other findings contrary to Neild see J. Johnston, 'The Price Level under Full Employment in the UK', in D. Hague, op. cit., and E. Nevin, 'The Cost Structure of British Manufacturing', *E.J.* 53 (1963), 642–64.

theory of *price* stability in the face of fluctuating demand and a
theory of *margin* stability are likely to be quite inconsistent. Second,
even if average cost pricing were applied ubiquitously and with a
rigid margin it could still give either type of result depending on
whether the margin was applied to 'standard' costs or to actual costs.
We cannot infer from Lund and Rushdy's argument that demand influences the pricing process, because they *assume* it is actual costs
which are the basis of the prices set. This we have seen is by no
means necessarily the case.[61]

There was however a more positive side to Lund and Rushdy's
study. Arguing that for both theoretical and technical reasons price
changes were to be preferred to price levels as the dependent
variable, they found demand variables to be significant in many
cases and inclusion of them to increase the squared correlation coefficient (though only on average from 0·59 to 0·65).

Representative of their results are the following two equations,
one without and one with their preferred demand variable (notation
changed).

$$\Delta P = 0\cdot566 + 0\cdot09 \; ULC_t + 0\cdot080 \; ULC_{t-1} - 0\cdot072 \; ULC_{t-2}$$
$$\quad (4\cdot55) \quad (2\cdot36) \qquad (2\cdot00) \qquad\qquad (1\cdot80)$$

$$\quad + 0\cdot082 \; MC_t + 0\cdot122 \; MC_{t-1} + 0\cdot092 \; MC_{t-2} \qquad \bar{R}^2 = 0\cdot86$$
$$\qquad (4\cdot10) \qquad\quad (5\cdot55) \qquad\quad (4\cdot84)$$

$$\Delta P = 0\cdot661 + 0\cdot056 \; ULC_t + 0\cdot047 \; ULC_{t-1} - 0\cdot088 \; ULC_{t-2}$$
$$\quad (5\cdot54) \quad (1\cdot47) \qquad (1\cdot21) \qquad\qquad (2\cdot31)$$

$$\quad + 0\cdot075 \; MC_t + 0\cdot123 \; MC_{t-1} + 0\cdot070 \; MC_{t-2}$$
$$\qquad (3\cdot99) \qquad\quad (6\cdot15) \qquad\quad (3\cdot63)$$

$$\quad + 0\cdot803 \; d_{t-1} \qquad\qquad\qquad\qquad\qquad\qquad \bar{R}^2 = 0\cdot883$$
$$\qquad (2\cdot66)$$

where d_{t-1} is a *labour* excess demand measure. Again demand is significant but undermines the actual unit labour cost variables and
makes little improvement on the correlation coefficient.

A more sweeping rejection of the view that demand does not

---

[61] Lund and Rushdy also argued that Neild's demand variable was mis-specified and
implied a distributed lag with *increasing* weights. McCallum however showed Neild's formulation to be correct even though it had increasing weights because they were applied to
excess demand in equations explaining price *levels*. See next footnote.

affect prices significantly comes from McCallum.[62] pointing out some weaknesses of Lund and Rushdy's price change equations,[63] he argued on the basis of a 'pure' model that prices are affected by excess demand *alone*, with costs influencing prices only in so far as they change supply conditions and so alter the level of excess demand. Regressing price changes on a distributed lag function of excess demand[64] showed the latter to be very significant and gave high correlation coefficients. In addition, with some distributed lag formulations, prices responded to excess demand much more rapidly than did excess demand in the labour market (which could well be a proxy for the *output* response to excess demand).

Bain and Evans noted that the results of Neild and of Godley and Nordhaus were directly contradicted by numerous Company statements to the effect that low demand greatly reduced prices.[65] They suggested that Godley and Nordhaus's correlation between actual and 'predicted' (average cost based) prices was not that good and noted in particular that the turning-points of the simulated series lagged behind the actual series. This they argued is to be expected of demand affects prices, because, for example, costs will respond only with a lag to a downturn in demand while prices would respond straight away. In addition, U.K. data are almost certainly subject to the limitation found by Stigler and Kindahl in the U.S., namely that actual transactions prices differ from quoted prices, the latter usually lagging in downswings.[66] Quoted prices might therefore move very closely with costs even though actual prices had already responded to demand changes. In their own tests Bain and Evans found capacity utilization to be important (though not greatly).

Finally, Scherer has pointed out that rigid adherence to full cost pricing could give rising prices in a recession,[67] and Eckstein and

---

[62] B. T. McCallum, 'The Effect of Demand on Prices in British Manufacturing: Another View, *R. Econ. Studs.* 37 (Jan. 1970), 147–56.

[63] These were (i) the demand parameters were very sensitive to specification, (ii) the wage parameter was very low, (iii) the constant in this equation implies an unexplained price *trend*, and (iv) there was first order serial correlation in 21 of 24 equations listed.

[64] The basic equation was:

$$\Delta P_t = 0 \cdot 2547 + 3 \cdot 775 \, d_{t+1} - 2 \cdot 856 \, d_t + 0 \cdot 7161 \, \Delta P_{t-1}$$
$$(0 \cdot 176) \quad (1 \cdot 05) \quad\quad (1 \cdot 15) \quad\quad (0 \cdot 116)$$

where d_t is excess demand in period t in the *labour* market. As this lags excess demand in the product market, d_{t+1} is a measure of excess demand in period t.

[65] A. D. Bain, J. D. Evans, 'Price Formation & Profits: Explanatory & Forecasting Models of Manufacturing Industry Profits in the UK', *Bulletin of the Oxford University Institute of Economics & Statistics*, 35, no. 4 (Nov. 1973), 295–308.

[66] G. Stigler, J. Kindahl, *The Behaviour of Industrial Prices*, National Bureau of Economic Research (New York, 1970).

[67] F. Scherer, *Industrial Market Structure and Economic Performance* (Chicago, 1970).

Fromm, and Lanzillotti *et al.* have suggested that target return pricing, particularly in concentrated industries, may result in *rising margins* in a recession.[68] Such behaviour by some firms would, at the aggregate level, tend to cancel out the more normal, opposite behaviour, thus diminishing the apparent importance of demand.[69]

Two other issues which should be mentioned briefly for the light they throw on the demand–price relation are those of 'administered pricing' and asymmetry in price sensitivity. The former stems mainly from the contention of Means that more concentrated industries have more inflexible prices because they are able to choose or 'administer' prices largely independent of the impact of general business conditions.[70] This debate has focused on two elements. First, do concentration variables have an impact when introduced into price equations? Second, and more in keeping with the thesis, is the response of price to cost and demand changes the same for low and high concentration industries? This topic, being concerned with the relation between industrial structure and performance, is mainly dealt with in Chapter 7, but it may be noted that most research in this field has either found no, or very little, sign of firms' ability to escape demand pressures.[71] Exceptions are a study by Levinson[72] and an important investigation by Eckstein and Wyss which found industries with $CR_4 \leqslant 35$ per cent to be competitive, those with 35 per cent $< CR_4 < 52$ per cent to be utilization-sensitive, and those with $CR_4 > 52$ per cent to be best explained by a target return thesis.[73] Earl's study, however, came up with partly contradictory results,[74] and the view that prices are 'administered' only in some industries (particularly steel in the

---

[68] O. Eckstein, G. Fromm, op. cit.; A. Kaplan, J. Dirlam, R. Lanzillotti, op. cit.

[69] For a detailed presentation, re-examination, and evaluation of a number of macro and micro price equations, see P. H. Earl, op. cit.

[70] See G. C. Means, *Industrial Prices and their Relative Inflexibility*, U.S. Senate Document 13, 74th Congress, 1st Session (Washington, 1935), for the first of a number of statements by him on this theme.

[71] See for example: A. C. Neal, *Industrial Concentration and Price Inflexibility*, American Council on Public Affairs (Washington, 1942); G. Stigler, J. Kindahl, 'Industrial Prices, as administered by Dr. Means', *A.E.R.* 63, no. 4 (Sept. 1973), 717–21; H. J. DePodwin, R. T. Seldon, 'Business Pricing Policies and Inflation', *J.P.E.* 71 (Apr. 1963), 116–27; L. Phlips, op. cit. Also L. W. Weiss, 'Business Pricing Policies and Inflation Reconsidered', *J.P.E.* 74, no. 2 (Apr. 1966), 177–87, for evidence that administered pricing occurs but is a temporary phenomenon.

[72] H. M. Levinson, 'Post War Movement of Prices and Wages in Manufacturing Industry', in *Study of Income, Employment & Prices, Study Paper No. 1* (Washington, 1959).

[73] O. Eckstein, D. Wyss, 'Industry Price Equations', in O. Eckstein (ed.), *The Econometrics of Price Determination*, S.S.R.C./Federal Reserve System (1972), 133–66. See also W. J. Yordon, 'Industrial Concentration and Price Flexibility in Inflation', *R. Econ. Stats.* 43, no. 3 (Aug. 1961), 287–94.

[74] See P. Earl, op. cit.

U.S.[75]) was further contradicted by Markham's results, which showed only 2 out of 9 concentrated industries clearly violating normal supply and demand effects.

The other issue concerns whether there is asymmetry in price behaviour. This might take two forms: (a) prices rise when costs rise, but do not fall when costs fall; (b) prices rise when demand increases, but do not fall when demand falls. Various theories (see Chapter 5) suggest this type of behaviour. However, the econometric evidence for neither is strong. Yordon did find some evidence of a 'materials ratchet', i.e. prices rising in response to an increase in material cost, though not to a decrease,[76] but McFetridge, Ripley and Segal, and Godley and Gillion have all tested for this effect in Canada, the U.S., and the U.K. respectively, and found it virtually absent.[77] On the demand side, both McFetridge and Eckstein and Fromm found that margins were reduced in recessions as much as they were increased in periods of rising demand.[78] The absence of a cost ratchet by itself is consistent with either a fairly rigid average cost pricing procedure, *or* high price sensitivity to intense competition, but the absence of demand-side asymmetry unambiguously supports the view that average cost margins are very dependent on demand conditions.

In general terms, this econometric work is largely consistent with both elementary theory and our previous conclusion that demand elements as well as cost elements are important in price setting. It therefore appears that the emphasis placed on average cost pricing after Hall and Hitch's work was in fact inappropriate. It arose because (a) as a pricing *procedure* it was in regular, systematic, and widespread use and because (b) as a result, the impact of costs on prices was immediately identifiable, whereas the impact of demand was allowed for by firms in a variety of less common, less formal, less systematic, and therefore less easily identifiable ways. In other words, as originally stressed, there is a large range of possible pricing situations, and while the influence of costs will tend to be similar across the whole range, allowing for considerable standardization in the method of incorporating costs, the influence of demand will differ widely with a consequent lack of standardization in the way demand is incorporated.

[75] J. Markham, 'Administered Prices and the Recent Inflation', in *Inflation, Growth and Employment*, Commission on Money and Credit (Englewood Cliffs, 1964).

[76] W. Yordon, op. cit.

[77] D. McFetridge, op. cit.; F. Ripley, L. Segal, op. cit.; W. Godley, C. Gillion, 'Pricing Behaviour in Manufacturing Industry', N.I.E.S.R. (Aug. 1965).

[78] D. McFetridge, op. cit., O. Eckstein, G. Fromm, op. cit.

5   INVENTORIES AND ORDER BOOKS

This conclusion is strengthened once we introduce the role of inventories and order books in price behaviour. Changes in them are frequently the immediate cause of demand (or supply) induced changes in price, and analysis of them helps to place price analysis in a dynamic context and conditions of uncertainty.

Production may loosely be categorized as 'production to stock' or 'production to order'. The latter implies commencement of production only after an order has been received, while the former implies production geared to maintaining a desired level of stocks (or inventories) from which shipments are dispatched when sales orders are received.[79]

With production to stock there will normally be relatively short unfilled order books or delivery lags, but a high inventory level, while with production to order, the inventory level will be approximately zero, but unfilled order books and delivery lags will be much longer. Production to order will tend to dominate where holding costs are high, where demand is highly unstable or intermittent, and where the product must meet particular specifications laid down by the individual purchasers;[80] the opposite conditions favour production to stock.[81]

The existence of inventories, delivery lags, and unfilled orders[82] serves several purposes. Firstly, they remove the necessity for production and/or pricing decisions to reflect demand changes either immediately or completely. Eckstein and Fromm's diagram[83] shown in Figure 4.1 indicates the possible reactions to a non-market clearing price *besides* price or production changes.[84] Order books and inventories therefore act as buffers,[85] allowing greater stability or smooth-

[79] The following analysis deals only with inventories of *finished* products. Stocks of raw materials and semi-finished goods raise additional problems which make the analysis more complex.

[80] In addition, wholesalers and retailers frequently take on the stock-holding role, thus allowing firms to produce to order despite different circumstances.

[81] V. Zarnowitz has examined the prevalence of both types of production in a number of industries. Not surprisingly, production to order dominated in durable goods, particularly such groups as primary metals, machinery, and transportation equipment. It also dominated over all, despite the dominance of production to stock in the non-durable goods. See V. Zarnowitz, 'Unfilled Orders, Price Changes and Business Fluctuations', *R. Econ. Stats.* 44, no. 4 (Nov. 1962), 367–94.

[82] In general, delivery lags and unfilled orders will be highly correlated. Rapid growth could undermine this, but probably only temporarily.

[83] O. Eckstein, G. Fromm, op. cit.

[84] The deviation of short-run demand from long-run demand seems *a priori* least likely to occur. Cancellation of orders will rarely be preferable to lengthened order books, and the reinstatement of cancelled orders may well be impossible.

[85] The stock buffer will, of course, not be available if production is all to order, nor the unfilled orders buffer if production is all to stock.

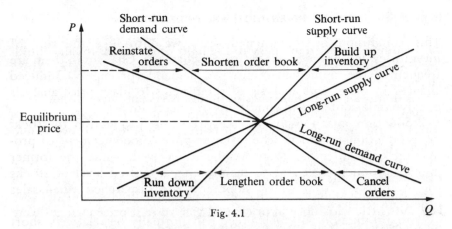

Fig. 4.1

ing of production[86] with consequent reductions in cost, and, if desired, greater stability of price. This may also reduce costs, namely those associated with changing price lists, but, more importantly, permits firms to adopt stable semi-collusive price policies in situations where an independent short-run profit maximizing strategy would generate instability, price wars, and reduced profits.[87]

Second, they permit a firm to largely ignore much of the uncertainty surrounding future consumer demand levels and timing of their purchases, competitors' behaviour, and other demand influences. Production and price decisions can be geared to variation in stocks and order books and in fact the timing and extent of demand shifts can be derived from these variations. Thus they provide useful information feedback signals while at the same time reducing the informational needs of firms.

In order to examine the implications for price setting, we need to analyse the relationships between price, orders, and inventories. As the diagram indicates, a price rise is an alternative reaction to extending the order book or running down inventories, and vice versa. These trade-offs imply an optimal level of unfilled orders and inventories. Too long an order book alienates customers more than the alternative of higher prices, while too short an order book results in less smooth production, higher costs, and therefore lower profits, despite higher prices. Similarly, too low a level of inventories will cause delivery delays at times and alienate customers more than

---

[86] But note Zarnowitz's conclusion that variations in inventory levels may have in fact destabilized production. See V. Zarnowitz, op. cit.

[87] This will be particularly true where there is oligopolistic interdependence coupled with different cost structures across firms. See F. M. Scherer, op. cit. for an elaboration of this point.

higher prices, while too high a level may again increases costs disproportionately more than prices. The optimal levels will of course vary from industry to industry in the light of customer loyalty, holding costs, the nature of the product, and the possible reactions to a change in price.

Assuming a firm initially has optimal orders and inventories, a rise in demand will generally generate rising prices, orders, and inventories in the new equilibrium, and empirically, therefore, we would expect and do find these effects to be correlated.[88] The main issue is the extent to which any demand shift is accommodated by each type of response. If the implicit cost of changing price is high, we would expect considerable variability of inventories, orders, and delivery lags, but little variability in price, and vice versa if price changes were inexpensive. Such an inverse relation between price fluctuation and order book and delivery fluctuation was empirically supported by Zarnowitz.[89] In a more limited investigation Hay found that only a very small percentage of the adjustment to demand changes was borne by price. He suggests however that there might have been more impact on price via cost changes if the demand levels examined had been nearer full capacity.[90] McCallum, adopting a different type of approach, emphasized that optimal inventory levels depend on price expectations. It will only be worth holding inventory while the gain from doing so—the difference between present and expected price per unit—is greater than the marginal cost of storage.[91] In equilibrium the two will be equal and the price level set becomes dependent on the level of inventory. He then found that for the U.S. timber industry the explanation of prices was much improved by adding inventory variables to pure excess demand equations.

The actual gains from greater price stability at the expense of changes in orders and inventories clearly depend partly on the expected elasticities of demand with respect to change in the three variables. This is an empirical matter on which it is not useful to theorize except in one respect. In a fairly competitive industry with established market shares, the change in price required consequent

---

[88] See V. Zarnowitz, op. cit.

[89] Ibid. This, incidentally, may well explain why Godley and Gillion found price responses clamped in engineering in comparison to other industries: see W. Godley, C. Gillion, op. cit. Zarnowitz also found price variability to be relatively much lower where production was mainly to order.

[90] G. A. Hay, 'Production, Price and Inventory Theory', *A.E.R.* 60 (Sept. 1970), 531–45.

[91] B. T. McCallum, 'Competitive Price Adjustments: An Empirical Study', *A.E.R.* 64, no. 1 (March 1974), 56–65. Changes in the level of storage costs are likely to have their main impact on the level of stock holding rather than on price levels. See A. Nevins, 'Some Effects of Uncertainty: Simulation of a Model of Price', *Q.J.E.*, 80, no. 1 (Feb. 1966), 73–87.

upon a demand shift can at best only be guessed at, depends on many unknowns, and may well precipitate instability and reductions in profit. The change in orders on the other hand requires no new action on the part of the firm and may reasonably be presumed to be matched by equivalent changes in the order books of competitors. In this case the elasticity of demand with respect to the lengthened order book is likely to be very low, with all firms quoting later delivery dates, and may well in fact be ignored. The path of price stability is therefore both safer and less demanding of market information.

Over all, the prevalence of production to order, the problem involved in changing price in a competitive (particularly oligopolistic) market, and the evidence available on the limited response of price as opposed to stock or order book changes, all support the view that in the short term, and perhaps over longer periods, price stability is both rationally desired and readily achieved in the face of demand fluctuations. This helps to explain the earlier conclusions that the effect of demand on price is often more difficult to identify and isolate than that of costs. The high degree of delegation of the pricing decision mentioned earlier can then be explained by the extent to which the process can become mechanical—basing price on cost, taking short-term demand changes on inventory and order levels, and changing price relative to cost when either low inventories or long order books indicate a significant shift of demand and the reduced risk of increasing price.

It may be added that marketing and product heterogeneity are likely to have similar effects. Both may be used as a means of avoiding price changes and in order to achieve and maintain a price-cost margin that would not otherwise have been feasible. These weaken the observed impact of demand on prices and margins respectively. In addition Cowling and Rayner found that demand for a differentiated product (tractors) was much more elastic with respect to a quality adjusted index of prices (in which differences in actual prices attributable to differences in quality are removed) than to actual prices.[92] This not only emphasizes the importance of demand but suggests that at the microeconomic level we should expect the relationship between demand and actual prices to be rather tenuous. If, as both Alfred[93] and Gabor and Granger suggest,[94] price is used as a guide to quality by consumers, then the traditionally

[92] K. Cowling, A. Rayner, op. cit.   [93] A. Alfred, op. cit.
[94] A. Gabor, C. W. Granger, 'Price as an Indicator of Quality. Report of an Enquiry', *Economica*, N.S. 33 (Feb. 1966), 43–70.

hypothesised relations between demand as measured[95] and actual prices may disappear altogether. Finally the fact that most firms are multi-product means that another variable—product range—is introduced, and, as with inventories marketing and product quality, allows firms more discretion to base price on costs, phasing out those products whose performance is unacceptable at that margin in favour of others.

It is therefore clear that the inclusion of such real-world phenomena as stocks, order books, delivery times, advertising, quality variations, and multi-product firms, gives a much more complex and realistic picture of firms' price behaviour. In all cases discretionary power over price is greater, but this increased power may be used in different ways. In general the lack of a clear or unified picture of the impact of demand on pricing methods noted earlier seems much more understandable in the broad context, and the greatly increased range of strategies that can be employed as alternatives to margin variation in the face of demand changes and market uncertainty make the general adherence to stable cost-based margins much more explicable. Finally, the difference between the businessman's description of pricing and economic price theory can be partly explained by the absence of these factors in price theory.

6 CONCLUSIONS

This chapter started with a simple theory of monopolistic pricing which incorporated profit maximization, downward sloping demand curves, and generalized cost structure, and which predicted price and margin sensitivity to cost and demand changes sometimes in unspecified ways. The empirical evidence subsequently reviewed shows that despite much diversity in pricing and widespread adherence to simple rules of thumb, prices and margins do respond to cost and demand changes in a manner generally consistent with that model. The existence of uncertainty does not generally seem to undermine the empirical validity of it. In the course of this it was seen that the objective of profit maximization should be interpreted in terms of the long run rather than the short run. Analysis of stocks, order books, etc. and brief consideration of non-price competitive variables all supported this and threw light on why demand effects have been more difficult to identify. The way is now clear to focus on the two main determinants of pricing in the typical oligopolistic industry. These are the direct interdependence of firms' prices and sales because of

[95] i.e. homogeneous units of heterogeneous products.

industrial concentration, examined in Chapter 5, and the influence of latent competition due to the existence of potential new entrants if supernormal profits are made. This is the theme of Chapter 6.

APPENDIX

The effect on prices and profit margins of changes in cost and demand conditions may be derived as follows:

1. A change in average cost.

(a) Average Variable Cost increases by a constant amount for all levels of output. This raises marginal cost by the same amount for all levels of output. Given a negatively sloped marginal revenue curve the profit maximizing output falls, provided the second-order conditions for profit maximization are met. With a negatively sloped average revenue curve price must then rise. Hence $\delta P/\delta AC$ is positive. However, in the expression

$$\frac{\delta P}{\delta AC} = 1 + \left(\frac{dAC}{dQ} - \frac{dP}{dQ}\right)\frac{\delta Q}{\delta AC} + Q\left(\frac{\delta(dAC/dQ)}{\delta AC} - \frac{\delta(dP/dQ)}{\delta AC}\right)$$

(i) $\dfrac{\delta(dP/dQ)}{\delta AC}$ equals zero, assuming a linear demand curve.

(ii) $\delta Q/\delta AC$ is negative (see above).

(iii) $(dAC/dQ) - (dP/dQ)$ is non-negative. This can be seen as follows:

$$MC = MR. \text{ Therefore } \frac{QdP}{dQ} + P = \frac{QdAC}{dQ} + AC$$

and assuming $P \geqslant AC$ we get the result that $(dAC/dQ) \geqslant (dP/dQ)$.

(iv) $\dfrac{\delta(dAC/dQ)}{\delta AC}$ is negative. This can also be shown very easily. We have seen above that the equilibrium value of Q falls as AC rises, and because dAC/dQ rises with Q if the AC curve is U-shaped, dAC/dQ falls as Q falls (AC rises) making $\dfrac{\delta(dAC/dQ)}{\delta AC}$ negative. Thus all algebraic elements in the original

expression are negative and $\delta P/\delta AC$ has a maximum limiting value of 1. Clearly if $(P-AC)$ falls as P rises, the percentage margin $(P - AC)/P$ falls.

(b) Fixed Costs rise by a given amount. As neither MC nor MR change, we get the familiar result that neither price nor output change. In terms of the original expression $\delta Q/\delta AC$ and $\dfrac{\delta(dP/dQ)}{\delta AC}$ are both zero and $\dfrac{\delta(dAC/\delta Q)}{\delta AC}$ equals $-(1/Q)$. This is because if fixed costs rise by X, the change in AC is X/Q. The change in dAC/dQ (which equals $(MC/Q) - (AC/Q)$) is $-(X/Q^2)$. Hence

$$\frac{\delta(dAC/dQ)}{\delta AC} = \frac{-(X/Q^2)}{X/Q} = -\frac{1}{Q}.$$

In the original expression therefore $(\delta P/\delta AC) = 1 + 0 - (Q/Q) = 0$. A rise in AC with constant P clearly reduces the profit margin both absolutely and as a percentage.

2. A change in demand.

(a) A change in the slope of the demand curve but with it still passing through the initial equilibrium point P,Q. As $MR = Q(dp/dQ) + P$ if the demand curve becomes steeper dP/dQ becomes more negative and MR falls. The profit maximizing output falls provided the second-order conditions are met. With a negatively sloped average revenue curve price must rise. As the original dP/dQ was lower (more negative) than dAC/dQ a further fall in dP/dQ means it is still lower than dAC/dQ and so P rises more than AC as Q falls. Thus the profit margin $(P-AC)$ rises, but the margin as a percentage of price may rise or fall. Letting the percentage margin be M, $\dfrac{dM}{dP} = \dfrac{AC - (dAC/dP)\,P}{P^2}$. This is negative only if $(dAC/dP) > (AC/P)$. Constant AC rules out this possibility.

(b) A rightward shift of the demand curve. This keeps dP/dQ constant but increases P for a given Q. Therefore MR rises and, as a result, if second-order conditions are met, the profit maximizing Q rises. What happens to price depends on the shape of the marginal cost curve. Assuming a linear average revenue curve given by $AR = a - bQ$ $b > 0$ and concentrating on marginal adjustments only so that we may use a linear segment of the marginal cost curve given by $MC = c + dQ$ $d \lessgtr 0$, the profit maximizing output is given by $Q = (a - c)/(2b + d)$. Therefore the profit-maximizing price is given by $P = a - b(a - c)/(2b + d)$ and $dP/da = 1 - b/(2b + d)$. This is positive except where $b > 2b + d$, i.e. where $d < -b$. For a maximum to exist at all we must have $d > -2b$ to ensure MR falling faster than MC. Thus, given our assumption, price will rise in response to a shift in the demand curve unless $-b > d > -2b$, i.e. where marginal cost falls faster than average revenue but not as fast as marginal revenue. The profit margin may rise or fall both in absolute and percentage terms depending on the shape of the average cost curve.

MARKET BEHAVIOUR: COMPETITION OR CO-OPERATION?

The purpose of this chapter is to examine the relationships between market concentration, market behaviour, and pricing decisions. The emphasis is on relationships between firms already in the market: the role of entry is the subject of the next chapter. The presumption in industrial economics has often been that the more concentrated the market, the more 'monopoly power' and hence the higher the price. This indeed holds for a monopoly, or for a formal cartel, but the situation in oligopoly is not so clear-cut. We can describe the nature of an *equilibrium* price in oligopoly if we make some assumptions about the behaviour of firms. Hannah and Kay[1] adopt the not unreasonable concept of a Nash equilibrium. Each firm maximizes profits, *given* the outputs of the other firms. Then the equilibrium is a set of outputs such that no firm in the market has an incentive to change its own ouptut. To illustrate this we utilize the model described in Chapter 3.[2] Let the market demand function $p = f(X) = f(x_1 + \ldots x_i + \ldots x_n)$ where x_i is the output of one firm and $\Sigma x_i = X$ is market output. Each firm has constant costs, c_i, which vary between firms. The profit for a firm i is given by

$$\pi_i = p \cdot x_i - c_i x_i$$

$$\therefore \frac{d\Pi_i}{dx_i} = p - c_i + x_i \frac{dp}{dX} \cdot \frac{dX}{dx_i} \text{ , where } \frac{dX}{dx_i} = 1 \text{, in equilibrium.}$$

Setting this equal to zero for a maximum, multiplying through by x_i, and summing over all firms gives:

$$px - \quad c_i x_i - pX\left(-\frac{X}{p} \cdot \frac{dp}{dX}\right) \quad \left(\frac{x_i}{X}\right)^2 = 0$$

[1] L. Hannah, J. Kay, *Concentration in Modern Industry* (London 1977), 11–12.
[2] This is the analysis of Hannah and Kay, following K. Cowling, M. Waterson, 'Price-Cost Margins and Market Structure', *Economica*, 43 (1976), 267–74. See Chapter 3, pp. 94–95.

Rearranging gives
$$\frac{pX - \Sigma \, c_i x_i}{pX} = \frac{H}{e}$$

where H is the Herfindahl concentration index, and e is the market demand elasticity. The ratio H/e determines the average price–cost margin in equilibrium. However the description of an equilibrium avoids the really fundamental question, which is how such an equilibrium might be reached in an oligopolistic market; that is the main concern of this chapter. Our starting-point is the 'evidence', culled from discussions with businessmen about pricing, that oligopolists are acutely aware of their interdependence. This evidence has been summarized in the descriptive theory of the kinked demand curve. The next section of this chapter will be concerned with the adequacy of this concept in reflecting the evidence. The second section then sets out a rather more formal analysis in which we examine the possibility that firms will act together to increase prices (if market conditions warrant) without any necessity for even an informal agreement. Finally the chapter looks at cartels.

1   THE KINKED DEMAND CURVE

The theory of the kinked demand curve was introduced almost simultaneously by Hall and Hitch[3] in England, and Sweezy[4] in America, in 1939. The former study was an interpretation of evidence collected from 38 businessmen concerning their pricing policy. Sweezy's formulation was directed to the widespread belief that prices in oligopolistic industries had exhibited rigidities, compared to other prices, during the 1930s.

The theory is illustrated in Figure 5.1. The presumption is that businessmen expect a price reduction to be followed, but not a price rise. Demand is, therefore, relatively inelastic downwards, the only expansion in demand coming from a constant share of a somewhat larger market. It is elastic upwards, however, as a unilateral price rise results for the particular firm in a greatly contracted share of a constant or slightly smaller market. The profit maximizing strategy is generally then to maintain price at its existing level, P^*. Quite large variations in marginal cost will not alter this, as there is a discontinuity in the marginal revenue curve, the length of which is a

---

[3] R. Hall, C. J. Hitch, 'Price Theory and Business Behaviour', in T. Wilson, P. W. S. Andrews (eds.), *Oxford Studies in the Price Mechanism* (Oxford 1951).
[4] P. M. Sweezy, 'Demand under Conditions of Oligopoly', *J.P.E.* 47 (1939), 568–73.

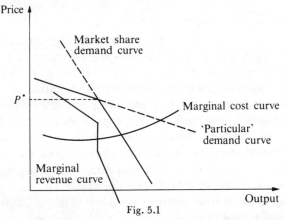

Fig. 5.1

function of the difference in the two elasticities.[5] Variations in demand would result in variations in stocks, order books, and eventually production, but not price, meaning that the curve shifted horizontally with the kink remaining at the same price level. It should be noted that this is only a theory of price stability—why a price, once set, might not change—rather than a theory of price determination. Nothing is said about why the existing price is at the level it is. Nevertheless, price rigidity would be an important aspect of price behaviour if found to be widespread.

In fact most investigations of this have come up with negative findings. Stigler[6] found that most price rises were followed in seven industries studied, suggesting that there was little basis for firms rationally to hold the expectation of not being followed upwards. In addition, price rigidity was greater under monopoly, where no kink could exist, than under oligopoly, suggesting that other explanations common to both structures exist. Simon[7] also found no evidence for the kink, prices being just as flexible in oligopolistic markets as monopolistic ones. Both studies were subject to some limitations. Stigler only covered two cases of monopoly, and it could not be ruled out that differences in the product between industries rather than differences in their structure might be the cause of the

---

[5] Marginal Revenue $= P(1 - (1/e))$. Therefore for a given price, the higher the elasticity of demand, the higher marginal revenue is. Therefore, very different elasticities give a very large discrepancy between marginal revenue for an upward price movement and for a downward one. A similar kink occurs at a limit price, because a price rise, though followed by everyone in the industry, precipitates new entry and consequent loss of market share. A price reduction does not, however, increase it. See J. Wenders, 'Collusion and Entry', *J.P.E.* 79 (1971), 1258–77. Limit prices are discussed in Chapter 6.

[6] G. J. Stigler, 'The Kinky Oligopoly Curve and Rigid Prices', *J.P.E.* 55 (1947), 432–49.

[7] J. L. Simon, 'A Further Test of the Kinky Oligopoly Demand Curve', *A.E.R.* 59 (1959), 971–5.

observed differences. Simon's study was based on business magazine advertising rates, but different readerships might make apparently oligopolistic competitors in reality minor monopolists. Primeaux and Bomball[8] attempted to overcome these difficulties by comparing the price behaviour of electric utilities in U.S. cities where they had a monopoly, with those in cities where a privately owned one was in duopolistic competition with the publicly owned one.[9] This avoided the data problems of the earlier studies, but again found unambiguous evidence that the monopolists' prices were more stable, that price increases were more often followed than not, and that price decreases were more often not followed.

Many explanations have been offered for this gap between a plausible theory and actual evidence:

(i) The finding that monopoly prices are more stable seems best explained by the fact that only shifts in cost or market demand will lead to price variations under monopoly, while demand shifts *between* firms could provide a third reason for price revision under oligopoly. It is, therefore, consistent with the evidence that the kink nevertheless operates to reduce the otherwise much higher variability of prices in oligopoly, but not so much that it matches the stability of prices under monopoly.

(ii) Effroymson[10] pointed out that the kinked demand curve is hypothetical; it represents the demand curve which an oligopolist *imagines* he faces. In general, price changes will only occur if the businessman believes, rightly or wrongly, that he has by some means circumvented the kink, for example by collusion. If price rises *are* followed or reductions *not* followed, this shows only that the mechanism used to circumvent the kink was successful. Observations that most price rises are followed may well not remove 'kink'-type expectations, but simply strengthen the belief that specific action needs to be taken if the kink is to be avoided. It is, therefore, the evidence for the *prevalence* of price changes under oligopoly, rather than the extent to which they are followed or not, which is harmful to the theory.

---

[8] W. J. Primeaux, M. R. Bomball, 'A Re-examination of the Kinky Oligopoly Demand Curve', *J.P.E.* 82 (1974), 851–62.

[9] They reject the view that the differences of ownership might by generating different objectives influence price behaviour, on the ground that the publicly owned utilities were roughly comparable to the privately owned ones in profitability. In fact the publicly owned ones were on average higher, suggesting that the existence of some monopoly utilities in the public ownership classification conferred some element of monopoly profits denied to the oligopolists.

[10] C. W. Effroymson, 'A Note on Kinked Demand Curves', *A.E.R.* 33 (1943), 98–109; 'The Kinked Oligopoly Curve Reconsidered', *Q.J.E.* (1955), 119–36.

(iii) The expectation that price cuts will be followed, but not price rises, is far from being the only plausible one in oligopoly. First, high demand conditions may well give Effroymson's reflex kink, shown in Figure 5.2. Belief in a widespread desire to raise

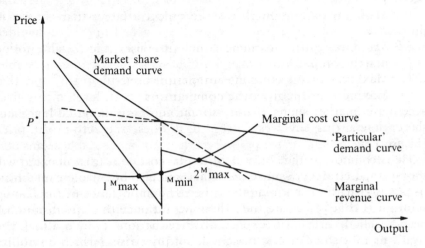

Fig. 5.2

price in reaction to increased demand, plus the likelihood of capacity constraints on competitors' ability to increase their output, will tend to generate the expectation that price rises *will* be followed and price reductions (if contemplated) will not. The existing price then represents a local profit minimization point (*MC* cutting *MR* from above) and a price change will probably occur. If costs are rising, a price rise is most likely; a shift upwards in the marginal cost will remove the right-hand profit maximization point ($_2M_{max}$).

Second, if full cost pricing is practised by oligopolists and known to be so by rivals, then a change in industrial costs may provide the basis for expecting consequent price changes to be followed. This possibility was noted by Hall and Hitch as an exception to the theory.

Third, it is not obvious that the strategy of matching price cuts and forgoing price increases is necessarily the profit maximizing strategy for the firm. A wide range of alternative strategies is possible and merits consideration. Consider, for example, the following list of possibilities suggested by Osborne.[11] He considered the behaviour of a duopoly with homogeneous product, equal constant marginal cost, and complete information. He then compared the returns

[11] D. K. Osborne, 'A Duopoly Price Game', *Economica* 41 (1974), 157–75.

from adopting 7 different non-collusive strategies.

(*a*) Maximize profit assuming competitor's output fixed[12] (Cournot[13]).

(*b*) Maximize profit assuming competitor uses rule (*a*) (Stackelberg[14]).

(*c*) Maintain current market share unless a larger share increases profit.

(*d*) Maximize profit assuming competitor uses rule (*c*) (Nichol[15]).

(*e*) Match competitor's price.

(*f*) Maximize profit assuming competitor uses rule (*e*).

(*g*) Maximize profit given the competitor's profit level, if this gives acceptable market share. If not, obtain minimum acceptable market share unless this involves losses. If it does, set zero-profit price (Bishop).[16]

He then showed that only if both players adopt (*g*) will each have the optimal strategy against the other and also be unable to improve its position without harming the other. The importance of the Bishop solution is that prices are fully flexible, but once the equilibrium has been reached, firms will expect price reductions (which attack the rival's market share) to be matched, but price rises (which do not reduce the rival's market share) not to be followed. The 'kink' expectations, being a function of the equilibrium, are not inconsistent with price flexibility. Whether the same conclusions would hold in oligopoly is not certain: but clearly the kinked demand curve strategy is not the only one for consideration in the next section.

Fourth, the theory ignores the possibility of reversing a price change should other firms not follow suit. Stigler[17] presented some evidence of firms behaving in this way, experimenting with price changes to see how the industry would react. This feature needs to be part of any theory of oligopoly pricing, and is given further consideration in the next section.

(iv) The analysis of Chapter 3 suggested that differentiation reduced the cross-elasticity of demand between products. Whether this

---

[12] If a rival faces capacity constraints this is a more rational assumption than is often made out. Repeated demonstration that the rival's output *eventually* changed would not make the expectation any more irrational, thus explaining the supposed lack of ability to learn by mistakes in the model.

[13] A Cournot, *Research into the Mathematical Principles of the Theory of Wealth*, translated by T. Bacon (Kelley, 1960), Chapter 5.

[14] H. von Stackelberg, 'Sintra teoria del duopolie e del poliopolio', *Rivista italiana di statistica* (1933).

[15] A. J. Nichol, 'Professor Chamberlin's Theory of Limited Competition', *Q.J.E.* 48 (1934), 317–37.

[16] R. Bishop, 'Duopoly: Collusion or Warfare?' *A.E.R.* 50 (1960), 933–61.

[17] Stigler, op. cit.

provides an 'escape' from the 'kink' depends on the number of near neighbours a product has in characteristics space. Fewness still leads to interdependence, unless the utility cost of movement in characteristics space is very high, or customers are clustered in characteristics space close to the different products on offer. Either of these features could be the result of advertising. It is evident that any complete theory of oligopoly pricing must incorporate the effects of product differentiation.

(v) Firms may utilize one of a whole range of possible devices for colluding over price. At one extreme there is 'focal point' pricing. No actual collusion of any type takes place, but all firms adopt a particular price because it stands out in some way as an 'obvious' price, and in the belief that rivals will do the same. The use of round sums or reliance on widely publicized data are examples of this. 'Price lining'—the use of a common (and usually 'focal point') price for a range of heterogeneous products—is a modification of this. Beyond this is a range of tacit understandings, informal arrangements, information agreements, various types of price leadership, and at the other extreme formal explicit collusion, often covering many aspects of competition besides price. Collusive solutions raise a whole new series of problems, for example the conditions under which secret price cuts will be detected, the dispersion of cost structures.

We conclude that the study of oligopolistic interdependence in pricing needs to be considerably more sophisticated than the theory of the kinked demand curve. Expectations, time, product differentiation, and the extent of collusion are essential ingredients for a comprehensive theory. In the next section of the chapter we indicate how these elements might be incorporated.

2   OLIGOPOLISTIC INTERDEPENDENCE AND PRICING

In this section five topics are covered. The first relates the consequences of a cut in price by one oligopolistic competitor to the degree of concentration and product differentiation. The second explores how a *rational* firm might approach the possibility of changing its price. In the third, learning from previous market experience is introduced, and its consequences for pricing examined. The fourth section introduces some examples, and discusses the market phenomena of leadership and information agreements. Finally we examine how 'industry social structure' can affect the pricing process and the nature of equilibrium.

(a) Price cuts and profits in oligopoly

We consider an oligopoly producing a broadly homogeneous product, though we will also assume that there is some slight differentiation (e.g. by means of brand names or location) which attracts customer loyalty. Each firm is considering whether to cut prices or to hold to the existing price for the product.[18] The *qualitative* situation facing each firm is illustrated in Figure 5.3 (quantitative aspects—e.g. market share—may differ between firms). Firms' variable costs are

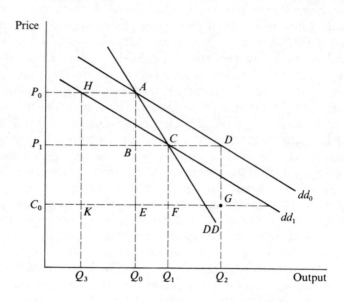

Fig. 5.3

constant at C_0 in the relevant range. The existing price is P_0. The oligopolist is considering a reduction in price to P_1. If he acts alone, then his market expands along his 'particular' curve (or dd_0 curve, adopting Chamberlin's terminology). The change in his profits is given by $\Delta\Pi_1 = BDGE$ minus P_0ABP_1.[19] Whether this is positive or negative depends not only on the elasticity of the demand curve, but also on the level of costs. Suppose, alternatively, that his price cut is matched by his competitors. Then he moves down his 'share' of the market curve (or DD curve, in Chamberlin's terminology). The change in profits is given by $\Delta\Pi_2 = BCFE$ minus P_0ABP_1. Again

[18] The profit outcomes of price increases can be deduced from a parallel analysis within same framework.

[19] An algebraic derivation of all the results is given in Appendix 1.

the size and magnitude of this change depends on the elasticity of the 'share' demand curve and the level of costs. Finally there is the possibility that the firm will decide to stay at price P_0, when all other firms go down to price P_1. In this case the firm will experience a loss of sales along the particular curve dd_1 (which is derived for other firms' prices of P_1). The change in profits is given by $\Delta\Pi_3 = P_0HKC_0 - P_0AEC_0$, which is always negative.

By inspection of the diagram we can see that in general $\Delta\Pi_1 > \Delta\Pi_2$. A larger output at the same price and variable cost must result in larger gross profits.

We can now consider three possible cases. The first is the case where $\Delta\Pi_1$ and $\Delta\Pi_2$ are both positive. This can only mean that MR exceeds MC whether the firm cuts price alone or whether all firms cut. Since we know that $\Delta\Pi_3$ must be negative we have the strong relationship that $\Delta\Pi_1 > \Delta\Pi_2 > \Delta\Pi_3$. So long as the firms are aware of the relevant elasticities of profit with respect to output they will all cut price. There is no reason why prices should not move down together without any need for conscious co-operation between firms.

A second case is where $\Delta\Pi_1$ and $\Delta\Pi_2$ are both negative. This is typically a situation where market demand is inelastic, and where price differentials lead to only a little switching of customers between firms. In this instance, declining profit indicates that MC exceeds MR when output is expanded. Indeed, it could be in the interests of all firms to raise their prices above P_0, unless that represents the profit maximizing price already (either because $MC = MR$ or because P_0 is the maximum price that can be charged without attracting new entrants, as analysed in the next chapter). There can be no doubt that price cutting is ruled out in this situation, unless a firm makes a mistake. Again there is no need for conscious co-operation to achieve this result.

The third case has attracted the most attention. This is where $\Delta\Pi_1$ is positive, $\Delta\Pi_2$ is negative, but larger than $\Delta\Pi_3$. The substance of this case is that a firm has an incentive to be the sole price cutter, but there will be an adverse effect on its profits if all firms cut. However it would be even more disadvantageous to be left as the sole firm maintaining a high price. Examination of this third case will occupy us in the rest of this section.

The precise values of the changes in profits are related to the degree of product differentiation and concentration in the market, which were explored in Chapter 3. We can summarize the conclusions relevant to the present analysis. We note that product differentiation makes the dd curve less elastic, the greater the disutility of movement in characteristics space for consumers, and the greater the concentration of preferences in the vicinity of existing products in that space. The effect then is on the values of $\Delta\Pi_1$ and $\Delta\Pi_3$: $\Delta\Pi_1$ tends to diminish and $\Delta\Pi_3$ to increase with increased differentiation. The relevance of the *DD* curve for a differentiated product depends mainly on the number of firms, when the number of characteristics exceeds four. Fewer firms and higher concentration increase interdependence of market 'areas' in characteristics space, and thus reduce the scope for independent pricing decisions along the *dd* curves. When the number of characteristics is less than four, the number of 'near neighbours' is *always* few, and hence interdependence is the rule, however large the number of firms.

The absence of differentiation implies that the *dd* curve becomes completely elastic. A price higher than the market will involve market share going to zero, and hence $\Delta\Pi_3$ is the sum of all current profits, which are lost. A price lower than the market will give an increase in output up to the firms' capacity, so $\Delta\Pi_1$ will be very large. Complete product homogeneity (i.e. no brand loyalty, goodwill, let alone product differentiation) implies that only one price can prevail in the market. The degree of concentration becomes the critical determinant of behaviour. High concentration implies that a single firm which expands output will have a non-negligible effect on market price, thus inviting output reactions from other firms. So the relevant curve must be the *DD* curve. Low concentration again would give the firm more independence of action.

In what follows we will confine our attention to markets that are characterized by high concentration, and hence interdependence. For the most part, too, we will assume some degree of product differentiation.

(b) Rational pricing decisions

We start with a model in which firms make the naive assumption that all other firms will maintain their price in the period for which a cut in price is considered. On that assumption the firm will cut price, hoping to increase its own profit. If all firms work on the same assumption, general price cutting occurs.

A more plausible assumption is that firms are aware of the alternative outcomes arising from various combinations of price cutting and maintaining price. They can be set out as a matrix of profit outcomes for the firm. This is a game theoretic situation. Every firm has a qualitatively similar profit matrix to work with, and each has to make a decision for the period in question. Examination of the possibilities makes it clear that a rational firm will cut price. For suppose

Profit change matrix		Other firms	
		Maintain	Cut
Firm	Maintain	0	$\Delta\Pi_3$
	Cut	$\Delta\Pi_1$	$\Delta\Pi_2$

the other firms cut price, then $\Delta\Pi_2$ is preferred to $\Delta\Pi_3$. Alternatively suppose the other firms maintain their price, then $\Delta\Pi_1$ is preferable to O. So to cut price is the 'dominant' or minimax strategy. Whatever the other firm decides to do, it gives greater profit than a strategy of maintaining price. We would therefore expect firms, even with awareness of the possibilities, to cut price and end up with $\Delta\Pi_2$. They could, of course, do better by agreeing to maintain the initial price. But within this framework this cannot occur if the firms are rational and overt co-operation is excluded.

We note that this result does not accord with the kinked demand curve, in that price cutting occurs. The reason is that the kinked demand curve analysis assumes that the *only* options are that both firms maintain price, or both firms cut. The choice is between a zero change in profits, and a negative change ($\Delta\Pi_2$), and hence no price cut occurs.

But the analysis does accord with the kinked demand curve hypothesis that prices will not be raised. The profit matrix is shown, qualitative values being deduced from a parallel analysis to that of Figure 5.3. The worst position for the firm is to raise its price, when others do not: $\Delta\Pi_4$ is negative. Profits would be increased ($\Delta\Pi_6$) if all firms

Profit change matrix		Other firms	
		Raise	Maintain
Firm	Raise	$\Delta\Pi_6$	$\Delta\Pi_4$
	Maintain	$\Delta\Pi_5$	0

raised price, but it would be even better for the firm if it could maintain a lower price when the others increased their prices ($\Delta\Pi_5$). So the ranking is $\Delta\Pi_4 < 0 < \Delta\Pi_6 < \Delta\Pi_5$. Hence if other firms increase their price then $\Delta\Pi_5 > \Delta\Pi_6$, so the firm should maintain price. If other firms maintain, $0 > \Delta\Pi_4$, and maintain price is again more profitable. In both cases the maintain price strategy dominates the raise price strategy, and so price will be maintained by the rational firm.

The major defect with the above approach is the inadequacy of its treatment of time. The firms make their decisions simultaneously and those decisions hold for the (timeless) period under consideration. But in practice firms are not tied by this pattern of decision making. A firm may wait and see what pricing decisions others make before making its own decision whether to change price or not. The effect of this amendment can be illustrated in a dynamic model of duopoly where the firms are assumed to make the same myopic assumption as above: i.e. that the other firm will not change its price. The analysis is best conducted in terms of Figure 5.4. (Some simple algebra is given in Appendix 2.) We

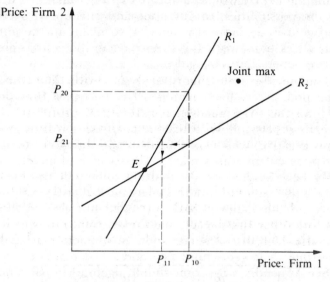

Fig. 5.4

introduce the concept of a reaction function. This expresses the profit maximizing price for one firm in terms of the 'given' price of the rival firm. For example, R_1 is the reaction function of firm 1 and shows the price which firm 1 will charge (to maximize profits) given a price quoted by firm 2. The sequence starts with firm 2 charging P_{20}. Firm 1 reacts by charging P_{10}, giving the appropriate price on his reaction function. Firm 2 reacts to that along its own reaction function R_2 and charges P_{21}. Firm 1 then moves to P_{11}. This process of price reduction continues until the point E is reached. This is the intersection of the reaction functions, and the sole price combination at which both firms are satisfied with the outcome.[20] We note, in passing, that this price combination represents a much lower profit level than is available from joint action by the firms to maximize joint profits.[21] The defect of this kind of model is obvious. After a few moves, the firm will *learn* that the other firm *does* react to price initiatives. It will become aware of a range of different possible reactions. Such awareness of different patterns over time will lead the firm to evaluate alternative streams of profit over time, rather than confining itself to immediate profit prospects. So the basis for pricing decisions must become more sophisticated. Further, the learning process will lead the firm to attach its own subjective *probabilities* to alternative reactions by other firms, and those probabilities may themselves change with accumulating experience. For analysis we will separate out these two aspects, leaving the probability approach to the next section of the chapter.

First, we examine the case where the oligopolistic firm is aware of the matrix of possible changes in profit following a price cut which we set out in the game theory analysis above. The firm has learnt that the price cut will be matched by the other firms at the next move.[22] So the firm makes the incremental profit $\Delta \Pi_1$, until such time as the others follow, when the change in profit is given by $\Delta \Pi_2$ (which is negative) which continues for all subsequent periods (unless further price cutting takes place). This stream of incremental profits can only be evaluated by discounting to obtain the present value. The size and magnitude of this incremental present value depends not only on the values of $\Delta \Pi_1$ and $\Delta \Pi_2$, but also on the length of time before other firms react, and the discount rate which is chosen. In general, a high discount rate and a slow reaction are favourable to price cutting: a low discount rate and a fast reaction are unfavourable. (See Appendix 3 for some simple algebra.) In particular we may note that where the time lag is 'zero', price cutting cannot be attractive at *any* discount rate. Zero has to be carefully defined in this

[20] Even simpler are the Bertrand price variation model and the Cournote model, both of which assume a completely homogeneous good. In the Bertrand case this leads to a situation where all the consumers switch to the lower-priced producer, whose identity alternates between the duopolists. In the Cournot case the relevant variable is output, assuming that the rival duopolist will not change his output. The model we are using is closer to the kind of price-interdependence and hence pricing behaviour, that we are trying to understand in this chapter.

[21] As, for example, in a cartel: see analysis later in this chapter.

[22] We return here, for simplicity, to the model which assumes that the best reaction to a rival's price cut is to match his cut precisely so that both firms end up with the same price. This is a special case of the more general model, set out in the reaction functions, where exact matching of prices is not assumed. However, the more general model would still generate the results that $\Delta \Pi_3 < \Delta \Pi_2 < 0$. The difference arises from the degree of differentiation of the products.

case. It does not mean instantaneous in a temporal sense: rather it requires that the price cut is recognized and matched before consumers recognize the price differential and switch their custom.[23] It may be objected that this analysis ignores the danger to the firm of being left as the sole firm that does not cut price. However this danger is mitigated by the firm's knowledge that other firms make the same calculation concerning a price cut as it has itself. Unless the other firms have a very different discount rate (we assume for the present that the length of the reaction lag is common knowledge), they will have the same reasons for not cutting. Further, even if a cut does occur, it is open to the firm which maintained its price to make a subsequent cut itself, so the consequences are somewhat less adverse.

The above analysis suggests that the time lag of reaction is the critical objective variable in the calculations of firms. So it warrants further examination. The length of the lag is dependent on how long it takes rivals to be aware of a price initiative by a firm, and how long it then takes for it to make a new pricing decision in the light of the new situation. We presume that the first is the most significant, and is dependent on the state of information in the market. Stigler[24] had pointed out that a firm which is attempting to cut price to increase market share and profitability is unlikely to broadcast the fact. List prices may not be changed at all: rather there will be secret price concession to major customers. Stigler suggests that rivals will learn about the secret price cut primarily from the effect on their own sales. They will be used to a certain variability in their sales, but too great a decline may exceed their estimate of normal variation and lead them to suspect a price cutter. This suspicion will be heightened if one other firm obtains a disproportionate share of the lost custom. Stigler casts this argument in a probability form. The firm sets arbitrary confidence limits relating to its own losses and other firms' gains of existing customers. He finds that a secret price cutter will be able to make greater gains without detection by the other when there are a larger number of sellers and when the amount of switching between sellers on the part of customers is high. If there is an inflow of new customers to the market the incentive to cut price (that is, the chance of being undetected as a secret price cutter) increases sharply with the number of sellers and with the rate at which new customers enter. Two more of Stigler's results are worth quoting.

---

[23] A more precise model would postulate a gradual shifting of custom to the lower-priced producer over time. Then the condition is that other firms cut before sufficient custom has switched to make the short-run gains from cutting outweigh the long-run loss of profit.

[24] G. J. Stigler, 'A Theory of Oligopoly', *J.P.E.* 72 (1964), 44–61.

The first is that if firms pool their information the probability of detecting a secret price cutter rises sharply. Alternatively if one firm has a large share of the market, the probability of detection again rises (the large firm may be thought of as the equivalent of several smaller firms pooling their information). The second is that repetition of the same pattern over time greatly increases the probability that a secret price cutter will be detected. Presumably the length of time required to establish the point is longer where the initial probability of detection is lower—i.e. in markets with many equal-sized sellers. It will be shortest in those markets with few sellers, or unequal-sized sellers.

Even if Stigler's theory is too sophisticated as a description of firm behaviour in oligopoly, the same conclusions as to the importance of market concentration can be derived from more pragmatic considerations. With fewer rivals a firm is more likely to be able to monitor their activities closely and to react rapidly to their changes in policy. As the numbers of rivals increase, the task becomes more difficult (and costly). It seems not unreasonable to assert that the length of the reaction lag will vary directly with the number of rivals.

We may also infer from the foregoing arguments that the reaction lag is likely to diminish as the size of the price cut increases. In terms of Stigler's argument, a larger price cut will generate a larger switch of custom in a given time period, and hence increase the probability of being detected.

We conclude from the above analysis that there is no reason for competitive price cutting to dominate oligopoly situations. A simple consideration of the possible profit outcomes over time can argue persuasively in favour of no price cuts. Firms appear to co-operate in maintaining the existing price. Our analysis therefore confirms the more impressionistic arguments advanced by expositors of the kinked demand curve. We must now ask whether the same considerations could lead firms to co-operate in *raising* price. Again, all we assume is that the individual firm can see the alternative scenarios clearly. It does not need to attach subjective probability weights to obtain the results below. That awaits the next section, which will deal specifically with that result of the learning process which enables firms to attach subjective probabilities to alternatives.

The profit matrix relevant to a rise in price is shown in the diagram. We assume that the market situation is such that $\Pi_1 > \Pi_0 > \Pi_2 > \Pi_4$. This corresponds exactly to the case we analysed above. Firms start with low prices, earning Π_2. The question is whther a move to a higher price, with higher profits Π_0, will take place if the firms act independently.

Profit Matrix		Other Firms	
		High P	Low P
Firm A	High P	Π_0 \ Π_0	Π_1 \ Π_4
	Low P	Π_4 \ Π_1	Π_2 \ Π_2

Suppose firm A does raise its price. How will the other firms react? We divide time into periods that correspond to the reaction lag of firms. We can compare two possible profit streams for the other firms:

Maintain low price: $\Pi_1, \Pi_2, \Pi_2 \ldots$ Profits rise to Π_1 for one period, but then fall back in the next period when A reduces its price not having been followed. All firms then continue at the same profit level as initially.

Raise price: $\Pi_1, \Pi_0, \Pi_0, \Pi_0 \ldots$ Profits rise momentarily to Π_1, but then fall back to Π_0 as the other firms follow firm A.

Since $\Pi_0 > \Pi_2$, the present value of the raise price response is higher. So we expect the other firms, if they act rationally, to make that response.

We must now turn to the initiator of the price rise, firm A, and ask whether there will be anything deterring the firm from raising price in the first place. The possible profit streams are:

(i) Maintain low price

$$\Pi_2, \Pi_2, \Pi_2 \ldots$$

(ii) Raise price, but reduce again when other firms do not follow

$$\Pi_4, \Pi_2, \Pi_2, \Pi_2 \ldots$$

(iii) Raise price: other firms follow

$$\Pi_4, \Pi_0, \Pi_0 \ldots$$

Given a reasonably low discount rate (calculated for the appropriate reaction lag periods), we may expect the present values to rank as follows:

$$(iii) > (i) > (ii)$$

But, given the previous argument concerning the reaction of other firms (and we assume that A is aware of the logic that we have applied to the other firms' response), possibility (ii) is ruled out. So there is a clear advantage in raising price.[25]

The critical objective variable here is again the length of the reaction lag. There is no problem of information about prices; firm A will presumably advertise the price rise generally to other firms, since it hopes to be followed. However there is one indeterminate feature. The other firms will wish to delay their price rise as long as possible, since $\Pi_1 > \Pi_0$, but not so long that firm A reverts to the lower price. This suggests that the rise in price will not occur unless each firm has a good understanding of how other firms operate, and of the policies that they are committed to pursuing. There is a further paradox arising from the analysis. While both firm A and the others benefit from firm A's price initiative, the other firms' gains will in fact be greater. So all firms will prefer to be followers rather than a leader. The only situation in which this is not true is when the reaction lag is 'zero' (defined as previously), so that all firms move to the higher price before the temporary price differential can affect market shares. Once again the resolution of this paradoxical situation depends as much on mutual understanding as on strictly economic variables. For these reasons a number of writers have advocated the examination of 'industry social structure' as an important non-economic variable. We return to this below.

(c) Pricing on the basis of experience

So far we have assumed that the experience of the market over time does no more than awaken firms to the logically possible alternative sequences consequent upon a price initiative by one firm. We have then examined the pricing decisions that a rational firm would take in the face of those possibilities. However for many firms the actual experience of the behaviour of rivals in the market may give more compelling reasons for believing that certain consequences will follow from a given price initiative. They will be less interested in whether their rivals are acting rationally in what they do. The form

[25] M. Shubik, *Strategy and Market Structure* (New York 1959), Chapter 10, is one source for this conclusion. He also provides less conclusive analysis of more complex situations.

that learning from experience is likely to take is that the accumulated history of the market will lead them to assign greater probabilities to some outcomes than to others.[26] For example a firm in a new oligopolistic market might experiment with price cutting. We recall that the change in profit expected is positive $(\Delta\Pi_1)$ if other firms maintain their price, and negative $(\Delta\Pi_2)$ if they cut. Other firms are also feeling their way in the market. After a few experiments the firm could attach subjective probability weights to the two alternative responses, e.g. λ as the probability that other firms maintain their price, $(1 - \lambda)$ as the probability that they cut. The expected gain from a price cut is then given by

$$E(\Delta\Pi) = \lambda \ \Delta\Pi_1 + (1 - \lambda)\Delta\Pi_2$$

So long as this is positive, a further price cut will be tried. The outcome of each experiment will alter the subjective probabilities gradually. In the case in point, we would expect λ to diminish over time, so that $E(\Delta\Pi)$ tends to become negative and price cutting experiments will cease.

Alternatively one could imagine the same logic being applied to experiments in price increases.[27] To begin with one would expect a variety of responses to a price initiative. However other firms would learn from the experience that a raise price strategy led to an increase in profits. They would more frequently respond in this way to future price initiatives. The initiator would in turn attach a higher probability to this outcome and attempt further price experiments, revising his subjective probability upwards all the time. The limit to this process would be when further price increases failed to increase profits for all members of the oligopolistic group. Then some firms would fail to match future price increasing experiments, and the price rise initiator would revise his probability estimate downwards. At some point the expected gain from further price increases would fall to zero and no further price change would occur. A period of price stability could follow, until a new element was introduced into the market situations, for example a threat of new entry or a change in demand conditions.[28] Then experimenting could begin again.

[26] The process of learning has been termed 'quasi-bargaining' by W. Fellner (*Competition among the Few*, London, 1949). The outcome he describes as a 'quasi-agreement'.

[27] R. M. Cyert, M. H. de Groot, 'Interfirm Learning and the Kinked Demand Curve', *J. Econ. Th.* 3 (1971), 272–87, have suggested an ingenious decision rule as to the size of price increase a firm will attempt in these circumstances, based on a subjective probability distribution of the highest price that other firms will match.

[28] S. A. Ross, M. L. Wachter, 'Pricing and Timing Decisions in Oligopoly', *Q.J.E.* 89 (1975), 115–37, analyse many of the issues raised in this section, with a model in which

Alternatively it may be just a matter of time. After a period of stability firms may forget the experience which led to the stabilization of the price and a new period of learning would be initiated. The learning theory suggested lends itself naturally to exploration by means of simulation. Simon, Puig, and Aschoff[29] have simulated a number of duopoly models in which the duopolists start with certain prior probabilities concerning their rivals' reactions to price initiatives and modify those in the light of experience. Each firm seeks to maximize the present value of its future profits at each stage in the game. The detailed results of the experiments cannot be reproduced here. However, there were two important general conclusions. The first was that the sequence generally begins with price cutting, but a change to a price increasing strategy takes over and the system converges to joint profit maximization. The second was that price cutting is more prevalent where the reaction lag of a competitor is longer.

(d) Price leaders and information agreements

We note that this pattern of stability following upon periods of instability and price experimenting is not infrequently described in case studies of oligopolies. The case of the U.S. cigarette industry is a widely reported example.[30] The early Tobacco Trust was convicted by the Supreme Court in 1911 for violation of the Sherman Act. It subsequently split into four companies, P. J. Reynolds, Liggett and Myers, P. Lorillard, and American Tobacco. The pricing policies of the big three, Reynolds, Liggett and Myers, and American, provide numerous illustrations of the type of pricing decisions we have postulated. Stigler lists the following changes:

28 September 1918. American Tobacco raised the price of Lucky Strikes from \$6 to \$7.5 per thousand. Rivals refused to follow. Price reduced to \$6 in November.

20 April 1928. Reynolds (Camels) announced a reduction from \$6.40 to \$6 per thousand, effective 21 April. American Tobacco followed on 21 April, Liggett and Myers on 23 April.

4 October 1929. Reynolds announced an increase to \$6.40 effective the next day. Rivals followed that day.

23 June 1931. Reynolds announced an increase to \$6.85 effective 24 June, and rivals followed that day.

the probability of a price initiative being matched is a function of time elapsed since the previous price change.

[29] J. L. Simon, C. M. Puig, J. Aschoff, 'A Duopoly Simulation and Richer Theory: An End to Cournot', *R. Econ. Studs.* 40 (1973), 353–66.

[30] Stigler, op. cit. (1947), and R. B. Tennant, 'The Cigarette Industry', in W. Adams (ed.), *The Structure of American Industry*, 4th edn. (New York, 1971), Ch. 7, 216–55.

1 January 1933. American Tobacco reduced its price to $6, effective 3 January, and both rivals followed that day.

11 February 1933. American Tobacco reduced its price to $5.50 and both rivals followed the same day.

9 January 1934. Reynolds increased its price to $6.10 and both rivals followed the same day.

A similar pattern has continued since, with two differences. First, the initiative in price increases has generally switched to American Tobacco since the Second World War. Second, the threat of antitrust proceedings has encouraged the firms to maintain at least an appearance of price diversity. Thus in July 1946 Liggett and Myers made an unsuccessful attempt to raise prices, though an initiative by American Tobacco in October was matched. In 1956 the same company tried a price rise of 50 cents per 1,000, but went back after two weeks when it was not followed. In 1965, Lorillard increased the price of filter cigarettes, and was followed by some firms but not others, notably American and Reynolds. So the price went back a month later.

Stigler reports similar experiences in six other cases, including cars and petroleum. Hession[31] has described price manoeuvring in the American metal container industry in the period 1958-9. A period of price war enabled the two major manufacturers to search for a new equilibrium, in a market situation characterized by the threat of entry by vertical integration on the part of the major canners. Once equilibrium was established in 1959, it remained stable for several years. More recently the U.K. Monopolies Commission did a study of uniformity in pricing or parallel pricing.[32] In addition to brief case studies of bread, electric lamps, gramophone records, petrol, and tyres, they suggested more generally that the phenomenon existed in a wide range of industries where seller concentration is high, new entry is difficult, product differentiation is only slight, and demand is inelastic. As far as they could judge, it could prosper without any collusion between the firms.

Reflecting on case histories of this kind, Markham[33] drew attention to the phenomenon of leadership in markets, the leader being the firm who took the initiative in making price changes which others then followed. He distinguished three types of leadership, and the conditions under which they might operate: dominant firm, barometric, and collusive price leadership.

Dominant firm leadership occurs in homogeneous markets where

[31] C. H. Hession, 'The Metal Container Industry', in Adams (ed.), op. cit., Ch. 9, 302–34.

[32] Monopolies Commission, *Parallel Pricing*, Cmnd. 5330, H.M. S.O. (London, July 1973).

[33] J. W. Markham, 'The Nature and Significance of Price Leadership', *A.E.R.* 41 (1951).

there is only one large firm whose actions can materially affect the market price, and a competitive fringe who take that price as given. The large firm then sets his price as a monopolist, taking into account the competitive supply at each price. When products are differentiated, the behaviour of the dominant firm is illustrated in Figure 5.5. The dominant firm chooses the price P_E, giving equilibrium at E on the reaction curve of the competitive fringe. E is the

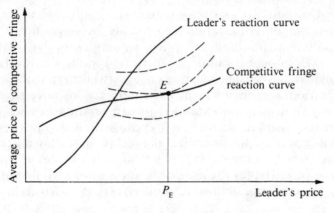

Fig. 5.5

dominant firm's highest profit point on that reaction curve. The possibility that other firms might try the same strategy *vis-à-vis* the dominant firm (the usual source of instability in such models) is excluded by the fact that each individually is small, and cannot therefore on its own affect the behviour of the leader. However we surmise that such a market structure is not common.

Markham's second category is barometric price leadership. It is distinguished by frequent changes in the identity of the leader, and by a less rapid adjustment of prices to any price initiative. The criterion for a price initiative to be followed is not the identity of the leader, but rather the degree to which the initiative reflects a felt change in market conditions or costs. Lanzillotti[34] suggested that such a situation could be competitive in its results, especially where the product is differentiated. His description of the U.S. hard-surface floor covering market in the period 1933–40 suggested that quite small firms could take the leadership on occasion. The only difference was that large firms were followed more promptly than small ones. A third category identified by Markham is a substitute for an

[34] R. F. Lanzillotti, 'Competitive Price Leadership—A Critique of Price Leadership Models', *R. Econ. Stats.* 39 (1957), 55–64.

overt collusive agreement. He suggested a number of characteristics of markets where this might occur. There should be few firms, each with a substantial market share, similar costs, and only slightly differentiated products. Given inelastic industry demand the actions of each firm could affect market price. A price leader in this situation could accurately reflect the conditions facing each firm, and so would be accepted by the other firms. The 'collusion' lies in their acceptance of his actions.

A second important institutional feature of oligopolistic markets is the existence of information agreements between firms, which clearly facilitate the kind of price adjustments that we have described. O'Brien and Swann[35] identify two kinds. Pre-notification schemes involve advertising of price changes well before they occur. Post-notification agreements involve the reporting of price changes as they occur. They may be extended to information besides prices, such as costs, market shares, and even technical advances. The obvious intention is to minimize the delay in following a price change, and to reduce the damage to a firm which makes an initiative which is not followed (in the pre-notification case, it could withdraw a planned price change before it took effect, if its rivals failed to react).

The unresolved question about price leadership and information agreements is the extent to which they represent an *additional* feature of oligopolistic markets, or whether they are simply the institutional reflections of a process that would occur in any case. Markham[36] and Oxenfeldt[37] both assume that price leadership is a significant addition to oligopoly, though only in the rather special dominant firm case is the effect clearly spelt out. O'Brien and Swann list various detriments from information agreements, for instance the disincentive to translate cost advantages (from innovation, for example) into price cuts, and the prevention of 'phantom' competition (customers lying about rival price quotations in an attempt to beat down the quotation from a firm). The implication is that these detriments would not occur without the agreements, and more competitive regimes would result. But the point is not established. One suspects that this approach to oligopolistic phenomena has gone as far as it can in classification of market institutions. To assess their impact we need a theory of oligopoly in

---

[35] D. P. O'Brien, D. Swann, 'Information Agreements—a Problem in Search of a Policy', *Manchester School* 34 (1966), 285-306.

[36] Markham, op. cit.

[37] A. R. Oxenfeldt, 'Professor Markham on Price Leadership: Some Unanswered Questions', *A.E.R.* 42 (1952), 308-84.

which 'the degree of co-operation' between firms is explicitly incorporated in the analysis. Attempts to do this are described in the next section.

(e) Industry social structure

An alternative approach to the oligopoly problem has been proposed by Phillips.[38] This approach sees the problem primarily in the context of interaction within small social groupings. Thus social variables are emphasized rather than the aspects of economic rationality described above. O. E. Williamson[39] followed this with a formal analysis of how these variables might interact. The three variables, he suggests, are (1) a performance variable for the group, (2) an 'adherence to group goals' variable, and (3) an inter-firm communication variable. These three variables are related as follows, where $\Pi =$ performance, $A =$ adherence, $C =$ communication, and $E =$ the exogenous environment (all values relating to the current time period).

1
$$\Pi = \Pi(A,E) \qquad \Pi_A > O \qquad \Pi_E > O$$

This expresses the idea that group performance improves with increased adherence to group goals and with the favourableness of the environment.

2
$$\frac{dA}{dt} = g(\Pi,C,A) \text{ with } g_\Pi, g_C, g_A \text{ all} > O$$

The relationship here involves increasing adherence over time in response to high levels of performance, communication, and adherence. The idea is that a successful co-operating group is likely to be self-sustaining: an unsuccessful one is likely to lose the loyalty of its members.

Equation 1 may be substituted into 2 to give

3
$$\frac{dA}{dt} = h(A,C,E) \text{ with all partial derivatives positive.}$$

The third relationship is

[38] A. Phillips, 'A Theory of Interfirm Organisation', *Q.J.E.* 74 (1960), 602–13.
[39] O. E. Williamson, 'A Dynamic Theory of Interfirm Behaviour', *Q.J.E.* 79 (1965), 579–607.

4          $$\frac{dC}{dt} = f(A,C)$$ with $f_C > O$ and $f_A > O$ for low A

                                              $f_A < O$ for high A

The interpretation of this is that inter-firm communication increases with adherence at low levels, but when loyalty is fully
established (high A) increased adherence involves less communication.

The outcome of the dynamic process described in these equations
does, of course, depend on the precise nature of the relationships.
Equilibrium exists when a pair of values A and C give $dA/dt = O$
and $dC/dt = O$, i.e. the system is in equilibrium with no tendency
to change over time. One possibility is shown in Figure 5.6, which

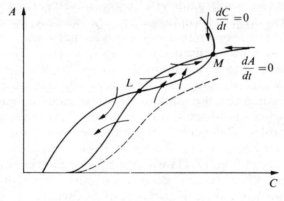

Fig. 5.6

is consistent with the equations (adapted from Williamson). Along
each phase line one of the endogenous variables is not changing:
at their intersection there is an equilibrium. The arrows indicate the
directions of change for non-equilibrium points. M is clearly a stable
equilibrium, while L is unstable. The interpretation of the diagram
is that over time in this industry there will be a tendency for adherence and communication to increase, until M is reached. But it is
important to note that this equilibrium may be dislodged by a sharp
decline in environment which would shift $dA/dt = O$ downwards
(see dotted line) until the curves become tangential and thus M is
an unstable equilibrium. At such a point the agreement breaks up
and adherence falls to O, though communication may not disappear.
The result is a decline in performance. However a recovery of the
environment (e.g. recovery in demand) could lead to rapid re-

establishment of co-operation within the group.

Development of this type of model could be extended in two ways. Williamson himself considers how industry structural variables may affect the position of the curves. For example, high barriers to entry improve performance and hence increase adherence: so the $dA/dt = O$ curve shifts upwards. Product differentiation on the other hand would drive a wedge between the firms and decrease adherence to group goals. A second development would involve the introduction of even more explicit behavioural material into the analysis. Phillips[40] sketches such a model following the March and Simon[41] organizational approach. The group of firms in the industry are constantly revising their profit aspirations in the light of experience. Failure to reach anticipated profit levels leads to search for new solutions. Search involves exploration of agreement with other firms, and so increases 'friendliness' in the industry, i.e. avoidance of price competition, and willingness to collude. A more friendly environment in turn leads to a better profit performance: and that tends to increase profit aspirations.

The difficulty is to give empirical content to these behavioural-type models. Williamson suggests that economic indicators could be used for performance. But 'communication' and 'adherence' variables present obvious difficulties in measurement. And this is *before* the usual variables of demand, supply conditions, barriers to entry, etc. are taken into account. But even if the empirical outlook is daunting, we should at least avoid the trap of treating oligopolistic groups too mechanically and deterministically. The 'social' framework of the industry has an importance of its own.

3   CARTELS

(a) Co-operation or cartel?

We have examined so far those factors in a market which will lead firms to co-operate in maintaining and raising prices without specific collusion taking place. In this section we will suggest reasons why firms might wish to go beyond quasi-agreements (to use Fellner's terminology) to a full formal cartel. We ignore for the moment the question of legal obstacles to such agreements. Later in the section we will discuss the effectiveness of cartels.

Quasi-agreements may be ineffective for a number of reasons.

[40] A. Phillips, 'Structure, Conduct and Performance—and Performance, Conduct and Structure', in J. W. Markham and G. F. Papanek, *Industrial Organisations and Economic Development* (Boston, 1970).
[41] J. G. March and H. A. Simon, *Organisations* (New York, 1958).

The first is that the preconditions may not be met, as described in previous sections. For example, if the reaction lag of the oligopolists to a price cut is too long, it may be worthwhile for one or more of the firms to undertake occasional price cuts to boost their market share. We recall that a long lag is likely where the number of firms is greater, and complete information about rivals is correspondingly difficult to collect. Combination in a cartel has two effects. The first is that pooling of information makes it much easier to detect a secret price cutter (Stigler's argument). The second is that in a cartel arrangement a central office or committee provides a single monitoring service for every member of the cartel, rather than each member incurring the costs of monitoring every other firm.

Secondly, a quasi-agreement may not permit full profit maximization, if firms' costs or demands differ substantially. We may illustrate the case of differing costs with a duopoly model in which the firms have equal shares of the market. The situation is shown in Figure 5.7.

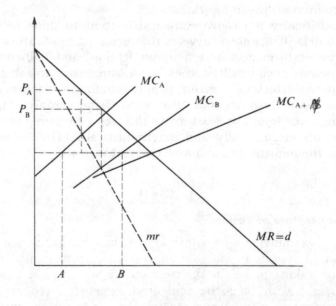

Fig. 5.7

Working with linear demand curves the marginal revenue curve for the industry as a whole, MR, is half the industry demand curve, and hence is the share demand curve for each firm, d. Then each firm has its own marginal revenue curve, mr, which is half that of the industry $MR = d$. The marginal cost curves of the two firms are given by MC_A and MC_B, while the supply curve for the industry is given by the horizontal summation of these two curves, MC_{A+B}. The difficulty is immediately apparent. Firm A would maximize profits with price P_A, firm B with price P_B. Neither of these prices will maximize industry profits. That can only be done by equating MC_{A+B} to industry MR and setting price accordingly on the *industry* demand curve (not shown in the diagram). But that implies unequal *shares* for firms, OA for firm A and OB for firm B, with consequently very different profits. Now this result could never be achieved by the process of learning described in previous sections. In particular firm B would not be willing to raise its price above P_B, for a further increase would leave it with $mr < mc$. Nor is firm A likely to reduce its output voluntarily to OA. The advantage of a cartel then is that it could achieve the profit maximizing solution for the industry as a whole. Then by means of side payments those firms whose profits rose on formation of the cartel could compensate those whose profits had fallen. The latter would, of course, defect from the cartel if they were not so rewarded for their reduction in output. In principle, at least, these matters could be sorted out by open negotiation between firms in the framework of a cartel.

In practice, though, a cartel may not find matters nearly so simple, and a number of other difficulties are likely to arise in its operation. The first concerns the definition of the product or products produced by the cartel. If firms are not permitted to compete on price they will seek to increase their share of the market by advertising, selling expenses, or differentiation of the product. The point is that cartel-determined quotas will be hard to enforce when a firm can claim that the public are showing a preference for its product. A particular example is the case where firms already have natural markets by virtue of high transport costs for the product, and the fact that they have an advantageous location *vis-à-vis* some geographical concentration in the market. The cartel may seek to eliminate such advantages, and thus permit the sharing of industry output on an agreed quota basis. The method adopted is the basing point system of pricing, whereby the price fixed for the industry is tied to a particular point or points of origin for each consignment. Then every consignment must be priced at the basing point price plus the cost of transport from that point (at freight rates agreed by the cartel). The possibility of regional competition for market shares on the basis of delivered prices is thus eliminated. Another example is where product differentiation involves differences in quality. The cartel may find it necessary to fix appropriate price differentials. But this will not solve the difficulty of long-term shifts in market preferences for different varieties of the same product.

A second type of difficulty in operating a cartel has been described by Fog.[42] He concluded that differences in policy were the greatest hindrance to successful cartels. Thus fundamental differences arose between cartel members on the question of short-run versus long-run profitability in a situation of potential entry. Large firms wanted lower prices because their view of the industry was more long run. They had larger resources committed to the industry and wished to maintain market shares. Because of these differences, negotiations between cartel members were the very opposite of joint action to maximize profits. Distrust, threatening, and bargaining were more frequent. It was even possible for a cartel to be used to promote competition within the cartel. He quotes the case of a cartel that had an unchanged price for ten years despite rising costs. The reason was that two large firms wanted a low price to drive smaller firms out of business! So they blocked any discussion on a new price.

The third practical problem is the appropriate action to deal with defectors. We have already suggested that the main deterrent to a defector is the ability of the cartel to detect the defection with a minimal time lag. That applies mainly to the case of a secret price cutter, where the cartel can react decisively by changing price. Orr and MacAvoy[43] have shown that a defection will always be worthwhile if the cartel reacts by matching the defector's price cut, after a time lag which is greater than zero. They argue that the correct procedure for the cartel is to fix their price to maximize profits, given the defector's price. The equilibrium is given by the intersection of the reaction curves of the cartel and the defector. Given that policy by the cartel, the would-be defector will have a higher present value if he stays in than if he leaves the cartel. This striking result derives from the assumption that the cartel sets a maximizing price initially (without fear of new entry), and that the defector sets a price which maximizes the present value of his future profits.

Osborne[44] has made a similar analysis, which can be illustrated by the case of a cartel facing a defector. The cartel sets market shares to maximize the total profit of the cartel. In Figure 5.8, x_1 and x_2 represent the outputs of the defector and the other firms in the cartel. CC is the contract curve, traced out by the points of tangency of the isoprofit curves of the two firms. Clearly the profit maximiz-

[42] B. Fog, 'How are Cartel Prices Determined?', *J.I.E.* 5 (1956), 16–23.

[43] D. Orr, P. W. MacAvoy, 'Price Strategies to Promote Cartel Stability', *Economica*, N.S. 32 (1965), 186–197.

[44] D. K. Osborne, 'Cartel Problems', *A.E.R.* 66 (1976), 835–44.

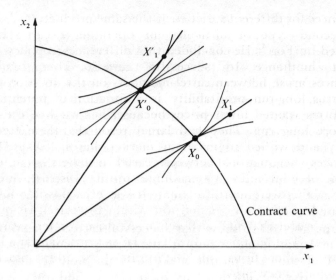

Fig. 5.8

ing function for the cartel must be on the contract curve. Assuming that cross-effects in demand are identical (i.e. the marginal effect on j's price of an expansion in output of x_i is equal to the effect on i's price of an expansion of x_j), Osborne proves[45] that the maximum

[45] There are firms j, i $(= 1 \ldots n)$, with profit functions F_j and inverse demand functions f_j. $x = (x_1 \ldots x_n)$ is the vector of outputs. $F_j(x)$ is concave and differentiable in x, x_j, and x_i. The profit function for the cartel $F(x)$ is the sum of all member profits $\sum\limits_j F_j(x)$.

Assume that cross-effects are identical,

i.e.
$$\frac{df_j}{dx_i} = \frac{df_i}{dx_j} \tag{1}$$

since $\dfrac{dF_j}{dx_i} = x_j \dfrac{df_j}{dx_i}$, then using (1)
$$x_i \frac{dF_j}{dx_i} = x_j \frac{dF_i}{dx_j} \tag{2}$$

x^0 maximizes $F(x)$ iff
$$\sum_{j=1}^{n} \frac{dF_j(x^0)}{dx_i} = 0,$$

or
$$\sum_{j=1}^{n} x_i^0 \frac{dF_j(x^0)}{dx_i} = 0 \tag{3}$$

profit for the cartel is at a point like X_0, where the tangent to the two isoprofit curves is a line through the origin (OX_0), which then defines the market shares of the two firms. The strategy to cope with a defector is then straightforward. If the defector expands his output, the cartel should expand output to maintain its market share, so that the new output position is at X_1. At that point, both the defector and the cartel have lower profits. This should deter the defector from making the first move. Suppose that the cartel made a mistake in fixing quotas, and was at a point like X'_0. Then the market share strategy will no longer avail to deter the defector. He will have every incentive to expand his output, since if the rest of the cartel maintain market shares, we arrive at X'_1 where the defector's profits are higher.

Osborne goes on to show that successful cartels depend on fairly precise information about output shares. In particular, ignorance of the level of industry output makes it impossible to maintain the cartel. An effective sanction may be harder to find where a defector is breaking rules concerning product quality or advertising. It is not clear that a cartel can take any *immediate* steps to counter such a move. The exception is a cartel that can apply a technical sanction outside the market. For example, the international airline cartel I.A.T.A. can exercise a technical sanction by persuading governments to withdraw rights of landing or of over-flying to an airline that does not toe the line. However few cartels can boast so effective a sanction. An alternative method of discipline is the use of fighting companies financed by the cartel to compete directly either with the recalcitrant firm or with a new entrant that is reluctant to join the club.

(b) Agreements on market sharing

Sometimes a cartel will give as its *raison d'être* the specific objective of sharing the market in an orderly fashion. There is no intention (they declare) of restricting output, and raising price, but rather there is a desire to share out the available demand, at a reasonable price. This is particularly the case where the market comes in large lumps, and where the method of selling is via a competitive tender. Industries which exhibit this pattern are large building contracts,

Using (2), (3) becomes $\sum_{j=1}^{n} x_j^0 \dfrac{dF_i(x^0)}{dx_j} = 0$ for $i = 1 \ldots n$.

This is the equation of a ray through the origin, illustrated in Figure 5.8 by the ray OX_0 tangential to the profit functions.

and the manufacture of heavy electrical equipment[46] (especially generators, large transformers, etc.). The problem of large lumps of demand is that a firm finds it difficult to obtain a steady flow of production orders. If it gets the price too high it may find itself for several months without any work to do; alternatively if it makes an error on the low side it may end up with contracts that it cannot finally fulfil in the allotted contract time. This situation is particularly likely to arise in situations where contracts are obtained by tendering. By its very nature this makes for the maximum uncertainty as to whether the firm will obtain a contract or not. Under these circumstances a market-sharing cartel is very attractive to the firms: the gain to profitability arises mainly from a steady flow of work and not from excessive prices. The firms agree among themselves on sharing the market and on the level of prices that should secure any given tender. Then each contract that becomes available is allocated to a firm which bids the agreed price, the other firms bidding a higher one, to maintain the appearance of competition (since such agreements are usually illegal). The main problem with these agreements is precisely that of the profit maximizing type of agreement: there is no obvious basis on which to fix the quotas of industry output. If, as before, the industry output is allocated on the basis of capacity, it becomes necessary to allocate capacity shares to the firms in the long run, so the cartel becomes interested in investment plans.[47]

(c) Fluctuation in industry demand

A further case where restrictive agreements are to be expected is where the industry experiences fluctuations in demand, and where individual firms have high fixed costs. (Any capital intensive sector is likely to have fixed costs as a major part of total cost.) The difficulties encountered in such a situation are illustrated by examining an oligopolistic industry where prices are fixed without a formal cartel agreement between firms. The relevant cost curves are shown in Figure 5.9.

[46] G. B. Richardson, 'The Theory of Restrictive Practices', *O.E.P.*, N.S. 17 (1965), 432–49; 'The Pricing of Heavy Electrical Equipment: Competiton or Agreement?' *B.O.U.I.E.S.* 28 (1966), 73–92.

[47] Under certain circumstances the cartel will develop solely as an investment cartel. This is where the growth in the market over time only allows a new plant to be established, presumably on a large scale, somewhat infrequently, e.g. a new oil refinery, or a new cement works. If all the oligopolistic firms made plans to invest simultaneously there would be gross over-capacity in the industry. So the cartel may share out the investment, allowing each firm to set up a new plant in turn. The result is a long-run constancy in the market shares of constituent firms.

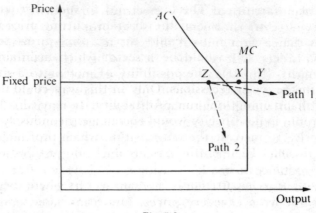

Fig. 5.9

Because of the high fixed costs and minimal marginal cost up to full capacity we show a steeply declining *AC* up to full capacity. The price we assume has been fixed by some price leader. This corresponds to the costs expected at usual operating output (say at *X*, about 90 per cent of firm capacity). Profits are determined by the barriers to entry to the industry. Suppose now that demand fluctuates. If it increases so that each firm would have a demand equal to *Y*, the firm will operate at full capacity and let some demand go unsatisfied. It is unlikely to put up the price to choke off the excess demand, for fear that its rivals would not do so. Then when industry demand slackened off again, it might find that it had lost the goodwill of its customers.

Suppose now that industry demand decreases so that the share of each firm is approximately *Z*. At this point all firms will be making losses: and given a steep *AC* curve the losses may be very considerable. Of course, the ability of the firm to take these losses will depend on how they financed the original investment. If this was financed from retentions they will be in no financial difficulty: but if the firm is highly geared, i.e. borrowed on debentures at a fixed interest rate, there is a danger that gross profit will be insufficient to meet the interest charges.

Now if we add to the above the assumption that the industry is relatively unconcentrated, there will be a strong temptation for an individual firm to break industry discipline and go it alone. The discipline of the kink may be weak, and it may be attracted by the possibility of following Path 1 in the diagram to obtain full use of its capacity and to escape from the unprofitable region. The danger is that its defection will be the signal for the start of a price war, with cut-throat competition. The logical end to such a sequence is that each firm follows Path 2 in the diagram, cutting price to marginal cost. In the long run we could expect some firms to leave the industry. The result would be a sector which maintained chronic undercapacity to avoid the possibility of moving to a situation like Z even in the worst recessions. Only in this way could the sector be sure of maintaining long-run profitability. It may also be the case that chronic undercapacity would encourage the industry to charge a higher price to increase the range within which profitable operation is still possible. High profit margins might be justified on the basis that the industry is risky.

The situation is particularly acute in sectors where the demand, as well as fluctuating, is also somewhat lumpy. This takes us back to the case considered in the previous section. The consequences for an individual firm may be so serious if it fails to obtain an order that it will be tempted, especially under the tender system, to undercut competitors in order to keep its plant in operation and earn *some* gross profit towards its fixed costs. In the case of non-homogeneous products, the temptation to claim that a particular project is a special case will be overwhelming, if the firm is short of work.

If the industry is highly concentrated, the firms will be well aware of the interdependency of their actions, and discipline is likely to be good even in the face of sharp fluctuations. However in the rather less concentrated case a formal cartel will be the answer to these problems. When industry output falls, the cartel will allocate available demand between the firms. Some restrictive agreements may also allow for an increase in prices when demand falls, so as to cover the higher fixed costs per unit.

The difficulties facing such a cartel are precisely the same as those facing the joint-profit-maximizing cartel. The cartel has to agree on market share, on prices and on products. Not only that, it must be flexible enough to adjust these in the face of fluctuating demand. Finally it must be able to enforce its decisions on members, or at least to obtain their acquiescence. On the other hand the cartel is not likely to face so serious a problem on entry to industry, unless it be dumping of products by foreign producers having a similar fluctuation in demand in their own home market. Such a short-term entrant will be particularly unwilling to enter the cartel.

(d) Evidence on collusion

In most advanced industrial economies, collusion is illegal. This makes it difficult to obtain evidence, especially in the United States, where penalties are substantial, and the Sherman Act has been enforced for many years. However, some idea of the extent of collusion in the absence of legal restraint can be derived from the experience of the U.K. In 1956 the Restrictive Practices Act required all agreements to be registered publicly. They were then assumed to be contrary to the public interest unless the parties to the agreement could show substantial benefits under a number of 'gateways' (e.g. public safety, countervailing power, unemployment, and exports). The benefits were required to outweigh the detriments. No less than 2,660 agreements were registered up to 1969, of which 1,240 were abandoned, 960 were varied to take them outside the scope of the Act, and 90 lapsed by effluxion of time. A certain number, which had been replaced by information agreements, were abandoned after an extension of the legislation to such agreements in 1968. Swann *et al.*[48] made a study of 40 which were affected by the legislation. They found that while 100 per cent coverage of industry output was not common, the agreements usually included all the largest firms, accounting for more than 80 per cent of sales. Outsiders usually did not have the capacity to upset the market, and imports were not a problem. The evidence suggested that the agreements were adhered to, since in most cases prices fell sharply when an agreement was abandoned or disallowed by the Restrictive Practices Court. Prices were broadly conventional, but only in a few cases were costs accurately determined. In most cases the prices reflected some sort of average cost for all firms, but this included the cost of plants that were in excess capacity. Certainly there was no pressure on inefficient producers. The objectives of the agreements were said to be 'reasonable' profit, with an orderly maintenance of market shares. Inevitably they became more exploitative in effect as costs fell, but prices were maintained to allow inefficient producers to retain their market shares. The effect of termination of the agreements was to promote price competition in about half the cases, with some sectors registering considerable price falls in price 'wars' that took from six months to six years to stabilize. The other half of the cases replaced the agreement with information agreements involving pre-notification of prices. When these too were made illegal in 1968, such schemes were replaced by post-notification of prices. The abandoning of restrictive agreements had the least effect in sectors with price leaders. Finally Swann *et al.* noted that mergers and innovation became important competitive weapons in a number of sectors, rather than outright price competition.

[48] D. Swann *et al.*, *Competition in British Industry* (London, 1974).

A second source of evidence is the work of Asch and Seneca[49] on the characteristics of collusive firms in the U.S. Their data were drawn from 51 firms that had been condemned for collusive practices under the Sherman Act of 1890, which prohibits contracts, combinations, and conspiracies in restraint of trade. These firms were compared with 50 non-colluding firms drawn randomly from the population of U.S. firms with Stock Exchange quotations. They found that colluding firms tended to have lower profit rates than their non-colluding partners, especially in producer goods sectors. The explanation advanced for this finding is that collusion is a *response* to low profitability. However, there may also be a bias in that data: only collusive agreements that fail to raise profitability are caught by the law, from information supplied by disenchanted conspirators! Asch and Seneca also analysed the relation between market structure and collusion. Collusion prone firms are (*a*) unprofitable firms that are also large or diversified, (*b*) consumer goods firms in high concentration sectors, (*c*) in high concentration sectors with low entry barriers. Collusion 'resistant' firms were small, specialized, fast-growing, and in advertising intensive sectors. Profitable firms tend not to collude, but the incidence of collusion among such firms increases with barriers to entry. They also investigated the success or otherwise of collusive agreements. The more profitable agreements were those of long duration, or in fast-growing sectors. The number of firms in the agreement had little effect.

CONCLUDING COMMENTS

Traditional oligopoly theory has rightly maintained that the price in an oligopolistic market is determined not only by the objective factors in the situation (e.g. barriers to entry) but also by the stance which the oligopolists adopt towards each other. Market behaviour and conduct towards each other determines whether the oligopoly will exploit the profit possibilities of the objective situation to the full. This chapter has examined the determinants of market behaviour. It has found that some variables in the situation are traditional economic variables, for example concentration. However we need to cast our net more widely than economics if we are to understand the situation fully. We have shown that co-operation in the market can develop simply from market experience, backed by a rational consideration of alternatives, without a cartel or even

---

[49] O. Asch, J. J. Seneca, 'Characteristics of Collusive Firms', *J.I.E.* 23 (1975), 223–37; 'Is Collusion Profitable?', *R. Econ. Stats.* 58 (1976), 1–12.

exchange of information being necessary. Indeed we see cartels as a solution to those situations where this process of learning from experience will not work. Cartels are much more likely to be preventive (i.e. to avoid uncomfortable periods of price cutting, especially in cyclical industries) than to have a deliberate intent to raise prices to full joint profit maximizing levels. Quite apart from legal obstacles and the limitations imposed by new entry, the problems of negotiations on market shares within the cartel are likely to prevent full exploitation of a monopoly situation.

APPENDIX 1.   PRICE CUTS AND PROFITS IN OLIGOPOLY

The demand facing the firm is given by

$$a - \beta p_0 + \gamma(p_0 - p_1)$$

where p_0 is the average price level charged by other firms, and p_1 is the price the firm is charging. α, β, and γ are parameters with positive values. Variable costs are constant at C per unit.

We examine the firm's profits, π, in four situations:

1. Initial situation, with all firms charging the same price.

$$\pi_0 = (\alpha - \beta p_0)(p_0 - C)$$

2. The firm is charging p_1, all other firms charging $p_0 > p_1$, i.e. the firm has cut price.

$$\pi_1 = (a - \beta p_0 + \gamma p_0 - \gamma p_1)(p_1 - C)$$

3. All firms cut price to p_1.

$$\pi_2 = (\alpha - \beta p_1)(p_1 - C)$$

4. The firm maintains price p_0, all other firms cutting price to $p_1 < p_0$,
$\pi_3 = (\alpha - \beta p_1 + \gamma p_1 - \gamma p_0)(p_0 - C)$

From these definitions we derive the following results which underlie the argument o the text.

$$\Delta \pi_1 = \pi_1 - \pi_0 = (p_1 - p_0)[\alpha - \beta p_0 - \gamma(p_1 - C)] \qquad \Delta \pi_1 > 0 \text{ if second bracket is negative}$$

$$\Delta \pi_2 = \pi_2 - \pi_0 = (p_1 - p_0)[\alpha - \beta p_1 - \beta(p_0 - C)] \qquad \Delta \pi_2 > 0 \text{ if second bracket is negative}$$

$$\Delta \pi_3 = \pi_3 - \pi_0 = (p_1 - p_0)[\gamma - \beta][p_0 - C] \qquad \text{Always} < 0.$$

$$\pi_1 - \pi_3 = (p_1 - C)(p_1 - p_0)(\beta - \gamma) \qquad \text{Always} > 0.$$

$$\pi_2 - \pi_3 = (p_1 - p_0)[\alpha - \beta p_1 - \gamma(p_0 - C)]$$

This is > 0 if second bracket is negative, which it is if second bracket in expression for $\Delta\pi_1$ is negative.

APPENDIX 2.   REACTION FUNCTIONS

We derive the reaction functions for an oligopoly, where one firm is pursuing an independent pricing policy, but other firms are acting together.

The demand curve for the single firm, X, is, as before,

$$\alpha - \beta p_0 + \gamma(p_0 - p_1)$$

The demand curve for the other firms, Y, as a group is,

$$A - B p_0 - D(p_0 - p_1)$$

X and Y set prices to maximize their profits on the assumption that the other firms' prices are given. We assume variables costs are zero.

$$\frac{\partial \pi_X}{\partial p_1} = \alpha - \beta p_0 + \gamma p_0 - 2\gamma p_1 = 0$$

$$\therefore \quad p_1 = \frac{\alpha - (\gamma - \beta)p_0}{2}$$

$$\frac{\partial \pi_Y}{\partial p_0} = A - 2B p_0 - 2D p_0 + D p_1 = 0$$

$$\therefore \quad p_0 = \frac{A + D p_1}{2(B + D)}$$

These give the equations for the two reaction functions for the case described in the text.

More general formulations would allow each firm to make allowance for some reaction from his rival to his own price initiative. We have

$$\pi_X = p_0 \cdot \phi_X \, (p_0, p_1)$$

$$\therefore \frac{\partial \pi_X}{\partial p_1} = \phi_X + p_1 \left(\frac{\partial \phi_X}{\partial p_1} + \frac{\partial \phi_X}{\partial p_0} \cdot \frac{\partial p_0}{\partial p_1} \right)$$

The second term in the bracket is the 'conjectural variation', i.e. the extent to which a reaction is expected to X's price initiative.

By analogy, we can write

$$\frac{\partial \pi_Y}{\partial p_0} = \phi_Y + p_0 \left(\frac{\partial \phi_X}{\partial p_0} + \frac{\partial \phi_Y}{\partial p_1} \cdot \frac{\partial p_1}{\partial p_0} \right)$$

which has the similar interpretation.

$$\frac{\partial \pi_X}{\partial p_1} = 0 \quad \text{and} \quad \frac{\partial \pi_Y}{\partial p_0} = 0$$

are the reaction functions of X and Y.

APPENDIX 3.
LAGS IN REACTION AND THE PROFITABILITY OF PRICE CUTTING

We compare the present value PV_0 of the profit stream arising from an unchanged price, with the present value PV_C arising from a cut in price that is matched after a lag T.

$$PV_0 = \int_0^\infty \pi_0 \, e^{-\lambda t} \cdot dt = \frac{\pi_0}{\lambda}$$

where λ is the appropriate discount rate

$$PV_C = \int_0^\infty \pi_1 \cdot e^{-\lambda t} \cdot dt + \int_T^\infty \pi_2 \cdot e^{-\lambda t} \cdot dt$$

$$= \frac{1 - e^{\lambda t}}{\lambda} \pi_1 + \frac{e^{-\lambda T}}{\lambda} \pi_2$$

The firm will cut price if $PV_C > PV_0$

$$PV_C - PV_0 = \frac{1}{\lambda}(p_0 - p_1)[\alpha - \beta p_0) + (p_1 - C)(\beta e^{-\lambda t} + \gamma - \gamma e^{-\lambda t})]$$

So the value of this expression depends on the value of the second bracket. The text concentrates on the length of the reaction lag T and the discount rate λ. So we rearrange to obtain

$$PV_C - PV_0 > 0$$

if

$$e^{-\lambda T} > \frac{\alpha - \beta p_0 - \gamma(p_1 - C)}{(p_1 - C)(\gamma - \beta)}$$

6

MARKET BEHAVIOUR: POTENTIAL COMPETITION

1 INTRODUCTION

The analysis so far has concentrated on competitive behaviour within a competing group of firms and has in general terms concluded that within the oligopolistic structure widespread in the western world mutually destructive pricing behaviour can usually be avoided with or without collusion. If this were the whole picture we could conclude that to a considerable extent firms acted as a monopoly to set price, sharing out the maximum profits thus generated according to market shares and cost structure. Competition might still be intense in a number of ways, for example non-price competition, efforts to increase efficiency and reduce costs, continual search for secret or open ways of circumventing the pressures towards price uniformity in quality adjusted terms, etc., but the monopolistic pricing model would still embrace the main characteristics of pricing. This however is to ignore the possibility of new competition from firms currently not producing competing products but attracted by the profits being made. This is an important element in structural change and the structural determinants of prices and profits, and it is to this we now turn.

If each time period were indpendent from all others in terms of industrial structure, pricing, and profits, then maximization of profit even in the long run would entail maximizing profit in each individual 'short-run' time period. In practice these conditions are rarely if ever met and the adoption of a long-term horizon which allows for changes in industrial structure through new entry involves rejecting the idea of short-run profit maximization in favour of maximizing the present value of the future stream of profits. This in turn represents the valuation of the firm, as the firm's only value to a wealth maximizer is in the profits it will generate. But viewing the firm as a value maximizer, while being theoretically more convincing and the natural result of the empirical evidence against short-run maximization so far discussed, raises two serious difficulties.

(i) If a value maximizing price is to be selected, then unless each period is quite independent of all the others the relationship between that price *and everything that influences profit in any future time period* must be known or estimated, including reactions of customers, competitors, potential competitors, future policy on advertising, the course of real incomes, etc., etc.

If there were a complete set of forward markets, then in principle firms could make contracts now which would settle all their future prices, sales, costs, etc., and the impact of current price on future profits could be identified. A value maximizing price could then be selected. In practice virtually no such markets exist and most of the factors that will determine the relation between current price and firm valuation are unknown, especially for the more distant future. Firms' executives then have to make estimates of them or simply ignore them, planning to adjust to them as they appear, for example new entrants. Alternatively they may use 'proxies' for them, for example market share as an indicator of a firm's power to increase profits in the future or maintain these profits if they are threatened. The difficulty for a firm is that different executives, regarding different influences as more important and adhering to different 'proxies', not unnaturally often come up with different price recommendations. The value maximization objective becomes inoperative in the sense that no price recommendation can be deduced without deciding these other matters; price policy becomes very sensitive to these, and the fact that all executives are pursuing value maximization guarantees neither agreement nor a particular price.

The analytical problem corresponding to this is that a theory may predict price behaviour on the basis of value maximization, but must inevitably include only some of the possible price/profit relationships and ignore others. The theory's usefulness is then often very dependent on whether this selection of influences has been made well, rather than on whether the assumption of value maximization itself is appropriate.

(ii) The second difficulty is that in an intertemporal context a discount rate is needed in order to calculate present values of alternative price strategies. This raises questions as to how the rate is determined, why it should be constant for different time periods in the future, and whether firms do in fact view the future this way. More serious, the presence of uncertainty about the future implies a 'risk' premium dependent on firms' attitude to risk. As this is normally unknown, it may be difficult to interpret price behaviour, even if it were known for which possible reactions to their price decision firms allowed and for which they did not.[1] For example a margin lower than the reciprocal of the elasticity of demand might simply be the predictable result of value maximization, or it might result from pursuit of a quite different objective.

The literature contains three different routes from here. The first,

---

[1] See A. Silberston, 'Price Behaviour of Firms', *E.J.* 80, no. 319 (Sept. 1970), 531–3, for elaboration of this point.

incorporating the reactions of oligopolistic competitors within the competing group, was considered in Chapter 5. The second incorporates the reactions of firms *not* currently in the 'neighbourhood'. This is considered below. The third rejects the value maximization assumption and examines pricing as part of the pursuit of quite different assumptions. This is picked up in Chapter 8, where firms are regarded as having sufficient discretion to pursue non-profit objectives.

The analysis of pricing when potential competition is introduced has involved two lines of approach. The first does not take product heterogeneity into account and regards new products coming into competition as being essentially the same as existing products.[2] The second does recognize product heterogeneity. We shall look at these in turn, noting the differences and similarities before coming to conclusions about this important determinant of price behaviour.

2   ENTRY-PREVENTION PRICING

The first step towards introducing the threat of potential entry into price theory was Harrod's distinction between (i) 'snatchers' who maximized short-run profits, careless of the impact on new entry because of their intention to leave after a short period of high profit, and (ii) 'stickers' who intended to remain in the industry, and therefore equated *average* cost and *average* revenue, to ensure no supernormal profits and no new entry.[3] The latter approach could, of course, explain average cost pricing, the margin being a 'normal' profit margin, but suffered from two gross simplifications in its assumption; first that all firms had the same cost structure, and second that potential entrants focused on whether *existing* profits were normal or not rather than on what profits might be *after* entry. Much of the later work focused on these two aspects. Bain provided a very useful starting-point in two ways.[4] First he listed the sources of barriers to new entry as:

[2] In this case we may talk of the firms as all being in the same industry rather than neighbourhood.

[3] See R. Harrod, *Economic Essays* (London, 1952). The more elaborate analysis developed by him was shown to be wrong by Pyatt, but Pyatt's own demonstration that a long-run profit maximizer would nevertheless maximize *short-run* profits, even though he knew this would cause new entry, depends crucially on his assumption that all firms have the same cost structure, i.e. firms either make normal profits for ever, or maximum short-run profits which are then competed down to a normal level by new entry. Clearly the present value of the latter stream of profits is higher. The possibility of more efficient firms entering destroys this line of analysis and it is not therefore pursued. See G. Pyatt, 'Profit Maximisation and the Threat of New Entry', *E.J.* 81 (June 1971), 242–55.

[4] J. S. Bain, *Barriers to New Competition* (Harvard University Press, 1956).

(*a*) Product Differentiation. This covers long-established preferences of buyers for existing products, sometimes sustained by continuous advertising of brands and company names; patent protection of products; product innovation through company Research and Development programmes; and control of particular distribution systems and retail outlets.

(*b*) Absolute Cost Advantages. This arises from superior production techniques either as a result of past experience, patented or secret processes; control of particular inputs required for production, be it materials, labour, management skills, equipment, etc.; and access to cheaper funds because existing firms represent lower risks than new ones.

(*c*) Economies of Scale. If these are important than a new entrant faces the dilemma of going in at a small scale and suffering a cost disadvantage or taking a very large risk by entering on a large scale. In addition, large-scale entry will disturb the existing situation, and may cause excess supply, lower prices, and retaliation. These effects will be exacerbated if (i) minimal optimal scale is a significant proportion of total industry demand and (ii) if the elasticity of demand is low, for then an addition to industry supply will depress prices more. (See below for a formal analysis of this.)

As an extension of this, Orr constructed a robust index of barriers to entry for all 71 Canadian manufacturing industries at the 3-digit level.[5] Each was a weighted average of capital requirements, advertising intensity, R and D intensity, profit rate variability and concentration if very high, where the weights were the coefficients on each variable when the rate of entry was regressed on them. This index was then very useful in subsequent econometric work (see Chapter 7).

Second, Bain constructed a four-way classification of industries covering the most important cases of entry barriers.

(*a*) Easy Entry. No competitor, actual or potential, has any significant cost advantage. Any attempt to earn supernormal profit will eventually fail, and no price above minimum average cost plus normal profit can prevent entry.

(*b*) Ineffectively Impeded Entry. Cost advantages do exist for some firms in the industry and can be used to obtain supernormal profits at prices which still prevent entry. However, the long-term gains are not sufficient to outweigh the current profits forgone, because entry is a slow process and/or firms have a relatively high discount rate.

(*c*) Effectively Impeded Entry. This is a similar situation except that

[5] D. Orr, 'An Index of Entry Barriers and its Application to the Market Structure-Performance Relationship', *J.I.E.* 23, no. 1 (Sept. 1974), 39–50.

here it *is* worthwhile for the firm to sacrifice short-run profits to prevent both entry and diminution of future gains.

(*d*) Blockaded Entry. The short-run profit maximizing price is itself not high enough to induce entry.

Only (*c*) necessarily involves non-short-run profit maximizing behaviour, but most of the emphasis has been on this case. Bain's evidence suggested that case (*a*) was comparatively unlikely, and more recently Wenders has shown, on the basis of plausible estimates of elasticities and entry barriers, that case (*d*) is very improbable indeed.[6] We shall look, therefore, at case (*c*) first, and then at more recent work which attempts to cover cases (*b*) and (*c*) together.

The first major contribution was made by Sylos-Labini,[7] but we shall adhere more to the presentation used by Modigliani in reviewing the work of Bain and Sylos-Labini.[8] Consider an industry producing a homogeneous product with a long-run average cost curve as shown by $LRAC$[9] in Figure 6.1 and industry demand curve DD. The 'Sylos postulate' assumes that potential entrants will expect firms already in the industry to maintain existing output levels if new entry occurs. This postulate, which is considered in more detail below, is best justified on the basis that firms operating fairly near capacity with high fixed costs will find contraction of output very unprofitable and expansion on a significant scale impossible for a considerable period. In this case, only the industry demand curve to the right of the existing price/demand point will be available to the new entrant. The entry-preventing price is the highest price consistent with no part of this residual section of the demand curve being profitable for the potential entrant. This can be found graphically by sliding the $LRAC$ curve and its axes horizontally rightward just until no part of the $LRAC$ curve touches the industry demand curve (shown by $LRAC'$ and $O'P'$). The entry-prevention price is then given by the intersection of the new axis $O'P'$ and the DD line. At this price the current output is OO', and this, via the Sylos postulate, is presumed to be pre-empted. Only output beyond O' is available for the new

[6] J. T. Wenders, 'Entry and Monopoly Pricing', *J.P.E.*, 75, no. 5 (Oct. 1967), 755–60. Osborne, in an interesting development, has argued that the output at an entry-preventing price will correspond to the Stackelberg output, i.e. the output chosen to maximize profits on the assumption that the other duopolist (i.e. the potential entrant) maximizes profit subject to the given output of the first one. Whether this blocks entry or not then depends on the marginal cost of the potential entrant. See D. K. Osborne, 'On the rationality of limit pricing', *J.I.E.*, 22, no. 1 (Sept. 1973), 71–80.

[7] P. Sylos-Labini, *Oligopoly and Technical Progress* (Harvard University Press, 1962).

[8] F. Modigliani, 'New Developments on the Oligopoly Front', *P.E.* 66 (June 1958), 215–32.

[9] This L-shape was found to be empirically valid by Bain, and is supported by much of the evidence reviewed in Chapter 2.

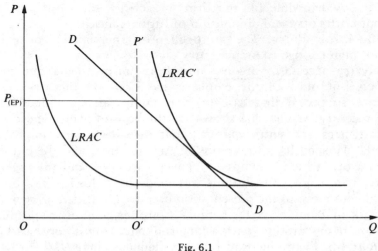

Fig. 6.1

entrant. If it enters, it will expand total industry output, depressing the price level. The industry will move down its demand curve, with the new firm meeting the increment of demand. However, $P_{(EP)}$ and O' have been chosen explicitly to ensure that no level of demand for the new entrant is sufficient to cover his costs, thus effectively impeding entry. A higher price, by reducing existing demand, would have made more of the demand curve available to the potential entrant ($O'P'$ and $LRAC'$ would have been further to the left) and a profitable entry could have been made at any level of output where DD was above $LRAC'$. Thus $P_{(EP)}$ is the 'limit price'. (A lower price would, of course, still discourage all entry, but would sacrifice profits needlessly.)

A special case of this can be put in a mathematical form which provides all the main implications of limit pricing. Suppose that current technology gives a cost structure as shown in Figure 6.2. There are different plant sizes each with its corresponding L-shaped short-run cost curve tangential to the $LRAC$ curve. Each has a minimal optimal output (i.e. extreme left-hand point of horizontal section), y beyond which average costs, AC, are both constant and a minimum for that plant size.

The demand curve is given by $P = a - bQ_D$ and potential entrants, it is assumed, will only enter if they can produce profitably at minimum cost for their plant size. (It is in this respect that the analysis is less general than the previous analysis.) If the ith firm is the potential entrant then the entry-preventing price $P_{(EP)} = AC_i + by_i$ (or, strictly, just below this). If the ith firm enters it will depress the

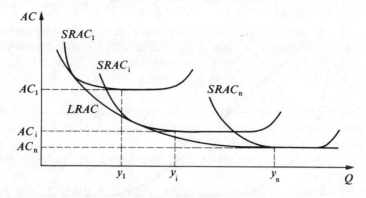

Fig. 6.2

price sufficiently to expand demand by the y_i units necessary for its minimum cost production. From the demand curve $\Delta P = b\Delta Q$ and as ΔQ is required to equal $+y_i$, $\Delta P = -by_i$.

The post-entry price becomes (just below) $AC_i + by_i - by_i$, which is just below AC_i, thus involving losses for the ith firm. Hence $AC_i + by_i$ is the limit price.

This may be rewritten

$$P_{(EP)} = AC_n + AC_i - AC_n + \frac{P_c}{P_c} \cdot \frac{Q_c}{Q_c} \cdot by_i$$

where AC_n is the minimum long-run cost. P_c is the competitive equilibrium price (equals AC_n) and Q_c is demand at price P_c. As

$$b = -\frac{dP}{dQ} \text{ for all } P$$

$$\frac{Q_c}{P_c} \cdot b = -\frac{dP_c}{dQ_c} \cdot \frac{Q_c}{P_c} = \frac{1}{E_c}$$

where E_c is the price elasticity of demand at the competitive equilibrium price. Assuming a constant elasticity ($E_c = E$) we may write

$$\frac{P_{(EP)} - AC_n}{AC_n} = \frac{AC_i - AC_n}{AC_n} + \frac{y_i}{Q_c} \cdot \frac{1}{E}$$

This says that the profit margin (expressed as a fraction of average cost rather than of price) for the largest firms will be dependent on:

(i) $(AC_i - AC_n)/AC_n$. This is an indicator of the extent of economies of scale, measuring the cost disadvantage of firms at less than minimum efficient size. Large economies will, therefore, allow a high margin.

(ii) y_i/Q_c. This is a measure of the minimal optimal output relative to the competitive output of the industry. Again if this is large a high profit margin will be possible.

(iii) $1/E$. The higher the elasticity, the lower the entry-preventing profit margin.

These are three main conclusions of Bain's study[10] and provide testable predictions about the impact of cost barriers on profits. In addition, the formulation gives an explanation for the size of the profit margin selected, if we presume that the largest firm with the lowest costs is the price leader in the industry.

This picture, though useful, is a highly simplified one, and many real-world factors can destroy it. A high degree of brand loyalty can mean much higher margins with no risk of entry, while a growing market will make entry easier unless the price is reduced, thus incidentally providing a further possible explanation for a lack of readiness to raise prices in an upswing (see p. 130).[11] The economics of 'sourcing'—new entry by a customer—will be markedly different as the new entrant then takes his market directly, and possibility of new entry by takeover, which avoids any creation of further capacity, means that limit pricing may be circumvented altogether. Nevertheless, the limit price approach is an important innovation and we briefly consider some issues inherent in the above analysis.

First, it requires a uniform price in a predominantly homogeneous product industry with significant differences in firms' costs. This strongly implies either a collusive group of firms, a price leader, or a 'dominant' firm (i.e. one which sets price and then meets all the demand not taken up by other firms in the industry at that price). Neither in the model nor in practice is there any easy way to determine market shares in the first two cases, where both price and total demand are already given.[12]

[10] Except that Bain focuses on the ratio of minimal optimal *scale* to market size, i.e. yn/Q. This only equals the above precisely if the potential entrant is a firm of size class n.

[11] For an Australian example of both factors, see M. A. Alemson and H. T. Burley, 'Demand and Entry into an Oligopolistic Market: A Case Study', *J.I.E.* 23, no. 2 (Dec. 1974), 109–24. Also see J. Bhagwati, 'Oligopoly Theory, Entry Prevention and Growth', *Oxford Economic Papers*, no. 3 (Nov. 1970), 297–310, for aspects of the theory of growth and entry prevention.

[12] See chapter 5, p. 168 for elaboration of the difficulties inherent in industry price setting with dispersions in cost.

Second, the analysis is dependent on significant economies of scale. If none exist then there is *no* price above that giving normal profit which will deter entry. In this case, profit maximization coupled with a steadily declining market share is the best possible strategy. Shaw provides evidence of an industry where entry prevention was too costly and so higher profits were aimed for and declining market share accepted, though combined with high advertising, some price reductions, and tight control of retail outlets to make entry as difficult as possible.[13]

The main difficulty, however, is with the Sylos postulate.

(*a*) If the potential entrant *does* enter then the rational action for the existing firms is to include the new firm in its cartel or price leadership policy and contract output somewhat.[14] In this way a higher profit could frequently still be made in comparison to those profits (quite possibly negative) resulting from a policy of maintaining previous output levels. Knowing this, the potential entrant may not be deterred by the Sylos-type expectations. In this case the only deterrent would be the threat of *irrational* behaviour.[15]

(*b*) New entry in fact only involves *someone* making losses. Whether it is the new entrant or not depends on whether it can capture any of the existing firms' demand, on relative costs, and on relative power to survive a loss-making period. This will depend mainly on its financial reserves and the existence of other profitable products. If the potential entrant is strong on these criteria, entry may not be deterred. A researched example of this is provided by Bevan's study of the entry of Imperial Tobacco into Smith's crisps market.[16] Though Smith's had been rather lethargic and were slow to react, it still cost Imperial £10 million to destroy Smith's dominant position, partly because of the advertising and product development war it sparked off. A company the size of Imperial could none the less achieve successful entry.

(*c*) Extending this approach if the new entrant is in the largest plant size class, then all firms will make losses, but the new entrant will generally make *smaller* ones than the price setter.[17] Both have the same price and the same average costs (higher than price) but the

[13] R. Shaw, 'Price Leadership and the Effect of New Entry on the U.K. Retail Petrol Supply Market', *J.I.E.* 23, no. 1 (Sept. 1974), 65–79.

[14] See J. T. Wenders, 'Collusion and Entry', *J.P.E.* 79, no. 6 (Nov. 1971), 1258–77, for a detailed analysis of the argument that existing firms would not find it profitable to maintain output at pre-entry levels.

[15] See F. Scherer, op. cit. 228–9, for discussion of this point.

[16] A. Bevan, 'The U.K. Potato Crisp Industry 1960–72: A Case Study of New Entry Competition', *J.I.E.* 22, no. 4 (June 1974), 281–98.

[17] This point is developed by J. Bhagwati, op. cit., 307.

new entrant has minimal optimal output whereas the price setter has this only in a limiting case, and othewise has a higher level, hence incurring the same margin of loss, but on a larger output.

(*d*) In addition, it may be asked why the price setter should not maximize profits most of the time, reducing price to the limit level only when the threat of new entry occurs. If the threat of shifting to a limit price is insufficient, the time taken for entry to actually occur would normally be sufficient to make the threat a reality. However Pashigian suggests that the cost of expanding output to the limit price level with a plant geared to the smaller short-run profit maximizing level might be very high, giving the new entrant considerable grounds for not expecting this reaction,[18] and in an oligopoly the problem of co-ordinating such a strategy might well be insuperable. Clearly further analysis of the entry decision is required before such problems can be dealt with fully,[19] but the conclusion appears to be that the limit pricing approach considered is unrealistic.

Such considerations, plus widespread evidence of firms failing to deter entry, have directed attention away from the decision on how to deter entry towards the decision as to what *rate* of entry to permit. This was strengthened by Osborne, who identified several industries where limit pricing *could* be practised, but where entry none the less occurred, i.e. cases of ineffectively impeded entry.[20] Pashigian's approach utilizes the fact that, at any time, limit pricing depresses current profits but, by reducing the eventual number of firms in the industry, gives rise to a higher stream of profits eventually.[21] Firms will maximize profits and permit entry until the present value of the future gains of limit pricing outweighs the current profit sacrifice, and then shift to limit pricing. This could be in the initial period, but it is argued (i) that the difficulty of identifying the product's profitability, preparing a substitute, and launching it will slow entry in the initial stages, and (ii) that maximum profits may be several times limit price profits. Both factors result in a short-run maximizing strategy and some entry. Over time both effects diminish, making rapid entry more probable and a switch to the limit price more profitable.[22] Pashigian adds that at this point, however,

[18] P. Pashigian, 'Limit Price and the Market Share of the Leading Firm', *J.I.E.* 16, no. 3 (July 1968), 165–77.

[19] For a probabilistic approach, introducing the subjective degree of risk aversion of fims, see D. Baron, 'Limit Pricing, Potential Entry and Barriers to Entry', *A.E.R.* 63, no. 4 (Sept. 1973), 666–74.

[20] D. Osborne, 'Rate of Entry in Oligopoly Theory', *J.P.E.* 72, no. 4 (Aug. 1964), 396–402.

[21] P. Pashigian, op. cit.

[22] See J. T. Wenders, op. cit., for a fuller analysis of the determinants of the optimal price/output strategy in an entry retardation context.

there may be a sufficient number of firms to prevent effective co-operation, and the price would not remain at the limit price, but continue on down to the competitive level. Against this, however, we may add that the probability of this occurring, which increases over time as more firms enter, may constitute a very strong reason to move to the limit price much earlier.

This approach seems a fruitful one, suggesting that many industries may rationally move from ineffectively impeded entry to effectively impeded entry. It retains, however, the simplification that only two price strategies are available, limit pricing and short-run profit maximization, with the number of new entrants a function of the period for which the profit maximizing price is maintained. Following Shaw's evidence it seems likely that firms may adopt intermediate price strategies to deter some entry,[23] thus hoping to retain longer terminal market shares and a more manageable industrial structure.

An early theory in this vein was that proposed by Worcester.[24] His starting-point is the observation that every product or sub-product must have been the initial product of a single firm. So where more than one firm produces, new entry must have occurred. The question is why the first firm 'permitted' this, and what determines the market shares of the individual firms. The explanation lies in Worcester's 'independent maximization hypothesis'. For simplicity, we again assume that costs are constant above a certain minimum economic size, and that the market demand curve is linear and does not shift over time. The situation is illustrated in Figure 6.3 where CC' is the cost curve and DD' is the demand curve. Now, according to Worcester's hypothesis, the first firm, A, faces the industry demand as a monopolist. He therefore equates marginal revenue and marginal cost and prices at P_A. Now in due course this profitable situation will attract a new firm, B. The reaction of A to new entry is to accept the new industry price, but not to change his output. So the demand curve for firm B is the marginal demand curve $P_A D'$, with marginal revenue curve MR_B. Firm B simply sets the best price for itself, i.e. P_B. Exactly the same occurs for subsequent entrants C and D until the new entry is prevented by considerations of minimum economic scale (the marginal demand for a new entrant would not enable it to cover its costs).

The advantages to the first firm are twofold. (i) It will have the largest market share. Colluding with new entrants to maintain a

[23] R. Shaw, op. cit.
[24] D. A. Worcester, *Monopoly, Big Business and Welfare in the Postwar U.S.* (Seattle, 1967), Chapters 5 and 6.

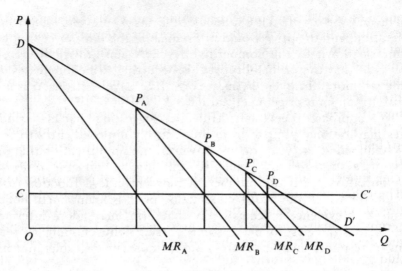

Fig. 6.3

monopoly price carries the disadvantageous implication that firm A will only have an equal share of the market with the new firms, instead of the virutal half-share that it retains by independent maximization strategy. (ii) It will have the largest profit. As all firms have the same price and average cost, profit is a linear function of market share. The difficulty with this model is that it suffers from the same sorts of criticisms as the Sylos-Labini approach described earlier.

In a more general form, however, there is considerable support for a type of 'entry-retardation' strategy. Firms frequently follow *Life Cycle Pricing*, the essence of which is the setting of a high margin in the early part of a product's life, reducing it progressively until a much lower, often minimum acceptable margin is reached in later years. This is not necessarily inconsistent with continuous short-run profit maximization if the elasticity of demand increases the longer the product has been in existence, but it does fit rather well with the idea of profit maximization giving way to limit pricing at the optimal point. In fact there is much evidence of firms first 'skimming' a market—i.e. charging a very high margin on a unique, small-volume product, then moving to a more 'penetration' oriented price which involves a much lower margin (conceivably even a negative one)[25] in order to rapidly expand the market, obtain substantial

[25] This would arise from so called 'predatory' pricing which involves firms in deliberately pricing at very low levels, frequently incurring losses, in particular markets at particular times to drive out competitors, thus allowing higher long-run profits. Examples of this do

economies of scale, and prevent or reduce entry. Market share and/or sales volume become vital objectives as firms attempt to move down their long-run average cost curves faster than their competitors in a form· of dynamic 'entry-retarding' pricing, the process ending in a stable, probably oligopolistic market where margins are relatively tight, where there is little scope for competitive price cutting, and competition is based more on advertising, product differentiation, etc. This more complex price policy encompassing profit maximization, limit pricing, market share objectives, and full cost pricing, but with variable margin, indicates the blinkering that may arise if a pricing model focuses specifically on one aspect of price policy only.

The other main development as a result of dissatisfaction with the logic of entry-prevention theory has been to recognize the indeterminacy that surrounds the entry decision. Caves and Porter argue, first, that a large number of factors come into the decision, including not only profits, and 'natural' barriers to entry, but also expected reactions, the behaviour of other (especially later) potential entrants, resources available to the entrant, and information costs.[26] Second, existing firms have a number of ways of deterring entry, including excess capacity, control of inputs, product differentiation, vertical integration, etc. The result is that barriers are significantly endogenous and that there is the same type of indeterminate oligopolistic game facing potential competitors as was seen to face actual oligopolistic competitors. The implication of course is that some game theoretic structure of the type examined in the previous chapter is required to explain entry behaviour.

Many testable predictions concerning the relationship between barriers to entry, profits, market share, and structural change over time arise from the limit price approach. In particular it suggests that if concentration is sufficient to generate some recognized pressure to price uniformity then profit margins and prices will mainly be determined by the extent of economies of scale implied by the industry's cost structure and other entry barriers. (See Chapter 7.) Interpretation of results is, however, difficult. For example, if high profits coincide with high barriers to entry, this might be because where there are low barriers *actual* entry reduces profits, or because higher barriers allow a higher limit price. Even if Blockaded Entry never occurs, the absence of entry may result from either limit pricing

exist, but it is probably an infrequent occurrence because the short-term costs may be very high and the long-term gains both uncertain and limited by the threat of subsequent new entry.

[26] R. E. Caves, M. E. Porter, 'From Entry Barriers to Mobility Barriers. Conjectural Decisions and Contrived Deterrence to New Competition', *Q.J.E.* 41, no. 2 (May 1977), 241–61.

or competitive pricing. Nevertheless, in providing a rational explanation for average cost pricing, non-short-run profit maximization, and many observed structure–performance relationships, the limit pricing approach is proving very fruitful.[27]

3 DIFFERENTIATED PRODUCTS: ENTRY AND PRICING

The above analyses either explicitly or by implication ignore product differentiation and are only capable of being applied if the price set is construed as an average of actual prices, the latter reflecting a dispersion of product qualities around the average. It has been seen, however, that the downward sloping demand curve can be and in fact is only appropriately interpreted as the demand curve facing a differentiated product. (See Chapters 1 and 3.) It is interesting to re-evaluate limit pricing in terms of the characteristics space analysis which lies behind the demand curve for a differentiated product.

Unlike the case of product homogeneity where entry involved a new firm making the 'same' product, it is not immediately obvious what entry into a differentiated product market means. But a non-rigorous view would be that entry occurs when a new product is located in characteristics space such that the demand facing existing products is significantly affected. The new product will obtain all the customers located in its area up to a distance determined by the preferences of customers and the nearness of existing products. The latter will in turn lose demand at existing prices.

Early analysis suggested that competing products would be located in pairs.[28] This can be seen in Figure 6.4. It would generally be more profitable for a product to locate at X, *next* to A, rather than at Y, because it means that the new product gains customers in the shaded area who would otherwise be nearer to product A. A subsequent new entrant would then have an incentive to locate immediately adjacent to one of the two existing firms, but a trio of firms would not result, as the middle one, having virtually no market, would either relocate elsewhere or start a leap-frogging movement with one other firm away from the remaining one. In either case we end up with pairs of firms located next to each other, which incidentally is far from the social optimum of even distribution if consumers are evenly distributed.

[27] It should be added that 'exit-promotion' is a similar sort of phenomenon, although generally outlawed. Williamson found an important case where large firms agreed with a trades union on higher wage rates in order to force smaller firms who could not obtain concomitant increases in productivity out of business. See O. Williamson, 'Wage Rates as a Barrier to Entry: The Pennington Case in Perspective', *Q.J.E.* 82, no. 1 (Feb. 1968), 85–116.

[28] See in particular H. Hotelling, 'Stability in Competition', *E.J.* 39 (Mar. 1929), 41–57.

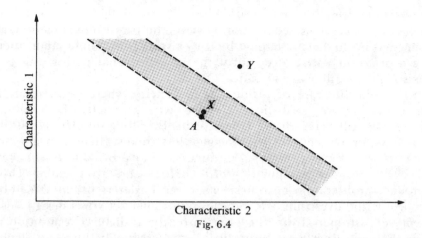

Characteristic 2
Fig. 6.4

If moving from Y to X loses some demand on the far side of Y because of other products located there, then X will not be the best point and some dispersion of products will occur. How spread out it will be, it is not in general possible to say.[29] Hay has shown that if products cannot relocate as new products enter then this also promotes a dispersion of products through characteristics space.[30]

Given a spread of products, how does a firm prevent entry in the sense of new products locating between it and its nearest rivals such that its demand is influenced? The answer to this has two parts.

(i) Just as in the case of homogeneous products, there are great difficulties in believing entry can be totally prevented by price policy. More specifically, assuming an even distribution of consumers: (*a*) If there are no economies of scale then there again can be no 'entry preventing price'. A new firm locating at a gap in characteristics space would have lower costs for the area around it irrespective of the size of the area and could, on entry, profitably undercut any price set by near rivals which was not below their own average cost. (*b*) If there are economies of scale then the market available to the new entrant could be made smaller than minimal optimum scale by appropriate prices of near rivals, thus preventing profitable entry. But, as in the Sylos-Labini model, if entry does none the less occur then existing firms will incur losses and the rational procedure for them, particularly if the new entrant is strong financially, is to raise

[29] For an analysis of various possibilities see B. C. Eaton and R. G. Lipsey, 'The Principle of Minimum Differentiation Reconsidered: Some New Developments in the Theory of Spatial Competition', *R. Econ. Studs.* 42, no. 129 (1975), 27–50.

[30] D. A. Hay, 'Sequential Entry and Entry Deterring Strategies in Spatial Competition', *Oxford Economic Papers*, 28, no. 2 (July 1976), 240–57.

price and accept the new rival. Knowing this, a limit price will not forestall entry. This would not however be true if consumers were bunched in the area occupied by the existing firm. There might then be a price such that after entry the new firm made a loss but the existing firm still made a profit.

(ii) Unlike the case of product homogeneity where entry retardation was the only realistic alternative, with product differentiation firms can still deter entry. They do this by filling up characteristics space with products such that the gaps left are insufficient to support output at or beyond minimal optimal scale at profitable prices even if existing firms maximize profits before and after entry. Thus product proliferation becomes a major entry deterrent, combined of course with advertising and other promotional activities designed to remove customers from the gaps currently available. In addition it can be seen that new entry will get increasingly more difficult, making early identification of opportunities—i.e. gaps in the market— important and entry into a well-established market very difficult. The implication for pricing is that firms have another reason to forgo using it as a means of deterring entry but to modify price policy if some reduction in the rate of entry is desired. Economies of scale may none the less permit higher profits through prohibiting entry into either a homogeneous or heterogeneous product market.

This picture can be extended to portray the view of industries adopted by Andrews and Brunner.[31] They recognized the widespread existence of product differentiation and multi-product firms, economies of scale and average cost pricing, inelastic industry demand but oligopolistic interdependence of groups within it, and elastic supply of products at a given price. This can be summed up as in Figure 6.5 which shows the cost curve for a single product, the locus of price–output points available to the firm, and the industry demand curve. To make the picture determinate we need to know first how far along the price–output locus a firm will locate. Profit maximization will mean it will move as far to the right as it can, and the constraint will be the few other firms producing a very similar product, at a very similar price. The fewer the rivals relative to demand the higher the profits possible. Second, we need to know why the locus is at the level it is. Andrews and Brunner suggest that this depends on the threat of 'cross-entry', that is, entry into the group of near rivals of a product made by a firm currently in another area of the market but not directly competing. This threat will as before depend on economies of scale, initial costs, appropriate

[31] P. W. S. Andrews, E. Brunner, *Studies in Pricing* (London, 1975). This collects together earlier work by the two authors.

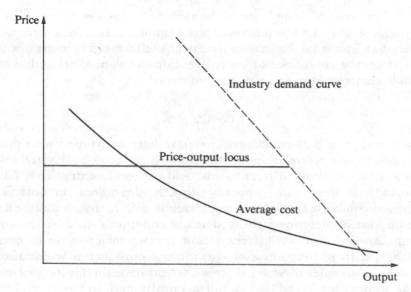

Fig. 6.5

expertise, consumer brand loyalty, etc., but typically these will tend to be much lower, given that the firm is already in the industry albeit not directly competing. For example, an established supplier of women's fashion shoes may offer no *actual* competition to producers of non-fashion women's shoes or children's shoes, men's shoes, football boots, etc., yet it could probably move relatively easily into any of these given its name and reputation, its existing machinery and expertise on leather processing, and so on. If profits become substantial in any of these areas it will enter, and thus reduce profit either by threat of cross-entry or actual entry.

This analysis has three important implications.

(i) First, it may be quite consistent that most firms only actually compete with three or four others in a subsection of an industry but none the less find their behaviour constrained by the structure of the industry as a whole. It may thus make sense to view for example the structure of the shoe industry as a determinant of shoe firms' performance even if many of the firms do not directly compete with each other.

(ii) Second, it will still be true that early entry will be desired, thus encouraging firms in the industry to proliferate products so as to be among the handful who are important in each subsection of the industry.

(iii) Third, the analysis suggests that fewness of firms and barriers to entry will both increase profitability. The complication is that it places considerable emphasis on barriers to (cross-) entry but this is a characteristic entirely *internal* to the industry. It is therefore possible that industrial concentration might affect price levels *via* its effect on the conditions of entry to localized sub-markets within the whole characteristics space of the industry.[32]

4   CONCLUSIONS

This chapter and the previous two have been concerned with price behaviour and its relation to the four main structural variables—costs, concentration, differentiation, and barriers to entry. They have shown that prices are generally directly dependent on cost and demand conditions and that concentration, differentiation, and entry conditions all determine those demand conditions. In addition cost structure and product differentiation are two major forms of entry barrier. If there were low concentration, no product differentiation, and no economies of scale, then we would have the limiting case in which prices are forced to their normal profit level. In fact it has been argued that typically there is product differentiation and that this alone makes supernormal profits possible. How large these are will, it is predicted, depend on the extent of product differentiation, the degree of concentration, and the height of barriers to entry. The first determines the relation between price and demand, the second determines the extent to which prices of competing products can be co-ordinated via market reactions or collusion, and the third determines the profit levels that a competing group can realize without it being undermined.

None of these relations is, however, rigid. Product proliferation will be likely to occur, undermining product differentiation advantages; high concentration operates primarily through perception of mutual interdependence by firms and these perceptions may be volatile in a changing environment; entry will rarely be prevented even if this is possible, and retarded entry may still be enough to put pressure on prices and profit levels.

These are the conclusions that emerge from examining the theory of price–structure relations. This provides the basis for the empirical examinations of structure–performance relations in the next chapter.

---

[32] For a more recent and more elaborate picture of cross-entry characteristics, see R. E. Caves, M. E. Porter, op. cit.

7

MARKET STRUCTURE AND PROFITABILITY

The theme of this part of the book is the constraints placed on the firm by the economic environment in which it operates at a given time. Thus in Chapter 2 we examined those elements that determine the unit costs of production of firms. In Chapter 3 we examined the basic market structure in which the firm operates, the size and number of competitors, and the existing degree of product differentiation. We follow the recent work on advertising in regarding it as an investment that builds up a 'stock' of 'brand loyalty' or 'goodwill', which is then an element in the market structure. In Chapters 4, 5, and 6 we combined these elements in the traditional analysis of pricing and price–cost margins. Thus the profitability of the firm is constrained by market limitations on the prices it can charge, and by the unit costs of its operations. If this analysis is correct, we expect to see strong links emerging empirically between current profitability and industrial structure. The purpose of this chapter is to examine the evidence on this matter.

The following pages are not intended to be an exhaustive review of all empirical work in this area. There simply is not room to quote every study and list its conclusions. Besides, the output of new studies is so great that any review would quickly be out of date. Rather we seek to examine the methodological problems, and to indicate the main areas of research, quoting studies as illustrative of these. We provide the student with a framework within which to locate the many studies and to relate them to each other, and we hope to arouse his critical faculties before he confronts the wealth of empirical detail. First, we summarize the main hypotheses about the determinants of profitability, and look at various definitions of profits and price–cost margins. Then we turn to the empirical studies of industry profitability in sections 3 and 4, and of firm profitability in section 5.

1 INDUSTRIAL STRUCTURE AND PROFITABILITY: A SUMMARY OF THEORY

Early oligopoly theory sought to explain inter-industry differences in profitability in terms of a single element of market structure—concentration. The reasoning was that the more concentrated the industry, the more likely it would be that firms would realize their interdependence and co-operate to raise prices. This theory has been described in Chapters 3 and 5. So the attempt was made to demonstrate empirical relationships between industry concentration and profitability. This theory continues to attract empirical investigations, and we summarize the main results in section 3 of this chapter.

The main alternative to this theory emphasizes the role of potential competition from outside the industry. Concentration is much less important: it only implies interdependence and avoidance of price competition, rather than specific collusion to raise prices, as in the older theories. The price–cost margin is determined by the conditions of entry, and this depends on the other elements of structure such as economies of scale, product differentiation, and brand loyalty. We summarize here the main results of the analysis of these theories in Chapters 4, 5, and 6. Relevant empirical work is discussed in section 4 of this chapter.

The primary constituents of industry structure which we examined in Chapters 2 and 3 may be summarized as scale (and notably scale in relation to industry size, measured by the proportion of industry output provided by a plant of minimum economic size), concentration, and product differentiation (including 'brand loyalty', measured by past and current marketing expenditures). Dichotomizing each of these aspects of structure into high (x) or low (o) values, we obtain the following the classification of possible market structures:

	Scale	*Concentration*	*Differentiation*
(1)	x	x	x
(2)	x	x	o
(3)	x	o	x
(4)	x	o	o
(5)	o	x	x
(6)	o	x	o
(7)	o	o	x
(8)	o	o	o

Examination of these possibilities enables us to eliminate (3) to (6) as *a priori* unlikely. Large scale is not consonant with low concentration, or vice versa. In fact the correlation between concentration and measures of scale has proved a serious handicap in econometric studies, as we shall see below. So we are left with cases (1), (2), (7), and (8), which we must examine in some detail.

(8). These are the structural conditions for perfect competition, which need not detain us.

(7) is of more interest. It reflects the kind of structure which is

the basis for the Chamberlinian analysis of monopolistic competi-tion.[1] Despite differentiation, low scale and low concentration mean that there is little price discipline: there are few barriers to entry, and new entry tends to eliminate abnormal profits.

(1) has monopoly as a polar case, but we are more interested in differentiated oligopoly. Firms have their own market demand curves, so there is little to be expected by way of intra-industry price competition. The main weapon of competition will be in marketing, and product diversification, as each firm attempts to find profitable areas in product space, or to lure consumers via advertising into the vicinity of their market.[2] The effect of a stock of advertising 'good-will' could be a powerful deterrent to entry. This might be due either to the advertising outlays which a new entrant might have to make to accumulate a sufficient stock, or to the existence of extra costs incurred in penetrating a market with a new brand over and above the recurrent advertising costs of existing firms. The first effect would increase the initial capital requirements of the entrant, with the additional hazard that this would be very risky capital, for if the venture failed there would be no 'asset' to sell at the end. In a world with bankruptcy this would be a serious disadvantage. The second effect simply gives established firms an absolute cost advantage over the new entrant.

This barrier will be in addition to that arising from large scale, which may have two effects. The first is the case of large scale in proportion to the market. If the entrant wishes to reach optimal economic size he may not find any part of the market where suf-ficient demand is available, unless he can oust an existing firm. But at sub-optimal scale, entry may be easy in some segment of the mar-ket. The second is that large absolute scale may require consider-able capital. This may be a barrier to entry, regardless of whether the firm will form a major part of the market.

(2) is the structure of a homogeneous oligopolistic industry. It is the type of industry that is the subject of oligopoly pricing models, and the Sylos-Labini–Bain[3] limit-pricing models. *A priori* one would expect that increasing scale will be associated with increasing con-centration and a greater entry barrier. The first will increase the oligopolistic interdependency and reduce the likelihood of intra-

---

[1] E. H. Chamberlin, *Theory of Monopolistic Competition*, 8th edn. (Cambridge, Mass., 1966).

[2] For a full discussion see Chapters 12 and 13.

[3] J. S. Bain, *Industrial Organisation* (New York, 1959), Chapter 8; P. Sylos-Labini, *Oligopoly and Technical Change*, trans. E. Henderson, Harvard Economic Series, 119 (Cambridge, Mass., 1962); F. Modigliani, 'New Developments in the Oligopoly Front', *J.P.E.* 66 (1958), 215–32.

industry price competition. The second will protect a high price against new entry. Finally we recall that large absolute scale (in terms of capital requirements) may of itself be a serious barrier to entry.

This brief catalogue of the possibilities suggests that we need to look at all three elements of market structure in the same analysis: product differentiation and concentration affecting the likelihood of intra-industry competition on prices and margins between existing firms: 'brand loyalty' and scale affecting the likelihood of new entry, or conversely the scope for entry-preventing pricing by the firms in the industry, against inter-industry competition. To put it very simply, structure controls not only the highest price that can be charged without inducing entry, but also the likelihood that existing firms will co-operate to realize this maximum price by avoiding price competition between them. The implied causal links can be summarized diagrammatically. The elements of structure listed in column 2 imply the influence on pricing in column 3, with implications for profits and price–cost margins in column 4. (Column 1 is discussed in the conclusions to this chapter.)

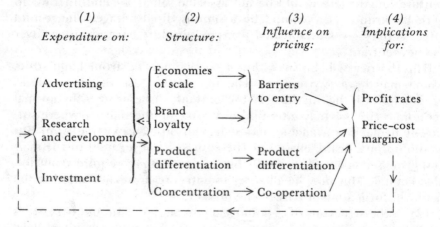

The implied direction of causation is shown by the solid arrows. It is these causal links that have been the subject of the empirical work which follows.

2 MEASUREMENT PROBLEMS: PRICE–COST MARGINS OR PROFIT RATES?

Before examining the alternative measures, we present some simple definitions.

R = revenue
C = cost

$C \quad = Kg + D$

$D \quad =$ direct cost

$Kg =$ capital costs on capital stock K, requiring a return g to cover depreciation (which depends on the expected life of the asset), interest, and risk premium appropriate to the industry.

The definition and measurement of revenue is unambiguous and need not detain us. However the other elements are not so simple: K, g, and D are far from being unambiguous.

D, direct costs, may involve two elements about which there is some doubt. The first is selling cost. There can be no doubt that some selling cost is simply concerned with delivery to the consumers and can be safely included with direct cost. However it has been strongly argued recently that advertising and other marketing expenditures seeking to differentiate the product should be properly regarded as capital expenditures building up a stock of 'goodwill'. In this case they should be valued as an accumulated capital stock in the same way as acquisitions of physical capital. The cost to the firm is not then the current outlay, but rather the interest, the risk premium, and the depreciation appropriate to advertising capital. The current outlay is a capital expenditure without significance for current profitability, just as current investment does not enter into the profit and loss account. The effect of making such an adjustment for advertising is considered later.

Second, it may be argued that some firms take some of their profits in the form of discretionary expenditures. For example, in a small firm, the owner-manager may take a larger salary than his contribution to output would justify. Stigler[4] has pointed out that unequal tax treatment of profits and salaries may lead to serious bias in U.S. figures for small companies. Alternatively the firm may absorb profit by increasing expenditure on items to satisfy the needs, or egos, of the managers, for example prestige offices, expensive company cars, generous expense allowances, etc. Unfortunately it is just not possible to distinguish these items from the returns that represent the true transfer earnings of the manager. However we should be aware of a possible bias in this regard.

The problems concerning K and g take us back to the difficulties expounded in Chapter 2. That is, there is no satisfactory measure for K, since there are no second-hand markets in which their opportunity costs may be evaluated as *assets*. The valuation of the *firm* may of course be given in the stock market, but if the firm is earning monopoly profits that will of course be allowed for in the market

[4] G. J. Stigler, *Capital and Rates of Return in Manufacturing*, N.B.E.R. (New York, 1963).

valuation. So we get a valuation of the firm (including its market position): not of the assets themselves. This has not prevented the use of such measures of capital in some studies! Historic costs of capital assets are not much more helpful: the questions of depreciation and true replacement cost are raised again. Finally there is no objective method for defining the proper g for a firm even if we could assign a correct value to the assets.

There are four possible simple measures which are used in these studies. They are defined in tabular form below:[5]

	Gross	Net
Profit on capital	$(1) \dfrac{R-D}{K}$	$(3) \dfrac{R-C}{K}$
Price–cost margin	$(2) \dfrac{R-D}{R}$	$(4) \dfrac{R-C}{R}$

Under fully competitive conditions, without any excess profits, these will tend to the following values.

	Gross	Net
Profit on capital	g	0
Price–cost margin	$\dfrac{Kg}{R}$	0

At first sight the gross measures look attractive from an operational point of view. Number (2) in particular appears to require no elements involving ambiguity in measurement. However this enthusiasm should quickly wane when one examines the specification of models to explain inter-industry variation in this as a dependent variable. The reason can be seen from our table of expected values under no-profit situations. For measure (1) the basic value is g, which will of course vary from industry to industry: it needs specific information about 'normal profits' (including depreciation and appropriate risk premia in each industry). And the denominator of the measure is the ambiguous measure of capital stock. Measure (2) eliminates the capital stock from the dependent variable, but adds it to the independent variables: the 'base' for each industry (i.e. the no-profit position) is Kg/R. We note in passing that it is quite in-

[5] *Gross* measures refer to the total returns to capital after direct costs, *net* measures to the returns to capital over and above 'normal' profit.

adequate to assume that g is invariant from industry to industry. Thus some studies employing measure (1) leave out any reference to g among the independent variables and some employing measure (2) use K/R (the capital–output ratio) as an independent variable, again ignoring variation in g. But there simply is no basis for the assumption that depreciation and risk premia are invariant between industries. At the best then this will introduce a lot of 'unexplained' variance into regression analysis; at worst there may be a serious bias in the results obtained.

So for greater conceptual accuracy we must turn to the net measures, and confront the measurement ambiguities already discussed, or include the same imprecise measures of K and g in the independent variables. Many empirical studies stop at a half-way house between gross and net measures by allowing for depreciation on capital.

$$\text{Let } g = \rho + \delta$$

where δ is the rate of depreciation of the capital stock, and ρ is the pure return on capital.

Then we may derive a further measure:

(5) $\qquad \dfrac{R - D - K\delta}{K} \quad$ which has a limiting value of ρ.

This is often expressed in its post-tax form:

(5a) $\qquad \dfrac{R - D - K\delta}{K}(1 - t) \quad$ where t is the corporate tax rate.

The numerator is the reported profits of the firm, after tax, and after allowance for depreciation. The limiting value of this expression is $\rho(1 - t)$.

Both these measures attract the same comment as measure (1) above. Explanatory variables ought to account for inter-industry differences in ρ. The after-tax measure is open to the major criticism that depreciation allowed for tax purposes need bear no relation at all to the *economic* depreciation of the capital stock due to wearing out or technical obsolescence. It is simply calculated on rules laid down by the taxation law, with no account taken of inter-industry difference in true depreciation. This obvious defect in the measure has not prevented its widespread use.

We must now consider the choice of profit or rate of return on capital measures (1) and (3), as against price–cost margin (2) and (4) measures. We will conduct the arguments in terms of the net measures only. We will signify (3) by g_K and (4) by M. Then

$$\frac{M}{g_K} = \frac{K}{R}$$

$$\therefore M = g_K \cdot \frac{K}{R}$$

Given that K/R, the capital–output ratio, can and does vary substantially between sectors, it is clear that M and g_K are very distinct as measures. One would not expect, *a priori*, any strong correlation between the measures. For example a low g_K associated with a high capital–output ratio could give a high M: and a high g_K could similarly be associated with a low M in a sector using little capital. The two measures are certainly not perfect substitutes. So the choice of measure must be made on the basis of the hypothesis being tested. The obvious choice is to use the margin of price over cost in those cases where the barriers-to-entry theory of the relationship of structure and profitability is being examined. The theory is about price exceeding cost: it is only indirectly a theory of return on capital. Further it is price–cost margins that are of interest in examining the allocative aspects of industrial structure. Thus Lerner's famous measure of monopoly[6] is (price minus cost)/price, which is precisely measure (2) deflated by output. On the other hand the attraction to entrant firms is not the size of the price–cost margin, but rather the return on capital which that margin represents. Thus a study of actual incentive to entry to an industry should use a rate of return measure. However that is more appropriate to the summing-up of Part III (Chapter 15). Again, any study of the advantages of size to a business would be more interested in the relationship between size and return on capital, rather than the *market*-oriented measure of margins.

3   CONCENTRATION AND INDUSTRY PROFITABILITY

The earliest empirical work on this relationship was that of Bain.[7] Using eight firm concentration ratios for a sample of 42 U.S. 4-digit

---

[6] A. P. Lerner, 'The Concept of Monopoly and the Measurement of Monopoly Power', *R. Econ. Studs.* 1 (1934), 157–75.

industries, he found that after-tax profits as a percentage of share-holders' equity averaged 11·8 per cent for those sectors with CR_8 greater than 70 per cent compared to an average of 7·5 per cent for sectors with lesser concentration. The argument since that study has sought to confirm the relationship between concentration and profitability, and to determine whether this is a continuous relationship, or whether there is a critical concentration level which leads to a sharp rise in profitability.

On the first point the single dissenting voice has been that of Stigler.[8] In a study of rates of return, he pointed out that very small firms produce a smaller proportion of the output of concentrated industries than of unconcentrated sectors. Hypothesizing that small firms are more likely to absorb profits in the form of larger salaries for owner-managers, he suggested that the unconcentrated sector would therefore show a lower profit rate. Indeed he found a negative significant correlation between the profit rate and the share of industry output accounted for by small companies. Using this relationship to adjust his profit rates he concluded that there was no relationship between adjusted profit rates and concentration. Kilpatrick[9] undermined this conclusion by demonstrating that the concentration ratio and the share of small companies are highly correlated: so Stigler's adjustment of the data removed the very element that he was seeking to relate to concentration. Accepting Stigler's contention that there was likely to be some bias in the reported profit rates for small firms, he eliminated these from his samples and examined the relationship between average profit rates and concentration for the large companies in each sector. He found that a relationship between concentration and profit rates did exist in 1950, 1956, and 1963, though the effect was not so clear in 1950. This confirms the findings of Weiss,[10] which also postulated a continuous relationship.

Parallel studies have been published on the relationship between concentration and price–cost margins. An important study was that of Collins and Preston[11] on 1958 U.S. data. Their dependent variable was (2) $(R-D)/R$. They include a measure of capital as an

[7] J. S. Bain, 'Relation of Profit Rate to Industry Concentration: American Manufacturing, 1936–40', *Q.J.E.* 65 (1951), 293–324.

[8] Stigler, op. cit.

[9] R. W. Kilpatrick, 'Stigler on the Relationship between Industry Profit Rates and Market Concentration', *J.P.E.* 76 (1968), 479–88.

[10] L. Weiss, 'Average Concentration Ratios and Industrial Performance', *J.I.E.* 11 (1963), 237–54.

[11] N. R. Collins, L. E. Preston, *Concentration and Price–Cost Margins in Manufacturing* (Berkeley, 1970).

independent variable. At the 2-digit level they found a positive association between concentration and their dependent variable. The association was continuous and significant, but not a 'strong' relationship. They then tested for industries at a 4-digit level within ten 2-digit groupings. The relationship continued to hold in six of these sectors, though variance explained never exceeded 25 per cent. In another four sectors the relationship was insignificant. These sectors were Textiles, Apparel, Machinery, and Chemicals. They argue that returns in the 4-digit sectors within these industries will tend to be equalized despite differences in concentration in the 4-digit sectors: the reason is that similarity of technology in the constituent 4-digit industries makes cross-entry relatively easy and profit rates are thus constrained. This result points the need for more complex models of industry structure and profitability. Rhoades and Cleaver[12] have repeated the Collins and Preston experiment with 1967 data. They plot average price–cost margins by four firm concentration ratio deciles, in 352 manufacturing sectors (U.S.). For CR_4 up to 50 per cent there is no clear association between concentration ratios and decile average price–cost margins. There is a sharp rise for $CR_4 > 50$ per cent but this does not increase much up to $CR_4 = 80$ per cent, when there is a further increase. This plot leads them to examine the relationship separately for CR_4 less than and greater than 50 per cent. They include among the independent variables the capital–output ratio (in value terms), and a dummy variable for differentiated goods sectors. The results confirm that CR_4 is not significant in explaining variation in price–cost margin in unconcentrated sectors, but has some significance in the more concentrated sectors. However it is quantitatively slight compared to the coefficient on the product differentiation variable. The discontinuity is confirmed by Meehan and Duchesneau,[13] who show that an eight firm concentration ratio of 70 per cent (as used by Bain) is a better discriminator than the equivalent four firm measure of 55 per cent.

The implications of the choice of CR_4 or CR_8 were taken up by Miller.[14] Following Collins and Preston, he defined the marginal concentration ratio MCR_8 as the share of firms ranked 5 to 8. He argued that these firms would have different effects on market competition, depending on the size of the four leading firms. In markets with a high CR_4 (> 60 per cent), a high MCR_8 would strengthen the

[12] S. A. Rhoades, J. M. Cleaver, 'The Nature of the Concentration Price/Cost Margin Relationship for 352 Manufacturing Industries, 1967', *S. Econ. Journal*, 40 (1973), 90–102.
[13] J. W. Meehan, T. D. Duchesneau, 'The Critical Level of Concentration: an Empirical Analysis', *J.I.E.* 22 (1973), 21–36.
[14] R. A. Miller, 'Marginal Concentration Ratios as Market Structure Variables', *R. Econ. Stats.* 53 (1971), 289–93.

'shared monopoly' behaviour of the market. MCR_8 would have no effect on the market outcome when CR_4 was low (< 30 per cent) because the sector was competitive anyhow. For intermediate values of CR_4 (30 per cent $\leqslant CR_4 \leqslant 60$ per cent) a larger MCR_8 would imply competitive pressure from medium-sized firms, and hence a reduction in profitability. Analysis of markets grouped according to these values of CR_4 gave some support to the last two suggestions, but not to the first. When $CR_4 > 60$ per cent, MCR_8 had a significantly negative sign. In interpreting these results, one recalls that there is no theoretical rationale for attaching particular significance to the first *four* firms, or to the second *four* firms. And the grouping of markets according to CR_4 is similarly arbitrary.

Studies in this area have been subjected to rigorous criticism by Ornstein[15] and Phillips.[16] Their argument that it is numbers of firms that determine the price–cost margin, rather than concentration, has been effectively answered by the work of Cowling and Waterson,[17] and Hannah and Kay,[18] reported at the beginning of Chapter 5. However they are right to point out that the theoretical links between concentration and price–cost margins are not established. The procedure of Cowling and Waterson does indeed give a definite theoretical conclusion, but a particular one. Their attempt to test it over time is not encouraging. They took as their dependent variable our measure (2), $(R-D)/R$, of the return to capital. They then took the ratio of this measure at two points in time (1958 and 1963) and regressed it on the ratio of the H-index for the industry (94 industries at Minimum List Heading level) at the same two points. Although the explanatory variable was significant and had the right sign, the very low R^2 ($0\cdot067$) was evidence that most of the variance in the dependent variable had not been explained.

A criticism of all studies of concentration and profitability is that other important variables are omitted, notably barriers-to-entry variables. Thus the exposition of Chapter 5 suggested that concentration was a help to co-operation between firms, so that prices could be raised. But in long-run equilibrium a limit is given by the entry-limit price. Failure to include entry variables will therefore bias the results of regression analysis of the relation of concentration and profitability in an unpredictable way. This is the substance of the

[15] S. I. Ornstein, 'Empirical Uses of the Price–Cost Margin', *J.I.E.* 24 (1975), 105–117.

[16] A. Phillips, 'A Critique of Empirical Studies of Relations between Market Structure and Profitability', *J.I.E.* 24 (1976), 241–9.

[17] K. Cowling, M. Waterson, 'Price–Cost Margins and Market Structure', *Economica*, 43 (1976), 267–74.

[18] L. Hannah, J. Kay, *Concentration in Modern Industry* (London, 1977).

criticisms levelled by Dalton and Penn[19] at previous studies. Including entry variables, they still found concentration to be important in a study of the profitability of 97 large food manufacturing firms. But they found only weak evidence for a dichotomous relationship below and above a critical value of $CR_4 = 45$ per cent. We return to the role of concentration variables in general studies of profitability and market structure in the next section.

Finally, both Ornstein[20] and Phillips[21] question the use of weighted averages of firm price–cost margins in cross-industry regressions. If, for example, there is a general tendency for large firms to be more efficient and profitable than small ones, then high concentration (large firms) will imply high profit margins, but not causally. Firm profitability is examined in more detail below.

4   STRUCTURE AND INDUSTRY PROFITABILITY

The first substantial test of the idea that profitability is determined by those elements of industry structure which affect entry into the industry was by Bain.[22] He examined the conditions of entry in 20 U.S. manufacturing sectors with respect to three types of barrier. These were, first, absolute cost advantages of existing sellers arising either from patented techniques or privileged access to resources: second, the existence of product differentiation, including patents, leading to established preferences of consumers for existing products: and third, the existence of scale economies, both in relation to industry size and in absolute terms. A careful study of these aspects for each industry led to a qualitative classification of industries according to barrier—'very high', 'substantial', 'moderate-to-low'. The eight firm concentration ratio for each sector was also calculated for 1936–40 and 1947–51. These data were then compared

[19] J. A. Dalton, J. W. Penn, 'The Concentration–Profitability Relationship: Is There a Critical Concentration Ratio?' *J.I.E.* 25 (1976-7), 133–42.

[20] We do not accept Ornstein's criticism that most studies have used a mis-specified equation. He argues that specifications of the form:

$$\frac{R-D}{R} = a + bCR_4 + c\frac{K}{R}$$

are incorrect, since dividing through by K/R gives the profit on capital $(R-D)/K$ as a function of $(CR_4 \cdot R/K)$, which has no meaning. He then argues for, and tests, a logarithmic relationship, reflecting the hypothesis that $(R-D)/K$ is a function of CR_4. But the theory leads to an explanation of the price–cost margin, *not* of the return on capital (as Ornstein's own theoretical summary makes clear).

[21] Phillips, op. cit.

[22] J. S. Bain, *Barriers to New Competition* (Cambridge, Mass., 1956).

with the average profit rate of each sector in the same periods. The profit rates were calculated for a few dominant firms only in each sector: Bain argued that these firms would be the ones to fix the limit price, since they would have achieved optimal scale and, as an oligopolistic group, would have the most to lose from new entry in the long run. Bain's result was that the main determinant of returns was barriers to entry. High barriers to entry lead to high profit rates, though the differences between 'substantial' and 'moderate-to-low' was not so clear. Seller concentration was not a good predictor of profitability: although high barriers were found to be roughly correlated with high concentration, some high concentration industries with medium-to-low barriers had notably lower profit rates. However *within* 'substantial' and 'moderate-to-low' categories there was a slight association of higher profit rates with higher concentration. Finally Bain identified product differentiation and advertising as the main causes of high barriers. Similar work by Mann[23] on data from 30 U.S. industries for 1950–60 confirmed Bain's results. Barriers to entry in each sector were assessed qualitatively as high, substantial, and moderate-to-low. Profit rates were defined as

$$\frac{\text{net income after tax}}{\text{net worth}}$$

(i.e. measure (5)), and calculated for the leading firms in each sector. The results are tabulated below for all industries, and for industries with $CR_8 > 70$ per cent.

Profit rates

Entry barrier:	All industries	Industries $CR_8 > 70\%$
High	16·4	16·4
Substantial	11·3	11·1
Moderate-to-low	9·9	11·9

The conclusion is that barriers are the main explanatory variable. The same variation in profit rates between different barrier-to-entry classes is found for highly concentrated sectors as for others. This conclusion is, however, weakened by the fact that CR_8 and the height of barriers tend to be correlated.

Subsequent work has sought to refine the analysis by substituting quantitative measures of various elements of market structure for

---

[23] M. Mann, 'Seller Concentration, Barriers to Entry and Rates of Return in 30 Industries', *R. Econ. Stats.* 48 (1966), 296–307.

the qualitative assessment of Bain and Mann and by the use of standard multiple regression technique to assess the statistical significance of various elements. A representative and comprehensive study of this kind is that of Comanor and Wilson,[24] which has formed the basis for much subsequent criticism and new empirical work. They seek to explain inter-industry variability in average profit rates by differences in concentration, barriers due to product differentation, barriers due to scale, and by differences in market growth. Some other studies have added to this list, but the main discussion has centred upon the correct measures for these elements.

(1) Concentration. Comanor and Wilson use two alternative measures: either the four firm concentration ratio, or a dummy variable distinguishing those sectors with $CR_8 > 70$ per cent from those with less.

(2) Product differentiation as a barrier to entry. This is central to their analysis, reflecting its importance in their empirical results. Taking their cue from Bain they argue that the main element in product differentiation is advertising, both as an indication of 'differentiability' of products, and as a measure of differentiation achieved. There are three possible barriers arising from this source.[25] The first is that existing firms have the benefit of brand loyalty, so that they have to advertise less to retain their customers than a new entrant to lure those customers away. Thus existing firms have an absolute cost advantage. Comanor and Wilson suggest that the ratio of advertising expenditures to sales is a proper measure of this. The second barrier arises from hypothesized economies of scale in advertising. It may be that a fixed 'lump' of advertising is necessary to reach a 'threshold' effective level. Alternatively the unit cost of advertising on TV or in the newspapers may be less for large advertising campaigns than for small ones. Either of these effects would increase the minimum economic scale for a new entrant. The third barrier arises from this: since part of the larger scale represents expenditure on advertising which creates no tangible asset, a new firm may find that its cost of capital is correspondingly greater, as well as requiring a greater initial capital outlay. The measure which Comanor and Wilson propose for these last two barriers is the average total advertising expenditure per firm among the largest firms in the industry accounting for the first 50 per cent of industry output.

[24] W. S. Comanor, T. A. Wilson, 'Advertising, Market Structure and Performance', *R. Econ. Stats.* 49 (1967), 423–40.

[25] Comanor and Wilson's analysis has been criticized by R. Schmalensee, 'Brand Loyalty and Barriers to Entry', *S. Econ. Journal*, 40 (1974), 579–88. See the further discussion in Chapter 12.

(3) Scale Economies. There are two barriers involved here. The first arises from the idea of minimum economic size, i.e. the minimum size at which a firm may achieve minimum cost operation as a percentage of industry size. This is clearly important in models of the Bain–Sylos-Labini kind. Comanor and Wilson use the average plant size of the largest firms accounting for the first 50 per cent of output (ranking firms from the largest to the smallest) as a measure of this. They find it correlates well with Bain's 'engineering' estimates of the variable. (It does however omit the important aspect of the rate at which costs increase at sub-optimal scale, which may affect entry prospects for smaller firms.) The second barrier arises from the absolute capital requirements of an entrant firm: as Bain suggested, a large capital requirement could be a barrier in itself even where it represented a rather small addition in industry capacity.

(4) Growth in industry demand. There is no theoretical agreement on this variable, apart from general agreement that it is likely to be of some importance. One may argue that rapid growth in demand will maintain pressure on capacity and thus tend to increase margins. Alternatively, Bain[26] has argued that in a situation of rapidly increasing industry demand, price discipline will be difficult to maintain, and margins will tend to be lower. Some oligopolists will be prepared to cut their margin in the hope of a larger share in the market growth. So the coefficient of industry growth may be either positive or negative depending on which of these effects predominates.

Comanor and Wilson tried a large number of alternative specifications involving these variables to explain profit rates in 41 sectors. The profit rate variable used was profits after taxes as a percentage of shareholders' equity, averaged within each industry (for large firms only) over the complete business cycle of 1954–7. A typical regression result was:

Constant	Advertising sales ratio	Absolute capital requirements (log)	Growth of demand	Concentration dummy: $CR_8 > 70\%$	Regional industry dummy variable	Corrected R^2
0·039	0·343	0·0105	0·015	0·0043	0·0278	0·40
t values	(2·7)	(2·8)	(1·4)	(0·3)	(1·5)	

Their major finding is that the advertising/sales ratio is consistently significant and important, this finding not being sensitive to

[26] J. S. Bain, *Industrial Organisation* (New York, 1959).

considerable changes in specification (e.g. a log linear form replacing a linear form, appropriate weighting to eliminate heteroscedasticity, substitution of dummies or alternative measures for the other independent variables). A secondary finding has implications for all studies of this kind: this is the fact of the high degree of collinearity between the other elements of structure, namely concentration, minimum economic size, and capital requirements, as indicated in the following regression result, with log CR_4 as the dependent variable:

Constant	Absolute capital requirements (log)	Economies of scale (log)	Regional industry dummy variable	Corrected R^2
3·85	0·244	0·238	−0·294	0·79
t values	(5·1)	(3·4)	(1·2)	

The implication of this is that regression equations including concentration and either minimum economic size or capital requirements cannot effectively separate out the two effects on profitability, as the theory requires. Generally speaking, the scale variables emerge as significant with concentration insignificant: but it is not safe to rely on this result. So the effect of concentration on profitability is still an open question. Finally we may note that in Comanor and Wilson's work the growth of the market variable is not significant.

Subsequent work has concentrated on refinement or extension of these results.

1. Weiss,[27] and subsequently Bloch,[28] have pointed out that the best approach to advertising expenditures treats them as an investment in the market. Hence the usual equation may contain two biases. First, the correct independent variable would be the accumulated 'stock' of goodwill arising from advertising in previous periods as well as the current one, with due allowance for depreciation. The current advertising outlay will only be a reasonable substitute variable if the level of advertising has been stable over an appropriate period. More seriously, if we treat advertising as a capital expenditure we need to adjust our profit measure by adding advertising expenditures back to reported profits, and by increasing the reported net worth of assets by the accumulated 'stock' of goodwill due to advertising. Since we will be increasing both the numerator and the denominator of the profit measure, we have no expectation as to the

[27] L. Weiss, 'Advertising, Profits and Corporate Taxes', *R. Econ. Stats.* 51 (1969), 421–30.
[28] H. Bloch, 'Advertising and Profitability: A Reappraisal', *J.P.E.* 82 (1974), 267–82.

direction of adjustment. And the adjustment itself is hard to carry out without some knowledge of the appropriate rate at which to depreciate advertising assets. This is the disagreement between Weiss and Bloch. Weiss uses a high depreciation rate, and finds that the advertising/sales ratio remains an important variable in explaining profitability.[29] Bloch uses a low figure of 5 per cent, and finds that the advertising/sales ratio becomes insignificant for his data sample.[30]

2. Caves *et al.*[31] have drawn attention to the mis-specification of the scale economies variable. The theory of Chapter 6 suggests three factors in the relation of scale economies to price–cost margins. The first is minimum economic size (MES) of plant relative to market output under perfect competition. A second is the cost disadvantage of firms at less than minimum economic size, and the third is the elasticity of demand for the new entrant. The second is usually ignored, though its importance has been stressed by writers on scale economies. Caves *et al.* hypothesize that a large MES will only be important if there are great cost disadvantages at lesser outputs. They define a variable which is the ratio of value added per worker in the smallest plants accounting for 50 per cent of market output to that in the largest plants accounting for the other 50 per cent of output. In their statistical analysis, MES only enters for a given sector if this ratio exceeds a critical value. They find that MES only becomes significant if the ratio exceeds 0·90, and gives the strongest result when the ratio is 0·80. This result may account for the failure of economies of scale variables (other than absolute capital requirements variables) to be significant in other studies.

3. Lustgarten[32] has pointed out that studies of market structure and profitability have concentrated on the supply side of the market

[29] This result is confirmed in L. W. Weiss, J. J. Siegfried, 'Advertising, Profits and Corporate Taxes Revisited', *R. Econ. Stats.* 56 (1974), 195–200, which is a reworking of Weiss's paper in the light of Bloch's criticisms.

[30] Bloch adopts 5 per cent depreciation on the following empirical basis. He examines the divergence of stock market values from book values of assets. He proposes that one systematic element in this divergence is the existence of a stock of advertising goodwill that does not appear in the company's asset sheet. Further, he finds for his sample of 40 firms that depreciating advertising expenditures at a rate of 5 per cent p.a. leads to the greatest reduction in the discrepancy between book values and market values. Two comments are in order. First, other studies of advertising have suggested that depreciation rates between 15 per cent and 60 per cent p.a. are appropriate. Second, Bloch's method is only correct if advertising goodwill is the sole reason for divergent book and market values: clearly it is not.

[31] R. E. Caves, J. Khalilzadeh-Shirazi, M. E. Porter, 'Scale Economies in Statistical Analyses of Market Power', *R. Econ. Stats.* 57 (1975), 133–40.

[32] S. H. Lustgarten, 'The Impact of Buyer Concentration in Manufacturing Industries', *R. Econ. Stats.* 57 (1975), 125–32.

to the neglect of buyer characteristics. The implicit assumption is that demand is competitive with a large number of small buyers. But in practice many manufacturing sectors are concerned with intermediate products sold to a few buyers in another sector. It is unlikely that oligopoly will lead to collusion among buyers, but major buyers will 'shop around' between sellers and thus put pressure on margins, especially where the average order is large. If buyers are concentrated, it is also likely that they will be keenly interested in what others are paying for essential components, particularly if they are selling to the same market. In an empirical study of price–cost margins in 327 U.S. producer sectors for the year 1963 he found that buyer concentration ratios and the average size of orders had a significant negative impact on margins, in a regression with the usual supply side structural variables.

4. An important extension of the model is the introduction of foreign trade in articles by Esposito and Esposito[33] and by Khalilzadeh-Shirazi.[34] The latter examined the level of price–cost margins in 60 U.K. manufacturing sectors, with particular reference to the effects of imports and exports. Clearly such an extension is essential for industrial analysis in an open economy like the U.K. The authors argue that imports represent the most immediate new entry threat in the domestic market, coming from established producers abroad who already have substantial home markets. Thus some of the barriers at least will not be operative, and a high level of imports will reduce domestic margins. Exports, on the other hand, represent goods in which the country has a comparative advantage, or where there is an absolute advantage in world markets based on successful product differentiation. So one expects a high export level to be associated with higher margins in the sector. Khalilzadeh-Shirazi regressed the gross price–cost margin (our measure (2)) on the capital–output ratio, structural variables, and imports and exports as a percentage of industry output. He also included a dummy variable for foreign direct investment, where foreign firms account for more than 10 per cent of industry output. His main regression result was:

Constant	Concentration ratio	Capital–output ratio	Growth of demand	Product differentiation	Minimum economic scale
6·36	0·008	0·083*	0·036	2·96**	0·821**

[33] L. Esposito, F. F. Esposito, 'Foreign Competition and Domestic Industry Profitability', *R. Econ. Stats.* 53 (1971), 343–53.

[34] J. Khalizadeh-Shirazi, 'Market Structure and Price–Cost Margins in U.K. Manufacturing Industries', *R. Econ. Stats.* 56 (1974), 67–76.

Imports	Exports	Foreign direct investment	Corrected R^2
−0·084	0·101*	0·34	0·536

*significant at 5 per cent level.   **significant at 1 per cent level.

This result confirms the *a priori* expectations concerning the signs of the coefficients. The foreign investment variable is not significant, though simple classification of industries suggests that those with more than 10 per cent foreign investment have average margins of 19 per cent compared to 14·9 per cent for the others. But these are also sectors with high entry barriers. The indication is that foreign investment is concentrated in the high profitability sectors.

5. A serious omission from most studies is some variable explicitly to account for differences in risk in different sectors, giving different normal profit levels. It is essential to distinguish this from profits arising from barriers to entry or collusion. Sherman and Tollison[35] have analysed the variability of profits due to output fluctuations and 'cost-fixity'.

$$\pi = pq - vq - F$$

where π = profit, p = price, v = variable costs, F = fixed costs, and q = sales volume. It follows directly that the variance of profits, σ^2_π, is given by

$$\sigma^2_\pi = (p - v)^2 \sigma^2_q$$

Output fluctuations are measured by σ^2_q: 'cost-fixity' by $(p - v)$. The implication is that the lower are variable costs as a proportion of price, the greater the variance of profits. Hence the greater the risk of the industry, and the higher its equilibrium profit rate.[36] This assumes that cost-fixity is technologically determined and not systematically related to output fluctuations (i.e. in industries with demand fluctuations entrepreneurs do not choose flexible plant).

This analysis has an important consequence. As we shall see in Chapters 12 and 13, the price–cost margin may be an important determinant of advertising and product differentiation activities,

[35] R. Sherman, R. Tollison, 'Technology, Profit Risk and Assessments of Market Performance', *Q.J.E.* 86 (1972), 448–62.

[36] In Chapter 14 we show that the correct measure of risk is the covariance of returns to assets in a sector with returns to a portfolio of assets in all sectors, optimally chosen to diversify away non-systematic risk. But if the variability of returns is mainly due to trade cycle factors affecting *all* sectors, the variance may be an acceptable proxy.

since a higher marginal profit rate makes it more worthwhile to extend these activities to give marginal increments of sales. Hence the significance and importance of product differentiation/advertising variables may simply reflect their role as proxies for 'cost-fixity'. Indeed Sherman and Tollison[37] claimed that reworking the Comanor and Wilson study, with cost-fixity variables included, reduced the significance of the advertising/sales ratio variable. The question of the direction of causation in advertising–profit relationships is more fully discussed in Chapter 12.

6. We note that the structure–profitability analysis pays scant regard to the question of behaviour which we examined at some length in Chapter 5. The main behaviour variable in the above analysis is the degree of concentration. This is taken as an indicator either of unwillingness to engage in price competition or of the propensity to collude. However Chapter 5 suggested that the matter is not nearly so straightforward. For example, Phillips[38] attacks the naivety of the traditional structure–goals–performance approach to the problem. He would wish to substitute a process of search by the firm over time seeking to improve its performance by acting on structure or by changing its conduct. The more the firm falls short of its profit expectations (or hopes) the more it will search for means to improve its position. The means it will use in oligopoly will include the attempt to form effective collusive agreements with the other firms in the industry: this in turn will feed back into performance, which will inspire further search if not satisfactory. Admittedly, in the long run, the industry may settle down at a point where all firms are satisfied with their current performance, and then links to industry structure will be more marked. But this 'state of peace' may be the exception rather than the rule.

Phillips followed up this criticism with his own empirical work. Instead of presuming a link between concentration and collusion, he incorporated actual evidence on the extent of price fixing agreements in U.K. industry in the period 1953–6. By attaching arbitrary weights depending on his subjective assessment of their effectiveness, he defined a new variable to measure the effectiveness of price agreements in 26 sectors reporting such agreements. He found that higher price–cost margins were associated with higher values of such variables, but the coefficients were not statistically significant. A

---

[37] R. Sherman, R. Tollison, 'Advertising and Profitability', *R. Econ. Stats.* 53 (1971), 397–405.

[38] A. Phillips, 'An Econometric Study of Price Fixing, Market Structure and Performance in British Industry in the 1950s', in K. Cowling (ed.), *Market Structure and Corporate Behaviour* (London, 1972).

difficulty with this approach is that in a highly concentrated sector collusive interdependence may not need anything so formal as a price agreement. So his data on price agreements may be a poor indicator of total collusive activity.

Asch and Seneca[39] compared the profit performance of 51 U.S. firms condemned for collusive activities in anti-trust cases, with a sample of non-colluding firms. They regressed profit rates on structural variables and a dummy variable which took the value of one for a collusive firm. They found that collusion had a negative coefficient, all other variables behaving as expected. The suggestion is that collusion is a response to low profitability. Alternatively, perhaps only ineffective collusive agreements are uncovered by the anti-trust authorities (e.g. from information supplied by a disaffected firm), and this has biased the result.

7. Two contributions have sought to interpret barriers-to-entry theory in more flexible terms, accepting that firms *will* enter profitable sectors though deterred in part by high barriers. Orr[40] investigated the rate of entry of firms into 71 Canadian manufacturing sectors (see above, p. 184). In his analysis firms are attracted by high profit rates and growth in the industry, but deterred by entry barriers represented by the usual structural variables—absolute capital requirements, advertising/sales ratio, R and D/sales ratio, profit risk (measured by the standard deviation of profit rates), and concentration. The fitted regression coefficients were taken as weights for different structural variables to derive a composite index of barriers to entry. The coefficients were (all negative since they *deter* entry):

Absolute capital requirements (log)	Advertising expenditure sales ratio	R and D expenditure sales ratio	Risk	Concentration
−0·24**	−0·13**	−0·07*	−0·08	−0·89**

**significant at the 1 per cent level.   *significant at the 5 per cent level.

Orr then related *profit rates* in each sector to the rate of growth of output and to the barrier index. He found that the index was a significant determinant of profitability only when it took a high value. Where barriers were low, the index was not significant.

A not unrelated approach has been taken by Stonebraker.[41] He

[39] P. Asch, J. J. Seneca, 'Is Collusion Profitable?', *R. Econ. Stats.* 58 (1976), 1–12.

[40] D. Orr, 'An Index of Entry Barriers and its Application to the Market Structure-Performance Relationship', *J.I.E.* 23 (1974–5), 39–50.

[41] R. J. Stonebraker, 'Corporate Profits and the Risk of Entry', *R. Econ. Stats.* 58 (1976), 33–9.

hypothesizes that the average profit of large firms in a sector is determined by the degree of risk facing an entrant, represented by the probability of earning less than the competitive rate of return, and the size of possible losses. These in turn are related to barriers to entry. Hence high barriers to entry increase entrant risk, and thus the existing firms can charge a higher price without attracting entry, since the probability of making a loss is too great. Stonebraker uses two measures of entrant risk. The first, 'risk', is the percentage of output on which less than competitive profit rates were obtained times the average shortfall of these returns below the competitive level. The second is the 'failure rate', the percentage of firms reporting negative net income. Both are found to be important determinants of profit rates:

Constant	Growth of the market	Risk	Failure	R^2
7·215	2·396	0·363	3.779	0·66
t values	(3·74)	(3·33)	(3·87)	

Furthermore, the risk measure is highly correlated with advertising expenditures and R and D expenditures (both as a ratio of sales) but not with scale variables.

5   MARKET STRUCTURE, MARKET SHARE, AND PROFITABILITY OF FIRMS

The studies discussed so far have concentrated their attention on the *average* profitability of various sectors. This reflects a theoretical presumption that prices are established within sectors with respect to the entry barriers. The role of concentration is as an indicator of the probability that firms will collude to raise price to the entry-limit level, and that they will act in concert in the face of new entry. Even within this framework one would expect profitability to vary between different sizes of firm in homogeneous sectors, due to economies of scale. In differentiated sectors without a single market price, the presumption of greater profitability with large scale is more doubtful. An alternative theoretical approach is to explain profitability in terms of competition between existing firms. Large market shares give firms some degree of 'monopoly' power over the market price. Further, the extent of rivalry in the market will affect the variability of returns to different firms, and hence their risk.

(a) The relationship between firm size and profitability

The empirical results under this head can be simply summarized. Two studies[42] examining an inter-industry cross-section sample of firms found a positive relation between size and profitability (using measures (1) or (3)) and also found that the variance of profitability decreased with size. However industry studies suggest that the positive relationship is due to an inadequate allowance for inter-industry differences in profitability. The study of 118 sectors by Marcus[43] showed that while there was a positive relationship in 35 sectors, there was a negative one in 9 sectors and there was no relationship at all in a further 74. Singh and Whittington[44] and Stekler[45] found that the *variability* of profits rates was larger for small firms than for large ones in the same sector. Singh and Whittington also found some evidence for persistence in firm profitability: above-average firms tended to remain above-average.

These results are not very helpful in terms of hypotheses. If we assume, with Marcus, that the structural factors affect small firms and large firms alike, we must look for explanations solely in terms of intra-industry factors. For example, in an oligopoly with an entry-deterring price, one would expect large firms to have a larger margin over cost than small ones, given scale economies. As we have already seen, there is no necessary relationship between margins and profit rates given a variable capital/output ratio. But while we would expect larger firms to be more capital-intensive and hence for a larger margin to represent no increase in profitability, it is unlikely that an increase in the capital/output ratio will *precisely* offset the increase in margin over cost to keep the rate of return constant. We have no evidence on this point. An alternative explanation is that costs are indeed constant for firms over a wide range of output. We should note that Marcus excluded the smallest corporations (assets less than ½ million dollars in 1959–62), as there was reason to expect a taxation bias in reported profits. So it may be that costs are constant over the range that he is testing. Finally, in a differentiated industry, it may be possible for small high-cost firms to maintain profitability by operating in segments of the market that accept higher prices. Clearly we cannot ignore industrial structure as an important determinant of firm profitability, and it is to studies of this kind that we now turn.

[42] W. L. Crum, *Corporate Size and Earning Power* (Cambridge, Mass., 1939); M. Hall, L. Weiss, 'Firm Size and Profitability', *R. Econ. Stats.* 49 (1967), 319–31.
[43] M. Marcus, 'Profitability and Size of Firm', *R. Econ. Stats.* 51 (1969), 104–8.
[44] A. Singh, G. Whittington, *Growth, Profitability and Valuation*, D.A.E. Occasional Paper, 7 (Cambridge, 1968).
[45] H. O. Stekler, *Profitability and Size of Firm* (Berkeley, 1963).

(b) Market structure and firm profitability

An article by Imel and Helmberger[46] of structure–profit relationships for 99 large firms in the U.S. food processing sector concentrates on the econometric problem arising from the use of firm data. In particular, where firms have markets in common (and if they are diversified they may have several) it is no longer safe to assume that the residual 'unexplained' error attached to each firm observation is independent of that of other firms. This will only be true where these residual errors relate solely to factors internal to the firm. But suppose one industry is unexpectedly profitable (that is, more profitable than the structural equation would predict): then all firms operating in that sector will have a positive component in their 'unexplained' profitability, and those components will be correlated between firms. Alternatively the success of one firm in a market may be at the expense of another firm which loses market share: then residual errors will be negatively correlated between firms. In these cases the assumptions for ordinary least squares (OLS) do not hold, and estimates based on them will be biased. The correct procedure is to use generalized least squares (GLS).[47] These matters are not merely of econometric interest. They show the importance of careful theoretical specification of the competitive situation in a market. Their results are correspondingly more worthy of attention. First, they classified industries on three different bases of increasing 'meaningfulness' in terms of markets. Comparison of results showed that the size of the estimated coefficients of structure and their statistical significance increased sharply as more 'meaningful' classifications were adopted. Secondly they found that variables representing product differentiation barriers (advertising/sales ratio and research and development expenditure/sales ratio) in each product market were invariably important and significant in explaining profitability. They found the usual problem of collinearity between concentration and minimum economic size variables. Third, they found that a 'market share' variable defined as the ratio of firm sales to the sales of the four largest firms in the industry performed well.

Articles by Shepherd[48] and Gale[49] have taken market share as being central to their analyses. Shepherd examined a sample of 210 firms taken from the Fortune 500 list. These firms will all, of course, be the dominant firms in their sectors. His starting-point is the

[46] B. Imel, P. Helmberger, 'Estimation of Structure–Profit Relationships', *A.E.R.* 61 (1967), 614–27.
[47] These matters may be pursued in the original article and subsequent exchanges.
[48] W. G. Shepherd, 'The Elements of Market Structure', *R. Econ. Stats.* 54 (1972), 25–37.
[49] B. T. Gale, 'Market Share and Rate of Return', *R. Econ. Stats.* 54 (1972), 412–23.

neoclassical presumption that increased market share implies greater profitability. So this is put into the equation together with the usual structural variables. His conclusion is that market share takes all the 'limelight' in explaining profitability. Structural variables, except perhaps for the advertising/sales ratio, are weak both as to magnitude and statistical significance. However, as Shepherd himself points out, the market share of the dominant firm may be reconstituted as a concentration ratio type of measure. In fact, we would expect the two to be highly correlated. We must suspect therefore that the market share variable is stealing the thunder of the theoretically more justifiable concentration and economies of scale variables. Gale explored the theoretical justification for market share variables in more detail. He suggests that a large share will have positive effects on profitability due to product differentiation advantages, bargaining power of a large firm in a collusive group, and economies of scale. But these effects are not independent of other variables. For example, increased market share will have little effect on profitability in an unconcentrated sector, but a considerable effect in a concentrated sector. Similarly, rapid growth of the market will tend to weaken the effectiveness of oligopolistic collusion. In a study of 106 firms he found strong support for these hypothetical interaction effects. Like Shepherd he concluded that market share is an important determinant of firm profitability.

(c) Risk and profitability of firms

A particular advantage of testing structure–profitability hypotheses with firm data is that risk can be accounted for more systematically. In the previous section we looked at risk arising from cost-fixity and the fluctuation in output at the market level. But that does not take into consideration the risk arising from fluctuating market shares due to competition within the market. A measure of the riskiness of the returns to a firm is the degree to which its returns vary with the returns on other assets over time.[50] If it is more variable then it has a higher risk, and hence will attract a premium on its profit rate (i.e. 'normal' profits will be higher). Bothwell and Keeler[51] have introduced this measure of risk as an explanatory variable for the price–cost margin in a sample of 158 U.S. firms for the period 1960–7, in an equation with dummy variables for substantial and high

[50] See Chapter 14 for an exposition of the capital asset pricing model on which this assertion is based.

[51] J. L. Bothwell, T. E. Keeler, 'Profits, Market Structure and Portfolio Risk', in R. T. Masson, P. D. Qualls (ed.), *Essays in Industrial Organisation in Honor of Joe S. Bain* (Cambridge, Mass., 1976), 71–88.

qualitative barriers to entry and with the concentration ratio (CR_4) as the other variables. They find that risk is a statistically significant variable. Thomadakis[52] has pioneered a new approach, looking at the stock market valuation rather than the profitability of the firm. His argument is that the difference between market value of a firm and its book value of assets can be explained by its monopoly position (measured by its market share, and the degree of concentration in the market) and by the risk of the market (in the sense defined above). Analysis of a large sample of large firms (from the Fortune 500 list, 1960-9) was not unfavourable to the hypothesis in that the explanatory variables were statistically significant. However much of the variance in valuation remained unaccounted for.[53]

6   CONCLUSIONS

The empirical work that we have reviewed in the previous three sections suggests that while structure does indeed explain a considerable amount of the variance in profitability between sectors, the relationship is far from being as precise as the theory would suggest. Some of this may be traced to the inadequacy of data, too high a level of aggregation, or to particular statistical problems arising from the collinearity of some of the explanatory variables. However, taking the evidence as a reasonable test of the theory, certain conclusions emerge. First, concentration seems to be less important as a determinant of profitability than structural variables intended to reflect barriers to entry. This confirms our theoretical conclusion that concentration leads to awareness of oligopolistic interdependence, avoidance of price competition, and willingness to act together, even in the absence of formal collusion. Hence concentration is a permissive factor, enabling firms to exploit the profit advantages afforded by the existence of entry barriers. Second, economies of scale variables are generally less important than product differentiation variables. Absolute capital requirements variables are better supported than minimum economic size of plant relative to market output. This suggests that the Sylos-Labini model of entry-deterring pricing in homogeneous goods industries is not widely applicable. In so far as scale is a barrier to entry it is because the initial capital

[52] S. B. Thomadakis, 'A Value Based Test of Profitability and Market Structure', *R. Econ. Stats.* 59 (1977), 179-85.

[53] For a more complex model of rate of return on equity, including the interaction of business risk (arising from the market) and financial risk (arising from decisions about debt and equity financing) see G. J. Hurdle, 'Leverage, Risk, Market Structure and Profitability', *R. Econ. Stats.* 56 (1974), 478-85. The results of this study suggest that market structure is the main determinant of the returns to equity.

requirements are too great, and presumably capital markets are imperfect. Third, the strength of the product differentiation variables (advertising/sales ratio and R and D expenditure/sales ratio, or dummy variables) supports the theory, advanced first by Bain, that product differentiation can limit the market available to a new entrant.

Where then does this leave the theory? First, it is essential to recognize that the majority of new entry will be cross-entry by established firms in other markets. The threat of new entry will thus depend on the number of firms who have access to similar technology (i.e. the firms in the *industry*, where that is defined in terms of technology rather than markets). In these circumstances a potential entrant is not likely to be deterred merely by scale and the market size, as in the Sylos-Labini model. He will be prepared to reckon on driving some other firm out of the market. But he may be deterred by lack of knowledge of the technology or of the market, especially where the products are differentiated and 'brand loyalty' is strong. Entry is then more than a matter of price: it involves the right product, marketed in the right way. That is more difficult to achieve and much more risky. Second, it seems right to develop the theory in terms of the risk faced by the entrant firm along the lines proposed by Stonebraker. Barriers are not *absolute* in the sense suggested by the theory. Rather they affect the probability that a new entrant will meet with failure.

However the structure–profitability approach is also subject to an important methodological criticism. That approach sees the firm constrained by the market structures as to the profits that it earns. The conditions in the markets are given to the firm, and it does the best it can for itself within that given environment. As far as the environment itself is concerned the firm is largely passive. At the most, an active policy involves entering into collusive agreements with other firms. Now this framework may be entirely adequate for the analysis of many small and medium-sized enterprises. However it is *not* satisfactory for the analysis of the large modern corporation. In Chapter 1 we added to the traditional analysis a more active aspect of the operations of firms. This consists of retaining some of the profits made in markets to use for the changing of conditions in those markets to suit the long-run purposes of the firm. Thus the firm may expend funds on physical capital to increase its capacity, on R and D to reduce the costs of production or to develop new products, and on marketing to alter market shares. This modern analysis is the subject of Part III of this book. It would however be foolish to ignore the possibility that these considerations may affect the outcome of the traditional analysis. For example, a large firm may precipitate intra-industry price competition deliberately to increase its own market share over a short period. This is a case where the *goals* of a large modern firm may differ from those of the traditional firm. A further query concerns the direction of causation that we are observing. In so far as large firms can materially affect market structure via their expenditures, there are causal links running *from profitability to structure*, as well as from structure to profitability as traditionally assumed. For example, it can be plausibly argued (as we shall see in Chapter 12 below) that profitability *leads* to more advertising expenditures, rather than the reverse causation assumed in the analysis above. This is shown in the diagram on p. 202 above as a causal link (dotted line) running from profits to the expenditures in column 1, and hence to market structure in column 2. This causal chain is discussed in Chapter 15, at the end of Part III. But we may note one study of that kind which succeeds in setting the structure–profitability approach on its head. Mancke[54] has simulated a model where investment outcomes are determined solely by chance, and the amount of investment is determined by retained profits. He finds that firm profitability is correlated with market share and size (as in Shepherd's study noted above). But of course there is no causal link involved, as the structure–profitability approach would require. Demsetz[55] has made a similar critique of models involving entry variables, arguing that *efficiency* of firms leads both to entry barriers and high profits, simultaneously within a market.

Furthermore, the links between the expenditures of column 1 and the market structure features of column 2 of the diagram on p. 202 are not solely from 1 to 2. The structure itself may be an important determinant of the type of expenditure that the firm will undertake. For example, high concentration may lead firms to avoid price competition, and seek to use advertising as a competitive weapon in differentiated sectors, or R and D expenditures aimed at cost reduction in the long run in a homogeneous sector. All these possibilities are examined in Part III. We conclude therefore that the structure–profitability approach is seriously deficient on its own. More complex causal links need to be taken into account. So an acceptance of the empirical evidence supporting the approach must be provisional, though we have no doubt that it is an important part of a more complete model.

[54] R. B. Mancke, 'Causes of Interfirm Profitability Differences', *Q.J.E.* 88 (1974), 181–93.
[55] H. Demsetz, 'Industry Structure, Market Rivalry and Public Policy', *J. Law Econ.* 16 (1973), 1–10.

PART III

The Behaviour of Firms

8

THE FIRM AND ITS OBJECTIVES

1 THE CONCEPT OF THE FIRM

The historical survey in Part I showed that industrial economics was able to escape the confines of the early theory of the firm and, by starting from a quasi-monopolistic view of firms, permitted a reintegration of deductive theory and systematic empiricism which had been one objective of Marshall's work. Based on a view of the firm as a representative quasi-monopolistic profit maximizing unit, Part II examined the structural conditions facing the firm and their impact on its conduct and performance. This, however, generated something of a paradox. For although the firm was presumed to react passively to its structural conditions in pursuit of profit maximization, the results indicated that, dependent on those conditions, firms might temporarily or permanently earn profits sufficiently large to make *active* and *non-profit maximizing* behaviour feasible. The firm in perfect or monopolistic competition had no discretion, because failure to maximize profits led to ultimate demise. But quasi-monopolists can, and it appears do, earn profits sufficient to permit discretion over the use of those profits and over whether to maximize profits at all. In addition, this active concept of the firm implies that short-term competitive conditions, the pressures they create, and the resultant performance of the firm are all ultimately to some extent endogenous.

All this naturally focuses attention on the firm itself and raises a number of interrelated questions to do with the nature of the firm, its objectives, and its behaviour. How strong is the firm's influence, how does it use its discretion to modify its competitive situation, what limits its power if it is not only independent market forces, and what are the ultimate determinants, internal and external, of its performance? If profit maximization is not essential, then why should we necessarily presume it? If we do not, then what alternative do we introduce? At a more fundamental level, what criteria do we use to judge which motivational assumption is most appropriate? Much of the diversity now existing in Industrial Economics arises from the fact that there are as yet no generally agreed answers to such questions.

That the active concept of the firm may introduce a large number of new issues is clearly seen if we recall the basic picture of the firm given in Figure 1.6. The generation of funds that cost and demand conditions permit can be used to alter those cost and demand conditions in a number of ways.

Investment in plant and expenditure and on process research and development determine the development of cost structure. Market investment and product research and development influence consumer preferences—one determinant of demand conditions— while merger and takeover are ways in which the size and number of firms—the other determinants—are modified. This chapter is a first step towards a view of the Firm that can incorporate such factors.

It will facilitate the structure and arguments of the chapter to start by asking *why* it might make sense to assume objectives other than long-run profit maximization. For the existence of discretion to pursue other goals does not of itself undermine the axiomatic arguments for maximization of net wealth which, in the present context, is the present value of the future stream of profits which will in the long run accrue to the firm. Four answers to this may be given, each of which raises the issue of what we mean by 'the firm' in industrial economics.

(1) First and most fundamental is the fact that *firms* cannot of themselves have objectives at all. Only people can have objectives. If the firm is either a one-man organization or regarded in some way as a single indivisible human decision-taking unit, then this creates no difficulties. Once we recognize that real-world firms are comprised of different parts each of which has many people in it, the issue is more complex. In particular it is necessary to examine why, if motivation is to be properly understood, individuals join groups within which production and selling are organized rather than negotiate ordinary market contracts between themselves; how the different participants—shareholders, managers, workers, etc.—relate to each other; and what they wish to get out of their membership of the firm.

(2) In support of this it is clear that there is a substantial discrepancy between many modern corporations characterized by size, market power, diversity, and complexity and the picture of the firm we have so far used. Much behaviour in such corporations is difficult to reconcile with simple profit maximization objectives. Crucial is the fact that the decision-takers are typically no longer the owners, and do not receive the profits, making it necessary to ask why they should bother about profits at all.

(3) Third, there is the existence of environmental uncertainty. This means that someone must bear the risks inherent in production and distribution—primarily the risk that products will not be sold as

expected and losses incurred as a result. With a one-man owner-manager firm it is clear that he will normally bear the risks and apart from putting the analysis into probabilistic terms the basic theory so far used might stand. But with managers and shareholders the important question arises as to who bears the risks. We shall see later (Chapters 14 and 17) that a perfect capital market *might* under certain restrictive assumptions transfer all risks from the decision-taking manager to the company-owning shareholder. In such circumstances, provided the manager still has the shareholders' interests at heart he becomes merely the executive arm of the entrepreneur-shareholder and we can maintain a view of 'the firm' as maximizing profits under uncertainty. In practice this type of situation rarely if ever exists. Even if capital markets were perfect a number of other very unlikely institutional arrangements are necessary if managers are to know precisely what evaluation shareholders place on uncertain outcomes. In the absence of these, managerial decision-takers, whether they wish to or not, have to take decisions incorporating at least partly their own risk evaluations. The prime example of this is their allocation of internal funds which, though owned by the shareholders, are in all but the most extreme circumstances used by managers with little or no direct reference to shareholders' preferences. Management shouldering of risk inevitably introduces managerial objectives into decision-taking and these may differ from the profit maximizing objectives of shareholders.

(4) Fourth, it is of interest to examine alternative objectives to see if they produce different predictions. If so, we have a basis for testing alternative motivational assumptions and the greater assurance for whichever objectives we incorporate in analysis as a result.

Against this background the chapter proceeds as follows: in section 2 we review the arguments for the profit maximization assumption so widely used in industrial economics, and some of the objections to them. This emphasizes some of the differences of view about the concept of the firm itself. We then go on to examine alternatives. This involves looking at the characteristics of real-world firms in section 3. Sections 4 and 5 examine different issues which the characteristics of real-world firms raise for economic theory.

2   THE PROFIT MAXIMIZATION ASSUMPTION

Five separate assumptions underlie the traditional view that firms are profit maximizers, and we will need to examine each of them during the course of this chapter.

(i) The assumption that there is something unambiguous and

potentially measurable which we can term profit and which it is assumed is maximized.

(ii) The 'black box' assumption that a firm acts as an indivisible decision-taking unit, behaving in the same way that an individual entrepreneur would behave, or at least in a way not significantly different, from the economic point of view. This is termed an 'holistic' concept of the firm; it precludes the necessity for examining the internal aspects of the firm—its personnel, organization, lines of communication, etc.

(iii) The assumption that the utility function of the firm as an indivisible decision-taking unit has only one variable in it, namely profit as unambiguously defined.

(iv) The assumption of rationality. A number of different concepts of rationality have been introduced into the literature of economics in recent years, but the normal conditions required for a decision-taker's behaviour to be described as rational are twofold:

(*a*) The decision-taker can weakly order the states of the world which can arise from his decision. This requires first that he can decide whether he prefers A to B, B to A, or is indifferent between them, and second that all such preference relations are transitive (preferring A to B and B to C implies preferring A to C).

(*b*) The decision-taker aims to maximize the utility he obtains from his decisions as between different states of the world.

(v) The assumption of complete, certain information.

These five assumptions logically entail the traditional picture of an holistic firm maximizing profits under conditions of complete certainty. This more general assumption has proved to be extremely resilient over a long period of time, and still forms the basis of much of the theorizing on the behaviour of firms.

There are a number of reasons, historical, methodological, and pragmatic for the utilization of this assumption over a period of 140 years or more, during the greater part of which it remained unchallenged. Each component assumption seemed either eminently plausible or reasonably justified by introspection or observation of typical owner-controlled firms. In most cases the assumptions were seen as uncontroversial abstractions of a very complex world which highlighted the main aspects. Increasingly, however, a major reason for using the holistic profit maximizing concept of the firm under certainty was its convenience. This had three elements. (i) It was simple to use both as a concept and as part of a model of firms' behaviour; it made economic analysis easier. Over the years, theories of the firm have become much more complex and this has partly been able to occur because of the simplicity of the motivational assumption. Any new factor that can be specified in profit terms can in principle be introduced. But these subsequent developments have themselves increased the incentive to maintain the motivational assumption which facilitated them. (ii) Maximization models were particularly well able to be handled by various standard mathematical techniques, especially differential calculus, and these were powerful tools for examining the propeties and implications of the models. (iii) If the assumptions were to be rejected there was a very serious problem as to what alternative, or set of alternative assumptions might reasonably and usefully be adopted. If for example the firm *didn't* behave as an indivisible unit, didn't maximize, didn't have complete information, etc., then what was it like and how should it be presumed to behave? Many alternative hypotheses are possible with initially little but the predilections of the theorist to act as a basis for selection.

One very obvious response to the last of these was to observe firms empirically in order to find out more about them. But it is at this point that the next reason for maintaining the profit maximizing assumption comes in. This argues that the assumption assists in the accurate prediction of economic behaviour, that the latter is the sole justification for a theory and the assumptions on which it is based, and that the criterion of testing the realism of the assumptions is a fallacious and/or meaningless one. As this argument has generated one of the longest-running controversies in recent economic discussion, and is very germane to our present purpose, it is necessary to survey the debate in more detail.

The main proponent of the view has been Milton Friedman. He argues that the profit maximization assumption is more convenient, precise, and economical than any alternative, but also puts forward two specific and related hypotheses.

(i) It is not meaningful to talk of the realism of the assumptions on which a theory is based, because theories, being abstractions, cannot exhibit nor are designed to exhibit complete realism, and '. . . the question whether a theory is realistic "enough" can only be settled by seeing whether it yields predictions that are good enough for the purpose in hand or that are better than predictions from alternative theories'.[1] Realism, he therefore argues, cannot be used in the assessment of an assumption, but only the predictive power of the theory that contains the assumption, and failure to appreciate this is, he states, the source of much irrelevant criticism of economics as unrealistic.

[1] M. Friedman, *Essays in Positive Economics* (Chicago, 1953), 41.

(ii) The second proposition is that there exists '. . . experience from countless applications of the hypothesis to specific problems . . . which reveals . . . the repeated failure of its implications to be contradicted'.[2]

We could expand on this statement of Friedman's position as follows. Clearly to say that a firm is a profit maximizer is, strictly speaking, absurd. As we have noted, firms do not have motives, only people do. A firm comprises many people each with a set of complex and largely unknown motives. Its behaviour depends on a whole host of influences, personal realtionships, perceptions, and so on. When we presume that a 'firm' is a profit maximizer we are really doing one or other of two things. The first is to presume that the behaviour of a firm or firms in the aggregate resembles *that which would occur if each was* an indivisible profit maximizing decision-taker. The test of the assumption is not therefore whether firms 'really' are profit maximizers, but whether the predicted aggregate behaviour occurs. This is Friedman's position. The second interpretation is not inconsistent with this, but goes somewhat further. It is put in its strongest form by Machlup. He argues that it is 'the fallacy of misplaced concreteness' to suppose that the 'firm' in the theory of the firm has anything to do with real-world firms.

The model of the firm in that theory is not, as so many writers believe, designed to serve to explain and predict the behaviour of real firms; instead it is designed to explain and predict changes in observed prices (quoted, paid, received) as effects of particular changes in conditions (wage rates, interest rates, import duties, excise taxes, technology, etc.). In this causal connection the firm is only a theoretical link, a mental construct helping to explain how one gets from the cause to the effect. This is altogether different from explaining the behaviour of a firm.[3]

On this argument it is even more true that the assumption of profit maximization can only be tested by the theory's predictions and not by any measure of the 'realism' of the profit maximizing 'firm'.

The Friedmanite position has been subject to a number of lines of criticism. The first of these suggests that it is not satisfactory from a methodological point of view to adopt predictive accuracy as the sole criterion for assessing a theory or its assumptions. Suppose for example, we *assume* that oligopolists always successfully collude on price, and therefore predict that their prices will be uniform, flexible, and move in line. Would we be satisfied by observing that this prediction was borne out if we *knew* that the firms observed had not

[2] M. Friedman, *Essays in Positive Economics* (Chicago, 1953), 41.
[3] F. Machlup, 'Theories of the Firm: Marginalist, Behavioural, Managerial', *A.E.R.* 57, no. 1 (Mar. 1967), 9.

in fact colluded? We might be satisfied on the ground that the oligopolies in the theory are mental constructs and the collusion assumption facilitates analysis by allowing us to work with the empirically observed uniform but flexible price level. But it would be neither strange nor meaningless to argue that the theory was not entirely unacceptable despite its accurate predictions, because its assumption was *false*, and hence did not constitute an *explanation* of the obseved phenomenon. We would still want to know *why* the predicted behaviour occurred and might well try to construct a theory to tell us why. The essential difference in the new theory would be that it would have an assumption that did not appear to be false. As Rotwein has argued, if predictions are based on unrealistic assumptions, then the theory does not have explanatory power and does not help to make the world more intelligible to us.[4] At the very least we would want to know why the discrepancies did not matter, which would again involve examining the realism of the assumptions.

In order to examine the validity of this attack it is necessary to note three things about it, and about the example. First, the example considered the case of a specific assumption being *false*, whereas the Friedman view is that the profit maximization assumption is an *abstraction* about firms. Melitz has argued that an abstraction need not involve falsity but only the distillation of a mass of characteristics into one (or more) summary characteristic.[5] Machlup would go further and argue that since the abstraction concerns hypothetical firms anyway it is neither true nor false. The alternative view is that theoretical assumptions are partly abstractions but may or may not be false. It follows that if a theory is to retain explanatory power its assumptions must either be true, or if they are strictly false it must be explained why this falsity does not undermine the theory. For example, it may be quite possible to explain why theories based on the assumption of decision-taking under certainty predict well, despite the existence of uncertainty. But if it is not possible, then the accuracy of the predictions does not mean we have fully understood what mechanisms are operating or why. If the profit maximization assumption abstracts from other motives that businessmen have, this may be quite acceptable. If businessmen do not in fact want or try to earn maximum profit, then theories based on profit maximization may be questioned irrespective of their predictive power.

[4] E. Rotwein, 'On the Methodology of Positive Economics', *Q.J.E.* 73, no. 4 (Nov. 1959), 554–75.

[5] J. Melitz, 'Friedman and Machlup on Testing Economic Assumptions', *J.P.E.* 73, no. 1 (Feb. 1965), 37–60.

The second point to note about the collusion example is that the assumption in it was behavioural, and therefore directly observable, whereas the profit maximization assumption is motivational and therefore not observable. As Archibald has argued, there is an obvious sense in which motivational assumptions are incapable of direct testing and so, unlike behavioural ones, can only be judged by their predictions.[6] The difficulty here is that at least some of the dissatisfaction with the profit maximizing assumption stems from the view that real-world firms do not appear to act in the way one would predict on the basis of that assumption. Thus the need to rely on predictions does not mean that observation of individual firms' activities can be ignored.

The third point about the example is that if the prediction were not borne out then we could reasonably infer that oligopolists did not successfully collude. But if predictions based on the profit maximization assumption are not borne out it may be that the assumption is wrong or it may be that some factor excluded from the theory does in fact have a significant effect. In practice there has tended to be a strong presumption in favour of the second, so that the profit maximization assumption is retained even if predictions based on it are *not* borne out. In this case assumptions about which characteristics of firms and markets to include in a theory are as important as those concerning motivation.

None of this undermines the need for testing of theory predictions. But it does suggest that the profit maximization assumption may reasonably be examined in terms of its 'realism' despite its being a motivational abstraction.

The second line of attack on Friedman's position is that theories based on the profit maximization assumption are not in fact good enough predictors. Much of the complexity involved in this issue can be quickly handled if we start by stressing that the profit maximization assumption has been used in most areas of economic analysis to help in answering a myriad diverse questions and that the accuracy of the predictions based upon it may be expected to vary according to the questions examined. As Machlup has stressed, within the scope of industrial economic behaviour alone there are many significantly different types of question we might wish to ask, but the traditional theory of the profit maximizing firm is only designed and equipped to deal with a relatively small number of them, albeit very important ones.[7] Given this, the question of adequate prediction splits into two

---

[6] G. Archibald, 'The State of Economic Science', *British Journal for the Philosophy of Science*, 10 (May 1959), 58–69.

[7] F. Machlup, op. cit., 9.

parts. First, is the theory of the firm a good enough predictor in areas such as price and output movements and other resource allocation questions in a market economy for which it has traditionally been used? Second, is it able to make good enough predictions in relation to the other questions we may wish to ask about firms' behaviour?

There is probably little argument over the second of these. Consider for example such issues as how the size of firms, their managerial structure, rate of growth, objectives, merger policy, market agreements, etc. are determined; how these affect their decisions concerning price, output, research, advertising, investment, decision criteria, and information systems; how these interact to determine firms' efficiency. In no case would economists want to preclude the possibility of the profit maximization assumption being the best one to make concerning motivation. Still less would they wish *per se* to rule out the construction of 'unrealistic' mental constructs to facilitate analysis. But there appears no good *a priori* reason to use the profit maximization assumption in preference to other possibilities, and no reason (irrespective of one's view on the debate over realism of assumptions) not to start in just the same way that the theory of the firm did, namely by constructing motivational assumptions on the basis of observation of the real world.

Whether the theory of the profit maximizing firm has been a good enough predictor in the more traditional areas of analysis is much more controversial. Friedman regards it as self-evident that it is (for reasons we shall come back to shortly) and does not therefore cite any evidence on the matter. Clearly we can never know whether one firm, or even an aggregation of firms is actually maximizing profit, indeed the concept is quite inapplicable without further restrictions being placed upon it (see later). This is irrelevant however, for it is with the market response to parametric changes that the traditional model is concerned. But it must be noted that factors such as barriers to entry and the separation of ownership and control have not only made suspect both the need and desire to maximize profits, but have also led to models where the output, price, and profit responses to a change in taxation, cost, etc. are *qualitatively* (i.e. different sign) as well as quantitatively different to that predicted by the profit maximizing model, with the question unresolved which approach is the better predictor.[8]

Friedman saw the assumption as self-evidently a good enough predictor, but he was writing in 1953. At that time the superiority

[8] Comparisons of predictions from different models are made below, pp. 271–275.

of the profit maximization assumption for predictive purposes probably *was* self-evident, because most of the work on alternative goals was of the descriptive case-study type with virtually no alternative theory developed to the point at which predictions could reliably be made, still less tested. Attacks on profit maximization based on casual or unsystematic observtion of actual behaviour could very easily have undermined the useful work done in the theory of the firm without replacing it by any workable or constructive alternative. It was not until later that alternative theories were developed which were, partly due to Friedman's views, explicitly capable of prediction, testing, and comparison with the traditional approach. These have all arisen from direct observation of real-world firms' characteristics, but have only recently been subject to more than casual testing and comparison with the profit maximization assumption. Even now it is still very debatable which motivational assumption is the best predictor. It seems reasonable to infer therefore that it is useful to build models based on alternative motivational assumptions, that real-world firms' behaviour is a fertile source for generating hypotheses, but that it is essential always to try to test the predictions of the models both absolutely and against a profit maximizing alternative.

3   CHARACTERISTICS OF INDUSTRIAL COMPANIES

Having described the basis of the profit maximization assumption and the reasons for its use, we have accepted the argument that it is nevertheless quite useful to examine alternatives to it. In fact there now exists a voluminous literature which directly or indirectly questions the profit maximization assumption, and the rest of this chapter is devoted to a summary of this literature and a review of the later and more promising developments.

First we briefly summarize some of the more important characteristics of the industrial companies whose objectives we shall be exploring.

(i) The most striking characteristic of firms at the present time is the dispersion of their size. At one extreme, in the U.S. in 1971 there were 83 non-financial corporations with sales over $1,500 million.[9] By 1976 there were 25 companies with capital employed in excess of $4,000 m.[10] in the U.S. In Europe there were a further 15 with assets in excess of $4,000 m., and 103 with assets in excess of

---

[9] See F. M. Scherer, *Industrial Market Structure & Economic Performance* (Chicago, 1973), Ch. 3, for a summary of other statistics.

[10] See *Times 1000*, 1976–7 (Times Books).

$1,000 m.[11] In 1968 the largest 200 in manufacturing in the U.S. accounted for 60 per cent of that sector's assets.[12] In the U.K. in 1976 there were 126 industrial companies whose capital employed exceeded £100 million, and the largest ten firms averaged over £1,500 m. assets each.[13] In 1968 the largest 100 firms in the industrial sector accounted for over 60 per cent of net assets in that sector and three-quarters of U.K. net output was in the hands of 1,275 firms. This represents a fall of almost two-thirds on the figure for 10 years earlier.[14] In 1972, the U.S. and the U.K. had 89 and 30 firms respectively in manufacturing employing over 40,000 workers, and the original six E.E.C. countries had another 32 such firms.[15] The largest corporations in the world have work-forces in excess of a third of a million people and sales in excess of the Gross National Product of many medium-sized countries.[16] More systematic figures indicating the extent to which net output has come to be dominated by large companies are given in Table 8.1.

At the other end of the scale are a large number of very small enterprises. In the U.K. in 1958, of over 80,000 establishments in manufacturing 80 per cent had less than 100 employees and together accounted for only 15·8 per cent of employment in that sector.[17] (If all businesses of any type are included then there were well over 2 million, of which 98·5 per cent had less than ten employees.[18]) In the U.S. in 1963 there were 121,000 establishments in manufacturing with less than ten employees, responsible for 2·4 per cent of manufacturing employment. In France, Germany, and Italy, where concentration of production is less evident, there were nearly 600,000 such establishments.[19]

An indication of the relative importance of large and small firms in the U.K. can be obtaned from the fact that in 1958 approximately 74 per cent of the 86,000 manufacturing establishments (nearly all

[11] See *Europe's 5000 Largest Companies* (London, 1975).

[12] See K. George, 'The Changing Structure of Competitive Industry', *E.J.* 82 (Mar. 1972), Supplement, 353-68.

[13] See *Times 1000*, 1971-2 (Times Books), and L. Hannah, J. Kay, *Concentration in Modern Industry* (London, 1977), 8.

[14] See K. George, *Industrial Organisation*, 2nd edn. (London, 1974), 34, and S. Prais, *The Evolution of Giant Firms in Britain*, N.I.E.S.R. (1976), 63.

[15] Ibid. 156.

[16] See F. Scherer, op. cit., and C. Tugendhat, *The Multinationals* (London, 1971).

[17] See M. Utton, *Industrial Concentration* (Harmondsworth, 1970), 59. Note that as one enterprise may control more than one establishment the number of enterprises is smaller, but as the vast majority of enterprises are very small single-establishment ones, the total number of enterprises is only approximately 25 per cent less (62,000 in 1968, see S. Prais, op. cit. 10).

[18] See M. Utton, op. cit., 56.   [19] See S. Prais, op. cit., 160.

TABLE 8.1

% Share of 100 largest firms in manufacturing net output.
U.S. and U.K.

	1909	29-30[a]	35	47-8[a]	53-4[b]	58	63	67-8[a]	70
U.S.	22	25	26	23	30	30	33	33	33
U.K.	15	26	23	21	27	32	37	41	41

a. Joint years indicate that U.S. figure is for first of the 2 years, and the U.K. figure for the second of them.

b. U.K. figure is for 1953, U.S. figure for 1954.

Sources: U.S.—S. J. Prais, *The Evolution of Giant Firms in Britain*, N.I.E.S.R., Appendix E, p. 213. U.K.—L. Hannah, *The Rise of the Corporate Economy* (London, 1977), Appendix 2, p. 216, and S. Prais, op. cit., p. 4.

Notes

(i) Department of Industry figures for 1963, 1968 and 1970 in the U.K. are 36·0%, 38·6%, and 37·7% respectively.

(ii) Equivalent figures for the share of net assets in manufacturing indicate even more dominance, being for example in the U.K. over 60 per cent in 1957 and approximately 75 per cent by 1969. For the whole industrial sector they were approximately 50 per cent and 64 per cent respectively. (See Hannah, op. cit., p. 166 and K. D. George, *Industrial Organisation*, 2nd edn. (London, 1974), p. 37.)

single-establishment enterprises) accounted for only 13·6 per cent of net output, while 9 per cent of them under the control of only 1½ per cent of manufacturing enterprises accounted for 60 per cent of net output.[20] In addition the number of small firms has fallen by roughly two-thirds in the period 1930–68.[21]

(ii) Associated with the large size of the companies which have increasingly dominated production are a number of other characteristics. The most significant is diversity of production, which can come about through mergers and acquisition, or through internal diversification. In the U.S. in 1968 the largest 200 firms were on average operating in 20 different 4-digit industries.[22] 322 were (in 1965) in at least 6 4-digit industries and 12 were in over 40 of them.[23] In 1963, 70 of the largest 100 manufacturing firms were amongst the 4 leaders in 4 or more industries.[24] In the U.K. in 1958, 60 per cent of manufacturing firms employing over 5,000 were

[20] See M. Utton, op. cit. 59. Each of these enterprises had on average 8 establishments under its control.

[21] See S. Prais, op. cit 10–11.   [22] See K. George, op. cit. 39.

[23] See C. H. Berry, *Corporate Growth & Diversification* (Princeton University Press, 1975). Scherer, op. cit., also provides a range of statistics for the 1950s and early 1960s.

[24] See K. George, 'The Changing Structure of Competitive Industry', *E.J.* 82 (Mar. 1972), Supplement, 353–68.

operating in at least 3 industries,[25] and in 1970, of the largest 100 manufacturing firms 94 per cent were to some extent diversified, of which only one-third could be categorized as 'dominant product' diversified firms.[26] Together they account for at least one-third of the output of half the 14 main manufacturing sub-sectors and at least a quarter in 10 of them.[27] In all, approximately 56 per cent of all manufacturing output was produced by firms in at least 2 industries.[28] In addition it must be remembered that even the 4-digit industry classification combines products that may not directly compete, being aimed at different segments of a market. For example, S.I.C. 3672 under the heading 'Other radio, radar and electronics capital goods' includes 'manufacturing radio and television transmitters, radio communication receivers, radar and electronic navigational aids, high-frequency heating apparatus, magnetic compasses and gyroscopes, X-ray apparatus and electro-medical equipment (which includes infra-red, ultra-violet, radiant heat, etc., lamps for diagnosis and therapy; electrical and electronic equipment for stimulation and massage; heart, kidney, and lung machines; sterilizing equipment and reading aids)'.

(iii) With size and diversity goes considerable organizational complexity. Each product line requires purchasing, employment, design, production, and sales functions to be carried out and integrated, and the different lines co-ordinated in terms of finance and investment. Marketing, research and development, and dividend policies all have to be fitted into the picture, quite apart from many other specialized accounting, legal, tax, and welfare aspects. Management therefore involves forecasting, planning, allocating, monitoring, and controlling in a highly complex environment.

As a result, formal structures of organization, communication, and responsibility are generally constructed, delineating tasks and their interrelation. This extends throughout the firm and is predominantly 'vertical' of hierarchical in the channels of communication and authority it establishes. At the same time informal structures of communication become established locally. These are more frequently 'horizontal' within the hierarchy of the firm and arise as required to facilitate integration of the many functions being simultaneously carried out. In both cases the primary function of many managers is the processing in one way or another of information through the organization.

[25] See L. Amey, 'Diversified Manufacturing Business', *Journal of the Royal Statistical Society* (Series A), 127, part 2 (1964), 251–90.
[26] See D. Channon, *The Strategy and Structure of British Enterprise* (London, 1973), 64.
[27] See S. Prais, op. cit. 8.   [28] See L. Amey, op. cit., calculated from Table 4, p. 265.

Most of the resulting decision-taking and information processing occurs in conditions of considerable uncertainty about the behaviour of consumers, suppliers, competitors, government, regulatory agencies, and frequently other parts of the same firm. As a result much management time is taken up with the process of seeking information on the activities of any or all of these other groups. This is costly in terms of time and money and therefore a process which itself is subject to economic resource-allocating decisions of some form.[29]

(iv) Virtually all firms initially were small, privately owned businesses. Thus nearly all medium- and large-sized firms (and many quite small ones) experienced substantial growth at some point, in the process of which they went through a stage of requiring more finance than they could obtain either internally from retained earnings, or by borrowing, for example, from banks. This led to the issue of equity shares conferring a part share in ownership of the firm to people not necessarily involved in the day-to-day or even strategic decisions determining the firm's development. This has now led to a situation in which ownership of a firm and effective control generally appear to have become largely divorced from one another. Thus it is not even certain that the objectives of the owners of a company are of any relevance at all to the company's behaviour and performance.

For any particular problem the most appropriate concept of the firm will be some abstraction of this complex picture. As seen earlier, the traditional approach abstracted from all internal characteristics and from diversity. The resulting indivisible single product unit was presumed to have one goal, and in as far as this could be interpreted as saying anything about real-world firms, it implied either that all members of a firm were profit maximizers, or the management control system employed was such as to ensure that no actions and decisions significantly diverged from the pursuit of profit maximization. But given the substantial proportion of production now controlled by very large, highly diversified corporations with complex organizational structures of decision-taking directly responsible to people other than the shareholders, and the trend towards such a picture even amongst smaller firms, it is not surprising that there has been a proliferation of new economic theories of the firm designed to incorporate some or all of these features. For ease of exposition the field can be divided into three issues, which we now consider: (*a*) How are firms organized? (*b*) What are their

---

[29] In addition the organizational structure of a company may itself be a main determinant of the objectives in practice pursued and the performance that results.

objectives? (*c*) What predictions do non profit maximizing models generate?

4   THE ORGANIZATION OF FIRMS

The large amount written in recent years about the behaviour of firms as organizations has come under several headings. These include Administrative, Bureaucratic, and Organization Theory, Social and Management Psychology, and Management Science, to name only some. Within this diverse literature it is useful to identify three qualitatively different approaches.

(i) The first, which started with the work of Taylor[30] and developed into the school of Management Science, was essentially normative, explaining how managers by the application of scientific principles could operate firms more efficiently in pursuit of various objectives. A large number of business problems, particularly in production, distribution, and finance, have been tackled using management science techniques.

(ii) The theory of bureaucracy, stemming from work by Weber[31] though having normative implications, was predominantly descriptive. This identified the defining characteristics of bureaucracies and examined how their behaviour and organization were related to their efficiency. Both approaches illustrate how organizational characteristics such as division of labour and specialization could overcome the natural limits on an individual's computational and decision taking ability, and Weber in particular concluded that techniques were available to put effective control of very large resources into the hands of a very few individuals at the top of a hierarchy.

(iii) Weber went further, however, in starting to examine the *reactions* of individual parts of an organization to the controls and procedures used to make it an efficient and integrated unit. It is this aspect which generally, under the heading of Organization Theory, has received most attention. Early studies illustrated clearly how organizational rules could generate rigidity and reduced efficiency, and more generally how decentralization, delegation, and specialization could bring about (*a*) an inability to compare performance of parts of the firm with its controllers' objectives, (*b*) subsequent commitment to 'localized' rather than company objectives, and (*c*) a consequent conflict between the objectives

---

[30] F. Taylor, *Scientific Management* (New York, 1947).
[31] M. Weber, *The Theory of Social & Economic Organisation* (Oxford, 1947).

of different sub-groups in the firm.[32]

Whereas the early work of Management Science (and much of its current analysis) viewed organizational behaviour as a mechanistic process in which the problem was the rational direction and co-ordination of the parts to maximize efficiency, organization theory has been primarily concerned with examining informal behaviour in organizations—the formation of informal groups, their objectives and comunication systems, the effect of these on performance and organizational efficiency—and the limits this places on the ability of organizations as a whole to act as a rational individual would with comparable decision-taking capacity. The formal organizational structure is no more than the 'field of play' for these considerations. Analysis proceeds partly through observations of actual organizations, including firms, and partly through laboratory experiments with small groups.

Once it is admitted that there is a multiplicity of decision-taking groups in an organization, and definite limits on the ability of those nominally in charge of the organization to control them, then it is no longer obvious what meaning to attach to the 'objectives of the firm' other than a combination of some sort of the many individuals involved. Whether these overlap sufficiently to give some sort of goal by consensus to the organization is an empirical matter, and much research by organization theorists has indicated that this rarely occurs.[33] In fact it is argued that individuals in organizations typically have individual goals which directly conflict with each other, and that the impact of this on the firm is a main determinant of the latter's behaviour and performance.

Two main issues have dominated investigation of the internal structure of firms and potential conflict of objectives between different sub-groups within them. The one which follows most immediately from the organization theory approach is that between managers charged with responsibility for different parts of, and different functions within, the firm (see p. 248). The more fundamental one, however, is the division in most large and medium-sized firms between the shareholders who own it and the managers who direct its operations. Two separate points are involved here.

(1) First, to what extent are the directors and/or managers who control a firm's day-to-day operations and geneally determine its

[32] The three main early studies were: R. Merton, 'Bureaucratic Structure & Personality', *Social Forces*, 18 (1940), 560–8. P. Selznick, *TVA and the Grass Roots* (Berkeley, 1949). A. Gouldner, *Patterns of Industrial Bureaucracy* (London, 1955).

[33] See J. March (ed.), *Handbook of Organisations* (Chicago, 1965), for a good selection of important articles in this field and summaries of empirical work carried out.

longer-term development owners of the firm? On this the evidence is fairly clear. Florence,[34] in a major study of share ownership in the U.K. since the war, found that the median value of the proportion of voting shares in the hands of the company's directors for a sample of 102 large firms was 3 per cent in 1936 and down to 1½ per cent by 1951. More recently, Prais found that, by 1972, in only 11 of the largest 100 U.K. manufacturing firms did directors own more than 10 per cent of the shares, and in 73 of them less than 2 per cent. A similar picture was confirmed in the U.S. Gordon,[35] in a study of 115 companies, found the median proportion of directors' shares to be 3½ per cent in 1939, and only two-sevenths of even this small proportion were held by directors with executive offices in the company. However, as Marris points out, in the typical firm directors rarely have negligible holdings, with fewer than one-third of all company boards holding less than 1 per cent.[36] The significance of this is examined below, but we may in passing point out that these relatively small percentages are predictable simply from comparing the typical size of a manager's wealth in relation to total company wealth. No general evidence is available concerning the proportion of company voting strength held by non-board managers, but this is very unlikely to alter the picture materially, despite the tendency for various managerial incentive schemes to generate increased holdings for any individual manager over his career.

(2) The second question follows from the first. Is there generally any other individual or group apart from the management with sufficient voting power to ensure that managers' decisions conform with the owners' wishes? This itself breaks down into two problems— what is the concentration of voting power, and what is the proportion of total votes necessary to enforce one's wishes? Several studies have empirically examined the former. The seminal work by Berle and Means[37] found that for 1929 in only 11 per cent of 200 large corporations did any individual person or group control more than 50 per cent, and in 44 per cent of the cases did not even have 20 per cent. By 1963 Larner[38] found that in only 2½ per cent of firms was there an individal majority holding and in only 15 per cent an individual or single group holding over 10 per cent of the total

[34] P. Sargent Florence, *Ownership, Control & Success of Large Companies* (London, 1961).

[35] R. Gordon, *Business Leadership in the Large Corporation* (Berkeley, 1961).

[36] R. Marris, *Economic Theory of Managerial Capitalism* (London, 1964).

[37] A. Berle and G. Means, *The Modern Corporation and Private Property* (New York, 1932).

[38] R. Larner, 'Ownership and Control in the 200 Largest Non-Financial Corporations 1929 and 1963', *A.E.R.* 56, no. 4 (Sept. 1966), 777-87.

voting strength. For 1937 the 'average' company, according to Perlo,[39] had the 20 largest shareholders holding 32 per cent of the votes, 980 holding the next 18 per cent, and 34,000 holding the remaining 50 per cent. A similar picture is seen in the U.K. Florence[40] found that in 1951 only 7 per cent of all U.K. companies with nominal issued share capital over £3 m. had a single majority shareholder, and that in only 5½ per cent of the rest did the largest 20 shareholders together have a majority position. For firms between £0·2 m. and £3 m. issued capital the corresponding figures were under 1 per cent and approximately 10 per cent. So strongly did such studies indicate a wide dispersion of shareholding and general lack of concentration of voting power that little further investigation has been done, and it has been widely accepted that control of managers by owners as a result of concentration of shareholdings is unlikely except in extreme circumstances. Yet such conclusions depend also on the second aspect—what percentage is *needed* for effective control? For the more widely shares are dispersed, the smaller the proportion necessary for control. Beed[41] argues that a proportion in the 1 per cent to 5 per cent range may be sufficient to exert influence on a board, perhaps through direct representation, if shareholding is as widely dispersed as the figures indicate. In that case the large majority of firms would contain an individual or cohesive group which could normally, through its ownership rights, dominate the affairs of the company. This would then mean that despite the separation of managers and owners, a small section of the latter could retain effective control. Most owners would be powerless, but not all of them, and managers could still be effectively directed by a small proportion of the owners.

Such reflections are made stronger if it is noted that frequently legally separate shareholdings with nothing to connect them as recorded are in fact used jointly. Relatives with different family names may together hold bigger blocks of shares than at first appears. A company may have an effectively controlling interest in another through a number of individual and apparently unrelated shareholdings.

But it is here that Marris's[42] argument based on Gordon and Florence's work must be recalled. Managers rarely have negligible shareholdings: 69 per cent of the boards examined in the U.K. had over 1 per cent of the shares, and 73 per cent in the U.S. On Prais's

[39] V. Perlo, *The Empire of High Finance* (International Publishers, 1957).
[40] P. Sargent Florence, op. cit.
[41] C. Beed, 'The Separation of Ownership from Control', *J. Econ. Studs.* 1 (1966), 29–46.
[42] See reference on p. 245.

figures even 40 of the largest 100 U.K. manufacturing firms came into the same category (in 1972).[43] Nor do they have to rely purely on their shareholding. Typically managers will make arrangements whereby any shareholder can place his voting rights at the disposal of a proxy voter amenable to the views of the management. Only in very extreme circumstances and in a company where *another* individual or group exists with a similar-sized holding to act as a focus of discontent is there much chance of a real proxy fight, and even then the management is generally in a much stronger position to argue its position. If, as Beed suggests, the diffusion of shareholdings permits holdings in the range of 1 per cent to 5 per cent to be effectively controlling ones, then it seems reasonable to conclude that managers often do retain effective control, as against the owners, and therefore do have considerable discretion to pursue their own goals.

One possible objection to this, increasingly raised, is that there is a trend towards institutional shareholding (pension funds, insurance companies, investment and unit trusts, etc.) and that the financial institutions concerned, by virtue of being more informed and more active in their investment behaviour, can exert more direct pressure on company managers to meet performance targets acceptable to the owners. The existence of such a trend in the U.K. is now fairly clear. Figures by Moyle show that the percentage of registered holdings of shares held by persons, executors, and trustees fell from 61·8 per cent in 1957 to 51·0 per cent in 1963, to 44·7 per cent in 1970, and to under 40 per cent by 1975.[44] Conversely the holdings of insurance companies, banks, pension funds, investment trusts, and other financial institutions rose from 28·3 per cent in 1957 to 41·1 per cent by 1970.[45] Dobbins and Greenwood, extrapolating past trends in the pattern of share acquisition and disposal, foresaw a 50 per cent share by 1977 and a 70 per cent share by 1990.[46] Personal ownership as a percentage has geneally been higher in the U.S. (e.g. 61·1 per cent in 1965), but institutional holdings have followed the same expanding pattern as in the U.K., with the share held by pension funds, investment and insurance companies rising from only 7·3 per cent of the total in 1950 to 19·1 per cent by

[43] S. Prais, op. cit. 89.
[44] The figures for 1957, 1963, and 1970 are from J. Moyle, *The Pattern of Ordinary Share Ownership 1957–70*, D.A.E. Occasional Paper, 31 (Cambridge University Press, 1971), 7. The 1975 figure is from *Economic Trends*, 287, H.M.S.O. (Sept. 1977), 96, and is on a slightly different basis.
[45] Ibid.
[46] R. Dobbins, M. J. Greenwood, 'The Future Pattern of U.K. Share Ownership', *Long Range Planning*, 8, no. 4 (Aug. 1975).

1968. It can be argued that the much more active policies of the U.S. institutions give them greater influence than is the case in the U.K., but to a great extent this simply reflects that *all* equity holders pursue much more active policies in the U.S., thus reducing the expected influence of the institutions.[47]

The difficult question is whether and to what extent this growing institutional ownership has been used to exercise effective control. In Germany, where 60 per cent of household savings flow through the banking system, institutional ownership has undoubtedly been used to manage companies.[48] Major banks hold at least one-quarter of many major corporations and typically have officials on the boards of the companies whose shares they hold.[49] But for various reasons institutions in the U.K. have remained more reticent, perhaps feeling that they have not the expertise to help manage nor the preparedness to take responsibility for the decisions taken. Instead it has been thought much easier to ensure only a relatively small holding in any one company and to sell this if performance appears inadequate.[50] Thus it is probably only via the threat of a falling share price rather than through active intervention that non-owning managers will generally be forced to adopt the owners' objectives if they differ from their own. Adherence to shareholders' wishes will therefore be ensured provided a market in corporate capital exists which is sufficiently efficient that the companies of managers who pursue non-wealth maximizing policies are bought up and the managers replaced.[51]

The other main issue is conflict within the management group itself. While the 'managerial' development described above has focused attention on the salaried managers who direct firms' operations, the 'behavioural' school has stressed that the managerial group itself is not cohesive and that the many different functions of management are likely to generate important divisions within it. The main contribution here has been the behavioural theory of the firm developed by Cyert and March.[52] At its most general level this argues that a 'firm' is a coalition of individuals, some organized into

[47] See R. J. Briston, *The Impact of Institutional Investors on the London Stock Exchange*, British Accounting & Finance Association, Occasional Paper, no. 1, Institutional Investors & the London Stock Exchange (1972), 13–14.

[48] See R. Dobbins, T. McRae, 'Institutional Shareholders and Corporate Management', *Management Decision* 13, no. 6 (1975), 390.

[49] Ibid.

[50] This pattern of behaviour may however change as bank loans become an increasing source of new funds for companies. There may also be a trend to fewer larger holdings to facilitate control.

[51] This issue is considered in more detail in Chapters 10 and 14.

[52] R. Cyert, J. March, *Behavioural Theory of the Firm* (Englewood Cliffs, 1963).

groups or sub-coalitions. In a firm these include managers, workers, shareholders, suppliers, customers, etc. According to the topic being studied we can identify major coalition members. Explicitly or implicitly a process of bargaining occurs continuously, in which 'side-payments'—salaries, commitments to particular lines of business or specific policies, etc.—are paid in order to induce others to join a particular coalition. This covers 'inducement' to join the firm and to stay in it, to pursue particular activities, and to agree to particular policies favoured by others. Cash payments become progressively less important as one moves through these phases.

This general framework, which could in principle be applied to any industrial economic problem, for example labour economics, in fact focuses, as far as price, output, and sales are concerned, on the managerial group, with all others presumed to join the coalition through provision of adequate side-payments. The bargaining process, however, does not eliminate all conflict within the managerial group. Cyert and March focus on five aims which they believe reasonably well represent the main organizational goals, normally operative. These are:

(i) Production goal. The desires primarily of the production side for stable employment, ease of scheduling, maintenance of adequate cost performance, and growth are all largely met by requiring that production does not fluctuate too much nor fall below an acceptable level.

(ii) Inventory goal. The desire primarily of the sales staff and their customers for there to be at all times a complete and convenient stock of inventory is largely met by keeping the level of inventory above a certain minimum figure.

(iii) Sales goal. The importance of sales for the stability and survival of the firm makes it an important goal for all firm members, but particularly the sale staff whose effectiveness is partly judged by their success in maintaining and expanding sales.

(iv) Market Share goal. This may be an alternative to the sales goal, particularly if market growth is important. Top management may adhere to it more because of the comparative performance measure element contained in it.

(v) Profit goal. Investment, dividends, and further resources for sub-units of the firm all require adequate profit. In addition profit is an important performance measure for top management.

It is clear that these may irreconcilably conflict when it comes to choosing price and output levels. Sales goals may require a lower price, the profit goal a higher one. Both sales and production goals may favour high inventories, profits a lower level, and so on. How are these conflicts dealt with? Cyert and March refer to four mechanisms.

(*a*) The objectives are stated in terms of aspiration levels, implying that business decision-takers do not maximize, but 'satisfice'—aim for a satisfactory 'aspiration' level. (The concept of satisficing is examined as part of the analysis of active decision-taking in Chapter 11.) This form of objective permits some quasi-resolution of conflict because frequently at any one time only one objective will be 'operative' in the sense of needing attention because it is not currently being achieved. Company decisions can then be directed to solving that problem without having to deal with the impact on other goals.

(*b*) As this implies, decision-taking is sequential. If a problem in the shape of an unfulfilled objective occurs, then 'problemistic search' occurs for a solution to the problem. If another objective subsequently becomes operative then it too generates problemistic search and a solution. But the pursuit of different objectives at different times reduces substantially the perceived conflict between different objectives.

(*c*) Organizational slack exists. This is the difference between the resources available and those necessary to meet the current demands of members of the coalition (firm). If performance becomes inadequate in terms of a particular objective it is generally possible for organizations to increase efficiency by utilizing slack resources. The existence of this slack frequently permits performance in terms of one objective to be improved without hitting performance in terms of another.

(*d*) The use of standard operating procedures. Many decisions are standardized and then operated by the department responsible for them to some extent irrespective of their consequences elsewhere. Acceptance of these standard procedures then circumvents much latent conflict. For example, if it is generally accepted that profit below some specified level is the signal for a rise in price this may avoid any conflict based on the adverse consequences for sales.

Two other mechanisms frequently operative in firms, though not relevant to the five-goal model referred to are, first, the statement of goals in non-operational form. For example the goal of greater efficiency would get 100 per cent support. It is only when specific decisions have to be taken that conflicts between more or less investment, more or less research, more or less employees, etc., all of which *could* increase efficiency, have to be dealt with. Second is the imperfect analysis of the ramifications of objectives such that the full (and conflicting) implications of a new activity or decision for existing policy are not realized or made explicit.

Few researchers who have observed firms or other organizations closely would deny that goal conflict does occur and that all of the above mechanisms operate to make the organization none the less viable and purposive. But this behavioural approach nevertheless faces theoretical, empirical, and methodological difficulties. Under the first heading a theory is required to explain what determines aspiration levels, how potential solutions to the problem of an unsatisfied goal are identified, selected, and in what order considered, and how such control mechanisms as the company's annual budget and allocation of funds fit into the picture. On the empirical side it is essential to identify the actual goals generally pursued. For clearly the five listed by Cyert and March do not allow us to investigate such matters as the division of funds between investment, dividends, and liquidity, between plant and equipment, research and development and advertising. Nor does it embrace elements in the desire for security such as diversification and merger. Equally difficult is the empirical identification of aspiration levels and the way they respond over time. In addition even the relatively simple model proposed by Cyert and March is only capable of analysis via computer simulation. This raises further difficulties as to the empirical identification of the systematic and general decision procedures used in firms and their computerization. But it is the methodological problems that have been focused on most. For example, it is not clear that aspiration levels permit unambiguous predictions to be made about business behaviour. There is virtually no recognition of the industrial structure and resulting competitive pressures which firms face. Most of all, the increased complexity of these models seems to *reduce* their generality of application, and it has been very difficult even to set up tests of their general predictive power (as opposed to very successful testing in simulation of particular individual decision processes).

All these and many other difficulties are recognized by Cyert and March in what may be seen as an important and stimulating integration of economics and organization theory. But while generally increasing understanding about firms' behaviour and providing a framework for extensive further research, yet it is still true that the behavioural approach has not entered the main stream of economic study of the firm because of the difficulties listed. Unless more general testable predictions can be generated it is likely that it will remain as an adjunct to more traditional heory in the analysis of detailed or individual decision problems, but not widely utilized for general analysis of firms' over-all performance.

Three ways of trying to integrate organizational characteristics into industrial economics have been explored. The first, due to

Simon,[53] is to argue that every operative aspiration-level goal pursued by a decision-taker represents a constraint on the set of decisions which are feasible. The 'goals of the organization' are simply all the constraints which must be satisfied, but we may wish to single out one constraint dimension at any one time to be maximized subject to the other constraints, instead of only satisfied. There is a clear parallel with linear programming, which in principle can be used in the formulation of such an approach. In practice models have generally only gone as far as recognizing some commonly held goal, usually profit, as a constraint on the pursuit of other goals.

A second possibility recently examined by Morris[54] is that for at least an important range of decisions—financial, investment, research and development—*final* decision-taking is very centralized. Lower-level managerial motivation cannot then have its influence through potentially conflicting decisions but through its effect on the many contributory decisions concerning information collection, processing, assessment, and transmission which provide the data for final decisions. Evidence strongly suggests systematic patterns of bias in these processes in the light of lower-level goals, which will have significant effects on both the final decisions and on company performance through time. This is often not recognized within the firm except in a very general way, however, because of the way in which the objectives of the board, the objectives of lower-level management, the information system connecting them, and the limits placed on the process by uncertainty interact. This approach re-emphasizes that it may be more fruitful to model firms 'as if' they were individuals with particular objectives, because their behaviour is partly the necessary consequences of organizational decision-taking processes rather than the pursuit of particular managerial objectives.

The third approach is primarily due to Williamson,[55] who has focused on the fact that two very different forms of formal organizational structure can be observed currently, and that the internal problems discussed above are only important in the older, unitary-form (or U-form) enterprise. This comprises a chief executive, with functional divisions—finance, production, sales, etc.—responsible to him for their respective functions as applied to all company products. This is a very common managerial structure for small and

---

[53] H. Simon, 'On the Concept of Organisational Goal', *Administrative Science Quarterly* (June 1964), 1–21.

[54] D. Morris, 'The Structure of Investment Decisions', unpublished D.Phil. thesis (Oxford, 1974).

[55] O. Williamson, 'Managerial Discretion, Organisation Form, and the Multi-Division Hypothesis', in R. Marris, A. Wood (ed.), *The Corporate Economy* (London, 1971).

medium-sized firms, and arguably the most appropriate form for such firms. But for large firms it leads to 'control-loss' as it becomes more and more difficult to transmit information reliably, co-ordinate all operations, prevent the aims of lower-level managers intruding, and therefore prevent the divisive effects examined by Cyert and March and others from occurring. In particular Williamson notes the need in larger U-form organizations for the chief executive to augment the top-level planning process with functional heads—sales director, production manager, etc.—and emphasizes that this changes the top level perspective from an enterprise-wide one to a collection of partisan and often conflicting views. There is less check on empire-building and related pursuits, and these 'dysfunctional' character-istics, as they are called, become significant. Nor does the stock market provide much check, partly because shareholders may accept performance far below maximum efficiency or profitability (espe-cially as they generally have little idea of what the latter is) but mainly because the only real checks—takeover or removal of directors—are so severe that they are generally unlikely to occur pro-vided performance is not disastrous. The threat of this has some con-straining effect, but it is arguably not great.

The other form,[56] the multi-divisional enterprise (M-form), arose in the U.S. out of the organizational problems caused by large size, in particular the pressure of work on senior executives faced with departmental and board responsibilities, the increased complexity of decision-taking, and the growing separation of different functions as information channels became unduly stretched. It replaced the U-form structure with, first, a general office with advisory staff, second, a series of operating divisions, for example one for each product, each with a head responsible to the general office, and third, functional departments as in the U-form enterprise responsible to divisional heads. These retained the rational division of decisions by function, but separated out these decisions from over-all respon-sibility for each product and from over-all strategy for the whole corporation. The result is that each division operates like a quasi-firm, but is responsible to the top board, which is free to concentrate on broad strategy and able, because of its separation from the divi-sions, to exert some control on them, not least through the advisory functions that the central staff provide.

The M-form has two main characteristics. First, it can circumvent much of the inefficiency of the U-form. It reduces the necessary communication network and separates out over-all integration from

[56] It has been found that there are a number of generally less successful intermediate organizational forms. See D. Channon, op. cit.

local operating problems. Second, it permits auditing of individual product lines, allocation of responsibility for their performance to individuals, and the insistence on such identifiable performance being up to a certain standard. This gives a very heavy incentive to divisional heads to avoid or neutralize the control-loss activities likely to occur within quasi-firms (which are individually U-form). This does not mean the M-form is always superior nor does it mean that the M-form removes all or even most of the control-loss problems of large organizations. But, Williamson argues, it does lead to the 'Multi-divisional hypothesis' that M-form enterprises will be better able to enforce the objectives of the top management which are likely to focus mainly on profits, as against the 'individualist' goals of lower management bent on expanding sales, growing faster, increasing expenditure on their own perquisites, and generally empire-building. In particular the M-form can permit control superior to that in the U-form because control is now internal and by informed managers rather than external and by uninformed shareholders. It can be fine-tuned, unlike takeover or removal of directors, and is much less costly, mainly because the information necessary for control is more easily and regularly available.

Evidence on organizational form is increasingly available. In France, Germany, Italy, the U.K., and the U.S. there has been a process of growing diversification which has been accompanied by a change from U-form to essentially M-form organization.[57] The latter provided the administrative mechanism necessary to control and make effective the great increase in diversification that resulted from the increased competition and uncertainty of the post-war world.

The growing importance of the multi-divisional form of organization has significant implications for company objectives. Williamson suggests that internal non-profit oriented organizational behaviour is relevant to the study of U-form enterprises and quasi-firms, but that the organizational complexities and personal goals can again be ignored when we analyse the economic behaviour of M-form enterprises. This would indicate that the neoclassical approach could be maintained for the latter despite their lack of similarity to the holistic firm on which that theory was based. There are however two problems about this. First, if the co-ordinating board of the M-form enterprise is comprised of non profit-receiving managers, then there may still be no reason to presume profit is anything more than a loose constraint on other more personal goals concerned, for example, with size, growth, and market domination. Second, such a group and even their advisory staff are heavily dependent on information

[57] See D. Channon, op. cit., Foreword, vi, and 238.

from the divisions. If, as has been suggested, dysfunctional behaviour occurs *vis-à-vis* centralized decisions through distortion of information supplied, forecasts made, etc., then even though the M-form is superior to the U-form enterprise the former may still end up taking decisions that reflect lower-level managerial preferences rather than higher-level objectives such as profit maximization.

To summarize this section, once we remove the 'black box' assumption we find a very complex world of individual motives contributing to sub-group goals which may or may not be consistent enough to generate a 'goal of the firm.' Whether this can be brought about or not depends in part on the formal structure of the organization, the information channels within it, the use made of them, and the mechanisms which are used to reconcile conflicting aims. The separation of managers and owners, the functional division of managers themselves, and the lack of knowledge about external and internal control mechanisms make it very difficult to identify clearly the effective motivation of a firm. What, however, it also indicates is serious doubt about how well the profit motive, still more that of profit maximization, is pursued or permitted to dominate. We therefore proceed to consider the many suggestions made as to the objectives firms appear to pursue and their initial implications.

5 FIRMS' OBJECTIVES

It is worth starting by noting that profit maximization is itself not unambiguous without further specification. Basic theory implies that the maximand is the excess of revenue over all costs, including opportunity cost and taxes in a static world in which either all factors of production are variable (long-term) or only some are variable (short-term). As such it first may clash with maximization in the long term of the rate of return on capital valued at historic cost—an objective inconsistent with the concept of 'rational economic man' but quite plausible none the less. Second, it is not directly related to accounting profit which ignores imputed opportunity cost, raising the possibility that 'true' profit is not maximized and/or regularly negative. But the most serious difficulty arises from the static framework within which it has generally been applied.

In response to the charge that static profit maximization (short- and long-run) could be shown to be descriptively and predictively false, most recent models have, as we have seen, tended towards a dynamic formulation in which it is the present value of the future stream of suitably discounted profits to infinity which is maximized. This led (see Chapter 6) to the conclusion that value maximization might well be an appropriate but inapplicable motivational assumption unless all main intertemporal relations were first identified correctly. But further ambiguity arises once we recognize that business activities, because they involve individuals, imply that individual time and effort are important inputs to the process of profit creation. This has three implications.

First, profit has to be defined as the excess of revenue over all costs including *imputed* wage costs for the owner-manager. Failure to include the latter would lead to the prediction that a profit maximizer would work up to 24 hours a day, 365 days a year as long as the marginal return was positive.

Second, recognition of the need for inputs of time and effort by an owner-manager suggests that it would be more reasonable to use a utility function containing both profit and leisure. This is one possible generalization of Hicks's argument that the main monopoly profit is a quiet life. But once leisure is an input (i.e. leisure is used up in the process of making profits) and also an element of the utility function, then profit maximization, even defined net of imputed wages, does not necessarily result from utility maximization. Profit (net of imputed wages) which was insufficient to compensate for leisure used up would be forgone. Ng has identified three situations in which the maximization of an owner-manager's utility dependent on his net income and leisure will lead to maximization of profit.[58] The most important[59] is when managerial services can be bought or sold freely, for then maximum utility is reached by pushing out a 'budget' line between income (profit) and leisure as far as possible—that is by maximizing profit—and then buying or selling management services (moving along the 'budget' line) to the point of maximum utility, tangent to the highest indifference curve. Of course, the owner-manager's profit net of the cost of hired managers is not now maximized, but the operations of the firm are exactly the same as if the owner-manager had been attempting only to maximize profit. Thus the possibility of hiring managers makes it acceptable to ignore the owner-manager's leisure propensities, provided the managers can fully duplicate the work which the owner would have done in their absence. Second, however, recognition of management inputs draws attention to the fact that managerial working time cannot be regarded as homogeneous. It may involve greater or lesser effort,

---

[58] Y. Ng, 'Utility & Profit Maximisation by an Owner-Manager: Towards a General Analysis', *J.I.E.* 23, no. 2 (Dec. 1974), 97–108.

[59] The second is trivial and the third utilizes an economically meaningful but largely inoperative definition of profit as net of the opportunity cost of leisure forgone.

with repercussions on profit, dependent on a firm's current performance.

Two similar approaches have been presented in the literature. First the existence of organizational slack (see p. 250) implies that profits are rarely maximized and that maximum profits are rarely pursued. Nearly all firms, if under severe pressure, can usually improve profits above what they would otherwise have been without recourse to more resources other than effort. Reder's famous example of the Ford motor company indicated that $20 m. (pre-war prices) was saved under the pressure of low profits.[60] This only arises because firms operate as if pursuing satisfactory rather than maximum profits. Unless it can be shown that over time these lead to the same result (see pp. 410–11), then the existence of slack in varying amounts makes the assumption of profit maximization more questionable.

Related to this, but not quite the same, is the concept of X-inefficiency referred to in Part II (pp. 67–70). This can be regarded as the difference between actual cost and minimum attainable cost, resulting from any reduction of the pressure on firms to apply maximum effort in pursuit of efficiency and profits. It is not the same as organizational slack because the latter is (directly related to) the difference between maximum performance and *acceptable* performance, whereas X-inefficiency is the difference between maximum and *actual* performance. None the less, they are both measures of 'reserve resources', will tend to increase or decrease together, and will both give rise to non-profit maximizing behaviour. Thus, although we may ignore leisure as a motive if salaried managers are available, we cannot ignore the fact that resources frequently are not fully utilized because of limits on the amount of effort which managers can or will supply.

The more prominent developments have not however been with regard to the constraint on profit represented by the desire for leisure or variability of effort, but in proposals for new components of the managerial utility function. In order to examine these systematically we first make a distinction. People's aims may be specified in two ways, first in terms of what they aim to achieve independent of the particular environment in which they find themselves: for example the desire for prestige. For the sake of clarity we will refer to these as *motives*. Second, aims may be formulated in terms of those things which will, in a particular situation, gratify these motives. A large staff, for example, will, in an organization,

[60]M. Reder, 'A Reconsideration of Marginal Productivity Theory', *J.P.E.* 55 (1947), 450–8.

generally enhance prestige. This we term an *objective* if it is still an immediate personal want within the framework of the organization (for example more investment funds for one's own department), and a *goal* if it is regarded as a characteristic of the organization as a whole, for example more profit. The borderlines between motives, objectives, and goals are not always precise, but the basic difference is reasonably straightforward. We look first at individual motives.

The best-known and most comprehensive statement in economics is given by Marris, who argues that the three dominant motives are income, status, and power.[61] These have been supported by a very large number of writers in psychology, economics, and organization theory. Barnard was one of the first to highlight management desires for these,[62] followed by Gordon, Galbraith, Williamson, and many others.[63] Few have ever questioned the existence of these as powerful motives, though there is disagreement as to their impact. In addition the aim of security has also been stressed heavily over the last few decades. Katona emphasized the importance managers attach to avoiding losses or retreats of any type (as opposed to the desire for gain or advance)[64] and the psychological need to avoid instability and uncertainty, while Baker very early on, and perhaps reflecting the 'quiet life' motivation of monopoly already mentioned, pointed out that much executive activity was designed to minimize worry.[65] Gordon specifically suggested that security in the form of avoidance of uncertainty was a dominant motive in business executives, and while Marris and Williamson both incorporate it, Cyert and March's behavioural theory has placed the greatest weight on it.

A number have wanted to add the desire for professional success. If success were seen as achieving what one wanted to achieve, then this would be a truism, but it is clearly not so intended. Rather it is the refutable proposition that there are certain specified signs of success, defined by the society in which one lives and the particular group within which one works, which people wish to obtain and be seen to attain. Marris in particular dwells on the difference between the traditional capitalist for whom the character of the goods and services he produces may well be an element in his utility function and the bureaucrat in the large modern corporation for whom the

[61] R. Marris, *The Economic Theory of Managerial Capitalism* (London, 1964).

[62] C. Barnard, *The Functions of the Executive* (Cambridge, Mass., 1938).

[63] R. Gordon, op. cit., Ch. 12 and 305–12; J. K. Galbraith, *American Capitalism* (Harmondsworth, 1963), 39–40; O. Williamson, *The Economics of Discretionary Behaviour: Management Objectives in a Theory of the Firm* (Englewood Cliffs, 1964), 50–2.

[64] G. Katona, *Psychological Analysis of Economic Behaviour* (New York, 1951), 204–6.

[65] J. Baker, 'How Should Executives be Paid', *Harvard Business Review*, 18 (Autumn 1939), 94–106;

major concern is the skill which he can bring to bear on a problem. In practice, salary, status, and power may well however be the main signs of 'success' in modern capitalism, making this additon redundant.

Many other motives have been suggested, including adventure, creativity, competitiveness or game playing, service, and social obligation. These are, however, less fully agreed and probably not pervasive. Indeed they are often the aim of management training programmes, suggesting that they are not very automatic or deep-rooted. Salary, status, power, and security therefore appear likely to be the motivational basis of most future developments in the theory of the firm.

There is less agreement about what goals and objectives these motives give rise to. The most frequently argued view is that they result in a desire for large size. We take the most controversial aspect of this first, the relation between managerial salary and company size. In a major study of executive compensation, Roberts found that salary levels appeared to be much more correlated with the size of firms as measured by sales than with profits, implying that the desire for increased salary would lead to greater emphasis on the pursuit of large size rather than large profits.[66] The empirical result was confirmed in a study by McGuire, Chiu, and Elbing, which found sales and executive compensation to be significantly correlated in five out of seven cases given, but profits and executive compensation not correlated at all.[67] Marris supported the view,[68] as did Patton.[69] In fact there appeared to be something approaching a consensus on the matter. Yet this position was open to strong criticism both theoretically and empirically. The first step on the empirical side was an extensive study by Lewellyn on compensation of top executives.[70] This analysed not only salary but bonuses, pension plans, deferred pay, profit sharing schemes, and stock options of the top 5 executives in 50 of the largest 500 U.S. firms. It came up with the surprising result that only about one-sixth of the top five executives' total remuneration came from salary, and less than one-fifth for the top executive. Dividends, capital gains, and other stock-based remuneration comprised most of their reward. This led Lewellyn and Huntsman to question the significance of the sales/

---

[66] D. Roberts, op. cit.

[67] J. McGuire, J. Chiu, A. Elbing, 'Executive Income, Sales and Profits', *A.E.R.* 52, no. 4 (Sept. 1962), 753–61.

[68] R. Marris, op. cit.

[69] A. Patton, *Men, Money & Motivation* (New York, 1961).

[70] W. Lewellyn, 'Management & Ownership in the Large Firm', *J. of Finance*, 24 (May 1969), 299–322.

salary correlation and they embarked on a study desinged to see if the picture changed when non-salary remuneration was included.[71] The results provided considerable surprise however. It was found that salary and bonuses *alone* were strongly correlated with profits and not at all with sales. The multivariate analysis consistently had the right sign for profits, but not for sales, and in addition showed the profit variable consistently to be significant, but not the sales variable. Furthermore, the correlation coefficient was in the range of 0·737–0·929 for the analysis. No improvement was found in the results when other elements of executive compensation were included.

Clearly these results needed some explaining, particularly as Lewellyn and Huntsman felt that the divergence of their results from those of McGuire, Chiu, and Elbing was too extreme to be explicable in terms of different sample or time period (they were in fact very similar). Instead they explain it in terms of econometric problems which their own study was designed to overcome. These were (i) that there is a high degree of collinearity between the independent variables of sales and profits used. The simple correlation coefficient between them was in fact found to be 0·9. (ii) Heteroscedasticity was also present—i.e. the error term was a function of (in fact proportional to) the dependent variables. Both problems were overcome by them by deflating all variables by the book value of total assets. Thus it appeared that a superior approach had shown profits to be much more important than sales in the determination of executive compensation even though only salary and bonuses were included. They explained the irrelevance of further components of compensation on the ground that they were correlated with salary and bonuses and/or too variable to have an identifiable effect.

Mason provides support for this in a number of ways.[72] He argued that much of the earlier work was cross-sectional, which seems irrelevant if the argument is that executives aim at large size to improve their salaries, and also very short-term, being generally for only one year. Even Roberts's time series analysis used only current profits, and this may clearly distort results if, as seems likely, any profit or sales effect is likely to be a longer-term and quite possibly cumulative one. Masson's own results showed that *changes* in compensation of the top 3 to 5 executives were not related to sales *changes* in a sample of 39 firms, but that executive compensation

[71] W. Lewellyn, B. Huntsman, 'Managerial Pay and Corporate Performance', *A.E.R.* 60, no. 4 (Sept. 1970), 710–20.

[72] R. Masson, 'Executive Motivation, Earnings & Consequent Equity Performance', *J.P.E.* 79, no. 6 (Nov. 1971), 1278–92.

was correlated with current plus lagged stock market share return. These studies and other supporting ones indicated that with regard to managerial objectives it is less important what proportion of a company's shares are owned by the management, but much more vital what proportion of the managers' remuneration depends on stocks and shares directly or indirectly. The division between ownership and control becomes much less important if managers, like the owners, primarily depend on profit for their compensation and therefore pursue profit goals. This has been further backed up by argument to the effect that the background, education, and wealth of senior managers gives them an affinity or community of interest with owners of wealth such that the legal separation of management and control is relatively unimportant.[73]

In fact the studies mentioned are themselves open to serious criticism and we therefore go a little further into what is a complex issue. First, it is very plausible to assume that executive compensation is made up of one part which is a function of size (sales) over a considerable period (see below for further justification for this) and another which is a function of profits over the current or last period. If so, *changes* in compensation would be much more correlated with changes in profits than with changes in sales, as Masson found, but general salary levels would still be much more heavily dependent on sales than on profits. Second, Meeks and Whittington go a long way towards reconciling the opposing evidence by examining in more detail the distinction between sales and change in sales (or growth) as independent variables.[74] They start by arguing that *absolute* differences in directors' pay will be associated with *absolute* differences in profit but *proportionate* differences in size. Thus an extra £10,000 profit will have an effect independent of current profit, but £100,000 increase in sales will add more to the pay of a director in a firm whose sales are £1 m. than in one where sales are £10 m. They therefore regress directors' pay on rate of return and the *logarithm* of firm size as measured by sales (other size measures did not materially alter the results). The results indicate that the size measure is a more reliable guide to pay than profits and that a shift from being average to (just) being in the top 5 per cent in terms of size has 5 times the effect (£10,000 as against £2,000) of such a shift in terms of profits. But they go on to point out that such a shift is quite feasible in terms of profit, but *not* in terms of size (such a

---

[73] See for example, T. Nichols, *Ownership, Control & Ideology* (London, 1969).

[74] G. Meeks and G. Whittington, 'Director's Pay, Growth and Profitability', *J.I.E.* 24, no. 1 (Sept. 1975). They also attack Lewellyn and Huntsman's method of deflating the variable in their econometric analysis.

shift implies a 750-fold increase in size). If, instead, *feasible* changes in both are focused on then it becomes clear that it is the *growth* rate that can vary widely across its sample range, not size; and their data show that shifts from zero to mean and mean to two standard deviations above it in terms of profit generally have a greater effect on the top manager's salary than equivalent shifts in growth rate. (Direct tests of the growth effect support this, though several difficulties mar the results.)

These results therefore suggest that salary is correlated much more with sales, but that changes in profit will have the bigger affect on salary. They therefore appear to break the link between the findings of the 'managerialists'—Roberts, McGuire *et al.*, Patton, etc.—and their conclusion that sales will become the dominant managerial objective. But this eclectic position can be challenged in two ways. First, as Meeks and Whittington themselves point out, increased salary as a result of higher profits lasts only while the profits continue to be earned, but with respect to growth there is a ratchet effect. The increased salary continues even if growth is subsequently zero, because sales then remain at their new high level. This makes the growth effect much more important.

Second, there are a number of reasons for suggesting that the correlation of salary with either sales or profits does not imply a corresponding incentive effect. These are:

(i) The causality may be in the opposite direction. A good manager will bring about good sales and/or profit performance and command a higher salary, but the resulting correlation does not imply that a manager of given ability can materially affect his salary by going for sales or profits at the expense of the other.

(ii) The studies have concentrated on the salaries of only the very top managers, either the individual with the highest remuneration or that of the top 3 to 5. Yet it is arguable that in the very large firms from which they come the power of this individual or group is to some extent circumscribed by other senior managers, by the limits to organizational control, and by their dependence on information from lower-level managers whose objectives may be rather different.

(iii) At lower levels the desire for salary will tend to be expressed as a desire for promotion. For many middle managers the link between their own actions and company performance, be it in terms of sales or profits, is frequently tenuous or difficult to discern and promotion is decided in terms of more immediate criteria such as clarity of thought and expression, energy, co-operation, etc., which may be directed to any of several main economic variables.

(iv) The correlation between sales and salary is probably the result of three very powerful forces. First, the need to offer a competitive salary at the lowest management level, where recruitment occurs; second, the severe limits to the span of control of any manager, which means larger firms need more hierarchical levels; third, the (almost) universal principle that a superior is paid more than his subordinates. The resulting salary structure may generate the desire to increase size and the number of hierarchies but it may also tend to separate performance from pay in the manager's view.

(v) Fifth, no study, except for the questionable one by Lewellyn and Huntsman, has yet been done which includes remuneration besides salary and bonuses. Given its quantitative significance, this is a severe gap.

(vi) Lower taxation of capital gains than of dividend income will increase the *shareholder*'s incentive for managers to reinvest at the expense of dividends and thus increase growth at the cost of a lower profit rate. The conflict between managers and shareholders could therefore disappear even if size is the main determinant of salary.

This debate raises another issue, namely the appropriate measure of profits. For if top management obtains the bulk of its remuneration from stocks and shares, it is dividends and capital appreciation that are important. Both are obviously dependent at least in part on profits, but are not identical with it. In as far as share valuation is a best estimate of the present value of current and future dividends and capital gains, profit could be replaced by share valuation as the presumed objective, but pursuit of size as measured by sales may be more of a constraint on maximization of stock market valuation than it is on maximization of profit. Not only may profit be sacrificed for the sake of sales, but the profits may be allocated more to retained earnings and less to dividends, thus further increasing investment, output, and sales at the expense of dividends and possibly therefore at the expense of share valuation.

Were salary the only reason to promote sales then we might conclude that the proportion of top management remuneration dependent on profits and the greater immediate effect profit seems to have as opposed to feasible growth both make the sales incentive effect relatively weak. But although the salary/sales connection has been the most studied it is quite possible that the main reason for pursuing a sales objective is its repercussions on status, power, and security. Status derived from managing a very large and therefore well-known company is almost certainly greater than that derived from high profitability provided the profit record is not notably poor. Power over resources—men, machines, and money—is undoubtedly determined primarily by size, and the power that comes from market dominance will be increased through larger size. Company survival and security is highest amongst the largest firms[75] and this may well reflect also on the security of individual managers. Monsen and Downs speculate that because shareholders are content provided their return is satisfactory, managers face an asymmetry in their rewards. Very good performance makes little difference, but bad performance can result in severe criticism, a bar to further advance, or even loss of position. This means that there is a great tendency to increase size because it reduces the variability of the returns made (see chapter 15):

In addition, large size may well decrease the probbility of new firms setting up in opposition, thus reducing uncertainty and competitive pressure, and increasing survival prospects. Indeed risk averse profit maximizers may well exhibit behaviour akin to sales maximization. In fact the desire to increase the size of operations seems to be a very powerful one in virtually all forms of organization, be they commercial, governmental, charitable, etc., and it is not surprising therefore if this is also the case in most firms.

All this strengthens the argument for seeing size as a dominant influence, but it is difficult to be very certain about such imponderables as status and power and the effect of such motivations. Furthermore, in a detailed study of the implications of different objectives (see below), Yarrow has argued that the people who rise to the top of large firms are likely to be risk averse, but that a high degree of risk aversion leads to behaviour more akin to *profit* maximization.[76] This is because aversion to risk entails aversion to avoidable non-maximization of profits with its attendant risk of takeover or removal. More generally it is possible to see both size and profit reducing insecurity directly; in the former case that associated with market and product risks, and the risk that insufficient opportunities for promotion will appear; in the latter case the insecurity associated with takeover or dismissal by shareholders. It is not self-evident which type of risk is most feared, nor even in general terms which is most likely to occur. Increasingly we are pushed into the view that both are important with no *a priori* way of assessing the priorities attached to them. How exactly they can be incorporated together in models of the firm we shall examine below.

A desire for size naturally implies a desire for growth, particularly if transfer of executives between companies is fairly limited. For any one time period they reduce to the same thing. But growth of firms,

[75] For evidence on this see G. Bannock, *The Juggernauts* (London, 1971).
[76] G. Yarrow, 'Managerial Utility Maximisation under Uncertainty', *Economica*, N.S. 40 (May 1973), 155–73.

which we examine in some detail in the next chapter, requires growth of available funds, of capital, of men, of demand, and the appropriate integration of these over time. Analysis of growth therefore requires a dynamic framework. This prevents direct comparison of growth models with the static ones examined below (although the latter have growth implications). In fact in a multi-period growth model context, the concept of size as a motive separate from that of growth has no meaning without further specification, and the only attempt to integrate size and growth objectives, by Solow, has focused on *initial* size and growth as the components of the utility function.[77] Solow himself does not see the development as very fruitful, but it seems possible at least that if there is a trade-off between initial size and growth then firms might attempt to move fairly quickly to a larger or smaller size and then adopt the long-run rate of growth which that size can permit. With this one exception, models have presumed either size or growth to be important, but not both. In that growth as an objective implies that size in many different time periods enters the utility function, it is to be preferred as an assumption to size in only one time period, but it is still limiting in the way in which it constrains the relative importance of different time-period sizes for analytical simplicity.

Yet the differences between size and growth objectives are not purely methodological. Growth even if from a small base and therefore small in absolute terms may well provide more utility than large size with no growth. This is partly psychological. Familiarity with existing positions of status and power generally reduces their utility and inspire the desire for new or more power, status, and salary. But it is also because if size is static then new opportunities are only realizable at the expense of some entrenched position, and actual reduction in status or power may be resisted very strongly indeed. Growth permits new opportunities to be acted upon without these opposing forces necessarily being triggered off. Frequently existing operations become institutionalized to the point where new activities can only occur against a background of growth. Marris goes further in suggesting that the norm of professional competence for managers includes organizing, and that absence of change, by reducing the need to organize, greatly reduces the kudos of the executive who presides over it.[78]

The emphasis on profit, size, growth, and security does not, of course, imply that no other objectives exist. Questionnaire

[77] R. Solow, 'Some Implications of Alternate Criteria for the Firm', in R. Marris, A. Wood (ed.), *The Corporate Economy* (London, 1971), 318–42.
[78] R. Marris, op. cit. 58–9.

investigations indicate the importance not only of these, but of other, sometimes vague, sometimes quite precise objectives. Cyert and March's market share and inventory goals are examples of the latter. The former are exemplified in Dent's survey, which found evidence of desires to provide a good product, 'stay ahead of the competition', provide employee welfare, and 'to be efficient'.[79] England found organizational and technical efficiency to be on a par with growth.[80] These goals tend to be ignored however, for various reasons. First, they are frequently 'contained' by the broader ones, for example, efficiency by profit. Second, they are suspect in some cases because of the public relations aspect involved in providing acceptable answers to questions about objectives. Third, objectives must be specified in a manner which is not so vague as to be inoperational, but not so detailed as to be inapplicable in anything but a very complex model. Meeting competition and maintaining inventory are examples respectively.

For all these reasons, and because analysis of growth requires examination of the co-ordinating activities of managers in a way that analysis of size does not, growth is generally the preferable objective on which to base non-profit maximizing models. None the less, as a transitional step we examine the three approaches to static size maximization so far developed and look at a number of important implications of them.

6   NON-PROFIT MAXIMIZING MODELS OF THE FIRM

The first is Baumol's familiar sales maximization model.[81] On the basis of casual empiricism Baumol thought managers appeared more concerned with sales revenue than with profits provided the latter were equal to or above some adequate level, and that beyond this minimum profit level, further increases in profit would be sacrificed if this permitted increased sales revenue.

His analysis commenced with the traditional apparatus as shown in Figure 8.1.

The total cost (TC) and revenue (TR) curves have the normal shape implied by the Marshallian analysis and the total profit (Π) curve indicates the difference between these two curves at any given output level. The profit maximizer would set output at Q_A, but the

[79] J. Dent, 'Organisational Correlates of the Goals of Business Management', *Personnel Psychology*, 12 (1959), 365–93.

[80] G. England, 'Organisational Goals & Expected Behaviour of American Managers', *Academy of Management Journal*, 10, no. 2 (1967), 107–17.

[81] W. Baumol, 'On the Theory of Oligopoly', *Economica*, N.S. 25 (Aug. 1958), 187–98.

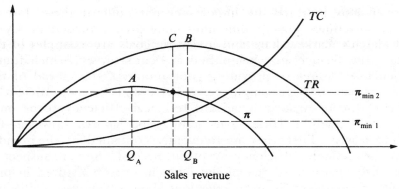

Fig. 8.1

sales revenue maximizer would choose output Q_B. The revenue maximizing output will always be above the profit maximizing output provided that total costs always rise with output, i.e. provided marginal costs are positive. For then at the profit maximizing output marginal revenue is positive and an increase in output would increase total sales revenue.

This so far presupposes no constraint on sales revenue maximization, but Baumol points out that the profits generated will have to meet some minimum profitability constraint. The factors determining this are not analysed, however. If in Figure 8.1 the constraint were to be at level Π_{MIN1}, the constraint would not be effective, as profits at Q_B are in excess of this. A constraint at level Π_{MIN2} however would be effective, preventing the firm from moving to point *B*, and forcing it to accept the highest revenue consistent with the constraint, namely point *C*, defined by the interaction of the total profit curve and the minimum profit constraint line. If the constraint were equal to, or above, maximum profit, then the sales revenue maximizer would choose the same output as the profit maximizer.

Baumol extends this analysis with two important and complementing modifications. First he views the objective as being *long-run* sales revenue maximization, and second he assumes that firms can use the profits in excess of the required minimum to influence the demand conditions facing the firm through marketing investment and product development. The demand curve moves outwards from the origin, and sales increase for any given price level. Given that any expenditure on advertising, etc. increases sales at any particular price, and therefore increases sales revenue, long-run sales revenue maximization requires that all profit in excess of the minimum be spent in such a way. It therefore follows that long-run sales revenue maximization will always lead to the profit constraint being operative. This is shown in Figure 8.2. This does not affect the conclusion

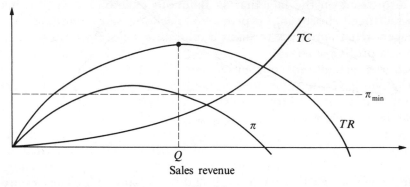

Fig. 8.2

that $Q_{SMAX} \geqslant Q_{\Pi MAX}$. It does mean, however, that a change in production costs, by altering profit, will generally lead to a change in price and output, whereas this would not be the case if actual profit were in excess of the minimum required.

This simple model has raised a whole range of questions in the theory of the firm, some of which cannot be adequately answered within the static framework of Baumol's model. For example, it directs attention to the decisions that determine the use of profits as between advertising, investment, and dividends, and indicates the importance of analysing the effect of advertising on sales revenue. More serious, it is difficult to give an adequate explanation of the size of the profit constraint in the Baumol formulation of the model, and it is the nature of the constraint, plus the predictions of the model, that have received most attention. The two are of course interdependent.

On the question of the constraint, Fisher, in reviewing Baumol's model, suggested that a different formulation was more plausible, namely that firms would try to maximize short-run profit, subject to a minimum sales or market share constraint.[82] The rationale for this was that firms would need a rule of thumb for trying to maximize long-run profit in uncertain or difficult-to-ascertain conditions with little knowledge of whether current and future profits were in conflict with each other. The implication of the rule was that increased current profit which did not reduce sales or market share

[82] F. Fisher, Review of W. Baumol, *Business Behaviour, Value and Growth*, in *J.P.E.* 68, no. 3 (June 1960), 314–15.

would not be seen as conflicting with long-run profit, whereas that which did would be seen·as being obtained at the expense of long-run profit, and therefore sacrificed. But this alternative formulation was also based on the fact that *all* Baumol's examples were of firms who sacrificed short-run profit to avoid declining sales, implying that managers felt themselves to be at a minimum sales constraint rather than at a profit constraint.

Osborne attempted, but unsuccessfully, to show that the two alternatives gave the same predictions.[83] But there were none the less several important consequences of his analysis and Fisher's reply.[84] First, there is no mechanism (nor is it easy to imagine one) to ensure that sales in excess of the constraint are forgone in favour of short-run profit, on a par with Baumol's advertising which ensures that all profit in excess of the constraint is forgone in favour of sales revenue. Clearly there are difficulties about the determinacy of a model where the constraint is not always effective. Second, even if sales are taken as a current proxy for future sales, it does not follow that either sales or current profits are necessarily the maximand with the other the constraint. Either formulation is plausible. Yet the two approaches cannot statistically be distinguished unless the constraint equation is known. Third, the stipulation of these constraints is rather unsatisfactory partly because more needs to be known about what determines their value, but mainly because it seems more plausible and more general to presume that *both* are constraints. This approach has been used in some cases,[85] but gives complete indeterminacy irrespective of whether it is feasible or not to meet the constraints. Another objection that has been made by Shepherd is that large managerial firms are, as Baumol himself argued, generally oligopolistic, and any resultant kinked demand curve would make profit and revenue maximization identical.[86] We have, however, seen that kinks are unlikely to last very long, or long enough therefore to make much difference to the long-term profit-revenue trade-off (see pp. 144–49).

Furthermore, different constraint specifications give different predictions. For example, Baumol's profit constraint implies cost minimization. But a rate of return on capital constraint, which may be much more plausible, implies higher than minimum costs.[87]

[83] D. Osborne, 'On the Goals of the Firm'. *Q.J.E.* 78, no. 4 (Nov. 1964), 592–603.

[84] F. Fisher, 'On The Goals of the Firm: Comment', *Q.J.E.*, 79, no. 3 (Aug. 1965), 500–3.

[85] See for example R. Wright, *The Investment Decision in Industry* (London, 1964).

[86] W. Shepherd, 'On Sales Maximising and Oligopoly Behaviour', *Economica*, N.S. 29 (Nov. 1962), 420–4.

[87] Note that such a constraint, combined with a fixed capital-output ratio, implies full cost pricing.

In particular Yarrow has presented a more plausible and more general constraint specification which generates quite different predictions from Baumol's model.[88] He argues that the constraint on managerial discretion to pursue a non-profit maximizing strategy is determined by the activities of wealth maximizing shareholders. The possibility of their removing managers or selling shares and creating conditions ripe for takeover means that there is a constraint on the *deviation* between the maximum stock market valuation and the actual one that results from the firm's behaviour. The size of the maximum deviation itself depends on the size distribution of shareholders and the cost of actual intervention to enforce policies acceptable to shareholders. A similar type of constraint specification applies if the threat to managerial discretion comes from a wealth maximizing firm contemplating a takeover.[89] In its most general form we have a model of the form:

$$\text{Maximize } U(x)$$

$$\text{Subject to } V(x,y) \geqslant V^*(y) - C$$

where x is a vector of utility-yielding decision variables
    y is a vector of parameters affecting market valuations
    $V^*(y)$ is the maximum valuation
and C is a parameter reflecting enforcement costs.

The dependence of the constraint on maximum valuation (or any proxy for it) reflects an opportunity–cost approach which is much more realistic than an arbitrarily given constraint, and Yarrow goes on to indicate the significance of the reformulation by examining the Baumol model with a constraint of the form

$$\Pi_{(q)} \geqslant \Pi_{(q*)} - C$$

instead of, as implied by Baumol

$$\Pi_{(q)} \geqslant Z$$

For simplicity, advertising is ignored, but the constraints still regarded as binding. Table 8.2 summarizes the predicted effect on

[88] G. Yarrow, 'On the Predictions of the Managerial Theory of the Firm', *J.I.E.* 24, no. 4 (June 1976), 267–79.

[89] It also applies if the threat is from another *utility*-maximizing firm provided only that the latter is at its own valuation constraint and the potential victim recognizes a sufficient rather than necessary constraint.

TABLE 8.2

	Profit-max. *Model*	*Sales-max.* *Baumol constraint*	*Sales-max.* *Yarrow constraint*
Increase in Lump-sum Tax or fixed cost	0	—	0
Increase in Profits Tax rate	0	—	+

output of various changes on the profit maximizing model, the sales-maximizing model with Baumol's constraint, and the sales maximizing model with Yarrow's constraint. The Baumol results follow from the fact that a rise in any type of cost or any type of tax will reduce profit below the constraint level and therefore require a reduction in output from the previous optimum to permit an increase in gross profit. Under the Yarrow specification managers are able to *expand* output as the profits tax rate increases, because the opportunity cost to shareholders of managerial utility maximization—that is, the extent to which post-tax profits are below their maximum—goes *down*. A lump-sum tax change on the other hand has no effect because it changes both $\Pi_{(q)}$ and $\Pi_{(q*)}$ by the same amount.[90] The same of course applies for any fixed cost change. Equally startling changes of prediction are then shown to occur with both the Williamson model (see below) and the Marris growth model (see Chapter 9), using which Yarrow examines the effect of changes in the cost of capital and the introduction of employee profit-sharing schemes.

Although these results indicate that the incidence of taxation will differ according to which model is correct, the most far-reaching conclusion is the most obvious, namely that price and output predictions are as much a function of the constraint specified as the maximand.

In an earlier article, Yarrow attempted to remove a constraint specification altogether by reinterpreting it.[91] He argued that in general there would be a continuous trade-off between managerial utility on the one hand and the probability of avoiding shareholder

---

[90] A simple example illustrates these. (i) Suppose maximum pre-tax profit equals £100, the tax rate equals 40 per cent, and the constraint is that no more than £24 of post-tax profit must be forgone. The minimum acceptable pre-tax profit is then £60, as this sacrifices £40 pre-tax profit which equals £24 post-tax profit. If the tax-rate goes to 50 per cent the minimum pre-tax profit falls to £52, sacrificing £48 pre-tax profit, but again only £24 post-tax profit. The fall in required pre-tax profit permits an expansion of output. (ii) If, with the same constraint and same maximum pre-tax profit, the tax is a lump-sum one, the minimum pre-tax profit is £76 irrespective of the size of the lump-sum tax.

[91] G. Yarrow, op. cit. 1973.

intervention and loss of management position on the other. The further the discretion to pursue non-profit maximizing was used, the greater the probability of failing to survive. Thus utility maximization under probabilistic uncertainty was a more general formulation which could avoid the need for a constraint specification separate from the utility function. The basic picture is summarized in Figure 8.3. The curve *AB* shows that the probability of surviving is greatest when sales revenue (or whatever utility-generating variable is selected) is at the level which maximizes profit ($q*$), but gets progressively lower as sales revenue rises above or below this level, because of the corresponding fall in profits. Line *CD* is an indifference curve for the managers, as between utility-generating sales revenue and the probability of being able to obtain that utility. Sales revenue q' is then chosen.[92]

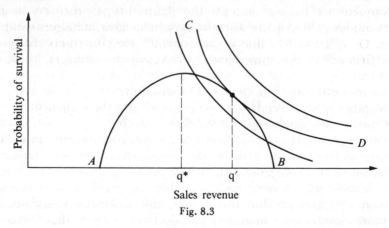

Fig. 8.3

Several predictions in comparative statics follow from this—in particular, and as confirmed by Yarrow's later article discussed above, that an increase in the profits tax rate will increase output. The reasoning is basically the same, namely that the higher profits tax rate *reduces* the difference between any actual post-tax profit and the maximum, hence increasing the probability of survival and permitting output expansion. A lump-sum change again has no effect.

It is not clear as yet whether this approach or the generalized constraint formulation is preferable and the difference in economic terms may not be great. More fundamental is Yarrow's demonstration of the dependence of prediction on the rather arbitrary selection

---

[92] Formally this is very similar to the Marris growth model described in detail in the next chapter.

of constraints. Yarrow's cannot be preferred just because it is based on managerial discretion and permitted deviations from profit maximizing behaviour. For example, if the probability of surviving is a function not of profits forgone but the *proportion* of profits forgone, then a rise in lump-sum taxes, as in the Baumol model, reduces output, while a rise in profits tax rate has no effect, as in the profit maximizing model.[93] Both differ from the Yarrow model. In fact a main determinant of whether a shareholder takes action is likely to be the proportion of his personal wealth in the particular firm. This is quite independent of the firm itself and unknown in general to the managers; hence the potential superiority of the probabilistic approach.

These developments of the Baumol model have focused on the constraints on managerial discretion to increase sales. The second development we look at accepts the Baumol-type profit constraint and examines in detail the discretionary behaviour managers exhibit. This is O. Williamson's line of approach.[94] He constructs the goals of the firm out of the immediate objectives of its managers. These he argues are:

(i) Salaries plus other monetary compensation.
(ii) Number of staff reporting to a manager and their quality.
(iii) Control over investment of the firm's funds.
(iv) Perquisites such as company cars, lavish offices, etc., in excess of those necessary for the firm's operations. This is a form of organisational or management slack (see p. 250).

All of the first three, and probably the fourth as well, are increased by large size, but this model, unlike Baumol's, focuses on the more immediate managerial objectives rather than size as measured by sales. The model is summarized in Figure 8.4.

Formally the utility function contains: (*a*) 'excess' expenditure on staff (S). This is the difference between maximum profit (Π_{MAX}) and actual profit (Π_A) as a proxy for (i) and (ii) above. Increases in S are assumed to increase output. (*b*) Management slack (M) which is

---

[93] Simple examples can again be used to illustrate these. (i) If maximum pre-tax profits are £100, the constraint is that post-tax profits must be at least 60 per cent of their maximum, and the profits--tax rate is 40 per cent, the minimum pre-tax profit is £60. This gives £36 post-tax profit which is 60 per cent of the maximum of £60. If the tax rate rises to 50 per cent, the minimum pre-tax profit is still £60. Post-tax profit is £30 which is 60 per cent of the maximum of £50. (ii) If, with the same maximum pre-tax profits, and same constraint, there is a lump-sum tax of £40, the minimum pre-tax profit is £76. Post-tax they are then £36 which is 60 per cent of the maximum post-tax profit of £60. If the lump-sum tax goes to £50, the minimum acceptable pre-tax profit rises to £80. This gives post-tax profits of £30 which are 60 per cent of the maximum of £50. The rise in profit would necessitate a fall in output.

[94] O. Williamson, op. cit.

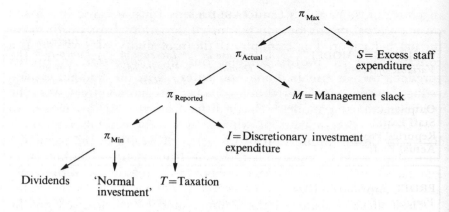

Fig. 8.4

absorbed as cost. This is the difference between 'actual profits' and 'reported profits' (Π_R), being in effect profits absorbed directly by the managers in kind. (c) Discretionary investment expenditure (I), i.e. the amount in excess of what is necessary to maintain profits at the minimum level acceptable to the shareholders (Π_{MIN}). Pursuit of all these is constrained by the need for reported profits to be acceptable. All this can be summarized as. follows, using the above notation and T for total taxes.

$$\text{Maximize } U = U(S,M,I)$$

$$\text{Subject to } \Pi_R \geqslant \Pi_{MIN} + T$$

$$\text{Where} \quad S = \Pi_{MAX} - \Pi_A$$
$$M = \Pi_A - \Pi_R$$
$$I = \Pi_R - \Pi_{MIN} - T$$

Apart from output (Q) the managers can select S, which together determine price and actual profits Π_A, and M which then determines Π_R. I is then uniquely determined because Π_{MIN} and T are given. The model is solved by substituting the equation for S, M, and I into the utility function and setting the partial derivatives with respect to Q, S, and M equal to zero. This shows that such a firm has higher staff expenditure and more management 'slack' in the form of perks than will a profit maximizer.[95] Williamson contrasts the two more starkly by deriving the two sets of results in Table 8.3.

[95] The managerial utility maximizer will still equate MC and MR however, in order to maximize the items S, M, and I which profits make possible.

TABLE 8.3

WILLIAMSON MODEL *Variable affected*	*Increase in Demand*	*Increase in Profits Tax Rate*	*Increase in Lump-sum Tax (or any fixed cost)*
Output	+	+	−
Staff Exp.	+	+	−
Reported Profit Actual Profit	−	−	+

PROFIT MAXIMIZATION *Variable affected*	*Increase in Demand*	*Increase in Profits Tax Rate*	*Increase in Lump-sum Tax (or any fixed cost)*
Output	+	0	0
Staff Exp.	+	0	0
Reported Profit Actual Profit	0	0	0

Taking each column in turn, an increase in demand increases output and staff expenditure in both models, but the possibility of increasing management slack reduces the ratio of reported to actual profits in Williamson's model, whereas it has no effect in the profit maximizing model because this ratio is *always* unity (zero slack). The tax effects are also different from the familiar ones of the profit maximization model. An increase in the profits tax rate penalizes reported profits and discretionary investment, leading to a reduction of them in favour of staff expenditure and slack, the former increasing output. A lump-sum tax simply raises the pre-tax profit constraint implied by the minimum required post-tax profit, squeezing slack, discretionary investment, and staff expenditure, which in turn reduces output. As an unavoidable (fixed cost) squeeze on companies probably does reduce slack, staff, and perks, while high proportionate tax rates probably do stimulte higher company staff and perks expenditure, the Williamson model seems quite realistic. Of course, the effects might be small, making the profit maximizing model more useful, but it is difficult to correctly identify slack, 'discretionary investment', and even 'staff expenditurures', still more to obtain data on all of them, in order to find out how significant are the effects. Anothe difficulty is again the static framework. How realistic, for example, is it to presume output and discretionary investment move in opposite directions in response to a changed tax rate? Then there is Yarrow's point again that the results crucially depend on the specification of the constraint. For example a Yarrow-type formulation implies that staff expenditure will not respond to a change in a lump-sum tax. Finally, there is Williamson's own argument that the M-form of organization may mean that such a model as this is relevant only to the quasi-firms it embraces and for short periods of time. In the longer term the internal and direct requirement for high profit performance may seriously undermine the scope for slack and unjustifiable staff expenditure, while 'discretionary' investment may only be maximized through maximization of reported profits. Over all, therefore, this approach appears to add to the factors likely to be important in firms' behaviour, but does not really itself provide the basis for a general 'managerial' theory of the firm capable of superseding the profit maximizing model.

7   CONCLUSIONS

This chapter has ranged rather widely over the very diverse literature on firms' behaviour and objectives. Our main conclusions are that:

(i) The internal structure of firms makes it necessary to examine models of the firm which incorporate non-profit maximizing objectives.

(ii) This is capable of producing a variety of models with notably different predictions from profit maximizing ones, and from each other.

(iii) The constraint on managerial motivation exercised by shareholders is equally important in explaining the behaviour of firms and in deciding on the most appropriate motivational assumptions to be made.

(iv) A desire for growth arising out of the advantages to managers of large size is the major addition necessary to the motivational assumptions on which theories of firms' behaviour are based.

The next chapter continues the analysis of the active firm by developing a model which recognizes these points.

THE GROWTH OF FIRMS

1 INTRODUCTION

This chapter has three main functions. First, it presents and examines in some detail a theory of what we have termed in Chapter 1 the active firm. This implies:

(i) Not only price/output decisions, but also finance decisions and firms' expenditure decisions must be incorporated. Under the finance heading are included decisions on how much to pay out in dividends and how much to raise through borrowing and the issue of new equity. Under the expenditure heading are included decisions on fixed capital investment, market investment, and research and development.

(ii) The theory must embrace the essential circularity of relationships involved in firms' behaviour. Demand and supply conditions which via price, cost, and output determine profitability are themselves affected by how those profits are utilized.

(iii) The theory must partly focus on the firm itself as an organization able to manipulate to some extent the competitive environment in which it finds itself, rather than as just a passive unit whose performance depends on various structural characteristics of the market of which it forms part. This naturally raises the difficult problem of identifying what constraints, if any, operate on such a firm, given that the traditional ones—consumer preferences, actual and potential competition, costs, and technology—are all manipulable by the firm itself.

Second, and in keeping with some of the arguments outlined earlier which led to more recent developments, the theory attempts to be more 'realistic' by encompassing many commonly observed characteristics of existing companies not included in the traditional approach. These characteristics have all been discussed previously (see in particular Chapter 1, pp. 20-5, and Chapter 8, pp. 238-43). Apart from the range of decisions incorporated and the active nature of the firm already referred to above, the major ones may be summarized as:

(i) The predominance of multi-product firms of very large size. This suggests that there may be no limit to the size of a firm in the long run. Only if there is a constraint on how rapidly a firm can expand would there then be any limit on its size and then only in the short run.

(ii) Most assets are controlled by managers in firms owned by share-holders. As we have seen this raises important new issues about the determination of policy and location of effective power within a firm. It also means that a firm has to be concerned with its performance not only in its product markets, but in the capital market also.

(iii) The possibility of takeovers occurring creates new opportunities for firms, but new constraints on its behaviour as well.

It should be reiterated, however, that complete 'realism' is neither possible nor desirable. The argument for trying to incorporate the above features rests on the belief that this will provide a more intelligible picture of the systematic aspects of firms' behaviour and a more fertile base from which to deduce testable hypotheses.

The third function of this chapter is to present a theory in which firms are characterized as trying to maximize their rate of growth rather than profit. The rationale for this was established in the previous chapter, where it was argued (*a*) that the desire for such things as salary, status, power, and security led to the pursuit of size in addition to, or at the expense of, profit, and (*b*) that the best way to allow for size when time enters the analysis is to presume a growth maximization objective. This also avoids the problem that size in the short term might be increased at the expense of size in the future (making a static size-maximization objective potentially very misleading). Remembering however the problems involved in switching from profit to other objectives, and the need to provide testable hypotheses, it will be important to examine how, if at all, the growth objective differs in its implications from that of profit maximization.

The next section presents the basic model of the growth of the firm, attributable to Marris. Sections 3–5 look in more detail at each of the main aspects of the basic model, namely the conditions and constraints on the demand side, the managerial side, and the finance side. Section 3 also tackles the difficult issue of methodology in this new approach, as this is far from uncontroversial in a number of respects. Section 6 reviews the growing body of empirical studies concerned with testing the impact of different motivational assumptions in general and the Marris model in particular.

2   THE MARRIS GROWTH MODEL

(a) The growth of supply and demand

In 1963 Marris presented a coherent and integrated theory of the growth maximizing managerial enterprise.[1] The presentation was

[1] R. Marris, 'A Model of the Managerial Enterprise', *Q.J.E.* 77, no. 2 (May 1963), 185–209.

subsequently modified by Marris,[2] and the new formulation, which we follow here, has become the standard one for analysis of the managerially controlled firm.

As in traditional theory it is useful to examine supply elements and demand elements and then put them together, but now it will be the *growth* of supply and *growth* of demand with which we shall be concerned. As a firm grows over the long term it will require more of all inputs, physical and human, to match increases in demand for its products. In trying to avoid both spare capacity and excess demand, senior management of a firm will spend considerable time on trying to bring not only existing supply of resources and the demands upon them into line, but also their future rates of growth. It therefore seems plausible to argue that in a growth context the equating of growth of supply of resources and growth of the demand upon them is an equilibrium condition.

This intuitive argument is much strengthened by two other factors. First, we are going to be concerned not with firms' growth in one year or over three years, but with the long-term trend rate of growth over a very long period. In this case, non-equalization of the growths of supply and demand would lead not just to spare capacity, for example, but *ever-growing* spare capacity. This is theoretically implausible, and empirically unsound. Second, to facilitate analysis, the Marris model is a *steady-state* one. That is to say, it is formulated in terms of a steady-state system in which all characteristics of the firm—assets, employment, sales, profit, etc.—are presumed to grow at the same constant exponential rate over time. Other potentially variable characteristics which are measured as ratios of two of these, e.g. the profit margin, the rate of return on capital, the capital–output ratio, then become constant and may be referred to as 'state' variables. The steady-state concept is not without its problems, and will be examined more fully later, but two points should be noted. First, it is the need to simplify the theory that leads to its introduction rather than any real-world characteristics it is wished to incorporate. In fact, corporations appear not to exhibit constant growth as defined, nor constant values of 'state' variables, and at best can only be interpreted as moving from one steady-state growth path to another. Second, the steady-state assumption is a very much stronger reason than the previous argument for assuming the equality of growth of supply and demand. Steady-state growth by implication continues at a constant exponential rate for ever. Once the firm has selected values for its decision variables, e.g. growth rate, profit margin, etc., the latter are presumed fixed and therefore must be

[2] R. Marris, *The Economic Theory of Managerial Capitalism* (London, 1966), 249–65.

such as to equate the supply and demand growth rates, if *permanently* growing excess capacity or demand forgone are both to be avoided.

The next step is to give precise meaning to the two growth rates introduced. This is straightforward on the supply side. As the firm's assets, of all kinds, and employment grow at the same constant rate, assuming constant factor prices the growth rate of productive resources can be measured by the rate of growth of the firm's asset base. The latter is defined as (i) physical assets; this includes fixed assets and stocks at replacement value,[3] (ii) financial assets (net) at current market value including cash, (iii) goodwill mainly generated by marketing expenditure etc., and (iv) know-how as a result of R and D expenditure.[4] The demand side is more problematical. For any one product with a specified price it is possible to define the growth of demand in physical units. But once we wish to introduce growth by diversification into new products we cannot use this approach. We can measure growth of demand as the growth of sales revenue, but in a real-world corporation this could easily cause distortion. The introduction of a product with a new ratio of capital employed to sales value would have different effects on the rate of supply and demand growth, and this could result from (i) a different capital–output ratio (output measured as value-added) or (ii) a different value-added to sales-value ratio as a result of more or less vertical integration. Fortunately these problems disappear in the steady-state system. Both ratios are constant and so demand as measured by sales value grows at the same constant rate as gross assets.[5]

(b) The growth-of-demand function

In identifying the main determinants of the growth of demand, Marris recognized that firms are usually multi-product and that diversification into new products is not just an important vehicle of competition, but the major engine of corporate growth. When a new product is introduced its subsequent performance may be categorized as being in one or other of two classes. In the first, sales start

---

[3] i.e. the estimated cost of replacing the assets at current prices. In a steady-state system with constant depreciation rate and inflation rate, this growth rate will be the same as that of fixed assets at written down historic cost book value (or any other generally used measure).

[4] The asset base may be referred to as 'capital' or 'capital employed', or gross assets.

[5] In fact such difficulties are also circumvented in that the demand side of the model is aggregated into a growth–profit relationship in which it is less important how growth of demand is measured than that the effect on profitability of a change in corporate growth *via the demand side* can be identified. This point however is more sensibly established later on.

from zero, increase somewhat as customers try the product and as a result of marketing efforts to launch it, but then level off as potential customers become aware that the product is not sufficiently competitive or attractive. After a while, sales start to fall back. The product is regarded as a failure and eventually withdrawn. This is shown by line *A* in Figure 9.1. The second alternative is that sales of the product rise quite strongly because it does meet customer needs competitively. A significant share of the product market is established and the successful diversification becomes a regular product-line for the firm. (If the product is entirely new the share may be

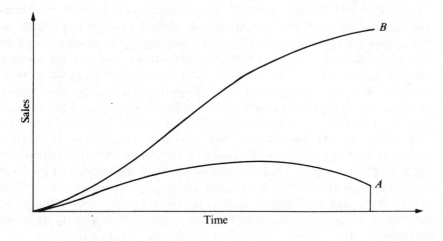

Fig. 9.1

100 per cent for some time, but in general, even with patent protection, imitations will be introduced which will result in a less than 100 per cent share of the effective market.) Eventually however the market share will tend to stabilize, primarily because of the greater inroads being made on competitors and the intensified competition by means of which they react. Beyond that time sales tend to grow only as fast as the over-all market. This is shown by line *B* which continues to rise but at a slower rate once market share has stabilized. In practice of course many products will follow some intermediate course, but the analysis is facilitated without any distortion by thinking in terms of diversifications which are either successes or failures.

In order to grow any faster than the rate of growth of the markets in which the firm establishes itself it must carry out further successful diversification. Thus we may write

$$g_D = f_1(\hat{d}) \tag{1}$$

where g_D is growth of demand and $\hat{d}$ is the rate of successful diversification. This may be regarded as holding even if the diversification results from other objectives than growth, for example the exploitation of higher profits in a new area, the need to diversify in order to provide more security against deterioration of business conditions in any one market, etc. The function f_1 reflects the nature of the market opportunities available and the rate of growth of the markets into which the firm diversifies.

(c) The growth-of-supply function

The rate of growth of assets equals the ratio of new assets acquired to existing assets. If new investment is regarded as covering the acquisition of all new assets, both fixed and current, the growth rate of assets becomes the ratio of investment to capital employed. This crucially depends on the finance available for new investment. There are primarily three types of source—retained earnings; new borrowing, be it non-marketable, e.g. from a bank, or marketable in the form of a new debenture or company bond; and the issue of new equity shares to new and/or existing shareholders. The latter may be individuals, financial institutions such as pensions funds, other companies, or even the firm's own managers and/or work-force.

Initially, suppose the firm has no recourse to external finance, i.e. borrowing or equity issue. The new investment then equals retained earnings. If the retention ratio, defined as the ratio of retained earnings to total earnings is denoted by r, profit by Π, and new investment by I (and ignoring tax complications),

$$I = r\Pi$$

and the growth of supply

$$g_s = \frac{I}{K} = r\frac{\Pi}{K} = rp$$

where K is the capital employed and p is the rate of return on capital. Thus the growth of supply of resources is a direct linear function of the rate of return on capital. Given that investment represents the employment of new funds and assuming that K is a measure of funds tied up in existing assets, g_s may also be regarded as the growth of supply of funds.

When external borrowing and new equity issue are introduced, the analysis, though less precise, is essentially the same. In this case the total funds that can be raised for new investment will exceed retained earnings, but will still over the long term be proportional to total earnings. This is because the higher the profits of a firm the more funds it will generally be possible to raise from external suppliers of funds.[6] Shareholders will expect a higher return in the long run and providers of loan capital will regard the company as subject to less risk of bankruptcy. Again by dividing through by capital employed we can see that the higher the rate of return on capital the higher the rate of growth of supply of funds. Thus we may write

$$g_s = \frac{I}{K} = \alpha \frac{\Pi}{K} = \alpha p$$

where the value of α indicates the amount of new investment financed per unit of profit earned.

How is the value of α determined? Clearly there is some absolute maximum in the sense that the retention ratio cannot be above unity and there will be limits to the amount of external finance that will be provided given the firm's profit rate. One might suppose that a management engaged in maximizing growth would set α equal to this maximum, but this is not in fact the case. Marris argued that each of the main ways of obtaining a higher α eventually has some disadvantages for shareholders. A higher retention ratio means lower current dividends and shareholders may not be indifferent to this change in the form of their earnings;[7] shareholders may estimate that managements with a higher rate of new equity issue will find it harder to utilize the proceeds as profitably as the funds could be deployed elsewhere; higher borrowing faces not only this problem but also that of saddling the firm with larger prior fixed charges in the form of interest payments due as a result of the borrowing. After a point therefore, a higher α results in the shares being less attractive than those of other companies. This implies a lower share price, making the firm more open to possible takeover by other companies. So the firm's management, concerned for its security and wishing to avoid the loss of its control and perhaps its salary, status, and power thereby, is faced with a maximum value of α denoted α^*, beyond which the risk of takeover becomes unacceptably high. We may therefore

[6] See Chapter 10 for elaboration of the supply of external funds.
[7] See Chapter 10, section 3.

write as the growth-of-supply function:

$$g_s = \alpha p \qquad \alpha \leqslant \alpha^* \tag{2}$$

where α^* is determined by the risk-averseness of the management, the shareholders' view of the riskiness of the financial structure of the firm, and the management's assessment of the likelihood of a takeover being embarked upon. (A more detailed and specific analysis of this occurs in section 5.)

(d) The cost-of-expansion function

Next we must ask what determines the rate of successful diversification. Given its value to management in generating growth of demand, what limits it? The answer is that there are significant costs attached to expanding by successful diversification and these costs of expansion all reduce the firm's rate of return on capital. To illustrate clearly the argument we will proceed in two stages. First the relationship may be written in a general formulation as

$$d = f_2 \frac{1}{P} \tag{3a}$$

By definition
$$P = \frac{\Pi}{K} = \frac{\Pi}{K} \cdot \frac{Q}{Q} = \frac{\Pi}{Q} \cdot \frac{Q}{K} = \frac{m}{v}$$

where Q is output, m is the profit margin, Π/Q, and v is the capital–output ratio, K/Q. Thus the cost-of-expansion function may be written as

$$d = f_2 \left(\frac{1}{m} \cdot v \right) \tag{3b}$$

Second, we may examine Marris's arguments concerning the two elements of this relationship and hence the view that, *ceteris paribus*, successful diversification and the rate of return on capital are inversely related. First, he argued that three factors were predominant in promoting growth through successful diversification. (i) Higher expenditure on advertising and other promotional and market activities though maybe facing diminishing returns would generally result in a higher growth rate for a firm by making more diversifications more successful than otherwise. (ii) Higher levels of expenditure on product (or process) research and development, would, by making products more suitable and more reliable, have a similar effect. (iii) Adopting a lower price than other firms would also enhance growth by attracting more customers. (The specific sense in which this is true is examined in more detail in section 3.) If the expenditures are regarded as capital costs then they result in a higher capital–output ratio. If they are regarded as a current cost they result in a lower profit margin, as does a lower level of prices. These confirm equation ($3b$). In all cases the rate of return on capital associated with faster successful diversification is lower,[8] as shown in equation ($3a$).

The use of the *ceteris paribus* assumption in the above argument must be explored a little. Clearly the taking-up of an opportunity of a new diversification into a very strong and buoyant market may permit faster growth of demand *and* higher average profit margins. But with any new opportunity, for a given profit margin there is a maximum to the growth of demand that can be generated. Faster growth than this via better utilization of the opportunity can only be achieved at the expense of the profit margin. Assuming that the firm will, for any profit margin, strive to obtain the maximum growth of demand consistent with that margin, we can infer that, *ceteris paribus*, growth of demand and the profit margin are inversely related.

Second, it must be asked what is happening to the firm's efficiency as the rate of diversification increases. There are, at any time, limits to the organizational and decision-taking capacity of managers. If they attempt to carry out a high rate of diversification then fewer management resources can be diverted to each one. This will result in the technical, financial, marketing, and development aspects of each one being less well researched or implemented, so that the proportion of failures may well rise. If this happens there may well be a tendency towards excess capacity in the firm, raising the capital–output ratio. Even in a steady-state system it would not be possible to avoid this by reducing the investment rate, because it will not be known in advance which diversifications will be failures.

In addition, there will be more errors of decision-taking. If too much capacity is created, the capital–output ratio will rise. If too little capacity is created, output will be constrained and the capital–output ratio will be at (or possibly slightly below) its normal planned level. On balance, therefore, bigger errors in investment planning will raise the capital–output ratio.

Finally, the firm may try to avoid these difficulties by recruiting new managers at a faster rate. This means that the faster a firm

[8] This is of course exacerbated if there are diminishing returns to diversification.

diversifies, the higher the proportion of managers who are relatively new to the firm and the shorter therefore the average length of service of the managerial group. This in turn will be one of the main determinants of the efficiency of the management. Again, therefore, after a point, adoption of a faster rate of diversification implies a lower level of managerial efficiency and, via the effects described above, a tendency to generate a higher capital–output ratio, as shown in equations (3a) and (3b).

(e) The complete model

We may now pull together the relationships of the last four sections. In equation form they are:

(1) $\quad g_d = f_1(d)$

(2) $\quad g_s = \alpha^* p$

(3) $\quad d = f_2\left(\dfrac{1}{p}\right) = f_2\left(\dfrac{1}{m} \cdot v\right)$

(4) $\quad g_s = g_d$

To solve the model, equation (3) as expressed in terms of the rate of return on capital, p, is substituted into (1), giving

(5) $\quad g_d = f_3\left(\dfrac{1}{p}\right)$

In other words, the growth of demand is an inverse function of the rate of return on capital because faster growth of demand via more rapid diversification either requires a lower profit margin, which lowers the return on capital, or leads to a higher capital–output ratio, which also lowers the return on capital or both.Equations (2), (4), and (5) together uniquely determine both the firm's rate of return on capital (profit rate) and growth rate.

Marris developed a very useful way of presenting the model diagrammatically, which follows directly from equations (2), (4), and (5), with the firm's growth rate plotted on the horizontal axis and profit rate on the vertical axis. As both the growth of demand and growth of supply are a function of only one variable, namely the profit rate, both can be plotted on this graph and their intersection identified. Figure 9.2 is based on Marris's diagram.

As it stands, the growth-of-supply function is the equation of a straight line through the origin. In practice a certain minimum profit rate would normally be necessary before any funds were made

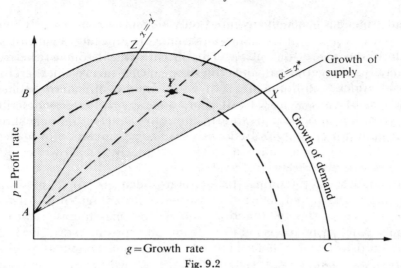

Fig. 9.2
Reproduced by permission of Macmillan, London & Basingstoke.

available for expansionary investment and therefore we draw the line
AX intersecting the vertical axis at a positive value. Its gradient is
$1/\alpha^*$.

As regards the growth-of-demand function, BC, the argument so
far has unambiguously generated an inverse growth–profit relationship. In fact Marris argued that at very low growth rates the
relationship would be direct, only becoming inverse after a certain
growth rate had been reached. The reasons for this are, first, that with
zero growth and no diversification at all, it is likely that some very
profitable opportunities are being missed. Increasing the growth rate
to a positive level might well increase the firm's average profit margin
because of the relatively high margin chargeable in the new market
by comparison with that in the current 'saturated' products. Second,
any successful diversification is likely to earn relatively high profits
in its initial stages when it has a temporary monopoly, with subsequent competition whittling the profits down. Some growth through
diversification (as opposed to none) has the consequence that there
will always be some product or products in the initial phase earning
temporary monopoly profit. This again suggests that moving from
zero to limited growth may increase profit by permitting higher
average margins. Finally, as was argued in Chapter 8, zero growth
may well present a very dull, stultifying, and rigid business environment which depresses managerial efficiency. This arises partly because
any switching of resources must be at the expense of others who
probably have an entrenched interest in preventing a reduction of
resources under their control, and also because the zero-growth

management is generally required only to repeat continuously fairly standard, well-understood, and unchallenging procedures which offer little or no scope for initiative. It is management of *change* that is generally recognized as the challenge facing management. Little kudos attaches to the manager of a stationary firm, indeed considerable loss of prestige may result. For all these reasons, some growth, by providing room for flexibility, initiative, exercise of managerial ability, and prestige, will frequently lead to a stimulation of management efficiency, and thus via previous arguments to a lower capital–output ratio and higher profit rate.

In Figure 9.2, therefore, the growth-of-demand curve shows the maximum growth of demand consistent with any given profit rate. The growth-of-supply function shows the maximum growth of supply that can be generated from any profit rate, given the characteristics which determine α^*. Their intersection at point X marks the unique steady-state balance growth/profit point, and nearly all the discussion of firms' growth rates can be interpreted as attempting to identify the factors which determine the location of this point.

Before proceeding to examine them in detail, it is necessary to add that Figure 9.2 may be reinterpreted in a rather more flexible and general manner. If a firm does *not* achieve maximum efficiency for any reason and gets less than maximum growth for any given profit rate, then the growth-of-demand curve on which it is in effect operating lies inside the one shown. Thus only points on or inside the function shown are feasible. On the supply size, management can in principle choose subject α to $\alpha \leqslant \alpha^*$, and by so doing determine the gradient of the supply-growth curve. Points below the line AX, reached only by adopting an α above α^*, are regarded as too risky, but if lower values of α than α^* are chosen then the supply growth curve becomes steeper,[9] giving a balanced growth point above the line AX. We may conclude that, dependent on efficiency and financial decisions, the management may locate anywhere within the shaded area, for example at point Y. If, however, the management wishes to maximize growth subject to the security constraint given by α^* then it will aim to achieve point X, the point in the feasible area furthest to the right.

The advantage of this approach is that we can now not only examine the effect of different degrees of efficiency, aversion to risk

---

[9] In fact a more detailed formulation of the growth-of-supply function suggests that changes in α shift the curve left or right rather than tilt it. However, no point of substance is involved and the same conclusions follow from either graphical presentation. See R. Marris, *The Economic Theory of Managerial Capitalism*, 252–3.

of takeover etc., but also consider different managerial objectives. For example, if management in more traditional manner wishes to maximize the rate of return on capital, then, with maximum efficiency, it will choose a rate of diversification and profit margin such that it locates at point Z and then take the financial decisions appropriate to a value of α' in the supply growth–profit relation. This would require a lower retention ratio, lower gearing (ratio of debt finance to total finance), increased financial security, and, according to Marris's original view, less fear of takeover arising from the depression of share prices.[10]

This then is the basic picture we shall develop. It indicates four main determinants of the firm's rate of growth. These are:

(i) The demand constraint that arises because costs of expansion reduce the profit margin and/or raise the capital–output ratio.

(ii) The managerial constraint that arises because of the deterioration in efficiency of managers as expansion becomes more rapid.

(iii) The financial constraint that arises because of the takeover threat that the sale of shares by shareholders creates or exacerbates.

(iv) The objectives that management pursue.

We may also add that the general level of managerial efficiency, independent of the rate of growth, and the general buoyancy of demand in the markets into which the firm diversifies will both have an impact because they will help determine how far out from the origin the effective demand growth curve is located. Each of these can now be examined in more detail.[11]

3   THE DEMAND CONSTRAINT

The idea incorporated by Marris that there would be a trade-off between the growth of demand and profitability was not itself new. Of two main antecedents, Baumol's work was the more specific.[12]

---

[10] It is shown later that this last condition does not necessarily follow.

[11] Note that the model has been developed independent of the *size* of the firm. Only in one article has the Marris model been reassessed with firm size introduced, but this rather speculative piece by Solow focuses only on initial size as a decision variable in addition to future growth, rather than on size as a general determinant of the growth rate. He finds that the Marris model amended to incorporate initial size cannot explain the initial scale of operations that would be adopted if it were a decision variable. This is because in the model adopted a larger growth rate can always be obtained by reducing the initial size. It is likely that different or more significant modifications will have to be made to the Marris model if it is to explain how size affects growth and therefore from what size a firm should choose to start its steady-state growth. See R. Solow, 'Some Implications of Alternative Criteria for the Firm', in R. Marris, A. Wood (ed.), *The Corporate Economy* (London, 1971), 318–42.

[12] W. Baumol, 'On The Theory of the Expansion of The Firm', *A.E.R.* 52, no. 5 (Dec. 1962), 1078–87. The other is J. Downie, *The Competitive Process* (London, 1958).

In attempting to move from his static sales-maximization model (see Chapter 8, pp. 266–8) to a dynamic growth maximization model he argued that too low a level of profit, by restraining the supply of finance, cut the firm's growth rate via the supply side, while too high a level of profit would result in a reduction in the 'magnitude of the firm's current operations'.[13] He concluded that 'the optimal profit stream will be that *intermediate stream which is consistent with the largest flow of output (or rate of growth of output) over the firm's lifetime*'.[14]

This conclusion that growth maximizing firms will not be profit maximizers accords with the implications of the Marris model depicted in Figure 9.2, and is central to the whole debate about whether managerially controlled firms do or do not act in the best interests of their shareholders. But J. Williamson has shown on the basis of a more detailed investigation of the Baumol model that a growth maximizing firm will *also maximize profits*.[15] The disparity arises because of an inadequate specification of the profit–demand relation in the Baumol model which leads to an error in his conclusion quoted above. Clearly it is important to identify the cause of this error and examine it in relation to the Marris model.

The problem essentially is that although it seems very plausible to suggest that a lower margin is necessary if faster growth of demand is to be generated, this does *not* follow from the traditional demand analysis for a single product. Given a normal demand curve, only very temporary growth of sales can be achieved by a price cut. Long-term growth (and *a fortiori* steady-state growth) requires continuous *shifting* of the demand curve, for example by marketing. The *growth* of demand may then be just as fast at a high price as at a low price. The market may be *smaller* in the former case, but have the same growth rate.

If the position of the demand curve is a function of the level of demand–growth-generating expenditure, then a similar difficulty exists. Over the long term the rate of growth of such expenditure must be the same as the rate of growth of profit and sales and this growth rate may be high or low irrespective of whether these expenditures are a high percentage of sales revenue (creating a large market but reducing the return on capital) or a low percentage (giving a small market with a higher return).

It can now be seen why the Baumol model is incorrect. A higher profit rate leads to a faster growth of finance, but does *not* inhibit

[13] W. Baumol, op. cit. 1086.   [14] Ibid. (our italics).
[15] J. Williamson, 'Profit, Growth and Sales Maximisation', *Economica*, N.S. 33 (Feb. 1966), 1–16.

the growth of demand. Thus, to maximize the rate of growth, managers would maximize the profit rate—the conclusion of Williamson which is so at odds with that of Baumol. Diagrammatically (see Figure 9.3) a high profit rate reduces current *size*, but generates

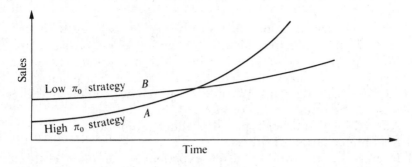

Fig. 9.3

faster growth (line A) and a low profit rate gives larger current size and a slower growth rate (line B). The *present value* of sales depends on the discount rate, and it is quite possible that an intermediate profit rate will maximize the present value, but the *growth* rate is unambiguously maximized by adopting the 'maximum current profit' strategy.

Thus the belief that a growth maximizer will behave differently from a profit maximizer requires the introduction of additional features to the analyses of the growth of demand, and Marris introduced two. These are the emphasis on growth through diversification and the development of a relationship between *current* price, marketing expenditure, etc., on the one hand, and the *future* rate of *growth* of demand on the other, which, while intuitively plausible, was the missing element in the Baumol model. To illustrate these it will be convenient to specify the rate of growth of the firm more precisely.

If the rate of diversification is d, if B is the proportion of successes, and the time periods are long enough for each new product to be revealed as a success or failure, then the rate of increase of products is Bd. If the rate of growth of existing products is x and the successful new products are assumed to be as successful as existing products,[16] then the rate of growth of the firm, g, is given by

$$g = x + Bd \qquad (6)$$

[16] Without this assumption it is not possible for both the diversifying firm *and* the markets it is in to have constant growth rates over time.

It follows, of course, that even if x and B are constant a faster rate of diversification, which it has been argued will lower the profit rate, will increase the firm's growth rate. But in addition Marris argues that both x and B will themselves rise as a result of higher levels of demand-generating expenditure and/or lower prices, as follows.

Very rarely will demand for a product grow as a result of a given number of consumers individually consuming ever-increasing quantities of a product. Generally it results from a progressively larger number of people becoming customers, each with a particular and roughly constant demand. Whenever a purchase is made it will generally be as the result of one or more of the following:

(a) Advertising and other types of product promotion.

(b) Recommendation of others.

(c) Interest in the product after experiencing another customer's purchase.

(d) Emulation of those in the same socio-economic group. This need not be conscious, but the result of a definite preference (e.g. for claret not bitter, or vice versa) as a result of familiarity with the product because of the frequency with which it is consumed in the consumer's socio-economic group.

(e) Habit, or experience of the satisfaction the product generates.

All of these, except the first, require that someone has previously bought the product. Marris therefore distinguishes two types of consumer—'pioneering' consumers, who come under category (a) and who do not require any previous acquaintance either with the product or another customer, and 'sheeplike' [sic] customers who initially purchase under categories (b), (c), and (d). All customers may then continue to purchase under category (e) and perhaps (d) as well.

The probability of a diversification being successful and therefore the value of B in equation 6 will depend on the number of pioneers obtained and the number of new customers they bring in. The rate of growth of demand for a successful product, and hence x, will also depend on the latter. If for example there are sufficient 'productive links' between pioneers and sheeplike consumers and subsequently between existing and further sheeplike consumers to obtain two new customers for every existing ten, then the rate of growth of demand will be twice as fast in a given market than if only one were obtained. Thus B, x, and therefore g are a function of the number of pioneers and the number of productive links established. These will in turn depend upon a whole range of social, economic, and demographic factors which we will assume are given, but also on:

(*a*) The intrinsic qualities of the product in relation to consumer needs (the latter themselves a function of socio-economic factors).

(*b*) The level and success of advertising and other marketing activities.

(*c*) The price charged.

Attempts to raise the former two and lower the third, it is assumed, will all tend to reduce the profit rate.

The central feature of this argument is that if the first two are high and the third low, it is less significant that more customers will be found than that (i) in a process of diversification more pioneering consumers will be found, and (ii) more customers *per existing customer* for the product will be found. The growth of the firm is then higher, but at the expense of a lower profit margin. Thus it can be established, on the basis of a dynamic theory of consumer behaviour, that the intertemporal relationship between *current* profit levels and *future* demand growth essential to the growth theory outlined, is plausible, but only in the context of diversification and/or consumer interactions as described above.

Once this is established then other reinforcing effects can be incorporated. In particular higher levels of marketing by generating faster growth are likely in an oligopolistic setting to precipitate a stronger reaction from competitors, meaning that still higher levels of marketing are required to maintain the growth rate. But three main points are by now clear. The demand growth–profit relationship is by no means obvious or derivable from standard demand theory. Second, it reinforces the view that marketing should be regarded as a capital good because it will have an effect on the sales of future time periods. Third, a dynamic theory of firm's growth appears to require a dynamic theory of consumer behaviour which is likely to more nearly mirror both actual behaviour and marketing managers' perception of the latter than traditional demand analysis.

In one respect the Marris model obviously complements the analysis of demand in Part II of this book in that it can give a clear picture of the factors which influence or determine the profit margin selected by a firm with some discretion over its prices.

None the less, it is the sharp contrast between the analysis of demand in this model and that pursued in Part II of this book which is most apparent, and requires some discussion. At least three problems are involved. First, there has been no reference to the *industry*'s behaviour as opposed to that of the *firm*. By itself this is not surprising. One rationale for the model was the existence of individual firms which could exercise considerable control over their environment and the consequent need to shift attention from the industry as a group of largely passive units to the firm as an active agent in its own right. In addition, the focusing of attention on diversification, now very prevalent amongst large firms in particular, indicates first that the concept of a firm being 'in an industry' is increasingly untenable, and second that firms' behaviour may be relatively less constrained by the development of the industry or industries in which they currently operate than traditionally supposed. None the less, there is a clear dichotomy between the view that performance is determined by the structure of an industry and the conduct that results from it, on the one hand, and the view now encompassed that firms can be analysed independent of industrial structure, on the other. Competitive behaviour is still included in the analysis of the firm above, in the sense that a lower profit rate can be construed as gaining a competitive advantage in terms of demand growth via price and marketing policy, but the profit rate nevertheless appears as a decision variable in the Marris model and not, as in Part II, the result of external factors rooted in the structure of industry.

Second, the role of new entry appears to be quite different. In the industry-based approach entry barriers were a structural feature that allowed higher profits to be made. In the firm-based approach entry barriers must be important because of the significance of diversification, but high barriers would presumably worsen the growth–profit trade-off and potentially *reduce* both the firm's growth rate and profit rate, i.e. the protection afforded to existing markets might well be more than offset by the barriers to diversification into new markets.

Third, nothing has been said except in passing about the existence of competitive interdependence as a result of the high concentration that may well exist in a whole series of markets into which the firm diversifies. At the simplest level, if the adoption of a lower profit margin, be it through lower price or increased selling exenditure, in order to achieve a higher growth rate, precipitates a similar reaction from rivals, then it would seem reasonable to argue that the lower margin will not generate the higher growth rate aimed for. If more rapid diversification, embarked upon as a vehicle of faster growth, brought about more intensive and retaliatory diversification into the same or similar markets by competitors, the same result might follow. Ultimately this difficulty turns out to be a special case of a more general problem concerning the determinants of the growth–profit relation facing the firm on the demand side.

To examine this we first need to return briefly to the characteristics of a steady-state system. Such a system does not strictly allow consideration of a firm which changes one or more of its decision variables. In the light of its objectives and its constraints, which partly reflect both management and shareholders' views about the future, the firm is presumed to fix its decision variables for an indefinite period. In practice of course the system is interpreted more flexibly. First, both decision and performance variables are regarded as long-run 'normal' values about which considerable stochastic variation may occur. Second, and more important, comparative dynamics are used not only to compare different firms, but also to infer how a firm's performance might be expected to change if it adopted significantly different values of its decision variables. Change through time is thus equated with switching from one steady-state growth path to another.

Despite these flexibilities of interpretation, however, the steady-state system does imply that particular values of decision variables now will be associated with a particular average rate of growth of the firm in the future. Any external disturbances which might lead to those same decisions giving a different growth rate have been ignored. In other words we have adopted the usual *ceteris paribus* assumption about the firm's economic environment when specifying the relationship between firms' decisions and their performance. But, as Marris points out, there is something rather strange about assuming that the environment is unchanged when the firm is explicitly assumed to be actively engaged in changing that environment in the light of its own objectives. He deals with this by postulating that firms face an immediate environment—demand curves, product preferences, etc.—which the firm can and does manipulate, and also a *super-environment* which is conceived of as a loose collection of general circumstances which place limits on the capacity of the firm to change its immediate environment. Thus, given such characteristics of a market as numbers of buyers and sellers, product differentiation, entry barriers, marketing, etc., a firm will in the short term be constrained by the immediate environment to a particular demand curve. Over the longer term, however, it will be able to change this continuously by manipulating the immediate environment by new product design, new advertising, etc. But there will be limits to how rapidly such changes can be accomplished because of consumer attachment to existing products, consumer resistance to marketing, less than complete information about prices and quality of products, etc., and because of the human and institutional limits which determine, for example, how rapidly managerial inefficiency increases as the diversification rate is raised. These factors, which if controllable at all are so only in the very long run, constitute the super-environment.

This concept permits more flexibility in the model, for although the super-environment is effectively exogenous it need not necessarily be constant. A firm experiencing increasing ease in recruiting suitable managers because of increases in appropriate training at universities, business schools, etc., or a firm in markets subject to long-term change in tastes would find the same decisions giving more rapid growth. Its super-environment would be improving and its demand-growth curve would be shifting outwards. Furthermore, given that multi-product firms do not cover all products, different firms may face different super-environments, and therefore different demand-growth curves.

The difficulty with all this lies in the fact that the super-environment ultimately *cannot* be regarded as exogenous because it depends on what other firms do. For example, suppose a high level of advertising, given the super-environment constraint, leads to a particular (high) growth of demand. If as a result firms in the aggregate pursue high advertising then this may well itself change the extent to which growth of demand *can* be generated by advertising. It might make consumers more susceptible to advertising or more resistant, but in either case the partial equilibrium view that there is a given relationship between current advertising and a constant growth of demand for a 'representative' firm is strictly untenable. Only if it could be established that the super-environment was not influenced by economy-wide changes brought about by the actions of the 'representative' firm (i.e. all firms) could the steady-state system be strictly adhered to. But in all three main areas—the markets for products, finance and managers—this is very unlikely to be true. Unlike the cost and market demand curves of traditional theory which were possibly independent of firms' behaviour, the underlying constraints of the super-environment are very clearly dependent on firms' aggregate behaviour.

Oligopolistic interdependence is simply the clearest case of the super-environment (and hence the position of the demand-growth curve) being ultimately endogenous, and the effect of firms' decisions indeterminate. While firms may grow at different rates as a result of different diversification rates, divisions of different firms in the same market have to grow at the same rate or one becomes progressively more dominant. Given the resources that large multi-product firms have at their disposal, this is likely to provoke a competitive reaction, altering the firm's demand-growth curve and therefore the result of the original strategy adopted. Marris began to deal with this difficulty by first statically analysing oligopolistic behaviour via game theory and suggesting that firms would reach a 'co-operative' solution which reflected their relative bargaining strength and comparative production advantages.[17] This static equilibrium then provided the basis for growth, with firms which were more successful in the static equilibrium growing faster and only the birth of new firms inhibiting a trend to greater concentration. Grabowski, on the other hand, concluded on the basis of a Cournot-type growth model with competitive reactions included that although levels of output were sensitive to a number of cost and demand parameters, the equilibrium growth rate of the firms depended only on the economy-wide growth rate and the extent to which there were or were not non-constant returns to demand-shifting expenditures.[18]

A framework which can encompass industrial structure, conduct and performance characteristics as well as those of the individual diversified firm, and incorporate an element of endogeneity in the super-environment, is depicted in Figure 9.4.

In the top left are summarized the main relationships examined in Part II, between technology, barriers-to-entry concentration,

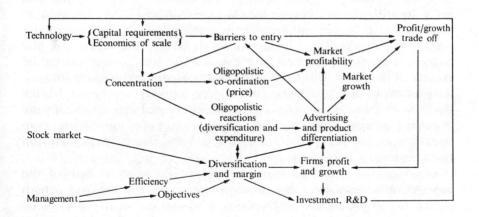

Fig. 9.4

[17] R. Marris, 'The Modern Corporation and Economic Theory', in R. Marris, A. Wood (ed.), *The Corporate Economy* (London, 1971).
[18] H. Grabowski, 'Demand Shifting, Optimal Firm Growth, and Rule-of-Thumb Decision Taking', *Q.J.E.* 84, no. 2 (May 1970), 217–35.

co-ordination, and profitability in industrial markets. The profit/ growth trade-off facing the diversifying firm depends on the opportunities for profitable growth through diversification that these markets present. This as shown therefore depends on the barriers that exist to entering, and the profit and growth possibilities once in the new market. The firm's actual profits and growth are determined by the point on the trade-off selected, which as we have seen depends on the diversification rate and profit margin selected. This in turn is a function of the firm's objectives and efficiency and the constraint imposed on them by the behaviour of the stock market and the threat of takeover. The decisions on diversification and margin both determine and are determined by reactions of competitors in oligopolistic industries. The component decisions of the selection of diversifiction rate and profit margin are as mentioned, marketing investment (advertising and product differentiation), physical investment, and research and development, all of which also depend on the supply of funds as determined by the firm's profits. Finally, the former tends to raise entry barriers and improve market profits and growth prospects, while the latter two have impact on the technical conditions underlying the markets concerned.

Several points are worth noting about this picture. First, the firm is construed as a multi-divisional (M-form) organization.[19] Each division is a 'quasi-firm'[20] or mini U-form traditional single-product firm, whose performance is largely dependent on the structure and conduct elements described in Part II. The firm as a whole is not restricted in this way and *its* profit and growth performance are only loosely constrained by these factors. The ultimate exogenous determinants of its performance are its objectives and efficiency and the degree of discipline imposed by the stock market—hence the increasing emphasis on these issues in industrial economics. There therefore turns out to be no necessary inconsistency between a structure–conduct performance approach to explaining market profitability and an objectives–diversification–expenditure approach to explaining firms' profitability. A smaller undiversifying firm can then be viewed as a special case in which diversification rate is set at zero. The profit–growth trade-off is restricted to such a firm's existing markets, and this may, though not necessarily, reduce profits to the point where demnd-generating and cost-reducing expenditure becomes inhibited.

Second, Figure 9.4 depicts the endogeneity of the super-environment. The profit–growth trade-off can be regarded initially

---

[19] See references to O. Williamson's work, p. 273.
[20] This is Williamson's term for the divisional units.

as given when, in conjunction with the firm's diversification and margin decisions, it determines the firm's profits and growth. But ultimately it is itself altered by the investment, R and D, marketing decisions, and oligopolistic reactions that result. Even though it is a partial equilibrium approach still, only the stock market and management characteristics are completely exogenous. As, however, even the shorter-term reactions to non-price behaviour seem frequently to be ignored (see Chapter 12 for further elaboration of this) it is *a fortiori* reasonable to view the firm as regarding the profit-growth trade-off it faces as given when it takes its decisions. It is only the very long-term repercussions which are strictly indeterminate within the Marris model, but not within one which reflected all the relationships of Figure 9.4. This framework therefore depicts the route by which the logical objections to the super-environment assumption might be overcome and by which the theory of the growth of the firm could incorporate—as the traditional theory of price has had to incorporate—oligopolistic reactions and interdependence, but in the context of multi-product firms and expenditure as well as price decisions.

4   THE MANAGERIAL CONSTRAINT

The next important element in the basic growth model was contained in the argument that there are at any time limits to the expansion that existing managers can achieve, but limits also to the rate at which the management can expand its numbers and thereby its managerial capacity. These two forces together generate constraints on growth in the form of expansion costs or, more specifically, increasing inefficiency as the growth rate is raised, which raises the capital–output ratio and depresses the profit rate.

By far the best-known examination of the managerial constraints on growth is that of Penrose,[21] and the impact of these constraints in growth theory is known as the 'Penrose effect'. She does not present a rigorous specification of her whole model either diagrammatically or mathematically, but at least some of the main points of her very detailed arguments concerning the managerial organization of growth can be summarized and presented diagrammatically (see Figure 9.5).

At any time a firm has certain productive resources—land, machinery, work-force, and, in particular, managers—the services of which are used to exploit the production opportunities facing the

---

[21] E. Penrose, *The Theory of the Growth of The Firm* (Oxford, 1959).

firm. The latter naturally depend on the financial and demand constraints facing the firm, but these are generally assumed away by Penrose as being either beyond the managerial constraint, or movable given sufficient managerial services. Each firm is regarded as unique because although firms may have similar resources, the services they can generate depend on the history of their use, experience of the past and present operations of the firms, etc., and so vary from firm to firm. Ability to exploit particular opportunities and even the perception of what opportunities exist are also determined by these historical factors, giving each firm unique productive opportunities.

There is no discussion of managerial objectives because it is assumed first that firms are profit maximizers, but second that this will be identical with growth maximization subject to all projects being profitable.[22] However, an additional and important incentive to growth exists because there are always unused productive services which, if they can be utilized in new projects, will generate more profit. These unused resources exist for three sorts of reasons. (i) The combination of a large number of particular indivisible resources will, unless the size of the firm is very large, mean that some are not fully utilized. In more real-world terms there will nearly always be some knowledge, experience, skill, etc. that one or more people in a firm have obtained that is currently underexploited. (ii) Increasing specialization of managerial functions may well exacerbate this effect. (iii) In the ordinary process of operating and expanding a firm, new productive services are continually being created through acquisition of new skills, information, etc. Furthermore, as the firm grows, obtaining new managers, new abilities, new information, so, the maximum services that the resources can generate increase. Any limit on the *scale* of possible operations recedes, and the issue becomes one of determining the limits on the rate at which the firm, in utilizing these services in innovation, diversification, and the like, can in fact grow.

We may construe the total managerial services needed by a firm at a point in time as partly required to run the firm at its current size, and partly required to carry out expansionary activities such as market research, product development, investment planning of cash flow, manpower, etc., with respect to new products and expansion generally. Initially we assume a constant managerial work-force. The firm will none the less be able to grow for two reasons. First, as each new project becomes established so its running becomes more routine and less demanding of managerial services. Thus a fixed

---

[22] Problems concerning this assumption are ignored as it is an unimportant aspect of the Penrose effect, and dealt with in detail elsewhere in the book. (See ch. 8.)

amount of managerial services for expansion through time will generate continuous growth. Second, there is a learning effect. As managers become more experienced at running the operations of their firm, so managerial services are released for expansion without any fall in the efficiency with which existing operations are run. If the amount of managerial services required to run the firm is directly proportional to the size of the firm, and the amount required for expansion is directly proportional to the absolute size of the expansion, then the firm's growth rate, assumed constant over time, cannot be above the rate of growth of managerial services provided by the constant managerial work force.[23]

Faster growth of the firm will require the recruitment of new managers. This relationship has the following characteristics.

(i) The more rapid the rate of increase of total managers employed, the higher the rate of growth of the firm.

(ii) This relation is subject to diminishing returns for two reasons:

(*a*) The managerial services *required* for a given absolute increase in size are assumed to increase the faster the growth rate. The problems of co-ordinating new activities with each other, and integrating them into the firm, are both greater per unit of increased output. The probability that new areas of operation will be entered, new managerial functions and expertise required, new methods tried, and new innovations incorporated are all greater if growth is rapid, and each of these is likely to increase the ratio of managerial services to the increase in output they bring about. The probability that the growth of the firm can occur through the exploitation of a particularly good opportunity, and in the absence of very strong competition, is reduced the faster the rate of growth being attempted. Thus in general more difficult business opportunities have to be embarked upon and/or more intense competition faced in the exploitation of those opportunities if the faster rate of growth is to be achieved, and this again increases the managerial services required per unit of increased output.

(*b*) The addition to total managerial services *provided* by each additional manager is assumed to *decrease* the faster the rate at which they are recruited. The addition to managerial services made

---

[23] If the firm's size in period t is Q_t and its growth rate is g, then size increases at rate g and size of absolute expansion increases at rate

$$\frac{[(1+g)^2 Q_t - (1+g)Q_t] - [(1+g)Q_t - Q_t]}{[(1+g)Q_t - Q_t]} = g$$

and so demand on managerial services for running and expanding the firm increases at rate g.

by a new manager will be greater the more managerial hours devoted to his training and the greater the degree of his integration into the managerial work-force. Both these will be reduced if the number of new managers is increasing rapidly.[24]

The arguments so far ars summarized by the line *AA* in Figure 9.5. The horizontal axis measures growth of the firm and the vertical axis the rate of increase of managers. Point *X* indicates that some growth is feasible even with a constant number of managers. The positive slope of line *AA* indicates that new managerial recruitment increases the growth of the firm. For the reasons given, however, additional growth per new manager falls, giving a progressively steeper curve.

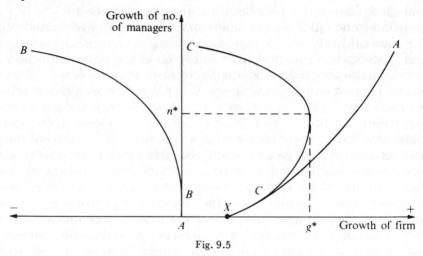

Fig. 9.5

(iii) Via another realtionship, however, an increase in the number of managers will tend to reduce the rate of growth of the firm. This is because the training of new managers and the integrating of them into the work-force occupies some of the time and effort of existing managers, thus reducing the managerial services available for expansion (assuming that the managers must maintain the current level of operations of the firm). This effect may be negligible if new managers are recruited at a low rate, but as the ratio of new managers to old increases, so the diversion of managerial time away from expansion activities is greater, and growth of the firm suffers. This is shown by curve *BB* in Figure 9.5.

[24] To see these points mathematically we may write $(dg/dn) = (dg/ds \cdot ds/dn)$ where g is growth of output, n is growth of new managers, and s is growth of managerial services. $dg/dn, dg/ds, ds/dn > 0$. As g and n rise dg/ds and ds/dn both fall bringing down the value of dg/dn.

The actual rate of growth of the firm for any given rate of increase in the number of managers is found by horizontally subtracting the effect shown by BB from that shown in AA, and this is given by the line CC. Hence the maximum rate of growth of the firm is g^*, and the optimum rate of growth of managers to achieve this is n^*.[25]

Penrose's work raises very significant problems for the theory of the firm. On the one hand her analysis is unrigorous yet complex. It focuses on variables which are not only relatively new to the theory of the firm, but difficult to quantify or even to formulate properly. Yet at the same time it suggests that the growth of the firm is determined by these variables and largely independent of the usual economic variables. In addition there are both theoretical and empirical reasons for believing that the Penrose effect *is* the major constraint on (and therefore determinant of) firms' growth. Allowing for diversification and a reasonably functioning capital market, it seems likely that growth could be very rapid indeed given the necessary managerial resources. Empirically both case study and econometric analysis support this view. Richardson[26] in a summary of the evidence obtained from a number of managers, found that none felt restricted by shortages of labour, materials, or equipment. Only two were held back purely by shortage of finance, and both were small and subsequently taken over. Only one felt a lack of suitable investment opportunities, and amongst the others firms' projects were in fact generally required to show relatively high rates of return to be accepted. Most expressed the view without hestitation that availability of 'suitable' management was the major check on expansion.

This shortage may partly reflect imperfections, in particular price rigidity, in the market for management skills, but also, it appeared, precisely the 'Penrose-effects' described above.[27] Particular emphasis

---

[25] Penrose also examines the effect of firm size on each relationship, but the over-all relation between size and growth is ambiguous. Reductions in managerial services required per unit expansion as a result of larger firms having a better-established name, using more capital intensive method, and expanding more by takeover will all push the line AA to the right. But at very large size such effects may cease to have further effect and managerial diseconomies as a result of control loss in a large firm may well shift AA to the left. Only if this is offset by the use of more sophisticated information and control systems, greater division and specialization of managerial labour, and recruitment of more able managers will the largest firms not suffer in this way. Finally, BB will tend to shift leftwards if for example it is proportionately more consuming of managerial services to integrate ten new managers into one hundred than two into twenty. This could arise if new contacts per new manager were (as is likely) to be higher in the former case.

[26] G. Richardson, 'The Limits to a Firm's Rate of Growth', *Oxford Economic Papers*, N.S. 16 (Mar. 1964), 9–23.

[27] Richardson pointed out that the more energetic managers would, paradoxically, notice the managerial constraint more because their efforts and aspirations would more readily bring them up against the constraint.

was also placed on the need for internal recruitment to the most senior posts to avoid the risk of having managers with little experience or knowledge of the particular company. The high rate of return demanded of prospective investment projects appeared to be an implicit recognition of the opportunity cost, in terms of lower managerial efficiency elsewhere, of taking on a new project, thus supporting the notion of an organizational determinant of the maximum rate of growth.

Shen, in an econometric study, argued that growth to larger size at the plant level, by permitting more economies of scale to be realized, higher profit to be made, and more advantage to be taken of the relative cheapening of capital to labour, would tend to sustain growth.[28] This he verified empirically, but none the less found that over-all growth in subsequent periods[29] tended to reverse, with initially high-growth plants becoming low-growth ones and vice versa. This effect, which showed up as a negative constant in the econometric determination of growth correlations between the two periods, he attributed to Penrose-type effects which compelled fast-growing organizations to slow down and permitted slower-growing ones to catch up.

Accepting then these Penrose-effects, the position of the demand-growth curve of Figure 9.2 can be regarded as partly (or for Penrose almost entirely) determined by the managerial constraint on growth. In its most extreme form the argument would suggest that the line becomes almost vertical, so that despite feasible shifts of the supply-growth curve to the right, no more growth would be forthcoming. Any attempt to grow faster would fail, while none the less pulling down the profit rate. Growth by merger becomes very attractive however as a means of greatly relaxing the managerial constraint by virtue of the reduction in demand on managerial services which mergers permit.

As with the intertemporal demand aspects of the last section, so with managerial constraints we again find that the theory of the growth of the firm depends in an important way on aspects of behaviour about which relatively little is known, but on to which growth theory focuses great attention. The virtue of the growth model is that it starts the process of integrating these new but central considerations into a single yet simple and systematic analysis of firms' economic behaviour and performance.

---

[28] T. Y. Shen, 'Economics of Scale. Penrose-Effect, Growth of Plants and Their Size Distribution', *J.P.E.* 78, no. 4 (July 1970), 701–16.
[29] Shen used 1948–53 and 1953–8.

5   THE FINANCE CONSTRAINT

The last two sections have established in more detail that, after a point, a higher growth rate can only be obtained at the expense of a lower profit rate. But if managers are not concerned with the profit rate *per se*, why should this bother them? The answer as we have seen is that it requires the supply-growth curve in Figure 9.2 to be pivoted clockwise (increasing the value of α) by increasing the retention ratio, the proportion of debt finance, or new issue of equity shares. This is nearly always *feasible*, if only by increasing retentions,[30] indicating, as Williamson has shown, that the growth of a firm could not be constrained by lack of finance while retaining less than all its earnings. But the depression of share prices which excess drawing on these sources brings about increases the threat of takeover and therefore makes it *undesirable* for managers to attempt to grow faster by such means. The self-imposed finance constraint is therefore dependent on the determination of the price of the company's shares and hence the total valuation of the company in the stock market. As Marris recognized very early on, a theory of the growth of the firm requires a theory of stock market valuation.

This is a matter of some complexity and controversy, and the issues will be examined in more detail in the next chapter on company finance. Some initial steps can, however, be taken. Shareholders we presume will only be concerned with current and future dividends, and with capital gains, as these are the only gains to them from holding shares. For the moment we assume away tax aspects which could affect shareholder preferences between dividends and capital gains, and simplify the analysis by using the steady-state framework. With a constant retention ratio, current dividends are determined by current profits, and the growth of dividends is determined by the growth of profits which equals the growth rate of assets.

Assuming the current price of each share equals the present value of current and future dividends per share plus capital sum accruing per share when the share is eventually sold, the current price of a share is[31]

---

[30] Very rarely will a publicly quoted company pay *no* dividend and then only temporarily.

[31] Discrete time analysis is used as dividends are normally paid at regular intervals, but the same conclusions apply if continuous time analysis is used.

$$S_0 = \sum_{t=0}^{t=n-1} \frac{K_0 p(1-r)(1+g)^t}{N(1+\delta)^{t+1}} + \frac{S_n}{(1+\delta)^n}$$

where S_0 is the present value of the share.
S_n is the share price when the share is sold in period n.
K_0 is the initial capital employed in period o.
p is the expected profit rate.
r is the retention ratio.
N is the number of shares, assumed constant.
g is the expected growth rate of the company.
δ is the discount rate.

The first term is the present value of the stream of dividends received from $t = 0$ to $t = n - 1$. Note that we presume the dividend to be paid at the end of each period. The second term is the present value of the share when sold at the beginning of $t = n$. If the dividend per pound of shares is constant over time then the share price must grow at the same rate as the dividend, i.e. at rate g.
Therefore $S_n = S_0(1+g)^n$

and $$S_0 = \frac{K_0 p(1-r)}{N(1+\delta)} \sum_{t=0}^{t=n-1} \left(\frac{1+g}{1+\delta}\right)^t + S_0\left(\frac{1+g}{1+\delta}\right)^n$$

Assuming $\delta > g$ (the share price is infinite otherwise)

$$S_0 = \frac{K_0 p(1-r)}{N(1+\delta)} \left[\frac{1 - \left(\frac{1+g}{1+\delta}\right)^n}{1 - \left(\frac{1+g}{1+\delta}\right)}\right] + S_0\left(\frac{1+g}{1+\delta}\right)^n$$

Regrouping the terms and simplifying gives

$$S_0 = \frac{K_0 p(1-r)}{N(\delta-g)}$$

The first thing to notice is that, given the simplifying assumptions made, the share price is independent of when the share is sold and hence of capital gains. At any time the share price represents the present value of the total dividend stream to infinity. The share price at time of sale reflects the *then* present value of all the dividends forgone by selling the shares before infinity. This greatly eases the analysis.

Second, the total stock market value, M, of the company will be[32]

$$M = NS_0 = \frac{K_0 p(1-r)}{(\delta-g)}$$

Suppose managers wished to maximize shareholder wealth. To find the growth rate they should choose, we differentiate the above equation with respect to g. Supply-growth and demand-growth functions can be summarized respectively as

$$g = rp$$

$$p = f(g)$$

Therefore

$$M = \frac{K_0\{f(g)-g\}}{(\delta-g)}$$

$$\frac{dM}{dg} = \frac{(\delta-g)K_0\{f'(g)-1\} + K_0\{f(g)-g\}}{(\delta-g)^2}$$

Setting this equal to zero gives

$$\{1-f'(g)\}(\delta-g) = \{f(g)-g\}$$

To find the rate of growth which satisfies this equation we note that it implies

$$f'(g) = \frac{\delta-f(g)}{\delta-g} = \frac{\delta-p}{\delta-g}$$

Thus the value of the company is maximized when the gradient of the demand growth curve is

---

[32] This formula is derived directly, ignoring capital gains, by G. Heal and A. Silberston, 'Alternative Managerial Objectives: An Exploratory Note', *Oxford Economic Papers*, 24, no. 2 (July 1972), 137–50. The following analysis comes from the same article.

$$\frac{\delta - p}{\delta - g}$$

The profit rate must be above the discount rate if the firm is to be profitable, i.e.

$$p > \delta - g$$

and so the gradient is both negative and fractional. Figure 9.6 reproduces the basic figure and plots this at point B. The management would select the retention ratio (and other financial variables) which gave supply-growth line S_2. Notice that this gives a higher growth rate (and lower profit rate) than a management trying to maximize the profit rate.[33] The latter would clearly locate at point A where

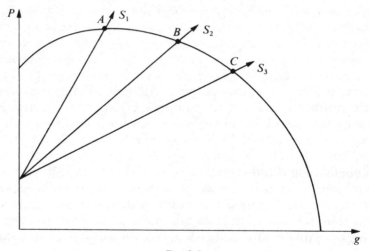

Fig. 9.6

[33] Marris argued that the maximum valuation ratio would in fact occur to the *left* of the maximum profit rate. This was based on the view that the valuation ratio would fall continuously as the supply-growth line shifted (not pivoted) rightwards because of the higher retention and gearing ratios this required. Thus the highest valuation ratio would occur on the upward sloping part of the demand-growth curve where the supply-growth line, being tangential to the demand-growth line, is as far to the left as possible. On this view, beyond the tangency point, even though growth rate *and* profit rate were rising the valuation ratio would fall because of the increase in retentions necessary to bring them about, and the accompanying increase in uncertainty. But as Heal and Silberston's expression for the gradient of the demand-growth curve shows, while a higher value of the discount rate may make the gradient positive, it is only at the cost of the discount rate exceeding the profit rate, implying long-run bankruptcy. Thus the uncertainty effect may push the maximum valution ratio point leftwards, but the latter is constrained to be at, or to the right of, the maximum profit rate point.

$$f'(g) = 0$$

Interest in the stock market valuation of the company arose because of its role as an indicator of the threat of takeover. In fact it is not the total value *per se*, but the value per unit of company assets which would be acquired in a takeover that is the effective determinant. We therefore focus on the *valuation ratio*

$$V = \frac{M}{K_0} = \frac{\{f(g) - g\}}{(\delta - g)} = \frac{p(1 - r)}{(\delta - g)}$$

illustrating that V depends positively on P, and g and negatively on r and δ. As K_0 is a parameter,[34] the decisions which maximize M will of course maximize V. In Figure 9.6, as the firm increases its value of of α, let us say by increasing the retention ratio, so, if it is operating at maximum efficiency, it will move along the demand-growth line. At first both growth rate and profit rate rise, current dividends and their prospective growth rise, and the valuation ratio increases. At some point the effect on dividends of a rising retention ratio offsets the rising profit rate so that current dividends fall, but the increasing growth prospects more than compensate and the valuation ratio continues to rise. Beyond point A, current dividends fall *both* because the retention ratio is rising *and* because the profit rate is falling, but it is only beyond B that the increasing growth rate fails to compensate and the valuation ratio begins to fall. If when the retention ratio reaches its security-constrained maximum the supply-growth line is S_3, then point C indicates the maximum growth rate. By this time the valuation ratio will have fallen below its maximum. Any higher growth rate makes the risk of takeover unacceptable.[35]

---

[34] If the value of the company as recorded in the company's accounts accurately reflects the present value of the future dividend stream, or indeed any other stock market based valuation, then the valuation ratio is always unity. In practice this will not be so generally, either because of the inaccuracy of accounting conventions or because the accounting value would not reflect the value of the assets as a 'going concern'. It is still true, however, that a higher valuation will, *ceteris paribus*, reduce the likelihood of takeover.

[35] Work by Singh reviewed in Chapter 14 (pp. 493–4) suggests that empirically the inverse correlation between valuation ratio and takeover is weak. This does not however undermine the theory above. The valuation ratio is (Stock Market Value (SMV))/(Book Value (BV)). The incidence of takeover will be a function of (Acquirer's Valuation (AV))/(Stock Market Value (SMV)). If the SMV is low because prospects are poor and the AV is even lower for the same reason, then, despite a low valuation ratio, takeover will not occur. If the SMV is high because of good prospects, but AV is still higher, perhaps because the acquirer envisages new management, new markets, or new finance being available, then takeover may occur despite a high valuation ratio. A rather weak inverse correlation between incidence of takeover and valuation ratio is to be expected therefore. It is none the less true for a

The relationship between the growth rate and the valuation ratio can therefore be summarized as in Figure 9.7, which again makes clear that different objectives will lead to different decisions by firms as to their growth and profit rates.[36] This in turn implies different rates of diversification, capital–output ratios, profit margins, retention rates, and so on.

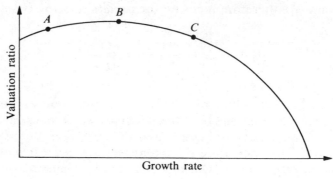

Fig. 9.7

This is the most general, and, as we shall see, most flexible presentation of the opportunities facing a firm. Note that a firm located at *A* would be under a bigger takeover threat than one at *B*, despite having a higher return on capital. It would need to *grow* faster, even though this reduced the profit rate, in order to reduce the threat of takeover. This gives some financial basis for believing that firms generally have to grow to survive as independent firms.

The introduction of a full valuation function to the analysis enables a more general model of management utility maximization to be formulated. As was seen in the last chapter, Yarrow showed that in models of managerial utility maximization subject to a constraint, the form of the constraint is crucial and that a fuller examination of managerial discretion under uncertainty implied a constraint formulation which related the value of the constraint variable to its maximum value.[37] Adopting a constraint of Yarrow's form we would have

company with given BV and AV that the higher the SMV the higher the valuation ratio *and* the lower the threat of takeover. It may be that a low SMV is nevertheless enough to discourage takeover of one firm whereas a high SMV does not prevent it for another, but, for both, the threat of takeover declines continuously as SMC and the valuation ratio rise.

[36] Note that if, as evidence suggests (see Chapter 11, p. 345), firms make lower returns on investment financed internally than that financed externally, then increasing the retention ratio may reduce the expected stream of earnings and hence directly reduce share valuation. Points *B* and *C* will then move nearer to *A*.

[37] See pp. 270–1.

$$\text{maximize } g = f(V)$$

$$\text{subject to } V \geqslant V^* - c$$

where V^* is the maximum valuation ratio and
    c is the cost of enforcement of shareholder preference.

This would directly tie the location of point C in Figure 9.6 and 9.7 to that of point B. The scope for increasing growth at the expense of the valuation ratio would then depend on such factors as the shareholders' access to company information and the number, size, and distribution of shareholdings. In effect c has replaced α^* as the parameter exogenous to the model.

This is still rather restrictive in that given there is managerial uncertainty about the value of c, management does not in fact face a rigid security constraint which determines the maximum permissible growth rate. Instead we may view managerial utility as having two arguments, the growth rate, which gives salary, status, power, etc., and the valuation ratio, which provides security from take-over. Beyond point B in Figures 9.6 and 9.7 there is a trade-off between growth and valuation. The more confident the management is that enforcement costs are high the further down the demand-growth and growth-valuation curves the firm will be moved. This is summarized in Figure 9.8, where the utility function

$$u = f(g, V)$$

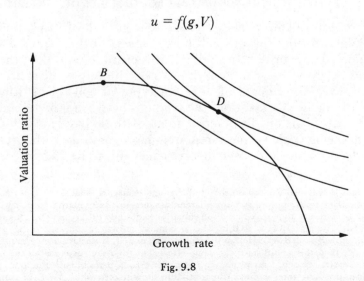

Fig. 9.8

is shown by indifference curves, the growth-valuation function

$$V = f(g)$$

portrays the trade-off between the two arguments of the utility function, and D indicates the point of maximum managerial utility. Shareholders, being interested only in valuation, would have horizontal indifference curves and naturally prefer point B at the peak of the growth–valuation curve. The discrepancy between B and D depends not only on c but on managements' degree of risk averseness in their assessment of enforcement costs.[38]

This formulation also allows us to introduce the idea that managers obtain some utility from their company's valuation independent of takeover threat, because of its role as an indicator of stock market approval.

Figure 9.8, though simple, is based on all the theoretical aspects so far considered. The position of the growth–valuation curve depends on all the constraints—demand, managerial, and financial—examined, while the shape and position of the managerial indifference curves reflects both managerial utility and managerial discretion. It is the fullest and most general statement of the theory of the growth of the firm.

6   EMPIRICAL EVIDENCE ON THE GROWTH MODEL OF THE FIRM

When we turn to empirical evidence on the growth of firms, there are many types of relationships and many aspects of the theory that can be examined and tested. In principle it is possible to look at the relationship of growth, profitability, and size, the rate of diversification and take-over, the impact of different types of control of firms, the effects of changes in taxation, the relations between growth and concentration, and so on. In practice some of these have faced insuperable problems, others have required more advanced theory than currently available, and some involve issues still to be examined. Here

[38] In fact it will also depend on shareholders' and managers' relative time-horizons and relative discount rates. The higher the shareholder discount rate relative to managers, the lower the growth rate that maximizes the valuation ratio, and the greater the constraint on management. The net effect is to bring the 'maximum' growth rate nearer to the valuation maximum growth rate. See G. Heal and A. Silberston, op. cit. If uncertainty causes discount rates to rise then this could have the same effect, but the result depends on the form of valuation constraint used. Yarrow shows that under certain plausible assumptions a rise in shareholder discount rates reduces the optimum growth rate while a rise in managerial discount rates raises it. See G. Yarrow, 'Management Utility Maximisation under Uncertainty', *Economica*, N.S. 40 (May 1973), 155–73.

we review the evidence with reference to one particular issue, namely the validity of the growth model presented earlier. More general evidence on the growth of firms is reviewed in Chapter 15.[39]

At first sight it seems a simple test to see whether owner-controlled firms (which might be presumed to pursue maximum rate of return on capital) have higher profit rates and lower growth rates than managerially controlled firms. This type of test was carried out in the U.K. by Radice.[40] He examined a sample of 86 firms from the food, electrical engineering, and textiles industries, but found that on average the owner-controlled firms (OCs) had higher profit rates (16·81 per cent against 12·40 per cent) *and* higher growth rates (10·42 per cent against 6·84 per cent) than the managerially controlled firms (MCs). The same pattern held for each industry except food, where the owner-controlled firms had a *lower* average profit rate and *higher* average growth rate. He also attempted to regress profit rates on control-type and industry dummy variables, initial size and growth rate for 68 of the firms.[41] This is hazardous because the two-way relation between profit rate and growth rate leads to simultaneous-equation bias. The results were relatively weak. Growth was found generally to be significant (though not for each industry), but in only one case (textiles) was the control-type dummy significant.[42] On average the results suggest that a 1 per cent increase in the growth rate is associated with a 0·4 per cent increase in the profit rate.

This study indicates not only that testing the growth model may be difficult econometrically, but also that the issues involved are quite complex. This can be illustrated using the basic diagram reproduced in Figure 9.9. If firms faced the same growth of supply (G_s) and demand (G_d) conditions, had the same objective, and were equally efficient in the pursuit of these objectives, then they would all have the same profit and growth rates as each other (point A). Table 9.1 indicates the predicted growth/profit relation for differences in each of these factors individually. Figure 9.9 identifies the points included in each relation.

This illustrates the following difficulties:

(i) The over-all growth–profit relation depends on which difference

---

[39] It is worth noting, however, that the general lack of correlation between firms' growth rates and their size (see ch. 15) is consistent with the model in that the latter has been developed independent of the size of the Firm.

[40] H. Radice, 'Control Type, Profitability & Growth in Large Firms', *E.J.* 81 (Sept. 1971), 547–62.

[41] The other 18 were not able to be classified as OCs or MCs reliably enough. The tests were run for all firms, for each industry, and then repeated for the OC and MC groups separately.

[42] The control-type dummy for all firms was, however, nearly significant.

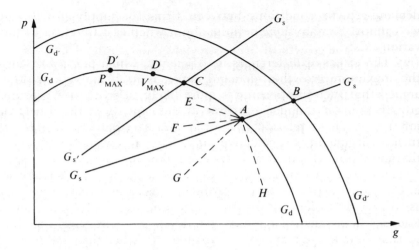

Fig. 9.9

TABLE 9.1

Difference between firms	Growth/Profit rate relation	Points Compared in Figure 9.9
Growth-of-Demand Conditions	direct	A–B
Growth-of-Supply Conditions	inverse	A–C
Objectives	inverse	A–D or D'
Efficiency	direct *or*	A–F, A–G
	inverse	A–E, A–H

dominates. Thus a direct correlation *might* be consistent with OCs *ceteris paribus* having higher profit rates and lower growth rates.
(ii) A multivariate analysis which attempts to identify the effect of control type should allow for the other three variables involved. For example Radice's industry dummy is a proxy for different demand conditions.
(iii) The four variables may themselves be correlated. As Radice points out, his sample contained only large firms in order to remove differences in behaviour due to large variations in size. But large owner-controlled firms are rather rare. In general they will have had either to have faced very buoyant growth-of-demand conditions or have been very efficient (or both) in order to become large without losing control as a result of going to the capital market. To take only the first of these, a growth-of-demand curve further out from the origin makes it quite possible for a firm to be at the peak of its curve and yet still have a higher growth rate than a firm beyond the peak on the lower curve. More generally, if there are differences in

demand-growth conditions between firms (or supply-growth ones) we cannot infer anything definite about whether differences of motivation exist.

(iv) The effect of differences in efficiency, which pull a firm inside the maximum growth-of-demand curve, is itself ambiguous. Marris argued that such inefficiency is more likely to give lower profit *and* growth than an abundance of one at the expense of the other, thus inferring a direct relation (*AF* or *AG* rather than *AE* or *AH*), but such an argument is speculative only. Even accepting this, it is clear that more powerful methods are required to test the theory.

These are by no means the only difficulties. We have already seen in Chapter 8 (pp. 244–8) the problem of accurately classifying firms as owner-controlled or managerially controlled. In addition, all Radice's firms, being large, had well-developed managerial structures, so that if it is the managerial bureaucracy rather than the board itself which effectively determines motivation then relatively little difference of performance would have been expected apart from the efficiency/demand-growth ones referred to. If Williamson's M-form[43] organization has re-established profit maximization, the MCs would become much more like OCs, while if owners want growth for capital gain rather than dividends because of differences in the way they are taxed, then OCs would become much more like MCs. If, as both Manne[44] and Hindley[45] have argued, a reasonable market in corporate capital exists, then the discretion available to managers to move down the growth-of-demand curve is circumscribed, especially if a Yarrow-type constraint formulation is appropriate, again making MCs like OCs.

Against the background it is not surprising to find considerable inconsistency between different studies. Monsen *et al.*,[46] in a study of U.S. firms, found that OCs had higher profit rates than MCs, but neither Larner[47] nor Kamerschen,[48] again using U.S. data, could find any difference between their profit rates. Holl[49] found for a sample of 183 firms in the U.K. that OCs had higher profit rates on average

[43] See pp. 252–5.

[44] H. Manne, 'Mergers & The Market for Corporate Control', *J.P.E.* 73, no. 2 (Apr. 1965), 110–20.

[45] B. Hindley, 'Separation of Ownership & Control in the Modern Corporation', *J. Law Econ.* 13, no. 1 (Apr. 1970), 185–222.

[46] R. Monsen, J. Chiu, D. Cooley, 'The Effect of Separation of Ownership & Control on the Performance of the Large Firm', *Q.J.E.* 82, no. 3 (Aug. 1968), 435–51.

[47] R. Larner, *Management Control & The Large Corporation* (1970).

[48] D. Kamerschen, 'Influence of Ownership & Control on Profit Rates', *A.E.R.* 58, no. 3 (June 1968), 432–47.

[49] P. Holl, 'Effect of Control Type on the Performance of the Firm in the U.K.', *J.I.E.* 23, no. 4 (June 1975), 257–72.

(16·9 per cent against 15·4 per cent) and lower growth rates (6 per cent against 8 per cent), but that there was substantial overlap between the two groups. When the effect of difference of market structure were allowed for, the difference between the groups disappeared, and the use of a restricted sample based on a tighter definition of owner and management control not only altered the ranking of growth-rate performance, but still did not allow OCs and MCs to be discriminated between.

Marris[50] had earlier argued that differences between firms in demand-growth conditions were more likely than differences in supply-growth conditions, because although large firms were often in very different *product* markets they were all more or less in the same *financial* market and facing the same sort of stock market constraint on their growth activities. In terms of Figure 9.9 this would make correlations along AB much more frequent than along AC. In addition, inefficiency at the expense primarily of growth (AF) was more likely than inefficiency at the expense primarily of profit (AG), because while both involve lower growth and profit rates, AG also involves a higher retention ratio unambiguously lowering the valuation ratio, while AF involves a *lower* retention ratio and hence some (or even complete) offset of the fall in valuation ratio that would otherwise occur. He concluded that correlations of the AB and AF form would be frequent, but of the AC and AG form infrequent.[51] He then set out to test this empirically by looking at correlations that existed in data provided earlier by Meyer and Kuh,[52] first deducing for AB, AC, AF, and AG whether the correlations between growth rate, profit rate, and retention ratio would be positive or negative and comparing these deductions with the evidence on the three variables. His results are summarized in Table 9.2.

While at first sight this suggests rather strong support for the Marris model, there are difficulties about it.

(i) The pattern of correlations inferred for AB is incorrect. Along AB, growth and profitability are positvely correlated as shown on Table 9.2, but the retention ratio, being constant along AB, is uncorrelated with either growth or profit rate. By not allowing for *non*-correlation (as opposed to positive or negative) and lumping AB with AF, the analysis obscures the significance of differences in demand-growth conditions. In practice there may be a justification for presuming a rising retention ratio as the demand-growth curve

[50] R. Marris, op. cit. (1963), 277–88.

[51] AE and AH were ruled out, as explained above, p. 315.

[52] Relating to 70 observations on 14 industries for 5 years from J. Meyer and E. Kuh, *The Investment Decision* (Harvard, 1957).

TABLE 9.2

	g, p	g, r	p, r	%
AB, AF	+	+	+	54
AC	−	+	−	13
AG	+	−	−	22
All other patterns				11

g = growth rate, p = profit rate, r = retention ratio.
+ indicates positive correlation, − a negative one.
Source: J. Marris, 'A Model of the Managerial Enterprise',
Q.J.E., 1963, vol. 44, No. 2, pp. 227–88.

shifts outwards. If the latter allows a firm to move from A to B then its valuation ratio unambiguously rises (high growth rate, high profit rate, same retention ratio). Given a Marris-type valuation ratio constraint this permits a rightward shift of the supply-growth line, increasing the growth rate and retention ratio at the expense of profit rate and bringing the valuation ratio back to its securely constrained value. Such synchronization of the supply-growth and demand-growth curves would then validate Table 9.2 and help provide further support for the model.

Whether such synchronization occurs is not known, but there is one argument each way at present. Against it is the argument that a constraint of the Yarrow-form (see p. 270) is more realistic. In this case a shift of the demand-growth curve by raising the *maximum* valuation ratio attainable would also raise the constraint value of it and *not* therefore permit an increase in the retention ratio. Supporting it is the fact that correlations between growth and profit rates may well be curvilinear as shown by the line AG in Figure 9.10 (see Chapter 15 for detailed evidence on the empirical relationship). This is what synchronization of shifts in the two curves would generate under a Marris-type constraint.

Initially at A, market prospects are poor, growth and profit rates are low, and there is virtually no prospect of the firm being able to sacrifice valuation for growth (A may indeed be the present-value maximization point.) This holds at B and C also, even though demand prospects are improving. After point C synchronization occurs as the higher growth and profit rates, by increasing the valuation ratio, permit a rightward shift in the SS curve. The profit-growth curve becomes much flatter until E is reached, where the retention ratio has risen so much that further rises in it would depress the valuation ratio even if associated with higher profit and growth

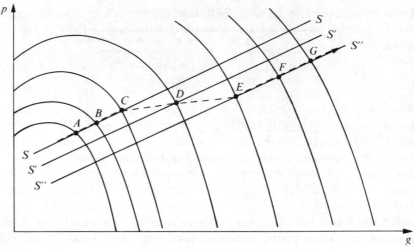

Fig. 9.10

rates. The supply-growth curve cannot shift further right without undermining security, and further shifts in the demand-growth curve generate points F, G, etc. AG then has the curvilinear shape referred to.

(ii) The second difficulty is that while the correlations discussed offer some support for the model depicted in Figure 9.9, like Radice's results they do not throw much light on managerial motivation. The analysis and evidence based on point A in Figure 9.9 could equally well have been based on point D, or even D'.[53] Thus they are equally consistent with firms' decision-takers pursuing present-value maximization or profit-rate maximization. Figure 9.10, however, is of some use here. If firms were profit maximizers or valuation maximizers, only a rather fortuitous series of shifts in the demand-growth curve (predominantly upwards first, then rightwards, then upwards) could generate the non-linear curve shown. Growth maximization, on the other hand, would give such a curve, provided that the valuation constraint is at least to some extent independent of its maximum value.

More significant, however, is Solow's argument that although growth and profit (and valuation) maximizers will choose different growth and profit rates, their *qualitative* reactions to such things as changes in taxes, discount rate, and factor prices will generally be the same.[54] This does not undermine the model as one in terms of which

---

[53] The only exception, and it is of little consequence, is that a correlation of the form AE could not be constructed from point D' as it would go outside the demand-growth curve.

[54] R. Solow, op. cit.

both objectives can be analysed, but may mean it is less important *where* on the growth-valuation curve a firm, in the light of its objectives, locates.

7   CONCLUSIONS

This chapter has provided a picture of the firm which incorporates most of the real-world features of firms discussed in Chapter 8 and all of the aspects of the firm initially outlined in Chapter 1. As a result the passive view of the firm has been modified, and so therefore has the original emphasis on the constraints imposed by demand and cost curves. Instead the stock market is seen as the major potential constraint on management, as the latter actively try, via their diversification, financial, and expenditure decisions, to obtain their optimum growth/profit combination. Size becomes a rather less important by-product of growth, performance in any market no more than one component element in determining the firm's over-all performance, and pricing only one part of an over-all set of interlocking corporate decisions. In the process of constructing this new picture of the firm it was necessary to set up a basic theory of stock market valuation, analyse managerial constraints on firms' behaviour, and develop a new approach to the theory of consumer behaviour. Each is an essential element in the explanation of the behaviour and performance of the active diversified firm.

Paradoxically one of the main issues which led to the construction of such a model—the type of company objective pursued—remains unresolved. While profit maximization appears less likely, there is little evidence to indicate unambiguously whether growth or valuation maximization is more prevalent or associated with particular types of company ownership. Whether growth and valuation maximizers respond differently to parametric chnges is quite likely to depend on the nature of the constraint hypothesized, as in earlier static models. But the basis for analysis which the over-all model provides may turn out to be much more important than the point on the demand-growth curve towards which the firm is presumed to aim. Thus, while there are still problems of the logic of the methodology, the inadequacy of empirical validation, and inferring of motivation from the evidence, the model none the less offers a good framework within which the various decisions of the firm can be examined.

10

COMPANY FINANCE

1   THE ANALYSIS OF FINANCIAL DECISIONS

Consideration of the model of the firm presented in the preceding chapter, and observation of the behaviour of actual firms both indicate that company finance is an important element in the understanding of industrial activity. Yet, as mentioned in Chapter 1, until very recently company finance was the object of quite separate study from price and output behaviour, and even investment behaviour. Even now the highly developed theoretical and empirical work on finance is often to be found in different journals[1] and separate texts,[2] and few industrial economics texts cover this area at all.

While an explanation for this is probably to be found in the fact that industrial economics largely grew out of the theory of the firm, it is none the less an unsatisfactory state of affairs. This is not only because financial behaviour is clearly a central feature of firm's development and performance, nor even just because senior management usually exerts its control through financial performance measures. Rather it is because, apart from technology and managerial objectives, the only completely exogenous constraint on the diversified firm is the stock market via its impact on company valuation and cost of funds. As a corollary, the need for and design of public regulatory constraint depends to a considerable extent on characteristics of the financial market as well as product markets.

In Part III of this book we make no claim to have fully integrated financial theory into models of firms' product market behaviour, nor have we attempted this. Rather we have been concerned to present some of the arguments and developments that have occurred in a fairly elementary way, so that the student of industrial economics will be fully aware of the issues involved, and at least some of the implications for industrial economics. It is perhaps advisable therefore at the outset to state briefly an outline of the issues and indicate where in Part III they are located.

Essentially there have been three strands of thought, as depicted in Figure 10.1.

---

[1] The main exception being the *American Economic Review*.

[2] There are now many texts on the subject, for example S. H. Archer, C. A. D'Ambrosio, *Business Finance: Theory and Management*, 2nd edn. (New York, 1972). Also very valuable is S. H. Archer, C. A. D'Ambrosio, *The Theory of Business Finance: A Book of Readings*, 2nd edn. (New York, 1976), which contains many of the most important articles.

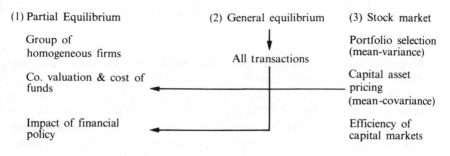

Fig. 10.1

Initially a partial equilibrium approach was adopted to tackle the question of how companies' financial decisions, particularly their decisions on dividend policy and the use of debt finance, influenced the cost of funds that they obtained for investment. This incorporates the issue of what determines a company's valuation, and so in terms of both content and method it is the approach that follows on most naturally from the previous chapter. Second, and more recently, partial equilibrium theorems concerning company valuation, the cost of funds, and the impact of financial policy have been re-examined within the context of a general equilibrium framework which embraces all transactions. In general terms this has bolstered the partial equilibrium conclusions, but emphasized more clearly the conditions under which financial policy is important and the conditions under which it isn't.

Largely separate from these developments, the behaviour of investors in a stock market was explored. This initially involved analysis of investor portfolio selection under uncertainty in terms of the mean and variance of returns from company shares (securities) and from combinations of them designed to maximize investor utility. From this developed the Capital Asset Pricing Model, which sought to establish how company financial assets were valued when the behaviour of all investors in the stock markets was taken into account. Of major significance was the conclusion that, because shares were valued by investors only in the light of the contribution they made to the mean and variance of a *portfolio* of shares, it was not the variance of a share return that mattered but only its *covariance* with other possible returns in the stock market.[3] In

---

[3] Whereas Variance is the Expected Value of the deviations of a variable from its mean squared, i.e. $E(x-\bar{x})^2$ where $\bar{x}$ is the mean of x, Covariance is the Expected Value of the product of the deviations from mean of two variables, i.e. $E(x-\bar{x})(y-\bar{y})$. A high positive value indicates that the two variables are strongly correlated; a high negative value indicates

addition, this model made it possible to examine the issue of whether the capital market is efficient or not as a market for ownership of capital assets.

More recently it has been seen that under certain conditions the conclusions of the partial and general equilibrium approaches can be generated from the mean-variance and capital asset pricing approaches, indicating that financial theory generally can be integrated and that a number of issues—the valuation of companies, the effect of financial policy, the behaviour of investors, and the efficiency of stock markets—can be properly linked together.[4]

In this chapter we mainly pursue the original partial equilibrium approach, review competing theories and survey empirical testing. This follows on easily from the introductory financial analysis of Chapter 9 and is the most appropriate, given the partial equilibrium emphasis of industrial economics to date. The chapter subsequently, however, presents a general equilibrium approach as an indication of the generality of the theorems discussed and of the direction that analysis may be more likely to follow in future. The third approach is presented in Chapter 14 where we adopt the perspective of the stock market to examine the issues of takeover and the efficiency of stock markets. Together these chapters should provide a reasonably broad review of the state of financial theory and evidence.

In considering the financial policy of firms, the basic diagram of Chapter 1 indicated that two decisions were central, namely:

(i) *The Retention Ratio (r)*—the proportion of earnings retained for investment. Both retentions and total earnings may be expressed gross or net of company tax, but we shall ignore tax aspects except when dealing with them explicitly. *The pay-out ratio* of dividends to earnings equals one minus the retention ratio.

(ii) *The Gearing Ratio (h)*—the ratio of debt finance to the total of debt plus equity finance. There are many forms of both debt and equity finance, but the essential difference between them is that the providers of debt finance obtain no ownership claim, whereas the providers of equity finance do. This ratio is to be distinguished from the leverage ratio (L) which is the ratio of debt to equity finance. The gearing ratio equals $L/(L + 1)$.[5]

---

that they are strongly inversely correlated; a low (positive or negative) value indicates little correlation, and a zero value indicates complete independence of the two variables.

[4] See for example M. E. Rubenstein, 'A Mean-Variance Synthesis of Corporate Financial Policy', *J. of Finance*, 28, no. 1 (Mar. 1973), 167–82.

[5] If D is debt finance, M is equity finance

$$h = \frac{D}{D + M}$$

In taking decisions on the retention ratio the company effectively determines its supply of internal finance, and indirectly therefore the proportion of its funds coming from external and internal sources. In taking decisions on the gearing ratio the company determines the proportion of its external funds coming from borrowing and equity.

These two decisions have traditionally been thought important because they together determine:

(i) The valuation ratio of the company (V). This we have seen is either the effective constraint on managerial behaviour and a co-determinant therefore of the firm's growth rate and profit rate, or itself part of the management's utility function.[6]

(ii) The cost to the firm of obtaining funds. Retentions, debt, and new equity finance all have different costs and the ratio (as determined by the retention and gearing ratios) in which they are combined also affects the cost of obtaining such funds. We shall therefore need to utilize again a theory of stock market valuation such as that introduced in Chapter 9, and provide an explanation of what determines the cost of different funds both individually and collectively.

Unfortunately, several issues in this area have been the subject of considerable controversy. Not only do different conclusons follow from different assumptions and specifications of financial models, but there are often difficulties in interpreting the empirical evidence designed to shed light on the issues. We shall, however, attempt as far as possible to provide a coherent picture of them and the conclusions which appear best supported.

The next section looks briefly at the flow of funds through a company, and section 3 at the costs of different individual sources of funds. This serves as an introduction to the four main sections, which review first the theory and then the evidence on the determination of both the retention ratio and the gearing ratio. At the end of the chapter are three appendices on accounting issues that arise in discussing company finance.

2   THE FLOW OF FUNDS

Figure 10.2 in very simplified form shows the main financial flows within a company with which we shall be concerned. Gross Trading

$$= \frac{D/M}{D/M + 1} = \frac{L}{L + 1}$$

Note that the term 'leverage' is sometimes used for the ratio of debt to total finance in the literature. Also shares are frequently referred to as stock. Such differences are generally correlated with the Atlantic.

[6] See pp. 308–10.

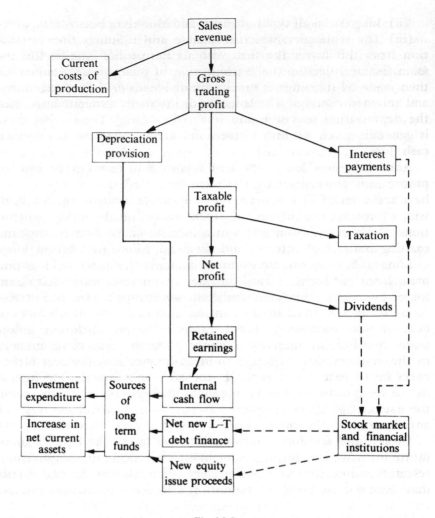

Fig. 10.2

Profit is that part of sales revenue remaining after paying current production costs,[7] and is split into three elements.

(i) Provision for depreciation of capital stock. This is a purely book-keeping operation. It identifies the part of gross trading profit estimated as necessary to cover the cost of the deterioration of machinery, plant, etc. Of itself this operation involves no flow of funds into or out of the company.

[7] The relationship between the flow of funds and accounting conventions is examined briefly in Appendix 1.

(ii) Interest on all types of short- and long-term borrowing.

(iii) The remainder, which is taxable profit. Subtraction of taxation from this leaves the firm with its net profit.[8] The first of the main financial decisions– the proportion of funds to be retained– is then made by splitting net profit into dividends paid to shareholders, and retained earnings. The total funds internally generated are then the depreciation provision and retained earnings. The sum of these is generally given the rather misleading term 'cash flow' or 'internal cash flow'.[9]

Adding in new long-term debt finance and new equity issue in proportions determined by the company's decision on gearing, we have the total of all long-term funds available to the company. Both will, of course, depend on the stock market's and financial institutions' views of the company, which in turn will be a function of the existing pattern of interest and dividend payments (dotted line).

Long-term debt finance normally includes three items: long-term bank loans (at fixed or variable rates of interest), other long-term loans, e.g. from other companies, the government, etc., and debentures, which are fixed interest marketable company bonds and are held by both individuals and institutions. Putting all these together under one heading therefore removes from the analysis differences in the marketability of long-term debt finance provided and differences in the extent to which the interest rate is variable. The item is net of repayment of outstanding loans. New equity proceeds covers the issues of all types of shares[10] to raise more finance, and is net of any repayment of capital.

These funds are shown as going into two uses. The first is expenditure on new investment, predominantly physical but also including research and development and marketing investment. Second, funds may be used to build up current (i.e. quickly realizable) assets–

[8] This is complicated by the fact that net profits are calculated after deducting tax *liability* whereas the cash flows in a company depend on actual tax *payment*. Typically these are not the same, as taxation is normally paid in arrears. See Appendix 1 for treatment of this problem.

[9] The fact that the depreciation provision is a source of funds should not be taken to imply that an increase in depreciation would make more funds available. Unless tax or dividends are changed, the increase in depreciation will be exactly offset by a fall in retained earnings. In fact lower tax and dividends may result but it is only in this way that increased depreciation increases the supply of funds.

[10] The main distinction is between *preference* shares, on which dividends are paid up to a specified amount before any dividends are paid to other shareholders, and *ordinary* shares, the most common form, which have no such priority. *Cumulative preference* shares carry the right to receive 'delayed' dividends not paid in previous years before any current dividend is paid to ordinary shareholders. Preference shares are more like debentures in that they are safer, prior charges on profit, but are still shares in that they confer an ownership stake and do not carry a legal right to payment.

mainly stocks and work-in-progress, financial assets, short-term loans to debtors, and cash balances—or to reduce current liabilities—mainly amounts owed to creditors, banks and other short-term loans. In either case the result is to increase *net* current assets.

A number of complications arise when it comes to recording the financial flows and financial performance of companies in a set of accounts. As nearly all empirical evidence on the economic behaviour of companies utilizes figures directly or indirectly derived from company accounts, this chapter contains three appendices on accounting. The first explains briefly the derivation of the usual format of company accounts and its relation to the flow diagram of Figure 10.2. It also gives aggregate figures for the component items as an indicator of the latter's relative magnitude. Appendix 2 identifies, on the basis of the accounts, some financial ratios commonly used to assess performance, including those with which we shall be concerned below. Appendix 3 identifies the difficulties that arise as a result of the impact of inflation on the conventional form of accounts, and presents some current proposals for improvement.

The main terms and ratios used in the text are given in Table 10.1 and are taken from a more complete list in Appendix 2.

TABLE 10.1

Stock Concepts	*Flow Concepts*	*Return Concepts*
Capital Employed, K	Gross Profit net of depreciation, Π	Rate of return on Capital $$p = \frac{\Pi}{K}$$
Debt Finance, D	Interest charges iD	Interest rate, i
Stock Market Valuation of Equity, M (= No. of shares, N times price of shares, S.		Earnings Yield $$y_e = \frac{\Pi - iD}{M}$$
Valuation ratio $$V = \frac{M}{K - D}$$	Dividends, d	Dividend Yield $$y_d = \frac{d}{M} = \frac{(\Pi - id)(1 - r)}{M}$$
Gearing Ratio $$h = \frac{D}{D + M} \text{ or } h' = \frac{D}{K}$$	Retention Ratio $$r = \frac{\Pi - iD - d}{\Pi - iD}$$	

Note: The two measures of the gearing ratio, both of which appear in the literature, are equal only when the valuation ratio (stock market value to book value of net assets, K-D) equals unity.

3   THE COST OF FUNDS

In this section we identify the cost of different individual types of finance as a basis for identifying the cost of finance when it is provided from a combination of sources.

The cost of short-term bank lending is generally very easy to identify, being based on the interest rate specified by the bank. The cost of such finance is not however equal to the interest rate because the interest paid is a tax deductible expense. If £100 of interest payable were to be avoided through repayment of a loan, the rise in *net* profits would not be £100 but only $(1 - t)100$ where t is the effective tax rate. This is the opportunity cost of the finance and measures its true cost.

Trade credit arises when there is either a discount for rapid payment or a cumulative charge for delayed payment. In both cases, delay in payment implies more funds for the company, but at a cost. The true cost is again identified after allowance for taxation. In some cases there is no charge made by a supplier for delayed payment, and so the cost of funds is technically zero. Companies may nevertheless want to impute a cost to delayed payment to suppliers because of the increased risk of slow delivery, higher prices, etc. Tax provisions also have zero cost because there is no charge for the delayed payment of taxation.

The annual charge for longer-term fixed interest loans is $iD_F(1 - t_0)$ where i is the interest rate, D_F the size of the fixed-interest debt, and t_0 the effective tax rate. The cost of the finance is $i(1 - t)$. In the case of marketable debt such as debentures the matter is more complicated. The rate of interest to the *debenture holder* is given by i' (ignoring taxation) in the expression

$$B_L = \sum_{t=L+1}^{t=L+m} \frac{bB_N}{(1 + i')^{t-L}} + \frac{B_N}{(1 + i')^m}$$

where m is the number of years to maturity, L the age of the bond when purchased, B_L the purchase price of the bond, B_N the terminal value, and b the nominal interest rate on the bond. But for the *company* issuing the debenture, it is given by i in the expression

$$B_0 = \sum_{t=1}^{t=n} \frac{bB_N}{(1 + i)^t} + \frac{B_N}{(1 + i)^n}$$

where B_0 is the issue price, n is the life of the debenture, and i is the cost of this form of finance. i only equals b if $B_0 = B_N$. Subsequent movements in B_t, the market price of the debenture, are *per se* irrelevant. If, however, the company is generally regarded as rather high-risk, then debenture holders will seek a high return, depressing the price of existing debentures. In the short term this does not affect the company, but over the longer term in which new issue of debentures occurs the price obtainable per new debenture issued, B_0, will be lower. From the above equation it is clear that this implies a higher value for b. Alternatively, to maintain the previous issue price $B_{t=0}$, i will have to be higher, which again implies a higher value for b. We can therefore assume that over the long term not only the yield for a prospective debenture holder but also the company's cost of debenture finance is inversely related to the price of debentures. Again, the company may add an imputed cost to b when raising debenture finance to allow for its subjective evaluation of the risk of default.

Turning to equity finance there are, as we have seen, three main forms: Retained Earnings, Depreciation Provision, and new Equity Issue, all of which are sources of funds owned by a company's shareholders. When a shareholder buys a share he obtains a claim to an uncertain stream of future returns, normally characterized by mean and variance of expected return. The combination of mean and variance of return that he requires in order to be willing to purchase the share depends on the return he can obtain from a riskless asset, and the mean and variance of return that he can expect from other shares that he could include in his portfolio. A rigorous derivation of this relationship is given in Chapter 14 (pp. 476–82) where the role of the stock market as a market in corporate ownership is examined. For present purposes all we need is the conclusion that for a given share, dependent on the risk and return characteristics of other assets, a shareholder will adopt a particular discount rate in evaluating the future stream of uncertain dividends which is a function of the riskiness of those dividends. For a given retention ratio this depends on three factors:

(*a*) The estimated variability of the future profit rate.

(*b*) The estimated likelihood that future share issues will decrease the dividend per share.

(*c*) The gearing ratio, which determines the degree of dividend variation for any variation in profit.

To see this, consider a company whose trading profit net of depreciation (and ignoring taxation) rises from Π_1 to Π_2. The proportionate increase in dividend is

$$\frac{(\Pi_2 - iD)(1 - r) - (\Pi_1 - iD)(1 - r)}{(\Pi_1 - iD)(1 - r)}$$

$$= \frac{p_2 K - p_1 K}{p_1 K - iD} = \frac{p_2 - p_1}{p_1 - i\dfrac{D}{K}}$$

This is unambiguously higher than the variation in profit $(p_2 - p_1)/p_1$, and rises as D/K rises.

Empirical support for this is provided by Ben-Zion and Shalit,[11] who show that the riskiness of shares is a function of the size (inverse) of a firm, its gearing,[12] and its dividend record. The last of these is associated with the firm's earnings stability and its success in hitting its dividend target as a result. The former two are not unrelated. Debenture finance appears to be more prevalent amongst large companies,[13] probably because, with a lower average variability of returns due to higher diversification, the likelihood that gross profit will be inadequate to cover interest charges in any period is lower for a given proportion of debt finance. The reduced threat of bankruptcy makes such finance cheaper for larger firms, and this provides the incentive to issue a higher proportion of debt finance.

Given the values of these determinants, the shareholder's discount rate is determined and represents the cost of equity finance which a company should utilize in its expenditure decisions if it wishes to maximize shareholder wealth.[14]

We can identify this cost of equity by recalling the expression for the stock market valuation of a company derived in Chapter 9 (p. 000).

---

[11] U. Ben-Zion, S. S. Shalit, 'Size, Leverage & Dividend Record as Determinants of Equity Risk', *J. of Finance*, 30, no. 4 (Sept. 1975), 1015–26.

[12] Note, however, that the relationship between share price volatility and gearing is a function of the term-structure of company debt, and this means it is theoretically possible for increased gearing to lower the volatility. See R. A. Haugen and D. W. Wichern, 'The Intricate Relationship between Financial Leverage and the Stability of Stock Prices', *J. of Finance*, 30, no. 5 (Dec. 1975), 1283–92. That firms are actively concerned with the term-structure of their debt, in order to minimize effective interest costs is shown by W. White, 'Debt Management & The Form of Business Financing', *J. of Business*, 29, no. 2 (May 1974), 565–78.

[13] See S. Prais, *The Evolution of Giant Firms in Britain*, N.I.E.S.R. (1976), 102.

[14] But see p. 331 for an exception to this.

$$M = \frac{K_0 p (1-r)}{\delta - g}$$

where δ is the shareholder's discount rate. Note that p is the expected profit rate of the company. Allowing for the possibility of interest payments out of gross profits, this expression becomes

$$M = \frac{(\Pi - iD)(1 - r)}{\delta - g}$$

Therefore $\delta = \dfrac{(\Pi - id)(1 - r)}{M} + g = \dfrac{d}{M} + g = y_d + g$

In other words, shareholders will buy or sell shares until the stock market valuation is such that dividend yield plus growth rate of the dividend[15] equals shareholders' required rate of return. Dividend yield plus growth rate of the dividend is then the most widely used guide to a company's cost of equity capital.

If the valuation ratio is unity, this expression becomes the *earnings yield*, as follows. New investment is internally financed investment, $r(\Pi - iD)$, plus that financed by new debentures, $\Delta X \cdot (D/X)$ where X is the number of debentures, plus that financed by new equity issue, $\Delta N \cdot (M/N)$ where N is the number of shares. The rates of increase of debt and equity finance are presumed equal. Thus

$$I = r(\Pi - iD) + \Delta N \cdot \frac{M}{N} + \Delta X \cdot \frac{D}{X}$$

and $g = \dfrac{I}{K} = rp' + \dfrac{\Delta N}{N} \cdot \dfrac{M}{K} + \dfrac{\Delta X}{X} \cdot \dfrac{D}{K} = rp' + g_n \cdot \left(\dfrac{M}{K} + \dfrac{D}{K} \right)$

where $p' = $ the post-interest rate of return on capital, $(\Pi - iD)/K$, and $g_n = $ growth of number of shares, $\Delta N/N$, and of the number of debentures, $\Delta X/X$. The discount rate on equity has to be amended to allow for the fact that future dividends are now shared with new

[15] It is presumed as in a steady-state system that dividends grow at the same rate as the company's capital employed.

shareholders, and becomes[16] $\delta + g_n$. Therefore

$$\delta + g_n = \frac{d}{M} + rp' + g_n \frac{M+D}{K}$$

If the valuation ratio is unity $M = K = D$ and $\Pi' = \Pi - iD$

$$\delta = \frac{d}{M} + rp' = \frac{\Pi'(1-r)}{M} + \frac{r\Pi'}{M} = \frac{\Pi'}{M} = y_e$$

This is frequently taken as the cost of equity finance.[17]

---

[16] The Present Value of the dividend per share equals

$$\frac{M}{N_0} = \sum_{t=1}^{t=\infty} \frac{d_0(1+g)^t}{N_0(1+g_n)^t} \cdot \frac{1}{(1+\delta)^t} = \frac{d_0}{N_0} \cdot \frac{1}{\delta + g_n - g + \delta \cdot g_n}$$

Ignoring $\delta \cdot g_n$ as being of an order of magnitude smaller

$$M = \frac{d_0}{\delta + g_n - g}$$

and, comparing this to the basic formula $d_0/(\delta - g)$ it is seen that the discount rate has become $\delta + g_n$.

[17] Note that this implies, and therefore only holds for

$$p' = y_e, \quad \text{i.e.} \quad \frac{\Pi'}{K} = \frac{\Pi'}{M}$$

If $p' \neq y_e$, then with internal financing

$$\delta = \frac{d}{M} + rp' \quad \text{and with} \quad p' = \frac{\Pi'}{K} \quad \text{and} \quad y_e = \frac{\Pi'}{M} \quad \text{we obtain}$$

$$\delta = y_e + r\Pi'\left(\frac{1}{K} - \frac{1}{M}\right) \quad \text{and} \quad \delta = p' + \frac{\left(\frac{K}{M} - 1\right)\Pi(1-r)}{K}$$

Therefore if $p' > \delta$, $(K/M) < 1$ and so $p' > \delta > y_e$.

This shows that when $p' > \delta$, the earnings yield understates the shareholder's discount rate. However, Lintner has shown that in a growth context, although counter-intuitive, the test discount rate for investment if the valuation of the company is to be maximized is *still* the earnings yield rather than the shareholder's discount rate. This is because the share valuation will continue to rise with new investment, provided the marginal internal rate of return is above y_e. For an elaboration of the theoretical significance of these issues see J. Lintner, 'The Cost of Capital and Optimal Financing of Corporate Growth', *J. of Finance*, 18, no. 2 (May 1963), 292–310.

As with debentures, the cost of equity finance, as measured by earnings yield, tends to be lower for larger companies.[18] This probably arises because of the importance of institutional shareholders in the stock market, who tend to prefer larger companies because of their need to deal in large amounts but in flexible markets. The greater security offered by larger companies could also be an explanation, but Davenport's study[19] indicated an inverse correlation between size and earnings yield after allowing for other factors including variability of earnings. In addition, issuing costs are subject to economies of scale, and quotation on a stock market itself greatly reduces equity yields through creating a broader and much more flexible market.

Several qualifications must be made to this basic picture of a company's cost of equity.

(i) Different shareholders may require different returns from a share either because they assess the latter's riskiness differently or because the rest of their portfolio has different risk/return characteristics. The latter could arise because shareholders have different estimates of the mean and variance of other shares, because of legal requirements concerning share purchase, because they face different tax schedules, etc. Some shareholders may therefore obtain a return in excess of their opportunity cost.

(ii) Retained earnings and depreciation provisions will be a cheaper source of finance than new equity issue because they avoid the administrative costs of equity issue.

(iii) Transactions costs imply a loss of anything up to 10 per cent in switching shareholdings, indicating that the return to an equity holder may to some extent fall below the latter's opportunity cost without precipitating a sale of shares.

(iv) If a company embarks on new investment which will provide the shareholder with a yield equal to his opportunity cost, δ, then provided the shares are valued 'correctly', $y_d + g = \delta$ and it does not matter whether exising or new shareholders purchase the shares. Both will earn or continue to earn their required return. But if for any of the reasons given the share price is undervalued, giving $y_d + g = \delta' > \delta$, then this is no longer true. If existing shareholders provide the new funds then the cost of capital should still be δ because although the rate of return will drop from δ' to $(a)\delta + (1 - a)\delta'$, where a is the ratio of new assets to old, the increase in the scale of operations will increase their total return. (This

[18] See S. Prais, op. cit. 109–12 for a useful summary of studies verifying this.
[19] M. Davenport, 'Leverage and the Cost of Capital: Some Tests using British Data', *Economica*, N.S. 38 (May 1971). 136–62.

is no different from moving down an investment schedule to the maximum profit point.) But if *new* shareholders provide the funds, all shareholders again earn $(a)\delta + (1 - a)\delta'$ but with no change in the existing shareholders' asset base. This then represents a gain to the new shareholders at the expense of the existing shareholders. In many cases this problem is largely avoided by making a 'rights' issue in which existing shareholders have the right to purchase the new shares if they wish. In this case, provided the new projects provide a return equal to or in excess of δ, the existing shareholders gain, and so δ is the cost of capital for both the company and the shareholders.

(v) Finally, it should be noted that taxation will of course frequently create differences in the effective cost of finance. For example, under some tax systems profits are first taxed (at rate t_c) and dividends are then also taxed (at rate t_p). If taxable profits is $\Pi - iD$, the amount of funds available to the shareholder to invest elsewhere, if this is all paid out in dividend payments, is

$$(1 - t_c)(1 - t_p)(\Pi - iD)$$

If these funds are retained, however, the funds available to invest on the shareholder's behalf are

$$(1 - t_c)(\Pi - iD)$$

The company could therefore invest to obtain a yield t_p per cent lower than the shareholder's opportunity cost and still be acting in the shareholder's interest.

For the most part we shall ignore these complications. In addition we will simplify by regarding M as equal to $K - D$. Ultimately these are only the stock market and the management's valuation of the net assets of the company respectively, and while stock market fluctuations and accounting conventions may generally cause them to diverge, for theoretical purposes they may be regarded as equal. (Clearly it will become an important distinction again in empirical work.) Hence we regard the cost of equity finance as

$$\delta = (d/M) + g = y_e$$

and the stock market valuation of a company as $M = \Pi'/\delta$.

The weighted average cost of capital when more than one source of funds is employed is the interest rate on debt times the proportion of finance raised in debt form, plus the yield on equity issued times the proportion of finance raised in equity form. This could be written as

$$w = \frac{iD'}{D' + M'} + \frac{y_e M'}{D' + M'}$$

where D' and M' are the market value of debt and equity at time of issue respectively, and w is the weighted average cost of capital. The ratio of $D'/(D' + M')$ need not of course be the same as the company's current ratio of debt to debt plus equity value at market value, $D/(D + M)$. Nor are these values constant over time, and so W_a cannot be directly found from observed values of $D/(D + M)$. But if over the longer term the company generally raises finance in a given proportion of debt to equity then $D'(D' + M')$ remains constant and will approximate to the long-run value of $D/(D + M)$. For specific finance-raising decisions D' and M' are the relevant amounts, but for analysis of long-term financial behaviour we may substitute D and M, and write $w = ih + y_e(1 - h)$.

We now go on to examine the central issues of how the retention ratio and gearing ratio affect the weighted average cost of capital and hence the appropriate discount rate for investment decisions.

4   THE RETENTION RATIO: THEORY

For simplicity we examine the retentions and gearing decisions separately. In this section we presume that the gearing ratio is optimal in that it minimizes the weighted cost of capital given the total funds raised by debt plus equity finance. Our concern is then over whether the cost of equity finance and the valuation of the company are a function of the retention ratio, and if so, how.

This is a question of considerable complexity and controversy both theoretically and empirically, and it will be useful to start at the point on which all agree. Modigliani and Miller (hereafter referred to as *MM*) have shown that under certain specific assumptions the valuation of a company is *completely independent* of its retention ratio.[20] The assumptions or conditions are:

(1) Perfect Capital Markets. This implies that no one buyer or seller of shares can affect their price: all traders have costless access to all relevant information: there are no transactions costs of any kind: there are no tax differentials between distributed or undistributed

[20] F. Modigliani, M. H. Miller, 'Dividend Policy, Growth & The Valuation of Shares', *J. of Business*, 34, no. 4 (Oct. 1961), 411–33.

profit for the company, nor between dividends and capital gains for the shareholder.

(2) Rational Behaviour. This implies preferring more wealth to less, and indifference as to the form of wealth or changes in it. £1 of dividends is valued identically to £1 of capital gain.

(3) Perfect Certainty, on the part of all investors regarding the future investment and profits of every company.

Under these conditions any reduction in dividend results in an exactly equal rise in capital gains as the valuation of the company rises to reflect the funds retained. Any shortage of funds as a result of higher dividends can be replaced immediately by a new issue of shares to the recipients of the dividends. Financial policy becomes irrelevant. MM show this formally as follows. Given the conditions listed, the return to a shareholder via dividends and capital gain from holding a share must in equilibrium be the same for all shares. Otherwise those with a lower (certain) return could be replaced by those with a higher (certain) return. This would lower the price of the former, and raise the price of the latter until the returns were equalized. We may therefore write

$$\frac{(d_t/N_t) + S_{t+1} - S_t}{S_t} = \beta \qquad (1)$$

where d_t is the dividend paid in the period t, S_t is the share price after d_{t-1} has been paid, and S_{t+1} is the share price after d_t has been paid. β is the total return from holding the share and is the same for all shares. Multiplying through by N_t and rearranging (remembering that $S_t N_t = M_t$) gives:

$$M_t = \frac{1}{1 + \beta}(d_t + N_t S_{t+1}) \qquad (2)$$

But

$N_{t+1} = N_t + \Delta N_t$ where ΔN_t is any new shares issued during period t at price S_{t+1}. Therefore $N_t S_{t+1} = N_{t+1} S_{t+1} - \Delta N_t S_{t+1} = M_{t+1} - \Delta N_t S_{t+1}$.

Therefore:

$$M_t = \frac{1}{1 + \beta}(d_t + M_{t+1} - \Delta N_t S_{t+1}) \qquad (3)$$

Now the company's need for new equity finance will be its investment in period t, given by I_t, minus the funds available from profits
in period t after payment of the dividend, i.e.

$$\Delta N_t S_{t+1} = I_t - (\Pi_t - d_t) \tag{4}$$

Substituting this in (3) above gives

$$M_t = \frac{1}{1 + \beta}(M_{t+1} - I_t + \Pi_t) \tag{5}$$

This indicates that M_t is independent of d_t and hence independent
of the pay-out (or retention) ratio. M_{t+1} reflects only future prospects beyond period t, Π_t depends on investment performance, and
I_t is independent of dividend policy because any shortage of funds
through payment of dividends is exactly made up for by the issue of
new shares. A similar equation can of course be derived for M_{t+1},
indicating that M_{t+1} is dependent on M_{t+2} but independent of d_{t+1}.
Similarly for M_{t+2}, M_{t+3}, etc., indicating that the market valuation
for any time period is independent of current and *all* future dividends.[21] As MM go on to say, the irrelevance of dividend policy is
'obvious' given the assumptions. In a rational and perfect economic
environment the 'real' variables, investment and profits alone determine stock market values, not the source of funds, nor the distribution of earnings, both of which are purely 'financial' aspects. A

[21] Substituting the equation

$$M_{t+1} = \frac{1}{1 + \beta}(M_{t+2} - I_{t+1} + \Pi_{t+1}) \text{ into (5)}$$

and substituting

$$M_{t+2} = \frac{1}{1 + \beta}(M_{t+3} - I_{t+2} + \Pi_{t+2}) \text{ into the resulting equation etc.}$$

gives
$$M_t = \sum_{t=0}^{t=\infty} \frac{1}{(1 + \beta)^{t+1}}(\Pi_t - I_t) + \frac{M_{\infty+1}}{(1 + \beta)^{\infty+1}}$$

The last term is effectively zero and the equation confirms the dependence of stock market
value on profits, investment, and stock market rate of return alone. Note that if $\Pi_t = \Pi_0$
and $I_t = I_0$ for all t this equation reduces to

$$M_0 = \frac{\Pi_0 - I_0}{\beta}.$$

shortage of funds through high dividend payments can always be made up through new equity issue, provided the prospective return is the same and shareholders are indifferent between dividends and capital gain.

It should be noted that although this argument permits replacement of funds paid out as dividends by new equity finance, the irrelevance of dividend policy to stock market valuation holds even if external financing is excluded. To see this we can recall the valuation formula

$$M = \frac{d}{\delta - g} = \frac{(1 - r)\Pi'}{\delta - rp'} \qquad (6)$$

where Π' and p' are profit and profit rate net of interest payments respectively. Differentiating with respect to r

$$\frac{dM}{dr} = \frac{-(\delta - rp')\Pi' + (1 - r)\Pi'p'}{(\delta - rp')^2} \qquad (7)$$

This gives the following results:

	dM/dr	*Optimal retention ratio*
for $p' > \delta$	+	1
$p' = \delta$	0	retention ratio irrelevant
$p' > \delta$	−	0

In the first and third cases the retention ratio *does* influence stock market valuation, but this does *not* in any way undermine the irrelevance of dividends *per se*. If all investment is internally financed then dividends compete with investment as a claim on funds and the dividend decision will determine the funds available for the firm to take up investment opportunities. With $p' > \delta$, retentions increase a shareholder's wealth by utilizing his funds in a higher yielding asset than available elsewhere. A dividend payment has the same effect if $\delta > p'$. The change in valuation reflects the shareholder's higher return from investment as a result of a change in the pay-out decision. Only if the return on prospective investment is exactly the same as the cost of the funds will changes in the volume of investment have no effect on share valuation, i.e. when $p' = \delta$. But this is the case where it is clear from the table that the retention ratio is irrelevant.

That the conclusion follows logically from the assumption is uncontroversial, therefore. Nor is there disagreement that perfect capital markets, rationality, and certainty do not completely hold in practice. The controversy arises over whether and to what extent the absence of these pure conditions makes dividend policy relevant or not, both in theory and in practice.

The first point of argument concerns the impact of introducing uncertainty into the model. At first sight it appears that earnings paid out as a certain dividend *now* will be preferred to an uncertain return from retention and reinvestment of those earnings in the future, but this is a simplistic and generally erroneous deduction. In particular MM argue that the existence of uncertainty does *not* alter the irrelevance of dividend policy. To establish this they first have to give a precise definition to the notion of rationality under uncertainty. This is done by introducing the concept of *symmetric market rationality*, which requires that

(1) Every investor is rational in the sense of preferring more wealth to less, irrespective of its form.

(2) Every investor *imputes rationality* to the market. This requires that in forming expectations an investor (*a*) assumes every other investor is rational, and (*b*) assumes every other investor imputes rationality to every other investor.

The proof of dividend irrelevance under uncertainty then follows a similar route to the proof under conditions of certainty. If a shareholder purchases shares at the beginning of period t he does not know what return he will obtain because he does not know the dividend he will receive, the profits that will be earned, nor the investment to be carried out. Irrespective of the price he pays for the share, the amount of wealth he will have at the end of period 1 per share is

$$\frac{\hat{d}_t}{N_t} + \hat{S}_{t+1}$$

where the circumflex indicates that the amount he will receive, for example as a dividend, is currently unknown. For the company's shareholders as a whole (i.e. multiplying by N_t), and noting $N_t = \hat{N}_{t+1} - \Delta\hat{N}_t$, we get a total value at the end of period 1 of $\hat{d}_t + \hat{M}_{t+1} - \Delta\hat{N}_t\hat{S}_{t+1}$. It is an accounting identity that

$$\Delta\hat{N}_t\hat{S}_{t+1} = \hat{I}_t - (\hat{\Pi}_t - \hat{d}_t)$$

and the total wealth at the end of period 1 is therefore

$$\hat{\Pi}_t - \hat{I}_t + \hat{M}_{t+1}$$

Although none of these is known, none depends on the dividend paid in period 1. For the first two terms this is true by assumption, and $\hat{M}_{t+1}$ is independent of $\hat{d}_t$ because it can only depend on prospects (be it of earning, investment, dividents) beyond period t. Thus the value of the shares now, M_t, is independent of $\hat{d}_t$.

By a similar argument, $\hat{M}_{t+1}$, though dependent on $\hat{\Pi}_{t+1}$, $\hat{I}_{t+1}$, and M_{t+2}, is independent of $\hat{d}_{t+1}$. Furthermore, under the assumption of symmetric market rationality it is *known* at time t that $\hat{M}_{t+1}$, whatever it turns out to be, is independent of $\hat{d}_{t+1}$. Hence M_t is independent of $\hat{d}_t$ and $\hat{d}_{t+1}$. Successive applications of the same argument show that M_t is independent of all future dividends, whatever value they may take.

The view that dividend policy is irrelevant under uncertainty has been attacked in a number of ways. Lintner argued that if investors, though they might have access to the same information, nevertheless had different subjective probability distributions of companies' prospects, then they would not be indifferent to dividend policy.[22] This is because retentions utilize the funds of *existing* shareholders, who have an expectation of gain from the company, whereas the payment of dividends accompanied by a new share issue in general requires raising funds from investors who currently do *not* hold the shares and who therefore have an expectation of loss from this company. To attract the latter to invest requires a low share price and so a lower stock market valuation. The prospect of new issues generating a fall in stock market value gives existing shareholders a rationale for preferring retentions.

MM however reject this simply by inviting one to repeat their proof for each individual investor and then to sum the results.[23] In other words Lintner's argument ignores the fact that in a perfect market *existing* shareholders having received a dividend would be ready to subscribe to the new issue of shares at current stock market prices because *their* estimate of the company's future by definition cannot be any different. Even if investors have different information or even no information at all, provided there is symmetric market rationality to ensure that future valuation is

[22] J. Lintner, 'Dividends, Earnings, Leverage, Stock Prices and the Supply of Capital to Corporations', *R. Econ. Stats.* 44, no. 3 (Aug. 1962), 239-69.
[23] F. Modigliani, M. H. Miller, 'Dividend Policy & Market Valuation: A Reply', *J. of Business*, 36 (Jan. 1963), 116-19. See footnote 1, p. 116.

independent of the current dividend, any individual investor will be indifferent between dividends and retentions and so will the market as a whole. Krainer has made this point more formally and more generally by introducing the investor's optimal consumption plan and arguing that, whatever the dividend policy of the company, a shortage of dividend income can always be met by a sale of shares, and an excess of dividend income can always be used to purchase the new shares that the dividend payment would make necessary.[24] The dividend policy itself is irrelevant.

Gordon pursued a different line of criticism.[25] Using the 'internal-finance only' model (see p. 337) and setting $p' = \delta$ to remove any investment effects, he argued that δ would itself be a function of r, and that a rise in r therefore, by raising δ, *would* change (reduce) share valuation. A reason for making δ a function of r is the 'growth stock paradox'. If a firm which restricts itself to internal finance alone pushes its growth rate higher and higher by successive increases in its retention ratio, then share valuation as shown by equation (6) rises further and further, becomes infinite, and then negative. The fact that this does not occur in practice suggests that δ may rise if r becomes very high. Gordon suggests two reasons.

(i) It would be reasonable because the dividend stream, having become more 'delayed' by an increase in the retention ratio, has become more uncertain.

(ii) More generally, if the discount rate used by shareholders to discount later returns is higher than that used to discount earlier ones, then a change in the stream of dividends which adds more weight to later time periods will raise the average value of the discount rate used and so lower the company's valuation.

As with Lintner's criticism however, this attempt to relate valuation to dividend policy is unsatisfactory. MM reject the first criticism, pointing out that for any future time period it is the size and uncertainty of *total* earnings (dividends plus retentions) with which the shareholder is concerned, neither of which are influenced by dividend policy if external financing is permitted.[26] It is not rational therefore to adopt a different discount rate if the retention ratio is altered.

The second argument was shown to be false by Brennan.[27] If all

[24] R. Krainer, 'A Pedagogic Note on Dividend Policy', *J. of Financial & Quantitative Analysis*, 6, no. 4 (Sept. 1971), 1147–54.

[25] M. J. Gordon, 'Optimal Investment & Financing Policy', *J. of Finance*, 18, no. 2 (May 1963), 264–72.

[26] F. Modigliani, M. H. Miller, op. cit. (1961).

[27] M. Brennan, 'A Note on Dividend Irrelevance and the Gordon Valuation Model', *J. of Finance*, 26, no. 5 (Dec. 1971), 1115–21.

investment is financed internally then a rise in the retention ratio permits extra investment each period. If this is ΔI_t for period t, the present value of this extra investment *in period t* allowing for different discount rates in different periods is:

$$\sum_{x=1}^{x=\infty} \frac{p'\Delta I_t}{(1 + \delta_{t+x})^x} - \Delta I_t$$

The present value *now* of all such future investment is

$$\sum_{t=1}^{t=\infty} \frac{\Delta I_t}{(1 + \delta_t)^t} \left(p' \sum_{x=1}^{x=\infty} \frac{1}{(1 + \delta_{t+x})^x} - 1 \right)$$

If $\delta_{t+x} = \delta$ for all t and x, then when $\delta = p'$ this expression is zero, confirming the earlier argument that investment effects are removed by setting $\delta = p'$. But if Gordon's view that $\delta_{t+x} \neq \delta$ for all t and x is admitted the expression is *not* in general zero *even if* $\delta_t = p'$. In other words the variation in valuation that arises from changes in dividend policy when the discount rate varies for different periods occurs because of the changes in the present value of company investment that accompany a different time profile of investment when the discount varies through time. The financial policy itself is again irrelevant. Keane reinforced this by showing that the change in valuation consequent upon the change in retention ratio would equally occur if there were no change in the retention ratio but a new share issue to finance the investment were announced,[28] thus illustrating that it was the investment, not the method of its financing, that caused the change in valuation. Thus it is not denied that discount factors may vary for different periods ahead (as a rising or falling function of the time interval), nor that a change in the retention ratio will generally change share valuation in such cases even if $\delta = p'$. What it shows is that the change in valuation is again a function of the change in investment rather than the change in dividend policy *per se*.

The conclusion so far therefore is that any effect of dividend policy on valuation is a result of accompanying changes in investment. If the latter is neutralized, MM's conclusion that dividend policy *per se* is irrelevant even under conditions of uncertainty is valid. Neither differences in shareholders' expectations, nor the use

[28] S. Keane, 'Dividends & The Resolution of Uncertainty', *J. of Business Finance and Accounting*, 1, no. 3 (Autumn 1974), 389–93.

of different discount rates for different time periods, nor restriction to internal sources of finance affect this conclusion.

Turning to the assumption of symmetric market rationality we find much less argument,[29] for while the conditions of symmetric market rationality might appear rather stringent Brennan has shown that much less restrictive assumptions than MM's still generate their conclusion.[30] Provided investors are rational in the ordinary economic sense, the MM conclusion requires only that M_{t+1} is independent of d_t. As long as (i) shares are valued only on the basis of future events, and (ii) some investors know this, then their arbitrage will force M_{t+1} to the value future events imply irrespective of d_t. Thus to deny the MM conclusion requires either that

(a) investors are not rational.

or (b) share prices depend on past events,

or (c) there are *no* investors who understand that shares only entitle one to future returns.

As virtually *all* models of market valuation exclude the first two and the third seems inherently very implausible, MM's conclusion seems more generally acceptable than their own initial specification would indicate.

The main difficulty lies with MM's third assumption—that of perfect capital markets. For once we admit imperfections to the analysis then it is obvious to all that dividend policy may be relevant, for a number of reasons given below. In addition however, once capital markets are recognized as imperfect, the existence of uncertainty *also* makes a difference. We review these points before proceeding to examine empirical evidence.

The main forms of imperfection are:

(1) Transactions costs. These include the legal, underwriting, and administrative costs of issuing shares and the brokerage charges on buying and selling shares. The result of these costs is that investors may well not be indifferent as between retentions on the one hand and dividends accompanied by purchase of newly issued shares on the other. Such costs are not however a sufficient condition for a change in dividend policy to affect share prices.[31] Each investor would be attracted to the shares of a company with his preferred retention ratio, such that the stream of dividend payments just met his stream of expenditures, thus eliminating these costs. A company changing its pay-out ratio would attract a different 'clientele', but

---

[29] But see W. Baumol, 'On Dividend Policy and Market Imperfection', *J. of Business*, 36, no. 1 (Jan. 1963), 112–15, and the reply by Modigliani and Miller in the same volume.

[30] M. Brennan, op. cit.   [31] See F. Modigliani, M. H. Miller, op. cit. (1961).

the valuation would again be independent of dividend policy. An investor unable to find his preferred pay-out ratio would buy combinations of shares with different pay-out ratios which together met his requirements. Only if there were heavy demand for extreme values of the pay-out ratio would the scarcity of the latter lead to a permanent premium or discount and so a change in valuation as a company changed its dividend policy.

(2) Limited supply of finance. Market imperfections may lead to new external finance being unavailable even though the expected return would be above the opportunity cost. If existing shareholders cannot or are not prepared to subscribe to new issues even though they will tolerate equivalent retentions, then, as Lintner argued (see above, p. 339), a high pay-out ratio will entail attracting new shareholders at lower share prices and hence lower valuation. These 'sweetening' prices may be necessary to attract attention, to overcome absence of information about the company, or to overcome less favourable judgements based on the same information as that available to existing shareholders. In each case the possibility of new shares being issued as a result of high pay-out ratios will make it rational for investors and managers to systematically prefer retentions to dividends. This type of effect is quite independent of any impact of investment changes on valaution.

(3) Information content of dividends. Given the existence of transactions costs, companies may rationally favour retentions and establish a normal pay-out ratio which just leaves them enough funds from retained earnings to finance their 'normal' investment. In addition this may become recognized in the market. If earnings then rise, investors may find out whether the (better-informed) managers judge this to be a transient or permanent change by seeing whether it results in an increase in dividends in an attempt to restore the normal pay-out ratio or not. A significant rise in dividends may therefore increase share valuation because of the higher earnings that the dividends are supposedly indicating. No such effect could occur in a perfect market with complete information. This phenomenon does not of course undermine the dividend irrelevance theorem. Any resulting empirical correlation between dividends and share prices is a result of the increased *earnings* expectation that the dividends indicate.

(4) Taxation. Three separate effects are involved.

(*a*) The existence of personal income tax means that not all dividends could be reinvested in the shares of either the same or a different company. By itself this implies an optimal retention ratio of unity until

$$p_2'(1 - t_d) > p_1'$$

where p_2' is the net profit rate in the best alternative investment, p_1' the net profit rate for the existing investment, and t_d the marginal tax rate on dividend income.

(b) On the other hand a capital gains tax will operate the other way. The net effect of the two tax rates will determine in conjunction with the investment opportunities available the optimal retention ratio. This is of course an empirical matter and has been different both across countries and over time. For all but those on the highest marginal income tax rates the net effect may be relatively small, in addition to which there are a number of institutional investors with sizeable investments which are tax exempt.

(c) If company taxation does not discriminate between retained profit and profit paid out as dividends then a company's tax liability is independent of its retention ratio and in an MM world the optimal retention ratio is determined by the investment opportunities facing the firm. If the company tax system does discriminate between retentions and dividends then, as King has shown, the production and investment decisions will not change nor will the optimal retention ratio.[32] In consequence, the higher the taxation of dividends relative to retentions,the lower will be the *net* pay-out ratio (given by the ratio of the net dividend to the sum of net dividends and retentions). The elasticity of the net pay-out ratio with respect to a tax discrimination variable $1/(1 + t_d)$ is shown by King to depend on the value of the variable itself and the optimal retention ratio.[33]

All of these cases deal with imperfections in the capital market. Equally important is the existence of substantial imperfections in product markets which permit managerial discretion, behaviour, and efficiency to intrude into the valuation–dividend relation.[34] This can happen in several ways.

(a) If full-cost pricing is employed and dividends are treated like interest charges as a 'cost of finance', then a change in dividends may change the company's earnings, and valuation thereby.

(b) If organizational slack is a function of the level of planned dividends then a change in the latter may influence earnings.

(c) If managers generally retain more funds than would be optimal for shareholders given the market imperfections that exist,

[32] M. A. King, 'Dividend Behaviour and the Theory of the Firm', *Economica*, N.S. 41 (Feb. 1974), 25–34.

[33] This he suggests may account for different empirical estimates of the elasticity in various studies which incorporate it as a constant.

[34] See J. E. Walter, 'Dividend Policy: Its Infuence on the Value of the Enterprise', *J. of Finance*, 18, no. 2 (May 1963), 280–91.

because their own goals favour excess liquidity, limited debt finance, and growth from retentions at the expense of profits, then a rise in dividends will move the pay-out ratio towards the shareholders' optimum and bring about a rise in valuation.

(*d*) Managers may utilize external funds more efficiently than internal ones because of the greater scrutiny of their plans by investors that a new issue often entails. Little and Rayner found some evidence to suggest that the average return to retained earnings was very low,[35] and in a more detailed study Baumol *et al.*[36] found the range of return to each form of finance dependent on the lags involved to be as follows:

Retentions	3%–4·6%
Debt Finance	4·2%–14%
Equity Capital	14·5%–20·8%

This pattern in itself is not surprising because the transactions costs of raising finance increase as we move down the table, but the figures still suggest that the absence of a 'market' test on retentions means that the latter may be used even though the shareholders' interest would have been better served by a dividend pay-out for reinvestment elsewhere. (Tax considerations might however negate this.) This would imply a preference for a high pay-out ratio on the part of a rational investor. (Whether in practice shareholders in a high-retention, high growth company systematically utilize a significantly higher discount rate is of course ultimately purely empirical.) A similar result follows if retentions are systematically used for more risky projects, though diversification could in theory offset this.

Given therefore the existence of market imperfections and uncertainty, share prices can be expected to fluctuate, dependent partly on 'real' variables such as investment and profits, and partly on dividends, both *per se* and as a guide to the real variables. Furthermore in many cases an individual investor will not know whether any given change in dividends or share price reflects real changes or not. Once this situation is recognized then we have a new set of reasons for believing dividend policy is important which could not apply in the case of perfect capital markets.

(i) **Risk averseness** will lead to a preference for stability of returns. Managers have considerable discretion to stabilize dividends but very little ability to stabilize stock market prices, leading to a preference for the former and a higher valuation for companies who can

[35] I. Little and A. Rayner, *Higgledy-Piggledy Growth Again* (Oxford, 1966).
[36] W. Baumol, P. Heim, B. Malkiel, R. Quandt, 'Earnings Retention, New Capital and the Growth of The Firm', *R. Econ. Stats.* 52, no. 4 (Nov. 1970).

maintain a higher proportion of their total return in this potentially more stable form.

(ii) The belief that a certain dividend now is preferable to the uncertain prospect of capital gain reflecting future earnings, which we saw was fallacious in a perfect market, can be rational under uncertainty once imperfections are admitted. Under these conditions dividends may well not be reinvested in the same firm and so a new equity issue might have to be made at lower prices to attract new shareholders.

(iii) Fluctuations in share price may inhibit consumption patterns if expenditure plans exceed dividend income at a time when share prices are very low. Prospects of future capital gain are unlikely to be such that they can be pledged as security for a loan. Even if they can be there is no limited liability provision, as there is with a company, to protect the individual's liability if he goes bankrupt.

To summarize, dividends are irrelevant in perfect capital markets irrespective of whether uncertainty exists, in the sense that a change in dividends with no change in investment will have no effect on valuation. With an imperfect capital market dividend policy may influence market valuation partly because it may lead to changes in investment policy (which does not negate the dividend irrelevance conclusion) but also directly. In either case shareholder wealth is influenced by the dividend decision, which is then a legitimate object of concern to managers. It is a purely empirical matter whether market imperfections have a significant and systematic effect one way or the other. It can only be determined by econometric analysis of dividend policy and valuation.

5   THE RETENTION RATIO: EVIDENCE

Early evidence on dividend policy took the form of correlating stock market valuation with dividends and retentions both separately and together.[37] Almost without exception these indicated that an increase in dividends would on average have a much greater effect on valuation than an increase in retained earnings, the latter effect in a number of cases being not significantly different from zero. If this is reliable, then given that transactions costs, taxation, and limita-

---

[37] See for example: G. R. Fisher, 'Some Factors Influencing Share Prices', *E.J.* 71 (1961), 121–41; M. J. Gordon, 'The Savings, Investment & Valuation of a Corporation', *R. Econ. Stats.* (Feb. 1962), 37–51; M. J. Gordon, 'Dividends, Earnings & Stock Prices', *R. Econ. Stats.* 41 (1959), 99–105; D. Durand, *Bank Stock Prices & The Bank Capital Problem*, Occasional Paper 54, N.B.E.R. (New York, 1957).

tions on the supply of finance are likely to favour retentions,[38] it appears that the explanation must be one or more of the following factors.

(*a*) The information content of dividends. Here there is important confirmation from a major study by Lintner,[39] who found that dividends could be explained very well by the following equation (our notation), which was based on extensive prior interviews.

For the *i*th firm

$$\Delta d_{it} = a_i + c_i[(1 - \hat{r}_i)\Pi_{it} - d_{i(t-1)}]$$

where a_i and c_i are constants and $(1 - \hat{r}_i)$ is the company's *target* pay-out ratio. This therefore says that the change in dividends is some fraction c_i of the difference between last year's dividend and this year's target dividend. c_i is a speed of adjustment coefficient. a_i might well be zero, but reluctance to cut dividends in any circumstances could statistically give it a positive value. This formulation reflected the following facts.

(i) The normal company decision variable is the *change in* (not the level of) dividends. This appears to be the result of inertia, conservatism, and shareholder preference for stability.

(ii) *Partial* adaptation of dividends to earnings because of the uncertainty over whether any change in earnings is permanent.

(iii) The importance of current earnings in determining current dividends.

(iv) The unimportance generally of other factors such as liquidity, debt position, etc. $(1 - \hat{r}_i)$ was of course itself dependent on a number of factors, the main ones being access to the capital market, management views on external financing, growth prospects, financial strength, competitors' $(1 - \hat{r})$ values, the tax structure, and estimates

---

[38] A study by Dhrymes and Kurz found that dividend policy depends on investment (a finding quite consistent with the MM thesis) and that investment depends on dividend policy (which is inconsistent with the MM thesis). Fama's study which finds the opposite (thus supporting MM) is strongly critical of the econometric aspects of Dhrymes and Kurz's refutation of MM, but in *either* event we would not expect a *positive* correlation between share price and pay-out ratio but only no correlation (Fama) or a negative one (Dhrymes and Kurz). See E. F. Fama, 'The Empirical Relation Between the Dividend & Investment Decisions of Firms', *A.E.R.* 64 (1974), 304–18; P. Dhrymes, M. Kurz, 'Investment, Dividends and External Finance Behaviour of Firms', in R. Ferber (ed.), *The Determinants of Investment Behaviour* (New York, 1967).

[39] J. Lintner, 'Distribution of Incomes of Corporations Among Dividends, Retained Earnings and Taxes', *A.E.R. Papers & Proceedings* (1956), 97–113; *idem*, 'The Determinants of Corporate Savings', in J. Heller *et al.* (ed.), *Savings in the Modern Economy* (University of Minnesota Press, 1953).

of the premium paid for stability.[40]

In testing, very high correlation coefficients were found; the period of adjustment seemed typically to be between 3 and 5 years; and the target pay-out ratio varied across firms from around 0·2 to 0·8 with an average somewhat over 0·5.

The importance of this is that if investors recognize that target pay-out ratios are constant over several decades, then a change in dividends will almost certainly have an information-content effect on company valuation.

A number of other studies have confirmed Lintner's conclusions, albeit with some modifications. Brittain found dividends to adjust slowly to net profit after tax and depreciation, but obtained an even better correlation with cash flow (i.e. profit after tax but *before* depreciation). This probably reflected the fact that with investment allowances operating, accounted profit is often a poorer guide to earnings patterns than cash flow.[41] He also found long-term trends in the target pay-out ratio between 1927 and 1960 with it falling (rising) as personal income tax rates rose (fell) and rising (falling) as interest rates fell (rose).

Darling also confirmed Lintner's results, but improved the correlation by replacing lagged dividends with lagged profits, suggesting dividends respond to the change in profits directly.[42] He also found cash considerations to be important, with depreciation provision, change in sales (as a guide to working capital requirements), and liquidity all apparently having some impact. Both studies were consistent with downward rigidity of dividends. Confirmation is also to be found in articles by Fama, and Fama and Babiak.[43]

In fact many companies do have explicit target pay-out ratios, and this is not surprising for established companies. Stability of investment and new equity and debt raising plans coupled with stable growth imply that all financing needs can be met with a constant pay-out ratio.[44]

Lintner also suggests that the dividend decision may take

---

[40] Dhrymes and Kurz later found pay-out ratios also to be a direct function of firm size (presumably because smaller firms have less easy access to the capital market), an inverse function of investment (which we would predict if new equity issue is partially or totally rejected), and an inverse function of long-term debt (probably as a result of attempts to reduce high debt levels by increasing financing from retentions). See P. Dhrymes, M. Kurz, 'On the Dividend Policy of Electric Utilities' *R. Econ. Stats.* 46 (Feb. 1964), 76–81.

[41] J. A. Brittain, *Corporate Dividend Policy* (Brookings, 1966).

[42] P. Darling, 'The Influence of Expectations & Liquidity on Dividend Policy', *J.P.E.* (June 1957), 209–24.

[43] E. F. Fama, op. cit. E. F. Fama, H. Babiak, 'Dividend Policy: An Empirical Analysis', *Journal of the American Statistical Association*, 63 (Dec. 1968), 1132–61.

[44] See J. E. Walter, *Dividend Policy & Enterprise Valuation* (Wadsworth, 1967).

precedence over investment where market imperfections tie the two together.[45] In such cases a shortage of funds for investment would lead to either new issues or abandonment of the investment rather than reduction of the dividend. This is likely to be a rare occurrence, however, because with dividends being more stable than earnings, retained earnings will rise disproportionately fast in an upswing, when investment is most likely.

(*b*) Stability of returns. The great stability of dividends to which these financial policies lead is well documented.[46] In an imperfect market and with risk averse shareholders this can explain a preference for high pay-out ratios.[47] Institutional shareholders in particular are often regarded as being especially concerned with stability of dividends, though survey evidence casts some doubt on the importance of dividends as opposed to over-all earnings and growth.[48] In addition, a high target pay-out will itself tend to indicate high stability of earnings (and dividends therefore) because the higher the target ratio the smaller the fluctuation which will reduce earnings below the target dividend. Walter found price-earnings ratios to be positively correlated with earnings stability and size of firm (which via diversification is likely to reduce earnings fluctuations) as well as the pay-out ratio.[49] Benishay found that stable dividends commanded a higher price, but that *in*stability of share price gave higher values.[50] He rejected however the view that a higher pay-out ratio would *per se* give a higher price–earnings ratio, despite the empirical correlation between them, on the grounds that if earnings were estimated inaccurately and were recorded at too low a value, both pay-out ratio and price–earnings ratio would be higher than otherwise, and thus be correlated, but this would not imply a preference for dividends. Similarly Friend and Puckett point out that

[45] Lintner, op. cit. (1956).

[46] See for example P. E. Hart, *Studies in Profit, Business Saving and Investment in the U.K. 1920–1962* (London, 1965). J. A. Brittain, Corporate Dividend Policy (Brookings, 1966); Lintner, op. cit. (1962).

[47] With extreme risk aversion all future profits and investment, however financed, would be discounted to zero, and so would expected share price variations in the current period. In that case the expected yield on a share would equal only the dividend yield for the current period and so the share price would be directly related to the current dividend.

[48] See R. Dobbins, T. McCrae, 'Institutional Shareholders & Corporate Management', *Management Decision*, 13, no. 6 (1975); R. J. Briston, 'The Fisons Stockholder Survey: An Experiment in Company-Shareholder Relations', *Journal of Business Policy*, 1, no. 1 (Autumn 1970); I. Friend, M. Puckett, 'Dividends & Stock Prices', *A.E.R.* 54 (Sept. 1964), 656–82.

[49] J. Walter, 'A Discriminant Function for Earnings–Price Ratios of Larger Industrial Corporations', *R. Econ. Stats.* (Feb. 1959), 44–52.

[50] H. Benishay, 'Variability in Earnings–Price Ratios of Corporate Equities', *A.E.R.* 51 (1961), 81–94.

if valuation depends on *normal* earnings, then temporary high earn-
ins give a low price–earnings ratio *and* a low pay-out ratio and vice
versa.[51] When they added a lagged share price variable to allow for
such short-run earnings variations, it in fact made retained earnings
more important than dividends, but this may just mean that lagged
share price is a proxy for dividends.

Other problems are that

(i) A high share price may itself encourage external financing and
hence lead to a higher pay-out ratio.

(ii) Higher commerical risk may be associated with both lower share
prices *and* lower pay-out ratios.

(iii) The econometric importance of retained earnings may be undermined if part of the future growth of the company is financed by
new equity.

(iv) 'Quality' shares of well-established companies may have higher
share prices *and* adopt higher pay-out ratios, but the two may not
be causally related.

(v) As dividends are measured precisely, any error in measuring
earnings will be carried as an error in retained earnings, tending to
reduce its coefficient in econometric analysis.

(*c*) Managerial behaviour. Finally, it must be remembered that the
previous section listed a number of reasons why companies may typically adopt pay-out ratios below those which, in the light of market
imperfections and uncertainty, shareholders regard as optimal. These
included managerial growth objectives, avoidance of transactions
costs, absence of a market 'test' on retentions, organizational slack
and consequent lower returns to retentions, etc. In addition, shareholders' discount rates may rationally be a function of the retention
ratio in imperfect markets under uncertainty. Therefore companies
with higher pay-out ratios may well command a share price premium.

This line of argument is strengthened by the fact that many investors retain their shareholding in a company over long periods.
For example, Briston and Tomkins found that 40 per cent of private
shareholders hold their shares for at least 10 years.[52] Although share
price movements will depend primarily upon the actions of those
investors entering and leaving the market, it seems likely that long-
term holders of shares are primarily concerned with the income
stream from dividends and therefore prefer the shares of companies
with high pay-out ratios and the higher earnings which may be associated with such a policy.

[51] I. Freind, M. Puckett, op. cit.
[52] R. Briston, C. R. Tomkins, 'Dividend Policy, Shareholder Satisfaction and the Valuation of Shares', *Journal of Business Finance* (Spring 1970).

In sharp contrast to all this is work by MM, who provide evidence that dividends are irrelevant.[53] They show that the value of a firm's equity is explained by its tax-adjusted net earnings, capitalization rate for firms of given commercial risk, firm size, and the existence of investment opportunities with a return above the capitalization rate, and that a dividend variable, while adding a little to the explanation if measured earnings are used, adds nothing to the explanation and has a negative correlation if an 'error-free' measure of earnings is used.[54] This was criticized in a number of ways[55] and in particular by Gordon and by Crockett and Friend, who both in effect argued that high gearing as a result of low risk would increase prior commitments on earnings and so lower dividends while also increasing the 'error-free' measure of earnings.[56] This would give a negative correlation between share price and dividends, but as *no* correlation was observed it implied that some offsetting factor was causing higher dividends to generate higher share prices, thus negating MM's conclusion. In addition Gordon points out that the main variable in the equation determining 'error-free' earnings is dividends, while two others—interest on debt and preference shares—are also correlated with dividends. It is not therefore surprising that dividends *in addition* to earnings adds little explanatory value.

Despite these criticisms, MM are not alone in finding dividends to be irrelevant. Higgins, in trying to take account of Gordon's criticisms, could find virtually no dividend effect.[57] In addition he found that if there was any correlation it appeared to be an *inverse* one between pay-out ratio and share price, despite examining an industry in which dividends are likely to be important and have considerable information content. Friend and Puckett, using a more rigorous statistical test, discovered little evidence that dividends were significantly more important in determining share prices than retained

[53] F. Modigliani, M. H. Miller, 'Some Estimates of the Cost of Capital to the Electric Utility Industry 1954-57', *A.E.R.* 56, no. 3 (June 1966), 333-91.

[54] The error-free variable is found by regressing earnings on a number of instrumental variables which are likely to be correlated with earnings, but not share price, and then using for each company an earnings figure calculated from the coefficients of this regression and the appropriate values of the instrumental variables. This in theory removes errors pertaining to individual companies in measuring earnings.

[55] See A. A. Robichek, J. McDonald, R. C. Higgins, 'Some Estimates of the Cost of Capital to the Electric Utility Industry 1954-57. Comment', *A.E.R.* 57 (Dec. 1967), 1278-88.

[56] J. Crockett, I. Friend, 'Some Estimtes of the Cost of Capital to the Electric Utility Industry 1954-57. Comment', *A.E.R.* 57 (Dec. 1967), 1258-67; M. Gordon, 'Some Estimates of the Cost of Capital to the Electric Utility Industry 1954-57. Comment', *A.E.R.* 57 (Dec. 1967), 1267-78.

[57] R. Higgins, 'Growth, Dividend Policy & Capital Costs in the Electric Utility Industry', *J. of Finance*, 29, no. 4 (Sept. 1974), 1189-1201.

earnings.[58] Kolin comes to the same conclusion,[59] as do Black and Scholes in a less reliable time-series study.[60]

A major difficulty with all such studies is that the share price is of course dependent on *expected* future values of earnings etc., but the latter are not directly observable. Malkiel and Cragg tried to overcome this.[61] Noting that in general expected earnings had in the past only been incorporated by assuming extrapolative expectations from past values, they developed a method tried previously by Whitbeck and Kisor utilizing security analysts' forecasting data.[62] A typical econometric result of Malkiel and Cragg's study was, for 1965,

$$\frac{P}{NE} = -15 \cdot 55 + \underset{(18 \cdot 69)}{2 \cdot 64} \, \bar{g}_p + \underset{(10 \cdot 09)}{20 \cdot 05} \, \frac{\bar{E}_{t+1}}{NE} - \underset{(0 \cdot 68)}{2 \cdot 04} \, \frac{D}{NE}$$

$$- \underset{(2 \cdot 99)}{7 \cdot 81} \, \frac{F}{E + F} + \underset{(2 \cdot 37)}{2 \cdot 64} \, Dum - \underset{(2 \cdot 78)}{17 \cdot 59} \, I_H \qquad \bar{R}^2 = 0 \cdot 78$$

where $\dfrac{P}{NE}$ is share price

is normalized predicted growth of earnings per share

$\bar{g}_p$ is average predicted growth of earnings per share

$\bar{E}_{t+1}$ is average predicted earnings for the next year

D is average dividends paid

$\dfrac{F}{E + F}$ is the gearing ratio

Dum   is an industry dummy variable

I_H is an instability-of-earnings index.

It should be added that gearing was insignificant in one of the 5 years tested and dividends were significant for 2 of the 5. Main conclusions from this study are:

(i) Expectational variables are generally superior to historical variables in explaining share price, P, with $\bar{R}^2$ on average about 0·75 in

[58] I. Friend, M. Puckett, op. cit.

[59] M. Kolin, *The Relative Price of Corporate Equity* (Boston).

[60] F. Black, M. Scholes, 'The Effects of Dividend Yield & Dividend Policy on Common Stock Prices & Returns', *J. of Financial Economics*, 1, no. 1 (May 1974), 1–22.

[61] B. G. Malkiel, J. G. Cragg, 'Expectations and the Structure of Share Prices', *A.E.R.* 60, no. 4 (Sept. 1970), 601–17.

[62] See V. Whitbeck, M. Kisor, 'A New Tool in Investment Decision Making', *Financial Analysts Journal*, 19 (May–June 1963), 55–62.

the former, but only 0·5 in the latter.

(ii) Combining them is slightly better still, with $\bar{R}^2$ about 0·8.

(iii) Long-term expected earnings growth seems to be very important, but so does the short-term figure as well.

(iv) Instability does seem to reduce share valuation.

(v) Dividends generally, though not always, were insignificant, offering some support for the MM thesis.

(vi) Though providing good fits, the equations were not very good predictors, possibly because valuation norms and principles themselves change from one year to the next.[63]

It is unfortunate, if understandable, that the evidence is rather more ambiguous on the most controversial variable in the equation, namely dividends.

Over all we can only conclude that the effect of dividend policy both *per se* and indirectly is still not satisfactorily quantified. This is mainly because so many of the relevant variables, particularly growth and profit expectations, risk estimates, true earnings, and discount rates are not directly observable. The evidence is however strong that companies do sequentially adjust towards target pay-out ratios, and the foregoing discussion suggests three determinants of these target ratios.

(i) They simply reflect the dividend consequences of stable growth and investment policies.

(ii) They reflect optimal values as determined by the tax structure.

(iii) They reflect the optimal trade-off between those factors discussed previously which favour a pay-out ratio of one and those which favour a value of zero. (Note, however, that this implies that one or more of these factors is a non-linear function of the level of dividends.)

Further empirical examination will be necessary to identify the relative importance of each and hence the extent and mechanism by which dividends influence share valuation.

6 THE GEARING RATIO: THEORY[64]

When we turn to the effect of gearing on a company's valuation and cost of capital, strong parallels with the discussion of dividend effects are immediately noticeable. First, it is clear that under certainty gearing can have no effect because under certainty a bond is no different from an equity. Both would have a known return and both

[63] The significance of the gearing variable is discussed in section 7.

[64] In this section we presume that the cost of equity finance is independent of the pay-out ratio in order to be able to simplify the analysis by ignoring the dividend decision.

would therefore sell at the same price per unit return. Second, on examining the effect of gearing under uncertainty we find two schools of thought, one with MM at the centre which claims that gearing has no effect on a company's cost of capital, and the other arguing the earlier traditional view more generally accepted in financial markets that gearing can and does have some effect.

The latter view can be seen very easily from the equation for the weighted cost of capital (writing y for y_e for simplicity)

$$w = \frac{iD}{D + M} + \frac{yM}{D + M}$$

If $y > i$ because investors require a higher average return from risky equity than riskless debt, then the higher the gearing the greater the weighting of i relative to y, and so with constant i and y the lower w will be. As we have seen, however, higher gearing raises the variability of y and increases the chance of default on the debt. The traditional view is that therefore, after a point, increasing gearing starts to raise both i and y in response to increased financial risks. Eventually this effect, which will tend to raise w, will dominate and the weighted cost of capital will rise. This is summed up in Figure 10.3, which indicates the optimal leverage ratio, $(D/M)^*$

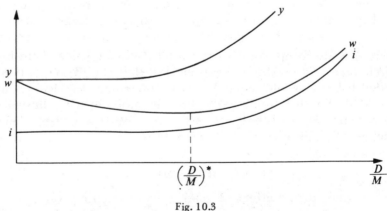

Fig. 10.3

MM on the other hand argued that the line ww is horizontal. Their original proof, which again presumed perfect capital market and rationality, was as follows.[65] Consider two companies in the same

[65] F. Modigliani, M. H. Miller, 'The Cost of Capital, Corporation Finance & The Theory of Investment', *A.E.R.* 48, no. 3 (June 1958), 261–97.

commercial 'risk class'.This implies that they are regarded by investors as having the same mean and variance of return.[66] One of the firms is geared, the other not. Profit, $\Pi_{(\Theta)}$, is a random variable such that each company makes profit $\Pi_{(\Theta)}$ if state of the world Θ occurs. The companies can then be described by the variables in Table 10.2.

TABLE 10.2

	·Company 1	Company 2
Value of Debt	D_1	—
Value of Equity	M_1	M_2
Total Value of Company	$D_1 + M_1$	M_2
Expected Profit*	$\bar{\Pi}$	$\bar{\Pi}$
Expected Rate of Return ($\bar{p}$)	$\bar{\Pi}/(D_1 + M_1)$	$\bar{\Pi}/M_2$
Cost of Capital (w)	$\dfrac{iD_1}{D_1 + M_1} + \dfrac{\bar{y}M_1}{D_1 + M_1} = \dfrac{\bar{\Pi}}{D_1 + M_1}$	$\dfrac{\bar{\Pi}}{M_2}$

*The bars indicate expected values.

If the pay-out ratio is 1 in both companies the income to a shareholder in Company 1 if state Θ occurs is given by

$$Y_1 = a(\Pi_{(\Theta)} - iD_1) \qquad (8)$$

where a is the proportion of the total company shares held by the shareholder, and making the assumption that $\Pi_{(\Theta)} > iD_1$ (otherwise limited liability would make Y_1 zero rather than negative). Suppose now that the shareholder sells his shareholding aM_1, borrows an amount aD_1 at prevailing interest rate i, and purchases shares in Company 2. The investor will be able to purchase a proportion of the shares equal to

$$\frac{aM_1 + aD_1}{M_2}$$

and his return from Company 2 after payment of interest on his personal borrowing will be

[66] We thus follow the usual assumption that only the mean and variance of return matter to an investor. It should be noted however thtat it is difficult to explain the poor mean performance of very high risk stocks except by reference to higher moments of the probability distribution of returns. See R. W. McEnally, 'A Note on the Return Behaviour of High Risk Common Stocks', *J. of Finance*, 29, no. 1 (Mar. 1974), 199–202.

$$Y_2 = \frac{a(M_1 + D_1)}{M_2}\Pi_{(\Theta)} - aiD_1 \tag{9}$$

This is unambiguously more than he was previously earning while

$$\frac{M_1 + D_1}{M_2} > 1$$

given that $\Pi_{(\Theta)}$, being above iD_1 is non-negative. The switch from the shares of Company 1 to Company 2 will raise M_2 and depress M_1. This arbitrage will continue until $Y_1 = Y_2$, when no further gain is possible. At this point

$$a(\Pi_{(\Theta)} - iD_1) = a\left(\frac{M_1 + D_1}{M_2}\right)\Pi_{(\Theta)} - aiD_1 \tag{10}$$

and therefore $M_1 + D_1 = M_2$.

Thus the gearing has not made any difference to the total valuation of the company, nor therefore to the cost of capital (see Table 10.2), which is seen to be completely independent of capital structure and equal to the cost of capital for a purely equity financed company in the same commercial risk class.

To construct MM's version of Figure 10.3 we need to find y, the yield on equity for a company. This is given by

$$y_j = \frac{\bar{\Pi} - iD_j}{M_j}$$

for the jth company.

But

$$\frac{\bar{\Pi}}{D_j + M_j}$$

is constant and equal to $\bar{p}$ (assuming the valuation ratio is unity), which in turn equals y_p, the yield if a company is financed purely by equity.

Therefore

$$y_j = \frac{y_p(D_j + M_j) - iD_j}{M_j} = y_p + \frac{D_j}{M_j}(y_p - i) \tag{11}$$

It is therefore equal to the discount or capitalization rate for a purely equity financed company in the same commercial risk class *plus* a premium equal to the debt–equity ratio times the spread between y_p and i. Figure 10.4 indicates the MM view.

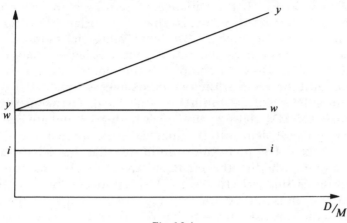

Fig. 10.4

MM's view is therefore that the option open to investors to carry out 'home-made gearing', i.e. the purchase of shares with personally borrowed funds, means that an investor can obtain through home-made gearing on an ungeared firm all the advantages that a geared firm tries to achieve. The result is that no firm obtains an advantage and all have the same cost of capital. The parallel with the MM view on retentions is that they again are identifying conditions under which purely financial characteristics cannot alter the cost of a firm's capital as determined by the 'real' (investment return) characteristics.

The MM model has generated much debate, in the course of which many aspects of it have been illuminated and the importance of it exemplified.[67] In the process it has been developed into a more general form which removes the need for a number of the restrictive assumptions on which it is based, and it is to such issues that we now move on.

---

[67] For example it has been examined in the context of depreciating assets; in an international context; dynamically such that optimal paths of financial structure change over time can be identified and valuation patterns over time examined. See in particular C. G. Krause, 'On The Theory of Optimal Investment, Dividends and Growth in the Firm', *A.E.R.* 63, no. 3 (June 1973), 269–79. Most important however is the incorporation of *risky* debt and this is examined later in the text. For analysis of the MM position in a growth context see P. Kumar, 'Growth Stocks & Corporate Capital Structure Theory', *J. of Finance*, 33, no. 2 (May 1975), 532–47.

(i) The model has been attacked on the grounds that Y_2 in equation (9) will end up higher than Y_1 in equation (8) because the *variance* of returns will be higher for the income Y_2.[68] Hence $M_1 + D_1$ would be higher than M_2 and the MM model would break down. Now while an alternative formulation can be constructed to support the MM view in which the variance of returns is the same in both companies,[69] the main point is that the variance of returns is *irrelevant*[70] to the argument. *Whatever* value the random variable $\Pi_{(\Theta)}$ takes the income Y_2 generated from it is higher than Y_1 while $M_1 + D_1 > M_2$. Thus Y_2 completely dominates Y_1 and is always preferred until the value of the two companies is equal.

(ii) Figures 10.3 and 10.4 illustrate that the difference between the traditional and MM views centres on whether a company can introduce *any* low cost debt into its financial structure without the yield on equity rising. The point above indicates that this debate does *not* revolve around whether the increased risk from low as opposed to zero gearing is subjectively regarded as significant, because the MM argument depends purely on arbitrage of investors irrespective of their evaluation of risk. But whether the irrelevance of leverage up to a point is found in practice or not *does* depend on whether the gains from such arbitrage are substantial enough, given market imperfections, for it to occur. If the gains from arbitrage are generally inadequate to cover transactions costs and the costs of gathering information about firms in the same risk class, or if institutional limitations on potential borrowers or lenders for home-made gearing are restric-

---

[68] The variance is larger because the random variable Π in equation (9) is multiplied by

$$\frac{M_1 + D_1}{M_2} > 1$$

thus increasing the variance. An alternative way of seeing this is to note that total gearing for the investor before switching

$$\frac{D_1}{M_1 + D_1}$$

and after switching

$$\frac{aD_1}{aM_1 + aD_1} \quad \text{is the same.}$$

Hence the percentage variability of the returns is the same but the average return is higher, and so the absolute variability (and hence the variance) is higher.

[69] See A. J. Heins, C. M. Sprenkle, 'A Comment on the Modigliani–Miller Cost of Capital Thesis', *A.E.R.* 59, no. 4 (Sept. 1969), 590–2.

[70] See F. Modigliani, M. Miller, 'Reply to Heins & Sprenkle', *A.E.R.* 59, no. 4 (Sept. 1969), 592–5.

tive,[71] then the process will be inhibited. The significance of this is less that it will halt arbitrage, as only a limited number of arbitrage operators are needed to equalize costs of capital. Rather it is that the process will be slowed somewhat, and this permits the company to gain from further gearing. Subsequent home-made gearing would not change the cost of the capital that had then been raised. It is not surprising therefore to find that home-made gearing appears not to occur on anything approaching the scale necessary to equalize the cost of capital.[72] Typically investors will choose investments by reference to industry and national prospects, past record, management reputation, particular factors like new products, etc., and invest on these bases *subject* to gearing being 'reasonable' or 'not excessive'. The fact that such appraisal is not generally accompanied by borrowing and investment in an ungeared company of the same risk class may reflect transactions costs but almost certainly also reflects the fact (or at least the belief) that no other company is in 'the same risk class' when this implies not just being in the same industry for example, but being of equivalent risk in terms of mean and variance of returns as determined by all the investment criteria listed above. This point is strengthened by the fact that firms often adopt rather conservative gearing ratios.[73] This makes the opportunities for gains through arbitrage small and therefore less likely to cover the search costs of finding an ungeared company in the same 'risk class'.

(iii) The home-made gearing example required $\Pi_{(\Theta)} - iD_1$ to be non-negative. This condition can be relaxed utilizing an alternative arbitrage example *but only if the investor can obtain limited liability for his personal loan if net profit is negative in the same way that a company does on its loans*, for example by pledging the company's shares as security for the loan.[74] (Negative net profit makes them worthless and results in zero loss when they are surrendered on default of the loan.) In this alternative example[75] an income of $a(\Pi_{(\Theta)} - iD_1)$ can be earned from an investment of aM_1 in the geared

[71] See D. W. Glenn, 'Super Premium Securities Prices and Optimal Corporate Financing Decisions', *J. of Finance*, 31, no. 2 (May 1976), 507–24. That some degree of segmentation of the capital market exists is supported by the fact that in practice the probability of loss over 8 years is much the same for bonds or equity despite the average equity return being 5·5 per cent better. Even over 1 year bond holders were forgoing 5·5 per cent to protect themselves from a 2·6 per cent chance of a maximum 24 per cent loss. See R. L. Norgaand, 'An Examination of the Yields of Corporate Bonds and Stocks', *J. of Finance*, 29, no. 4 (Sept. 1974), 1275–86.

[72] See for example A. Merrett, A. Sykes, *The Finance and Analysis of Capital Projects* (London, 1963), and D. Durand, 'The Cost of Capital, Corporation Finance and the Theory of Investment: Comment', *A.E.R.* 49, no. 4 (Sept. 1959), 639–55.

[73] Because the consequences of bankruptcy are generally more serious for managers than for an investor holding a portfolio of shares. See below for consideration of bankruptcy.

[74] See later, p. 360, for indications of the importance of this assumption.

[75] See F. Modigliani, M. H. Miller, op. cit. ('Reply to Heins & Sprenkle').

firm. Consider now an investment of aM_2 in the geared firm accompanied by personal borrowing of aD_1. The net income is again $a\Pi_{(\Theta)} - aiD_1$. Hence arbitrage will bring aM_1 and $aM_2 - aD_1$ into equality again giving $M_1 + D_1 = M_2$ *whatever*[76] the value of $\Pi_{(\Theta)}$.

The proviso above is however crucial. If it is admitted that companies but not investors enjoy limited liability then the possibility of negative net profit destroys the arbitrage argument. For if $\Pi_{(\Theta)} < iD_1$ then the investor carrying out home-made gearing receives no dividend and has to pay his interest charges, ending up with an income of $-aiD_1$. Had the investor remained with the geared company, limited liability would have restricted his loss to zero. Thus where $\Pi_{(\Theta)} < iD_1$, the investment aM_1 has a higher return than an investment aM_2 accompanied by personal borrowing of aD_1. Hence $M_1 + D_1 > M_2$ and a geared firm has a lower cost of capital, as in the traditional model.[77] It therefore makes a difference whether investors are institutions with limited liability or individuals without such protection.

(iv) The possibility of bankruptcy has other impacts on the MM model besides that on the process of arbitrage. In particular the market rate of interest i will tend to rise with gearing because of the higher risk of default. For the weighted average cost of capital to remain constant, the equity yield curve in Figure 10.3 would then have to *fall* as gearing increased despite higher risk of loss. MM suggested that in the absence of enough risk lovers arbitrage would bring this about. In other words if the equity yield curve *didn't* fall as the interest curve rose then the weighted cost of capital would rise and investors could earn this higher return by selling shares in other companies and buying debt and equity *pro rata* in the highly geared company. This would raise its equity valuation and lower its equity yield. This, however, is incorrect reasoning. As Robichek and Myers point out, this would imply a *marginal* rate of interest above the yield on equity, which with perfect markets and risk-averse investors is inconsistent if debenture holders have a prior claim on company assets.[78] In addition, this MM argument appears to forget that the returns in

---

[76] Thus personal limited liability implies that gearing is irrelevant even if gross profits are negative.

[77] In the original home-made gearing example Y_2 no longer dominates Y_1 because some values of $\Pi_{(\Theta)}$, namely those below iD_1, result in $Y_1 > Y_2$. Thus it can no longer be inferred that $M_1 + D_1 > M_2$. For elaboration of the impact of risky bonds see R. W. Resek, 'Multidimensional Risk and the Modigliani–Miller Theorem', *J. of Finance*, 31, no. 1 (Mar. 1970).

[78] A. A. Robichek, S. C. Myers, *Optimal Financing Decisions* (Englewood Cliffs, 1965). Proof: Let $D + M = V$, therefore $wV = iD + yM$. Therefore $Vdw + wdV = Ddi + idD + Mdy + ydM$. But in the MM model, w and V are constant so that this equals zero. Also $dD = -dM$ as debt is substituted for equity. Therefore $Ddi + idD + Mdy - ydD = 0$ and $y = i + D(di/dD) + M(dy/dD)$. Now i', the marginal rate of interest equals

the model are *expected* returns. If the nominal interest rate on so-called 'riskless' debt finance rises as gearing increases, it is because the high gearing makes the debenture risky. Boness has shown formally that if investors are risk-neutral then the *expected* interest rate remains the same.[79] The expected income from equity is definitionally the expected income of the company minus the expected interest payment, i.e.

$$yM = p(D + M) - \hat{i}D \tag{12}$$

where $y, p, \text{and } \hat{i}$ are *all* expected rates.

Therefore
$$y = p + \frac{D}{M}(p - \hat{i}) \tag{13}$$

which is MM's formula except that $\hat{i}$ replaces the actual interest rate i. If there is no risk of default, $\hat{i} = i$. Given some riskiness on debentures, however, i rises, but $\hat{i}$ remains the same provided investors are risk-neutral. Rearranging equation (12) gives

$$\frac{D}{D + M}\hat{i} + \frac{M}{D + M}y = p$$

and hence the weighted cost of capital is still, as MM concluded, constant.

If however investors are generally risk-averse (and cannot remove risk by diversification of their share portfolios across negatively correlated investments) then increased gearing by increasing risk of default *would* raise $\hat{i}$.

(v) The MM conclusion requires that investors can borrow at the same interest rate as companies. If the former have to pay more, then in equation (10) $M_1 + D_1 > M_2$ when $Y_2 = Y_1$, and so the geared company will have a higher valuation and lower weighted cost of capital. But this may frequently be the case, partly because

$$\frac{d(iD)}{dD} = i + D \cdot \frac{di}{dD}$$

Therefore
$$y = i' + M \cdot \frac{dy}{dD}$$

So, for $\frac{dy}{dD}$ to be negative $i' > y$.

[79] A. J. Boness, 'A Pedagogic Note on the Cost of Capital', *J. of Finance*, 19, no. 1 (Mar. 1964), 99–106.

individual investors often do not, like companies, have limited liability and more generally because their credit rating will be weaker. Also personal loans may have conditions attached which make them imperfect substitutes for company debt. These points are weakened however to the extent that one group likely to engage in home-made gearing are institutional investors, for whom they probably do not hold.

The significance of bankruptcy and differences in credit rating have both been emphasized by Stiglitz,[80] utilizing a similar type of argument but within a general equilibrium framework. In this model it is demonstrated that, given one general equilibrium in which the supply and demand for both debentures and equities are equal, there is always another one in which a firm has changed its gearing, but all company valuations, the profit rate, and interest rate are the same as before. Suppose, for example, that firm 1 removes its debentures. An individual can always ensure the same income for any state of the world Θ as before by borrowing $(D_1/M_1)M_1^j$ where D_1 and M_1 are the initial debt and equity values of firm 1 and M_1^j is the jth individual's holding of equity in the firm. His new equity holding is then

$$M_1^j + \frac{D_1}{M_1}M_1^j = \frac{M_1^j}{M_1} \cdot V_1$$

where V_1 is the value of the company before and after the financial policy changes. Hence the jth individual holds a proportion M_1^j/M_1 of the shares of firm 1. His gain in earnings is

$$\frac{\Pi_1 M_1^j}{M_1} - \frac{(\Pi_1 - iD_1)M_1^j}{M_1} = \frac{iD_1}{M_1}M_1^j$$

which exactly equals the cost of his loan. He will no longer have an interest income from firm 1, iD_1^j, but will have switched this holding into other bonds to earn the same interest. The over-all demand for bonds will therefore be the same, but so will the supply, because the personal borrowing of the j individuals

$$= \sum_{j=1}^{j=n} \frac{D_1}{M_1}M_1^j = D_1$$

---

[80] J. Stiglitz, 'A Re-examination of the Modigliani–Miller Theorem', *A.E.R.* 59, no. 5 (Dec. 1969), 784–93.

which exactly replaces the reduction in borrowing by firm 1. The demand for equity will have increased by a factor of V_1/M_1, but as V_1 is the (unchanged) value of the company after removing its gearing, so has the supply (either through the issue of new shares or an increase in retentions to replace the debt finance). Hence all markets clear and the existence of the new equilibrium is established. Stiglitz later extended the analysis to a multi-period one and in similar fashion demonstrated that all financial decisions of companies would be irrelevant again because of the ability of investors to 'undo' the changes firms could bring about.[81]

This general equilibrium approach has two important implications. First it does not require certain assumptions previously necessary.

(*a*) After all financial changes each individual's income generated by state Θ is exactly the same as before. Therefore the model is independent of risk assessment which can be entirely subjective. Firms do not therefore need to be regarded as being in the same risk class, nor identical in all non-financial aspects.

(*b*) All transactors must face the same prices but the capital market does not need to be perfectly competitive. Thus the fact that a firm raising more debt may have to pay a higher interest rate does not negate the proof, if it occurs because its debt raising increases the *market* rate of interest.

Second, the analysis indicates the conditions under which the financial policy would *not* be irrelevant. The first two of these reinforce earlier conclusions.

(*a*) Bankruptcy. If this is a possibility then there will be some states of the world in which the cost of an individual's personal loan is $(iD_1/M_1)M_1^i$ but his increased earnings are zero. The theorem then breaks down. Stiglitz has identified a number of special cases where the threat of bankruptcy does not undermine the irrelevance of financial policy. These include cases where the ratio in which different risky assets are purchased by different individuals is the same (as is implied by the capital asset pricing model, see pp. 474–82)[82] and where financial intermediaries can be established costlessly.[83] It may be added that reserve funds, further borrowing, depreciation allowances, and sale of assets may all be utilized to avert bankruptcy, and as the consequences for the management concerned are so much

[81] J. Stiglitz, 'On the Irrelevance of Corporate Financial Policy', *A.E.R.* 64, no. 6 (Dec. 1974), 851–66.

[82] For a demonstration of the MM thesis utilizing this model of the stock market see R. S. Hamada, 'Portfolio Analysis, Market Equilibrium & Corporation Finance', *J. of Finance*, 24, no. 1 (Mar. 1969), 13–31.

[83] Also where the number of firms is equal to or greater than the number of states of nature, as this establishes an Arrow–Debreu market: see pp. 582 and 586.

greater than for the typical investor holding a portfolio of shares, companies may well maintain very low gearing ratios, thereby minimizing the prospect of bankruptcy.

(b) Credit conditions. As before, if individuals face different terms from those faced by companies, because they can borrow less, have to pay more, are subject to different tax provisions, or incur different transactions costs, then gearing will affect the cost of capital. Partly this just reflects the higher probability of default by individuals and so is part of the general problem of bankruptcy.[84]

(c) If the real return expected is thought to depend in some way on a company's debt policy, then gearing may influence the cost of capital, for example if high gearing causes investors to fear that in a bad year investment opportunities will have to be forgone, then this may cause a rise in the cost of capital as investors sell shares. Conversely if debt finance is though to be used more efficiently than retained earnings, then gearing might lower the cost of capital.

(d) Interest is normally a tax deductible cost, so that the introduction of taxation in the model lowers the true cost of debt finance. The MM theorem instead of giving $\Pi_j/(M_j + D_j)$ = constant for all j in a given risk class gives $\Pi_j^T/(M_j + D_j)$ = constant for all j in the risk class, where Π_j^T is the return gross of interest, but net of taxation. As an increase in gearing normally lowers the tax bill and increases Π_j^T, the valuation of a company will increase with gearing and so lower the cost of capital.[85]

(e) Imperfections in the capital market such that a claim on the same expected income stream can sell at more than one price will negate the theorem. This does not preclude bonds selling at different prices given that, with the possibility of bankruptcy, they are risky to different degrees (and hence not the same). Nor does it preclude lending and borrowing between transactors at different rates because they are subject to different degrees of risk. But if for example transactions costs make a given transaction profitable for one potential

---

[84] The effect may however be small if investors can 'undo' reduced company borrowing by reducing their own bond holdings rather than home-made gearing. See J. Stiglitz, op. cit. (Dec. 1974), 862.

[85] If, however, capital gains tax is lower than that on interest received by investors by an amount sufficient to offset the corporate tax on earnings, then, allowing for personal taxation, retained earnings will be cheaper and gearing can increase the cost of capital. Formally, if $(1 - t_c)(1 - t_{cg}) > (1 - t_y)$ where t_c is corporate tax, t_{cg} is capital gains tax, and t_y is unearned income tax, then retained earnings will be cheaper than debt capital. (This presumes that capital gains exactly equal the rise in retained earnings as a result of lower interest charges.) For a full analysis of the effect of taxation when risky debt is present see V. L. Smith, 'Default, Risk, Scale and the Homemade Leverage Theorem', *A.E.R.* 62, no. 1 (Mar. 1972), 66–76; D. P. Baron, 'Default Risk, Homemade Leverage and the Modigliani–Miller Theorem', *A.E.R.* 64, no. 1 (Mar. 1974), 176–82; idem, 'Firm Valuation, Corporate Taxes and Default Risk', *J. of Finance*, 30, no. 5 (Dec. 1975), 1251–64.

purchaser but not for another then investors may not always be able to re-establish their opportunity set.

Over-all it seems reasonable to conclude that with the possibility of bankruptcy existing, with taxation generally favouring debt capital, with divergence of credit constraints, and in the absence of fully offsetting financial moves by investors because of transaction and information costs, the weighted cost of capital curve will, as in the traditional theory, be U-shaped. But the potential weakness of these factors in capital markets characterized by conservative gearing ratios and financial intermediaries able to issue their own debt, reduce information costs, and gain tax advantages means that there is likely to be a substantial range of gearing ratios over which the cost of capital varies relatively little.

7   THE GEARING RATIO: EVIDENCE

MM backed up their theoretical reasoning by regressing (i) earnings yields on the debt–equity (leverage) ratio, and (ii) the weighted cost of capital on gearing for electric utilities and oil companies (separately).[86] They found statistical confirmation for their argument that equity yields rose with leverage and by an amount necessary to maintain a roughly constant cost of capital. They subsequently adopted a rather more sophisticated two-stage instrumental variable approach, and in a study of the U.S. electric utility industry found gearing (and dividend policy) to be irrelevant.[87] Further support came from Robichek *et al.*, who found a statistically significant correlation between leverage and the cost of capital.[88] There are however a number of problems which not only throw doubt on these results, but also create severe difficulties for any empirical testing in this area.

(i) Other studies have come up with different results. For example Brigham and Gordon found that although earnings yield did rise with

---

[86] F. Modigliani, M. H. Miller, op. cit. (*A.E.R.* 1958). Utilities have been used because they avoid tax complications, though there is some controversy over whether a pre- or post-tax model should be used. See E. J. Elton, M. J. Gruber, 'Valuation and the Cost of Capital for Regulated Industries', *J. of Finance*, 26, no. 3 (June 1971), 661–70; M. J. Gordon, J. S. MacCallum, 'Valuation and the Cost of Capital for Regulated Industries—Comment', *J. of Finance*, 27, no. 5 (Dec. 1972), 1141–6; E. J. Elton, M. J. Gruber, 'Valuation and the Cost of Capital for Regulated Industries—Reply', *J. of Finance*, 27, no. 5 (Dec. 1972), 1150–5.

[87] F. Modigliani, M. H. Miller, 'Some Estimates of the Cost of Capital to the Electric Utility Industry 1954–57', *A.E.R.* 56, no. 3 (June 1966), 333–91. For a series of criticisms of the method used, and reply, see *A.E.R.* 57 (1967), 1258–1300.

[88] But the result held only for *book* values of debt and equity, not *market* values. See A. A. Robichek, R. C. Higgins, M. Kinsman, 'The Effect of Leverage on the Cost of Equity Capital of Electric Utility Firms', *J. of Finance*, 28, no. 2 (May 1973), 353–68.

leverage it was not enough to fully offset the cheaper cost of debt, and so the weighted cost of capital still fell as gearing was increased.[89]

(ii) Evidence presented by Weston showed that leverage and growth of earnings per share were negatively correlated,[90] suggesting that firms with rapidly rising earnings had less need to raise debt finance. Now rapid earnings growth prospects will tend to raise share values, hence reducing the cost of equity as measured by the earnings yield. Thus we would expect the earnings yield and leverage to be directly related empirically quite independent of any home-made gearing effects. Weston therefore re-tested the electric utility industry (over a later period) and found that if growth of earnings per share was added as an explanatory variable then leverage had little effect on equity yields, and as a result *did* have a significantly negative effect on the cost of capital.

(iii) More generally *anything* exogenous to MM's model which raises equity values will tend to reduce measured leverage *and* equity yields, generating a correlation which has nothing to do with home-made gearing. It is also possible that gearing will for example be increased just *because* equity yields are currently high. Again the statistical correlation does not reflect any neutralizing arbitrage. The plausibility of this is increased when it is noted that the weighted cost of capital curve reflects the activities of the *providers* of finance. If the curve does have a downward sloping section for the reasons given, and if, as mentioned before, managers are more risk-averse because they are managing one company rather than a diversified portfolio, then they will tend to maintain gearing ratios below the 'optimum'. These can then be increased if a rise in equity yields makes the cost of a conservative gearing ratio too high.

Some of these problems of statistical testing arise partly because of the use of *market* values of debt and equity in calculating gearing.[91] Barges[92] used book values in the cement, railroad, and department-stores industries to circumvent this and found evidence to support the traditional view. Book values are not however without their drawbacks, often being arbitrary and unreliable, out of date, and uncorrected for inflation.

(iv) The significance of bankruptcy has already been emphasized.

[89] See E. F. Brigham, M. J. Gordon, 'Leverage, Dividend Policy and the Cost of Capital—Reply', *J. of Finance*, 23, no. 1 (Mar. 1968), 85–103.

[90] J. F. Weston, 'A Test of Cost of Capital Propositions', *S. Econ. Journal*, 30, no. 2 (Oct. 1963).

[91] See pp. 328 and 334.

[92] A. Barges, *The Effect of Capital Structure on the Cost of Capital* (Englewood Cliffs, 1963).

Given that debentures are in fact risky, then it is to be expected that earnings yields will rise as companies gear up. Again this does not imply home-made gearing. A horizontal weighted cost of capital curve could then be interpreted as showing that the gains from using low-cost debt are just offset by the increase in the cost of equity capital as a result of the greater risk of bankruptcy.

(v) If firms in an empirical test are in the same risk class, and factors such as taxation determine an optimal gearing ratio, then we would expect firms over-all to cluster around a point. But most evidence, including MM's, shows wide disparities of gearing values. This suggests that different companies in the same industry are effectively in different risk classes. If so, then statistically there is no reason to expect a U-shaped relationship between the cost of capital and gearing even if the traditional view is correct. It may therefore be that a series of U-shaped cost curves should be drawn, one through each of the points in MM's graph, rather than trying to fit one line to all of them. This would result in *no* cross-sectional correlation, and correlation coefficients of 0·12 and 0·04 in MM's study tend to confirm that much is missing in the explanation of the cost of capital figures. But if firms facing high U-shaped curves systematically pursue more nearly optimal gearing ratios as a result, then there would be a tendency towards a horizontal weighted cost of capital line.

8 CONCLUSIONS

Although there has been much controversy over the role of corporate financial policy we can draw the following conclusions:

(*a*) Under the assumptions of a perfect capital market and rationality, financial policy is irrelevant, both under certainty and uncertainty.

(*b*) Inability to observe many of the relevant variables, coupled with other estimation problems, means that there is still no universal agreement on the empirical question of whether market imperfections are sufficient to significantly undermine this irrelevance conclusion in practice.

(*c*) The great concern shown by company managers to get their financial policy 'right' should not be taken to imply that financial policy must be 'relevant'. The irrelevance theorems *depend* on the notion that such participants in the capital market are constantly attempting to take advantage of any discrepancies that arise between the actual and potential costs of capital.

(*d*) The two main issues when considering the effect of gearing are the threat of bankruptcy and the effect of taxation. The four main issues when considering the dividend policy are the effect on the supply of finance for investment; the implications for managerial performance; information effects; and tax aspects.

(*e*) There is little theoretical or empirical support for the view that financial policy has very considerable effects on the cost of capital to a firm. This suggests that no great discrepancy will result if investment and financing decisions are treated separately.

APPENDIX 1

Figure 10.5 is a modified version of Figure 10.1 in the text and shows all the main sources and uses of funds separately. Most of it is self-explanatory or follows from the text of the chapter, but certain notes to it are necessary.

(i) Creditors are regarded as a source of funds because they have provided goods and/or services but not yet received payment. They are therefore regarded as having received the payment and lent it back again to the company. Thus trade credit received is, like a loan from a bank, a source of funds. In a similar way debtors are a use of funds.

(ii) The distinction between short- and long-term loans is of course in practice blurred but usually dealt with by adopting an arbitrary period for delineating the two. (Often one year, as that is the normal period covered by company accounts.) The distinction is none the less vital, not only because the company must stand ready at all times to cover short-term liabilities, but also because, as we shall see, companies are often assessed by their record of performance in using profitably those long-term funds made available to them by shareholders and suppliers of long-term debt finance.

(iii) Any funds flowing into the 'funds available' box flow out to the right as a use of those funds or remain as cash. But such cash is, like a financial asset, a current asset. As such it is regarded as flowing into the 'cash balance' box and is therefore treated as a current asset. If other uses of funds exceeded all the sources shown then this would be a negative flow and the reduction in current assets resulting from the depletion of cash balances would be the additional source of funds, but shown as a *negative use* of funds. At its simplest the planning of cash flow requires first that for any time period the sources, including any run-down of cash, are sufficient for all planned uses, particularly those legally required such as payment of suppliers, interest payments, etc. Second, it requires that over the longer term the supply of funds is adequate to meet the uses. Variations in the amount of cash held clearly only deal with short-term discrepancies between other sources and uses.

There are 3 main types of accounting document which describe different aspects of this flow of funds diagram. The first, normally required in law to be published annually, is the *Profit and Loss Account* or *Income and Appropriation Account*. This is essentially a statement of the top half of Figure 10.5. Its typical format is shown in Table 10.3, which gives a simplified aggregate profit and loss (or appropriation) account for 1972 for all U.K. companies in manufacturing, construction, distribution, transport, and property with net assets above £2·0 million or gross profit above £200,000 in 1968. There is one important discrepancy between the cash flows of Figure 10.5 and the accounting terms of

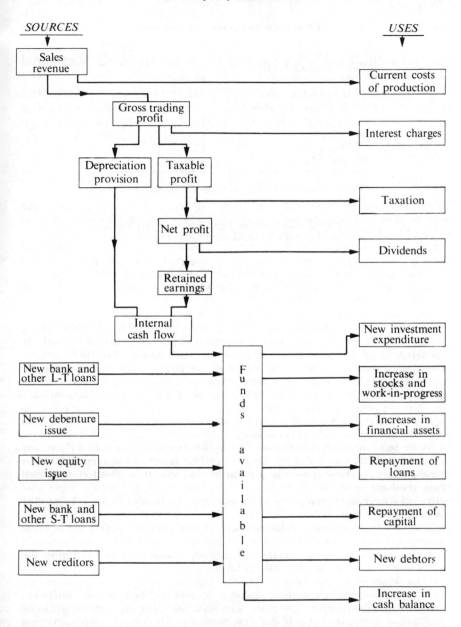

Fig. 10.5

TABLE 10.3 (figures in £ millions)

Sales Revenue		54 663
Gross Trading Profit		7127
Depreciation	1763	
Interest Charges	838	
Profit before Taxation		4526
Taxation	1624	
Net Profit		2902
Dividends	1342	
Retained Profit		1560

Source: *Business Monitor, Company Finance*, 6th issue, H.M.S.O. (1975).
Notes:
(1) 1972 was chosen as giving a more typical distribution of the sums involved than later years for which figures are available.
(2) The table omits income of approx. £330 million from financial investments, expenditure of approx. £340 million on hire of plant and machinery, and income of approx. £270 million from net disposal of capital.

Table 10.3. In order that the figure for net profit in the Profit and Loss Account should indicate the increase in owners' wealth net of *all* costs and liabilities, the tax figure is the tax *liability* incurred on the profit made. This will be different from the actual tax *payment* outflow of Figure 10:5 because, with tax normally paid one year in arrears, the current year's tax payment will be last year's tax liability. If tax paid is less than the current tax liability (as would normally be the case if taxable profits are on a rising trend) then part of taxable profits becomes a tax *provision* which is in the short term a source of funds over and above retained profit net of tax liability.

A second document which some but by no means all companies provide is a statement of *Sources and Uses Of Funds*. This is a more general summary of Figure 10.5. The typical format is as shown in Table 10.4. This follows directly from the table except that

(i) Sales Revenue minus Costs of Production is shown as Gross Trading Profit net of depreciation.

(ii) New long-term loans, debenture and equity issue are shown net of *re*payments.

(iii) Increases in short-term loans and creditors are subtracted from both sides and hence show up as negative uses of funds.

(iv) Increases in Stocks, Financial Assets, Debtors, and Cash are all uses which increase the company's current assets. Increases in Creditors and Short-term loans are sources (negative uses) which increase the company's current liabilities. The former minus the latter is then the increase in *net* current assets fof the year and is given this title in Table 10.4.

Both statements presented so far are *flow* statements, showing various financial flows occurring during the course of one year. The third statement is the Balance Sheet and is a *stock* concept. It shows the value of various company assets and liabilities outstanding at the end of each financial year and is, like the Profit and Loss Account, legally required to be published. To obtain this we first

TABLE 10.4

Sources of Funds	Uses of Funds
Gross Trading Profit after Depreciation	Interest Paid
Depreciation Provision	Tax Paid
New Long-Term Loans (Net)	Dividends Paid
New Debenture Issues (Net)	Investment Expenditure
New Equity Issues (Net)	Increase in Net Current Assets
	= Increase in
	Stocks
	Financial Assets
	Debtors
	Cash
	− Increase in
	Creditors
	Short-term loans

subtract depreciation, interest, tax, and dividends from both sides of the Sources and Uses table. This gives:

Sources	Uses
Retained Earnings	Investment Expenditure
New Long-Term Loans (Net)	− Depreciation
New Debenture Issues (Net)	Increase in Net Current Assets
New Equity Issue (Net)	

As these two columns give the same total in any given time period, the sum of each for all time periods in the past up to the date of the Balance Sheet will also be equal. The sum of all previous earnings is termed *the reserves*. They do not of course constitute a reserve in the sense of a fund that can be drawn on, all these earnings having previously been used in one or more of the ways described under 'uses'. The sum of all periods' new long-term net loans is the total outstanding *long-term loans* on the date specified. Similarly the sum of all net new debenture issues is the total *debentures* still outstanding. The total outstanding equity issue is generally split into two parts. The first, the *share issue at par value* is the nominal or face value of the shares issued, while the other, the *share premium*, is the difference between the par value and the funds actually received when the shares were issued. This depends on the price at which the shares were actually sold and is generally positive.

On the right-hand side, the totals are, first, the total expenditure on capital minus the accumulated depreciation. This is the current 'written down' book value of the company's *fixed assets*. Second, the total of all increases in net current assets is total net current assets, i.e. *current assets* minus *current liabilities*. The total of either column is known as *capital employed* and is the most common measure of the resources available to the company over the long term with which to earn profit.

Thus the Balance Sheet generally looks as shown in Table 10.5. The figures relate to the same coverage as in Table 10.3 and are for the end of the companies' financial year 1971/2.

TABLE 10.5

£ millions		£ millions		
Share Issue (par value)		Fixed Assets (Book Value)		22 136
Share premium	8345	Current Assets		
Reserves	14 677	Stocks	11 812	
Debentures		Debtors	12 222	
Other Long-Term Loans	6615	Financial Assets	2682	
Tax Provision[1]	1392	Cash	2797	29 513
Minority Interest in[2]		— Current Liabilities		
Subsidiaries	1173	Creditors	10 686	
		Short-Term Loans	5567	
		Dividends, Interest &		
		Tax Currently Due[3]	3194	19 447
Capital Employed[4]	32 202	Capital Employed		32 202

Source: *Business Monitor, Company Finance*, 6th issue, H.M.S.O. (1975).
Notes:
  (1) See p. 370 for explanation of this item.
  (2) This shows that part of the aggregate capital employed which is in the form of assets in other non-controlled companies. Being included in the 'uses' side as part of fixed assets, net current assets, etc. it must be added to the 'sources' side to achieve balance.
  (3) These are liabilities now incurred but not yet paid.
  (4) By adding current liabilities to both sides, an older but still used form of Balance Sheet is obtained. The 'uses' side is then known as 'Assets' and the 'sources' side as 'Liabilities'. The Share and Reserves items are liabilities of the *company*, as a legal entity, to its *owners*. The other items are all different types of liability to lenders of funds.

While the Balance Sheet provides evidence on the relative importance of different sources of funds over the past, it does not indicate which sources are currently the most utilized. In fact in recent years only a very small proportion of funds has been raised by the issue of new equity or debentures in the stock market in the U.K. This is illustrated in Table 10.6, which shows the percentage of total funds available to U.K. industrial and commercial companies from each source and for each use.

The implication of these figures is that the role of the capital market in the U.K. in supplying new funds to firms with good investment prospects is very limited. This might be because companies wish to avoid issuing costs, the risk of a new issue failing, close stock market scrutiny, the dilution of management stock holdings, or higher taxation of shareholders' return via dividends than capital gain.[93] This has been challenged, however, as a rather misleading statement by Prais.[94] He looked at the contribution of different sources of funds to the increase in *net* assets. Retentions were calculated net of depreciation and stock appreciation (that element of profit due to an increase in the price of stocks) and found to contribute approximately 60 per cent (excluding acquisition) and new issues (equity and debenture) about 40 per cent. This emphasizes (*a*) the extent to which internal sources are required for replacement and main-

[93] See W. Baumol, *The Stock Market and Economic Efficiency* (Fordham University Press, 1965).
[94] S. Prais, *The Evolution of Giant Firms in Britain*, N.I.E.S.R. (1976), 126-30.

TABLE 10.6

Percentage of total sources and uses for U.K. Industrial and Commercial Companies

Sources	1970	1971	1972	1973	1974
Ordinary Shares	0·6	2·2	3·2	0·7	0·3
Debentures (and Preference Shares)	2·5	3·2	2·9	0·3	—0·4
Total New Issues	3·1	5·4	6·1	1·0	—0·1
Bank Borrowing	18·2	10·9	30·1	31·4	31·4
Internal Sources	52·9	55·6	48·7	48·6	53·4
Other[1]	25·8	28·1	15·1	19·0	15·3
Uses					
Gross fixed investment			36·2	30·5	37·6
Increase in Stocks etc.			9·0	22·7	38·8
Acquisition of financial assets			40·5	38·1	18·8
Other[2]			14·3	8·7	4·8

Sources: *Financial Statistics*, C.S.O. (Apr. 1975) and *Economic Trends*, H.M.S.O. (Sept. 1977).
Notes:
   (1) Includes capital transfers and overseas sources.
   (2) Includes taxes on capital and unidentified uses.

tenance of stock levels under inflationary conditions, and (*b*) the dependence of companies on borrowing, which does not increase net assets.

APPENDIX 2

Many useful ratios can be derived from the Balance Sheet and Profit and Loss Accounts, which indicate different aspects of a company's performance. They can be read off from Table 10.7, which also defines the various symbols used. The figures included are those implied by Tables 10.3 and 10.5 and are given pre-tax and post-tax in that order where applicable.

   The main financial performance ratios are:

(i) Rate of Return on Capital Employed. This measures the profitability of the capital employed.

(ii) Return on Net Worth. The denominator, net worth, represents the total assets available to the owners of the company after all liabilities to others have been settled. The numerator, net profit, is the income (increase in assets) for the year net of all claims. The return on net worth is therefore a measure of the return attributable to the shareholders (owners) of the company earned by the management.

(iii) Ratio of Long-Term Debt to Net Worth is a measure of the risk to which providers of debt finance are exposed. $1 - (D/C)$ indicates the extent to which the net assets of the company could fail to realize their book value if sold and

TABLE 10.7

Stock Concepts	*Flow Concepts*	*Return Concepts*
Capital Employed (K)	Gross Trading Profit Net of Depreciation (Π)	Rate of Return on Capital Employed ($p = (\Pi/K)$) (17·3%, 12·1%)
Long-Term Debt (D)	Interest Charges (iD)	Interest rate (i)
Net Assets or Net Worth ($C = K - D$)	Net Profit ($\Pi - iD$)	Return on Net Worth $$p' = \frac{\Pi - iD}{K - D} \quad (19·6\%,\ 12·6\%)$$
Ratio of Long-Term Debt to Net Worth $$\left(\frac{D}{K - D}\right) \quad (27·7\%)$$	Ratio of Times Covered (Π/iD) (6·4, 4·5)	
Number of Shares Issued (N)		Earnings per Share $$\frac{\Pi - iD}{N}$$
Share Price (S)		
Stock Market Valuation of Equity ($M = N \times S$)		Price–Earnings (P.E.) Ratio $$\frac{M}{\Pi - iD} \quad (8·8,\ 13·8)$$
	Dividend, d.	Dividend Yield $$y = \frac{(\Pi - iD)(1 - r)}{M}$$ (Post-tax 3·4%)
Valuation ratio $$V = \frac{M}{C} = p'\frac{(1 - r)}{y}$$ (1·6)	Retention Ratio $$r = \frac{\Pi - iD - d}{\Pi - iD}$$ (34·5%, 53·8%)	Earnings Yield $$y' = \frac{(\Pi - iD)}{M}$$ (11·3%, 7·3%)
Gearing Ratio $$h = \frac{D}{D + M} \quad \text{or} \quad h' = \frac{D}{D + C}$$ ($h = 17.3\%, h' = 25·8\%$)		

Notes:

(1) The two measures of the Gearing Ratio, both of which appear in the literature, are identical only when the valuation ratio is unity.

(2) The P.E. ratio is based on $M =$ £40,000 million. This is derived from earnings yield figures given in *Financial Statistics*, Central Statistical Office, H.M.S.O., no. 117 (Jan. 1972).

still cover all outstanding debt.

(iv) Ratio of times covered is another view of debt finance providers' risk. $1 - (iD/\Pi)$ is a measure of the extent to which profit could fall without impairing the company's ability to meet its interest payment commitments. In that higher gearing generally raises (iii) and (iv) it is a main determinant of debt-providers' risk.

(v) Earnings per share. This figure multiplied by a shareholder's number of shares indicates the full income obtained in the year by the shareholder.

(vi) Price–Earnings (P.E.) ratio. This shows the number of years necessary for earnings per share at their current rate to sum to the current share price. By itself the figure is well-night meaningless but is in principle a useful basis for comparing the earning power of different shares per pound invested. In practice it has severe limitations, because a high P.E. ratio may indicate that a strong rise in earnings is forecast while a low one may be the result of very bad prospects and consequent collapse of the share price.

(vii) Dividend Yield. This measures the last dividend paid as a percetage return on the current equity value of the company. It measures the dividend-earning power per pound of the shares if the last dividend were to be maintained.

(viii) Earnings Yield. This is similar except that it includes all earnings attributable to the shareholders whether they are paid out as dividends or not.

(ix) The price of the share. Changes in this indicate the opportunities for capital gains that have occurred.

(x) Valuation ratio. This indicates the current value which the stock market places on the net assets of the company. A value in excess of unity indicates that the net assets as a going concern are worth more than the sum of their individual written-down book values.

Thus we have 2 over-all management performance ratios, 2 long-term debt security measures, 5 equity return measures and a management security-from-takeover measure. A final common measure, this time of short-term insolvency, is the 'current ratio' of current assets to current liabilities. Generally this covers assets and liabilities realizable within a year, and unless the company has secured a source of further short-term finance on demand a current ratio below one indicates a very exposed position. A liquidity ratio of highly liquid current assets to total current liabilities gives an even shorter-term view of the company's ability to meet a possible run on its current assets.

APPENDIX 3

In nearly all countries, but particularly the U.K., there has been for many years a growing dissatisfaction with the accounting procedures used because they give a seriously distorted picture of a company's true position in times of inflation. This appendix is not intended to be more than a very brief introduction to the issue. The difficulties may be summarized under four headings.

1. Depreciation

Depreciation provisions are normally based on the Historic Cost (actual purchase price) of assets and are such as to total up to the historic cost figure over the estimated life of the assets. While the total depreciation provision in a company in any one year will normally provide funds for expenditures unconnected with the assets to which they pertain, over the long term and in the absence of inflation the funds from this source will equal the funds required to maintain a constant physical capital stock. Under inflationary conditions the accumulated depreciation on each item of equipment will be less than the cost of replacing it with identical equipment, and so over the long term the funds from depreciation provisions will be inadequate to maintain the company's capital stock. Part of so-called profit has therefore to be used even to maintain the company in its current form in physical terms. This raises first the theoretical problem that measured profit no longer corresponds to true income, the latter being defined as that which can be distributed without reducing the company's wealth and hence its ability to carry on its business. Second, there is the practical problem that a company may appear to be profitable but be unable to finance replacement investment, still less expansionary investment.

2. Stock Appreciation

When supplies are purchased they are for accounting purposes regarded initially as being part of the 'cost of goods sold' in the same time-period. If at the end of the period some goods embodying those supplies have not been sold then the cost of the supplies is deducted from 'cost of goods sold', does not enter the Profit and Loss Account, and constitutes the 'closing stock' figure in the Balance Sheet for the period. These stocks are then available for use in the production of the next period's sales, appear as 'opening stock' of the next period, and are regarded as part of that period's 'cost of goods sold'. Thus the cost of goods sold equals:

Opening Stock
+ Purchases
− Closing Stock

A problem then arises in determining which part of the inputs purchased throughout the year is presumed used first and which, because it is used later, is regarded as part of closing stock. In nearly all cases it would be very difficult and costly to actually identify the date and cost of purchase of the physical materials used in current sales, and in some cases, such as paint from large storage containers, impossible.

The usual procedure is that known as First-in-First-out (F.I.F.O.), in which materials are presumed to be used up in the order that they were purchased. In general this means the cost of goods sold includes all the opening stock purchased in the (or any) previous year, and the earlier purchases of the current year. The closing stock subtracted includes the latest purchased stock.

Suppose now that the opening and closing stock are physically similar, but inflation has occurred within the year—it is then the lowest cost materials which are included in the 'cost of goods sold'. Profit is therefore calculated on the basis of a cost of supplies which no longer applies. Part of this accounted profit will be absorbed in physically replacing the stock used up by new stock at higher prices. This 'stock appreciation' element is not true profit as it cannot be distributed without the firm beginning to run down its scale of operations. This is seen most clearly by the fact that if the firm sells goods embodying previously purchased stock and simultaneously replaces the stock at new higher prices, the net addition to the firm's cash balance will be less than the accounted profit by an amount dependent on the rise in prices of the stock regularly purchased. If inflation is rapid and profit margins narrow, the stock appreciation element can be a very substantial part of profit as conventionally accounted.

3. Asset Value Appreciation

If inflation increases the value of a company's fixed assets then this too is excluded on traditional historic cost accounting procedures. The statement of net worth is therefore artificially low and the measurement of rate of return on capital employed artificially high.

4. Monetary Liabilities

This is the most controversial aspect. If a liability of £100 is incurred at 10 per cent then neither the debt outstanding nor the interest charge per annum is affected by inflation, and it has been argued that no change in company accounts is necessary therefore. On the other hand however, there is a clear sense in which a firm with a fixed interest liability is better off in real terms as a result of inflation. Conversely a firm which holds a given sum of money throughout a period of inflation will be worse off in real terms at the end of the period.

The over-all result is that companies may well be showing apparently healthy rates of return, but be unable to maintain their level of operations and be going steadily into insolvency.

In the U.K. two approaches to the problem have been presented, which though fundamentally different in concept become much more similar in practice. One, recommended by an independent Committee of Enquiry[95] under the chairmanship of F. Sandilands, is known as Current Cost Accounting (C.C.A.) or Replacement Cost Accounting. This starts by classifying gains into realized and unrealized 'holding' gains (the difference between measured value of an asset and its original cost); operating gains (the difference between the amounts realized for a company's output and the 'value to the business' of the inputs used by the company in generating those amounts); and extraordinary gains (which are similar to operating gains except that they are realized on items which do not form part of the company's output). The report then adopts Hicks's definition of profit[96] as 'the maximum value which the company can distribute during the year and still expect to be as well off at the end of the year as it was at the beginning'. In order to determine how 'well-off' the company is, it is necessary to value its capital in some way. Four possible ways are:

  (i) Historic Cost.
  (ii) 'Value in Purchase'—Replacement Cost.
  (iii) 'Value in Use'—Present value of cash flows obtainable.
  (iv) 'Value in Sale'—Net realizable value.

On the basis that the appropriate concept of value is the 'value of assets to the business' and that this is given by the 'deprival value' or maximum loss that the company will suffer if deprived of the asset, number (i) is irrelevant. Of the other three, the report tends to favour replacement costs. If either the present value or the net realizable value is highest, then on being deprived of the asset the company would replace it (for use or resale respectively) and the loss would be the replacement cost. Only if the latter were the highest would the company not replace the asset, and the cost to the company if deprived of the asset would be the higher of the other two. On this basis the report favours measuring fixed assets as the written-down (or written-up in the case of appreciation) value of

[95] *Inflation Accounting. Report of the Inflation Accounting Committee* (Sandilands) Cmnd. 6225, H.M.S.O. (Sept. 1975).
[96] J. R. Hicks, *Value and Capital*, 2nd edn. (Oxford, 1946), 172.

their replacement cost, the latter being found for the company by reference to a price index of assets for the industry in which it operates. Stocks, it is recommended, should be based on replacement cost or net realizable value, whichever is the lower. Again a price index of stock prices may be necessary to calculate these values if stock is not turned over rapidly. Although such changes allow for changes in the price of assets over time, the unit of measurement by which the current value of assets to the business is measured is still money in the ordinary sense. On this basis monetary assets, it is recommended, should not be adjusted. Over-all it regards only operating gains as profit and in particular excludes the holding gain of stock appreciation.

Most criticism of the report has centred on its treatment of monetary assets, but a more fundamental set of criticisms has been made by Scott.[97] His two main criticisms are, first, that the report confuses two concepts of gain. The first, the 'gain' concept, is 'the discounted net present value of all future cash flows at the end of the year, less the discounted net present value of the future cash flows at the beginning of the year, plus the net cash flow arising within the year after making adjustments for the introduction of new capital during the year', which is one definition used in the report. The second, the 'standard-stream' concept is similar to that sometimes employed in the report to describe operating gains and is defined as 'the maximum amount which could be taken out of the enterprise by the owners in a given period without impairing their ability to take the same amount out in all future periods of equal length'. These two under certain circumstances are different;[98] in particular, if prices are expected to rise, then the standard stream concept requires that the holding gains arising from the increased present value of assets should be included, just as the holding *losses* arising from the decreased present value associated with the depreciation of capital equipment are negatively included.

The second and equally serious criticism is that standard stream income must be seen as a *real* income concept. The ability to take out a constant *monetary* amount from an enterprise during inflation, especially if the latter is rapid, would clearly not be a useful guide to distribution. This then means that the concept has to be formulated in purchasing power terms. Additionally Scott argued that historic cost is the correct basis for calculating depreciation provided the depreciation funds can be used to earn the same rate of return as the asset concerned; also that the 'deprival' value approach is neither justified by the report nor in fact superior to the 'economic' (present) value basis.

Despite these points it seems quite likely that the Sandilands recommendations will generally be implemented, except possibly in respect of monetary items where its views, based on the failure to recognize that the standard stream income removable every year must be in real terms, fail to allow for a central impact of inflation.

The other main proposal put forward by the accountancy profession itself[99] is known as Current Purchasing Power (C.P.P.) accounting in the U.K., and General Price-Level or General Purchasing Power accounting in the U.S. The

[97] M. Scott, *Some Economic Principles of Accounting: A Constructive Critique of the Sandilands Report*, Institute of Fiscal Studies Lecture Series, no. 7.

[98] Examples given are when the interest (discount) rate used to calculate present value changes, and when price expectations change. Neither of these, however, requires that holdings gains be included.

[99] *Accounting for Changes in the Purchasing Power of Money*, Accounting Standards Steering Committee Exposure Draft, no. 8 (Jan. 1973).

essential point of these systems is that conventional entries in company accounts are converted to take account of inflation *not* by assessing the current value of an asset either in purchase, use or sale but by assessing *the current purchasing power of the money previously spent in acquiring an asset.* Thus historic cost values again have to be converted, but this time by a price index reflecting the change in the *general* price level since the purchase occurred.

This, however, was criticized and rejected by the Sandilands report on several grounds, including, first, that it introduced an unsatisfactory new measuring rod, namely 'purchasing power units' rather than money, second, that it did not indicate the value of the business, third, that it did not indicate the impact of inflation of the business, and finally that the resulting measure of profit might not be fully distributable.

11

INVESTMENT EXPENDITURE

1 INVESTMENT DECISIONS

At the macroeconomic level, the determinants of investment expenditure have been very thoroughly studied. At the level of industries and individual firms they have, until recently at least, been much less well explored. Given the central role of investment decisions in determining a firm's success or failure, growth and general development, it is somewhat surprising that relatively little attention has been paid within the discipline of industrial economics to this aspect of firms' behviour. This situation probably arose because of the great emphasis placed in the early theory of the firm on the determination of prices and the role of market structure and the price mechanism in determining the allocation of resources. Investment expenditure entered this picture only in so far as it was necessary to establish a particular short-run average cost curve in order to attain the profit maximizing point on the long-run average cost curve. Although various writers, in particular Fisher[1] and the Lutzes,[2] examined and developed the optimality conditions for investment decision-taking, this aspect was largely treated as subsidiary to that of studying determinants and effects of market structure and the nature of the competitive process. Furthermore, this emphasis persisted once empirical investigation started at the microeconomic level, with firms' pricing behaviour being investigated far more thoroughly than their investment decision behaviour.

In recent years, however, this situation has begun to change with increasing emphasis being placed on the determinants of investment at a more microeconomic level, the nature of the investment decision process, and the impact of government policy on investment. This has come about for two reasons. First the 'active' approach to understanding firms' behaviour, with its emphasis on long-term balanced growth, product innovation and development, has given, at least by implication, a central role to firms' investment expenditure. A company's investment expenditure decisions in their broadest sense allocate the dominant proportion of its cash flow, determine in which markets it will operate, and are a major factor in the success or failure of its operations. Essentially they implement

[1] I. Fisher, *The Theory of Interest* (New York, 1930).
[2] F. Lutz and V. Lutz, *The Theory of Investment of the Firm* (Princeton, 1951).

the management's plans for developing the company at the desired rate of growth and in a way which balances the demand for products and the capacity to supply over time. The basic diagram in Chapter 1 illustrates the central role of investment in this process, and the growth models of Chapter 9 embody this.

Second, empirical testing of macroeconomic investment functions has provded difficult and often rather inconclusive. As more information at the level of the firm or the industry has become available, so it has become possible to supplement such studies by more disaggregated ones, especially as the main theories of investment behaviour which have been tested at the aggregate level have been based on views about how the individual firm would be likely to determine its investment. The result is that there is now a sizeable body of literature on this topic, the results of which are well worth incorporating into the context of industrial economics. It should none the less be stressed that although for most firms their investment decisions are generally the most important, most centralized, documented, and most analysed of all the decisions they have to take, yet, paradoxically, their investment is frequently very volatile, unsuccessfully forecast, and not easy to influence.

To begin the detailed examination of firms' expenditure decisions we first present a simple framework within which the various aspects of importance can be incorporated. While this is primarily designed with plant and equipment investment in mind, it is in general terms applicable to the other two major types of capital expenditure, namely research and development and market investment[3] which are examined in the following two chapters. This framework is represented in Figure 11.1. The box represents the firm. Its external business environment comprises demand conditions—primarily the price, quantity, and marketing trade-off opportunities it faces in various markets—and supply conditions—primarily the cost and availability of capital, labour, materials, and funds. Both are of course influenced by government fiscal, monetary, prices and incomes, and exchange rate policy.

Investment decisions initially require forecasts to be made of all such variables, and these forecasts provide the basic supply and demand information on which the decisions will depend. This information will include, or in some way embody, risk and/or uncertainty elements, and all three aspects will be processed and analysed in the generation of the data on the basis of which the decision will be taken. In general, specific criteria will be used to evaluate the data,

[3] Note that although market investment may be *accounted* as a current cost its economic characteristics are akin to a capital expenditure.

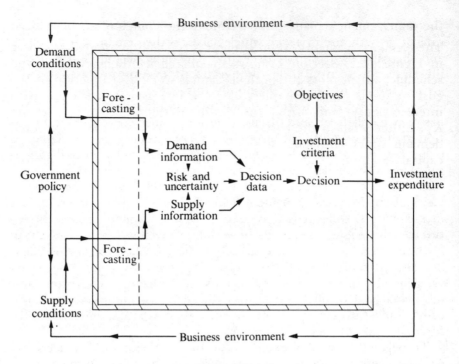

Fig. 11.1

based on or derived from the firm's main objectives. The decisions which result will determine the investment expenditures made, which in turn will help shape the future business environment of the firm.

Potentially all parts of this framework are important influences on investment decisions. In the following sections we adopt the approach implied by the main contributions to our understanding of investment. Initially, therefore, we abstract almost entirely from the 'internal' aspects of investment decisions deriving the basic theory of investment under very simplified conditions. Section 3 presents the main empirical findings when various versions of the basic theory are tested. Increasingly this has led to the inclusion of forecasting, risk, and uncertainty elements of the investment decision process in econometric analysis. Section 4 focuses on the impact of government policy, primarily in the U.S. and U.K., on investment. Finally, Section 5 explores the investment decision process itself, in particular the investment criteria adopted by firms, their information processing and decision taking, in an effort to account for those variations in investment that remain inadequately explained by statistical analysis.

2   THE BASIC THEORY OF INVESTMENT

The elementary theory of investment is typically presented as shown in Figure 11.2. Section 1 shows the marginal efficiency of capital schedule, which plots the optimal capital stock as a function of the cost of funds (in the simplest case the interest rate). Starting with interest rate i_1 and MEK_1 the optimum capital stock is given by K_1^*. Either a fall in the cost of capital to i_2 or a change in expected demand which shifts the schedule to MEK_2 will generate a desired capital stock of K_2^*. If the capital stock was initially $K_1 = K_1^*$ desired

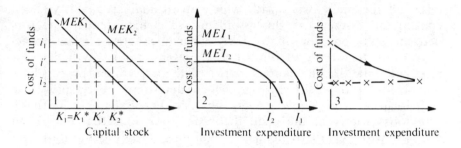

Fig. 11.2

investment equals $K_2^* - K_1$ as this is the increase in the capital stock necessary to bring the firm back into equilibrium. Conceivably this could occur in one time period, but typically there will be expansion costs which limit the rate at which the investment can be made while maximizing profits. In Section 2 MEI_1 is the marginal efficiency of investment schedule which shows how much investment it would be profitable to carry out in the *current* time period for different levels of cost of funds *given* that the capital stock is initially at K_1. (The horizontal scale is greatly extended for graphical clarity.) The *MEI* is probably horizontal for low levels of investment, indicating that some of the desired investment can be carried out without any change in the cost conditions faced by the firm. Increasingly, however, as the rate of investment is increased so expansion costs will intrude. These arise because of the problems of integrating large amounts of capital quickly and getting them operational, and because the capital goods industry will prefer to be geared to produce at a long-run steady rate to avoid the worst effects of cyclical demand fluctuations. More rapid production will generally mean a higher price to cover higher production and/or higher finance costs and consequently a lower return to the purchaser of the equipment.

Initially the *MEI* is located at MEI_1 cutting the vertical axis at level i_1 because initially it is only at level i_1 that the demand for investment is zero. In the familiar Fisher analysis a fall in the interest rate to i_2 generates investment of I_1, increasing the capital stock to K'. The *MEI* shifts to MEI_2 because at K' the capital stock would be optimal for interest rate i', and only at *that* rate would there be no further demand for investment. Because i_2 still prevails there is invesment of I_2 in the second year, increasing the capital stock further towards K_2^*, etc. Section 3 plots the empirical relation between investment and the cost of capital funds.

Although much too simple to be of any direct use this figure raises all the main issues with which investment studies have been concerned. These are the problems of what demand factors determine the position of the *MEK*; what in practice are the characteristics of the supply of funds here represented only by the interest rate; and what are the characteristics of the adjustment process here portrayed by the *MEI* diagram which determine how rapidly the actual capital stock converges on the desired capital stock. We therefore look briefly at the main theoretical positions that have been adopted with regard to demand conditions, supply conditions, and the adjustment process.

(i) *Demand factors*

The simplest starting-point is a strict neoclassical interpretation of the basic theory generally associated with Jorgenson. Factor prices and ratios are presumed fully flexible and all markets are assumed to be perfect. Then the necessary condition for an optimum capital stock is that the additional capital cost of increasing the capital stock equals the additional revenue it generates, i.e.

$$cdK = pdQ$$

where p is the price of output and c is the implicit price of the service derived from capital.

Therefore
$$\frac{dQ}{dK} = \frac{c}{p}$$

A Cobb–Douglas production function is then introduced.

$$Q = AK^\alpha L^\beta$$

so that the marginal product of capital

$$\frac{dQ}{dK} = \alpha A K^{\alpha-1} L^\beta = \alpha \frac{Q}{K}$$

Hence the optimality condition is

$$\frac{c}{p} = \alpha \frac{Q}{K}$$

where α is the elasticity of output with respect to capital. The desired capital stock is given therefore by

$$K^* = \alpha \frac{Qp}{c}$$

and the desired capital stock is proportional to the value of output deflated by the price of capital services. This indicates the two most common main determinants of investment hypothesized, namely ouptut, Q, and p/c, the relative price of output to capital services. In practice there have been three approaches involved.

(*a*) Much early analysis of investment ignored the effect of relative prices, regarded Q as exogenously determined, and hence was based on the equation

$$K^* = \alpha Q \tag{1}$$

where α is the desired or necessary capital–output ratio. In effect the elasticity of capital with respect to output is 1, and with respect to relative prices zero.

(*b*) The second we may term the 'strict' neoclassical approach which constrains the elasticity of capital with respect to both output and relative prices to be unity. The basic equation is then as given originally

$$K^* = \alpha \frac{Qp}{c} \tag{2}$$

In testing, Q is again generally regarded as being exogenous, but strictly for a neoclassical firm Q is endogenous and a function of relative prices. If this were to be incorporated, desired capital stock would be a function of relative prices only.[4]

(c) A more general neoclassical approach which does not constrain the values of the elasticities, i.e.

$$K^* = f\left(Q, \frac{p}{c}\right) \qquad (3)$$

In addition this may embody the price of labour relative to capital and output prices.

So far nothing has been said about the timing relationships involved in the derivation of desired capital stock. Typically investment is an extended process with substantial lags between recognition of an opportunity to invest and a decision to invest; between the decision and commencement of investment expenditure; and between then and the completion. This has two major implications for even the most basic investment functions. First, investment now is a function of *expected* desired capital stock. Second, the latter must be formulated and is usually thought to depend in some way on past values of the independent variables which determine the desired capital stock. The latter then becomes a function of one or more past values of the independent variable(s). There is considerable discretion over the choice of a specific lag structure. At one extreme a number of past values of the independent variable may be selected on the basis of theory or goodness of fit, with no constraint on the relative weighting of the past values, for example for output as the determinant of desired capital stock.

$$K_t^* = \alpha[\lambda_1 Q_t + \lambda_2 Q_{t-1} + \lambda_3 Q_{t-2} \cdots \qquad (4)$$

At the other extreme the weights may be constrained to be a progression (generally geometric), for example

$$K_t^* = \alpha[\lambda Q_t + \lambda^2 Q_{t-1} + \lambda^3 Q_{t-2} \cdots \qquad (5)$$

The former is potentially more flexible but reduces degrees of freedom and may face severe problems of multicollinearity. The latter can generally be reformulated to contain only one or two past values but imposes a weighting that may be inappropriate. In practice a compromise is usually effected. One method is to use the Koyck transformation or some modification of it. This adopts the structure

[4] For elaboration of this point see R. M. Coen, 'Tax Policy and Investment Behaviour: Comment', *A.E.R.* 59, no. 3 (June 1969), 370–9, and H. I. Grossman, 'A Choice–Theoretic Model of an Income–Investment Accelerator', *A.E.R.* 62, no. 4 (Sept. 1972) 630–41.

$$K_t^* = \alpha(1 - \lambda)[Q_t + \lambda Q_{t-1} + \lambda^2 Q_{t-2} \cdots \tag{6}$$

Rewriting this for period $t - 1$ and multiplying by λ gives

$$\lambda K_{t-1}^* = \alpha(1 - \lambda)[\lambda Q_{t-1} + \lambda^2 Q_{t-2} \cdots$$

When subtracted from the equation for K_t^* this gives

$$K_t^* = \alpha(1 - \lambda)Q_t + \lambda K_{t-1}^* \tag{7}$$

If capital stock in the previous period is assumed to have been optimal then this provides a very simple and readily testable equation from which both α and λ can be derived. Greater flexibility can then be achieved by applying independent weights to the first one or more terms and the Koyck formulation thereafter, for example

$$K_t^* = \alpha[aQ_{t-1} + (1 - a)(1 - \lambda)(Q_{t-2} + \lambda Q_{t-3} + \lambda^2 Q_{t-4} \cdots \tag{8}$$

Another approach is to use a distribution of weights where each weight is a function of several parameters of the distribution, thus permitting some degree of flexibility in the determination of different weights.

(ii) *Supply factors*

The naive model introduced only the interest rate on the supply side. This ignores first that equity financing as opposed to borrowing may be significant and second that the availability as well as the cost of funds may be important. Such considerations have focused attention first on equity yield as component of the cost of funds and variables closely associated with it, in particular the valuation of a company and profits; second on the flow of internally generated funds in the belief that the supply of funds schedule may have an actual or imputed discontinuity in it at the point where internal funds are exhausted. But it should be noted that if the marginal cost of funds schedule has any positive slope then in principle investment will be responsive to changes in the flow of internal funds if these are regarded as a cheaper source.

(iii) *The adjustment process*

The basis of most work has been the flexible accelerator formulation

$$I_t = \beta(K_t^* - K_{t-1}) \tag{9}$$

where β is a speed of adjustment coefficient. If, for example, this is combined with equation (1) we obtain

$$I_t = \beta(\alpha Q_t - K_{t-1}) \tag{10}$$

which is the familiar capital–stock adjustment model of investment. This illustrates that investment functions can be interpreted in terms of capacity utilization. If α is constant over time, capital in $t - 1$ was optimal, and full adjustment occurs in one period, i.e. $\beta = 1$, we have

$$K_{t-1} = K^*_{t-1} = \alpha Q_{t-1}$$

and $$I_t = \alpha(Q_t - Q_{t-1})$$

which is the crude accelerator model.

Two difficulties arise once the adjustment process is introduced. First it is no longer consistent, as was done in relation to equation (7), to assume that the previous capital stock in $t - 1$ was optimal. This suggests that it is better to use a specific distribution of weights to derive the optimal capital stock if the number of lagged terms is to be kept manageable. Furthermore, even if this problem is ignored, combining equations (7) and (9) gives

$$I_t = \beta[\alpha(1 - \lambda)Q_t + \lambda K_{t-1}]$$

$$= \beta(1 - \lambda)(\alpha Q_t - K_{t-1})$$

This precludes β, the speed of adjustment, and λ, the expectational lag parameter, being identified separately, though for testing and prediction this type of formulation may be acceptable.

The second issue is whether a coefficient of adjustment is sufficient to embrace the adjustment process or whether the costs of adjustment which determine the rate of investment are dependent on additional variables that must be added to the equation. In particular, if external finace costs more than internal finance then the cost of adjustment will depend not only on the adjustment speed but on the supply of internal funds. A further complication is that because costs of adjustment (and uncertainty) cause a slow adjustment of capital to demand changes, short-run changes which are not regarded as invalidating firms' long-run output hypotheses may have no effect at all.[5]

[5] See E. M. Birch, C. D. Siebert, 'Uncertainty, Permanent Demand & Investment Behaviour', *A.E.R.* 66, no. 1 (Mar. 1976), 16–27.

To summarize, in moving from elementary theory to testable models of investment, it is necessary to select the determinants of K_t^* to be tested in equation (9) and a lag formulation. The main options in selecting determinants of the optimal capital stock are:

Demand	*Relative Prices*	*Internal Funds*	*External Funds*
Change in output	Implicit price of	Retained Earnings	Interest rate
Capacity Utilization	capital services	Depreciation	Rate of Return
	Product Prices	Tax Liability	Value of company
	Wage Rates	Liquid Assets	Share Prices

The main reasons for continuing ambiguity about the determinants of investment are to be found in this multiplicity of potential determinants, the complexity of the investment process, the significance of expectations, and the timing of the adjustment process.

Finally, it should be noted that this all relates to the determination of changes in the capital stock, i.e. net investment. To explain gross investment expenditure figures we need to add in replacement investment. This is generally presumed to be a constant function of the existing capital stock, thus making the basic equation

$$I_t = \beta(K_t^* - K_{t-1}) + \delta K_{t-1}) \tag{11}$$

where δ is the rate of depreciation of the capital stock. Note, however, that this presumes a unit coefficient of adjustment on replacement investment which may well not be appropriate. The alternative would be

$$I_t = \beta[K_t^* + (\delta - 1) - K_{t-1}] \tag{12}$$

3 EMPIRICAL STUDIES OF INVESTMENT

It is essentially an empirical matter which of these determinants is most important in explaining investment behaviour, and many investigations have been made at both micro- and macroeconomic level. Here we shall be concerned only with studies of investment of the firm and industry, for although the theory may be applicable at both levels there is no necessary reason to expect the main determinants to be the same at both levels. Interest rate effects might for example be swamped by demand effects for each firm individually, but the former dominate at aggregate level if changes in demand are predominantly switches from one firm to another within a relatively unchanging aggregate.

Historically, four stages can be identified in the analysis of investment. The first, corresponding to the original elementary theory, viewed interest rates as the prime determinant of investment. Keynes of course utilized this type of relation in the *General Theory*, though he did not distinguish the marginal efficiencies of capital and investment, with the result that the analysis saw levels rather than changes in interest rates as the main influence. This stage is now largely of historical interest only.

In the second stage, in the 1950s and early 1960s, opinion moved quite strongly away from emphasis on interest rates and in favour of changes in demand or capacity utilization as the main factor influencing investment. This arose partly because of negative evidence with regard to interest rates and partly because of much positive econometric evidence with regard to the more sophisticated demand and capacity models. We consider these in turn.

Several case-study investigations were important in establishing the view that the cost of funds had relatively little impact in the U.K. The Oxford Economists' Research Group, carrying out some pilot interviews and then a survey questionnaire in the late 1930s, found almost unanimous agreement that short-term interest rates were unimportant in influencing fixed or stock investment. Few of the businessmen thought even the long-term rate of interest important.[6] At most only 13 per cent of 309 replying firms saw cost of funds as an influence and this was sometimes via the liquidity or asset value effect on company bond holdings. Availability as opposed to cost of funds was sometimes important, but the two factors together still influenced less than 20 per cent of the firms which replied.

A member of the group, Andrews, working later with Brunner on U.S. investment, again found little impact of the cost of funds, but availability as potentially very important.[7] The Radcliffe report inquiries in 1958 generally confirmed the picture for the U.K.,[8] with only between 6 per cent and 11 per cent of firms affected, as did a survey by Corner and Williams.[9] In this only about 3 per cent had abandoned projects due to high interest costs, though 13 per cent had delayed them. In the U.S. Ebersole[10] could find little

---

[6] P. W. S. Andrews, J. E. Meade, 'Summary of Replies to Questions on Effects of Interest Rates', *Oxford Economic Papers* (Oct. 1938), 14–31, and P. W. S. Andrews, 'A Further Enquiry into the Effects of the Rate of Interest', *Oxford Economic Papers* (Feb. 1940), 32–73.

[7] P. W. S. Andrews, E. Brunner, *Capital Development in Steel* (Oxford, 1952).

[8] (Radcliffe) *Report of Enquiry into the Working of the Monetary System in the U.K.*, H.M.S.O. (1959).

[9] D. C. Corner, A. Williams, 'The Sensitivity of Business to Initial and Investment Allowances', *Economica*, N.S. 32 (Feb. 1965), 32–47.

[10] J. F. Ebersole, 'The Influence of Interest Rates upon Entrepreneurial Decisions in Business—A Case Study', *Harvard Business Review*, 17 (Autumn 1938), 35–9.

evidence for interest-sensitivity of investment, and Mack none at all.[11] Her study, like those of Heller *et al.*,[12] de Chazeau,[13] and Eisner,[14] noted the emphasis on internal financing with its consequent availability considerations, but all found hardly any attention at all paid to the cost of funds when the funds were externally raised.

A study by Gort[15] also found interest rates to have had little effect on the amount or timing of investment,but adds that this was at least in part due to the view that action by the U.S. authorities would rule out big fluctuations. Thus when more financing was necessary, share yields and prices, gearing and retention ratios would be more significant, with the implication that cost of equity could not necessarily be ignored. But even here the difficulty of issuing stock at depressed prices may be essentially a problem of availability rather than cost of funds.

Most of these studies found depreciation/cash flow, or liquidity considerations to have an impact, further emphasizing availability effects. But more important, nearly all the interview/survey inquiries found support for a sales- or capacity-based model, as did a comparison of different models at the firm level carried out by Cannon via case-studies.[16] Thus over all there was considerable support for the view that expected demand was crucial, availability of finance of some significance, and the cost of funds of virtually no significance.

This picture was further supported by the early econometric evidence, which attached increasing importance to the sales/capacity approach. Although the earliest studies, in particular Tinbergen's pioneering work on investment in railroads, found the relationship to be weak,[17] these utilized the crude accelerator, which as we have seen is excessively restrictive. Studies since then have tended towards a capital stock adjustment model, not least because it allows for differences in capacity utilization. Chenery, looking at 6 U.S. industries, compared the two formulations, confirmed Tinbergen's result that

[11] R. Mack, *The Flow of Business Funds & Consumer Purchasing Power* (New York, 1941).

[12] W. Heller, F. Boddy, C. Nelson, A. Upgnen, *The Minneapolis Project: A Pilot Study of Local Capital Formation* (University of Minnesota, 1950).

[13] M. G. de Chazeau, 'Regularisation of Fixed Capital Investment by the Individual Firm', in N.B.E.R., *Regularisation of Business Investment* (Princeton University Press, 1954), 75–106.

[14] R. Eisner, 'Interview & Other Survey Techniques and the Study of Investment', in N.B.E.R., *Problems of Capital Formation* (Princeton University Press, 1957), 513–83.

[15] M. Gort, 'The Planning of Investment: A Study of Capital Budgeting in the Electric Power Industry', *J. of Business*, 24: Apr. 1951, 79–95 and July 1951, 181–202.

[16] C. Cannon, 'Private Capital Investment: A Case Study Approach towards Testing Alternative Theories', *J.I.E.* 16–17 (1966), 186–95.

[17] J. Tinbergen, *Statistical Testing of Business Cycle Theories*, Vol. I, *A Method and its Application to Investment Activity*, League of Nations (Geneva, 1938).

the crude accelerator did not work well, and found the capacity version to be more successful.[18] Monro also, using data similar to Tingerben, found a capacity formulation to work much better.[19] Several subsequent studies all found strong evidence for a capacity formulation of the stock adjustment principle (see for example those of Kisselgorf and Modigliani,[20] Taitel,[21] and in a non-econometric study, Gordon[22]). Koyck, using his distributed lag function, found a strong sales effect, with the capacity version generally stronger than the pure sales one, and the effect being more rapid in periods of expansion and in faster growing industries.[23] Also, Bourneuf[24] using capacity utilization measures and Eisner[25] using sales in real terms both found such variables to work reasonably well.

Equally important in studies however is the general lack of significance of interest rate variables. Kisselgorf and Modigliani for example found neither stock market prices nor interest rates to be important or even have the right sign. Meyer and Kuh, whose approach is examined in more detail below, could find no significant interest rate effect,[26] and while some of Tinbergen's results indicated a negative interest elasticity in the U.K., it did not apply in the U.S., France, or Germany. Virtually all the other studies either did not find, or did not investigate the effect of the cost of funds. Only Klein of the early econometric researchers found interest rates to be important and even here different specifications made them insignificant or of the wrong sign.[27]

With regard to availability of funds, particularly internal funds, the

[18] H. B. Chenery, 'Overcapacity and the Acceleration Principle', *Econometrica*, 20 (Jan. 1952), 1–28.

[19] A. S. Monne, 'Some notes on the Acceleration Principle', *R. Econ. Stats.* (May 1954), 93–9.

[20] A. Kisselgorf, F. Modigliani, 'Private Investment in the Electric Power Industry and the Acceleration Principle', *R. Econ. Stats.* 39 (Nov. 1957), 363–80.

[21] M. Taitel, *Profits, Productive Activities and New Investments*, T.N.E.C. Monograph 12 (Washington, 1941).

[22] R. Gordon, in E. Lundberg (ed.), *The Business Cycle in the Post-War World* (New York, 1955). This is an example of the accelerator being much more important at the industry level, due to switches in demand, than at the aggregate level.

[23] L. M. Koyck, *Distributed Lags and Investment Analysis* (Amsterdam, 1954).

[24] A. Bourneuf, 'Manufacturing Investment, Excess Capacity & the Rate of Growth of Output', *A.E.R.* 54, no. 5 (Sept. 1964), 607–25.

[25] R. Eisner, 'Realisation of Investment Anticipations', in J. Duesenberry *et al.* (ed.), *The Brookings Quarterly Model of the U.S.* (North Holland, 1965).

[26] J. Meyer, E. Kuh, *The Investment Decision* (Harvard University Press, 1966).

[27] L. Klein, *Economic Fluctuations in the United States 1929–41*, Cowles Commission Monograph 11 (New York, 1950). However, a study of individual firms by Eisner, contrary to his other studies, found the rate of return, as a guide to the cost of equity, important but not capacity utilization. See R. Eisner, 'A Permanent Income Theory of Investment', *A.E.R.* 57, no. 3 (June 1967), 363–90.

evidence was more mixed, with some studies, particularly those of Tinbergen, Klein, Meyer and Kuh, and Eisner finding profit and/or internal cash flow important, and others, such as Grunfeld[28] and Taitel, rejecting such correlations.

Two reactions to these views occurred. The first was to attempt to explain why the cost (and/or availability) of funds might not have the effect previously hypothesized. Amongst such explanations have been:

(i) Great uncertainty about the future makes the internal rate of return highly uncertain. As such, relatively much smaller fluctuations in interest rates have little impact.

(ii) The use of very unsophisticated investment decision procedures means that comparison of project returns with the cost of funds doesn't happen.

(iii) The long-term horizon of investment projects means that firms may react to high interest costs by borrowing short and rolling over the debt at a later date when interest rates have fallen.

(iv) On short-term projects the elasticity of present value with respect to interest rates is rather small, while the long planning period on long-term projects undermines the significance of current interest rates.

(v) If full cost pricing is employed and interest regarded as cost, firms may believe that profitability will not be impaired by higher borrowing costs.

These all suggest that businessmen simply ignore the cost of funds for one reason or another. Another set of reasons argues that although they recognize the cost, investment still does not respond to changes in interest rates.

(vi) It is the *expected* pattern of interest rates rather than current or past ones that matters.

(vii) The internal rate of return may frequently be above the opportunity cost of internal funds, but below the cost of external funds, making the availability of internal funds the key supply side determinant.

(viii) The variations which occur in interest rates may be relatively much less significant than the variations in, for example, demand, especially if the former is calculated in real terms.

(ix) Any artificial control of supply of funds, such as a refusal to issue new equity, may create excess demand for funds, which will in turn make only its availability and not its cost important.

(x) Richardson has argued that firms are typically very short of

[28] Y. Grunfeld, 'The Determinants of Corporate Investment', in A. C. Harberger (ed.), *The Demand for Durable Goods* (Chicago University Press, 1960).

managerial resources to deal with the expansion which investment brings forth.[29] Thus most projects have a high opportunity cost in terms of other possible projects forgone. Therefore internal rates of return a long way above borrowing costs are required in order to allow for this, with the result that interest rates themselves have less impact.

(xi) Finally, in this group, Yarrow has shown that the Marris growth model coupled with high interest rates and a constraint formulation as specified in Chapter 8 (see p. 270) may result in a 'backward sloping' interest–investment function.[30] Shifts in the growth–valuation curve as a result of higher interest rates may be such that *more* growth can be obtained with the same sacrifice of valuation as before, inducing expansion investment. The cost of funds is included in the relevant calculations, but the growth objective undermines the negative effect of higher interest rates on investment normally predicted.

No doubt some, if not all of these factors do operate to reduce or negate the effect on investment of the cost of funds. Nevertheless, it is the second reaction which has become much more widely accepted in recent years. This argues that the cost of funds *is* important, but for various reasons its impact is particularly hard to isolate. This approach has led to a series of criticisms of both the case-study and econometric studies and the use of more sophisticated techniques to identify the impact.

On the critical side, it is now widely recognized that interviews and surveys, though being useful, are very suspect ways of actually testing theories of behaviour. Individuals may not always be aware of the wider or longer-term influences determining their decisions and many may quite genuinely never consider the cost of funds, being only one member of a large group of decision-takers who contribute to a decision. In addition, as Eisner argues, economic relationships cannot be identified by majority voting; if just 5 per cent of investment decision-takers are influenced by interest rates the latter may none the less *at the margin* be a crucial determinant of investment.[31] Finally, it may well be that other variables which are taken into consideration when decisions are taken themselves reflect the cost of funds. Higher interest rates may well squeeze cash flow and lower net profits, and if the latter influence decisions then the cost of funds may have an impact.

[29] G. Richardson, 'The Limits to a Firm's Rate of Growth', *Oxford Economic Papers*, N.S. 16 (Mar. 1964), 9–23.

[30] G. Yarrow, 'On the Predictions of Managerial Theories of the Firm', *J.I.E.* 24, no. 4 (June 1976).

[31] Eisner, op. cit. (1957).

Such points place a greater emphasis on econometric testing at the firm and industry level. But here too many objections have been raised to the early studies.

(i) Investment rises as the economy expands because of demand effects, but typically this causes interest rates to rise as the demand for funds rises. It is not surprising therefore that there might be little evidence of a negative investment–interest relation even if one did exist, and a simultaneous equation system would need to be developed to test the one relation amongst all the others. This may mar the results of, for example, Meyer and Kuh, and Kisselgorf and Modigliani. Of course this argument can work two ways. Rising stock market valuation in a boom may well result in a lower cost of equity when investment is rising, but *not* represent a causal relationship between the two.

(ii) Firms normally face a whole range of short- and long-term debt and equity finance instruments, and they can within limits change the proportions in which they are employed. Thus particular measures of the cost of funds may vary markedly from the true weighted cost of capital which particular firms face. In addition it is not immediately clear what opportunity cost is imputed on retained earnings given that this depends on estimates of risk. These rationally may vary systematically, the risk premium being lower in the boom when interest rates as measured are higher.

(iii) Investment is a function of disequilibrium in the capital stock. Just as it will therefore be a function of changes in demand so it will in theory be dependent on changes in, rather than levels of, the cost of funds, be this measured by interest rates, equity yields, etc. This has not always been recognized in econometric testing. The exception is that a lower cost of funds by generating a larger capital stock will cause replacement investment to be at a higher level subsequently.

(iv) The use of different sources of funds at different times is likely to make the investment–interest relation vary over time and thus be harder to identify econometrically. This gives rise to, amongst others, the 'bifurcation' hypothesis that the cost of funds might be important in the boom when external funds are being used, but not in the recession. In fact the theory is suspect unless opportunity costs are ignored, and may be dominated by 'synchronization' effects as cash flow rises strongly in the boom. Despite early evidence of different determinants of investment at different stages of the cycle, later work, which to some extent has overcome the econometric problems, has tended to reject the bifurcation thesis.

(v) The role of internal funds, and especially profits, is particularly difficult to isolate. Depreciation allowances may well reflect accounting procedures and the tax system and not therefore give a true guide to internal funds at all. Similarly, because of accounting procedures, net profit can frequently be much higher than the funds actually available as a result of profitable operations. Also, the latter is likely to rise with demand, so that it may well play the role of a proxy for demand growth. In fact correlations between investment and profits, even where the latter is lagged, cannot distinguish whether profits are acting as a supply of funds in an imperfect capital market, a proxy for demand, or an expectational variable indicating future expected profit. In general it seems unlikely that firms would forgo future profits from investment just because past profits were poor. In addition the effect of demand is likely to be the same for large and small firms, bu the effect of the availability of funds is likely to be different and more acute for smaller firms. Finally, if profits fall because of rising *non-capital* costs, investment may be induced by factor substitution which will cloud the relationship between investment and profits. For such reasons, correlations between these variables are generally regarded as picking up far too many influences to be directly useful in explaining, predicting, or controlling investment.

Such difficulties have resulted in a third stage of investigation. This has involved a number of increasingly more sophisticated studies using eclectic models in which both supply and demand aspects are incorporated in an attempt to isolate and identify the effect of the supply side more clearly. Several alternatives have been tried. A major study by Meyer and Kuh[32] analysed data on investment by over 700 firms for the period 1946–50. They carried out a large number of correlations between investment and a series of potential individual determinants, constructing their final tests on the basis of this first exercise. Their main finding was that neither interest rates nor the cost of labour was important but that stock market price was; that in a boom the capacity utilization model fitted best, but that in the recession it was internal cash flow (profits and depreciation) that appeared to determine investment; that neither liquidity *stock* variables nor a crude accelerator explained investment; and that the so-called senility effect—firms with already older plant doing *less* investment—dominated the opposite 'echo' effect. Their results led them to hypothesize an Accelerator–Residual Funds theory in which investment was geared to gross profit minus 'conventional' dividends, but with discrepancies from this being generated by pressure on capacity as a result of increasing sales.

[32] Meyer and Kuh, op. cit.

Meyer and Glauber[33] appeared at first to confirm this for the period up to 1958, and in addition were able to reject the view that the profit element in cash flow was only important because it was a guide to, or correlated with sales. This was because the 'residual funds' variable (profit plus depreciation minus dividends and working capital) fitted better and was not correlated with sales. However, more specific testing resulted in the evidence being much less clear-cut, with no specific role for deprecation, changes in stock market prices no longer significant, the profit varible still subject to theoretical objections, and with the evidence for cyclical alternation between capacity utilization and residual funds models being no longer supported.

Finally, Kuh,[34] examining 60 firms over 20 years, could no longer substantiate the model, with external finance disturbing the investment–residual funds relationship and the capacity model regularly appearing superior to models based on lagged profits or internal cash flow.

Despite failure in establishing this particular approach to combining supply and demand elements, a series of eclectic models have found both capacity and cost of funds variables to be simultaneously important and there is now widespread agreement that both are important. This is partly because of the increased attention that has been paid to developing superior lag structures to reflect both the expectational and adjustment elements in the investment process. Evans found that an equation with capacity lagged one quarter, output lagged five and six quarters, corporate cash flow and interest rates lagged the same amount, share prices lagged one and two quarters, and the capital stock lagged five and six quarters, worked well.[35] In general, however, liquidity and interest rate variables were much less significant than capacity and sales variables. Of special note in this study is Evans's double distributed lag in which typically there is a peak impact on investment from output, capital stock, cash flow, and interest rates lagged five quarters, and another peak impact from output lagged one quarter. The former reflects the investment decision and allocation of funds, the later reflects last-minute modifications in the light of unforeseen changes in capacity utilization.

Anderson obtained not dissimilar results using a more conventional

[33] J. Meyer, R. Glauber, *Investment Decision, Economic Forecasting & Public Policy* (Harvard University Press, 1964).

[34] E. Kuh, *Capital Stock Growth: A Micro-Econometric Approach* (North Holland, 1967).

[35] M. K. Evans, 'A Study of Investment Decisions', *R. Econ. Stats.* 49, no. 2 (May 1967), 151–64.

single peaked lag structure.[36] Capacity utilization was very significant, but so also was the interest rate. Various measures of the availability of finance, including internal funds, government bonds held, tax provisions, and debt raising capacity proved relatively insignificant. Finally Resek obtained good results when regressing investment on output and the change in output (all deflated by capital stock) and interest rate and a variable derived from the marginal cost of funds curve incorporating retained earnings and the debt-asset ratio.[37] Although econometric difficulties arose, share prices when added were also important. Over all, Resek's results represent one further step from Evans's results to Anderson's in that although capacity and interest rates are again the main determinants, the latter is now the stronger one. Debt capacity as a measure of availability of funds is again much less important. The share price variable is interesting because it further supports the view that the cost of external funds is significant.

In so far as data permits econometric inferences to be made, such studies indicate that demand variables, cost of funds variables, and expectational and adjustment factors as embodied by the lag structure are all significant, with only the availability of funds being a dubious determinant. The caveat above is necessary because of the problems of identifying proper lag structures and of multi-collinearity between the independent variables, because different studies tend to result in different elasticities of investment with respect to its determinants, and because of the generally poor level of prediction as opposed to data fitting that even very sophisticated equations generally give on industry and firm's investment. All these can seriously weaken the inferences drawn.

Another approach to the testing of investment theory is sufficiently different from those previously mentioned to constitute a fourth stage in estimation. This is mainly due to Jorgenson and utilizes the strict neoclassical approach outlined on p. 385, of the form

$$K^* = \alpha \frac{Qp}{c}$$

Ignoring taxation, the price of capital services, c, is the cost of depreciation and the cost of capital funds appropriate to the capital

---

[36] W. H. L. Anderson, *Corporate Finance and Fixed Investment: An Econometric Study* (Harvard, 1964).

[37] R. W. Resek, 'Investment by Manufacturing: A Quarterly Time Series Analysis of Industry Data', *R. Econ. Stats.* 48, no. 3 (Aug. 1966), 322–33.

goods supplying these services. Therefore

$$c = q(\delta + r)$$

where q is the price of capital goods, δ the rate of depreciation, and r the cost of capital as measured by the rate of return. To the extent that there are capital gains from a rising price of capital equipment to offset this cost of capital services, this may be rewritten

$$c = q(\delta + r - \frac{\dot{q}}{q})$$

Thus the function for gross investment is again

$$I_t = \beta(K_t^* - K_{t-1}) + \delta K_{t-1}$$

where

$$K_t^* = \alpha \frac{Q_t P_t}{q_t\left(\delta + r_t - \dfrac{\dot{q}_t}{q_t}\right)}$$

This directly incorporates a measure of the cost of funds which is not simply (and inappropriately) the interest rate; the price and volume of output; and the price of capital goods. The cost of other inputs is indirectly included in that a change in them changes the factor price ratio, hence the optimal point on the production function and so the marginal product of capital. Within the neo-classical assumptions this only occurs if the marginal product of other inputs changes.

Such an approach can be evaluated only by its predictive power rather than the 'realism' of its assumptions. Potentially it has a draw-back in the shape of the neoclassical assumption of a perfect capital market which collapses all difference of internal and external financing and a spectrum of finance costs into a single figure equal to the firm's rate of return on capital, but whether this 'MM' view of the world creates distortion is really an empirical matter. It may not be serious, particularly if the model is applied to large firms with easy access to the capital market.

Jorgenson and Siebert[38] have tested this model with data from 15

[38] D. W. Jorgenson, C. Siebert, 'A Comparison of Alternative Theories of Corporate Investment Behaviour', *A.E.R.* 58 (1968), 681–91.

of the largest 500 firms in the U.S., and Jorgenson and Stephenson[39] with data from 15 sub-industries. The former study found the neoclassical model, with and without capital gains included, to be superior to models based only on a simple accelerator, expected profits, and on liquidity. The latter study confirmed the neoclassical as superior to the accelerator and liquidity models. Against these Schramm found little relative price effect when applying the neoclassical approach to French data irrespective of whether it was the relative price of capital services and output, wages and output, or wages and capital services.[40]

The neoclassical approach has been subjected to some criticism. Elliott, reworking Jorgenson and Siebert's analysis for a much larger sample of 184 firms, found little difference between the neoclassical, accelerator, and liquidity models on time series data, and on cross-sectional that the ranking of the models was Liquidity, Accelerator, Expected Profits, and Neoclassical model last.[41] Coen has argued that by using the Cobb–Douglas production function, Jorgenson *et al.* restrict the elasticity of substitution between capital and labour to unity.[42] This creates three difficulties. First, as the elasticity of demand for capital with respect to its price equals the elasticity of substitution[43] it is not appropriate to restrict the latter to unity when the former is being investigated. If unity is too high a value the model will overstate the sensitivity of desired capital to changes in its implicit price. The empirical testing simply gives the lag distribution of the desired capital stock. Second, retesting by Coen of the neoclassical model using a CES production function gave better results when the elasticity of substitution was constrained to be 0·2 and progressively worse results as its constrained value was set nearer and nearer to unity. Third, he attacked another study, by Jorgenson and Hall, on the grounds that their own results were

[39] D. W. Jorgenson, J. A. Stephenson, 'Investment Behaviour in U.S. Manufacturing 1947–60', *Econometrica*, 35, no. 2 (Apr. 1967), 169–220.

[40] R. Schramm, 'Neo-classical Investment Models and French Private Manufacturing Investment', *A.E.R.* 62 (1972), 553–63.

[41] J. Elliott, 'Theories of Corporate Investment Behaviour Revisited', *A.E.R.* 63, no. 1 (Mar. 1973), 195–207.

[42] R. M. Coen, 'Tax Policy & Investment Behaviour: Comment', *A.E.R.* 59 (1969), 370–9. Combining a Constant Elasticity of Substitution production function with $dQ/dK = c/p$ gives $k^* = \alpha^\sigma (p/c)^\sigma Q$ where σ is the elasticity of substitution. Clearly, if σ is one this becomes the equation used by Jorgenson *et al.*

[43] If $K^* = \alpha^\sigma (p/c)^\sigma Q$

$$\frac{c}{K}\frac{dK^*}{dc} = \sigma\alpha^\sigma \frac{p^\sigma}{c^{\sigma+1}} Q \cdot \frac{c}{\alpha^\sigma(p/c)^\sigma Q} = \sigma$$

inconsistent with a value as high as unity.[44] Jorgenson and Hall have replied not that a value of unity has any theoretical superiority, but that a series of tests using the CES production function have found approximately this value.[45]

The main difficulty however is that the equation for desired capital stock results in the latter being regressed on a composite variable, pQ/c. Thus the three variables, price, quantity, and cost of capital services, are constrained to have the same proportionate effect, and it is not then possible to distinguish the output and relative price effects on desired capital stock. Using Jorgenson's data, Eisner and Nadiri[46] found the unconstrained estimate of the elasticity of capital stock with respect to the price of capital services to be around 0·2 but the elasticity with respect to output to be much higher and in some cases above 0·7. The response to changes in relative price was also much slower than the response to changes in Q, and as the lag structure employed by Jorgenson *et al.* precludes any short-term response, Eisner and Nadiri argue that the measured impact of output changes will be reduced.

In opposition to this Bischoff has suggested that there are econometric drawbacks to the Eisner and Nadiri analysis[47] and in a separate study finds results much more sympathetic to the neoclassical assumptions.[48]

A very thorough study utilizing a generalized neoclassical approach but incorporating other elements as well was carried out by Flemming and Feldstein.[49] Their five main relaxations of the strict neoclassical model were (i) to allow for a non-unitary elasticity of substitution; (ii) to allow for expectations about output based on long-run output growth; (iii) to decompose the cost of using capital services in order to permit the different components to have

[44] R. E. Hall, D. W. Jorgenson, 'Tax Policy & Investment Behaviour', *A.E.R.* 57 (1967), 391–414.

[45] See also D. W. Jorgenson, 'Econometric Studies of Investment Behaviour: A Survey', *J. Econ. Lit.* 9 (1971), 1111–47. This surveys various attempts to measure the elasticity of substitution and also studies which have investigated whether the constant returns to scale assumption employed is valid. See A. B. Treadway, 'On Rational Entrepreneurial Behaviour & the Demand for Investment', *R. Econ. Studs.* 36 (1969), 227–39 for discussion of costs of adjustment with non-constant returns to scale.

[46] R. Eisner, M. I. Nadiri, 'Investment Behaviour & Neo-Classical Theory', *R. Econ. Stats.* 50 (1968), 369–82.

[47] C. W. Bischoff, 'Hypothesis Testing and the Demand for Capital Goods', *R. Econ. Stats.* 51 (1969), 354–68.

[48] C. W. Bischoff, 'The Effect of Alternative Lag Distributions', in G. Fromm (ed.), *Tax Incentives and Capital Spending* (North Holland, 1971).

[49] M. S. Feldstein, J. S. Flemming, 'Tax Policy, Corporate Savings and Investment Behaviour in Britain', *R. Econ. Studs.* 38 (1971), 415–34. This and the 3 previous articles can all be found in J. Helliwell (ed.), *Aggregate Investment* (Harmondsworth, 1976).

different weights; (iv) to allow for long-run changes in the availability
of internal funds (in the event that they are viewed as the cheapest
source of funds); and (v) to introduce a multiplicative error term.
Hence instead of using

$$K_t^* = \alpha \frac{P_t}{c_t} Q_t + u_t \qquad (i)$$

they use

$$K_t^* = \alpha^\sigma \left[\left(\frac{p}{c} \right)' \right]^\sigma Q_t' v_t$$

where $(P/c)'$ is the decomposed relative cost of using capital and
incorporating internal funds, and Q_t' is a function of the trend of
output and its expected long-run growth. Investment is then the
usual weighted function of past desired capital stock, minus actual
capital stock.

This was tested for aggregate investment, so that the results are
not comparable with those previously considered, but it is none the
less worth noting, first, the approach, which is the most widely em-
bracing to date, and second, three conclusions. These are (i) that the
elasticities for components of the cost of capital services differ
greatly; (ii) relative price changes were insignificant, possibly because
they do not closely determine the expected relative prices on which
decisions might be based; (iii) the elasticity of substitution was much
lower than unity. However, they point out that this result and the
accompanying low elasticity of capital with respect to the price of
capital services are observed parameters. There is no necessary reason
to infer that technology is necessarily not of the Cobb–Douglas form.
It may again be that current changes in the observed values are not
closely related to changes in the relevant expected values or even that
there is a behavioural relation different from that implied by technology because of non-optimal behaviour.

Another difficulty that has been raised is the general one of distinguishing demand, cost, and availability effects. Jorgenson himself
argued that in those few studies where availability of funds was significant it might well be that it was a proxy for expected demand
(seen most clearly in the case of rising profits). Similarly Eisner and
Nadiri argue that any relative price effect on investment may well
just be picking up the response to rising equity values as expected
output rises. There is some support for this in that the response to
the interest rate alone, for which this problem may be less severe,
tends to be much slower.

Most studies have utilized data on investment and on current and lagged values of hypothesized determinants, but the latter are of course frequently only proxies for *expected* values. Some studies have tried to improve understanding by working directly with expectational variables. There are three types of approach.

(i) Variables such as unfilled orders and stock market prices can be used on the assumption that they give a more direct indication of business expectations. Evans[50] has shown, however, that the former probably reflects current rather than expected future sales (it tends to be significant only where current sales, because of large sales fluctuations, are not significant). Stock market prices on the other hand have generally been found important, but as noted before it is not always clear whether this is because rising share prices indicate the expectation of higher profits and/or higher output, or because they lower the weighted cost of capital.

(ii) The second approach has been first to relate investment *intentions* data to explanatory variables, and second, relate realized investment to the intentions data and changes occurring since the intentions were recorded.[51] Though generally applied at the macroeconomic level this has also had some success at industry level,[52] and offers some hope of circumventing the worst aspects of the lag structure and multicollinearity in investment functions.

(iii) The third approach has been to focus on expectations more explicitly. Helliwell and Glorieux constructed a model in which investment was related to future expected desired capital stock where the latter was derived from expectations that had extrapolative and regressive elements and incorporated trend growth effects also. The results suggested that the extrapolative element was much stronger, although evidence was ambiguous as to how rapidly each effect decayed over time. This approach was then used to fit and forecast investment, with encouraging results. Flemming and Feldstein on the other hand found that deviations from long-term trend are not extrapolated but regarded more as cyclical deviations from it. More recently Birch and Siebert[53] have found evidence to

[50] M. K. Evans, *Macroeconomic Activity* (New York, 1969).

[51] See for example F. Modigliani, H. Weingartner, 'Forecasting Uses of Anticipatory Data on Investment & Sales', *Q.J.E.* 72, no. 1 (Feb. 1958), 23–54. R. Eisner, 'Expectations Plans and Capital Expenditure: A Synthesis of Ex Post and Ex Ante Data', in M. J. Bowman, *Expectations, Uncertainty & Business Behaviour*, Social Science Research Council (New York, 1960).

[52] M. Foss, V. Natrella, 'The Structure & Realisation of Business Investment Anticipations' in N.B.E.R., 'The Quality and Economic Significance of anticipating Data' (New York, 1960).

[53] E. M. Birch and C. D. Siebert, 'Uncertainty, Permanent Demand and Investment Behaviour', *A.E.R.* 66, no. 1 (Mar. 1976), 15–27.

support Eisner[54] that sales expectations data have some role in explaining investment over and above that provided by current and lagged values. Although at an early stage, investigation of the link between past values and the expected values that determine decisions is clearly a vital element in understanding the process of investment.

To conclude this section, despite a large amount of research the results are not entirely satisfactory in certain ways. Estimates of the impact of different determinants vary considerably, prediction is much weaker than data fitting, expectations are difficult to incorporate, the lags involved complicate estimation, and econometric problems abound. None the less, there is now reasonable evidence at the level of the firm and the industry that expected capacity utilization and the cost and availability of different sources of funds all have an identifiable effect on investment. Models emphasizing only one aspect have generally been superseded and attention centres more on the relative importance over time of the different determinants, the correct identification and measurement of them, and the most suitable incorporation of decision lags and expectational aspects.

4   GOVERNMENT POLICY IMPACT

So far we have been concerned with the impact of the business environment on investment decisions and its consistency with the standard investment model. Another way of examining the applicability of the model is to observe the impact of government policy designed to influence investment decisions. Investment allowances and grants and changes in corporation tax rates, etc. can all change the cost and availability of funds and the expected net profits from investment, so all should be important determinants if the model is substantially correct. The evidence not surprisingly tends to mirror the more general testing reviewed in section 3, with case studies and early econometric evidence largely finding rather weak effects, but more recent econometric studies finding stronger and sometimes very strong impact.

In the first category the Radcliffe inquiry[55] found that incentives caused favourable changes for 23 per cent of the companies asked and unfavourable ones for 14 per cent. In Hart and Prussman's[56]

---

[54] R. Eisner, 'A Permanent Income Theory for Investment', *A.E.R.* 57 (June 1967), 363–90.

[55] Radcliffe Report, op. cit. (1959).

[56] H. Hart, D. Prussman, 'An Account of Management Accounting and Techniques in the S.E. Hants Coastal Region', *Accountants' Journal* (Jan. 1964).

study the figure was up to 36 per cent, but in that of Corner and Williams[57] tended to be about the 20 per cent level. McKintosh's[58] detailed case-studies revealed a similarly small role for government investment incentives. Like those of Corner and Williams his results indicated that it was firms who were under strict finance constraints who responded most, but in contrast to the other studies suggested that small firms responded more than large firms, because of their more limited access to funds.

Several reasons have been put forward to explain limited effects of policy.

(i) The incentive system at least in the U.K. has been changed too frequently for decision-takers to rely on it when making decisions now about investment which will only occur some time into the future. On average the system has been changed about once every four years and has included initial allowances (higher depreciation in first year offset by lower depreciation later), investment allowances (higher depreciation in first year, not offset later), investment grants, and 'free' (100 per cent) depreciation. All these as well as the system of corporate taxation may be expected to have both expected return incentive effects and cost/availability of funds effects.

(ii) The use of pre-tax criteria by some firms, and

(iii) The use of crude rules of thumb rather than D.C.F. procedures. Barna, for example, in detailed case-study work, found approximately two-thirds of companies not using quantitative post-tax criteria,[59] while Cannon discovered that even when figures were formally required to be presented before investment proposals could be approved they none the less quite often were not provided.[60]

(iv) The interdependence of projects in a long-term investment programme, such that the latter predetermines the former and restricts any incentive influence on decisions about individual projects.

(v) The risk and uncertainty surrounding projects. Typically a 5 per cent sales forecast error will change a D.C.F. internal rate of return by a far greater amount than an investment incentive such as has generally been used in the past.

(vi) Pursuit of objectives other than profit, in particular growth.

(vii) Finally, Harcourt demonstrated that allowing for factor intensity the impact of various types of investment incentive systems

[57] Corner and Williams, op. cit.

[58] A. McKintosh, *The Development of Firms* (Cambridge, 1963).

[59] T. Barna, *Investment & Growth Policies in British Industrial Firms*, N.I.E.S.R. (Cambridge, 1962).

[60] C. Cannon, 'The Limited Application of Minimum Profitability Requirements to Capital Expenditure Proposals', *J.I.E.* 15, no. 1 (Nov. 1966), 54–64.

coupled with alternative investment decision rules could be in some cases perverse.[61]

None the less it is difficult to believe that such factors as the seven listed above are an adequate explanation. Increasingly firms, particularly large ones, do use post-tax D.C.F. criteria at least in conjunction with other criteria. In addition incentives will normally have an effect even if pay-back or rate of return criteria are used. If individual projects are necessary parts of an integrated programme it is not clear why the programme as a whole should not be influenced by the incidence of taxation and incentives. Investment for growth subject to a profit constraint should in theory respond to incentives that modify profit and hence the constraint. Even the popular view that inherent uncertainty swamps marginal incentive effects is of doubtful validity by itself. If a risk premium is added to a minimum acceptable internal rate of return figure, then a bigger incentive will still normally move projects previously unacceptable into the acceptable range. If a mean-variance approach is applied, the higher mean values resulting from the incentive should increase investment also.

It is not perhaps therefore surprising that most recent econometric studies have found taxation and incentives to have had some effect. Agarwala and Goodson fround that changes in initial and investment allowances, taxation, and investment grants all had effects on investment via both liquidity and profitability, but that the former was much more important.[62] For example the first-year response of investment to a change of five percentage points in initial allowances might be only 1 per cent, but in year two with liquidity effects also operating it was nearer 5 per cent. Their estimation procedure is, however, rather crude, essentially regressing investment on the rate of return and cash flow. In view of the many interrelations between variables previously discussed, an examination of the impact of incentives within the context of a fully derived model of the inestment process is to be preferred.

Hall and Jorgenson, using the strict neoclassical model, found tax effects to be very strong in the U.S.[63] For example they calculated that the accelerated depreciation of 1953 and the 1963 tax credit on investment were each responsible for around 10 per cent of the gross investment then occurring, in the latter case this representing between 40 per cent and 50 per cent of net investment. However,

[61] G. Harcourt, 'Investment Decision Criteria, Investment Incentives & the Choice of Technique', *E.J.* 78, no. 309 (Mar. 1968), 77–95.

[62] R. Agarwala, G. C. Goodson, 'An Analysis of the Effects of Investment Incentives on Investment Behaviour in the British Economy', *Economica*, 36 (1969), 377–88.

[63] R. E. Hall, D. W. Jorgenson, 'Tax Policy & Invesmtent Behaviour', *A.E.R.* 57 (June 1967), 391–414.

the tax effects all work by changing the value of the cost of capital services and Hall and Jorgenson's estimates of the impact rely on the assumption that the elasticity of demand for capital with respect to the cost of capital services is the same as for the elasticity with respect to the composite variables pQ/c. As we have seen, this is suspect, with some evidence to suggest that the impact of c is much below that of Q. On the basis of the unconstrained estimates of the elasticity by Eisner and Nadiri, the impact needs to be divided by about six.[64] Further tests by Eisner support the view that the impact is small.[65] Coen, using both a flexible accelerator formulation and a modified one to include cash flow as a determinant of the speed of adjustment, found that only between 30 per cent and 40 per cent of the tax saved as a result of tax changes in the U.S. in the early 1960s came through as increased investment,[66] and an investigation carried out by Eisner and Lawler[67] of replies to survey questionnaires about the impact of various tax measures also generally indicated a smaller response, though the validity of the replies is dubious. This in turn, however, was contradicted by Bischoff, who, using a general neo-classical formulation, found that, at least for the investment tax credit, more investment resulted than the tax saved.[68] The still more general approach of Feldstein and Flemming already discussed also found a significant impact of investment allowances and tax changes, this time in the U.K., though in this study the effect can also operate by inducing higher retentions. In fact, their results suggested that about two-thirds of the increase in retentions as a result of a greater incentive to retain earnings was offset by a reduction in the use of external finance. The elasticity of demand for capital with respect to a direct measure of internal funds was however low and insignificant, suggesting that it is only long-run changes in the retention ratio as a result of tax changes that have an impact. It should be added, however, that King,[69] using a vintage model of investment behaviour, found only about half the impact of tax allowances found by Feldstein and Flemming. An important difference between the studies which King points out is that he uses the tax rate on retained

[64] See R. Eisner, 'Tax Policy & Investment Behaviour: Comment', *A.E.R.* 59, no. 3 (1969), 379–88.

[65] Ibid.

[66] R. M. Coen, 'Effects of Tax Policy on Investment in Manufacturing', *A.E.R.* 58 (1968), 200–11.

[67] R. Eisner, P. J. Lawler, 'Tax Policy and Investment: An Analysis of Survey Responses', *A.E.R.* 65, no. 1 (1975), 206–12.

[68] C. W. Bischoff, 'The Effect of Alternative Lag Distributions', in G. Fromm (ed.), *Tax Incentives and Capital Spending* (North Holland, 1971).

[69] M. A. King, 'Taxation & Investment Incentives in a Vintage Investment Model', *Journal of Public Economics*, 1 (1972), 121–47.

profit only rather than on dividends as well. This, as noted before (p. 344), is because the optimal investment policy should be independent of the pay-out decision.

Over all it seems clear that tax policy does have an effect, but that the magnitude of impact in the past and even more the forecast effect of tax and incentive changes is extremely uncertain. In many ways this is a reflection of the complexity and consequent ambiguity involved in isolating and measuring the many determinants of investment. But it also suggests that it is worth examining in more detail the nature of the investment decision process itself, in an attempt to understand why such a central, carefully considered, and well-documented process should be so difficult to forecast. It is to this that we finally turn.

5   THE INVESTMENT DECISION PROCESS

So far the picture underlying the analysis of investment has been fully consistent with that shown in Figure 11.1. Demand conditions, Supply conditions, Government Policy, and elements of forecasting have all been included in the determination of investment decisions. However, two internal characteristics of the firm's decision process have been largely ignored. First, the role of risk and uncertainty has been almost entirely ignored except in so far as it creates the need for slow adjustment to only the longer-term trends discerned in short-term variations in variables. Second, company objectives and the investment criteria derived from them have been mentioned only in passing, except to presume behaviour consistent with profit maximization. This reflects very largely the literature on investment, but is a cause for concern given the arguments of Chapters 8 and 9 which suggested alternative specifications of objectives for firms actively engaged in determining their own business constraints. It is at least possible that part of the difficulty in explaining investment at the level of the individual firm and even at industry level can be attributed to these issues. Here we consider three sources of 'noise' in the analysis of investment.

(I) Traditionally, risky situations, defined as those in which only the parameters of a probability distribution of possible outcomes are known, have been dealt with by assuming that decision-takers maximize Expected Value. But a large number of examples, especially insurance, gambling, and the St. Petersburg Paradox,[70] led to the rejection of this in favour of the assumption that decision-takers

---

[70] The Expected value of a gamble in which one receives 2^i pence where i is the number of times a coin is tossed until it comes down heads is

maximize Expected Utility, i.e.

Maximize
$$EU = \sum_{i=1}^{i=n} \mu_i U_i$$

where μ_i is the probability of U_i being achieved,
U_i is the utility derived from the outcome i valued in money terms at V_i. Therefore $U_i = fV_i$.

This modification generated no conceptual difficulties provided that utility was measured cardinally, but became largely inapplicable once utility was regarded as an ordinal measure.[71] While all the main decision–theoretic conclusions that were derivable from the cardinal approach were subsequently derived from the ordinal, and eventually by reference only to choice behaviour,[72] none the less virtually no developments took place with regard to the analysis of risky choice until the 1940s because of the lack of a measure of utility that could be used in the calculation of Expected Utility.

The ordinal and revealed preference approaches to decision-taking had the advantage of being based on very unrestrictive axioms, but with the publication of Von Neumann and Morgenstern's classic work on decision-taking[73] it became clear that the switch from cardinal to ordinal utility was by no means as necessary as had been supposed. They constructed a utility index essentially by first arbitrarily assigning utility values to two outcomes; second, finding different probability-times-outcomes between which decision-takers were indifferent where one of the outcomes had an assigned utility value; and then deriving the utility measure of the other outcome

$$\sum_{i=1}^{i=\infty} (\tfrac{1}{2})^i 2^i$$

which equals infinity, but no one would pay any finite sum to play. See D. Bernouilli (translated by L. Sommer), 'Specimen Theoriae Novae de Mensura Sortis', *Econometrica*, 22, no. 1 (Jan. 1954), 23–36.

[71] Note, however, that as early as 1933 Lange had demonstrated that being able to judge whether the difference in utility between two outcomes was greater, the same, or less than the difference in utility between two other outcomes was sufficient to be able to measure utility cardinally. See O. Lange, 'The Determinateness of the Utility Function', *R. Econ. Studs.* 1 (1933), 218–25.

[72] See P. Samuelson, 'A Note on the Pure Theory of Consumer Behaviour', *Economica*, N.S. 5 (1948), 344–56.

[73] J. Von Neumann, O. Morgenstern, *The Theory of Games and Economic Behaviour* (Princeton, 1944).

by equating the two Expected Utilities.[74]

A number of attempts have been made experimentally to measure utility functions[75] and Grayson constructed utility functions for oil industry decision-takers, afterwards using them for selecting 'correct' decisions based on maximizing Expected Utility in subsequent decisions.[76] These, however, like the Von Neumann and Morgenstern approach, are based on objective probabilities, i.e. the frequency distribution to which outcomes approach as a number of repetitions of an 'experiment' tends to infinity. This is now generally rejected, first because decisions are determined by subjective probabilities, which measure the degree of belief in the likelihood of an outcome and may or may not conform to objective probabilities. Second, because the frequency distribution concept is inapplicable in unique choice situations. Models based on maximizing Expected Utility where subjective probabilities are employed are known as Subjectively Expected Utility (SEU) models.

Not until 1957 was it realized that subjective probabilities and utility could be measured simultaneously, utilizing a method first proposed by Ramsey in 1926.[77] From subsequent testing it appears that much decision activity can be understood as an attempt to maximize SEU and also that the typical utility function is, as previously theorized, non-linear. In fact that results can be shown to be generally consistent with a modified version[78] of the double inflected utility function proposed by Markowitz[79] (and derived from an early formulation by Friedman and Savage[80]) which is necessary if the utility function is to be bounded and able to explain insurance and gambling. This is shown in Figure 11.3. The regions where the second derivative is positive explain why the Expected Utility of a gamble can be positive despite negative Expected Value (subjective

[74] If a decision-taker is indifferent between outcome V_1 with probability μ_1 and outcome V_2 with probability μ_2 then writing $V_1\mu_1 = V_2\mu_2$ and letting V_2 (e.g. 5p) equal 1 utile, then $V_1 = V_2\mu_2/\mu$, and hence as a value assigned to it. In practice Von Neumann and Morgenstern used composite gambles but this example conveys the basic idea. Note that although their utility measure was like cardinal utility in that it was unique up to a linear transformation, it was not like it in viewing utility as a psychic quantity or as corresponding to some introspectively observable phenomenon. Rather it could just be used in conditions of risk to predict decisions assuming consistency on the part of the decision-taker.

[75] See for example F. Nosteller, P. Nogee, 'An Experimental Measure of Utility', *J.P.E.* 13 (Oct. 1951), 371–404.

[76] C. Grayson, *Decisions Under Uncertainty* (Harvard, 1960).

[77] See D. Davidson, P. Suppes, S. Siegel, *Decision-Taking: An Experimental Approach* (Stanford, 1957). Also F. Ramsey, 'Truth & Probability', in F. Ramsey, *The Foundations of Mathematics and Other Logical Essays*, ed. R. B. Braithwaite (London, 1931), 156–98.

[78] See D. J. Morris, 'The Structure of Investment Decisions', D.Phil. Thesis (Oxford, 1974).

[79] M. Markowitz, 'The Utility of Wealth', *J.P.E.* 60, no. 2 (Apr. 1952), 151–8.

[80] M. Friedman, L. Savage, 'The Utility Analysis of Choice Involving Risk', *J.P.E.* 56, no. 4 (Aug. 1948), 279–304.

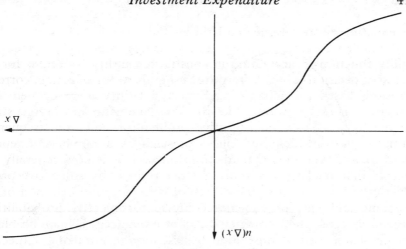

Fig. 11.3

or objective) and why the Expected Disutility of a large loss can be greater than the disutility of an insurance premium despite having a lower Expected Value.

The significance of these developments is that if

(i) an investment decision-taker's utility function is double-inflected, as both theory and evidence tend to suggest, and

(ii) the subjective probability distribution is of a standard form, for example the normal distribution,

then the resulting function relating SEU to outcomes may well be double-peaked, as shown in Figure 11.4.[81] Which peak is the global maximum and hence which investment decision is taken is a function of the relative positions of the utility and probability functions, and relatively small shifts in the latter as a result of changing expectations can cause the decision-taker to make a large and discrete switch in intended investment.[82] This type of instability has been verified empirically in investment decisions by Cannon.[83]

[81] See D. J. Morris, op. cit. This type of function also permits a reconciliation of satisficing and maximizing.

[82] Note that there has also been considerable elaboration of a 'Potential Surprise Function' first proposed by Shackle as a non-probabilistic way of analysing investment decisions uncer uncertainty, i.e. where not even the parameters of a probability distribution are known. This can also explain instability and insensitivity of investment decisions, but has found little application so far. Shackle rejected the view that the analysis could be represented in terms of the probabilistic approach. See G. Shackle, *Expectation in Economics* (Cambridge, 1952), and G. Shackle, *Uncertainty in Economics & Other Reflections* (Cambridge, 1955).

[83] C. Cannon, 'Private Capital Investment: A Case Study Approach Towards Testing Alternative Theories', *J.I.E.* 16, no. 3 (July 1968), 186–95.

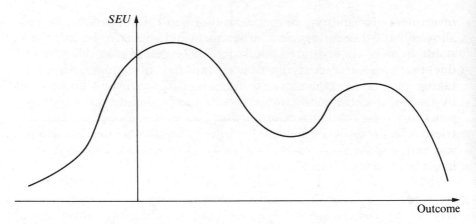

Fig. 11.4

Such potential instability in situations of unique choice can seriously interfere with the determination of the optimal capital stock, the smooth process of adjustment to it, and the sensitivity of decisions to fiscal changes. These will in turn make it more difficult to isolate investment determinants at the microeconomic level and predict on the basis of them. (Industry level functions may avoid these problems if such effects are swamped by the aggregation of a substantial number of independent firms, but not necessarily.)

(II) Whether market structure affects the instability of investment has been much theorized about. Scitovsky thought a more perfectly competitive market would experience more instability because firms would ignore the effect of their cumulative investment on prices.[84] Richardson supported the view that oligopoly would see more stability on the grounds that quasi co-operation or collusion would operate to ensure over-all equating of demand and supply capacity.[85] Against this Duesenberry thought oligopolistic competition via investment would be destabilizing,[86] and Bain argued that concentration and resulting high profits coupled with low barriers to entry would cause many entries and exits and hence destabilize investment.[87] This, however, seems difficult to maintain for more than a few industries in the light of the results of Chapter 7.

Finally, Scherer,[88] noting these alternative views, regressed

[84] T. Scitovsky, *Welfare and Competition* (London, 1951).
[85] G. B. Richardson, *Information and Investment* (Oxford, 1960).
[86] J. S. Duesenberry, *Business Cycles and Economic Growth* (New York, 1958).
[87] J. S. Bain, *Barriers to New Competition* (Harvard, 1956).
[88] F. Scherer, 'Market Structure and the Stability of Investment', *A.E.R.* 59 (May 1969), 72–9.

investment variability on concentration and found that, having allowed for other influences,[89] investment did appear to be more unstable in more concentrated industries. He suggested that this may be due to the greater centralization of industry investment decision-taking in a more concentrated industry and confirmed his results by finding that the prediction errors of the Jorgenson and Stephenson study (discussed in section 3) were greater in concentrated industries. A later study by Scherer indicated that the greater instability was not due to the greater 'lumpiness' of investment as a result of larger economies of scale in concentrated industries.[90]

(III) Turning to the question of firms' objectives, here too there are reasons to think that characteristics of the decision process may reduce the correlation between external variables and investment decisions. Although the latter are highly centralized within a firm and taken in the light of generally well-established criteria derived from the objective of profitability, the process of identifying investment opportunities and obtaining and processing the necessary information is highly diffused through a firm and itself has a bearing on the determination of investment. First, the criteria for identifying investment opportunities are frequently derived, either explicitly or implicitly, from the over-all profit and/or growth objectives of the fim, for example excessive capacity utilization, rising production costs and/or interruptions to production, maintenance of product cycles, etc., rather than profit and growth criteria themselves. This occurs partly because of the decentralization of functions within a firm and partly because the more general criteria of profit and growth often cannot be applied when first identifying possible investment opportunities at a rudimentary stage. Thus the selection of projects for investigation is largely, if not totally, independent of, for example, investment incentives which operate via their effect on quantitative profitability calculations.

If the subsequent evaluation of the project were purely a matter of specifying objective estimates with which to calculate post-tax profit, then incentives would still have an impact at this second stage. But typically estimates are partly forecasts and partly targets, often in practice representing attempts to identify a set of project figures which are both *feasible* and *profitable*. If such a set cannot be found then the project will normally be dropped. But feasibility depends on views concerning what future actions can be taken by one or more departments in a company to achieve the condition necessary

[89] Variability of demand, capital–output ratio, industry, size, and industry-type.
[90] F. Scherer, 'Investment Variability, Seller Concentration, and Plant Scale Economies', *J.I.E.* 22 (1973), 157–60.

for adequate profitability to result. Thus a project less likely to meet minimum acceptable profit levels, but none the less thought desirable for the company when judged by the initial criteria in terms of which the project was first identified, may well be formulated in quantitative terms no less attractive than other projects. This can be justified by the belief that many aspects of a project are partly endogenous and therefore a function of the 'effort' assigned by one or more departments involved in collecting data for forecasting. This potential bias of information can be greatly magnified, first if the project meets more personal criteria such as the desire for divisional expansion, smooth production, higher performance products, increased security, etc., and second because many involved in the estimation procedure will become associated with the project and its success or failure. The very large element of uncertainty that surrounds most individual projects and estimates facilitates this form of information distortion. This will frequently be subconscious, but in more extreme form can result in the provision of data that will maximize the probability of a project being accepted on profitability grounds by the board where the desirability of the project is based on the more decentralized criteria initially derived from the profitability objective. Investment incentives may be included in the former but generally do not make any difference to the latter and potentially more dominant decision criteria.

Several predictions arise from this picture, all of which have been observed in practice.[91] First, projects submitted for approval generally more than just meet the formal investment criteria specified. Second, realized profitability will on average be below estimated profitability despite risk-aversion being likely to generate the reverse. Third, small changes in the environment which move a project from the desirable to undesirable category in terms of decentralized criteria are likely to cause much bigger variations in the data from which profits are estimated, in order to bring about a halt to the evaluation or approval process. Fourth, where companies use multiple investment criteria, estimates of a project would normally demonstrate its acceptability on all of them, thus greatly diminishing the significance of more sophisticated criteria. Finally, investment incentives would generally be regarded as having only a limited effect on whether a project was approved or not.

Two main consequences follow. The first is that a number of

---

[91] See for example R. Cyert, W. Dill, J. March, 'The Role of Expectations in Business Decision-Taking', *Administrative Science Quarterly* (Dec. 1958), 307–40; D. J. Morris, op. cit.; C. Cannon, op. cit. and 'The Limited Application of Minimum Profitability Requirements to Capital Expenditure Proposals', *J.I.E.* 15, no. 1 (Nov. 1966), 54–64.

decentralized non-profit criteria which are derived from a profit objective but are none the less different from it, and which generally are more readily satisfied by growth, become important determinants of investment decisions via their impact on information processing. In terms of Figure 11.1 we require a new link running from objectives to the provision of supply and demand information. Second, and as a result of this link, the direct impact of external variables is modified and that of tax and incentive changes reduced. Only where such changes alter the flow of funds to a firm facing a finance supply constraint will the above effects be by-passed and effects of tax changes be readily identifiable. This is consistent with the findings of McKintosh,[92] Agarwala and Goodson,[93] and Feldstein and Flemming.[94]

6   CONCLUSION

In conclusion the last section offered some possible contributory explanations as to why investment has been so difficult to predict and influence, and why therefore there is still headway to be made towards agreement on the determinants of investment. None the less, there is increasingly a pattern running through the econometric results despite still wide differences of theoretical approach. The last section also suggests that, in as far as investment decisions are a major vehicle by which companies allocate or re-allocate resources internally between different products, they are likely to be a less rapid and less effective alternative to the process of direct competition than sometimes presumed. Investment is none the less the major way by which firms determine their size, growth, markets, products, and costs. The investment decision process described is also in principle the way in which funds are allocated across physical investment, research and development investment, and marketing investment. In practice the latter two may become so uncertain and incapable of objective assessment that very crude rules of thumb, for example regularly allocating a given percentage of sales revenue to each, are necessary to make any allocation at all. They are none the less long-run alternative uses of funds and it is to the more specific characteristics of marketing and research and development investment that we turn to next.

---

[92] A. McKintosh, op. cit.   [93] R. Agarwala, G. C. Goodson, op. cit.
[94] M. S. Feldstein, J. S. Flemming, op. cit.

MARKET INVESTMENT

A second way in which firms can use their available funds to further their profit and growth objectives is expenditure on marketing their products. Marketing can be broadly defined to include all aspects of selling the product once it leaves the plant where it is made. The product may be differentiated by distinctive packaging, distinctive sales outlets, or distinctive 'after-sales' service. Changes in these specifications are indeed important, but we prefer to see them as product innovation (where 'product' includes all these aspects), which will be discussed in the next chapter. The objective of the firms is to adjust the nature of their products to obtain the best market 'area' in product characteristics space (see Chapter 3). The other side of marketing, which will occupy us in this chapter, is concerned mainly with advertising. The proportion of total marketing expenditures spent on advertising is variable between products. Backman[1] quotes the examples of marketing expenditures on breakfast cereals and biscuits in the U.S. in 1964, which were respectively 27 per cent and 24·3 per cent of sales. Advertising contributed 14·9 and 2·2 percentage points to these totals, suggesting that the marketing *mix* was very different. There are also great variations within a single product market. Avon is an extreme example of a cosmetics firm that uses no advertising, but relies solely on local 'agents' for home sales. Other cosmetics firms depend more on advertising to promote their products. The purpose of advertising, given the specification of the product in all objective respects and given prices, is to increase the number of consumers who will prefer that product to its competitors. This may happen in two rather different ways, though it may in practice be difficult to distinguish these. One way is purely informative. The consumers have their indifference maps in goods characteristics space. But they will not be able to exercise their choices wisely unless they are aware of the existence and location of all competing products in that space. The alternative is the use of advertising to influence the shape of the consumers' indifference map in characteristics space, so as to increase the strength of their preference for the firm's products, and to increase the psychic cost to them of moving to an alternative product. The distinction between these

[1] J. Backman, *Advertising and Competition* (New York, 1967), 17–21.

two aspects of advertising is thought to be important in assessing the desirability or otherwise of advertising.[2] Information is essential to the functioning of markets, but persuasive advertising could be thought to be less desirable in welfare terms. Discussion of this issue must wait to Chapter 17. In practice, the distinction is hard to make. How, for example, could one decide whether repetitive advertising of the same product was primarily to *remind* forgetful consumers of the existence of the product, or to persuade them by repetition that that was the product they really wanted? But in what follows we will find the theoretical distinction valid.

We use the term market 'investment' because recent theoretical and empirical work has shown that advertising expenditures contribute to a stock of 'goodwill', which has a life persisting beyond the current period. The suggestion is that current market conditions are affected by the stock of goodwill to which current advertising expenditure makes a contribution which 'decays' gradually over time. So an investment framework seems appropriate, especially since we are considering advertising as an alternative use of funds to investment in physical capital or research and development.

1   A MODEL OF ADVERTISING EXPENDITURES

The optimal advertising decision for the firm was explored in a seminal article by Dorfman and Steiner.[3] In this section we present their model in the form provided by Schmalensee,[4] together with various extensions due to Schmalensee and Arrow and Nerlove.[5]

We assume that the firm can purchase advertising messages at a unit cost of T per message. These messages, A, enter the demand function for the output of the firm in the general form

$$Q = Q(A,P) \qquad \frac{\delta Q}{\delta A} > 0 \qquad \frac{\delta Q}{\delta P} < 0$$

where Q is quantity demanded and P is the price.

Costs, apart from advertising, are a function of output $C[Q]$. Then the profit function of the firm, Π, can be written,

[2] L. G. Telser, 'Advertising and Competition', *J.P.E.* 72 (1964), 537–62.

[3] R. Dorfman, P. O. Steiner, 'Optimal Advertising and Optimal Quality', *A.E.R.* 44 (1954), 826–36.

[4] R. Schmalensee, *The Economics of Advertising* (Amsterdam, 1972).

[5] M. Nerlove, K. J. Arrow, 'Optimal Advertising Policy under Dynamic Conditions', *Economica*, N.S. 29 (1962), 129–42.

$$\Pi = PQ(A,P) - C[Q(A,P)] - AT$$

Differentiating with respect to A, and setting this equal to zero to obtain the profit maximizing condition for advertising messages purchased, we have,

$$\frac{\delta \Pi}{\delta A} = \left(P - \frac{\delta C}{\delta Q}\right)\frac{\delta Q}{\delta A} - T = 0$$

$$\therefore \frac{AT}{PQ} = \left(\frac{P - (\delta C/\delta Q)}{P}\right)\frac{A}{Q}\cdot\frac{\delta Q}{\delta A}$$

(handwritten margin notes:)
$AT = \left(P - \frac{\partial c}{\partial q}\right)\frac{\partial q}{\partial A}$
$\frac{AT}{Pq} \quad \frac{A}{Pq}\left(P - \frac{\partial c}{\partial q}\right)\frac{\partial q}{\partial A}$

This can be interpreted as requiring the ratio of advertising expenditures to total sales to be determined by the price–cost margin (expressed as a proportion of the price) and the response elasticity,

$$a = \frac{A}{Q}\cdot\frac{\delta Q}{\delta A} \text{ of sales to advertising.}$$

If the firm fixes *price* so as to maximize its profits, then the price–cost margin is equal to $1/E$, where E is the price elasticity of demand. Substituting in the above condition we obtain:

$$\frac{AT}{PQ} = \frac{a}{E}$$

i.e. the advertising–sales ratio is given by the ratio of the advertising elasticity, and the price elasticity of demand.

Dorfman and Steiner present this result in a slightly different form. Rearranging the above condition we obtain:

$$E = \frac{P}{T}\cdot\frac{dQ}{dA}$$

The right-hand side of this equation is the marginal value product of an extra unit of expenditure on advertising.

There are two major defects of this simple model, which have prompted extensions. The first defect is that current advertising enters directly into the demand function rather than indirectly via the accumulation of a stock of goodwill acting on demand. The second is that the reactions of other firms are not accounted for. To keep the exposition simple we examine these two extensions separately.

The idea that advertising contributes to a stock of goodwill was suggested by Arrow and Nerlove.[6] This requires an amendment to the optimal condition described above. The effect of extra advertising expenditure has to be considered over time, so the firm's discount rate, α, must enter the calculation. Further, that effect decays over time at a rate, δ. So the *long-run* elasticity of output with respect to advertising is given by

$$a^* = a \int_0^\infty e^{-(\alpha+\delta)t} dt = \frac{a}{\alpha + \delta}$$

In its simple form, the Arrow–Nerlove condition can be obtained by substituting a^* for a in the Dorfman–Steiner condition to give:

$$\frac{AT}{PQ} = \frac{a^*}{E(\alpha + \delta)}$$

However, Cable[7] has pointed to the lack of symmetry in this formulation. Logically one should also consider the long-run elasticity of demand with respect to a price cut, and replace E (the short-run elasticity), with E^* in the formulation.

The reactions of other firms may take the form of either price variation or advertising reactions. The former can be incorporated in two ways. Classical oligopoly theory introduces the concept of conjectural variation into the firm's calculation of its price elasticity of demand. That is, the firm takes into account the likely changes in other firms' prices in response to its own price initiatives. This can be formalized as follows, where Po is the price charged by other firms

$$\hat{E} = \frac{P}{Q} \left(\frac{\delta Q}{\delta P} + \frac{\delta Q}{\delta Po} \cdot \frac{\delta Po}{\delta P} \right)$$

[6] Arrow and Nerlove, op. cit.
[7] J. Cable, in K. Cowling (ed.), *Market Structure and Corporate Behaviour* (London, 1973), 105–24.

The second term within the brackets expresses the 'conjectural variation'. This extended elasticity is the appropriate one for the firm's advertising decision. We note that it is 'subjective' in that it expresses what the firm *thinks* other firms will do.

However, we would argue that the elasticities approach to pricing in oligopoly has not been particularly fruitful (see Chapter 5). It is better therefore to use the price–cost margin as the analytic variable since it is known to be determined by more than just elasticity and cross-elasticity of demand.

Advertising reactions are more amenable to the cross-elasticities approach.[8] We redefine the demand curve for the firm to include other firms' advertising, $\bar{A}$, as a variable.

$$\Pi = P \cdot Q(A, \bar{A}, P) - C[Q(A, \bar{A}, P)] - AT$$

$$\frac{\delta \Pi}{\delta A} = \left(P - \frac{\delta C}{\delta Q}\right)\left[\frac{\delta Q}{\delta A} + \frac{\delta Q}{\delta \bar{A}} \cdot \frac{\delta \bar{A}}{\delta A}\right] - T = 0 \text{ for a maximum}$$

$$\therefore \frac{AT}{PQ} = \left(\frac{P - (\delta C/\delta Q)}{P}\right)\left(\frac{\delta Q}{\delta A} \cdot \frac{A}{Q} + \frac{\delta Q}{\delta \bar{A}} \cdot \frac{\bar{A}}{Q} \cdot \frac{\delta \bar{A}}{\delta A} \cdot \frac{A}{\bar{A}}\right)$$

$$= \left(\frac{P - (\delta C/\delta Q)}{P}\right)[a + \bar{a}\eta]$$

where $\bar{a} = \dfrac{\delta Q}{\delta \bar{A}} \cdot \dfrac{\bar{A}}{Q}$ elasticity of demand with respect to other firms' advertising.

$\eta = \dfrac{\delta \bar{A}}{\delta A} \cdot \dfrac{A}{\bar{A}}$ elasticity of response of other firms' advertising with respect to own advertising.

This formulation is perhaps the most useful for studying the market determinants of advertising. The elasticities can be interpreted as long-run in the Arrow–Nerlove sense as required. It would be possible to formalize yet further to incorporate a time lag in the reaction of other firms to the firm's advertising campaign (compare the incorporation of a time lag in the reaction to a price cut discussed in Chapter 5). But we will not pursue that here.

We conclude from this model that the ratio of advertising expenditure to sales is determined by the price–cost margin, the elasticity of

[8] Schmalensee, op. cit.

demand with respect to own advertising and other firms' advertising, the advertising response of other firms to own advertising (the advertising 'conjectural variation'), the rate of decay of 'goodwill' stock, and the firm's discount rate. In what follows we present an amalgam of further theorizing and empirical tests of this theory. The further theorizing suggests how the explanatory variables listed here may be related to the nature of the product or market conditions.

2   ADVERTISING AND THE NATURE OF THE PRODUCT

In this section we concentrate on the determinants of the elasticity of response of demand to the firm's own advertising, a. Similar considerations will affect $\bar{a}$, response to other firms' advertising. To do this we need to distinguish between different effects of advertising. Information advertising, according to Telser,[9] can serve a number of functions. The first is identification of the existence of a seller. A second, applicable to differentiated products, is some indication of the characteristics mix embodied in a product. The third is the identification of the quality of a product by means of a brand name. Without this information the consumer is not able to make choices. Persuasive advertising goes beyond this in an attempt to change consumers' preferences. The question of informational advertising has been treated by Ozga[10] and Stigler.[11] The situation facing the firm is as follows. Consumers will not know about firms' products unless they are told. The primary source of information must be issued by the firm itself, though this information may well be passed on between potential customers. There is a relationship between the amount of advertising that a firm does in a given period, and the proportion of the potential market who will receive the information (Stigler suggests that the relationship is characterized by diminishing returns). At the same time, a number of potential customers who received the information in previous periods will forget what they were told. Finally, the identity of the potential customers will itself be changing. In each period new customers will enter the market. Others will leave, being no longer interested in purchasing the product.

Let the potential market size be N. Let a proportion C of these be reached when advertising is at a level A, where $C = f(A)$. Assume that a proportion b are 'new' customers, either entering the market for the first time, or customers who were in the market before but

[9] Telser, op. cit.
[10] S. A. Ozga, 'Imperfect Markets through Lack of Knowledge', *Q.J.E.* 74 (1960), 29–52.
[11] G. J. Stigler, 'The Economics of Information', *J.P.E.* 69 (1961), 213–25.

have forgotten all they may have heard and so are in a practical sense 'new'. Starting from scratch, in the first period CN customers will be informed by advertising. In the second period there will be three categories of informed persons:

$C(1-b)N$ First-period customers still informed.

CbN 'New' customers informed.

$CN(1-C)(1-b)$ First-period customers, who were neither informed, nor left the market, but are informed in the second period.

Total $= CN[1 + (1-b)(1-C)]$

In the kth period this becomes:

$$CN[1 + (1-b)(1-C) + \ldots (1-b)^{k-1}(1-C)^{k-1}]$$

For large k (i.e. after a large number of periods), this can be approximated by

$$\frac{C}{1-(1-C)(1-b)}N = \lambda N$$

where λ, the proportion of the potential market who are informed, is a function of both C and b.

$\times$ We must now consider how this fits into the elasticity formulation, a. The definition $a = (A/Q)(\delta Q/\delta A)$ must be expanded to

$$a = \frac{A}{Q} \cdot \frac{\delta Q}{\delta \lambda} \cdot \frac{\delta \lambda}{\delta C} \cdot \frac{\delta C}{\delta A}.$$

$\delta Q/\delta \lambda$ measures the response of demand to an increasing proportion of informed customers in the potential market, and is presumably positive. $\delta C/\delta A$ measures the effectiveness at the margin of an extra unit of advertising in terms of increasing the proportion of the potential market that is informed. This is likely to be positive, though possibly diminishing. We return to both these aspects below. For the present, we concentrate on the value of $\delta \lambda/\delta C$, which is positive.[12] A larger value, *ceteris paribus*, leads to more advertising. Our interest is in how its value changes with changes in C and b. We note first that $\delta\lambda/\delta C$ is a diminishing function of C. Increased effectiveness in informing the potential market involves diminishing returns in the proportion of the market that is so informed in the long run. The response of $\delta\lambda/\delta C$ to changes in b is ambiguous, but it is generally positive unless b is large in comparison to C. The interpretation of this result is that in general an increasing 'turnover' of potential customers in the market leads to an increase in advertising. However, as the turnover becomes larger in relation to the 'reach' of advertising, then a point is reached where the optimal level of advertising diminishes. From Stigler's model we may derive the following example. Suppose that advertising informs 25 per cent of the potential market in a given period. Then as 'turnover' in the potential market increases up to $33\frac{1}{3}$ per cent, optimal advertising will be greater. But beyond that level, optimal advertising diminishes. The point is simply that a rapid turnover in the market destroys the cumulative effect of informative advertising, so less advertising will be done.

The results of Stigler's analysis receive some confirmation in work by Doyle. He showed that greater frequency of purchase of an item was correlated with a smaller advertising/sales ratio. There are two elements in this. The first is that when goods are purchased frequently the identity of the potential market is unlikely to change rapidly between periods. The second is simply that people are much less likely to forget information which frequent purchases will constantly recall to mind.

So far we have concentrated on the informative aspect of advertising. However the type of product is clearly a determinant of the effectiveness of persuasive advertising. Again, a full treatment would

---

[12] The results in this paragraph are obtained from the evaluation of the appropriate first and second derivatives of λ. They are:

$$\frac{\partial\lambda}{\partial C} = \frac{b}{(C + b - Cb)^2} \qquad \text{which is } > 0$$

$$\frac{\partial^2\lambda}{\partial C^2} = \frac{2b(1-b)}{(C + b - Cb)^3} \qquad \text{which is negative since } 0 < C, b < 1$$

$$\frac{\partial^2\lambda}{\partial C \cdot \partial b} = \frac{C - b + bC}{[C + b - Cb]^3} \qquad \text{which is positive if } C - b + bC > 0$$

$$\text{i.e. if } \frac{1}{b} > \frac{1}{C} - 1$$

demand an excursion into consumer behaviour, but Doyle[13] suggests two reasonable generalizations from experience. The first is that if goods are low-priced in relative terms, consumers will be less willing to shop around (since search is time-consuming and the gains will be small anyway) and so are more vulnerable to persuasive advertising. For high-priced goods, more care will be exercised and advertising will be less persuasive. Doyle found this to be confirmed by the evidence. His second generalization is that persuasive advertising is likely to be more effective where the consumer has no means of evaluating the product. Thus most consumers would find it hard to evaluate independently the many different makes of washing machine that are available (even with the help of consumer magazines). So they are more open to persuasion. But a product which is made to a standard specification (e.g. steel rods or a basic chemical) requires no evaluation by the consumer, and attempts by a firm to persuade customers that their standard product is 'better' are not likely to be successful. Nelson[14] makes the same distinction in terms of 'experience' and 'search' quality goods. 'Experience' qualities are those that can only be ascertained after purchase, and will therefore affect repeat purchases, but not first-time buyers. 'Search' qualities are in principle determinable prior to purchase, and hence are not amenable to misleading advertising. The demand for experience quality goods is more likely to be affected by advertising. The central issue is how easily the firm can create preferences which did not exist before, or can change pre-existing preferences. And that depends on the receptivity of the potential market and on the 'strength' of existing preferences. While economic variables such as Doyle suggests are of some importance here, social and psychological variables are quite possibly more significant.

We recall from section 1 that the effectiveness of advertising depends in part on how long it remains persuasive, that is the rate of depreciation of the stock of goodwill. As in the case of informational advertising there are two elements in this—the rate of turnover in the potential market, and the 'forgetfulness' of customers. Peles,[15] for example, analysed the lagged impact of advertising on sales of beer, cigarettes, and cars. He deduced from the regression equations that goodwill generated by beer advertising depreciated at 40–50 per cent

[13] P. Doyle, 'Advertising Expenditure and Consumer Demand', *O.E.P.* N.S. 20 (1968), 395–417.

[14] P. Nelson, 'Advertising as Information', *J.P.E.* 82 (1974), 729–54.

[15] Y. Peles, 'Rates of Amortisation of Advertising Expenditures', *J.P.E.* 79 (1971), 1032–58.

per annum, cigarette advertising 30–50 per cent, and cars 100 per cent. In the case of beer and cigarettes, the main feature is forgetfulness, but for cars the outcome arises from the turnover in the market, since last year's potential customers are unlikely to be still in the market this year.

A number of studies have emphasized the role of advertising in launching new products, so that the amount of advertising devoted to the product may be variable over the product life cycle. Diffusion of a new product can be described by a learning process by which consumers learn to consume new products, largely by imitating each other. Initially when a few consumers are buying the product (the 'pioneers', in Marris's terms)[16] the imitative effect is small and growth is slow. Eventually, however, the proportion grows and hence the size of the 'bandwagon' effect, so demand enters an explosive phase. Finally there is a slowing down in growth as the market approaches saturation and the remaining non-purchasers are harder and harder to attract. The rate of learning is determined by two features. First, the price of the product. A high price will act as a deterrent to rapid spread of the innovation. For this reason, firms follow a new product pricing cycle, starting off with a high price to cover high costs at low initial output, and then bringing down the price as the idea catches on. The second determinant is advertising, which has a major role in convincing the 'pioneers', and then in persuading others to follow. The firm may concentrate advertising in the early stage in order to build its market share. Once a stock of goodwill is established, a much lower advertising/sales ratio may suffice to keep that share. This suggests that the over-all advertising/sales ratio in an industry may be determined by the rate at which new brands or products are launched. Backman[17] has drawn attention to the high turnover of brands in drugs, grocery products, deodorants, cigarettes, soaps and detergents, hair preparations, toothpaste, and breakfast cereals. These are all product classes characterized by high advertising/sales ratios. Lambin[18] found the same correlation between advertising/sales ratios and the rate of product diversification over time in his study of 16 product classes in 8 West European countries.

Estimates of the advertising elasticity, a, have been obtained in a

---

[16] R. Marris, *The Economic Theory of Managerial Capitalism* (London, 1964), Ch. 4.
[17] Backman, op. cit. 60–79.
[18] J. J. Lambin, *Advertising, Competition and Market Conduct in Oligopoly over Time* (Amsterdam and Oxford, 1976).

number of studies.[19] Metwally's study[20] of three brand leaders in the Australian soap powder market will serve as an illustration of the method. His preferred model was:

$$q_t = \alpha_0 + \alpha_1 q_{t-1} + \alpha_2 p_t + \alpha_3 s_t + \alpha_4 v_t$$

where the variables are defined as follows: each is expressed as a share or proportion of the industry total, and transformed to a log-scale:

q_t output
p_t price
s_t own advertising
v_t rivals' advertising.

Lagged values of all the explanatory variables were also added to the equation, to capture the long-run effects of advertising. Estimates of the elasticities for the three brands are tabulated in Table 12.1.

TABLE 12.1

	Brand A	Brand B	Brand C
Price elasticity of demand	−2·533	−2·493	−2·886
Advertising elasticities of demand { short-run	0·041	0·036	0·038
long-run	0·137	0·133	0·158
Optimal advertising/sales ratio calculated from coefficients	0·054	0·053	0·055
Actual advertising/sales ratio	0·059	0·043	0·043

The uniformity of the results for the three brands is encouraging to the thesis that *a* is determined by the nature of the product. It is notable that the advertising elasticities are small compared to the price elasticities. Optimal advertising/sales ratios can be computed from these estimates using the formula:

[19] Early studies are reviewed by Schmalensee, op. cit. See also K. Cowling, J. Cable, M. Kelly, T. McGuinness, *Advertising and Economic Behaviour* (London, 1975), Ch. 4; Peles, op. cit.; M. M. Metwally, 'Profitability of Advertising in Australia: A Case Study', *J.I.E.* 24 (1976), 221–31, for other studies similar to those reported in the text. Lambin, op. cit., has a full discussion of specification and estimation of advertising equations.

[20] M. M. Metwally, 'Advertising and Competitive Behaviour of Selected Australian Firms', *R. Econ. Stats.* 57 (1975), 417–27.

$$\frac{AT}{PQ} = \frac{a^*}{E}$$

where a^* is the long-run advertising elasticity and E is (minus) the price elasticity of demand. These optimal ratios are shown in the table, and are encouragingly close to the actual advertising/sales ratios for the three brands.

Lambin[21] has presented the most comprehensive set of estimates of advertising elasticities. He found that brand advertising had a significant positive effect on current sales and/or market shares for 52 out of 65 brands, and in 23 out of 24 markets that he investigated. Short-run elasticities had a mean value of 0.101: the largest was 0.482, and 60 per cent were less than 0.1. The mean long-run elasticity was 0.228 (with a standard deviation of 0.226). Comparison of optimal and actual advertising/sales ratios suggested significant deviations in a few brands, but over all the two were fairly close.

3 ADVERTISING AND MARKET STRUCTURE

In this section we concentrate on the relationship between market structure and the coefficient η—the conjectural response of other firms' advertising to a change in advertising by the firm. The problem is similar to the one we examined in Chapter 5 where we were discussing oligopolistic responses to price changes by other firms. The argument there was that concentration increased the degree of interdependence between firms (in the sense that one firm's policy change had a greater impact on other firms), *and* that it enabled firms to keep a much closer watch on each other. So a reaction to a price change became more certain. We then went on to show how firms would become aware of the self-defeating nature of price cutting strategies and could even co-operate in raising prices. We might wish to argue an analogous case for advertising. The more concentrated the industry, the more certain that advertising initiatives would be matched and hence rational oligopolists would desist from a self-defeating escalation of advertising costs. However, advertising in fact is a different matter for two reasons. The first is that a price cut can be carried out very rapidly. An advertising campaign on the other hand takes time to mount. So there is bound to be a time lag before other firms can retaliate to an advertising initiative by a firm. The second is that while there can be no doubt about a matching price cut, a firm may well believe that it has a particularly successful

---

[21] Lambin, op. cit.

advertising campaign, which other firms will not be able to match.

A number of recent studies have specifically investigated the existence of rivalry in advertising. Metwally[22] made a study of the two leading brands in the Australian cigarette, washing powder, and toothpaste markets. He estimated demand functions for each of the firms, including both own advertising and the rival's advertising as explanatory variables. The evidence suggested that advertising was reciprocally cancelling: i.e. own advertising and rivals' advertising had equal, but opposite, effects on sales. However the reaction function suggested somewhat less than a matching of expenditures on advertising, with response coefficients varying from 0·16 to 0·72. Precise matching would give coefficients of unity. In a subsequent study,[23] described above, he examined the three leading brands of soap powder. The leading brand's advertising initiatives attracted an immediate response from the other brands equal to slightly over 50 per cent of its own increased expenditures. But for the second and third brands (by market share), the reaction was approximately 27 per cent and 11 per cent. Again rival advertising expenditures had equal but opposite effects. So the net returns to advertising were much less for the brand leader than for the other two.

These results have been confirmed by the major study by Lambin[24] of 107 individual brands in 16 product classes in 8 West European countries. The particular contribution of his work is that oligopolistic rivalry can involve a mix of price, advertising, and quality 'weapons'. He found that rival brand advertising had a negative effect on the firm's sales or market share. The average short-run elasticity was −0·108, compared to 0·101 for own advertising. And in most sectors, the two were reciprocally cancelling. Lambin also found that positive advertising reactions were observed in 7 product markets. The mean value was 0·471, with only one exceeding unity, which would imply escalation of advertising in the market.

The conclusion from Metwally's study,[25] described above, is particularly interesting. We saw in section 2 that the actual advertising/sales ratio was closely approximated by the optimal ratio, derived from estimates of the long-run advertising elasticity and the price elasticity of demand. But the advertising elasticity did *not* incorporate the reactions of other firms, which other evidence from the study suggested was substantial. The tentative conclusion is that the firms ignored rivals' reactions in making advertising expenditure decisions. This conclusion is supported by the results of Lambin[26]

---

[22] Metwally, op. cit. (1975).   [23] Metwally, op. cit. (1976).   [24] Lambin, op. cit.
[25] Metwally, op. cit. (1975).   [26] Lambin, op. cit.

and Cowling *et al.*[27] It may be interpreted in terms of the model of section 1. The firm must know that η is large, since it has had experience of rivals' advertising reactions. But it must also believe that a (the elasticity of sales with respect to own advertising) exceeds $\bar{a}$ (the elasticity with respect to other firms' advertising). If it does not believe something like this, $(a - \eta \cdot \bar{a})$ has a value which tends to zero, as η tends to unity, and so little advertising will take place. If, on the other hand, all firms believe in their own advertising effort, each firm will have a high personal a, and believe $\bar{a}$ to be negligible. Hence a great deal of advertising will take place. Nor will they necessarily learn from experience, since any firm may indeed have had a specially successful campaign at some stage, and may hope to repeat it. If this line of reasoning is correct we would expect advertising intensity to be highest in most concentrated industries for a given value of a, because the response coefficient, η, is likely to be high. In less concentrated oligopolies, the build-up of competitive advertising is probably much less because η is smaller, and firms react less to others' initiative. However, we would also expect the value of a itself to vary with the degree of concentration. If there are many competing products, consumers are less likely to be able to make a complete comparison of available brands and so will rely on advertising. If there are few products available, a complete search is possible and persuasive advertising will be less effective.

Unfortunately we have no method of deciding *a priori* what will be the result of combining these effects. But Cable[28] and Sutton[29] have suggested that advertising expenditures will rise to a peak at intermediate levels of concentration and decline again for the most concentrated sectors. Before we turn to the empirical evidence on this point, we should also note the view that concentration also enters via the determination of the price–cost margin. We saw in Chapter 3 that it was possible to derive, under special assumptions, a relationship between the degree of concentration, and the Lerner index of monopoly, which is $1/E$. If the firm acts like a monopolist *vis-à-vis* its demand curve, then this is also equal to the price–cost margin as a proportion of price in situations of constant cost. We make the further assumption that E declines as the industry becomes more concentrated. As we showed in section 1, with this formulation of the Dorfman–Steiner theorem we have $A/S = a/E$ where both a and E are functions of concentration. Cable argues that the resultant

---

[27] K. Cowling, J. Cable, M. Kelly, T. McGuinness, op. cit.   [28] J. Cable, op. cit. (1973).
[29] C. J. Sutton, 'Advertising, Concentration and Competition', *E.J.* 84 (1974), 56–69; W. D. Reekie, R. D. Rees, C. J. Sutton, 'Advertising, Concentration and Competition: an Interchange', *E.J.* 85 (1975), 156–76.

relationship will again show a peak for A/S at intermediate concentration levels. However, the postulated relationship between concentration, E, and the price–cost margin can claim little weight, being based on a too simplistic theory of pricing in oligopoly markets.

The relationship between industrial concentration and advertising has attracted a number of empirical contributions, the interpretation of which has led to no little controversy. The two major issues seem to be (i) the shape of the relationship: is it linear, or does it have an inverted U-shape, with advertising intensity having a peak at intermediate concentration levels? (ii) is it a general relationship for *all* industries, or does it apply only to those products that are inherently 'advertisable'? Our theoretical analysis suggests that in each case we should expect the second option to apply, i.e. the relationship is non-linear and applies only to a restricted class of products. And that is what the empirical analysis confirms. Telser,[30] for example, tested a linear model with data drawn from 42 consumer industries. He found little relationship, which is scarcely surprising if the underlying relationship is curvilinear. Mann *et al.*[31] carried out the same analysis for a sample of 42 firms in 14 4-digit S.I.C. industries, where products are highly advertised. They found a significant associaion of the advertising/sales ratio and concentration. But their sample was strongly criticized by Ekelund and Maurice, and by Telser,[32] on the grounds that it was restricted to firms with high advertising/sales ratios in highly concentrated sectors, and not therefore typical.

Cable[33] and Sutton[34] have investigated the non-linear relationship for carefully selected products which are heavily advertised. Their evidence supports the inverted-U hypothesis. Sutton fitted a quadratic function to a sample of U.K. consumer industries. His equation was:

$$A/S = -3 \cdot 1545 + 0 \cdot 1914c - 0 \cdot 0015c^2$$
$$t\text{-values} \qquad (3 \cdot 71) \qquad (3 \cdot 51) \qquad \bar{R}^2 = 0 \cdot 34$$

This implies a maximum value of A/s ($2 \cdot 95$ per cent) where the concentration ratio (c) is about 64 per cent, and a zero value at $c = 19$ per cent. Fitting a linear regression to the same data gave a very poor result ($\bar{R}^2 = 0 \cdot 01$). The model did not work for a sample of producer

[30] Telser, op. cit.

[31] H. M. Mann, J. A. Henning, J. W. Meehan, 'Advertising and Concentration: an Empirical Investigation', *J.I.E.* 16 (1967), 34–45.

[32] H. M. Mann, J. A. Henning, J. W. Meehan, L. G. Telser, R. Ekelund, J. Maurice, 'Symposium on Advertising and Concentration', *J.I.E.* 18 (1969), 76–104.

[33] J. Cable, op. cit. (1973).   [34] C. J. Sutton, op. cit. (1974).

goods industries. Cable's sample was 26 narrowly defined U.K. markets; all products were low-priced, frequently purchased consumer goods, mainly foodstuffs but also household non-durables and pharmaceutical products. He finds advertising intensity reaching a maximum at $H = 0.40$, which is a typical duopoly situation with two large firms and a string of small ones. This result may also explain why a linear hypothesis is successful for a sample of industries or firms where advertising is important. So long as industries with $H > 0.40$ are not present, the linear model will approximate the part of the relationhip where advertising and concentration increase together.

However a contrary result has been achieved by Reekie[35] in a response to Sutton's work. His sample was 63 consumer non-durable goods, all low-cost basic household items, sold through grocery stores. For each market he calculated the *brand* concentration. He found no association of A/S with concentration so measured, either in a linear or curvilinear equation. However it is not clear that brand concentration is an appropriate measure in terms of the theory we have advanced above. A firm with several different brands is not likely to allow brand managers to engage in mutually destructive advertising of its own products.

4 ADVERTISING AND PROFITABILITY

A third element in the equation for optimal advertising expenditure set out in section 1 is the size of the price–cost margin. *Ceteris paribus*, higher profit margins are associated with more advertising. The intuitive reason for this is that higher profit per unit makes the return on increased sales by advertising more attractive.

The profit margin as defined in the model excludes expenditure on advertising. However Needham[36] has shown that the correlation beween the advertising/sales ratio and the price–cost margin still holds when advertising expenditures are added to unit costs. The starting-point is the optimal advertising equation for the firm:

$$\frac{AT}{PQ} = \left(\frac{P - AC}{P}\right) a$$

which assumes constant returns to scale in production (over the range in which firms are operating, so marginal cost (MC) = average

[35] W. D. Reekie, op. cit.
[36] D. Needham, 'Entry Barriers and Non-Price Aspects of Firms' Behaviour', *J.I.E.* 25 (1976-7), 29–43.

cost (AC)), and constant costs (T) in advertising.

The profit margin $(P - AC)/P$ covers both advertising expenditure (AT/PQ), and the true profit margin (Π/PQ). So we may write

$$\frac{\pi}{PQ} = \frac{P - AC}{P} - \frac{AT}{PQ}$$

Substituting from the optimal advertising equation:

$$\frac{\pi}{PQ} = \left(\frac{P - AC}{P}\right)(1 - a).$$

Schmalensee[37] extends this result to the return on capital (π/K):

$$\frac{\pi}{K} = \frac{\pi}{PQ} \cdot \frac{PQ}{K} = \frac{PQ}{K} \cdot \left(\frac{P - AC}{P}\right)(1 - a).$$

For given a, it is apparent that the advertising/sales ratio will be highly correlated with both the profit margin (π/PQ) and the return on capital (π/K), since they are all related to $(P - AC)/P$. By appropriate substitution we can write the optimal advertising equation in terms of either π/PQ or π/K. Assuming that a, and the capital–output ratio do not vary between firms, we may follow Schmalensee in aggregating all three conditions across all firms in a market. Then precisely the same correlations will be evident, with the direction of causation running from the profit rate or profit margin to the advertising/sales ratio. The remaining question is what determines the profit rate, which was the subject of Chapter 7.

But the causation may also run in the other direction. Advertising can build up a stock of goodwill that makes entry to the industry harder, and enable firms to earn greater profits. This further possibility is not accounted for in the advertising model we have been using and so warrants further discussion. The simplest case has been analysed by Comanor and Wilson.[38] They suggest that the main barrier to a new entrant is the cost of market penetration in a market that is heavily advertised. They argue that existing firms will have to

[37] R. Schmalensee, 'Advertising and Profitability: Further Implications of the Null Hypothesis', *J.I.E.* 25 (1976), 45–54.

[38] W. S. Comanor, T. A. Wilson, 'Advertising, Market Structure and Performance', *R. Econ. Stats.* 49 (1967), 423–40.

spend less on recurrent advertising to protect their established brands than a new entrant who is trying to gain a market for the first time. This is illustrated in Figure 12.1. The costs of existing firms, including their recurrent advertising to protect their brands, is given

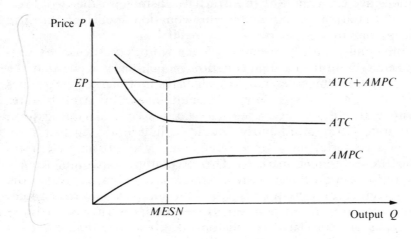

Fig. 12.1

by *ATC*. In addition a new entrant faces market penetration costs of *AMPC*, which rise with the size of market required. So the new entrant has costs *ATC* + *AMPC*. The entry-preventing price is at least *EP* and may be more if the minimum economic scale of an entrant (*MESN*) is a significant proportion of industry size (i.e. new entry would depress the industry price). Alternatively, and more in keeping with the treatment of advertising as creating a stock of goodwill, the problem facing the new entrant is to build up his own stock. This may require a substantial initial outlay in addition to the recurrent expenditure on advertising to keep the stock of goodwill at a given level. The effect of this is to raise an additional entry barrier. Williamson[39] has extended this model by considering the case where increased advertising by existing firms increases the market penetration barrier, thus shifting up the *AMPC* curve and raising the limit price. Then the existing firms have to choose an optimal level of advertising, trading off the cost of further advertising against the returns in terms of a higher limit price.

These theoretical investigations suggest that we need to treat correlations between advertising and profitability with great caution. In our discussion of the subject in Chapter 7 we suggested that the

[39] O. E. Williamson, 'Selling Expense as a Barrier to Entry', *Q.J.E.* 77 (1963), 112–28.

causation ran from goodwill to the price–cost margin. That causal link does have an adequate theoretical base. However, the alternative link from profitability to advertising is equally possible, always assuming that the product is 'advertisable', i.e. $(a - \eta\bar{a})$ is not zero in the subjective estimation of the firms. To distinguish the two directions of causation in a simultaneous equation model of the firm (with appropriate lag structures) is more difficult.

Vernon and Nourse[40] attempt to cope with the difficulty by testing a reduced form of a two-equation model. They argue that the *aggregate* advertising/sales ratio of all firms in a market determines profit rates via the effect on entry conditions, and that profit rates determine the *firm*'s advertising/sales ratio. Hence a reduced form equation for firm profitability should include both the firm's advertising/sales ratio, and the weighted industry advertising/sales ratio in the firm's product markets. Their tentative conclusion from a study of 57 firms in consumer non-durable product classes is that the main direction of causation is from the industry advertising/sales ratio to the firm's profit rate. But the firm and industry advertising/sales ratios are correlated (correlation coefficient is 0·62 for their sample), so it is difficult to distinguish the two effects.

An alternative approach to advertising and profitability has been suggested by Horowitz.[41] Assume that the firm faces a stochastic demand curve, and that advertising helps to reduce the variance of sales at any particular price. If the firm is risk averse (in the sense that it weighs variance of returns adversely), then it will spend on advertising simply to reduce the variance of its returns, and hence enhance its valuation. Schramm and Sherman[42] have extended the analysis to a case where the firm can adjust its advertising outlays in the light of current fluctuations in demand, rather than having to make a single decision as in the Horowitz model. The firm can then choose how much fluctuation in profit it is prepared to accept. Dehez and Jacquemin[43] have generalized the Horowitz model to include the possibility that firms will cope with fluctuations in demand by adjusting both advertising and price. Whether the firm will advertise more or less than the equivalent firm with certain demand depends on the relative advertising and price elasticity of demands. No definite conclusions can be drawn from this analysis.

[40] J. M. Vernon, R. E. M. Nourse, 'Profit Rates and Market Structure of Advertising Intensive Firms', *J.I.E.* 22 (1973–4), 1–20.

[41] I. Horowitz, 'A Note on Advertising and Uncertainty', *J.I.E.* 18 (1970), 151–60.

[42] R. Schramm, R. Sherman, 'Advertising to Manage Profit Risk', *J.I.E.* 24 (1976), 295–311.

[43] P. Dehez, A. Jacquemin, 'A Note on Advertising Policy under Uncertainty and Dynamic Conditions', *J.I.E.* 24 (1975), 73–8.

Intuition would suggest that fluctuating demand could generate high advertising expenditure to reduce profit variability. But whether it would be sufficient to give the industry a lower risk rating, and hence a lower equilibrium profit rate, is not clear. So no direct correlation of advertising/sales ratios and profit rates can be deduced. Whether advertising does reduce variability of sales is not decided by the evidence one way or the other. Reekie[44] looked at advertising and market share data for 63 sub-markets in foodstuffs, medicaments, kitchen and household supplies, and toiletries. He found that advertising and the mobility of market shares were positively associated in foodstuffs and toiletries markets, but not in the others.

Telser[45] examined the behaviour of market shares of leading brands for food products, household cleaning materials, and cosmetics. Cosmetics are highly advertised, food products not at all, with household cleaning materials in between. He found that market shares were most unstable for cosmetics, and most stable for food products, a result which he linked to the greater brand and product innovation in cosmetics. But we do not have evidence as to how volatile the market shares would be in the absence of advertising. One could argue that preferences are much more stable for food products than for cosmetics, where the objective qualities of different products can scarcely be evaluated. From another study, of cigarettes, Telser[46] does accept that repetitive advertising reduced brand switching by consumers and thus reduced variability in sales.

It is possible however to pursue the logic of section 3 above, and imagine a situation where competitive advertising in an oligopoly could be destabilizing with respect to market shares. We saw there that competitive advertising could arise simply because firms believed that their own advertising would be more successful than any (lagged) response from other firms. If that supposition were at least sometimes true, it is possible that market shares could switch sharply between firms as first one and then another conducted a successful campaign to which the others were unable to reply immediately. Reekie[47] has noted that this offensive use of advertising is likely to be particularly associated with product innovation in differentiated markets. We shall return to the subject of fluctuations in market share in Chapter 15, but one particular causal sequence can usefully be mentioned here. Suppose that advertising does lead to greater fluctuations in market share (when associated with innovation, for

---

[44] W. D. Reekie, 'Advertising and Market Share Stability', *S.J.P.E.* 21 (1974), 143–58.
[45] Telser, op. cit.
[46] L. G. Telser, 'Advertising and Cigarettes', *J.P.E.* 70 (1962), 471–99.
[47] Reekie, op. cit. (1974).

example). The effect on one firm may not be systematic, but it is for the industry as a whole. Over time some firms are likely to grow larger (a run of successful advertising campaigns) while others lose out. Hence concentration is likely to increase, *because* of the advertising intensive nature of the industry. This reverses the direction of causation assumed in our discussion of the optimal advertising equation in section 3 above. We should also note that concentration may be one of the determinants of the price–cost margin, though this possibility was rather discounted in Chapter 7.

5   ADVERTISING COSTS AND EFFECTIVENESS

The model we presented in section 1 makes the assumption that the unit costs of advertising messages are constant. Schmalensee[48] examined advertising rates for television and newspapers and concluded that the assumption of constant costs is probably valid. Certainly he could find no evidence of pecuniary economies of 'scale' in advertising rates which would give an advantage to the large advertisers. Blair[49] comes to a different conclusion about rates on the basis of evidence presented to the U.S. Senate Subcommittee on Antitrust and Monopoly in 1966, concerning the costs of TV advertising. He concludes that the published rates are misleading, since major discounts are not publicized. He also suggests that larger advertisers had privileged access to the more favoured times on television.

An alternative possibility is that while rates for advertising are constant, their 'effectiveness' in terms of the number of 'messages' transmitted to consumers is related to the scale of advertising. Lambin[50] noted that small brands in his sample tended to keep their share of advertising substantially higher than their share of the market. The ratio of the two shares was 1·59. He argued that this was an indication of a 'threshold' effect in the advertising response curve. A certain minimum level of advertising was necessary before sales were affected. Above the threshold the response was positive, but diminishing, for which two reasons may be advanced. First, more advertising may seek to 'reach' more potential consumers. There is evidence from advertising practice that such an increase in advertising may encounter diminishing returns. The reasons for this are straightforward. Suppose a product is aimed at a particular type of consumer. Then the obvious first place for advertising is in a magazine that

---

[48] Schmalensee, op. cit.
[49] J. M. Blair, *Economic Concentration* (New York, 1972).
[50] Lambin, op. cit.

many of that type of consumer will read. If the advertiser wishes to increase his reach he will then have to extend his advertising to other magazines, perhaps less relevant to his potential customers. The point is that fewer readers of these magazines will be potential customers: the medium for his advertising is less effective, since more readers will not be interested in his advertisement. But it is unlikely he will pay less for the advertisement itself. Second, more advertising may be attempted by increasing the frequency of advertising in the most effective medium. The more frequent the advertisement the less likely that any potential customer will be ignorant of the product, either through not having seen the advertisement, or through forgetting it. Examination of Stigler's model[51] suggests strongly that there are diminishing returns to frequency (section 2 above), and Schmalensee shows this to be confirmed by empirical evidence.

The weight of the evidence then suggests that at least from an informational point of view there are likely to be diminishing returns to increased advertising scale, and hence increasing costs for advertising 'messages' which are effective. An increasing marginal cost for advertising messages would lead the optimizing firm to purchase fewer than in the case of ~~constant~~ costs.

6   CONCLUSIONS ON ADVERTISING AND THE FIRM

The large number of possible causal sequences between advertising and other market structure variables, which we have explored in this chapter, is inevitably somewhat confusing. The simultaneous effect of all the relationships needs to be assessed jointly. The framework set out by Strickland and Weiss,[52] with its associated econometric tests, serves to bring all the analysis together. Using the same elements as we have discussed in the previous sections, they postulate a three-equation system.

(1) The optimal advertising equation.

$$A/S = f_1(C, M)$$

where A/S is the advertising/sales ratio, C is the concentration ratio, and M the price–cost margin. Following the theory of section 3, they include C^2 to capture the inverted-U relationship of A/S and concentration. To this they add three 'nature of the product' variables: CD/S, the share of total sales going to consumers (who are more

[51] Stigler, op. cit.
[52] A. D. Strickland, L. W. Weiss, 'Advertising, Concentration and Price–Cost Margins', *J.P.E.* 84 (1976), 1109–21.

likely to be influenced by advertising than industrial customers); Gr, the growth rate of the industry; and Dm, a dummy variable for durable goods (less likely to be sold by persuasive as opposed to informative advertising).

(2) Determinants of concentration.

$$C = f_2(A/S, MES).$$

This reflects the reasoning at the end of section 4, that advertising may lead (over time) to concentration. MES is the minimum economic scale of plant as a fraction of industry output. These variables are further discussed in Chapter 15.

(3) Determinants of the price–cost margin.

$$M = f(A/S, C, k/S, GD, MES)$$

This is the kind of equation for explaining the margin, which was discussed in Chapter 7. k/S is the capital–output ratio (a determinant of the price/variable-cost ratio). GD measures the degree of geographical dispersion of the market, which may enhance the effect of concentration. MES is included as a scale-economy barrier to entry. We note that A/S is part of the margin, M, so it should enter with a coefficient which exceeds unity.

A linear form of this model was tested for 408 4-digit S.I.C. U.S. manufacturing industries in 1963, both by ordinary least square and two-stage least squares methods. The results are given in Table 12.2, for the latter method. Strickland and Weiss note that the superior econometric technique made little difference in the equations with A/S and C as dependent variables, but the equation for M was notably different. This suggests that single equation tests of the advertising–profitability relationship are unreliable. In the A/S equation all the coefficients but one had the expected signs and were significant at least at the 5 per cent level. The curvilinear relationship with concentration is confirmed, A/S taking a maximum at $CR_4 = 57$ per cent. The growth of the market has a positive and significant coefficient, perhaps reflecting advertising related to innovation. The C equation also fulfils expectations: both A/S and MES appear as important determinants of the level of concentration. The least satisfactory equation is that for M. Neither concentration nor scale economies are significant, and the A/S coefficient exceeds unity by an amount that is barely significant ($t = 1.91$). A tentative deduction is that this aspect of advertising is less important than the other two, which concentrate on the reasons why firms find it worthwhile to

TABLE 12.2

	Dependent variables		
	A/S	C	M
Constant	−0·0245	0·2591	0·1736
	(−3·86)	(21·30)	(14·66)
C	0·073		0·0377
	(2·84)		(0·93)
C^2	−0·0642		
	(−2·64)		
M	0·0544		
	(2·01)		
CD/S	0·0269		
	(8·96)		
Gr	0·0539		0·2336
	(2·09)		(2·61)
Dm	−0·0018		
	(−0·93)		
A/S		1·5347	1·6256
		(2·42)	(5·52)
MES		4·169	0·1720
		(18·84)	(0·92)
k/S			0·1165
			(7·30)
GD			−0·003
			(−2·79)

Source: A. D. Strickland, L. W. Weiss, 'Advertising, Concentration and Price–Cost Margins', *J.P.E.* 84 (1976), pp. 1109–21. Table 2. © 1976 by The University of Chicago. All rights reserved.

advertise their products, as part of their general market strategy of growth (and as an alternative use of funds to investment in physical capital or research and development).

We conclude from the analysis of the chapter that in theoretical terms there is a distinction between 'informational' and 'persuasive' advertising. The former is necessary for many goods, if customers are to be aware of the existence of the product. As Stigler[53] points out, the only alternative is the development of some single localized market or markets where sellers can exhibit their goods and buyers can inspect a particular good; so long as this place is sufficiently well known, advertising can be dispensed with. But in the absence of

[53] Stigler, op. cit.

localized markets it will be worthwhile for the firm to engage in disseminating information about its products. How much advertising they do, of this kind, depends largely on the characteristics of the product and the product market—specifically the turnover of potential customers, the frequency of purchase, and the absentmindedness of consumers. It is also related to the returns to increased advertising in terms of 'reach' and 'frequency'. A particularly important case of informational advertising will be its use in association with the launching of a new product or brand. In fact Telser[54] sees advertising as a means of *promoting* competition by enabling the entry of new products to monopolized markets. However, that is to ignore the other, persuasive, use of advertising. We have seen that this type of advertising will *not* occur unless the product is basically 'advertisable'. In crude terms, that is when the preferences of consumers in quality or characteristics space are not strongly based in objective assessments of the products. Of course, this will vary 'in degree' between differing products. But it is this quality of being 'advertisable' in differing degrees that has hindered empirical work in this field. Given that a product is 'advertisable' (measured in terms of the response coefficient of demand to own advertising), then we may explore the effect of market structure and firm profitability on the level of advertising that will occur.

[54] Telser, op. cit.

RESEARCH AND DEVELOPMENT, AND INNOVATION

In the two previous chapters we considered how the firm could change its situation in a market by expanding its output capacity or by advertising. In this chapter we concentrate on a third major use of funds by firms, allocation of funds to research and development with a view to developing new processes or new products. The objective of the firm is to change the conditions under which it operates in markets. Research and development expenditure is thus an important part of the competitive strategy of the firm. It may also be the basis for growth by diversification.

The structure of the chapter is as follows. In the next section we provide some definitions of terms. In section 2 we look at R and D expenditure as an investment, from the point of view of the firm. Section 3 discusses sources of funds. In section 4 we look at the R and D process itself before moving in sections 5 and 6 to the evaluation of innovations. Section 7 examines the innovating firm, and section 8 examines the rate at which innovations diffuse between firms.

1 DEFINITIONS

The literature is bedevilled by lack of clear definitions of terms. Those definitions we adopt here can hold no claim to the unanimous support of writers in this area. They are provided as the basis for the discussion in subsequent sections, and to clear up some minor theoretical issues.

Technological change: inventions leading to change in blueprints for:

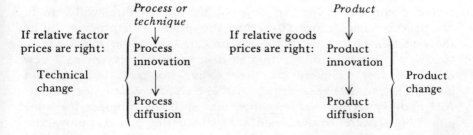

We define *technology* as information: the specifications (in the engineering sense) for a product or a process. It must be more than just an idea. It must be something, which, if built or produced according to specification, will 'work'. The technology at any time is the 'book' of specifications or blueprints. If an invention has not reached the blueprint stage then it is excluded from technology. It is the task of R and D to bring such ideas to the blueprint stage. A change in the 'book' of blueprints is a *technological change*.

Not all technology will be in use at any time. Some techniques will be technically inefficient in the sense that they use more of all factors of production than some other techniques. The isoquant in Figure 13.1 gives the technically efficient frontier of all possible

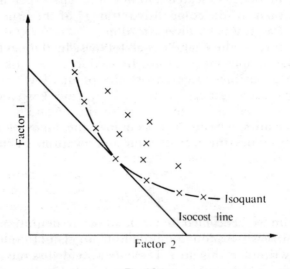

Fig. 13.1

techniques using the two factors. The points lying outside the frontier represent blueprints that would do the job, but which nobody would contemplate when setting up a new plant. Not all techniques on the frontier will be used at a given time. The relative prices of factors (represented by the slope of the isocost line) will lead to one process having lower costs than the others. This process will be the one utilized in new plants. A *process innovation* may arise in two ways. It may result from a shift in relative prices giving a new minimum cost technique on the existing isoquant. This will not involve R and D expenditure, as the technology will not change. Alternatively technological change may shift the isoquant (or some points on it) nearer to the origin, thus stimulating process innovation.

Innovation refers to the first use of the new technique. Over time use of the technique will diffuse to other firms. *Technical change* includes both innovation and diffusion.

There is no parallel distinction between available and efficient product technology, since it would be difficult to exclude some products on engineering grounds alone. But once again the choice of products depends on relative prices. A product may be so expensive or have such an undesirable specification that no market for it exists. A product change may be stimulated either by an addition to technology or by a change in relative prices. The change in relative prices may arise directly from a change in consumer preferences, or it may arise from changes in the cost of making different products (in which case process innovation leads directly to product innovation). Innovation again refers to the first producer of a product. Diffusion refers primarily to diffusion of use among consumers rather than diffusion of production among firms. Innovation and diffusion together constitute *product change*.

2 · R AND D EXPENDITURE AS AN INVESTMENT DECISION

The main elements in the Research and Development expenditure decision can be drawn from Figure 13.2, which is an expanded version of the relevant sections of Figure 1.6.

First, we note that R and D expenditure is competing for a share of the total supply of funds with market investment and investment in physical plant. Orthodox investment analysis would predict a three-way split of the funds so that marginal returns in each use were equalized, with an appropriate provision for risk in each case. However the discussion of Chapter 11 showed that this was a gross oversimplification. The R and D project passes through the same complex decision matrix as other investment decisions.

Second, the R and D investment decision involves two sorts of forecasts. The first, shared with advertising and physical investment, is the prospective stream of returns expected in the market or markets. There will naturally be a greater degree of uncertainty about these forecasts, especially where a new product is contemplated. But the firm will also have to make some sort of estimate as to whether the project will be a technical success, and what the costs of R and D are likely to be. The point is that R and D activity is merely a means to an end. In the diagram the expenditures are made on R and D inputs, e.g. scientists, research facilities, and materials. The R and D 'Black Box' represents the production function by which these inputs are transformed into R and D outputs—technological change

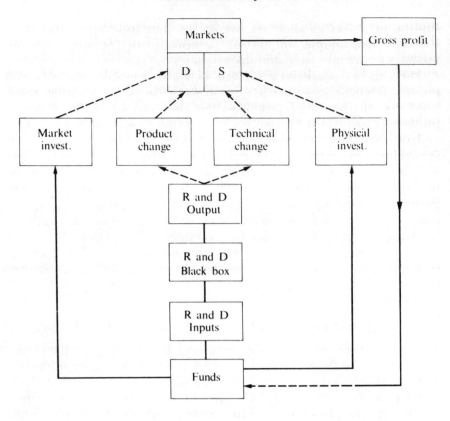

Fig. 13.2

in the form of new products or processes. These then have to be submitted to the test of market profitability.

Given these special problems of forecasting the outcome of R and D projects it is interesting to note how firms actually evaluate projects and how accurate their forecasts are. Freeman[1] draws on various sources to show that engineers and R and D scientists are usually far too optimistic about the likelihood of success in a project, and about the costs and length of time of development. Managers believe that market prospects are even more difficult to estimate than technical outcomes, and their evaluations tend to be pessimistic. As a result the choice of projects may owe more to the 'animal spirits' of the entrepreneur and R and D scientists than to any sophisticated technique of appraisal such as discounted cash flow. The pessimism of managers about market prospects tends to favour R and D into processes rather than products. There is also a tendency to emphasize

[1] C. Freeman, *The Economics of Industrial Innovation* (Harmondsworth, 1974), Ch. 7.

routine projects with a small innovative content. Mansfield[2] found that one large R and D intensive company had made an accurate estimate in two-thirds of the R and D projects it undertook. Schott's survey[3] of 81 U.K. firms showed that of all R and D projects completed or abandoned by these firms in 1972, 91 per cent had been successful in reaching their initial objective. This evidence suggests rather careful choices of projects initially.

Third, we note that R and D expenditures must be viewed in the context of the growth of the firm. Profits generate the funds for R and D expenditure. But R and D expenditure also provokes changes in the firms' market positions, and thus generates profits. The causation runs in both directions.[4]

3   FINANCE FOR R AND D

Because of the high degree of uncertainty in R and D projects, it is not surprising that virtually all expenditure is financed out of retained profits. Galbraith[5] concluded that the profits earned by large monopolistic corporations would be a major source of funds for R and D, and that this could lead to the pre-eminence of such firms in innovation. In the United States in 1970 firms of 10,000 or more employees accounted for 83 per cent of total R and D expenditures; and the largest 100 firms accounted for 79 per cent of R and D expenditure, but only 39 per cent of employment.[6] Certainly profits often emerge as a strong variable in time series analysis of firms' expenditures on R and D. Grabowski[7] found that profits lagged by one year were a significant determinant of R and D expenditure at the firm level in three sectors, chemicals, petroleum refining, and drugs. But R and D has to compete with other expenditures out of

---

[2] E. Mansfield, *The Economics of Technological Change* (London, 1969), Ch. 3.

[3] K. Schott, 'Investment in Private Industrial Research and Development in Britain', *J.I.E.* 25 (1976), 81–99.

[4] Anticipating the analysis of subsequent sections to some extent we may note the work of Branch, 'Research and Development Activity and Profitability', *J.P.E.* 82 (1974), 999–1011, on this point. He examined the experience of 111 large firms in 7 U.S. sectors in the period 1950–65. He tested a simultaneous equation model where (i) current profits are determined by, among other variables, patents registered by the firm in previous periods, and (ii) lagged profits in turn determine R and D activity and hence patents registered. The first equation of the pair was strongly significant in all 7 sectors, suggesting a strong link between profits and previous R and D activity. The second equation, relating current R and D effort to previous profits, was also significant in 4 sectors, but not in chemicals, pharmaceuticals, or non-ferrous metals.

[5] J. K. Galbraith, *The New Industrial Estate*, 2nd edn. (London, 1972).

[6] Freeman, op. cit. 201–2.

[7] H. G. Grabowski, 'The Determinants of R and D in Three Industries', *J.P.E.* 76 (1968), 292–306.

retentions. Survey work, for example by Mansfield[8] in the United States, suggests that firms often use a rule of thumb in allocation of funds to R and D. The typical target allocation is a percentage of sales which is determined with reference to the industry average. This would suggest a 'bandwagon' effect in R and D allocations with firms following each other, given the opportunities existing in the industry. The idea of long-run adherence to a rule of thumb is supported by the econometric work of Mueller[9] on the expenditure decisions of 40 large U.S. manufacturing firms. In the long run, advertising, physical investment, and R and D expenditure had constant elasticities with respect to the total supply of funds. But he did find evidence of switching of resources between selling expenditure and R and D expenditure in response to opportunities in the short run. Adherence to rules of thumb in allocations to R and D certainly reflects the uncertainty attached to the outcomes. Given that returns are difficult to estimate and that the extra technical uncertainty makes it impossible to compare those returns with other expenditures, a rule of thumb may be the best that a firm can do.

4   THE RELATIONSHIP BETWEEN R AND D INPUTS AND OUTPUTS

Identification of the R and D production function presupposes that we can effectively identify and measure the inputs and outputs to the process. Inputs present the lesser difficulty since one can rely on objective measures such as expenditure or the number of scientists and engineers employed. The output of R and D can only be measured in terms of patents or by the number of 'significant' inventions. Comanor and Scherer[10] defined a number of shortcomings in patent statistics. First, they found evidence in the United States of a secular decline in the propensity to patent innovations, particularly since 1940, largely due to the legal factors affecting patents (e.g. anti-trust legislation) and to the expense and difficulty of registering a patent. Second, they found that there was more patenting of products than of processes. Processes can be protected by careful industrial secrecy and security. Products can be bought and copied. Third, the propensity to patent varies greatly between industries. It is relatively easy to patent the formula for a drug. It is much harder to patent an invention like the ball-point pen in a way that will exclude competition. Fourth, the propensity to patent also varies

---

[8] Mansfield, op. cit.

[9] D. C. Mueller, 'The Firm Decision Process', *Q.J.E.* 81 (1967), 58–87.

[10] W. S. Comanor, F. M. Scherer, 'Patent Statistics as a Measure of Technical Change', *J.P.E.* 77 (1969), 392–8. In this chapter we *assume* the existence of a patent system. Patent systems are fully discussed in Chap. 17 section 8.

between firms in an industry, according to size. Large firms will rely on their market and technological dominance to protect their innovations. Small firms will patent to avoid their idea being pirated by a large firm with more resources to exploit it. Finally, it is said that patent statistics do not reflect the 'quality' of the innovations. For example, drug firms may patent a range of chemical substances *Fencing in* around the one drug that is useful, to prevent other firms from producing a near chemical substitute. However Comanor and Scherer are not convinced that we can distinguish 'important' inventions to obtain a more convincing measure of innovation. There is no reason why we should not use patent statistics in the aggregate as a measure, though not for inter-industry comparisons. There are obvious limitations too in using patent data at the level of the individual firm where differences in patent quality may be critical.   -

Research has suggested that the productivity of R and D efforts may be related systematically to three factors, the scale of the operation, the 'technological opportunities' of the sector, and the management of the firm. We look at these in turn.

A priori, there are a number of reasons why a large R and D effort might be more effective than a small one in terms of output of information. Indivisibilities in equipment may lead to economies of scale. The pooling of risks from undertaking several projects simultaneously may lead to a steadier flow of innovations, and also enable firms to undertake more speculative R and D. Parallel teams working on the same or similar projects will be able to share ideas more readily. Large R and D efforts may well attract better scientists because they provide a better working environment and a wider range of projects. Fisher and Temin[11] have explored this Schumpeterian hypothesis of a relation between size and effectiveness. They point out that there are two separate assertions involved. The first is that there are economies of scale within the R and D Black Box itself. The second is that a given size of Black Box will be more efficient in a large firm than in a small one. The only systematic test of these two separate hypotheses has been provided by Mansfield,[12] using evidence from 35 firms in chemicals, petroleum, glass, drugs, and steel. Holding firm size constant, he found a linear relationship between inputs and R and D outputs with evidence for scale economies in the Black Box only in the case of chemicals. On the second his evidence suggested that a given R and D effort was likely to be

[11] F. M. Fisher, P. Temin, 'Returns to Scale in R and D: What does the Schumptereian Hypothesis imply?', *J.P.E.* 81 (1973), 56–70.
[12] E. Mansfield, *Industrial Research and Technological Innovation* (New York, 1968), Ch. 2.

more effective in a medium-sized firm than a large one. Scherer[13] analysed R and D inputs and patents for 448 of the Fortune 500 list of companies in the United States in 1955. He found that inventive inputs (scientists) increased less than proportionately with firm size.[14] Patents, on the other hand, had a phase of increasing returns with respect to firm size (up to firm sales of $500 m. in 1955) but thereafter increased less than proportionately. Fisher and Temin show that this evidence is not sufficient to test either of the two hypotheses separately, but there is clearly no support for a general Schumpeterian hypothesis that size is good for R and D expenditure and effectiveness. Scherer suggests that one explanation of his results may be the greater involvement of large companies in government-sponsored R and D where patents are not important.

'Technological opportunities' are difficult to define objectively, but there is good reason to believe that there is a distinction between science-based industries and more traditional industries. A number of studies have made attempts to incorporate this factor into explanations of inter-industry differences in employment of R and D inputs. Scherer[15] divided industries into four classes, general and mechanical, electrical, chemical, and traditional on the basis of their technologies. These groupings were represented by dummy variables in a regression equation to explain variations in the employment of scientists and engineers in 58 United States industries (1960). He concluded that technological opportunity was indeed very important. A rather different proposal was examined by Baily.[16] He suggested that a period of rapid innovation in a sector could deplete the possibilities and thus reduce 'technological opportunity' in the sector for a number of subsequent periods. He found some rather weak support for this idea in a study of the United States pharmaceutical industry.

The third suggestion concerning the efficiency of R and D efforts seeks an explanation in a number of variables internal to the firm or to the R and D unit. The argument is that R and D is a very complex

[13] F. M. Scherer, 'Firm Size, Market Structure, Opportunity and the Output of Patented Innovations', *A.E.R.* 55 (1965), 1097–1125.

[14] W. S. Comanor, 'Market Structure, Product Differentiation and Industrial Research', *Q.J.E.* 81 (1967), 639–57, confirmed this result in a study of 21 U.S. 3-digit sectors. He examined the elasticity of numbers of research personnel with respect to size of firm. In 14 he was not able to reject the hypothesis that the elasticity was unity. In the other 7 sectors it was significantly less than unity, implying that research intensity diminished with size of firm.

[15] F. M. Scherer, 'Market Structure and the Employment of Scientists and Engineers', *A.E.R.* 57 (1967), 524–31.

[16] M. N. Baily, 'Research and Development Costs and Returns: The Pharmaceutical Industry', *J.P.E.* 80 (1973), 70–85.

matter involving a wide range of managerial, behavioural, and socio-logical influences. The attempt to identify a production function is misguided. Rather we must look carefully at the way in which R and D is performed within the firm. The danger with such an approach is that it may simply become anecdotal and fail to pinpoint important aggregate relationships. The problem is familiar to us from the study of pricing. The description of pricing given by case studies of indivi-dual firms is not necessarily an aid to understanding the more general determinants of prices and profit margins. An excellent example of a case study approach that avoids being anecdotal is the report on Project SAPPHO.[17] This was concerned with innovations which reach the stage of being marketed. It suggested that there is a threshold size both of firm and of R and D unit which is a pre-requisite for a firm entering the innovation race. Further it found evidence that successful innovation had its roots in two features of the R and D effort. The first was the size of team associated with each project, which indicated the firm's degree of commitment to it. The second was the degree of linkage to the outside scientific com-munity (e.g. in universities and other research establishments), not science in general, but specifically with scientists working in fields related to that of the innovation.

Up to this point we have assumed that the major contribution to R and D is made by units within firms. However this conclusion has been challenged by a number of writers. Jewkes *et al.*[18] have em-phasized the contribution of individual inventors to the list of important inventions in the twentieth century. Hamberg[19] reports tht only 7 out of a total of 27 'major inventions' in the period 1947–55 came from the R and D units of firms. Peck[20] shows that only 17 out of 149 major inventions in the aluminium industry came from major firms in the period 1946–57. The explanations for these results are various. Companies seek a short pay-off period for projects and they avoid uncertain major projects, preferring to con-centrate on small improvements in processes and products. In parti-cular the close links of R and D to production and sales may absorb their energies in minor projects and leave little time for imaginative ones. Team research in large R and D units tends to suppress the ori-ginality of more creative scientists. And even if some new idea does emerge, the firm as a whole may be unwilling to embrace it if it

[17] Science Policy Research Unit, *Success and Failure in Industrial Innovation*, Centre for Study of Industrial Innovation (London, 1972).

[18] J. Jewkes *et al.*, *The Sources of Invention*, 2nd edn. (London, 1969).

[19] D. Hamberg, *Essays in the Economics of Research and Development* (New York, 1966).

[20] M. J. Peck, *Competition in the Aluminium Industry* (Cambridge, Mass., 1968).

means a major upheaval in production or marketing. While all these points may be valid (and we may well be sceptical about the definition of 'major inventions'), there is excellent evidence to suggest that the twentieth century has seen a major shift in emphasis in R and D away from the small independent inventor or firm to the more professional R and D of the major companies.[21] Even where an invention originates outside a major firm, it usually requires the expertise of a large R and D unit to develop it. Occasionally the inventor may be able to grow his own firm on the basis of such an invention and thus acquire the necessary size of operation to exploit it.

5   MARKET STRUCTURE AND THE VALUATION OF R AND D OUTPUTS

(a) Process innovation

For the sake of clarity in exposition we have separated out the process by which R and D generates new technology and the market evaluation of that technology. But clearly new technologies are of no use to the firm unless they further the market aims of the firm. It is to this issue that we now turn. Our starting-point is the Schumpeterian hypothesis that a monopoly firm has a greater demand for innovations because its market power increases its opportunity to profit from them. This assertion has generated a debate about the relative merits of innovation in pure monopoly and perfect competition. We briefly summarize this debate before proceeding to a discussion of innovation in oligopoly.

Arrow[22] considers the gains to the originator of a technical innovation, in monopoly and competition. Assume first that the originator is a firm *within* the industry. The effect of the technical innovation is to reduce marginal costs—from OC to OC' in Figure 13.3. The monopolist was making a profit of A when costs were OC. When marginal cost falls to OC', his profit rises to B. So his incentive to innovate is the net addition to profit or $(B - A)$. For the competitive firm the initial cost and price is OC, and there are no excess profits. One firm in the industry then makes a technical innovation and licenses all the other firms in the industry. If the patent can be successfully protected, and if the innovating firm exploits his monopoly of the information to the fullest extent, it can gain B in licence fees. Therefore, Arrow concludes, the competitive situation gives a greater incentive, since the return is higher. We may note however

---

[21] This emerges very clearly from Professor Freeman's account of the rise of science-related technology: see Freeman, op. cit., Part One.

[22] K. Arrow, 'Economic Welfare and the Allocation of Resources for Invention', in *The Rate and Direction of Inventive Activity*, N.B.E.R. (1962).

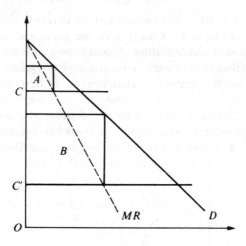

Fig. 13.3

that an *existing* patent-holder in a competitive industry would have
no more incentive than a monopolist, since he will have been earning
A from licences on the previous patent. The alternative assumption
is that the patent-holder is outside the industry, for example a
research institute. For perfect competition the gains are as before,
provided the research institute was not the previous patent-holder,
in which case the gains are $(B - A)$. For a monopoly structure the
patent-holder must be careful to charge a lump sum licence fee and
not a royalty per unit of output. The latter would enter the monopolists marginal cost with the result that he would reduce output and
royalties would be less. The maximum lump sum royalty that the
monopolist will be prepared to pay is $(B - A)$. We conclude that a
competitive situation provides more incentive to a new patent-
holder who can effectively license the use of his invention.
Demsetz[23] has argued that this conclusion is inavlid, on the grounds
that output in the monopolistic sector *prior* to the innovation is
less than that in the competitive sector. To compare like with like,
one should compare monopolized and competitive sectors with the
same initial output. But this is an arbitrary requirement. A given
sector will have a *given* demand curve, and hence different outputs
under competition and monopoly. If one is interested in the incentive to innovation in that sector as it is, one cannot require outputs
to be the same prior to innovation.

[23] H. Demsetz, 'Information and Efficiency: Another Viewpoint', *J. Law Econ.* 12
(1969), 1–22.

Oligopoly is a more realistic market setting for the analysis of the returns to innovation. In Chapter 5 we saw that interdependence tended to rule out intra-industry price competition. So R and D expenditures (together with advertising) provide an alternative means of competing. We shall also see that they reduce new entry competition.

Competition between firms can be generated either by new processes or new products. Returns to process innovation are illustrated in Figure 13.4. The initial price and output equilibrium of the firm

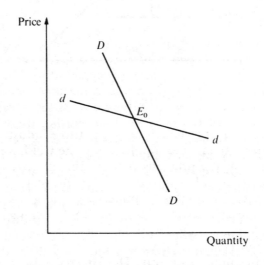

Fig. 13.4

is at E_0. Following the analysis of Chapter 5 we recall that the firm faces two demand curves. One, the DD curve, is a share of the market curve reflecting the demand for the firm's output when all firms move their prices together. The other, dd curve is the situation when the firm changes price on its own, other firms not changing their prices. We now consider the effect of a reduction in costs for the one firm brought about by a process innovation. The very *least* that the firm will gain is an extra profit per unit at the same price and output. However if the dd curve is elastic, the firm will increase its profit by reducing price and increasing its market share. The elasticity of the demand curve will depend on two things: the homogeneity of the products of the firms, and the number of firms.[24] For a given product the cross-elasticity of demand will be highest where there are few firms, since the customers will be able to obtain price quotations

[24] For a full explanation, see Chapter 3.

from all suppliers. The reason for lowering price in this case is that the innovator knows that his competitors cannot match his new price, since their costs are higher. Of course, they will have every incentive to apply their own energies to cost reduction. But there will inevitably be some delay. The returns to the innovator then are the discounted present value of the stream of additional profit up to the time when other firms can match its costs. That of itself would be a considerable incentive where the estimate of the time lag is long.

The relationship between the returns to process innovation and market structure has two aspects. A situation with fewer firms leads to an increase in the elasticity of the *dd* curve, and therefore, *ceteris paribus*, implies a larger increment to the profits of the successful innovator. But it also increases the degree of interdependence between the firms, and will lead them to match expenditures as a defensive measure. The matching of expenditures however by no means implies that firms view them as cancelling each other out (as in the case of a price cut not based on cost differences). If they did, presumably less R and D would be done. Rather there is the uncertainty attached to R and D expenditures which always leads a firm to hope that it may be able to innovate more effectively than its rivals, and the knowledge that a cost advantage once gained cannot be immediately matched. Thus an *offensive* R and D programme will be evaluated *without reference* to rival R and D expenditures. It will be based on a subjective estimate of the probability of successful innovation, and on a rather short period over which incremental profits would be available. There is a tendency then for the level of R and D expenditure to be set by the offensive strategy of the most optimistic firm. Other firms match this expenditure in self-defence.

Rivalry will also lead oligopolistic firms to speed up the introduction of process innovations. Barzel[25] analysed a simple model in which the innovator is able to license his process to his rivals at a fixed fee, h, per unit, which represents the cost saving achieved by the innovation. The market demand X is growing at a fixed rate, ρ so $X = X_0 e^{\rho t}$. The innovation has a fixed R and D 'investment' cost of I. The firm has a discount rate, r, and chooses the innovation date T so as to maximize the present value of revenue minus R and D cost:

[25] Y. Barzel, 'Optimal Timing of Innovations', *R. Econ. Stats.* 50 (1968), 348–55.

$$\text{Present value of innovation} = \int_t^\infty hX_0 e^{-(r-\rho)\tau} \cdot d\tau - I e^{-rt}$$

$$= \frac{hX_0 e^{-(r-\rho)t}}{r-\rho} - I e^{-rt}$$

This has a maximum, when

$$hX_0 e^{-(r-\rho)t} = rI e^{-rt}$$

i.e. when

$$\hat{t} = \frac{\log r + \log I - \log(hX_0)}{\rho}$$

Now, although this gives the maximum return on the innovation, the present value will be positive for a range of t which is less than the optimal $\hat{t}$. Rivalry between firms may then lead the firm to innovate earlier, when t is less than $\hat{t}$, to forestall the possibility that a rival will be able to obtain the patent first.

(b) Product innovation

For an analysis of product innovation in oligopoly, we use the concept of 'product characteristics' space developed in Chapter 3. The idea is that a differentiated product is distinguished from others by having a different mix of characteristics desired by the consumers. Consumers are thought to have rather diverse tastes spread out in characteristics space. All other things being equal, including price, consumers will purchase the commodity whose specification is nearest to their preferred point in characteristics space. On this basis the market is divided into market areas or shares. An example is given in Figure 13.5, with existing products X_1 to X_4. The purpose of product innovation then is to produce a new product with characteristics that will enable it to occupy a 'gap' in the market. The point X is a likely product in this case, if we assume that the preferences of consumers are evenly spread out in the characteristics space. A single firm may innovate in several segments of the market to build up a significant market share with several differentiated products.

The conclusion that product innovation increases the market share of the firm in a differentiated market permits an obvious analytic parallel with the effect of advertising, though the underlying con-

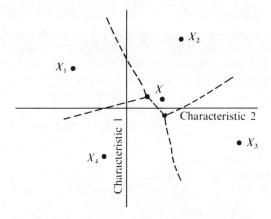

Fig. 13.5

sumer behaviour is obviously different. This has been developed by Needham.[26] Let the market share of the firm be given by

$$Q = Q(P, X, \bar{X})$$

where P is the price of the products, X is the number of products produced by the firm, and $\bar{X}$ is the number of competing products. Assume that the costs of production are given by $C[Q]$, and that each new product involves a constant cost R in research and development. Finally, let each product become obsolete over time (changes in the tastes of consumers) at a rate δ, and let the firm's discount rate (cost of capital) be α. Then the present valuation of the firm, V, is given by

$$V = \int_0^\infty (PQ - C[Q])e^{-(\alpha + \delta)t} \cdot dt$$

Let the firm now consider the incremental value of an additional product in the market, given that the costs of developing such a product are R. We use the notation ΔX to indicate an additional product. Let us suppose that it is located at X in characteristics space in the diagram, and that it is successful in attracting a proportionate share of the market. Initially then the innovator's share will go up.

[26] D. C. Needham, 'Market Structure and Firms' R and D Behaviour', *J.I.E.* 23 (1974–5), 241–55.

However the success of the product may attract imitation by other firms, who will produce a similar product after some time lag, k periods in length. This may not completely restore the old market shares, but at least the innovator will see some of his gains eroded.

The gains before successful retaliation are given by:

$$\left(P - \frac{\Delta C}{\Delta Q}\right)\frac{\Delta Q}{\Delta X}\int_0^k e^{-(\alpha+\delta)t}\cdot dt$$

The gains thereafter fall back to

$$\left(P - \frac{\Delta C}{\Delta Q}\right)\left(\frac{\Delta Q}{\Delta X} + \frac{\Delta Q}{\Delta \bar{X}}\cdot\frac{\Delta \bar{X}}{\Delta X}\right)\int_k^\infty e^{-(\alpha+\delta)t}\cdot dt$$

So the change in the value of the firm is given by adding these two expressions together and subtracting the R and D outlay to give:

$$\frac{\Delta V}{\Delta X} = \left(P - \frac{\Delta C}{\Delta Q}\right)\frac{\Delta Q}{\Delta X}\int_0^\infty e^{-(\alpha+\delta)t}\cdot dt$$

$$+ \left(P - \frac{\Delta C}{\Delta Q}\right)\left(\frac{\Delta Q}{\Delta \bar{X}}\cdot\frac{\Delta \bar{X}}{\Delta X}\right)\int_k^\infty e^{-(\alpha+\delta)t}\cdot dt - R$$

For this to be positive (i.e. for the R and D outlay to add to the valuation of the firm), we must have

$$\frac{RX}{PQ} \leqslant \left(\frac{P - \Delta C/\Delta Q}{P}\right)\left[\frac{\Delta Q}{\Delta X}\cdot\frac{X}{Q}\int_0^\infty e^{-(\alpha+\delta)t}\cdot dt\right.$$

$$+ \frac{\Delta Q}{\Delta \bar{X}}\cdot\frac{\bar{X}}{Q}\cdot\frac{X}{\bar{X}}\cdot\frac{\Delta \bar{X}}{\Delta X}\int_k^\infty e^{-(\alpha+\delta)t}\cdot dt\Bigg]$$

In the limit, across all lines of a firm's operations, we expect the strict equality to hold, i.e. all R and D projects are undertaken which give a return exceeding the firm's cost of capital. We can then interpret the equation as an expression for optimal outlays on R and D. The analogy with the case of advertising becomes clear.

Looking at the right-hand side, the first bracket is the price–cost margin (for a constant cost industry). The second bracket contains two terms. The first is the present value to the firm of the increased market share arising from the marginal new product, which we will term q^*. The second term is negative and reflects the impact of other firms' retaliation. $(\Delta Q/\Delta \bar{X})(\bar{X}/Q) = \bar{q}$ is the (arc) elasticity of the innovator's market share with respect to retaliation by the other firms.

$$\frac{X}{\bar{X}} \cdot \frac{\Delta \bar{X}}{\Delta X} \int_k^\infty e^{-(\alpha+\delta)t} \cdot dt$$

reflects both the degree of retaliation (how many new products, $\Delta \bar{X}$, will be produced to counter the innovation ΔX) and the time lag, k, before this occurs. We summarize this term by η. Making these substitutions we have:

$$\frac{RX}{PQ} = \left(\frac{P - \Delta C/\Delta Q}{P}\right)(q^* + \bar{q}\eta)$$

Our particular interest is whether q^*, $\bar{q}$, and η can be expected to vary systematically with market structure. First we note that q^*, and hence $\bar{q}$, are likely to vary mainly with the number of products. When there are few products a new one is likely to pick up a substantial share of a differentiated market. However, as the number of products increases, the size of 'gaps' in the market diminishes, and hence the share accruing to a new product.[27] This suggests that there is a limit to the degree of product proliferation in a market. Of course, the *number* of *products* is not necessarily related to the number of *firms* in any direct way. So the value of q^* and $\bar{q}$ will depend on the 'age' of the market, rather than the number of firms. η however will definitely depend on the number of firms (as in the case of advertising), though the matter is not simple. It might be thought that the fewer the firms (and hence the greater the interdependence) the greater would be the reaction, since firms would be

---

[27] For a discussion of entry into the spatial analogue of products characteristics space, see D. A. Hay, 'Sequential Entry and Entry-Deterring Strategies in Spatial Competition', *O.E.P.* 28 (1976), 240–57. The limit to the process is when no 'gap' is sufficient to cover the costs of producing a further product.

particularly sensitive to market share losses inflicted by a new product. However the very fact that products are located in characteristic space inevitably implies that a new product will impinge primarily on a few neighbouring products, and not on the market shares of all products. Hence even if the differentiated sector has a large number of firms, it is likely that a new product will provoke a sharp reaction from firms that are producing closely similar products, even if not from the majority of firms. There is however the possibility that they *cannot* react at all. This could occur if the new product neatly filled a 'gap' in the market, leaving no other 'gap' nearby in which a competitive product could be launched.

The lag before a retaliatory product can be launched is also unlikely to bear any relation to the market structure, for the same reason. Where there are a large number of competing products, a firm will need to watch developments mainly in the vicinity of its products, so that the information advantages of few firms will not be important here.

The determinants of the retaliation lag must be sought in the R and D production function. Freeman[28] has made a useful distinction between 'offensive' and 'defensive' innovation. Retaliation falls into the second category. Firms whose innovation is defensive can choose between seeking a licence from the 'offensive' firm, and making their own product. Wilson[29] has suggested that this choice depends on the nature of technology and the complexity of the product. If the sector is one with high technological opportunities arising from scientific and technical advance, the defensive firm is more likely to seek a licence from the innovator. It simply may not be possible to match the R and D effort of the 'offensive' firm. The latter may be willing to offer licences in cases where the defensive firm has a decisive advantage in marketing, for instance a specialized or geographical market. On the other hand, a differentiated product with a large number of characteristics is much easier to imitate without infringing patents. The defensive firm can profit from the mistakes (e.g. in design) made by the innovating firm, and can carry out simple modifications or improvements without a major R and D effort. In a study of 350 large U.S. firms, Wilson found that expenditure on royalties in 1971 was positively related to technological opportunity, and negatively related to product 'complexity' (as a measure of differentiation), as the above arguments would suggest. A further consequence is that in either the case of a licence or the

---

[28] Freeman, op. cit.
[29] R. W. Wilson, 'The Effect of Technological Environment and Product Rivalry on R and D Effort and the Licensing of Innovations', *R. Econ. Stats.* 59 (1977), 171–8.

case of a product imitation, the lag in retaliation need not necessarily be long.

Rivalry in R and D may also stimulate increased expenditure as rival firms race to get a patent first on a new product.[30] This point has been discussed by Scherer,[31] and Kamien and Schwartz.[32] Scherer introduced the notion that the expected completion date of an R and D project could be brought forward by increased expenditure, but with diminishing returns. Hence the present value of development costs are a decreasing function of the time period involved. Increasing time spent on the project however increases the probability that a rival firm will win the race to the patent office. Rewards are higher to the first firm to patent. Under these circumstances, it is plausible that firms will tend to shorten their projects. Kamien and Schwartz argue that the expected completion period for projects that are undertaken will be shortest when the probability of a rival's success is neither too high nor too low. Too high a probability would discourage a firm from starting on a project: too low would provide no incentive to hurry.

The final element in the equation for optimal R and D expenditures is the price–cost margin. In the analysis of advertising we assumed that this was determined by the barriers to entry to the market, including advertising itself. However in a differentiated market there is some doubt as to whether entry-deterring pricing is appropriate. The reason is that if a 'gap' in the market is sufficiently large new entry will occur in that gap. If there is no gap entry will not occur, since a new entrant could not pick up a sufficient market. Each product then can be priced by reference to its own demand curve alone. The appropriate profit maximizing price–cost margin is equal to the reciprocal of the demand elasticity. That demand elasticity in turn reflects two factors, the number of competing products in the neighbourhood of the good, and the strength of consumers' preferences for particular bundles of characteristics (see Chapter 3). So there is no reason to relate this elasticity to the number of firms, rather than the number of products.

[30] The effect of monopoly on product innovation is discussed by P. L. Swan, 'Market Structure and Technological Progress: The Influence of Monopoly on Innovation' *Q.J.E.* 84 (1970), 627–38, and L. J. White, 'A Note on the Influence of Monopoly on Product Innovation', *Q.J.E.* 86 (1972), 342–5, with 'Rejoinder' by P. L. Swan, 346–9. The conclusion is that monopolies have no incentive to delay innovation once a new product is developed. But the incentive to do R and D may well be less. These results are of no relevance to oligopoly.

[31] F. M. Scherer, 'Research and Development Resource Allocation under Rivalry', *Q.J.E.* 81 (1967), 359–94.

[32] M. I. Kamien, N. L. Schwartz, 'On the Degree of Rivalry for Maximum Innovative Activity', *Q.J.E.* 90 (1976), 245–60.

We may summarize the analysis as follows. As the market fills up with products so the cross-elasticities will increase and price–cost margins will fall. Similarly the values of q^* and $\bar{q}$ will decrease with an increase in the number of products. The value of the whole expression

$$q^* + \bar{q}\eta$$

depends on the degree of reaction to any given product innovation, and on the lag before that reaction becomes effective. Neither of these is primarily related to the number of firms, though there is some element of oligopolistic rivalry involved.

(c) Evidence on market structure and R and D

The theory outlined above suggests that market concentration will be an important determinant of expenditure on R and D, though the relationship will not be so direct for product R and D in differentiated sectors. Scherer[33] tested the theory for 58 U.S. industry groups (1960). His explanatory variables were the weighted concentration ratios of all 4-digit S.I.C. industries included in the group, dummy variables to distinguish four classes of 'technological opportunity', and dummy variables for durable/non-durable and consumer/producer goods categories. The dependent variable was the ratio of employment of scientists and engineers to total employment in each sector. Although the over-all explanation was good (the equation explained about 70 per cent of the variance in the dependent variable), the concentration variable was significant only at the 10 per cent level.[34] The 'technological opportunities' variables accounted for much of the explanation. An attempt to introduce a squared concentration term to pick up non-linearities in the relationship also failed to find statistically significant coefficients, though the signs of the coefficients suggested a relationship concave to the concentration axis. The main difficulty with interpreting these results is that concentration and the technological opportunities variables are themselves highly correlated.

The alternative to industry studies is an examination of the determinants of R and D expenditure by individual firms, seeking a test

[33] F. M. Scherer, 'Market Structure and the Employment of Scientists and Engineers', *A.E.R.* 57 (1967), 524–31.

[34] Concentration was a stronger explanatory variable in log linear equations of the same variables, but the specification is inappropriate since it requires that employment of scientists and engineers tends to zero whenever concentration does, whatever the technological opportunities.

of Scherer's hypothesis of rivalry between firms. Rosenberg[35] has suggested that while average expenditure on R and D depends on the degree of concentration in the sector, the expenditure of a firm is also influenced by its market share. A firm with a large market share will have less incentive than a small one, since its share is already large. A study of 100 large U.S. firms (from the Fortune 500 list) gave some support to this hypothesis. A more direct test of the rivalry hypothesis has been provided by Grabowski and Baxter,[36] in a study of R and D expenditures over time by 8 leading U.S. chemical firms. They found clear evidence that firms responded to the R and D initiatives of other close rivals by increasing their own expenditures with a lag of one year. The main other determinant was found to be cash flow.

6 OTHER FACTORS IN THE EVALUATION OF R AND D

(a) New entry competition and barriers to entry

We have already touched upon the possibility that firms in a differentiated market will proliferate products to fill up 'gaps' in the market and thus deter new entry. The gain arises primarily from the retention of a large market share, in this case protected against new entry rather than from incursions by existing firms. However the analysis is the same as before. Process innovation may involve larger scale of operations and thus increase the minimum economic size for a new entrant. In the Bain–Sylos-Labini model (see Chapter 6), the firms in the industry can then enjoy a larger margin of price over cost. The R and D expenditures themselves may constitute a further barrier to entry. Suppose that there is a minimum level of expenditure (presumably over time) before any R and D effect begins to produce new ideas. Then a new entrant will have to incur that block of initial expenditure before he can hope to enter and obtain returns. The difficulty is then the familiar one of imperfection of the capital market. The prospective entrant is not likely to be able to borrow to finance the initial R and D, or if he can it will be at a very high cost given the risk. The danger is, of course, that the money may all be spent without any worthwhile innovations being made.[37]

[35] J. B. Rosenberg, 'Research and Market Share: A Reappraisal of the Schumpeter Hypothesis', *J.I.E.* 25 (1976), 101–12.

[36] H. G. Grabowski, N. D. Baxter, 'Rivalry in Industrial Research and Development: An Empirical Study', *J.I.E.* 21 (1973), 209–35.

[37] Precisely the same point was made about advertising expenditure in the previous chapter.

Comanor[38] looked at the relation between R and D and barriers to entry rather differently. He made the suggestion that where existing barriers to entry were high, firms in the industry would have a reduced incentive to engage in R and D, either to reduce costs or to differentiate the product, since their profits would already be high. However the analysis of the previous section casts doubt on this suggestion, since firms will still be competing for market share. The suggestion could only be right where the primary purpose of R and D was to create barriers to entry. Not surprisingly Comanor was unable to find empirical support for the idea.

(b) Growth of the market

Schmookler[39] has presented a historical analysis of the relation between output growth and the number of patents registered in four U.S. markets—railways, horseshoes, petroleum refining, and construction. He found over long time periods that the series were closely correlated, with the important proviso that in virtually every case variations in output were found to *lead* variations in the numbers of new patents. This suggests that R and D effect is committed where the growth prospects are good and profits are likely to be high (this applies as much to individual inventors as to industrial R and D). Further, intensive use may stimulate dissatisfaction with products and processes on the part of producers and consumers, and thus lead to new thinking.

(c) Diversification of firms

The more diversified a firm is, the more likely that some R and D output will find a use in one of the existing markets of the firm. A single product firm may well reject R and D leads that do not relate directly to its own operations, with the consequence that they are not followed up. Scherer[40] found that the number of patents produced by 448 firms (drawn from the 1955 Fortune 500 list) was correlated with the number of industries (at approximately MLH level) in which they operated. At a more disaggregated level Grabowski[41] studied the R and D expenditures of large firms in three industries. Diversification, measured by the number of 5-digit industries in which each firm was involved, was significant for chemicals and drugs, but not for petroleum. There is, however, as Scherer points out, a query as to the direction of causation in these studies.

[38] W. S. Comanor, 'Market Structure, Product Differentiation and Industrial Research', *Q.J.E.* 81 (1967), 639-57.

[39] J. Schmookler, 'Economic Sources of Inventive Activity', *J. Econ. Hist.* 22 (1962), 1-20.

[40] Scherer, op. cit. (1965).   [41] Grabowski, op. cit. (1968).

Innovation is a major vehicle for growth of the firm by diversification into new markets. So a large number of patents may reflect the process of diversification, rather than a given level of diversification being an incentive to patenting.

7   THE INNOVATING FIRM

Schumpeter's original hypothesis linked size of firm and innovation for three distinct reasons. First, only a large firm could bear the cost of R and D programmes. Second, a large and diversified firm could absorb failures by innovating on a wide front. Third, it needs some element of market 'control' to reap the rewards of innovation. These three possibilities have been explored in the previous sections of this chapter. Here we will summarize the evidence as it relates to Schumpeter's hypothesis. First, we found that the flow of previous profits is an important determinant of expenditure on R and D, but there is no strong evidence to suggest that large firms spend proportionately more than small ones among those firms that actually do R and D. Second, there is no strong evidence of increasing returns to R and D itself, though *a priori* there are good reasons (e.g. indivisibilities, better scientists) for expecting it. Third, there are theoretical reasons for expecting concentration to be a determinant of R and D expenditure, though these relate more to the rivalry of oligopolistic competition than the incentive of assured markets in 'monopolized' sectors. Within such a market, the R and D efforts of a particular firm will depend also on the competitive stance adopted by the firm. Some may adopt an 'offensive strategy', in an attempt to lead the market. According to Freeman,[42] such firms will maintain good contacts with basic science (possibly having their own 'in-house' basic research), will be R and D intensive compared to their rivals, and attach importance to securing patents. R and D personnel will also be involved in marketing. The defensive firm, on the other hand, will simply seek to match the product and process innovations of other firms, accepting that it will lag in those areas, but relying on strength in some other area, for example, marketing. But the distinction between 'offensive' and 'defensive' strategy firms is not necessarily to be made on the basis of size. Rosenberg's evidence[43] suggests that larger firms may have a lesser incentive. Fourth, diversification does give the innovating firm a wider choice of markets, and thus reduce the risks of R and D.

It is not therefore surprising that the size of firm is in practice an important determinant of R and D. Freeman[44] shows that R and D

---

[42] Freeman, op. cit.   [43] Rosenberg, op. cit.   [44] Freeman, op. cit., Ch. 6.

programmes are highly concentrated in all O.E.C.D. countries, with the top 100 programmes accounting for as much as 80 per cent of total R and D expenditure. These programmes are to be found in firms with more than 5,000 employees, while most small firms do no R and D in any formal sense. Small firms have contributed (along with private inventors) disproportionately to the number of inventions. But it has been left to larger firms, with their greater resources, to bring inventions to innovation. Freeman studied 1,100 innovations in 50 U.K. industries, in 1945–70, and found that no less than 80 per cent were accounted for by firms with over 1,000 employees. However he also found that the pattern varied between industries. In some sectors, such as aerospace, motor vehicles, pharmaceuticals, and dyestuffs, all the innovation was by large firms. In others, small firms had a more proportionate share of innovation.

So we accept that the Schumpeter hypothesis is not disproved by the evidence, though we might wish to explain the causal links slightly differently, especially the effects of market structure. However, existing studies can be effectively criticized for their concentration on a single aspect of the relationship of R and D expenditure and market structure. This is a model where R and D expenditure/innovation at the level of the market is explained by (i) technological opportunity, (ii) the degree of product differentiation, (iii) concentration leading to rivalry, and (iv) industry profitability, both as a source of funds and as an incentive. For an individual firm, its own expenditures relative to the industry average will be determined by the strategy that it adopts. But two other causal links are at least plausible.[45] The first relates the profitability of a market to the barriers to entry created by a high level of R and D expenditure. Process innovation, especially linked to patents, may effectively debar entrants. Product innovation may fill up the characteristics space, and thus deter entry. The second relates the level of concentration to R and D expenditures in the past, and will be explored in Chapter 15. The correlation of 'technological opportunity' variables and concentration, noted by Scherer,[46] is particularly noteworthy. Until these relationships are systematically incorporated in the analysis, the results reported in this chapter can only be regarded as provisional.

[45] The argument is developed by analogy with the case of advertising. See the exposition of Weiss and Strickland's work in the previous chapter, section 6 (L. W. Weiss, A. D. Strickland, 'Advertising, Concentration and Price–Cost Mrrgins', *J.P.E.* 84 (1976), 1109–21.

[46] Scherer, op. cit. (1965).

8   DIFFUSION OF NEW TECHNIQUES

This section examines the rate at which an innovation spreads to other firms. Evidence suggests that this can be very variable. An early example was given by Salter.[47] In U.S. blast furnaces the average productivity of plant was only at half the level of the 'best practice' technology—i.e. that of new plants. It took 15 years for average productivity to reach the best practice level in a given year. In a more recent study of the processes in nine sectors across a number of countries, Ray[48] found that the rate of diffusion of new technology varied markedly between sectors, and between the same sector in different countries. He noted particularly that 'pioneer' countries with new technology tended to have slower diffusion rates. Romeo[49] examined the rate at which numerically controlled machine tools were adopted in ten different sectors. He took the average time lag for firms to move from 10 per cent to 60 per cent numerically controlled, and found it varied from 2·3 years for industrial instruments to 6·1 for aircraft engines, and 6·5 for farm machinery. Furthermore, the lag can differ substantially *within* firms, as Mansfield[50] showed for the introduction of diesel locomotives in U.S. railroads. Such examples have prompted a number of studies of diffusion.

The theory of technical diffusion was thoroughly explored by Salter.[51] He constructed a simple theory on the following assumptions: (i) the embodiment assumption that all innovation requires investment in new physical capital; (ii) a competitive market with static demand; (iii) information on the new technique is free: there is no patent system. The theory is most easily expounded diagrammatically (see Figure 13.6). The initial situation is given by the intersection of demand and supply curves. The supply curve is shown as representing the labour cost only of different plants or groups of plants labelled according to the vintage of capital they incorporate. The newest capital is represented by 1, the oldest by 6. The assumption is that labour costs will be less on the newer stock.

Suppose now there is an innovation with total costs (including capital costs) less than the labour costs of vintages 5 and 6. In a competitive market, with information on the innovation freely available, the market price will fall to the total cost of the latest

[47] W. E. G. Salter, *Productivity and Technical Change*, 2nd edn., with addendum by W. B. Reddaway (Cambridge, 1966).

[48] G. F. Ray, 'The Diffusion of New Techniques: A Study of Ten Processes in Nine Countries', *N.I.E.R.* 48 (1969), 40–83.

[49] A. A. Romeo, 'Interindustry and Interfirm Differences in the Rate of Diffusion of an Invention', *R. Econ. Stats.* 57 (1975), 311–19.

[50] E. Mansfield, *Industrial Research and Technological Innovation* (New York, 1968).

[51] Salter, op. cit.

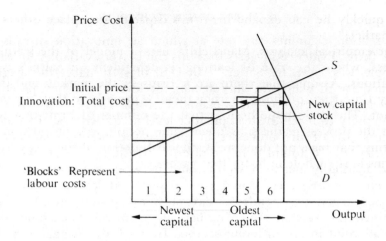

Fig. 13.6

technique. The new capital stock will replace vintages 5 and 6, plus the slight increment in industry demand derived from the elasticity of the demand curve. However, the vintages of capital 1–4 will continue in operation. The reason is that at the new price they continue to earn quasi-rents over labour costs. There would therefore be no economic rationale in abandoning them until they wear out or until a further change in techniques so reduces cost that they too are eliminated by competitors.

The conclusion of this analysis is that diffusion of the new techniques will be limited by economic factors, and not only by ignorance. The amount of new capital incorporating the new techniques will depend specifically on the degree of cost reduction leading to retirement of obsolete capital and on the small degree of expansion in output due to demand elasticity. We can extend the analysis to monopoly, noting that a monopolist will take on less capital stock since he will expand along the marginal revenue curve, not along the demand curve. Further, existence of patent fees will increase the current costs of using the new technique, and will reduce the degree to which it is adopted. The assumption of a static demand is unrealistic: an innovation will diffuse more rapidly in a growing market. Finally we note that the rate of diffusion depends on the owner of the patent, where a patent can be enforced. He may for example use his cost advantage to drive competitors out of business (assuming that the labour costs of some of these exceed his total cost with the new technique). The rate of diffusion then depends on how quickly he can expand his firm's capacity to replace others in the market.

For empirical analysis, Mansfield[52] uses a model of the learning process, where the 'rate of learning' is dependent on Salter's considerations. Assume that there are n firms in the market, and that at any time t, m_t of these are using the new process, so that $(n - m_t)$ are not. The basic hypothesis is that the number of firms that will adopt the process in the subsequent time period, as a proportion of all firms that have not done so, is a linear function of the proportion of firms in the whole industry that have: i.e.

$$\frac{m_{t+1} - m_t}{n - m_t} = \psi \frac{m_t}{n}$$

where ψ is a constant. Then we can approximate

$$\frac{dm_t}{dt} = \psi \frac{m_t}{n}(n - m_t)$$

Integrating, and recalling that the initial value of m_t was zero, we obtain

$$m_t = \frac{n}{1 + e^{-(k + \psi t)}}$$

where k is the constant of integration, or as a proportion of the firms in the industry:

$$\frac{m_t}{n} = \frac{1}{1 + e^{-(k + \psi t)}}$$

The empirical justification for this model is that it generates an S-shaped logistic curve which accords well with the observed pattern of diffusion of innovations over time. That is, a slow start, a rapid middle phase, and a long slow tail of technical laggards (see Figure 13.7). The precise position of the curve is determined by the value of the parameter ψ, which is the 'rate of learning'.

This model has generated a number of studies of the value of ψ,

[52] Mansfield, op. cit., Ch. 7.

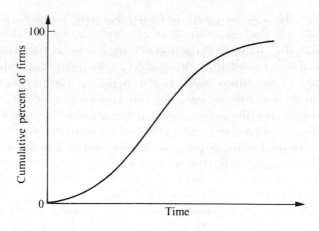

Fig. 13.7

derived by fitting logistic curves to the actual diffusion paths of various innovations. Mansfield's own work concerned diffusion of innovations in coal-mining, iron and steel, brewing and railroads. He hypothesized that ψ was determined by (i) the extent of the cost advantage over existing methods, (ii) uncertainty, (iii) rate at which initial uncertainty is dispelled by evidence of successful use, (iv) the size of the initial capital investment required. For analysis he reduced this to a size variable, and a profitability variable based on the 'payback' periods estimated by the firms. He found that these two variables could explain a great deal of the variance in ψ. He had insufficient evidence to test various subsidiary hypotheses, for example that ψ is smaller (diffusion is slower) if the innovation replaces equipment that is very durable, or that ψ is larger if the market is expanding rapidly. Romeo[53] adopted the methodology developed by Mansfield in a study of the diffusion of numerically controlled machine tools among 152 firms in 10 U.S. industries. He sought to explain variations in ψ between industries by a concentration variable, a scale variable and a variable for expenditure on R and D. Concentration was measured by the number of firms, and the variance of the logs of their size. It was expected that the first would have a positive relation with the rate of diffusion, whereas size inequality would be an inhibiting factor. Expenditure on R and D was expected to make firms more receptive to new ideas, and thus speed up diffusion. These expectations were confirmed. It was particularly notable that concentration, in its inequality aspect, was a deterrent

[53] Romeo, op. cit.

to diffusion. In a subsequent analysis, Romeo[54] added the date of introduction of the innovation as an explanatory variable, on the grounds that the rate of imitation *generally* has been speeding up over time. Metcalfe[55] found that the size of investment required, and the profitability of the innovation, as measured by the payback period, were the main determinants of the rate of diffusion of innovation in the Lancashire textile industry in the U.K. More puzzling is the evidence for different rates of diffusion of innovations in the same sector but in different countries, as discovered by Ray.[56] Globerman[57] addressed himself to this question in a study of the rate of diffusion of numerically controlled machine tools in the tool-and-die industry in the U.S. and Canada. He found that the rate of diffusion for the U.S. was approximately four times the ψ for Canada. He concluded that much of the difference could be explained by the relative sizes of firms and their degree of specialization. U.S. firms were larger and more specialized, so that they had the longer production runs to justify the more specialized technology. This rather particular explanation is not of much help in explaining the more general differences uncovered by Ray for other sectors.

A second question raised by diffusion concerns the types of firms that are quick to adopt new technology. Mansfield[58] suggested that size of firm was the main determinant, given the profitability of the innovation. Larger firms are more able to meet the conditions for any particular innovation, and so their speed of response is likely to be faster. He tested this hypothesis for 14 innovations in coal, iron and steel, brewing, and railroads, and found that the elasticity of the time lag with respect to firm size was of the order of −0·4, i.e. a 10 per cent increase in size was associated with a 4 per cent reduction in the time lag between the initial innovation and the time it was adopted by the firm. Carter and Williams[59] had earlier suggested that managerial attitudes were also a determinant of the willingness to adopt new techniques quickly. This suggestion was taken up by Mansfield,[60] Globerman,[61] Metcalfe,[62] and Romeo.[63] Attention has

---

[54] A. A. Romeo, 'Rate of Imitation of a Capital-Embodied Process Innovation', *Economica* 44 (1977), 63–70.

[55] J. S. Metcalfe, 'Diffusion of Innovation in the Lancashire Textile Industry', *Manchester School*, 38 (1970), 145–62.

[56] Ray, op. cit.

[57] S. Globerman, 'Technological Diffusion in the Canadian Tool and Die Industry', *R. Econ. Stats.* 59 (1975), 428–34.

[58] Mansfield, op. cit., Ch. 8.

[59] C. F. Carter, B. R. Williams, *Investment in Innovation* (London, 1958).

[60] E. Mansfield, 'Industrial Research and Development: Characteristics, Costs and Diffusion of Results', *A.E.R. Papers and Proceedings*, 59 (1969), 65–79.

[61] Globerman, op. cit.   [62] Metcalfe, op. cit.   [63] Romeo, op. cit. (1977).

been focused on the age of the firm's top manager, and on his education, or on the number of scientists and engineers employed by the firm, but there is little empirical support for the hypothesis.

One important determinant of the rate of diffusion, which has not yet been discussed, is the impact of the patent system. Taylor and Silberston[64] obtained information from 44 U.K. companies in five research-oriented U.K. industries.[65] In respect to questions concerning the granting of licences, only 3 out of 26 respondents said that they had refused to grant a licence in the 1966–8 period. But at least half the firms acknowledged that there were some patents for which they would not grant licences if they were asked. Outright refusals of patents were uncommon in the chemicals and pharmaceuticals sectors largely because firms were willing to *exchange* information, granting licences reciprocally. Taylor and Silberston conclude that large firms had a reasonable approach to licensing, especially where the licence was requested by foreign firms not operating in the U.K. domestic market. Scherer *et al.*[66] found a similar pattern in a survey of American firms. Large firms adopted a more liberal attitude than small ones, though most firms agreed that there were certain important patents that they would not be willing to license. But as Taylor and Silberston note, refusal to grant a licence seldom has a serious impact on competitors. Usually firms were able to find a substitute technology, or were prepared to purchase a key component from the patent-holder. Imitative R and D was concentrated on product differentiation. This survey evidence accords well with the data on licensing of innovations presented by Wilson.[67] He argued that licensing was an alternative to R and D. Firms would seek licences for major technical advances, rather than trying to market the original innovation from their own R and D. But they would use R and D to create differentiated products in sectors characterized by complex products (i.e. ones involving combinations of already known features in different characteristic mixes). An analysis of 350 large U.S. firms showed that royalty spending was positively related to technological opportunity variables, reflecting the importance of the patents in those sectors. But R and D expenditure was positively related to the 'complexity' of the product specification, as expected. The conclusion is that the

---

[64] C. T. Taylor, Z. A. Silberston, *The Economic Impact of the Patent System* (Cambridge, 1973).

[65] Similar work is reviewed by F. M. Scherer, *The Economic Effects of Compulsory Patent Licensing*, New York University Graduate School of Business Administration, Centre for the Study of Financial Institutions, Monograph Series in Finance and Economics (1977).

[66] Ibid. 56.   [67] R. W. Wilson, op. cit. (28).

existence of patents is not likely to be a serious barrier to the diffusion of technology between firms in general, though there may be specific examples of refusal to grant licences where it is.

MERGERS AND THE STOCK MARKET

In the three previous chapters we described the ways in which the firm can use accumulated funds to escape the constraints of its existing cost structure and market share. It can invest in new capacity, it can put resources into R and D, and it can spend on marketing its products. In each case the firm acquires and organizes new factors of production. The purpose of this chapter is to explore the alternative possibility that the firm may acquire resources already organized in the form of a firm by merger or takeover.[1] The purchase of a 'going concern' will always have some attractive features. A merger will involve none of the delays that may arise in the execution of an investment programme. There will probably be less risk, as the acquiring firm can draw on the experience of the acquisition. This is particularly true where the firm is using acquisition to overcome a barrier to entry into a sector into which it wishes to diversify. A merger will also enable the firm to grow without increasing the total capacity in a sector. These issues will be explored in more detail below.

Merger activity has played an important part in the development of firms in all the advanced capitalist economies. The merger movements in the U.S. and the U.K. have been fully described elsewhere.[2] Two points of interest can be drawn from these studies. First, merger activity tends to follow a cyclical pattern with periodic booms in merger activity followed by more quiescent periods. Second, these booms are correlated, though not precisely, with the cycles in general economic activity and the cycle in stock market prices. Nelson[3] suggests that, in the U.S., merger activity peaks before the stock market, with the trade cycle lagging both. These results have led a number of writers to propose a 'macroeconomic' theory of merger activity.

[1] We do not propose to distinguish in this analysis between 'mergers', signifying a voluntary amalgamation of the firms, and 'takeover', which implies an unwilling partner. Casual observation suggests that the difference between the two does not have an economic significance. It may simply reflect a clash over the ownership or control of the joint assets, which may be as much attributable to differences in personality of managers and owners as to anything else.

[2] R. L. Nelson, in W. W. Alberts, J. E. Segall, *The Corporate Merger* (Chicago, 1966), 52–66; K. D. George, Z. A. Silberston, 'The Causes and Effects of Mergers', *S.J.P.E.* 22 (1975), 179–93; G. D. Newbould, *Management and Merger Activity* (Liverpool, 1970).

[3] Nelson, op. cit.

At first sight the timing of the merger and stock market cycles seems a little curious. As the stock market rises and falls, so will the values of both acquirers and victims. Discrepancies in stock market valuation are likely to be greatest when share price movements are greatest, that is in the rising and falling periods, not at the peak or trough. This could explain the greater merger activity in the upswings, but not the lack of activity in downswings. The lack of conventional financial reasons for the merger booms has led to the formulation of theories[4] that emphasize the state of business confidence or expectations. The starting-point for such theories is that the rise in general economic activity creates disequilibrium in product markets. At the same time expectations about conditions are generally favourable. Mergers are the first stage in the attempt to reach a new equilibrium, especially since they can quickly become effective. And they increase the firm's size, and hence its sense of security and its base for undertaking the risks of internal growth. Once mergers are undertaken by a few leading firms, they become 'fashionable', according to Newbould.[5] Mergers create more uncertainty for the firms that have not been involved in merger themselves. Some evidence for this kind of explanation of merger booms is given by George and Silberston.[6] They point out that merger booms were much more violent in the U.S. than in the U.K. prior to 1956. The reason they suggest is that restrictive agreements between firms in the U.K. (curtailed in 1956) permitted an orderly response to changed market conditions, so that the merger response was not necessary.

Even if the timing of merger activity can be explained in the above terms, it still leaves open the need to develop a microeconomic explanation of mergers. This will survey the causes and consequences of mergers at the level of the firm. The exposition will emphasize analysis rather than description, so it may seem unduly abstract to those who have observed the in-fighting of an actual merger situation. The framework for all arguments to be presented is the functioning of the capital assets markets. The most evident of these markets is the stock market, in its day-to-day operations. In Chapter 10 we discussed the role of capital markets in supplying new funds to firms with good investment prospects. But new issues are generally a minor part of the operations of a stock market. By far the most important activity is trading in the shares of existing companies, representing the transfer of part of the ownership of the company from the seller to the buyer. The stock market acts as a market for the 'second-hand'

[4] M. Gort, 'An Economic Disturbance Theory of Mergers', *Q.J.E.* 83 (1969), 624–42.
[5] Newbould, op. cit. [6] George and Silberston, op. cit.

bundle of assets that each firm represents. Not every firm is 'quoted' of course, but the same principles apply to unquoted companies, except that in the case of an entirely private company there may be no shares as such and acquisition must involve the whole firm. The value of an asset reflects the market's evaluation of the prospects and risks of holding it. This is explored in the next section of the chapter, and forms the basis for the analysis of mergers in the subsequent sections. First we examine the gains from horizontal and vertical mergers in those cases where pre-merger firms are utilizing their resources efficiently in the interests of their owners. Second we look at the special case of conglomerate mergers under the same assumptions of efficiency in both the asset market and the firm. A third motive for merger is that a firm is able to identify merger bargains in the form of firms that are not using profitable resources efficiently. We are interested in this possibility not only from the point of view of the growth and diversification of the firm, but also because the fear of takeover has been identified by Marris as constraining firms to use resources efficiently and as a limitation in the pursuit of managerial objectives. In other words, if this takeover constraint is dominant, it will cast light on the effectiveness of the stock market as an instrument of economic efficiency, transferring assets from ineffective managements to more efficient ones. Finally, section 5 deals with the possibility that the managers of firms can pursue a merger policy to suit their own objectives, without regard to the best interests of the share-holders. We would emphasize that this classification of motives for mergers need not be exclusive in any particular merger. A merger may contain real possibilities of economies deriving from integration of the firms' activities, may involve increased efficiency in the use of resources formerly misused by one of the firms, and at the same time be motivated by a managerial growth objective. The classification serves only for pedagogic purposes.

1   THE STOCK MARKET VALUATION OF FIRMS

The valuation of risky assets involves a number of issues that are not yet fully resolved, either empirically or theoretically. An asset (e.g. a share in a firm) gives a prospect of returns over time. The market evaluation of that stream of returns involves both the rate of time discount, and another factor to allow for the riskiness of the un-certain returns. The most complete theoretical construct is the capital asset pricing model associated with the names of Sharpe,

Lintner, and Mossin,[7] and surveyed in Jensen.[8] We will set out this model first before proceeding to more empirical matters.

The theory makes seven assumptions of greater or less importance. All asset holders are single period expected utility of wealth maximizers who choose their asset portfolios on the basis of mean and variance of return. They can borrow or lend at a risk-free interest rate. They have identical subjective estimates of the means, variances, and covariances of returns in all assets. And they are price takers, so that the asset markets are perfectly competitive. The quantities of assets are fixed. All are perfectly divisible and perfectly liquid, i.e. they are all marketable without transactions costs. Finally, there are no taxes.

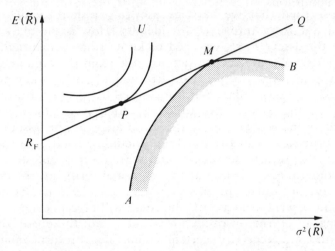

Fig. 14.1

We begin the analysis with the hypothetical exercise of constructing varying portfolios of risky assets and determining their mean return $E(\tilde{R})$ and their variance of return $\sigma^2(\tilde{R})$. From this exercise we can derive a frontier of efficient portfolios, those portfolios which involve the least risk for a given level of return. The frontier is shown in Figure 14.1 by the line AMB, appropriately shaded to show that it is a frontier of the set of all portfolios. We now identify the return R_F on the ordinate, as the return to the same wealth invested in the riskless asset. Given the assumption that the individual asset holder can lend or borrow at this rate, it is apparent that his

[7] W. F. Sharpe, *Portfolio Theory and Capital Markets* (New York, 1970); J. Lintner, 'The Valuation of Risk Assets and the Selection of Risky Investments in Stock Portfolio and Capital Budgets', *R. Econ. Stats.* 47 (1965), 13–37; J. Mossin, 'Equilibrium in a Capital Asset Market', *Econometrica* 34 (1966), 763–83.

[8] M. C. Jensen, 'Capital Markets: Theory and Evidence', *Bell Journal* 3 (1972), 357–98.

most efficient portfolio must lie on the line $R_F MQ$, which he reaches by appropriate combinations of investment in the risk-free asset and the market portfolio of risky assets denoted by M. For example, the asset holder with preference function U will hold his wealth in the combinations denoted by the point P, i.e. the proportion $R_F P/R_F M$ in the risk-free asset. The important point to note is that whatever the utility function of the asset holder he will always hold his risky assets in the proportions given by the market portfolio at M. Furthermore there is a unique price of risk in this model given by the slope of $R_F MQ$, which indicates the rate at which the market is willing to trade extra risk for increased return. We will call this price of risk Θ.

Suppose then that we have an asset (e.g. a share) which gives an expected but risky return D_j (dividends). How is the market likely to value the asset? First, we need to know what adjustment will be made for risk. We derived a price for risk from the argument above, but that price was for the risk attached to the market portfolio. So the risk of a particular asset is measured by its contribution to the variance of the market portfolio of which it is one element. In statistical terminology, this is the covariance of the asset's returns with all other assets in the portfolio (including itself!), or the degree to which the returns are correlated with returns on other assets.[9] This is sometimes described as the 'systematic risk' of the portfolio. There may, of course, be unsystematic variable elements in the return on the asset, but in a portfolio these will be cancelled out by the unsystematic returns on other assets and do not therefore contribute to portfolio variance. The 'certainty equivalent' return on an asset j, then, can be derived by subtracting from the dividend return its

---

[9] In the figure, the returns over time to one dollar invested in the market portfolio are shown by M. Share A gives returns which vary *less* than the market portfolio, though the time pattern is the same. It therefore contributes less to the variance of returns on the market portfolio than share B, which gives returns with a greater variability. The *covariance* of B with the market portfolio is greater than the covariance of A.

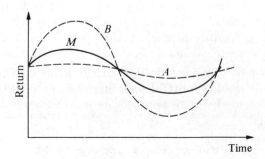

covariance with the market portfolio multiplied by the market price
of risk;

i.e. $\bar{D}_j - \Theta \, \text{cov}(\tilde{D}_j, \tilde{D}_M)$

where the bar indicates the mean return, and the tildes indicate
random variables. Thus $\text{cov}\,(\tilde{D}_j, \tilde{D}_M)$ is the covariance of the random
return with the random return on the market portfolio $\tilde{D}_M$. Having
converted the return to its 'certainty equivalent', the valuation of the
asset is simply derived by discounting at the risk-free rate R_F as if it
were a certain stream of returns over time. So the valuation V_j is
given by

$$V_j = \frac{1}{R_F} \, [\bar{D}_j - \Theta \, \text{cov}(\tilde{D}_j, \tilde{D}_M)]$$

The simplicity of this model is appealing, not least since the main
elements can be identified empirically, when the equation is cast in
the form of a rate of return to one unit of wealth invested in the
risky asset. The return then comprises two elements. The first is the
risk-free interest rate. The second is an addition for risk, the product
of the market price of risk, and the covariance of the asset's return
with the market portfolio,

i.e. $\qquad E(\tilde{R}_j) = R_F + \Theta \, \text{cov}(\tilde{R}_j, \tilde{R}_M)$

Recalling that $\quad \Theta = \dfrac{E(\tilde{R}_M) - R_F}{\sigma^2(\tilde{R}_M)}$, we can substitute

$$E(\tilde{R}_j) = R_F + [E(\tilde{R}_M) - R_F] \, \frac{\text{cov}(\tilde{R}_j, \tilde{R}_M)}{\sigma^2(\tilde{R}_M)}$$

$$= R_F + [E(\tilde{R}_M) - R_F] \cdot \beta_j.$$

The value of β_j, the contribution of the asset's covariance to the
variance of the market portfolio, is derived by regressing the asset
yields on the yields from an appropriate market portfolio, over time.
Then the test is

$$\bar{R}_j = \gamma_0 + \gamma_1 \beta_j + \epsilon_j$$

where γ_0 and γ_1 are regression coefficients, and ϵ_j is a random error term. The expectation is that $\gamma_0 = R_F$ and $\gamma_1 = (\tilde{R}_M - R_F)$. However Jensen's careful review of empirical work suggests that the model is not entirely satisfactory. The coefficient γ_0 is usually too large, while γ_1 is too small when compared with appropriate observed values. Furthermore, the equation explains more when an additional variable, the own-variance of the asset's yield, is added to the regression. Within the strict logic of the simple capital asset pricing model, the own-variance should not appear at all. The strict assumptions of the model can be relaxed in various ways to make them more acceptable (see Jensen's article), but none of these amendments alters the basic conclusion that in a perfect equity market it is the covariance rather than the own-variance which should determine asset prices and yields. Perhaps the most important amendment is that of Lintner,[10] who introduces heterogeneity of expectations. The effect of this is that the 'separation theorem' no longer holds, i.e. the existence of a single market portfolio held by all asset holders (though in different proportions). $E(\tilde{R}_j)$, $\mathrm{cov}(\tilde{R}_j, \tilde{R}_M)$ and Θ all are complex weighted averages involving the individual utility functions of asset holders. The frontier of efficient portfolios will vary between asset holders depending on their expectations. Hence the point M will represent a different portfolio for each, and individual share portfolios will differ. Reasons for the empirical inadequacies of the capital asset pricing model may be sought in three areas. First, the actual asset markets may not be efficient at reflecting the real variables like returns and risk, and instead may be subject to 'errors' arising from the operations of the asset markets themselves (e.g. speculation, transactions costs, monopoly positions in the market for assets). It is not difficult to imagine that such imperfections could exist. However we need to know whether in practice they grossly distort the relationship between returns and asset prices. Second, the capital asset pricing model may presume a skill in portfolio analysis which exceeds that of operators in the market. If the actual asset holders form their portfolios on a less sophisticated system (e.g. evaluating assets on the basis of own-variance) then this will be reflected in empirical asset values. Third, there may be uncertainty as to what properly constitutes the earnings of an asset, in particular what weight should be attached to retentions, and what allowances to make for new issues and new debt in valuing the firm. We will now take these three issues in more detail.

The issue of efficiency in the capital markets has been surveyed by

[10] J. Lintner, 'The Aggregation of Investors' Diverse Judgements and Preferences in Purely Competitive Markets', *Journal of Financial and Quantitative Analysis*, 4 (1969).

Fama.[11] He defines an efficient capital market[12] as one where the prices of shares fully reflect all available information. He identifies three potential sources of inefficiency: (a) transactions costs; (b) information not being freely available to all asset holders; (c) some asset holders are better at interpreting available information than others. The weak form of the efficient market hypothesis asserts that a portfolio holder cannot use past and current share price information to earn a return consistently greater than a holder who uses a random method to choose a portfolio with the same risk. One test is to examine whether share price changes follow a random walk with serial covariances zero between all successive time periods; i.e. changes in share prices in one time period are not systematically related to changes in previous time periods. The idea is that the market adjusts to the flow of information coming to it. If the information comes randomly, then one expects the share price to reflect the latest 'news', rather than any previous patterns of share price movements. If price changes are related between time periods, a portfolio holder who understood this pattern could make an excess return. Most evidence suggests that one-period covariances are zero, but it is possible to discern some more complex relationships over greater lags. However the transaction costs involved would swamp any excess return. An alternative test is to examine market trading rules which have been proposed by transactors. In principle these could only be effective if price changes follow some specific pattern over time. Again no 'rule' appears to be profitable once transactions costs are considered. The 'semi-strong' form of the hypothesis suggests that the prices of shares will always reflect all publicly available information. The test is to examine the reaction of share prices to new information, for example dividend announcements as an indicator of firm performance, profit figures. Allowing for the fact that some 'insiders' may have information before it is made public, the evidence is that the market adjusts swiftly and completely to the information. Finally, we may look at the 'strong' form of the hypothesis: that share prices reflect accurately all *relevant* information whether public or not. The implication would be that even 'insiders' would not be able to make a return exceeding the market return. On

[11] E. Fama, 'Efficient Capital Markets: A Review of Theory and Empirical Work', *J. of Finance, Papers and Proceedings*, 25 (1970), 383–423.

[12] This notion of efficiency is primarily concerned with the functioning of the asset market. It does not extend to the broader notions of the asset market promoting efficiency on the real side of the economy (a) by transferring ownership of existing assets to those who will produce the most from them, (b) by allocating new savings to the most efficient investment uses. Though these latter concepts of efficiency could not be attained without an 'efficient capital market' in the more limited sense intended here.

the face of it this seems unlikely. Some individuals are bound to have privileged access to information, and to be able to use it. However that may be insignificant if their numbers are few and the information lag to the general public is short. Collins[13] produced evidence to show that share prices did not reflect fully the situation of the firms. He examined the share prices of diversified companies where the breakdown of profits between sectors of the company only became available after aggregate profit figures were declared. He found that the breakdown gave a better indication of profit potential but this potential was *not* reflected in share prices until it became public at a later date. This strongly suggests that share prices do not reflect the circumstances of the firms fully and accurately. We shall return to this below. Given this situation one would expect some portfolio holders to obtain above average returns simply because they have better information. For example, unit trust managers should surely do better than he market. However Jensen's work[14] reaches the surprising conclusion that on the average they perform less well than the market, even before expenses are taken into account. We conclude that ignorance may lead to a less than perfect correlation between asset prices and the underlying real returns of the firms, but that this divergence is not systematically exploited by any group of operators in the market.

Our second query about the capital asset pricing model concerns the realism of the model as a description of actual portfolio behaviour. Whatever the normative merits of the model, it may well be that holders of shares are more simplistic in their evaluation of alternative portfolios. One particular theory, advanced by Modigliani and Miller,[15] is that holders group shares according to their risk class, all shares in the same class having the same risky pattern of returns. Then the returns to all shares in that class are discounted at a rate ρ, which is the market rate appropriate to that class. Exactly how ρ varies between classes is not made clear: it has no particular theoretical basis. It is not necessarily inconsistent with the capital asset pricing model, if it is made clear that the risk which matters is the contribution of the shares in a class to market portfolio variance, and if the grouping of shares in classes is done on the basis of *perfect* correlation of their returns.[16] A little algebra makes this clear.

[13] D. Collins, 'SEC Product Line Reporting and Market Efficiency', *J. of Financial Economics*, 2 (1975).

[14] M. C. Jensen, 'The Performance of Mutual Funds in the Period 1945-64', *J. of Finance* 23 (1968), 389-416.

[15] F. Modigliani, M. Miller, 'The Cost of Capital, Corporation Fir ance and the Theory of Investment', *A.E.R.* 48 (1958), 261-97.

[16] As Modigliani and Miller presume.

Capital asset pricing model

$$V_j = \frac{1}{R_f}[\bar{D}_j - \Theta \operatorname{cov}(\tilde{D}_j, D_m)]$$

$$= \frac{\bar{D}_j}{R_f}\left[1 - \Theta \frac{\operatorname{cov}(\tilde{D}_j, D_m)}{\bar{D}_j}\right]$$

For all firms in the same risk class, so defined, the term in square brackets is a constant, λ.

Risk class approach $\qquad V_j = \dfrac{\bar{D}_j}{\rho}$

The two are equivalent if $\qquad \dfrac{1}{\rho} = \dfrac{\lambda}{R_f}$

However the risk class approach can also be based on the more traditional (naive?) analysis where the risk class is determined by each share's own variance of returns.[17] Perhaps the results of the tests of the capital asset pricing model can be best interpreted as evidence that shareholders *do* take account of own-variance in assessing the value of a share. This may reflect either inability to diversify fully to a market portfolio position, or ignorance of the effects of portfolio diversification. Either way the model is not redundant yet.

The third issue arises from the definition of the earnings of an asset, particularly as these are split between retentions and dividends. This issue was discussed in detail in Chapter 9 (pp. 334–353). Comparison of internal and external financing of growth showed that, in a market without taxation and the threat of bankruptcy, the valuation in the case of growth by new issues is identical to the valuation in the case of retentions financing. We are operating in a Modigliani–Miller 'world' where the finance of the firm is irrelevant to its valuation (and its operations). The explanation is that a national asset holder is quite indifferent as to dividends or capital gains. If the firm pays low dividends, and he needs cash, he can simply dispose of a part of his holding. If on the other hand the firm pays out everything in dividends and finances itself by new issues, the asset holder who prefers to accumulate can simply subscribe for the new issues.

[17] A. A. Robichek, S. C. Myers, *Optimal Financing Decisions* (Englewood Cliffs, 1968), Ch. 3.

Unfortunately we have to leave the subject of a firm's market valuation without any very firm conclusions. The capital asset pricing model does not seem to correspond exactly to the actual process of asset valuation in stock markets. The risk class approach leaves the discount rate unexplained. The market seems to show a definite preference for dividends, so the strategy adopted by the firm in its financing decisions is not unimportant. Perhaps the most useful result for what follows is the conclusion that a semi-strong concept of market efficiency seems to apply. That is, however the market values assets, it certainly responds quickly to changes in the published information about the firms. The lack of response to unpublished information suggests that we may be able in some cases to drive a wedge between the market value of an asset and the real valuation of the firm that it represents. This is clearly important for the consideration of merger activity.

2　MERGERS IN A CAPITALIST UTOPIA

The purpose of this section is to set out the reasons for merger activity in a pure capitalist world. This is the traditional theory of merger activity which occupies a major part in the literature.[18] We describe the hypothetical conditions as a capitalist Utopia for the following reasons. First, managers are assumed to be entirely efficient in the use of resources. There is no X-inefficiency or slack in the internal allocation of resources, and those resources are deployed externally in the most profitable markets from the firm's point of view. Second, the managers are willing instruments of the shareholders and implement the shareholders' utility functions in assessing different profit streams over time, so that the market valuation of the firm is maximized. Third, the market valuation of the firm is an entirely accurate reflection of the current and future earnings potential of the firm. There is no ignorance and no uncertainty (though there will of course be risk). Finally, we assume that in merger activity the managers of both firms are acting in the best interests of the shareholders: this requires that the market valuation of the merged firm, V_m, shall exceed the sum of the market valuations of the pre-merger constituent firms, $\sum_i V_i$. Under the conditions set out this can only be a reflection of an increase in the *real* evaluation of the assets.

On this basis we may classify the pure theory of merger under three separate heads:

[18] W. W. Alberts, J. E. Segall, *The Corporate Merger* (Chicago, 1966).

1. Increased market power. If the two firms are operating in the same market, a merger will increase market concentration and give the merged firm greater market power. This is a much more rapid path to market dominance than a competitive war between the firms, and it has the advantage of not increasing the total capacity in a market that may not be growing very much. However we saw in Part II that increased concentration does not by itself necessarily increase profitability in the market. That depends on the willingness of other oligopolists to collude, and on the barriers to entry to the sector. The increased concentration simply makes collusion easier by reducing the number of degrees of freedom in the search for collusive agreements. Also a larger firm may be able to dictate industry policy. On the other hand, increased concentration consequent upon a merger may also bring disadvantages. It may upset a rather delicately balanced oligopolistic agreement, and lead to a period of oligopoly war. And in an economy with a policy of intervention in market structure, such a merger may be frowned upon by the Monopolies Commission, leading to subsequent uncertainty. We conclude that there may well be gains from increased concentration in the market, but such gains are by no means inevitable.

2. Reduction in advertising and other promotional expenditures. Even if increased market power does not, of itself, increase profit margins, a merged firm may be able to reduce competitive expenditures on advertising and promotion, especially where the merger enables some amalgamation of product lines. Once again the outcome depends not only on the action of the two firms, but also on the reactions of other competitors in the oligopolistic markets, as we saw in Chapter 12.

3. Increased efficiency. In the literature, the advantages on the cost side are graphically described as 'synergism' or the '2 + 2 = 5 effect'. This brings us back to all the topics that we examined in detail in Chapter 2: so we will simply recall some of those arguments.

(i) It may be possible to realize production economies, due to economies of scale. But these are not available in the short run, since merger will simply bring together two small plants of sub-optimal size. The gain must be in the long run when the total production can be concentrated in a single plant, and economies can be realized thereby.

(ii) Indivisible or spare resources. One or both firms may own a particular resource that they cannot use to the full, and which because of indivisibilities cannot be reduced in size. Then a merger may enable the resources to be fully utilized, allowing their fixed costs to be spread and economies thereby obtained. The most frequently cited example is management, especially in cases where a good manager is not given sufficient scope by the operations of a small firm. A merger will enable him to exercise his talents on a larger bundle of resources, and economies arise from disposing of otiose managers. Exactly similar arguments can apply to other under-utilized resources; for example, a large piece of plant which a single firm cannot use to capacity, or a chain of sales outlets which would benefit from a wider range of product lines, or a network of salesmen.

(iii) Economies in R and D. This was dealt with in detail in Chapter 13. The advantages of a joint R and D programme may arise via economies of scale or by better utilization of spare resources as outlined in (i) and (ii). However we may add to this the advantage of pooling of risks in a larger effort, and the effect already noted that larger R and D efforts are on average able to attract better research and engineering personnel.

(iv) Economies in obtaining finance: for this we refer back to Chapter 10, where it was shown that large companies may have advantages in raising funds. The first is that they tend to be better known (though this will not be important in the capitalist Utopia we are currently assuming). The second is that resort to the capital market incurs transactions costs, some of which are fixed. So unit costs will be lower for larger issues.[19]

(v) Elimination of transaction costs. This again refers to issues that were discussed in Chapter 2. A merger that involves vertical integration may reduce costs by replacing market transactions between firms, by planning and co-ordination within firms. Market transactions involve management time, in searching for information, in carrying out negotiations, and in accounting time in making payments between firms. The merged firm will have access to better information at a lower cost, since it is easier to monitor activity within a firm than to obtain information about the activities of a separate firm (the cost of industrial espionage may be very high). Production relations between input–output divisions of a firm can be carried out on the basis of production management fiat. Stock may be at a lower level over-all, since flows between sectors can be more certain as they are under one control. So there is a saving in working capital costs. Finally there may be specific technical economies, for instance when hot materials can be passed between processes, thus saving energy costs in reheating.

We may now return to our initial question and ask why the firm

---

[19] In the U.S. there are also certain tax advantages in mergers, since the combined firm may write off accumulated losses against the profits of the merged firm.

should seek to obtain the advantages listed under 1 to 3 above by the process of merger, rather than be creating their own new resource combinations. It has already been noted that merger will be chosen in those cases where the purpose is to increase market share, since the competitive process would result, at least in the medium time horizon, in the creation of additional capacity. The second advantage of merger is that it enables a firm to overcome a barrier to entry of a sector into which it wishes to diversify. The alternative is a costly competitive war. Third, there are no delays involved in a merger, whereas it may take considerable time to plan and carry out an investment programme. Fourth, there will probably be less risk in the purchase of a 'going concern' with a proven performance in the market. Finally, the advantage of merger may be the acquisition of a particular resource in another firm, which may not be available to a new entrant to the sector.

By its very nature, evidence on these types of mergers is not available in any systematic form. Each particular instance must be examined on its own evidence. However if the types of benefits described above are a major motive for merger we would expect firms to take care in assessing the potential gains before the merger takes place, and to take steps to improve the use of resources, or to exploit markets, in the post-merger period. Newbould[20] concentrated on these two points in a study of 38 firms that were involved in a number of mergers in the late 1960s. His data came from interviews with the managers involved in the mergers. He found that the pre-merger analysis by the firms was often extremely sketchy. In no case of takeover was there a careful analysis of the assets of the 'victim', or of how they might contribute to the joint firm. This negative result accorded well with the motives for merger activity that were expressed. These rarely related to specific objectives: in many cases the firms had no better reason for merger than that everybody else was doing it at the same time. Merger was a fashionable entrepreneurial activity. In the post-merger phase only half the firms took specific steps to create 'synergy' or to improve the use of assets. And in these cases the improvement was not the result of a systematic programme, but piecemeal as the occasion arose. The main recorded economies came from the merging of administrations, and the joint use of selling outlets. The largest specific economy was the merging of central administration, which often involved the disposal of a valuable office block in London or another big city, as well as the reduction in joint staffs.

Newbould's rather negative results are backed up by a number of

[20] Newbould, op. cit.

studies of the performance of merging firms. Hogarty,[21] in a study of 43 firms that were heavily involved in mergers in the period 1953-64, found no evidence that the return to shareholders in dividends and capital gains exceeded that for other firms in the same sectors over the same period. Indeed rather the reverse was true. Twenty-one firms were clear 'failures' in that they performed much worse than the industry average: only three chalked up clear successes. Much the same was true in Utton's study[22] of the profit and growth performance of 39 U.K. companies which were heavily involved in mergers in the period 1961-5. Neither during the merger period, or in the period 1966-70, was there any evidence of a superior performance. Lev and Mandelker[23] examined matching pairs of firms (in respect of size nd industry), one firm in each pair having experienced a single merger. In this way they were able to compare the performance of each pair, both before and after the mergers. They examined thirteen measures of performance relating to profitability and growth. On none was the difference between the firms statistically significant.

In a more comprehensive study, Meeks[24] examined the profitability performance of firms before and after merger, for 233 U.K. acquisitions in the period 1964-72. The cases were chosen so as to give at least three years prior to the merger, and a number of years after the merger, in which no other acquisitions were made by the firms. Profitability was measured with reference to the average for the industries in which the firms operated, so as to remove cyclical influences. His substantive finding was that, apart from the year in which the merger occurred, profitability showed a mild but definite decline. He also found that the acquirers were significantly more profitable than other firms in their sector, prior to merger. This makes it less likely that merger was a response to deteriorating conditions in the industry, the effects of which were mitigated by the merger. The alternative conclusion, that merger *causes* bad performance, seems the more convincing.

[21] T. F. Hogarty, 'The Profitability of Corporate Mergers', *J. of Business*, 43 (1970), 317-26.

[22] M. A. Utton, 'On Measuring the Effects of Industrial Mergers', *S.J.P.E.* 21 (1974), 13-28.

[23] B. Lev, G. Mandelker, 'The Microeconomic Consequences of Corporate Mergers', *J. of Business*, 45 (1972), 85-104.

[24] G. Meeks, *Disappointing Marriage: A Study of the Gains from Merger*, University of Cambridge, Department of Applied Economics, Occasional Paper No. 51 (Cambridge, 1977).

3 THE CONGLOMERATE MERGER

The classical theory of mergers discussed in the previous section meets its most serious objection when confronted by the evidence of recent merger activity in the U.S. and U.K. Lintner[25] reports that in the period since 1950, culminating in the 1966–8 merger boom, about 80 per cent of the mergers in the U.S. could be classified as conglomerate. The classification was not particularly strict, so it is possible that there were links in production or distribution involved in a number of these cases. But the evidence is sufficient to draw attention to the 'pure' conglomerate merger, where the firms are in different industries with no possible links.

For purposes of analysis, we retain the assumption of the previous section: the capital market is efficient in the information sense, and the firms seek to maximize the utility of the shareholders. A popular explanation for the conglomerate merger is that the merger reduces risk.

We define for a firm both a mean or expected return, μ, and a probability distribution of returns which may be described entirely by the variance σ^2. We should note that ignorance or uncertainty, which we have excluded by our assumption in this section, would make it impossible for managers or shareholders to know the values of these parameters. An elementary theorem in statistical theory enables us to predict that to the extent that returns to independent firms are non-correlated, the creation of a single diversified firm leads to a reduction in the variance of total cash flow. This can be most easily illustrated by considering the merger of two firms with identical pre-merger μ and σ^2. The expected return, μ_m, of the merged firm is, of course, 2μ. The variance of these returns is given by

$$\sigma_m^2 = \sigma_i^2 + \sigma_j^2 + 2r \cdot \sigma_i \sigma_j$$

where i and j refer to the pre-merger firms and m to the merged firm. r is the coefficient of correlation between the two profit streams, and can take values between $+1$ and -1. If $r = 1$ then a positive or negative deviation in firm i returns is paralleled by an identical variation in the profits of firm j. In this case $\sigma_m^2 = 4\sigma^2$. This means that the expected returns to the merged firm are exactly the sum of the expected returns of the constituent firms, and the spread of returns (measured by the standard deviation σ_m) has also doubled.

[25] J. Lintner, 'Expectations, Mergers and Equilibrium in Purely Competitive Securities Markets', *A.E.R. Papers and Proceedings*, 41 (1971), 101–11.

There has been no reduction in the variability of the earnings stream expressed as a ratio of the average return. (This measure is the co-efficient of variation, a normalized measure of variability.) However, for $r < 1$ it is clear that $\sigma_m^2 < 4\sigma^2$. Specifically when $r = 0$, i.e. the two profit streams are completely independent of each other, $\sigma_m^2 = 2\sigma^2$. So the return has doubled, but the standard deviation increases by only $\sqrt{2}$, so the coefficient of variation diminishes by a factor of $1/\sqrt{2}$. Finally if $r = -1$ the two streams move in precisely opposite directions: a positive deviation in firm i is exactly offset by a negative deviation in firm j. In this unlikely case, the variance of the returns falls to zero. Obviously in all cases where $r < 1$, the merger reduces the variability of profits and thus the risk attached to the earnings stream by shareholders. The result is that the market attaches a smaller risk premium in discounting the earnings of the merged firms so that V_m is greater than $\sum_i V_i$. Furthermore the firm will benefit in the long run from having a lower cost of new capital if it needs to raise outside finance. So the merger would seem to be in the interests of the shareholders.

That is what Levy and Sarnat[26] describe as the 'uneasy case for conglomerate mergers'. The reason for their unease is that the argument completely ignores the theory of asset pricing. If we adopt the capital asset pricing model all gains from this type of merger should have been already achieved by shareholders who will hold the 'market portfolio' where unsystematic risk is already diversified away. The argument will have weight only if the stock market is imperfect in some way, or if shareholders are not rationally following the precepts of the model. However we noted above that both of these are likely. Information in the market is not complete, and shareholders appear to discount on the basis of variance of returns to a share even though they should not do so if they were more skilful portfolio analysts. First, not all companies are quoted, and in the case of private companies the ownership may not be divisible (too few shares, if indeed shares are issued at all). In which case it is an 'all-or-nothing' merger. Second, small shareholders may not be able to diversify fully because of indivisibilities in shares, and because transaction costs of small dealings may be prohibitive. Third, we may relax our assumption of perfect knowledge in a capitalist Utopia, and admit that for many small investors the attraction of a blue-chip investment like I.C.I. is that the managers will have greater expertise in choosing where to diversify than a small investor. The

[26] H. Levy, M. Sarnat, 'Diversification, Portfolio Analysis and the Uneasy Case for Conglomerate Mergers', *J. of Finance* 25 (1970), 795–802.

argument is analogous to that for unit trusts, which are another means of doing the same thing.

Fourth, Lintner[27] points out that the fact that not every shareholder has every share in his portfolio leads to identifiable merger gains within the capital asset pricing model framework. His contention is that many conglomerate mergers will increase the *number* of shareholders in the merged firm compared to either of the constituent firms. This would happen, for example, if the merger is financed by issuing new equity of one firm to the shareholders of the other firm which is taken over. In so far as the shareholders of j previously had no stock in i (and vice versa), the creation of the merged firm will reduce risk for them all. The value of the shares will then exceed the pre-merger valuations. Fifthly, Lewellen[28] has added a further element to the situation. Suppose that the pre-merger firms have some debt finance. Then the lenders to the firm are interested in the possibility that the firm's net income may be so low as to lead to a default on interest payments (technical bankruptcy). This will determine the amount of finance that the firm can borrow. Now consider a merger between two such firms. The probability of default is clearly affected, so long as the income streams of the firms are not perfectly correlated. Suppose, after the merger, that the income stream of one constituent firm falls below the default level. Unless the other part of the firm simultaneously experiences difficulties, the losses on one side can be made up by the income on the other side of the firm, and default is avoided. Lewellen contends that the merged firm will in these circumstances have a credit 'limit', which exceeds the sum of the debt capacity of the two pre-merged firms. In a world of corporate taxation, with debt interest being tax deductible, debt finance is cheaper than equity, and it follows that the merger will reduce the cost of capital to the firm. Hence the market valuation should rise. Higgins and Schall[29] have modified this conclusion by pointing out that part of the gain from merger should also come in the form of a lower interest rate on debt. But that will only be available if the merged firm is able to retire all the old debt without penalty, and reissue at a lower interest rate. Finally, we may relax our assumption that mergers are always undertaken in the interests of shareholders. Even if shareholders may have fully diversified portfolios, it may still be in the interests of the managers to pursue the greater stability of earnings from a diversified firm. The reason is

[27] Lintner, op. cit. (*A.E.R. Papers and Proceedings*, 1971).

[28] W. G. Lewellen, 'A Pure Financial Rationale for the Conglomerate Merger', *J. of Finance* Papers and Proceedings, 26 (1971), 521–37.

[29] R. G. Higgins, L. D. Schall, 'Corporate Bankruptcy and Conglomerate Merger', *J. of Finance*, 30 (1975), 93–113.

simply that a steady stream of profits makes it easier to pay steady dividends, and reduces the possibility that things will go wrong leading to the dismissal of the managers.

The performance of firms involved in conglomerate mergers has been subject to some empirical investigation. A study by Reid[30] suggested that conglomerate performance after merger indicated the pursuit of managerial rather than shareholder utility. Conglomerates were distinguished by higher growth in sales, assets, and employment, rather than by a growth in market values of shares or other indicators of profitability. This result was disputed by Weston and Mansinghka[31] in an interchange with Reid. They compared the performance of 63 conglomerate merger firms with 2 control groups, for the period 1958–68. They concluded that the conglomerates were inferior to the other firms in 1958 on measures related to shareholder objectives, for example return on assets and the ratio of debt to net worth. However by 1968 they had caught up, and performance of the two groups was not distinguishable. Their explanation for conglomerate mergers was that they were embarked upon by firms whose traditional products were in declining markets. They were a defensive measure to maintain corporate profitability. This explanation is attractive, though it does not explain why the conglomerate merger should have become *so* popular in the 1960s. Nor does the evidence give any support to the proposition that mergers brought benefits to shareholders in the performance of their shares. Mason and Goudzwaard[32] collected questionnaire data for 22 U.S. firms that accounted together for 194 mergers in the period 1962–7. The performance of the conglomerates was matched with simulated portfolios that mirrored their asset structures. Despite the fact that 1962–7 was a boom period for conglomerates, the return on assets, and the returns to investors were higher in the simulated portfolios. Haugen and Langetieg[33] examined 59 industrial mergers in the period 1951–68. Each case was paired with two other non-merging firms with characteristics as close as possible to those of the merged firms. The performance of both was compared for 36 months before and after the merger, using the analytic framework of the capital asset pricing model. There was no evidence that merger affected the

[30] S. R. Reid, *Managers, Mergers and the Economy* (New York, 1968).

[31] J. F. Weston, S. K. Mansinghka, 'Tests of the Efficiency Performance of Conglomerate Firms', *J. of Finance*, 26 (1971), 919–36.

[32] R. H. Mason, M. B. Goudzwaard, 'Performance of Conglomerate Firms', *J. of Finance*, 31 (1976), 39–48.

[33] R. A. Haugen, T. C. Langetieg, 'An Empirical Test for Synergism in Merger', *J. of Finance*, 30 (1975), 1003–14.

risk attached to the shares, compared to the performance of the portfolio of non-merging firms.

4 MERGER BARGAINS

We have already discussed the role of the stock market and other financial markets in transferring the ownership of capital assets. The hypothesis of this section is that mergers are a means of reallocating capital assets to to those managers who will make better use of the resources. The motive for merger then is the gains to be made from taking over poorly utilized assets and using them more effectively. Two types of 'inefficiency' can be distinguished, with the help of the relationship of firm valuation to growth rate of the firm derived from the analysis of Chapter 9. This relationship is shown in Figure 14.2. It assumes that a firm is utilizing all its resources efficiently to

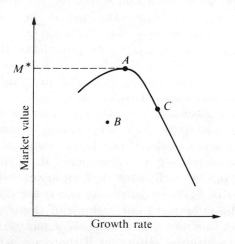

Fig. 14.2

reach points on the frontier. The point A, corresponding to valuation M^*, represents the optimal point for a firm that is maximizing shareholder utility (i.e. shareholders' preferences for dividends and capital growth are incorporated in the valuation formula). The first type of inefficiency is where a firm is operating *within* the frontier at a point such as B. The assets could be used more effectively to produce both more growth and a higher valuation. The firm's failure to do so may reflect a deliberate policy on the part of the managers of eating up profits by expense preference as identified by Williamson.[34] Expense

[34] O. E. Williamson, *The Economics of Discretionary Behaviour* (Chicago, 1967).

accounts, large bureaucratic staffs in prestige office blocks, and managerial sloth constitute the main elements of this. However a similar failure may be due to ignorance on the part of management as to the true value of the assets. For example, a manufacturing firm may be situated on a central-city site which could be more profitably used for offices or shops: but ignorance and inertia may prevent the manager from transferring the business to a cheaper industrial site and selling off the land. Such firms will be an attractive victim for takeover. The buyer will make his gain by eliminating the waste of resources: i.e. moving the firm to the growth–valuation frontier.

A further possibility is that identified by Marris.[35] Suppose a firm is pursuing managerial growth objectives. Then it may operate at a point like C, using resources efficiently, but sacrificing some market valuation for growth. The firm may then become an attractive take-over victim. The buyer will simply reduce the growth rate of the firm, and increase profitability. The gain is the increase in market valuation to M^*. Marris sees the existence of this possibility as acting as a constraint on its actions. He postulates either a fixed take-over constraint (a minimum M below which takeover becomes inevitable) or, more reasonably, that the probability of takeover increases as the valuation decreases.

If either of these reasons for takeover exists we would expect the performance characteristics of the victim firms (V) to differ markedly from those of other firms in the same industry (S). In the case of expense preference and managerial slack this should appear as V having lower growth rates and/or lower valuations than S, prior to merger. The case of ignorance about the value of assets may not appear in the same way. The essence of the situation is that the market valuation and the book value of assets do not reflect their value in an alternative use. However if there are gains from mergers of this kind it should show up in a before and after merger comparison of the acquiring firm. It is difficult to obtain data to test this possibility. The merged firm cannot be 'unscrambled' statistically to determine the post-merger performance of the constituent firms, and it is not possible to determine what the performance of the two parts would have been in the absence of a merger. The Marris hypothesis predicts that the V will have higher growth rates, but lower valuations than S.

The comparison of the performance of S and V has been the

---

[35] R. Marris, in R. Marris, A. Wood (ed.), *The Corporate Economy* (London, 1971); G. M. Heal, Z. A. Silberston, 'Alternative Managerial Objectives: An Explanatory Note', *O.E.P.* N.S. 24 (1972), 137–50.

subject of two thorough studies with U.K. data, by A. Singh[36] and by Kuehn.[37] Singh studied all the takeovers or mergers in the period 1954–60 in five U.K. sectors: food, drink, electrical engineering, clothing and footwear, and engineering. He examined a number of indicators of firm performance, at first separately and then in a multivariate analysis[38] of differences in V and S. He defines as his indicators four possible alternative measures of profitability, the growth of assets, and the valuation ratio. The last is the ratio of the stock market value of assets to the reported book value of the assets. In a perfect world these two valuations should be the same. The firm would revalue assets on the basis of their profit potential, and if the same information were available to stockholders they would evaluate the shares on exactly the same basis. In fact, on all these measures taken individually S did better than V on average. But although there was an absolute difference in means, the spread of the values for S and V was so great that the difference in means is not significant, and no single measure is a good discriminate of S and V firms. Nor did a multivariate analysis of the same performance variables improve the degree of discrimination. In fact, the best discriminant of S and V firms was found to be size, which is not, of course, an indicator of performance. The probability of being a V is about the same for small and medium firms, but it is much lower for large firms. But for a *given size class* in an industry, profitability is the best indicator of the probability of being taken over. Singh examines this indicator over two-year and six-year periods. On a two-year profitability basis, the level of profitability has no significant effect on the chances of being a V, except for those firms in the lowest decile of profitability for which the probability is significantly higher, and those in the highest decile for which the probability is notably less. Over a six-year period, the distinction was between those firms with above average and those with below average profitability: the latter were twice as likely to be V firms as the former. Thus the evidence suggests that there are some mergers that are attributable to this reason: but it also suggests that the 'discipline' imposed by the stock market is weak. In particular a large firm is quite likely to survive even if it is somewhat incompetently managed. The message for managers who wish to keep their jobs is that they should make their firms as large as possible. A good profit performance is not necessarily a good protection for a small firm.

[36] Ajit Singh, *Takeovers* (Cambridge, 1971).

[37] D. A. Kuehn, *Takeovers and the Theory of the Firm* (London, 1975).

[38] A group of firms (V) may not be clearly distinguishable from others on the basis of *one* characteristic alone, but may be so distinguished when a number of characteristics are examined simultaneously.

In a subsequent study of mergers in the 1967–70 merger boom, Singh[39] examined the same performance variables as in the 1955–60 study. In this period profitability appeared to be a rather better discriminant of S and V, a *fall* in profitability being particularly associated with V. However the broad conclusions of the previous study were confirmed: the stock market acts as a weak discipline for unprofitable firms, and size is the main deterrent to takeover bids. Kuehn's study[40] was a more direct attempt to test the Marris hypothesis alone, so it concentrated in the first place on the valuation ratio and secondly on the financial performance variables that underlie that ratio. The merger experience in 66 industrial sectors in the period 1957–69 provided the data. Although there was a difference in valuation ratios between S and V taken as a whole, it was a weak discriminant between the two groups. Disaggregation to the underlying financial variables—profit rate before tax, growth rate of assets, retention ratio and liquidity ratio—gave weaker results.

5   MERGERS FOR GROWTH

The previous section concluded that stock market discipline of inefficient and managerial firms is weak. The firm can pursue its own (managerial) objectives with the minimum of constraints. So we can now turn to our last motive for merger, and hypothesize that mergers are part of the growth strategy of managerial firms. The theory of Chapter 9 restricted itself to 'internal' growth. The main limits to growth were the trade-off between growth and profitability, involving both the market position of the firm and its managerial capacity to generate growth, and the possible constraint on funds. We examine these constraints now for the firm that seeks to grow simply by taking over existing firms, rather than by the creation of new assets for itself.

A firm that grows by merger does not face the same restrictive trade-off between growth and profitability. There will be many more projects available to it, and those projects need not involve a diminution of profitability. For example, the firm can expand in its existing markets simply by taking over the market share of other firms already in those markets. This will involve no reduction in profit rate: indeed it may lead to a rise in profit rate as we suggested under section 1 above. No reduction in prices, and no expensive selling campaign will be necessary. Furthermore the firm can diversify,

[39] Ajit Singh, 'Takeovers, Economic Natural Selection and the Theory of the Firm', *E.J.* 85 (1975), 497–515.
[40] Kuehn, op. cit.

without expensive R and D in a new product area, by taking over an existing firm in that area. Nor need any management problems arise *à la* Penrose.[41] The acquiring firm can take over an existing management and continue to give it independence in managing the affairs of the firm. Indeed management problems are only likely to arise where there is an attempt to integrate the operations of the acquired firm at a level which goes deeper than having a common letterhead. The effect of merger then is to shift the opportunities curve to the right. Presumably it is not all gain—we would expect there to be diminishing returns to such a process (there may not be too many suitable victims, and there may be managerial problems eventually)—but it will be a substantially larger range of possibilities than are available to the internal growth firm. The effect on profitability does, of course, depend on the price the firm has to pay for its acquisitions. We may consider three possibilities.

The first is that the acquisition is a well-managed, profit maximizing firm, operating at the peak of the growth–valuation function. Heal and Silberston[42] have pointed out that even in these circumstances the growth-by-merger firm will be willing to pay more than the existing market valuation. The reason is simply that the acquiring firm, because it is a growth firm, will probably apply a lower discount rate (have a longer time horizon) than the current shareholders and so value the firm more highly. So long as the acquiring firm does not have to pay much above the pre-bid market valuation there should be no decline in its profitability. It will not of course be particularly worried by the lower growth profile of the acquired firms, as it is aiming to grow by acquisition anyway. If it does acquire a growth firm, the second possibility, it will presumably wish to cut back its growth pretensions; and a growth firm will be attractive because of its lower market valuation. But to change the policy of an acquisition may require management time, and this it will be reluctant to divert from acquiring new companies. The third possibility is that the victim will be an inefficient firm—i.e. one that is operating *within* the growth/valuation frontier. But again the acquisition of such a company might prove expensive in managerial time. This brief survey of the possibilities suggests that growth-by-merger firms will be interested in firms falling into the first category. They will not be primarily interested in the economies or market power that may be forthcoming. Nor will they wish to spend much managerial time on rectifying inefficiencies. But they may take such gains, on an *ad hoc* basis, where opportunity arises. This pattern of

[41] E. Penrose, *The Theory of the Growth of the Firm* (Oxford, 1959).
[42] Heal and Silberston, op. cit.

behaviour seems to be consistent in the findings of Newbould[43] reported earlier.

However one particular type of gain does seem to be particularly relevant to the type of managerial firm we are considering. Previously we raised the point that conglomerate mergers would reduce the variance of firms' earning streams, but suggested that this was not necessarily attractive to shareholders who could create their own diversified portfolio to suit their own preferences. But it is certainly very attractive to *managers*, for whom the shareholder point is irrelevant. Managerial firms may seek conglomerate mergers to reduce the variability of their cash flow, and thus reduce the risk to themselves of major fluctuations in corporate income.

We have indicated that the trade-off between growth and profits may be substantially shifted for the growth-by-merger firm. We now need to consider the supply of funds for merger. If the firm carried out its merger policy with retentions alone, the relaxation on the opportunities side would be unimportant. But the situation changes if the firm can acquire others by offering its own shares in exchange, in appropriate proportions to the valuation of the existing shares. Even if such a deal has some cash element the quantity of funds required is only a fraction of the total deal. Of course, it can get the best out of such an arrangement if the value of its own shares is relatively high. So it will deliberately adopt a policy of high pay-out and low retentions to keep the share price high. There are two possible objections to this procedure. The first is that shareholders in the victim firm may not be willing to accept shares in a merged company. There is no reason why their returns should be higher. However they may see some virtue in holding shares in a larger company; the earnings stream may be more stable and the shares may be more marketable. Second, they may change from a significant shareholding in a small company to an insignificant holding in a large one. Exactly the same objection may be raised by the existing shareholders of the acquiring firm about the dilution of their ownership. However, given the weakness of control of shareholders in modern firms, the management can probably afford to ignore such objections simply because shareholding is so diffused. No shareholder has enough votes or the power to remove them from office. So they may pursue managerial objectives undisturbed. Besides, the shareholders may enjoy the illusory psychic benefit of owning shares in a 'growth' firm. It is an illusion, because the number of shares is growing at the same rate as the firm.

If these deductions are correct, we have the following results for a

[43] Newbould, op. cit.

growth-by-merger firm compared to the managerial firm described above. We assume that no purely profit maximizing firms exist, and that all firms are managerial to some extent, i.e. they sacrifice some profits to faster growth. First we expect the growth-by-merger firm to grow faster than its internal growth counterpart. Second, the growth-by-merger firm will have a lower retention ratio. Third, the firm will have a higher valuation ratio (stock market valuation to book value of assets), due to its policy of keeping share prices up by a high dividend. Finally, we expect the firm to have a slightly higher profit rate than the average firm. These results would be hypothetical only, were it not for the works of Kuehn.[44] He examined 117 U.K. companies which had been involved in 3 or more takeovers in the period 1957–69 and compared their performance characteristics with the median characteristics of all firms in their sectors.[45] A simple sign test showed that a significant proportion of the 117 firms differed from the median for their industry on all performance indicators except profit rate, and the deviations were in the direction suggested by the hypotheses above.

Meeks[46] provided further support for the financing hypothesis. He examined the average contribution of retentions and external finance to growth by investment in new fixed and working capital, and to growth by merger, for those members of the U.K. quoted company population which survived from 1964 to 1971. Retentions financed 59 per cent of net investment, and 77 per cent of gross investment. But acquisitions were 72 per cent financed by new issues. Meeks notes that new issues in such circumstances avoid the uncertainties attached to selling equities for cash to finance new investment. The 'price' can be fixed in the merger deal, on a share-for-share basis, and, of course, the 'project' is a company with a known earnings record, and is therefore less uncertain.

Two further questions raise themselves. The first is why some firms can undertake growth in this way, and not others. We would seek the explanation in two areas. Some firms may have sufficient majority shareholdings to make the dilution of ownership by issuing new shares an unattractive proposition. This is particularly so in the case of owner-managed companies. We will only expect this model when share-ownership in the firm is widely diffused and divorced from management. Further we note that this type of operation

---

[44] Kuehn, op. cit., and in K. Cowling (ed.), *Market Structure and Corporate Behaviour* (London, 1972), 19–37.

[45] It should be noted that, although we are using Kuehn's data, our theoretical analysis does not exactly correspond to his, though it is not dissimilar. The reader is urged to read Kuehn's analysis for himself.

[46] Meeks, op. cit.

requires far more financial skill than strictly managerial skill. So we would expect only a few entrepreneurs to have the skill or the taste for it. It would not appeal to a management that was more concerned with production problems. The second question is whether there are limits to firm growth by this method. In the long run the answer would seem to be no, unless and until managerial talent is diverted to reorganization and restructuring in the merged companies. Then their energy may be diverted from further take-overs. We should note that the first stage in these mergers, that of putting different firms under the same legal heading, has virtually no *economic* significance in terms of resource allocation. It does however concentrate considerable economic power in the hands of the managers. And if they do eventually set about integrating the operations there may be very significant effects in terms of economies, market power, and possibly direction of capital flows beween sectors of the same company.

6   CONCLUSIONS

We can draw two conclusions from the material of this chapter. The first concerns the information efficiency of the stock market. We are not yet clear how the market values an asset: it is obvious that the full capital asset pricing model is not adequate as a descriptive model. But it is certain that share prices systematically reflect the dividends and retentions policies of the firms, and that prices adjust rapidly and smoothly to changes in published information. Second, the evidence supports the view that merger is an important route to achieve the managerial objective of growth. There is little evidence that mergers lead to substantial real or pecuniary advantages. Nor does the evidence support the view that takeovers are the symptoms of a healthy stock market discipline which takes assets away from incompetent or wrongly motivated managers. Rather the reverse seems to be true: stock market discipline is astonishingly weak. Finally, while conglomerate mergers may bring some specific gains to shareholders, the major motive once again seems to be managerial in terms both of growth and security for the managers.

15

THE DEVELOPMENT OF FIRMS,
AND MARKET AND INDUSTRIAL STRUCTURE

In this chapter we draw together a number of strands from Parts II and III of this book, and assess the effects of firms' actions on the development of market structure and aggregate industrial structure over time.

In Part II we examined the behaviour of the firm within a given market structure. The direction of causation assumed was primarily from market structure to profits. At any point in time, the firm is a bundle of assets, the size and quality of which determine the costs of production. The firm faces a given degree of concentration and product differentiation in the markets within which it is deploying its assets. Given these constraints the firm sets price to maintain its position and profitability. A price that is too low will lead to unprofitable price competition within the market. A price that is too high will lead to new entry, and rapid erosion of its market share and profit margins. In Part III we have analysed the more active element in firm's behaviour. The market structure and its own asset structure are no longer 'given': it is those very elements that the firm is trying to change to its own advantage. The previous chapters have catalogued the ways in which the firm may try to do this, especially by utilizing retained profits. Investment in physical capital, research and development, marketing and advertising expenditures, and merger, are all means to changing the firm's position and hence the structure of markets. The chapter assesses the joint impact of these interdependent elements upon the structure of markets. The literature has concentrated particularly on the relationship between the growth of individual firms and the degree of market concentration. The discussion has included the impact on structure of the entry of new firms, and of the 'death' of existing firms by merger. Changes in structure then 'feed back' into the discussion of Part II: the analysis of profitability in different market structures.

A second thread of analysis observes that vertical integration and diversification are the major elements in the growth of very large firms in advanced Western economies. The result is not merely high concentration in individual markets, but also a very great concentration of the assets of the entire industrial sector in the hands of large diversified firms. The process by which this concentration of economic 'power' has occurred will occupy us in the second half of this chapter.

A.   MARKET STRUCTURE

The evidence for both the U.S. and the U.K. suggests that market concentration does change substantially over time. We assume that we can identify 'markets' by the finer classifications of the Standard Industrial Classification, and we ignore the caveats of Chapter 3 about the suitability of different concentration measures. Mueller and Hamm[1] present evidence on the four firm concentration ratio in 166 4-digit U.S. industries for the period 1947–70. The average CR_4 (weighted by value added) rose by 3·9 percentage points, but this conceals a much greater variation between sectors. Eighty-six sectors experienced increases, and included many consumer products. Seventy-four sectors, with a majority in producer goods, showed decreases. Blair[2] analysed similar evidence for 209 U.S. 4-digit industries, 1947–67. Thirty-nine sectors changed by less than 3 percentage points either way. Of the remainder, 95 showed increases in concentration ratio of more than 3 per cent, and 75 of less than 3 per cent. The U.K. experience has been more dramatic in the 1950s and 1960s. George[3] analysed the five firm concentration ratio in 209 product classes 1958–63. He found that the average (unweighted) CR_5 had gone up from 54·4 per cent to 58·9 per cent over the period, reflecting an increase in concentration in two-thirds of the product classes. Food and drink, textiles, vehicles, leather, clothing and footwear were the sectors particularly affected. The largest increases in CR_5 tended to be found in those product classes with low initial CR_5. Sawyer[4] confirmed George's analysis, by drawing concentration curves for 117 sectors in 1958 and 1963. Ninety-one showed an unambiguous increase in concentration, 13 a decrease, and 12 were ambiguous because the concentration curves for the two years crossed. In the next five years, up to 1968, there was intense merger activity in the U.K. George was able to analyse 150 industries. The average CR_5 rose by another 6·5 percentage points, representing increases in 102 sectors. In 61 of these the index rose by more than 10 percentage points. These reflected those

[1] W. F. Mueller, L. G. Hamm, 'Trends in Industrial Market Concentration', *R. Econ. State.* 56 (1974), 511–20
[2] J. M. Blair, *Economic Concentration* (New York, 1972).
[3] K. D. George, 'A Note on Changes in Industrial Concentration in the U.K.', *E.J.* 85 (1975), 124–8.
[4] M. C. Sawyer, 'Concentration in British Manufacturing Industry', *O.E.P.* N.S. 23 (1971), 352–83.

sectors where merger activity had been most intense: metals, electrical engineering, vehicles, textiles, leather, clothing and footwear, and bricks. All these recorded changes in concentration reflect the actions of the individual firm in the sectors involved. In the next section we will set out a framework within which the joint impact of these actions can be analysed.

1   STOCHASTIC MODELS OF FIRM GROWTH, AND MARKET STRUCTURE

The simplest hypothesis concerning the development of market concentration over time is suggested by a casual inspection of the data on firm sizes. In virtually all cases the data exhibit a similar pattern: the size distribution of firms is highly skewed with a few large firms, rather more medium-sized firms, and a large 'tail' of small firms. Such a size distribution is approximated by a number of related skew distributions[5] of which the lognormal is the most familiar, and may be used for purposes of illustration. The common feature of these distributions is that they may be generated by a stochastic process in which the variate (in this case the size of firms) is subjected to cumulative random shocks over time. The implication would seem to be that the size distribution of firms at a given point in time is the product of a series of random growth patterns in the history of the market.

The process of random growth leading to a lognormal distribution was first described by Gibrat,[6] and his formulation is termed Gibrat's Law of Proportionate Effect. We can imagine the growth of a firm being made up of three effects. The first is a constant growth rate (of the market), which is common to all firms. Let X_t be the firm size at time t, and let α be the constant growth rate. Then we have:

$$\frac{X_{t-1}}{X_t} = \alpha$$

The second element is a systematic tendency for the growth of a firm to be related to its initial size:

$$\frac{X_{t+1}}{X_t} = \alpha X_t^{(\beta-1)}$$

[5] H. A. Simon, 'On a Class of Skew Distribution Functions', *Biometrica*, 42 (1955), 425–40. J. Aitchison, J. A. C. Brown, *The Lognormal Distribution* (Cambridge, 1957).
[6] R. Gibrat, *Les Inéqualités économiques* (Paris, 1931);

The effect of initial size on growth is determined by the value of β. For $\beta = 1$, the exponent of X_t is zero, and so size has no effect on growth. For $\beta > 1$, large firms grow faster than small ones, and vice versa for $\beta < 1$. The latter is termed 'regression': the tendency for a variate to return to the mean size of the population. The third element is a random growth term, ϵ_t, which again enters the growth equation multiplicatively:

$$\frac{X_{t+1}}{X_t} = \alpha X_t^{(\beta-1)} \epsilon_t$$

or $\log X_{t+1} = \log \alpha + \beta \log X_t + \log \epsilon_t$.

Gibrat then made two strong assumptions. The first is that $\log \epsilon_t$ is normally distributed with zero mean and variance σ^2, and that it is independent of the initial size of firm.

The second is the requirement that the mean proportionate growth of a group of firms of the same initial size is independent of that initial size. In terms of the above formulation we require $\beta = 1$, and to make the point more sharply we will assume that the mean growth rate for all size classes of firms is zero ($\alpha = 1$).

We may now apply elementary statistical theory to determine the variance of the firm size distribution over time, assuming an initial variance which we will write Var $(\log X_t)$. After one period we have,

$\log X_{t+1} = \log X_t + u_{t+1}$, where $u_{t+1} = \log \epsilon_{t+1}$

so $\mathrm{Var}(\log X_{t+1}) = \mathrm{Var}(\log X_t) + \sigma^2$

and after n periods

$\log X_{t+n} = \log X_t + u_{t+1} + u_{t+2} + \ldots + u_{t+n}$

so $\mathrm{Var}(\log X_{t+n}) = \mathrm{Var}(\log X_t) + n\sigma^2$.

The outcome of this stochastic process is a variance that increases steadily over time. Hence, concentration has increased.[7] The only

[7] We should note L. Hannah and J. A. Kay's (*Concentration in Modern Industry*, London, 1977) objection to the use of variance of logs of firm sizes as a measure of concentration. It is possible to find cases that represent increases in concentration according to their criteria and yet show a diminution in the variance measure. The reason is that the measure is one of *inequality* of firm sizes, and not of concentration. The exposition in the text is intended as an illustration of the concentrating effects of the operation of a stochastic process. It should not be taken as support for a particular measure of concentration.

factor that could militate against such a result, as Prais[8] points out, is the existence of 'regression' ($\beta < 1$) in a strong enough form to counteract the exploding variance of the random process.

To test this hypothesis of the formation of industrial structure over time two types of information have been investigated. The first is to see how closely the behaviour of firms accords with the assumptions of the theoretical model. The second is to examine how closely actual size distributions of firms conform to the lognormal distribution.

Evidence on the first point is variable. An early study by Hart[9] of U.K. firms in brewing, cotton spinning, and soft drinks showed that the average growth of firms in each size class was independent of size. There was no tendency for large firms to grow faster than small ones. On the other hand the variance of growth rates was not independent of size class in brewing and soft drinks. In the former case the variance decreased with size; in the latter it increased. Hymer and Pashigian[10] presented results for 10 2-digit industries 1946–55. They too found that average growth rates were not related to size, while variance was. But they claimed the rather stronger result that the variance declined monotonically with size. A further study was that of Singh and Whittington,[11] who examined the growth experience of 2,000 quoted (and hence the larger) firms in 21 U.K. sectors 1948–60. They found that there was a mildly positive relationship between size and growth rate, and that the variance of growth rates diminished with size in each sector. But they did not find the smooth diminution of variance with firm size reported by Hymer and Pashigian. Further they found some evidence of serial correlation in growth rates: above-average growth firms tended to remain above average. Finally, we may note the results of Mansfield[12] for firms in the U.S. steel, petroleum, tyres, and car industries. For all firms that remained in the industry during his period of observations he found that the smaller size classes of firm had *higher* mean growth rates and a greater variance than large firms. Excluding those firms that were less than Bain's estimates of minimum economic size for the industry in question he found that the mean growth rate was now

[8] S. J. Prais, 'A New Look at the Growth of Industrial Concentration', *O.E.P.* N.S. 26 (1974), 273–88.

[9] P. E. Hart, 'The Size and Growth of Firms', *Economica*, N.S. 29 (1962), 29–39.

[10] S. Hymer, P. Pashigian, 'Firm Size and Rate of Growth', *J.P.E.* 70 (1962), 556–9.

[11] A. Singh, G. Whittington, *Growth, Profitability and Valuation*, D.A.E. Occasional Paper 7 (Cambridge, 1968); 'The Size and Growth of Firms', *R. Econ. Studs.*, 42 (1975), 15–26.

[12] E. Mansfield, 'Entry, Gibrat's Law, Innovation and the Growth of Firms', *A.E.R.* 52 (1962) 1023–51.

constant across all size classes, but the variance still declined.

These results indicate that the simple formulation of Gibrat's Law does not hold generally. However Ijiri and Simon[13] have shown that relaxation of the strict assumptions still leaves a stochastic process that will generate distributions in the same family as the lognormal distribution, for instance the Pareto or Yule distributions. For example, they adopt the assumption that the aggregate of firms in a particular size stratum has an expected percentage change which is independent of size. This amendment can accommodate the observed decrease in variance of firm growth rates with size.

A systematic relationship between size and growth can be incorporated in the analysis. (Kalecki:[14] the exposition here follows Hannah and Kay.[15]) When β is not equal to unity, the growth equation is, writing L_t for log size at time t:

$$L_t = (1 - \beta)\bar{L} + \beta L_{t-1} + u_t$$

where $\bar{L}$ is a constant. It can be shown by induction[16] that

$$L_t = \bar{L} + u_t + \beta u_{t-1} + \beta^2 u_{t-2} + \ldots + \beta^t u_0$$

Thus L_t remains as the sum of the independent random variables, u_t, and the distribution tends to lognormality, with a variance determined by the value of β, and by the variance of the u_t.

Serial correlation (i.e. persistence in a firm's growth rate over a number of periods) can also be modelled. We assume a linear relationship of the following form, where the value α indicates the degree of persistence in growth rates between one period and the next:

$$L_t = L_{t-1} + \alpha(L_{t-1} - L_{t-2}) + u_t$$

[13] Y. Ijiri, H. A. Simon, 'Business Firm Growth and Size', *A.E.R.* 54 (1964), 77–89. 'Effects of Mergers and Acquisitions on Business Firm Concentration', *J.P.E.* 79 (1971), 314–22; 'Interpretation of Departures from the Pareto Curve Firm Size Distribution', *J.P.E.* 82 (1974), 315–31.

[14] M. Kalecki, 'On the Gibrat Distribution', *Econometrica*, 13 (1945), 161–70.

[15] Hannah and Kay, op. cit.

[16] A proof by induction proceeds as follow. Assume the result:

$$L_t = \bar{L} + u_t + \beta u_{t-1} + \beta^2 u_{t-2} + \ldots + \beta^t u_0$$

$$\therefore L_t - \beta L_{t-1} = (1 - \beta)\bar{L} + u_t,$$

which is the growth equation. The result is consistent with the assumptions about growth. An analogous argument gives the result for serial correlation.

Induction again gives the result:

$$L_t = u_t + (1 + \alpha)u_{t-1} + (1 + \alpha + \alpha^2)u_{t-2} + \dots$$
$$+ (1 + \alpha + \alpha^2 + \dots + \alpha^t)u_0$$

which again is lognormal, since the u_t etc. are normally distributed independent random variables. The variance of the resulting distribution depends on α. Ijiri and Simon[17] have used computer simulations to generate distributions from more complex patterns of serial correlation. They found that a large number of cases approximated the Pareto distribution. In the same article Ijiri and Simon also investigated the effects of new entry. The strict Gibrat process described above is amended by the addition of a constant birth-rate of new firms into the lowest size class. This gives

$$F(i) = Ai^{-(\rho+1)}$$

where $F(i)$ is the rank of firm of size i, A is a constant, and ρ is a constant which depends on the rate of entry of new firms. This is a Pareto function, and is approximated by the Yule function for large i. Finally Ijiri and Simon[18] tackle the question of mergers and acquisitions. If the probability that a firm will disappear through merger is independent of size, and if the probability of any firm gaining via merger is independent of size, an initial Pareto distribution of firm sizes will remain a Pareto distribution with the same value of its parameters over time. More systematic tendencies, for instance for small firms to be at greater risk of takeover, can be accommodated within a more general stochastic model by appropriate probability weightings.

The second test of the stochastic hypothesis is to compare the actual size distribution of firms with that predicted by the statistical model. There have been two studies along these lines. Quandt[19] examined the size distribution (measured in assets) of firms in 30 4-digit S.I.C. U.S. sectors. A sophisticated econometric treatment including tests of goodness-of-fit and on the randomness of the residuals led to the conclusion that a Pareto distribution was acceptable description of the data in only 6 cases. Silberman,[20] in a similar study of the lognormal distribution fitted to 4-digit data, concluded

[17] Ijiri and Simon, op. cit. (1974).   [18] Ijiri and Simon, op. cit. (1971).
[19] R. E. Quandt, 'On the Size Distribution of Firms', *A.E.R.* 56 (1966), 416–32.
[20] I. H. Silberman, 'On Lognormality as a Summary Measure of Concentration', *A.E.R.* 57 (1967), 807–31.

that the distribution was frequently a rather poor fit. Two conclusions are drawn from these results by these writers. First, there is no reason to accept the very specific model of firm growth that underlies the lognormal and associated distributions. Second, that we should not expect a model which ignores the underlying cost conditions and market structure to be a good predictor of market concentration. It is to these objections that we now turn.

First, we note that there is a general 'Gibrat effect' which exists quite independently of the precise assumptions set out above. Any dispersion in the growth rates of firms will tend to increase concentration over time. Prais[21] gives a simple example. Assume an initial population of 128 firms each with 100 employees. The growth process is very simple: in each period half the firms remain unchanged in size, while a quarter increase and another quarter decrease by 10 employees. At the end of the first year, 32 firms have 110 employees, 64 have 100, and 32 have 90. At the end of the second year, there are 8 with 120 employees, 32 with 110, 48 with 100, 32 with 90, and 8 with only 80. The distribution gets wider every year, and the concentration ratio increases. The assumption of absolute increments of growth in each year is not as appealing as the proportionate growth rate assumed above. But there is clearly no need to be tied to the lognormal distribution.

Second, the stochastic hypothesis can be seen to incorporate systematic cost and market effects in a number of ways. Let us suppose that a simple Gibrat process *is* operating: since concentration is observed to vary between industries we must ascribe this to inter-industry differences in growth rate variance or alternatively to the age of the industry (since variance at time n is equal to the initial variance $\text{Var}(\log X_t)$ plus $n\sigma^2$ where σ^2 is the variance of growth rates in each period). So we must look for the structural reasons lying behind the differences in variance. Nor perhaps should we be too worried about the divergence of actual structure from a theoretical distribution: after all, the theoretical distribution is a limiting distribution as the number of time periods tends to infinity. In a short time horizon, quite large deviations from the theoretical distribution are not unlikely. Again we may wish to look for structural explanations of observed deviations from Gibrat's rule. One example is the observed decreasing variance with size. Hymer and Pashigian[22] have shown that this cannot be explained solely by regarding large firms as agglomerations of small firms with identical mean growth rates and variance. The lower variance of the large

[21] S. J. Prais, *The Evolution of Giant Firms in Britain* (Cambridge, 1976), 26.
[22] Hymer and Pashigian, op. cit.

firms is less than that expected on the basis of the law of large numbers. So a structural reason has to be found. The simple stochastic hypothesis can also be easily amended to include the birth of new firms. There is no reason why we should not look for *structural* reasons lying behind the rate of birth of new firms, arising out of our theory on barriers to entry. We have seen that it is perfectly possible to incorporate systematic size/growth effects. The main structural variable here would be the minimum economic size for a viable production unit in each sector. Finally, we will want to amend our view of the process of growth to include the possibility of growth by merger within a particular sector. These structural matters are the main substance of the rest of the chapter.

However, we shall not abandon the stochastic hypothesis, and this calls for some justification. We may write the growth equation for a firm in size class i at initial time t as

$$\frac{X_{i,t+1}}{X_{i,t}} = f(S_{i1}, S_{i2}, S_{i3} \ldots S_{ik}) \cdot u_{it}$$

where $S_{i1} \ldots S_{ik}$ are k structural variables relating to size class i and u_{it} is an error term. In a deterministic model $u_{it} = 0$. The industrial structure would evolve over time in response to the structure determining variables S. The interaction of these variables would determine whether the structure was constantly changing or whether it would eventually settle to a long-run dynamic equilibrium. Now suppose we allow for some uncertainty with $u_{it} \neq 0$. The outcome is now the result of interaction of deterministic and random elements. One possible interaction is the case where the increase in variance due to random shocks over time is offset by the phenomenon of regression (a systematic tendency for large firms to grow more slowly than small ones).

What justification is there then for continuing with the assumption that the random error term is still substantial, even when structural factors are included? One argument is simply the empirical matter that our understanding of the growth of firms is at best imperfect: the size of the error term is simply a measure of our ignorance. It is the 'unexplained variance' in econometric terminology. The counter to this argument is that ignorance should be dispelled, not allowed to remain. However, the matter is clarified by considering the possible explanations for the residual variance. If we have included in the equation all variables relating to the industry, and all variables relating to size classes within the industry, the residual variance must be traced back to the firms themselves. Specifically we return to the view of Chapter 2 that every firm is a *unique* bundle of resources. Hence we expect the growth response to differ between firms for which the structural variables (e.g. size class) were identical. This then is the source of error. The growth of the individual firm may indeed be determined given its internal structure and given the market structure variables. But a model of industry structure over time that included all the factors internal to the firms would cease to be a useful model. It would merely be a catalogue of each firm's growth history. It is more economical in model building, and more illuminating, to allow a substantial stochastic element in the model, so long as it is not forgotten in interpreting results that the residual variance is important in its own right as an indicator of internal factors in the growth of firms. For the individual firm, as the previous chapters of Part III attest, the growth process is very far from being an entirely random process.

2   INTER-INDUSTRY DIFFERENCES IN GROWTH RATE VARIANCE

Greater variance in the growth rate of firms in an industry will, *ceteris paribus*, lead to great dispersion of firm sizes over time, and hence an increase in concentration. We must therefore seek evidence on the stability of market shares in different markets. One hypothesis is that the nature of competition in the market is of critical importance. Oligopolistic rivalry in expenditures on advertising and product innovation was discussed in Chapters 12 and 13. Metwally[23] and Lambin[24] have both found evidence of firms reacting to rivals' advertising initiatives over time. Indeed, both suggest that these expenditures are reciprocally cancelling over a long period, so the incentive must come from the short-run gains in market shares that firms hope to make. They are always hoping that their rivals will not be able to match them in advertising effectiveness. A similar pattern of rivalry in R and D has been discussed by Grabowski and Baxter[25] in a time series analysis of R and D expenditures in U.S. chemicals, though the matching of expenditures was not so exact as those found for advertising. If the firms' expectations of gains in market shares are to be fulfilled, we will expect to observe fluctuations in market shares in those advertising

[23] M. M. Metwally, 'Advertising and Competitive Behaviour of Selected Australian Firms', *R. Econ. Stats.* 57 (1975), 417–27.

[24] J. J. Lambin, *Advertising, Competition and Market Conduct in Oligopoly over Time* (Amsterdam and Oxford, 1976).

[25] H. G. Grabowski, N. D. Baxter, 'Rivalry in Industrial Research and Development: An Empirical Study', *J.I.E.* 21 (1973), 209–35.

and R and D intensive sectors. This view gains credence from Telser's study[26] of market shares in food, soap, and cosmetics. The last two are much more heavily advertised and characterized by frequent brand changes. They also exhibit much less stable market shares than in food markets. In an article tracing the changes in market shares in various Australian sectors, Alemson[27] also found that competition via selling expenditures and product change led to fluctuating market shares, even where price agreements were in existence. The point is particularly clear for his studies of the cigarette and chocolate market.

Reekie[28] examined market share stability in 63 sub-markets in the U.K. food, medicaments, kitchen and household sppplies, and toiletries sectors. He found that market share mobility (measured by the standard deviation of firms' sales from their mean sales) was positively associated with advertising in foodstuffs and toiletries, but the relationship was weakly negative in the other sectors. Finally, Backman[29] showed that high advertising intensity tended to be associated with a rapid turnover of brands in a number of consumer non-durable sectors such as deodorants, soaps and detergents, and toothpaste. These also experienced fluctuations in market shares. Against these studies we set the results of Gort,[30] who studied the actual market shares of the largest 15 firms in 205 U.S. manufacturing sectors in 1947 and 1954. Stability coefficients were calculated for each sector by regressing market shares in one year against market shares in the other year. He found that high values of these coefficients were strongly associated with product differentiation. Other possible determinants of stability in market shares are not well researched. Gort found that stability was strongly associated with a high concentration ratio: a result that may be attributed to collusive oligopolistic behaviour in a concentrated market. He also found that stability was associated with slow growth in the industry. This last result is supported by some findings of Singh and Whittington.[31] They examined the 'mobility' of firms within the industrial structure by examining the changes in size rankings of firms in the industries over time. The smallest changes in rank occurred in the industries with the lowest growth.

The evidence on variability of market shares is not conclusive.

---

[26] L. G. Telser, 'Advertising and Competition', *J.P.E.* 72 (1964), 537–62.
[27] M. A. Alemson, 'Demand, Entry and the Game of Conflict in Oligopoly over Time: Recent Australian Experience', *O.E.P.* N.S. 21 (1969), 220–47.
[28] W. D. Reekie, 'Advertising and Market Share Mobility', *S.J.P.E.* 21 (1974), 143–58.
[29] J. Backman, *Advertising and Competition* (New York, 1967).
[30] M. Gort, 'Analysis of Stability and Change in Market Shares', *J.P.E.* 71 (1963), 51–61.
[31] Singh and Whittington, op. cit. (1975).

However a number of studies have gone a further step to associate R and D intensity and advertising intensity with changes in concentration, assuming variability of market shares as the explanation of the link. Weiss[32] analysed the changes in concentration 1947–54 and 1954–8 in 87 4-digit U.S. manufacturing industries. In the first period he found that the sharpest increases in concentration occurred in the consumer durable and durable equipment industries. These are the sectors where vigorous product competition is most common. However the same was not true of the second period. More recently Mueller and Hamm[33] carried out an analysis of changes in CR_4 in 166 U.S. 4-digit industries for the period 1947–70. Explanatory variables in the regression analysis included the industry growth rate, the initial level of concentration, and the degree of product differentiation (dummy variables for 'medium' and 'high' degrees of differentiation). The 'high' product differentiation variable had a coefficient of 16·5 percentage points for the period 1947–70, indicating an important contribution to the changes in concentration in those sectors. A parallel study by Dalton and Rhoades[34] for slightly different time periods reached an identical conclusion about the significance of product differentiation. Prais[35] however showed that in the period 1958–68, concentration rose faster in the less advertised sectors than in a number of highly advertised sectors in the U.K. His explanation is that the latter had already reached a high level of concentration (the average CR_5 was 82 per cent in 1958), and large increases were not possible. Admittedly tentative, these results should make us cautious about the interpretation of the studies reported in Chapters 12 and 13, which purported to find empirical support for a causal link from market structure *to* expenditure on R and D and/or advertising. Causation may well run in both directions, and this could not be settled except by recourse to a simultaneous equation model.

3   SCALE ECONOMIES, GROWTH AND CONCENTRATION

The theoretical reason for seeking an empirical relationship between the extent of economies of scale in a sector and the growth of firms and concentration needs no great elaboration. Economies of scale refer not only to the minimum size for least cost operations, but the whole shape of the curve up to that point. The level of costs at

[32] L. W. Weiss, 'Factors in Changing Concentration', *R. Econ. Stats.* 45 (1963), 70–7.
[33] Mueller and Hamm, op. cit.
[34] J. A. Dalton, S. A. Rhoades, 'Growth and product differentiability as factors influencing changes in concentration', *J.I.E.* 22 (1973–4), 235–40.
[35] Prais, op. cit. (1976), 83–4.

sub-optimal scale will be an important determinant of the 'surviv-ability' of small plants. This was discussed in Chapter 2. Here we are interested in two further aspects. The first is the effect of scale on the growth of firms: in terms of the discussion of section 1, we are considering the effect on the value of β. The second is the effect of scale on concentration, given the market size.

It is indisputable that the variance of growth rates is larger for small size classes of firms. This has been explained by Hymer and Pashigian[36] as the response of small firms to sub-optimal scale. They suggest that small firms have to go out of business, because of their small size. Hence some firms succeed in this programme, while others decline and eventually disappear. Mansfield[37] found, in his study of the growth experience of firms that managed to *survive*, that the growth rate of the smallest firms was on average greater than that of larger firms. This is consistent with the 'grow or go out of business' hypothesis of Hymer and Pashigian.

Other studies of the relationship of average growth rates to size of firm were reported above in section 1 of this chapter. The most reliable study (in terms of industry coverage and number of firms) is that of Singh and Whittington,[38] who found a slight positive rela-tionship between size and growth in 21 U.K. sectors, 1948–60. This suggests that economies of scale are not a strong determinant of growth rates of different firms.

An explanation for this has been advanced by Shen.[39] He used data for output, capital, and labour in c. 4,000 manufacturing plants in Massachusetts in each of the years 1935–59. The plants were grouped in 14 2-digit industries. He fitted an average expansion path for the manufacturing activity in each sector in each of 4 sub-periods, each path characterized by fixed elasticities (not propor-tions) between inputs and outputs. He then derived an expression for the elasticity of profit with respect to scale of output, following the analysis of Steindl.[40] The rate of profit is given by revenue, Q, minus variable cost, C, divided by capital stock, K:

$$\pi = \frac{Q - C}{K}$$

[36] Hymer and Pashigian, op. cit.   [37] Mansfield, op. cit.

[38] Singh and Whittington, op. cit. (1975).

[39] T. Y. Shen, 'Economies of Scale, Expansion Path and Growth of Plants', *R. Econ. Stats*. 47 (1965), 420–8; 'Economies of Scale, Penrose Effects, Growth of Plants and their Size Distribution', *J.P.E.* 78 (1970), 702–16.

[40] J. Steindl, *Random Processes and the Growth of Firms: A Study of the Pareto Law* (London, 1965).

Let C/Q and K/Q be the functions of scale, S, $F(s)$ and $\phi(s)$ respectively.

$$\therefore \qquad \pi = \frac{1 - F(s)}{\phi(s)}$$

$$\therefore \qquad \frac{d\pi}{ds} \cdot \frac{1}{\pi} = \frac{F'(s)}{1 - F(s)} - \frac{\phi'(s)}{\phi(s)}$$

$(d\pi/ds)(1/\pi)$ is the required profit elasticity. Shen's empirical results suggest that along the expansion path $F'(s)$ and $\phi'(s)$ are negative in most of the industries. So the majority of the firms are operating under conditions where the profit rate is an increasing function of scale. The incentive for increased scale applies to all firms. So Shen argues that mean growth rates will be the same for firms of all sizes. But the greater the returns to scale, the greater dispersion of firm sizes is to be expected. However, there are other factors militating against increasing concentration. The main one is the Penrose effect, which Shen adduces as the reason for the observed negative correlation between growth rates in successive long periods. Despite the profit incentive, rapid growth is a strain on the managerial resources of the firm. These issues were fully explored in Chapter 9.

Such systematic size–growth relationships as do exist can be very easily handled within the framework of stochastic processes. In an early contribution, Adelman[41] suggested that the development of industry structure could be studied by use of Markov chains. The main element in the analysis is a transition matrix: the rows represent initial size classes, the columns, size classes in the next period. Each entry in the matrix is then the probability that a firm in size class i in the initial period will have moved to size class j in the next period (where j can be a smaller class, a large class, or the same class). The transition probabilities can be appropriately weighted to reflect a particular hypothesis concerning the relation of size and growth. The development of industrial structure over time is found by taking some initial size distribution of firms and postmultiplying by the transition matrix. A second period vector of firm size distribution results. This procedure may be repeated indefinitely to generate the structure over time. Furthermore, so long as the transition matrix is a regular stochastic matrix,[42] the size structure will

---

[41] I. G. Adelman, 'A Stochastic Analysis of the Size Distribution of Firms', *J.A.S.A.* 53 (1958), 893–904.

[42] That is, one where a firm starting in size class i has a non-zero probability of moving to size class j in a finite number of periods.

tend to a long-run equilibrium state: that is, a vector of sizes which when post-multiplied by the transition matrix gives the initial vector again and is therefore invariant over time. Adelman calculated some probabilities for the U.S. steel industry on the basis of past growth experience. These probabilities were then used to simulate the development of the industrial structure over time. It was claimed that the results were not inconsistent with observed trends in the structure, in particular the growth in firm sizes without any appreciable increase in concentration (as determined by movements in the Lorenz curve).

(The second aspect is the long-run relationship between economies of scale and concentration,)the result of the growth process described above. The first exploration of the topic was by Bain.[43] Studies of economies of scale in 20 U.S. manufacturing industries gave estimates of the market share of an optimal size plant and firm in each sector. He then compared this with the average market share of the top four plants in each sector in 1947. He concluded that actual concentration went beyond that required by optimal scale considerations in 13 out of the 20 sectors. Only a rough correlation between economies of scale and observed concentration was evident. Pashigian[44] has also demonstrated a relationship between economies of scale and industry concentration. First, he examined the hypothesis that observed differences in concentration between industry are due to chance. His method was to generate the parameters of the (lognormal) distribution of *all* firms in *all* manufacturing sectors in the U.S. Suppose now that n firms are randomly selected from this population of firms, and are called an 'industry'. Then it is possible to derive a relationship between the size of the sample and the expected concentration ratio (four firm) of that sample. The concentration ratios of the hypothetical 'industries' based on a random sampling were compared with actual concentration ratios in 4-digit sectors. The result was an unequivocal rejection of the hypothesis that observed concentration ratios could arise simply from sampling the total population of firms. The actual concentration ratios were consistently less than those expected from random sampling. This is the consequence of firm sizes within actual industries being more uniform than the random sampling hypothesis would imply: there is a systematic tendency for sectors to have their own optimal size ranges of firms. Given this result, it is not surprising that Pashigian found that he was able to explain much of the variance in four firm

[43] J. S. Bain, 'Economies of Scale, Concentration and the Condition of Entry in 30 Manufacturing Industries', *A.E.R.* 44 (1954), 15–39.

[44] P. Pashigian, 'The Effect of Market Size on Concentration', *I.E.R.* 10 (1969), 291–315.

concentration ratios in 90 sectors, by variables reflecting minimum economic size as a proportion of the total market. Sawyer[45] reports similar results for 117 U.K. sectors in 1958 and 1963. However, he uses as his measures of optimal size indices derived from the actual size characteristics, notably the reciprocal of the Herfindahl index. This reduces the value of his results.

Weiss[46] sought an explanation of changes in concentration 1947–54 in 85 4-digit U.S. industries in terms of changes in the 'optimal' size of plant. His assumption is that changes in optimal plant size will be reflected in changes in the size of the 'mid-point' plant. Half of the output comes from plants larger than the mid-point plant and half from smaller plants. Concentration is affected by the change in optimal size relative to industry size. So the independent variable is defined as

$$P = \frac{1954 \text{ mid-point plant size}}{1954 \text{ industry size}} \bigg/ \frac{1947 \text{ mid-point plant size}}{1947 \text{ industry size}}$$

The dependent variable, C, is the ratio of CR_4 in 1954 to CR_4 in 1947. The regression equation was:

$$C = 0 \cdot 295P + 70 \cdot 19 \quad r = 0 \cdot 51$$
$$(3 \cdot 14)$$

This gives some support for the hypothesis that economies of plant size are important determinants of concentration.

In his more recent comparisons of industrial concentration in 2-digit manufacturing sectors, Pryor[47] found that concentration ratios showed remarkably similar patterns, despite great differences in market size. Indeed for the U.S., France, West Germany, Italy, Japan, and the Netherlands he concluded that there were no statistically significant differences in the concentration ratios in 20 sectors. The relationship of concentration ratios in the U.S. and the U.K. was not so close, though still significant at the 5 per cent level. The U.K. tended to have high concentration values compared to the U.S., for U.S. industries with low concentration, and vice versa. Pryor also demonstrates that the average size of establishment in manufacturing is highly correlated with market size indicators. So is the number of

[45] Sawyer, op. cit.   [46] Weiss, op. cit.
[47] F. L. Pryor, 'An International Comparison of Concentration Ratios', *R. Econ. Stats.* 54 (1972), 130–40.

enterprises with multiple establishments. So, as one would expect from the two previous results, is the average size of enterprises or firms.

However we must be cautious about ascribing too much of concentration to the effect of scale economies. In a study of differences in industrial structure between the U.K. and the U.S. in the 1950s, Bain[48] noted no systematic relationship between concentration in the two countries in 32 industries. One would expect concentration to be much higher in the U.K., given its smaller market size, if economies of scale were the explanation (this does, of course, ignore foreign trade). And this was precisely the case for *plant* concentration, which was on average 34 per cent higher than in the U.S. The conclusion is that the extent of multiplant operations by firms is more important than economies of plant size in explaining concentration. For example, Prais[49] found that the increase in concentration in 74 U.K. industries 1958–68 had a correlation coefficient of 0·50 with the increase in multiplant working. But this cannot be solely attributed to economies of scale at the firm level. In 10 out of the 12 industries studied by Scherer *et al.*,[50] the market share of the top 3 producers in each industry greatly exceeded the share required to exploit multiplant economies of scale (see Table 2.5, p. 56). These economies of scale included the possible advantages of size in marketing and R and D discussed in Chapters 12 and 13. We conclude that there are real inter-industry differences in concentration, but these cannot be solely attributed to inter-industry differences in scale economies. But the similarities revealed by international comparisons encourage us to seek for explanations that are industry specific.

4   TECHNICAL CHANGE, PRODUCT CHANGE, AND CHANGES IN CONCENTRATION

In section 1 we referred to the possibility of serial correlation in the growth of firms. There is little evidence on this point. Singh and Whittington,[51] in their study of 2,000 firms in 21 U.K. sectors 1948–60 found that firms with an above (below) average growth performance in the first six years tended to have the same in the subsequent six years. The reasonable inference is that 'success breeds

---

[48] J. S. Bain, *International Differences in Industrial Structure* (New Haven, 1966).
[49] Prais, op. cit. (1976), 69.
[50] F. M. Scherer, A. Beckenstein, E. Kaufer, R. D. Murphy, *The Economics of Multiplant Operations* (Cambridge, Mass., 1975).
[51] Singh and Whittington, op. cit. (1975).

success'. The implications of such a phenomenon for concentration were spelt out in section 1: concentration would increase rapidly over time.

The basis for 'success breeds success' models of firm growth is the two-way causation running from growth to profits and from profits to growth, spelt out in Chapter 9. The level of profits provides retention finance and attracts external finance for growth. Growth itself produces profits, though the opportunities open to each firm are constrained by the growth-of-demand function. Firms with particularly good management, or better market opportunities, will be less constrained than others, and hence will have higher growth rates *and* profit rates. This is Eatwell's explanation[52] of the positive relationship between profits and growth of firms over a number of years, observed by Singh and Whittington.[53] The implication of this analysis for the development of market structure over time requires specific consideration here. The particular case to be discussed is technical change and product change arising from R and D.

Downie[54] suggested a systematic tendency for technical change to lead to increased concentration. The main focus of his analysis is the supply side, so the relationships for demand, pricing, and profits are deliberate simplifications. First, we have a price equation implying a full cost pricing model. The price is set by adding a 'normal' profit margin to the weighted average of firms' costs. The profit function for each firm then follows, as the difference between the firm's average cost and the market price, multiplied by its output. Firms only continue in existence so long as profits are greater than zero. This determines at any time the number of firms, n, that are in the industry. Since each firm in the market has the same industry price, we assume that every firm has an equal share of the market.

The second, and more important part of the model, concerns the way in which average costs will change over time. The change in average costs per unit time in firm j is determined by the resources devoted to investment in physical capital I_j, and to investment in research and development R_j, in the same period. The more the firm spends the more its costs decline. I_j is determined directly as a given proportion of profits. But investment in R and D is determined by two factors, the availability of funds from profits, and by the incentive to innovate arising from an awareness that the firm's costs differ

[52] J. Eatwell, 'Growth, Profitability and Size', Appendix A of R. Marris, A. Wood (ed.), *The Corporate Economy* (London, 1971).

[53] Singh and Whittington, op. cit. (1968).

[54] J. Downie, *The Competitive Process* (London, 1958).

from the industry average. The last assumes that a high cost firm will make a special effort to reduce its costs by searching for lower cost techniques.[55]

Putting these elements together, we can discern two ways in which the current level of costs in firm j affects the rate of change in those costs over time. The first is the 'transfer mechanism' described by Downie: a firm with below-average costs will have higher profits, will therefore spend more on new equipment and on R and D, with a consequent decrease in its cost. The second term is Downie's innovation mechanism: high costs are an incentive to search for techniques which will reduce average cost. The typical situation, Downie suggests, will have the transfer mechanism outweighing the action of the innovation mechanism: in this case lower cost firms will have average costs which decline faster than high cost firms. If the industry starts out with a number of firms with different cost structures, it is clear that over time the least cost firms will have a faster decline in costs than high cost firms. As a result the weighted average costs of the industry will decline, and, hence via the price equation, the industry price. The decline in price will squeeze out the least efficient firms, thus decreasing the number of firms in the industry and hence the market share of each surviving firm. So concentration will inevitably increase. On the other hand a strong innovation mechanism could lead to a narrowing of cost differentials between firms, without any reduction in the number of firms, so concentration would not increase over time. This mechanistic and highly simplified model is intended as an illustration and should not be taken too seriously empirically. But Downie claims that a process similar to this can be observed in the development of industrial structures over time, so the model may have more than heuristic value. To make it operational one would need to have empirical evidence on the nature and parameters of the behavioural equations.

Shen[56] explored some of the issues raised by the Downie model in his analysis of c. 4,000 Massachusetts manufacturing firms, 1935-59. We explained above how he derived an expansion path for each of 14 sectors. He then classified plants into 5 technology classes for each industry, in terms of their position in input–output space with respect to the average expansion path. He found a high association (Chi-squared) between a plant's technology class and its growth rate.

---

[55] R. R. Nelson, S. G. Winter, H. L. Schuette, 'Technical Change in an Evolutionary Model', *Q.J.E.* 90 (1976), 90–118, postulate a similar mechanism in their model of technical change. Low profitability leads firms to search for more profitable techniques of production.

[56] T. Y. Shen, 'Competition, Technology and Market Share', *R. Econ. Stats.* 50 (1968), 96–102.

But he did not find evidence of persistence: technological mobility tended to be very high. One reason for this was the importance of the vintage of the technology employed in a plant. He compared the expansion paths of 1935 plants with those of plants started after 1935. The elasticity of output with respect to labour inputs was higher in the 'new' plants in 10 out of the 14 sectors. Hence the old plants were at a disadvantage in a period of rising labour costs.

Finally we note the impact of product innovation on market shares. Menge[57] drew attention to the elimination of small car producers in the U.S. despite no aggressive price cutting by the large companies. He argued that the competitive weapon employed was the style change. Each style change requires new dies. For large volume producers these would wear out with production over a much shorter period than for a small volume producer. So unit costs are lower for large volume producers who change styles frequently. A small producer either incurs higher per unit die costs or cannot keep up with consumer demand for changing styles. Either way the small producer will be squeezed out of business.

We conclude that technical and product change are capable of creating systematic growth advantages for certain successful firms. Whether this is completely offset by other factors is not clear from the evidence. But if it is not, we would expect serial correlations in firms' growth rates over time, and hence increasing concentration.

5   NEW ENTRY AND THE DEVELOPMENT OF MARKET STRUCTURE

So far we have considered mainly the development of industrial structure arising from differential growth of firms within the industry. We must now turn our attention to those factors determining the number of firms in an industry over time. In this section the emphasis will be on new entry: in the next section we will look at exit due to merger.

The traditional theory on barriers to new entry[58] emphasized price setting to exclude new entrants altogether. More recent developments in theory have pointed out that it may be in the best interests of the firm to set a rather higher price in the short run and accept some new entry in the long run. The presumption is that the rate of entry will in some way be determined by the industrial structure.

An early contribution to this is the theory of industrial structure

[57] J. A. Menge, 'Style Change Costs as a Market Weapon', *Q.J.E.* 76 (1962), 632–47.
[58] F. Modigliani, 'New Developments in the Oligopoly Front', *J.P.E.* 66 (1962), 214–32.

proposed by Worcester.[59] His 'independent maximization hypo-thesis' was described in Chapter 6. Here we are interested in the im-plications for market structure, so we reproduce the relevant part of the analysis. Firms enter a market one at a time, each acting as a profit maximizer given the output of previous entrants. For simpli-city, we assume that costs are constant above a certain minimum economic size, and that the market demand does not shift over time. The situation is illustrated in Figure 15.1, where c' is average cost

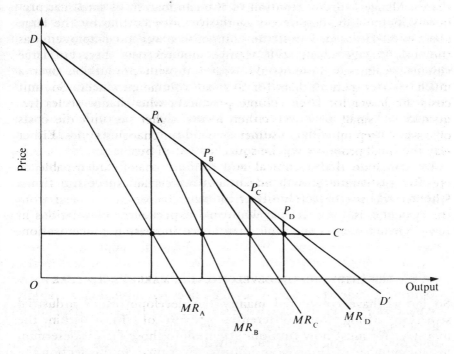

Fig. 15.1

above minimum economic size and DD' is the demand curve. The first firm, A, faces the industry as a monopolist: he equates marginal revenue and marginal cost and prices at P_A. The second firm, B, then faces the marginal demand curve, $P_A D'$ (since firm A does not reduce output, but simply allows the price to fall), with marginal revenue curve MR_B. So firm B prices at P_B. Exactly the same occurs for subsequent entrants C and D etc., until new entry is prevented by considerations of minimum economic scale. The end result of this process involves specific market shares. Firm A will have an

[59] D. A. Worcester, *Monopoly, Big Business and Welfare in the Postwar US* (Seattle, 1967), Chapters 5 and 6. © 1967 by the University of Washington Press.

output half the competitive output, Firm B will have $\frac{1}{4}$, Firm C $\frac{1}{8}$, and Firm D $\frac{1}{16}$. This follows directly from our assumption of a linear market demand curve. So in terms of industry output firm A will provide $\frac{8}{15}$, firm B $\frac{4}{15}$, firm C $\frac{2}{15}$, and firm D $\frac{1}{15}$. It is simple to calculate the market shares for any final total number of firms in the industry. All firms do, of course, have the same margin. So the larger profits of the first firm come from having a larger market share albeit at a low margin.

On the face of it this does not seem to be a very convincing argument. But the implications for industrial structure ensures its retention as a possibility. For the size structure that it predicts is common among the 3 or 4 leading firms in U.S. manufacturing sectors (1954) according to the evidence Worcester presents. (Further, the size structure would accord well with an observed lognormal distribution of firms.) Leading firms of approximately equal size were very uncommon. Where firms were closer in size there was evidence of collusive market sharing. Furthermore the hypothesis predicts an equilibrium profit margin for the industry that is due to barriers to entry. So it is also consistent with the body of evidence relating profit rates to entry barriers. The hypothesis cannot be regarded as proven but nor can it be easily rejected.

In further, theoretical development, Worcester dealt with alternative demand configurations. It is not hard to see that a demand curve which was convex viewed from the origin would imply a size structure in which the second firm was more than half the first in size, and the third more than half the second, and so on. The alternative would be a concave function in which sizes diminished more rapidly. Demand *shifts* over time are less easily accommodated. It depends on the ability of firms to expand to meet growth. It is not entirely obvious that they will obtain the growth in precise proportion to their initial market share. And, of course, a growing market may make it easier for firms to enter at the margin.

This point was examined by Kamerschen,[60] following earlier studies by Nelson[61] and Shepherd.[62] His sample was U.S. 4-digit S.I.C. industries: 177 for the whole period 1947–63, and rather more of them for shorter sub-periods. He regressed the change in concentration ratio on the growth rate of each sector. He found a significant negative relationship for the whole period, but no relationship in the

    [60] D. R. Kamerschen, 'Market Growth and Industry Concentration', *J.A.S.A.* 63 (1968), 228–41.

    [61] R. L. Nelson, 'Market Growth, Company Diversification, and Product Concentration', *J.A.S.A.* 55 (1960), 640–9.

    [62] W. G. Shepherd, 'Trends of Concentration in American Manufacturing, 1947–58', *R. Econ. Stats.* 46 (1964), 200–12.

short sub-periods. Addition of a 'net entry' variable (the percentage increase in the number of firms) to the regression equation made the growth rate insignificant even for the whole period. He concludes either that the relationship only holds over long periods, or that the relationship has become systematically weaker over time. Dalton and Rhoades[63] have reached a similar conclusion for the period 1954–67, with a sample of 187 4-digit S.I.C. U.S. industries. Over the whole period growth had a negative effect on concentration, but for the shorter period 1963–7 the relationship was positive. The explanation offered is that in the short periods large established firms are best placed to take advantage of market growth, but in the long run they cannot prevent entry. They also found that a dummy variable for consumer goods had a positive effect on the change in concentration.

A study by Orr[64] is a full articulation of a barriers to entry model in which entry is induced in the long run by a profit level exceeding the 'no-entry' profit rate arising from market structure. Thus the model is developed in two equations. The first is

$$\pi^* = f_1(X, K, C, A, R.)$$

where π^* is the long-run equilibrium profit rate predicted on the basis of entry barriers, such as market share of a plant of minimum economic size (X), capital requirements of such a firm (K), industry concentration $(C$, a dummy variable for high concentration), and advertising and research and development intensity variables $(A$ and $R)$. The second equation is

$$E = f_2(\pi - \pi^*, \dot{Q}, S, r)$$

where E is the rate of entry, π is the observed profit rate in the sector (so $\pi - \pi^*$ represents the profit gap above the no-entry barrier), $\dot{Q}$ is the past industry growth rate of output, S is the total *size* of the industry, and r is a measure of risk. Orr then substitutes the first equation into the entry equation to get a testable model. On a test on 71 sectors he finds that such a model accounts for about 43 per cent of the variance in entry rates between 71 Canadian manufacturing sectors:

[63] Dalton and Rhoades, op. cit.
[64] D. Orr, 'The Determinants of Entry: A Study of the Canadian Manufacturing Industries', *R. Econ. Stats.* 56 (1974), 58–66.

π	Q	$\log K$	A	R	r	C	$\log S$
0·03	0·01	−0·24**	−0·13**	−0·07*	−0·08	−0·89**	0·51**

**significant at 99 per cent level   *95 per cent level.

Capital requirements, advertising, and concentration emerge significantly as reducing entry, but neither the profit rate nor the growth rate are significant as inducements to entry. Given Orr's results, we would expect industries with high entry barriers to be particularly protected against declines in concentration. Duchesneau[65] argues that where barriers are substantial or low, firms maximize profits by setting high prices and accepting new entry over time, so concentration will decline. But where barriers are high, the market can be successfully protected against entry. In a study of 24 4-digit U.S. industries, 1947–67, he found strong support for this view. Changes in concentration were significantly and negatively related to initial concentration levels, but a dummy for high barriers had a large positive coefficient (representing a gain of about 16 percentage points in CR_4 over the period in industries with high barriers). Mueller and Hamm[66] analysed a sample of 166 4-digit S.I.C. industries over the longer period 1947–60. They used a product differentiation dummy variable instead of the more general qualitative entry variable, but again found it made a positive contribution to changes in concentration (16·5 percentage points on average, 1947–60). The size of the product differentiation effect suggests that it is acting on concentration in two separate ways. First it is a deterrent to entry. Second, it contributes positively to concentration as described in section 2 above.

A study by Guth[67] switches attention from the dynamics of entry to the long-run equilibrium concentration to be expected in an industry where there are substantial entry barriers. He examines particularly the role of advertising in determining new entry. His first hypothesis is the conventional one that advertising raises the barriers to entry. He also argues that it will increase concentration, for two reasons. The first is that product differentiation makes it difficult for small firms in the industry to grow very much and that it is a particular barrier to large-scale entry. Secondly, successful differentiation will enable market leaders to obtain and hold a large market share. So one would expect advertising and concentration as

[65] T. D. Duchesneau, 'Barriers to Entry and the Stability of Market Structure: A Note', *J.I.E.* 22 (1973–4), 315–19.
[66] Mueller and Hamm, op. cit.
[67] L. A. Guth, 'Advertising and Market Structure', *J.I.E.* 19 (1971), 179–98.

measured by the four firm concentration ratio to be highly correlated. His second hypothesis derives from the finding that high advertising barriers are correlated with high profits (Comanor and Wilson[68]). This will, of course, make the industry extremely attractive to new entrants. Given the industry structure, large-scale entry will not be possible, but differentiation of products may enable a small firm to find a niche in the market. So his second prediction is that there will be a fringe of small firms in the market. Combining this with a large market share for a few leading firms we have the outcome that the Gini coefficient (a measure of relative firm size) will be high. Tests of these two hypotheses revealed little support for the first: concentration ratios were better explained by economies of scale variables. But the second hypothesis was upheld by a strong statistically significant relationship between the Gini coefficient and the advertising/sales ratio (for 35 U.S. 3-digit industries in 1958 and 1963).

6 MERGERS AND MARKET CONCENTRATION

Merger is the last of the determinants of industry structure over time that we must consider. The role of merger in industrial concentration is receiving increasing attention from economists, and the view is now emerging that merger activity is the major contributor to observed trends in concentration. The reasons for merger activity were fully explored in Chapter 12: here we look solely at their impact on industrial structure.

The idea that merger should increase concentration is not particularly startling theoretically. The main interest is in the empirical contribution of merger to observed concentration changes. So the emphasis is on techniques of measurement. The first systematic study at an industry level is that of Weiss,[69] tracing the effect of mergers on observed concentration ratios in 6 U.S. sectors. Four firm and eight firm concentration ratios were calculated at approximately 10-year intervals between 1930 and 1960: the precise dates were determined by data availability. All mergers in this period in the industries were traced. Then the changes in concentration were apportioned (by means of indices) to merger, internal growth, entry of new firms, exit from the industry, and a residual described as displacement, which allowed for changes in the identity of the top firms

[68] W. S. Comanor, T. A. Wilson, 'Advertising, Market Structure and Performance', *R. Econ. Stats.* 49 (1967), 423–40.
[69] L. W. Weiss, 'An Evaluation of Mergers in Six Industries', *R. Econ. Stats.* 47 (1965), 172–81.

in each time period. The method of calculating the components seems entirely reasonable. At first it seems as though merger contributes the largest components to increasing concentration. But as Weiss points out, his method may overstate the contribution, since mergers frequently involve the displacement of other leading firms, particularly in the case of the four firm concentration ratio. The problem is the use of the concentration ratio as the fundamental measure of concentration. Allowing for this bias, merger appears to be no more important as a source of concentration than are exit and internal growth. Only entry is unimportant.[70] Recent studies for a sample of 30 U.K. product groups by Hart, Utton, and Walshe[71] do however give greater weight to mergers in 10 sectors; but suggest that a further 11 sectors experienced increasing concentration which cannot be attributed to merger. In a study of 150 U.K. product markets, George[72] found that the largest increases in concentration ratios during the 1960s were associated with those sectors where merger activity had been most intense.

The most extensive investigation of the role of merger in changes in concentration in Britain has been carried out by Hannah and Kay,[73] for the period 1919–76. Their analysis has two drawbacks which should be mentioned at the start. The first is that they confine themselves to quoted companies (with a few major exceptions), thus excluding many medium and small businesses from consideration. Secondly, the level of aggregation is high: the analysis is conducted at the 2-digit S.I.C. level. But they did have a complete set of information relating to mergers, which had been lacking in previous studies.[74] And they use a superior index of concentration: the numbers equivalent form of the Herfindahl or entropy measure. They examined three periods. In the first, 1919–30, they found that concentration increased substantially due to both merger and internal growth. In the period 1930–48, concentration fell somewhat in all sectors (i.e. the numbers equivalent measure rose). Merger was not important in this period.

Results for the period 1957–69 are tabulated in Table 15.1. They are derived by merging the firms of 1957 with their subsequent

[70] An application by J. Muller ('The Impact of Mergers on Concentration: A Study of Eleven West German Industries', *J.I.E.* 25 (1976–7), 113–32) of Weiss's technique to 11 4-digit S.I.C. West German sectors also found that merger was the major contribution to increase in CR_4 and CR_8 in the period 1958–71, though internal growth was also important in explaining changes in CR_8.

[71] P. E. Hart, M. Utton, G. Walshe, *Mergers and Concentration in British Industry*, N.I.E.S.R. (Cambridge, 1973).

[72] George, op. cit.   [73] Hannah and Kay, op. cit.

[74] Notably the study of Hart and Prais, 'The Analysis of Business Concentration', *J.R.S.S.* 119, Part 2 (1956), 150–91.

Table 15.1. *Source of Changes in Concentration in U.K. Industry 1957–1969*

S.I.C. Industry group	Measure	1957	Change due to merger	Change due to internal growth	1969
III Food	(i)	62·1	+12·9	+ 5·5	80·5
	(ii)	28·3	− 9·9	− 1·7	16·7
	(iii)	19·6	− 5·9	− 0·9	12·8
IV Drink	(i)	40·8	+45·4	+ 1·0	87·2
	(ii)	55·7	−41·6	− 0·4	13·7
	(iii)	23·5	−14·5	+ 0·1	9·1
V Tobacco	(i)	100	−	−	100
	(ii)	2·9	− 0·6	− 0·0	2·3
	(iii)	1·9	− 0·2	+ 0·0	1·8
VI Chemicals	(i)	80·6	+ 2·0	+ 3·8	86·4
	(ii)	10·6	− 2·3	+ 0·2	8·5
	(iii)	3·8	− 0·3	+ 0·1	3·6
VII Metal Manufacture	(i)	58·7	+16·7	− 1·1	74·3
	(ii)	28·8	−15·9	+ 3·5	16·4
	(iii)	13·4	− 8·0	+ 2·5	7·9
VIII Non-Electrical Engineering	(i)	39·0	+ 6·0	−12·9	32·1
	(ii)	74·4	−19·3	+21·7	76·8
	(iii)	24·5	− 3·3	+27·5	48·7
IX Electrical Engineering	(i)	60·4	+22·0	− 1·2	81·2
	(ii)	33·0	−21·5	+ 4·0	15·5
	(iii)	17·3	−12·4	+ 2·9	7·8
X Shipbuilding	(i)	80·3	+10·5	+ 2·5	93·3
	(ii)	15·1	− 4·4	− 1·3	9·4
	(iii)	10·7	− 2·4	− 1·5	6·8
XI Vehicles and Aircraft	(i)	67·2	+20·0	− 1·4	85·8
	(ii)	25·7	−14·2	+ 1·3	12·8
	(iii)	15·7	− 8·6	+ 1·0	8·1
XII Metal goods n.e.s.	(i)	67·2	+12·8	− 2·9	77·1
	(ii)	20·8	− 8·5	+ 2·5	14·8
	(iii)	6·5	− 1·8	+ 1·2	5·9
XIII Textiles	(i)	55·9	+23·4	− 5·1	74·2
	(ii)	47·2	−32·0	+ 2·4	17·6
	(iii)	15·5	− 9·4	+ 0·6	6·7

Continued over

Table 15.1 *(cont.)*

S.I.C. Industry group	Measure	1957	Change due to merger	Change due to internal growth	1969
XVI Building Materials	(i)	71·2	+ 3·2	− 9·4	65·0
	(ii)	19·3	− 2·7	+ 1·3	17·9
	(iii)	9·6	+ 0·5	+ 2·1	11·6
XVII Paper and publishing	(i)	63·6	+16·1	− 1·6	78·1
	(ii)	27·7	−11·5	+ 1·3	17·4
	(iii)	11·3	− 2·9	+ 0·7	9·1

Source: L. Hannah, J. Kay, *Concentration in Modern Industry* (London, 1977), pp. 89–91. Measures of concentration: (i) CR_{10} per cent; (ii) numbers-equivalent form of the entropy measures; (iii) numbers-equivalent form of the Herfindahl index. The properties of the three measures are discussed in Chapter 00. Note that a decrease in (ii) and (iii) is a sign of increasing concentration. Reproduced by permission of MacMillan, London and Basingstoke.

merger partners in the next 13 years. This gave by comparison with the actual 1957 population an estimate of the effect of merger on concentration. Any residual between this and the actual change in concentration 1957 to 1969 was attributed to 'internal growth'. The overwhelming importance of merger is evident from the table. Only in Non-Electrical Engineering is internal growth important, reflecting a decline by a dominant firm. And only in Building Materials is there ambiguity about the effect of merger. In general, internal growth is of minor importance, sometimes contributing to an increase in concentration, sometimes to a decrease. The uniform pattern across all sectors leads Hannah and Kay to seek a general explanation for mergers in this period, rather than industry specific explanations.

B INDUSTRIAL CONCENTRATION

As firms grow, they tend also to diversify. Diversification may involve expansion into new product lines, or it may come from vertical integration, back into supplying sectors or forwards into distributing sectors. So the large modern firm typically will be operating in several markets. As far as a single market is concerned, we are interested only in that part of the firm which operates in that market. The alternative is to ignore the markets in which firms operate, and look at their total size. Interest in this matter has come as much from those who wish to stress the political implications of concentrations of economic assets in a few companies, as from other economists who observe uneasily that resources are allocated by managers *within* large companies with very little 'discipline' enforced by markets. The size of firms, and the implications for the goals they pursue, were discussed in Chapter 8. Here we confine our analysis to changes in aggregate concentration over time.

Much of the attention has been focused on changes in the share of the largest 100 manufacturing businesses in net output or in assets of the manufacturing sector. The estimation of these shares from data that are at best imperfect before the Second World War has attracted a great deal of discussion.[75] To avoid confusion it is convenient to concentrate on the estimates made by Prais,[76] which are plotted in Figure 15.2. The most notable feature of the graphs is the very sharp rise in concentration in the U.K. in the period

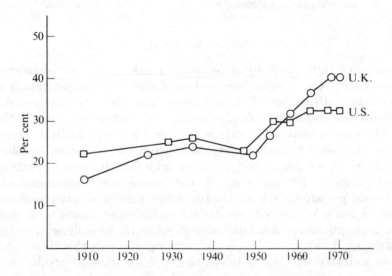

Fig. 15.2. Share of the hundred largest enterprises in manufacturing net output, U.K. and U.S. Source: J. Prais, *The Evolution of Giant Firms in Britain* (Cambridge, 1976), Chart 6.1, p. 140.

[75] Prais (op. cit., 1976), Appendix A for the U.K. and Appendix E for the U.S., gives an extended discussion. Other valuable sources for the U.S. are Blair, op. cit. 60–71, Scherer, *Industrial Market Structure and Economic Performance* (Chicago, 1970), 43, N. R. Collins, L. E. Preston, 'The Size Structure of the Largest Industrial Firms, 1909–1958', *A.E.R.* 51 (1961), 986–1011, and for the U.K., S. Aaronovitch, M. Sawyer, *Big Business* (New York), 1975), Ch. 6. The estimates given by Hannah and Kay, op. cit., for the U.K. refer only to the assets of the quoted manufacturing sector, and are correspondingly much larger than the estimates for the share of the 100 largest corporations in net output of the whole sector.

[76] Prais, op. cit. (1976).

1949–70, a rise which is not paralleled in the U.S. experience. The other main feature is the dip in concentration in the decade spanning the Second World War, which is evident in both countries. In neither country can the current level of concentration be explained by plant size. The concentration ratio of the largest 100 plants has remained stable at 9–10 per cent in both countries over a large number of years. This suggests that multiplant operation is extensive, and that is confirmed by the data for the largest 200 manufacturing enterprises in the U.S., which had an average of 45 plants each. In the U.K. the degrees of multiplant operation has risen rapidly for the 100 largest enterprises, from 27 in 1958 to 72 in 1972. It is notable that in employment terms the average size of plant has fallen from 750 to 430 employees in the same period.

That, briefly, is the evidence on changes in aggregate concentration. Now we turn to explanations.

1   DIVERSIFICATION AND VERTICAL INTEGRATION

The study of both diversification and vertical integration has been hampered by lack of data. So our knowledge of these matters is at best sketchy. Difficulties of making measurements of vertical integration have been emphasized by Adelman.[77] A suggested measure is the ratio of value added to sales for a firm (or sector). In a sector without vertical integration, each firm would buy in semi-finished inputs from other firms, add to value added in its own operation, before selling to the next stage in the production process. So the ratio would probably be low. On the other hand a sector which was integrated back to primary materials would have firms with high ratios. Unfortunately, the ratio also depends on how close the firm is to primary production. Adelman's example makes this clear. Consider an industry with three firms, one at each stage of production, primary, manufacturing, and distribution, each contributing one-third of total value added. Assuming that the firm in primary production requires no material inputs, its ratio will be 1·00. The manufacturing firm will have a ratio of 0·5 and the distributor of 0·33. But our intuition is that the degree of vertical integration is the same in every sector. An alternative measure suggested by Adelman is the ratio of inventory (or work in progress) to sales. His argument is that the longer the production line, the larger the number of processes and hence the more work in progress. This measure is not distorted by 'nearness' to primary production, but

[77] M. A. Adelman in G. J. Stigler (ed.), *Business Concentration and Price Policy*, N.B.E.R. (Princeton, 1955), 318–21.

there are likely to be major inter-industry differences related as much to the nature of processes and the valuation of materials as to the degree of vertical integration.

Difficulties of measurement are no doubt one reason for the lack of systematic study of vertical integration, though its importance in particular cases has been stressed by Blair.[78] Gort[79] made an analysis of vertical integration in 111 large U.S. corporations. He distinguished for each firm those production activities which were subsidiary to the main activity, and either supplied inputs to that activity or were supplied by it. The ratio of employment in these subsidiary activities to total employment was taken as a measure of vertical integration. Petroleum firms were found to have the highest index (67 per cent). At the other end of the scale came firms in transportation equipment (9·7 per cent) and electrical equipment (12·8 per cent). He also found a weak rank correlation (0·37) between firm size and his measure of vertical integration. Unfortunately there is no evidence on changes in vertical integration over time at the firm level. We therefore have no indication as to what extent the rise in aggregate concentration can be attributed to this source.

For diversification our information is rather more detailed. A study by Houghton[80] of the 1,000 largest U.S. corporations in 1962 analysed the number of product lines (5-digit S.I.C.) in which each firm was operating in 1950 and 1962. The information is summarized in Table 15.2. There is a clear indication of a rapid increase in

Table 15.2.

Number of product lines	Number of firms in each class	
	1950	1962
1	78	49
2–5	354	223
6–15	432	477
16–50	128	236
>50	8	15

diversification: the number of firms with 16 or more product lines virtually doubled over the period. Gort[81] also reported on the diversification activities of his sample of 111 large U.S. firms. He noted

[78] Blair, op. cit., Ch. 2.
[79] U.S. Senate, Committee on the Judiciary, Subcommittee on Anti-trust and Monopoly, Hearings, Economic Concentration: evidence of M. Gort, pp. 673–6.
[80] Ibid., evidence of H. F. Houghton, pp. 155–8.
[81] M. Gort, *Diversification and Integration in American Industry* (Princeton, 1962).

an increasing tendency to choose new product lines outside the firm's primary 2-digit sector. In the period 1950–4, no less than 68 per cent of the additional products were in 2-digit industries other than the firms' primary operations.

For the U.K. more recent evidence is available.[82] Prais[83] noted that large enterprises tended to grow by diversification rather than within sectors. Data were available on the diversification of output in 51 industrial sectors for all U.K. manufacturing enterprises employing more than 5,000 people in 1958 and 1963. In 1958 there were 180 such companies, with an average diversification of 6·6 industrial groups. Thirty-eight enterprises were completely specialized. By 1963, there were 210 firms in this category, but only 19 were specialized in one sector and the average diversification had risen to 7·5. A recent study by Utton[84] of the largest 200 U.K. manufacturing enterprises in 1974 provides further insights into diversification in 121 industrial sectors (3-digit S.I.C.). On average the five primary activities of each firm accounted for 89 per cent of their employment, and the most important activity of each firm for 57 per cent. Thus the diversification of activities is highly skewed. To cope with this Utton proposes a summary measure of diversification.[85] He plots an enterprise cumulative diversification curve (see Figure 15.3). Industries in which the firm operates, i, are ranked in order of their employment. The proportion of employment in each sector p_i is cumulated vertically. The index used is twice the area above the diversification curve, which is given by:

$$W = 2 \sum_{i=1}^{n} i p_i - 1$$

This index has the useful property that it takes the value 1 when the firm is completely specialized, and the value n when the firm has its activities equally spread among n sectors. Hence any value for a particular firm can be interpreted as a 'numbers equivalent'. The weighted average value of this index for the 200 enterprises was

[82] Other studies are: L. R. Amey, 'Diversified Manufacturing Businesses', *J.R.S.S.* 127 (1964), 251–90; P. K. Gorecki, 'An Interindustry Analysis of Diversification in the UK Manufacturing Sector', *J.I.E.* 24 (1975), 131–43; J. Hassid, 'Recent Evidence on Conglomerate Diversification in UK Manufacturing Industry', *Manchester School*, 43 (1975), 372–95.

[83] Prais, op. cit. (1976).

[84] M. A. Utton, 'Large Firm Diversification in British Manufacturing Industry', *E.J.* 87 (1977), 96–113.

[85] Measures of diversification are discussed in P. K. Gorecki, 'The Measurement of Enterprise Diversification', *R. Econ. Stats.* 56 (1974), 399–401.

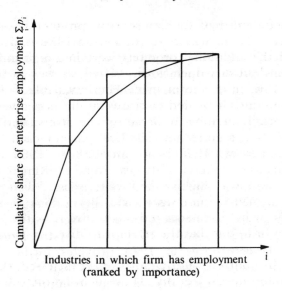

Fig. 15.3

4·39. Within the sample, there was clear tendency for the index to decrease with the ranking of firms. Finally the evidence suggested that about two-thirds of the average firm's diversification is into sectors with close technical or marketing links with the primary industry in which it operates.

The explanation of diversification as a means to growth received attention in Chapter 14. Here we report some empirical analyses of the phenomenon. An early study by Amey[86] found that diversification by firms was correlated with the size of enterprise, and the employment of scientific manpower in the sectors into which the firm was diversifying. But diversification was only weakly correlated with growth in these sectors. Gort's analysis[87] confirmed the finding on the R and D intensity of sectors into which firms diversify.

The useful study of Berry[88] seeks to link diversification to firm growth. He constructed diversification indices for 460 large U.S. corporations in 1960 and 1965. The index was defined as

$$D = 1 - \sum_i h_i^2$$

[86] Amey, op. cit.   [87] Gort, op. cit. (1962).
[88] C. H. Berry, 'Corporate Growth and Diversification', *J. Law Econ.* 14 (1971), 371–83.

where h_i is the value of the firm's output in sector i as a proportion of the total value of the firm's output. This 'Herfindahl' type index of diversification has the advantage of taking into account the size of the firm's output which is diversified, as well as the number of sectors into which it is diversified. The index takes a value of 0 for the single product firm, and increases as the firm diversifies equally into an increasing number of sectors. Berry calculated this index for 2-digit and 4-digit industrial classifications for each firm. He then regressed firm growth 1960–5 on a number of variables, including the observed changes in the two indices. The 4-digit index had a positive coefficient and was highly significant. The 2-digit index had a negative sign but was not significant. Berry took these to indicate that fast growth was associated with diversification on a *narrow base* by the firm, but that the attempt to diversify more broadly was a hindrance to growth.

Studies by Sutton and Grant[89] have stressed the managerial motivation for diversification. They identify three basic elements. The first is the growth rate of existing product lines. Where these are low or falling the firm has an incentive to seek new, faster-growing sectors to expand into. A second is firm expenditures on 'innovation', both R and D and the marketing of new products. Sutton describes this as 'market pull'. R and D may identify new product lines with high potential, even if existing products are satisfactory. Firms will diversify to take advantage of these opportunities. Third, they will diversify to reduce market risks. Attempts to test these hypotheses did not prove encouraging. The current growth of the firm was positively correlated with diversification, marketing expenditures negatively—the reverse of the theoretical expectations.

2 CONCENTRATION

The development of the aggregate distribution of firm sizes can be easily fitted into a stochastic model. Each firm is subject to a wide range of influences on its growth performance, depending on its particular resources and the conditions in each of the markets in which it operates. Comparing one firm with another chosen at random we have no reason to believe that there will be any systematic differences in their growth performance, except for the possibility that size and growth go together. The rate of entry of new firms will not be determined by a particular industrial structure. And

[89] C. J. Sutton, 'Management Behaviour and a Theory of Diversification', *S.J.P.E.* 20 (1973), 27–42; R. M. Grant, 'On the Theory of Diversification: A Comment', *S.J.P.E.* 21 (1974), 77–83.

we will not expect any variable except size to be a systematic determinant of takeover buyers and victims. Since most of the studies consider the size distribution of the top firms only (e.g. Fortune 500 or all firms with stock market quotations) we must also allow for 'deaths'—firms which drop out of the lists for reasons other than merger. But again we would expect no variable but size to influence the probability that a firm will die. So the main discussion on overall concentration concerns the degree to which concentration changes over time can be attributed either to the Gibrat effect, or to systematic size effects, or to merger.

Simon and Bonini[90] analysed data for the Fortune 500 Corporations 1954-6. Transition matrices by size classes for 1954-5, and 1955-6, indicated that the average growth rates of firms was independent of size, and that the variance was also independent of size. Assuming a constant birth-rate of new firms the transition probabilities would generate a Yule distribution of firm sizes over time. Simon and Bonini proceeded to fit this distribution to the data and pronounced themselves satisfied with the statistical fit. Collins and Preston[91] carried out a similar exercise for the 100 largest corporations in manufacturing at approximately 10-year intervals since 1919. For each 10-year period they constructed transition matrices for firm sizes, and derived from this a probability matrix. This was then used to predict the 1958 structure. There was a marked tendency for concentration to be less than that actually observed. They suggested a number of reasons for this. First, the number of entrants and exits declined steadily over time. Second, the mobility of firms in the structure of firm sizes diminished. Third, there was an unspecified increase in concentration due to merger. A study by Ijiri and Simon[92] concentrated on explanations for the observed departures from the strict Pareto curve. The actual size distribution for 831 large U.S. corporations (Fortune list) in 1969 showed a pronounced pattern of deviations for intermediate-sized firms. For example, the actual size of the 100th-ranked firm was approximately twice the size predicted by a fitted Pareto curve. They show that this can be explained by merger activity. Small firms are more likely to be victims than large ones. They are also more likely to register substantial growth by merger. Ijiri and Simon compare the 1969 size distribution of firms with what it could have been had no mergers

[90] H. A. Simon, C. P. Bonini, 'The Size Distribution of Business Firms', *A.E.R.* 48 (1958), 607-17.
[91] N. R. Collins, L. E. Preston, 'The Size Structure of the Largest Industrial Firms, 1909-58', *A.E.R.* 51 (1961), 986-1011.
[92] Ijiri and Simon, op. cit. (1974).

taken place, and conclude that mergers are largely responsible for the observed deviations.

Turning now to the U.K. context, there have been a series of studies by Hart and Prais[93] on the quoted company sector. These studies emphasize the role of the Gibrat effect. Merger is not considered separately, possibly because the data series for mergers was inadequate. It is another random factor in the growth of firms, though it may be systematically related to the size of firm. In the latest study by Prais,[94] the emphasis is on the phenomenon of 'regression': the tendency for the rate of growth of a firm to be related to its size as measured by $(\beta-1)$ in the growth equation:

$$\frac{X_{t+1}}{X_t} = \alpha X_t^{(\beta-1)} \epsilon_t$$

(The properties of this equation were discussed at the beginning of the chapter.) In the period prior to the Second World War $(\beta-1)$ had the value -0.02. But this 'regression', the tendency of large firms to grow more slowly than small ones, was not sufficient to outweigh the Gibrat effect, so concentration increased at a moderate rate. Prais suggests that a value of -0.10 would have been needed to prevent an increase in concentration. In the war period, 1939–50, there was exceptionally strong 'regression', with $(\beta-1)$ equal to -0.23, and deconcentration was the result. Finally, in the post-war period, the growth of large firms is particularly favoured with $(\beta-1)$ having a positive value, possibly as large as $+0.12$. Between 1949 and 1970, aggregate concentration rose from 22 per cent to 41 per cent, measured by the share of the 100 largest enterprises in manufacturing net output. About half of this rise can be attributed to the systematic factors favouring the growth of large firms.

The explanation of this pattern of increasing concentration is given by Hannah and Kay[95] largely in terms of merger waves, though they do not entirely rule out a separate Gibrat effect arising from internal growth alone. Their analysis is restricted, with one or two exceptions, to the assets of the quoted company sector. They calculate the contribution of mergers to aggregate concentration in 3 periods, 1919–30, 1930–48, and 1957–69. The contribution of merger in each period is found by calculating the beginning-of-period

---

[93] P. E. Hart, S. J. Prais, 'The Analysis of Business Concentration', *J.R.S.S.* 119, Part 2 (1956), 150–91; S. J. Prais, 'A New Look at the Growth of Industrial Concentration', *O.P.E.* N.S. 26 (1974), 273–88; P. E. Hart, 'Business Concentration in the UK', *J.R.S.S.* 123, Series A (1960), 50–8.

[94] Prais, op. cit. (1976) Chapter 2.   [95] Hannah and Kay, op. cit.

concentration measure, as if all the mergers which took place in subsequent years took place at the beginning of the period. The difference between this and the actual concentration measure then is taken as the contribution of mergers. Any remaining change in concentration over the whole period is attributed to 'internal growth'. Their results for CR_{100}, and numbers equivalents for the entropy and Herfindahl measures are given in Table 15.3. The interpretation of

Table 15.3.

Period	Measure	1919	Change due to merger	Change due to internal growth	1930
1919–30	(i)	56·4	+ 16·1	+ 4·9	77·4
	(ii)	395	−212	− 49	135
	(iii)	144	− 73	− 27	44
		1930			1948
1930–48	(i)	65·7	+ 1·9	− 10·7	56·9
	(ii)	254	− 26	+152	380
	(iii)	50	− 1	+ 48	97
		1957			1969
1957–69	(i)	60·1	+ 15·2	− 0·4	74·9
	(ii)	324	−152	+ 14	326
	(iii)	92	− 28	+ 6	71

Source: L. Hannah, J. Kay: *Concentration in Modern Industry* (London, 1977), Table 5.1, p. 65; Table 5.3, p. 73; and Table 6.1, p. 86.
Measures: (i) CR_{100}; (ii) numbers-equivalent form of entropy measure of concentration; (iii) numbers-equivalent form of Herfindahl index of concentration.
Note: The data series for 1919–30 are not fully compatible with those for 1930–48.
Reproduced by permission of MacMillan, London and Basingstoke.

the results is unequivocal. In the period 1919–30, both mergers and internal growth contributed to increasing concentration, but mergers were three or four times as important. In the period 1930–48, mergers are unimportant, but internal growth is a powerful deconcentrating force. Finally, in the last period, 1957–69, mergers are the cause of the sharp rise in concentration, internal growth having a negative effect, albeit a very slight one. A separate analysis was carried out for 1919–30 and 1957–69, in order to test for the Gibrat effect. The method used was to simulate the development of the industrial structure on the computer, using the *ex post* distribution of growth rates of firms not involved in merger in the period as an *ex ante* probability distribution applied to the initial population of firms. They concluded that a significant Gibrat effect leading to concentration in both periods could not be excluded, though it was not able to account for more than a small part of the observed increase in concentration. Merger was still the dominant influence.

The explanation of the growth in concentration in the post-war period must lie with the various factors affecting the growth of firms described in Chapters 9 to 14, especially the role of merger. One negative conclusion is that there are no limits to the size of firms in terms of diseconomies of scale. There are only limits to the rate of growth (the Penrose effect), and these possibly do not apply to merger. The size of giant firms greatly exceeds the scale necessary for full exploitation of scale economies. The evidence of Chapters 12 and 13 suggests that no significant advantages are likely to accrue in terms either of marketing or R and D. The feature stressed by Prais[96] is the advantages which large firms have in raising finance. This arises in the U.K. not so much from the cost of capital, but its availability. He argues that the post-war period in Britain has seen the growing influence of institutional investors, representing pension funds and insurance companies. They have tended to lend mainly, if not exclusively, to the very largest companies, both debt and equity finance. The reason for their choice is the marketability of the stocks, since they are interested in portfolio management and not the operations of the companies themselves. Large firms have therefore been able to get all the finance they need, and have also found it relatively easy to issue new equities in exchange for the equity of acquisitions. While these factors may have been permissive towards the growth of large firms, it still does not explain why the managers of these firms sought size, usually by conglomerate diversification. The answer must lie in the managerial objectives being pursued, which were discussed at length in Chapter 8. Size and growth are being sought for their own sake. Finally the reader may inquire why the same pattern is not evident in the U.S. The answer seems to lie with differing policies towards mergers. The U.S. authorities have been generally hostile towards mergers of any kind, while policy in Britain has been, at the very least, permissive towards them.[97]

---

[96] Prais, op. cit. (1976) Ch. 5.

[97] See Blair, op. cit., Ch. 22, Scherer, op. cit. (1970), Ch. 20, for a discussion of the U.S. policy stance. The one exception seems to have been conglomerate mergers. See A. Sutherland, *The Monopolies Commission in Action*, D.A.E. Occasional Paper 21 (Cambridge, 1970), for a discussion of the U.K. policy in practice.

PART IV

Issues for Public Policy

The purpose of this part of the book is to examine the principles that lie behind public policy towards the private, capitalist sector in a modern economy in the light of the evidence about the behaviour of firms collated in the previous chapters. In doing this we shall avoid the exhaustive presentation of legislation and cases that is a feature of much writing in this field, for example Scherer, George, Rowley.[1] Such analyses are already available. What is not available is a clear presentation of the case for or against intervention. Nor has there been a systematic investigation of different policy instruments and their effects (apart from the institutional or legal embodiments of such instruments in different economies).

The application of public policy involves three steps. The first is the establishment of criteria of performance. Society must be able to express, in a sufficiently detailed manner (generalities will not do), what it expects of the private productive sector. Second, the criteria must be used to identify areas where the private sector is failing to perform properly. Third, the government must have policy instruments to cajole, persuade, or force the private sector to amend its ways, or at least to mitigate some of the consequences of its socially undesirable behaviour. It is as well to make clear at this point that we exclude from government action the possibility that the state will take full control of a sector in nationalization. The policy solutions that we consider stop short of that point.[2]

Our discussions fall naturally into two parts. The first concerns the role of public policy in the matters discussed in Part II of the book—market structure, prices, and profits. This has been the traditional area for public policy intervention in industry. The second part looks at public policy issues arising in the context of Part III— the growth and diversification of firms. Public policy in this area has lacked coherence, both in establishing criteria and in co-ordinating instruments of policy. Of course, actual policy questions will not be so tidy. To take one example, a proposed merger may have policy implications under both headings: it may involve an increase in market power and scale of operations, thus involving the monopoly

---

[1] F. M. Scherer, *Industrial Market Structure and Economic Performance* (Chicago, 1970), Chs. 17–22; K. D. George, *Industrial Organisation*, 2nd edn. (London, 1974); C. K. Rowley, *The British Monopolies Commission* (London, 1966).

[2] This does not reflect ideological commitment on the part of the authors to the continued existence of the private sector. It is simply a matter of space. To include the option of nationalization would involve first an examination of the positive economics of the nationalized sector, and second a full exposition of the various rules that have been suggested as guidelines for the operation of such industries. The second topic has been very fully explored in recent years with the revival of interest in applied welfare economics. The first has sadly been almost totally neglected, except for descriptive work on the performance of the nationalized industries and the policies that have been pursued.

policies relevant to Part II, and it may also involve questions of firm growth and investment in R and D which are relevant to public policy questions in the context of Part III. Throughout Part IV we assume a familiarity with the evidence on market structure and performance contained in Part II, and that on behaviour of firms in Part III. It is to that evidence that the public policy questions are addressed.

16

PUBLIC POLICY TOWARDS MARKET STRUCTURE, CONDUCT AND PERFORMANCE

The chapter begins with a description of welfare economic analysis in its application to the problems of market structure, conduct, and performance (sections 1 to 3). The next two sections present some empirical analysis concerning the extent of the problems. The last part of the chapter (sections 6 to 8) sets out the policy options.

1 THE STATIC PARETO FRAMEWORK

Our reason for starting with the Paretian framework is the importance of this paradigm in economic analysis. The agnosticism of the late 1950s concerning this paradigm has crumbled,[1] and has been replaced by a guarded optimism associated with the development of cost–benefit analyses, and particularly with the feeling that the problem of the second-best (see the next section) is not so intractable after all. As we shall see, the difficulties seen by earlier writers have not been resolved by any means. But neither has the desire to provide prescriptive solutions, especially for public expenditure, been assuaged. Graaff's plea for purely positive economics has fallen on deaf ears. It is a moot point as to whether economists have taken it upon themselves to assume the role of prescriptive philosopher-kings, or whether their political masters have refused to accept advice in the form of choices for action rather than a prescription for action. Whether we like it or not, prescriptive or normative economics still lies at the heart of economic analysis. Our best course, therefore, is to understand the bases for such economic prescription so that we may criticize it intelligently. Certainly neither of the authors is satisfied with the ethical basis of normative economics, and we suspect that many of our readers will wish to make their own judgement. With this caveat we may proceed to analysis.

The Pareto principle is deceptively simple. It states that an economic change is desirable if the satisfaction or utility of one group in society can be increased leaving the rest of society as well off as before. The implication of this principle is that an optimum

[1] Compare J. V. Graaff, *Theoretical Welfare Economics* (Cambridge, 1957) with D. Winch, *Analytical Welfare Economics* (Harmondsworth, 1971).

position has been reached when no such change is possible, i.e. when an increase in the utility of one group can only be achieved at the expense of the utility of another. A major objection to this principle must be stated immediately. It is that the Pareto principle, to be useful, must assume that one person's utility is not affected by the utility enjoyed by another. If, for example, someone else's utility enters into my utility function so that I am depressed when his utility increases relative to mine, and presumably so that I am happier when his utility decreases in relative terms, the Pareto principle becomes impossible to implement. An economic change can only be desirable under these circumstances if everybody's satisfaction is increased in such a way as to leave the relative positions unchanged. So we can only proceed by affirming the Pareto principle in a situation where envy is declared to be irrelevant.

The application of the Pareto principle to the analysis of production and exchange is well known, and we will only state the results here.[2] Consider first the conditions for society to be on its production frontier. The purely formal conditions are the same for any pair of factors, or a pair of goods, or a factor and a good. Denote any such pair by x_i and x_j. Then efficiency requires $\partial x_i / \partial x_j$ to be the same throughout the economy. Consider for example a case where i is a good and j is a factor. If $\partial x_i / \partial x_j$ were not equal in all firms where i was transferred into j, then it would increase output, to transfer resource i from the firm where its marginal return in terms of output j was smaller, to the other firm. Only where the marginal rates of transformation are equal is there no scope for such Pareto improvements. An analogous argument holds for the optimal conditions of exchange. If $(\partial U / \partial x_i) / (\partial U / \partial x_j)$ is not equal for all households (consumers and factor owners), then exchange at the margin will increase welfare.

Finally, the 'top level' optimum requires that the marginal rate of transformation in production should equal the marginal rate of substitution in consumption. Suppose the marginal rate of substitution of x_i and x_j is one for one, and that the marginal rate of transformation is one x_i for two x_j. Then producers could reduce production of x_i by one unit, and make two more x_j. Of these only one x_j is needed to compensate consumers for the loss of x_i. The other is available to make everyone better off. In principle then a rearrangement of production can increase welfare, whenever the marginal rates of transformation and substitution are not equal. Hence the condition.

---

[2] We assume a familiarity with the basic technique and results of welfare analysis.

Unfortunately these conditions relating to production and exchange are not unique. They supply only the necessary conditions for an optimum organization of production and exchange. This matter can be illumined by a diagrammatic analysis. In Figure 16.1, *TT* is the production frontier of the society representing the maximum outputs of Good II available given varying outputs of

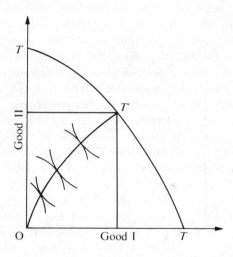

Fig. 16.1

Good I. At all points on the frontier the marginal equivalences relating to production are satisfied. We now consider the output mix of *T'*, and construct a consumers' Edgeworth–Bowley box relating to the distribution of those outputs between consumers *F* and *G*. (The box is drawn within the production frontier with one corner at the origin and the other at the output point *T'*.) Now fulfilment of *all* the Pareto conditions requires that the distribution of goods between *F* and *G* should be *on* the contract curve (to satisfy the marginal conditions for exchange), and *at* a point on the contract curve where the consumers' marginal rate of substitution is equal to the marginal rate of transformation of Good II for Good I at *T'*. This condition may be satisfied at a number of points on the contract curve, or at none at all. In general, we do not know. Clearly though, if we examine each possible output mix on the production frontier in turn we are likely to find a large number of situations which will satisfy the Pareto conditions. Each situation will be distinguished by the level of utility which it gives to the two consumers.

For the sake of diagrammatic completeness we may depict these possibilities as a welfare frontier (see Figure 16.2). This represents the envelope of all Pareto optimal possibilities with regard to production and exchange. At any point on the frontier the full Pareto conditions are fulfilled. The obvious question is: at which point should society be? And that is a question to which there is no answer unless

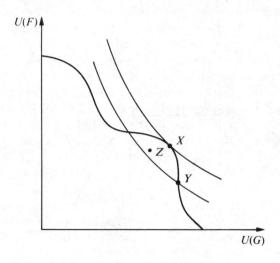

Fig. 16.2

one is prepared to postulate the existence of a Bergson–Samuelson social welfare function which gives an ordering of different distributions of utility as between members of the society. Then we may identify the point X as representing society's best position. X does correspond to a particular point on the production frontier of society, and to a particular distribution of outputs between consumers. In that sense the whole system is determinate, *once* the social welfare function is specified. The possibility of defining the social welfare function lies beyond the scope of our discussion, though we will have occasion to return to the topic. However we may draw one very significant negative conclusion from the analysis. That is, without a social welfare function, or some other proposition concerning the distribution of welfare, we cannot be content solely with satisfying the production and exchange conditions to reach the welfare frontier. Thus, in the diagram, point Y on the frontier is clearly inferior to point Z which lies *within* it (some of the marginal equivalences are not satisfied).

2   THE SUPPOSED OPTIMALITY OF PERFECT COMPETITION

The basic Pareto conditions, as we have discussed them above, are entirely independent of the economic organization. It would be possible for them to be used as principles of production and exchange in an entirely planned economy. They are by no means only of relevance to market economies. However, since we are interested in the performance of market capitalist economies, we will follow the traditional course of applying them to a competitive system. This is not because we have any illusions about the perfectin of competition but because it is a useful introduction to some aspects of the policy debate.

The 'proof' of the optimality of perfect competition is well known, and we will only sketch an outline here. Suppose that all firms in the economy are profit maximizers, and suppose that all consumers are utility maximizers. Suppose further that all factors and all good are traded in perfect markets, in the sense that all firms and all consumers are price takers. Consider first two goods, with competitive prices. Then all firms engaged in production of these goods will set the marginal rate of transformation of one good for another equal to the price ratio. To fail to do so would involve a sacrifice of potential revenue (and hence profit, given the outlays on factors). Furthermore all consumers, in maximizing their utility, would set the price ratio equal to the marginal relative utility of the goods, assuming that they consume them both. The outcome is that the price ratio determines the equality of the marginal rate of transformation and the marginal relative utility throughout the economy. The Pareto conditions relating to exchange, production, and exchange-and-production are simultaneously fulfilled. It needs little imagination to extend the same analysis to the trade-offs between factors and goods, and factors and factors for all firms and all consumers. All the criteria for a Pareto optimum will be fulfilled. Furthermore, since firms all purchase their factors in competitive markets, and sell their output in competitive markets, there will be no scope for internal inefficiency in the operation of firms. Firms of sub-optimal size, or inefficient deployers of factors, will be eliminated in the long run by this inability to earn normal profits.

The deficiencies of this beautiful picture of the 'invisible hand' in action are well known, so we will only refer to them briefly here. First, there is every reason to doubt the dynamic efficiency of competition: this is a theme to which we return in the second chapter of Part IV. Second, in the real world, we cannot declare external effects in production to be of no importance (as we have arbitrarily declared in the case of externalities in consumption). Congestion, pollution, and noise have found a well-deserved niche in welfare economics, as in public policy. Third, there is the whole range of public goods where the exclusion principle for a private market cannot apply. Further, there is the problem posed by indivisibilities or increasing returns to scale where satisfaction of the $P = MC$ rule is not compatible with supply by the private sector. All these cases have been analysed,[3] and solutions of greater or lesser practicability have been proposed. We cannot pursue this theme here, though a full 'competitive' solution to the optimal allocation of society's resources does presuppose that these questions can also be optimally resolved.

Much more serious is the question of whether a full competitive solution would necessarily be optimal. Returning to the analysis of the previous section we see that satisfaction of the Pareto conditions via a competitive price system only provides *an* optimum in the sense that we arrive at the welfare frontier. But this is *not* sufficient to reach the optimal point on that frontier as determined by the social welfare function. Indeed it would be the merest fluke should a competitive price system take us to that point. There are two routes out of this impasse. The first is that society should make its social welfare function explicit. The policy recommendations which would flow from this depend largely on how far the institutional framework and the distribution of resource ownership is taken or given. One extreme, involving in all probability major institutional and social change, would be the identification of the best point on society's welfare frontier. Policy would then proceed on two fronts: first, the implementation of a competitive economy in the private sector subject to appropriate adjustments to allow for the problems outlined above. Second, a redistribution of factor ownership to ensure that competitive returns to factors lead to the desired distribution of income. A second extreme is to accept the current distribution of factor ownership, but introduce redistributive taxation, again in conjunction with a competitive economy. Ideally the taxation should be lump sum to avoid disturbance of the marginal condition. Then the cost to society would be only the resources involved in collection of the tax and redistribution. But virtually any feasible tax would involve a price distortion so that the relevant consumer trade-off would not reflect the true opportunity cost to society. At which point we have abandoned the first-best Pareto solution to the problem, and we must look to second-best theory (see the next section of this chapter).

[3] See for example, R. S. Millward, *Public Expenditure Economics* (London, 1971).

The second route shows a much closer correspondence to the ideals of a traditional capitalist society. This is to assume that the distribution of factor ownership, however it may have come about, is of itself just, or at least that the state should not concern itself with income distribution. Instead the criteria of efficiency becomes the sole guide to policy. There is no question of choosing a point on the welfare frontier. A competitive price system will ensure that the Pareto efficiency criteria are fulfilled. The distribution of income is determined by the initial distribution of factor ownership and by the prices of factors that are thrown up by the competitive system. We shall refer to these assumptions as the 'capitalist assumptions'. There can be little doubt that they have been a powerful force in shaping policy towards the private capitalistic sector in Western economies, which has been largely directed to the evaluation of industrial performance in terms of efficiency, with equity considerations ignored. Industry has dictated that it should be judged in terms of volume of production, not the distribution of production.

The main defect in the approach to policy outlined above is its 'all-or-nothing' character. The analysis of the second-best[4] has shown that achieving a competitive solution in one sector of the economy is of no avail if price distortions continue to exist in other sectors. Or to be more precise, we have no *general* basis for a belief that it will improve the allocation of resources. It may, or it may not, depending on the precise circumstances, including all relevant cross-elasticities of supply and demand between the sectors involved. The destructiveness of this conclusion to any idealist solution is evident. Even the most devoted 'capitalist' will scarcely push for total abolition of all taxation except of a lump sum nature. And the reformer who wishes to couple a competitive solution with an equitable distribution of income is in even greater difficulty.

Fortunately the very theory that has dealt such a body-blow to idealist–reformist programmes for ameliorating the industrial sector has also provided a way forward. Any total solution to the problem of policy towards the private sector must be discounted, but second-best theory has paved the way for a piecemeal approach, very much at the micro level. It has focused on the welfare gains and losses arising from a particular economic change, and has set about the complex question of how to measure these gains and losses. The key to the analysis is the reintroduction of consumer surplus (and related producer surplus) measures of welfare.

[4] R. Lipsey, K. Lancaster, 'The General Theory of the Second Best', *R. Econ. Studs.* 24 (1956), 11–32.

3   A PIECEMEAL APPROACH

Harberger[5] has put the case for a piecemeal approach to problems in applied welfare economics, and has made a plea that the economics profession should standardize the procedures which it applies in each case. Public investment projects, pricing in the public sector, taxation policy, and policy towards the private sector could then be approached with a common set of tools. We will examine his proposals first, and then examine some of the implications.

He suggests three basic postulates as a basis for applied welfare economics:

(*a*) The competitive demand price for a given unit of output measures the value of that unit to the demander.

(*b*) The competitive supply price for a given unit measures the value of that unit to the supplier.

(*c*) When evaluating the net benefits or costs of a given action (project, programme, or policy), the costs and benefits accruing to each member of the relevant society should normally be added without regard to the individual(s) to whom they accrue.[6]

Harberger then derives a consumer surplus measure by expanding the utility function of the individual by Taylor's expansion. Let the consumer's utility function be,

$$U = U(X_1 \ldots X_n)$$

then $$\Delta U = \sum_i U_i \Delta X_i + \tfrac{1}{2} \sum_i \Delta u_i \Delta X_i,$$

neglecting higher order terms.

Assuming that the consumer maximizes his utility in the face of market prices $P_1 \ldots P_n$, then we have $U_i = \lambda_0 P_i^0$ where U_i is the marginal utility of good i, P_i^0 is the price, and λ_0 is the marginal utility of income at the given level of utility.

Now $$\Delta U_i = \lambda_0 \Delta P_i + P_i^0 \Delta \lambda + \Delta P_i \Delta \lambda$$

Substituting back into the expression for welfare change we may approximate,

[5] A. Harberger, 'Three Basic Postulates for Applied Welfare Economics: An Interpretive Essay', *J. Econ. Lit.* 9 (1971), 785–97.

[6] Again, equity considerations are pushed into the background, though in principle gains and losses could be given welfare weights with regard to the individuals to whom they accrue.

$$\frac{\Delta U}{\lambda_0 + \frac{1}{2}\Delta\lambda} \approx \sum_i P_i^0 \Delta X_i + \frac{1}{2} \sum_i \Delta P_i \Delta X_i$$

For any one good i experiencing a rise in price of P_i we can illustrate these terms very simply (see Figure 16.3). The first term is the surplus loss to consumer which would appear in usual national income measures as initial price times the reduction in quantity—the rectangle $BCDE$. The second term is the 'welfare triangle' ABC

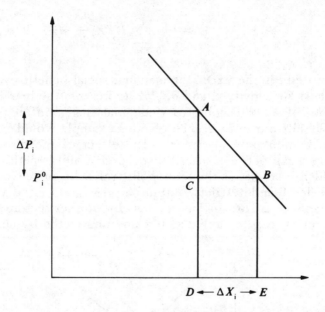

Fig. 16.3

which measures the additional losses in welfare arising because consumers value intramarginal units of the good more highly than the marginal unit.

From a technical point of view the most useful contribution here is that the formulation does not depend on the constancy of marginal utility of income. This was the problem with the Hicksian measures. Instead the change in utility is explicitly translated into money terms by dividing by $\lambda_0 + (\Delta\lambda)/2$: this is the midpoint value of the marginal utility of income over the range of change.

Applying postulate (c) we may aggregate the money values of welfare changes given by this expression over a number of consumers.

Before we leave this expression for welfare change we should heed
Harberger's warnings that the Taylor approximation is only correct
for small changes in X_i, and that the ignoring of higher terms is a
fairly gross simplification unless the underlying utility functions
are linear or quadratic.

Harberger's second major technical contribution was to point out
that the consumer surplus technique can be easily extended to
general equilibrium. He proposes to measure the welfare effect of
some price distortion, Z^*, by the expression

$$W = \int_{Z=0}^{Z^*} \sum_i D_i(Z)\frac{\partial X_i}{\partial Z}dZ$$

D_i represents the excess of marginal social benefit over marginal
social cost in activity i, and $\partial X_i/\partial Z$ represents the marginal change
in output of X_i in response to a marginal change in the price distortion dZ. For our purposes, an obvious example would be the existence of a monopoly in sector i. The effect of the distortion is to
open up a gap between marginal social cost and benefit in that sector, which increases as the monopolist raises his price from the competitive level and restricts output. So for good i the welfare loss
is the familiar $\triangle ABC$, in Figure 16.4. In another sector, j, there is a
distortion D_j (e.g. a tax) that remains unaffected by changes in Z.

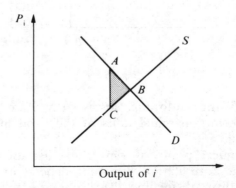

Fig. 16.4

However the change in the price of good i has cross-effects on both
the supply and demand curves in that market (see Figure 16.5).
Assume that i and j are complements on both the supply and demand

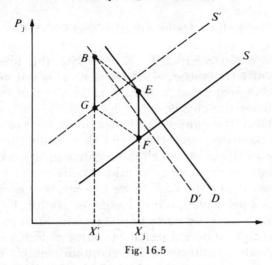

Fig. 16.5

sides. As the price rises in sector i the demand curve shifts to D' and the supply curve to S'. As a result, output falls from X_j to X'_j, the distortion D_j remaining constant. The welfare loss is the area $BEFG$, and represents the expression

$$\int_{Z=0}^{Z^*} D_j \frac{\partial X_j}{\partial Z} \cdot dZ.$$

Similar expressions and their geometric counterparts exist for *all* goods j^*, and for completeness all other sectors in the economy need to be included. However in a particular case the task may not be so herculean. As Harberger points out, the secondary welfare effects in other markets will only be significant in cases where both D_j and $\partial X_j/\partial Z$ are large. In other words, in all the other markets where distortions exist we need only be concerned if the cross-elasticity of supply or demand is substantial. This is not to under-estimate the measurement difficulties that remain; but it does at least reduce the problem to more manageable proportions.

The major problem that remains is whether postulate (c) is accept-able. It is the equivalent to the 'capitalist assumptions' of the idealist approach to policy. Efficiency is the only criterion for policy, and the distribution of income is of no interest. In principle, one could introduce equity considerations by distinguishing the gains and losses by reference to the individuals or groups in society to whom they accrue. A social welfare function, or welfare weights, would then be needed to assess the gains and losses. Alternatively, one could operate with the Kaldor–Hicks criterion, which is that a change in policy resulting in some gains and some losses is acceptable so long as the gainers could adequately compensate the losers and still remain better off. Of course, if compensation is not actually paid, we are back to the capitalist assumptions. However if compensation has to be paid for the change to be acceptable, then policy recommendations about the proposed change must *include* the method compensation payment, and this must then enter the second-best analysis of the situation on which the recommendation is based. The objection to introducing equity considerations is the practical one of complication. It may be hard indeed to measure even total gains and losses from a particular policy change: to ask for the distribution of gains and losses may be quite impracticable. So it may be better to adopt the escape route suggested by Turvey[7] in his discussion of pricing in nationalized industries. The economist simply assumes that income distribution is the function of another branch of policy. This approach will not be satisfactory to those who see the effect on income distribution as *the* objection to monopoly. It would be helpful to have some estimates of how great the effect might be. But it is unlikely that elimination of monopoly would represent a major step towards a more equal distribution of income, given that the distribution of factor ownership was unchanged. For this reason we accept the simplification proposed by Turvey and concentrate on allocative efficiency.

The following sections of this chapter are mainly concerned with the identification of socially undesirable behaviour in private good markets in the light of our discussion of welfare criteria. That is followed by a discussion of policy options. However we would emphasize that resolution of these more practical problems cannot be divorced from the more abstract discussion of the first three sections of this chapter. Policy analysis and prescription must have its roots in some form of welfare analysis.

4   THE PROBLEM OF MONOPOLY

The monopoly problem is the traditional area of policy towards the private sector. By 'monopoly' we mean those situations where there is thought to be a significant deviation of price from marginal cost:[8] as we saw in Chapters 5 and 6, this may characterize a wide range of oligopoly situations. The deviation of price from cost is a definite

---

[7] R. Turvey, *Economic Analysis and Public Enterprise* (London, 1971).

[8] This is not intended to include the case of 'externalities', which arise when private and social costs (or returns) diverge.

sign of failure in the market for an idealist, and constitutes a signal
for an appropriate partial analysis for piecemeal policy. In the first
case the deviation is a sign that the marginal relative utility between
the good in question and at least leisure is not equal to the marginal
rate of transformation. In the second the deviation suggests that
marginal social benefit is not equal to marginal social cost.

There have been a number of attempts to quantify the losses
arising from monopoly. The pioneer study was that of Harberger,[9]
who examined the evidence relating to 73 sectors in the U.S. manufacturing sector in the period 1924-8. His approach was to examine
the partial equilibrium welfare losses arising in each sector.

The method of calculation can be illustrated by Figure 16.6, and
by some simple algebra taken from Scherer.[10] Suppose that the

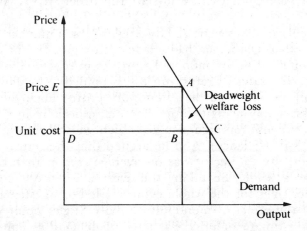

Fig. 16.6

demand curve is linear over the relevant range. Then the deadweight
welfare loss is given by the area of $\triangle ABC$. This is approximated by
$W = \frac{1}{2}\Delta P \cdot \Delta Q$ where ΔP and ΔQ are measured as deviations from
competitive price and output. We define the relative price distor-
tion as

$$M = \frac{\Delta P}{P}$$

[9] A. C. Harberger, 'Monopoly and Resource Allocation', *A.E.R. Papers and Proceedings*, 44 (1954), 77-8.
[10] F. M. Scherer, *Industrial Market Structure and Economic Performance* (Chicago, (1970), 401-2.

so the elasticity of demand, $\epsilon = (\Delta Q/Q)/M$

$$\therefore \Delta P = MP \text{ and } \Delta Q = MQ\epsilon$$

Substituting this in the expression for deadweight loss yields $W = \frac{1}{2}(PQ)\epsilon M^2$.

Harberger proceeded by calculating the deviation of industry profit rates from the average for all manufacturing. These deviations were then translated into dollars of 'excess profits' and expressed as a proportion of sales to give the value of M. The elasticity of demand was assumed to have a value of unity, so the deadweight loss is simply $\frac{1}{2}M^2$ times the value of sales. The sum of these losses across all sectors gave the welfare loss. On the assumption that all the output was sold in consumer markets, and none in intermediate markets, this gave a maximum welfare loss of the order of 0·1 per cent of G.N.P.

This calculation was criticized by Stigler[11] on a number of counts. He argued that Harberger had made quite insufficient allowance for the capitalization of monopoly profits in reported asset values. So the observed rates of return on assets tended to be unduly equal. Furthermore he observed that monopoly profits might be absorbed by unnecessary payments to other factors, especially in the form of managerial expense (an argument to which we will return in our discussion of X-inefficiency). And he argued that the return on capital in the manufacturing sector was on average greater than that in the economy as a whole. So taking the average for the manufacturing sector rather than for the whole economy led to a systematic underestimate of the effect of monopoly. Finally Stigler pointed out that Harberger's estimate of price elasticity of demand as unity was not consistent with monopoly profit maximization. These criticisms led to a new estimate by Schwartzman[12] for the U.S. in 1954. He avoided the use of rates of return by going direct to evidence on price–cost margins, and he allowed for demand elasticities up to 2. Despite these improvements he was unable to increase his estimate of welfare losses to more than 0·1 per cent of G.N.P. in 1954.

Worcester[13] made a further estimate for the U.S. in 1958 and 1969, using data from the Fortune 500 list of firms, rather than industry data as in previous studies. Industry profit rates tend to bias downwards the estimates of welfare loss, because the high profits of

[11] G. J. Stigler, 'The Statistics of Monopoly and Merger', *J.P.E.* 64 (1956), 33–40.

[12] D. Schwartzman, 'The Burden of Monopoly', *J.P.E.* 68 (1960), 627–30.

[13] D. A. Worcester, 'New Estimates of the Welfare Loss to Monopoly: United States 1956–69', *S. Econ. Journal*, 40 (1973), 234–45.

'monopolistic' firms are offset by low profits from failing firms. However, even assuming that the 'degree of monopoly' observed in the largest firms was typical of the whole manufacturing sector, Worcester was unable to get a welfare loss estimate much greater than 0·3 per cent. Cowling and Mueller[14] have attempted to circumvent the requirement to assume the elasticity of demand. Instead they argue that the price–cost margin is equal to the reciprocal of the elasticity of demand facing the firm, i.e. $\epsilon = 1/M$. So the welfare loss becomes:

$$W = \tfrac{1}{2}(PQ)\epsilon M^2 = \tfrac{1}{2}(PQ)M$$

which is one-half of the profit of the firm. Using firm data for both the U.S. and the U.K. gives welfare losses substantially greater than those previously reported (about 4 per cent in the U.S. and 10 per cent in the U.K. of the output of the manufacturing sector). But the derivation of the elasticity of demand from the price–cost margin implies a theory of oligopoly pricing which is rather unlikely (see Chapter 5).

It is worth entering a caveat about the methodology involved in these studies. Our second-best analysis of welfare gains and losses in the previous section should have alerted us to the difficulties involved in treating each monopolized sector in isolation without reference to other sectors with substantial cross-elasticities of demand or supply. Suppose for example that there is a group of sectors with very high cross-elasticities between them, but zero cross-elasticities with all other goods. Then if one of the constituent sectors is monopolized it may be necessary for the other sectors to be monopolized as well. Such a pricing pattern would ensure the right output mix from the group of sectors. The group as a whole would have a completely inelastic demand curve, so that the total output of the group would be reduced only a little and the welfare loss would be small. But if the Harberger estimation is applied to each sector in turn, each of which may have a considerable elasticity of demand (if it could be estimated), a sizeable 'welfare loss' could be calculated. Bergson[15] has made a particularly sharp critique of the Harberger method. To illustrate his contention that cross-elasticities cannot be ignored, he examines an economy with a welfare function that is made explicit in the form of a constant elasticity of substitution function with the goods as arguments. He shows that for simple economies with a small number of goods, and with given

[14] K. Cowling, D. C. Mueller, 'The Social Costs of Monopoly Power', *Economic Journal*, December 1978.

[15] A. Bergson, 'On Monopoly Welfare Losses', *A.E.R.* 63 (1973), 853–70.

price–cost ratios for each good, the welfare loss is highly sensitive to changes in the elasticity of substitution between goods. The conclusion is that the partial equilibrium estimates of welfare loss may be hopelessly erroneous.[16]

Posner[17] has argued that all previous studies have erred in their concentration on the minor welfare loss arising from the welfare triangle. His contention is that all monopoly profits are gained by some expenditure, from advertising to bribing government officials to grant a monopoly. He assumes that obtaining a monopoly is a competitive activity, so the cost of being a monopolist is exactly equal to the expected profit of being a monopolist (all abnormal profits having been competed away by rivals contending for the monopoly). Further he assumes a perfectly elastic long-run supply of all inputs used in obtaining monopolies, and that the costs involved in obtaining a monopoly situation have no socially useful by-products. Under these assumptions the loss to society of monopoly is equal to the welfare triangle (*ABC*) *plus* the whole of the firms' profit (*ABDE*) in Figure 16.6. The profit represents the return on the resources used to obtain the monopoly position. Not surprisingly this approach gives much larger empirical estimates of welfare loss. (Cowling and Mueller[18] estimate losses in excess of 10 per cent for both the U.S. and the U.K.) Posner's assumptions are no doubt exaggerated. For example, some monopoly positions are based on successful innovation, and we would surely not wish to regard expenditure on R and D as having 'no socially useful by-products'. But his ideas will not allow us to rest with the conclusion that monopoly losses are negligible.

The market structure and conduct conditions under which price may exceed marginal cost were fully discussed in Chapters 5 to 7. Barriers to entry of some kind are a necessary condition. These may be either temporary (in which case the possibility of excess profits is in the short run only), or more permanent (advantages arising from economies of scale, goodwill, product differentiation, or restricted access to specialized resources). Whether the possibility of profits is exploited depends in part on market structure, and in part on conduct. The conduct point is clear in the case of a formal cartel or a firm. Less obvious is the co-operation between firms that may develop in a highly concentrated market (see Chapter 5). We should

[16] But see the comments of R. Carson, 'On Monopoly Welfare Losses: Comment', *A.E.R.* 65 (1975), 1008–14, and Worcester 'On Monopoly Welfare Losses: Comment', *A.E.R.* 65 (1975), 1015–23, for a criticism of Bergson's conclusions.

[17] R. A. Posner, 'The Social Costs of Monopoly and Regulation', *J.P.E.* 83 (1975), 807–27.

[18] Cowling and Mueller, op. cit.

note immediately the problem for anti-trust policy that arises from a consideration of these conditions: only a few situations have any obvious *institutional* form, which can be made the target of policy. The easiest target is the price-fixing agreement or formal cartel. Vertical integration backwards to monopolize a source of supply or forwards to control selling outlets (described in the anti-trust literature as 'foreclosure', 'exclusive dealerships', etc.) may also be obvious targets, though the possibility of new entry may vitiate the attempt to earn monopoly profits in such cases. But these cases are only a minor part of the problem. The emphasis on institutional forms in actual policy has unduly narrowed the discussion.

5   PRODUCTIVE EFFICIENCY[19]

The smallness of the estimates of welfare loss from misallocation of resources formed the starting-point for Leibenstein's seminal article on X-efficiency.[20] Bringing together scattered evidence on the internal efficiency of firms he suggested that the losses of output due to the failure of firms to operate on their production frontier were much more serious than the allocative losses arising from monopoly. He also argued that X-inefficiency would be associated with non-competitive market structures. In an article with Comanor[21] he outlined the implications of this for the measurement of welfare losses.

In Figure 16.7 M is the monopoly price and C_m and C_c represent costs under monopoly and competition respectively. Now the usual measure of welfare loss is the triangle ABC. However the addition of X-inefficiency in the form of a divergence between monopoly and competitive costs implies a larger welfare loss represented by the triangle ADE. And to this must be added the resource waste implied by $C_m BDC_c$, which is likely to be the largest element, according to Comanor and Leibenstein. The normal caveat about second-best applies to the welfare loss as usual, but the resource waste is an unequivocal loss. Furthermore they point out that elimination of the allocative inefficiency may be possible without any transfer of resources between sectors. Efficient redeployment of the wasted resources $C_m BDC_c$ within the sector may be sufficient to expand output to the competitive level q_c. However, as Ng and Parish[22]

---

[19] This section presupposes the discussion of costs and efficiency in Chapter 2.

[20] H. Leibenstein, 'Allocative Efficiency versus X-Efficiency', *A.E.R.* 56 (1966), 392–415.

[21] W. Comanor, H. Leibenstein, 'Allocative Efficiency, X-Efficiency and the Measurement of Welfare Losses', *Economica*, N.S. 36 (1969), 304–9.

[22] R. Parish, Y. Ng, 'Monopoly, X-Efficiency and the Measurement of Welfare Loss', *Economica*, N.S. 39 (1972), 301–8.

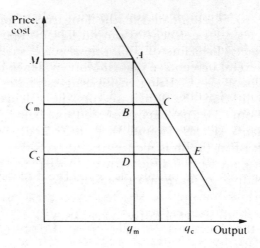

Fig. 16.7

have pointed out, it may be wrong to attribute all of the higher costs to inefficiency in resource use. One possibility is that monopoly rents are shared out between shareholders, managers, and workers, instead of being reported as profits. Alternatively the firm may pay more for its inputs than is necessary—thus transferring some of the monopoly profits to its suppliers. Third, we could consider the case of the owner-manager with leisure as one argument of his utility function. Then the level of costs in the firm may represent his own trade-off between leisure and more profit. The gain to society from lower costs may have to be offset by his loss of leisure in bringing about a reduction in costs. The welfare gain is then no longer unequivocal.

Sadly, all these arguments must remain at the level of speculation since we have no better evidence on the matter than was available at the time Leibenstein originally wrote.

Another area of possible public policy interest is the use of resources in bundles that are less than the optimum scale. From the point of view of measurement this takes us back to all the problems that were surveyed in Chapter 2, as to what is the meaning of optimum scale. The usual criterion is to ask how many firms of a size consonant with minimum costs are needed to serve a particular market. However, that criterion will be inadequate in the case of differentiated products. Be that as it may, there are clearly a large number of sectors with sub-optimal capacity, which does not seem to be eliminated in the long run. Thus Bain[23] suggested that at least 20 per cent of output in U.S. manufacturing in 1954 was produced in plants of sub-optimal scale, sufficient to raise their costs by several percentage points. More evidence has been compiled recently by Weiss.[24] Using engineering estimates of minimum efficient scale in 35 U.S. 4-digit sectors, he calculated a simple average of about 50 per cent of output being produced in sub-optimal plant. He also found that the extent of sub-optimal capacity was least in the most concentrated sectors, with obviously disturbing consequences for anti-trust. Steep cost curves, large market size relative to minimum economic size, and geographically large markets (low transport costs) were also correlated with a low proportion of sub-optimal capacity.[25]

In the next three sections we will look at the options for policy.

6   WORKABLE COMPETITION AND NON-DISCRETIONARY ANTI-TRUST

The originator of the concept of 'workable competition' was J. M. Clark.[26] He observed that it was unreasonable to expect the *structure* of the manufacturing sector of an advanced economy to conform to the textbook standard of perfect competition, but claimed that benefits would accrue to society if some means could be found of influencing oligopoly *behaviour* so that performance conformed to competitive standards. This idea, if not Clark's original formulation, has remained very influential both in policy itself and in academic discussions of policy.[27] So we must subject it to some critical attention.

One justification for the principle might be of the form that, *ceteris paribus*, more competition is better than less competition. However this simply ignores the problem of the second-best, as we saw earlier in this chapter. So unless one is to claim that competition is *per se* good, workable competition is only acceptable as part of an all-or-nothing Paretian policy package. The policy must set out to deal with *all* cases of market failure simultaneously. And even then one must make the capitalist assumption that income

[23] J. S. Bain, 'Economies of Scale, Concentration and the Condition of Entry in Twenty Manufacturing Industries', *A.E.R.* 44 (1954), 15–39.

[24] L. W. Weiss, 'Optimal Plant Size and the Extent of Sub-Optimal Capacity', in R. T. Masson, P. D. Qualls (ed.), *Essays on Industrial Economics in Honor of Joe S. Bain*, Ch. 7, pp. 123–42.

[25] Z. A. Silberston, 'Economies of Scale in Theory and Practice', *E.J.* 82 (1972), 369–91, has used engineering estimates for U.K. sectors to estimate the extent of sub-optimal capacity.

[26] J. M. Clark, 'Towards a Concept of Workable Competition', *A.E.R.* 30 (1940), 241–56.

[27] Scherer, op. cit., Chs. 19–21 (for U.S. examples).

distribution is of no importance, so that formal Pareto efficiency is all that matters. So the theoretical foundations of the concept do not seem at all secure.

In operation the concept requires the identification of all types of structure, market conduct, and performance that would produce substantial deviations of price from marginal cost. Rules are formulated to define the limits of acceptable structure, conduct, and performance. An investigatory body is then empowered to investigate possible breaches of these rules, and legal or administrative sanctions are applied to eliminate the undesirable features. Examples of such action are the prevention of mergers which will increase market power, the prohibition of growth in market share beyond a given point (and forced division of firms where the market share is too great), and the banning of collusive agreements. However this intervention is intended very much as a last resort. The hope is that a clear definition of the ground rules will enable the private sector to operate efficiently *without* intervention from government.

Sadly, the state of economic analysis, as described in Part II of this book, is simply not adequate for so complicated a task. For what we need is not merely generalizations about structure–conduct–performance relations, but some hard empirical evidence. And Chapter 6 suggests that such evidence is not available yet. Sosnick[28] has provided a most helpful survey of the literature, including a list of qualitative elements that might be included in setting up a 'workably' competitive norm. He sets the requirements out under three heads:

(1) Structure:
>   (i) An appreciable number of firms with no single one dominant.
>   (ii) Moderate and price sensitive quality differentials in the products offered.
>   (iii) No artificial barriers to entry.
>   (iv) Adequate access to information.

(2) Conduct;
>   (i) Some uncertainty as to whether a price reduction will be met.
>   (ii) No collusion: but 'conscious' rivalry between firms.
>   (iii) No unfair, exclusionary, or predatory tactics.
>   (iv) Sales promotion not to be misleading.

[28] S. H. Sosnick, 'A Criticism of the Concepts of Workable Competition', *Q.J.E.* 72 (1958), 380–423.

(3) Performance:
- (i) Operations should be efficient.
- (ii) Promotion expenses should not be excessive.
- (iii) Profits should be sufficient to reward investment and to encourage innovation.
- (iv) Prices should not intensify the cyclical problem.
- (v) The range of qualities should be responsive to consumer demand.

The imprecision of these requirements emphasizes the problem of a workably competitive approach to policy. We simply do not have the knowledge to give quantitative content to the structural requirements under (1), and it is difficult to give any operational content at all to some of the requirements listed under (2) and (3). The ideal would be clear quantitative guidelines on industrial concentration, economies of scale, and product differentiation under 'Structure', associated with specific proscription of unacceptable conduct. It would then be possible to dispense with the performance category altogether. And this is no doubt the objective towards which the academic proponents of workable competition are striving. However this will always be inadequate, since such an approach assumes that it is possible to define situations that are oligopolistic and yet perform according to the competitive ideal, without any further intervention. Further, the ideal solution for firms with declining cost curves would involve them in making losses, since marginal cost is always less than average cost. This applies to all cases where the required scale does not exhaust possible economies. For these reasons, Markham[29] proposed that workable competition protagonists should shift their ground. Instead of a set of specific norms, he suggested that each situation should be investigated on its merits, and that it should be declared 'workable' if there is no policy change which could lead to an unequivocal improvement. If categorical norms are required they should be in the form of prohibitions on certain market behaviour, for example no collusion. But this approach involves the abandonment of the all-or-nothing objective, which can be the only justification of workable competition as promulgated by Clark. Markham's suggestion is much more at home in the piecemeal framework to which we turn below.

Recently the whole idea of non-discretionary anti-trust policy has been revived, but with a very different intellectual base to that proposed by Clark. It arises from Leibenstein's observation on the

---

[29] J. W. Markham, 'An Alternative Approach to the Concept of Workable Competition', *A.E.R.* 40 (1950), 349–61.

size and the incidence of X-inefficiency.[30] He relates X-inefficiency
particularly to the degree of external motivation and stimulus. In
a competitive environment each firm will constantly be comparing
its own cost performance with that of competition. If its performance falls short it will institute active search for new methods with
lower costs. By contrast, a firm in a monopolistic sector has no direct
standard of comparison, and there is no pressure on it to improve
its performance in terms of costs. Thus inadequate profitability can
be rectified by raising prices, a course of action which is not open
to the firm in a more competitive environment. The aim of a workable competition policy then is to provide for the maintenance of
competitive pressures on the firms to avoid X-inefficient operations.
The case for this has been put by Crew and Rowley.[31] However, the
same problem of giving quantitative content to such a policy
remains. How many competitors are necessary to maintain the external motivation to efficiency? How does the policy cope with natural
barriers to entry due to economies of scale and inelastic demand
curves? Is it sufficient to ban overt collusion to avoid a market-
sharing 'quiet life' solution for an oligopoly? We simply do not
know. We even lack quantitative evidence for the presumption that
X-inefficiency is a more serious problem than allocative inefficiency.

Though the policy predates the development of the 'workable
competition' doctrine, we will take the U.S. anti-trust policy, particularly the Sherman Act of 1890, as the most notable example of its
application.[32] To some extent this is to distort the historical record.
Neale suggests that the development of the policy owes little to
'workable competition' or any other economic rationale. '. . . The
rationale of anti-trust is essentially a desire to provide legal checks
to restrain economic power and is not a pursuit of economic
efficiency as such. Consequently, the question asked is not whether
anti-trust decisions lead to the greatest economic efficiency, but
whether it can be said, given the non-economic reasons for anti-trust
policy, that these decisions do any serious harm.'[33] If Neale is

[30] H. Leibenstein, op. cit. (1966); 'Organisational or Frictional Equilibria, X-Efficiency
and the Rate of Innovation', *Q.J.E.* 83 (1969), 600–23; 'Competition and X-Efficiency',
J.P.E. 81 (1973), 765–77.

[31] M. A. Crew, C. K. Rowley, 'Antitrust Policy: Economics versus Management Science'
(Moorgate and Wall Street, 1970), 19–34.

[32] United States anti-trust law and cases are all surveyed in A. D. Neale, *The Anti-trust
Laws of the U.S.A.: a Study of Competition enforced by Law*, 2nd edn. (Cambridge, 1970);
F. M. Scherer, *Industrial Market Structure and Economic Performance* (Chicago, 1970),
Chs. 19–21; J. M. Blair, *Economic Concentration: Structure, Behaviour and Public Policy*
(New York, 1972), Ch. 21; C. Kaysen, D. F. Turner, *Anti-trust Policy: An Economic and
Legal Analysis* (Cambridge, Mass., 1959). R. A. Posner, *Anti-trust Law: An Economic
Perspective* (Chicago and London, 1976), presents an economic perspective.

[33] Neale, op. cit. 489.

correct, then there will be little economic insight to be gained from a detailed examination of case law, except for the intrinsic interest of the case studies of particular industries. However if one *was* to seek an economic justification of the *per se* approach of U.S. antitrust it seems likely that some concept of workable competition would be invoked. It is on that basis that we discuss the U.S. situation as an exemplification of 'workable competition', while eschewing a lengthy description of cases.

Section 1 of the Sherman Act proscribes 'every contract, combination . . . or conspiracy in restraint of trade or commerce . . .'. This includes price-fixing, and any form of output quota, which would be an essential feature of any successful cartel (see Chapter 5). As interpreted by the U.S. Courts, this section has come to represent a *per se* prohibition of agreements. The judgement of the Supreme Court in the Trenton Potteries case (1927) makes this clear:[34]

The aim and result of every price-fixing agreement, if effective, is the elimination of one form of competition. The power to fix prices, whether reasonably exercised or not, involves power to control the market and to fix arbitrary and unreasonable prices. The reasonable price fixed today may through economic and business changes become the unreasonable price of tomorrow. Once established, it may be maintained unchanged because of the absence of competition secured by the agreement for a price reasonable when fixed. Agreements which create such potential power may well be held to be in themselves unreasonable or unlawful restraints, without the necessity of minute inquiry whether a particular price is reasonable or unreasonable as fixed and without placing on the Government in enforcing the Sherman Law the burden of ascertaining from day to day whether it has become unreasonable through mere variation of economic conditions.

This position was strongly confirmed in the Socony–Vacuum Oil case in 1940, and has remained established ever since.[35] As a result, formal cartels are not a feature of U.S. markets. But one may doubt that co-operation between firms has disappeared entirely. Blair[36] suggests that agreements may continue, but the evidence for them is more carefully concealed by the firms concerned. For example, the conspirators in the heavy electrical equipment case in 1960 were alleged to have gone to great lengths to conceal the evidence of their meetings and telephone contacts.[37] In the absence of such evidence, the only other basis for an indictment is evidence of parallelism in pricing. But our discussion in Chapter 5 showed this to be insufficient to establish overt collusion: the same parallelism could arise in any concentrated oligopoly, or where a dominant firm acted as a price leader, without any collusion at all. The evidence of Asch and

[34] *U.S.* v. *Trenton Potteries Co.*, 273 U.S. 392 (1927), at 397.
[35] See the survey of cases in Neale, op. cit., Part I, Chs. 1, 2.
[36] Blair, op. cit. 580–5.   [37] Blair, op. cit. 576–80.

Seneca[38] is open to the interpretation that collusion is a sign of failure to co-operate successfully. The arbitrariness of an anti-trust rule based on a particular institutional form is evident in this case.

Section 2 of the Sherman Act makes it an offence to 'monopolise, or attempt to monopolise . . .' any market. Since the Alcoa case (1954),[39] this section has had the effect of a *per se* restriction on the attainment of monopoly power, whether or not the power was exercised.[40] The difficulty is the definition of monopoly power: what is the relevant market? What is the critical level of market share at which a firm becomes a monopoly? In the aluminium case the judgement favoured a narrow definition of the market (definitely excluding the substitutes for aluminium), and identified a threshold of 60-64 per cent of the relevant market. However the cellophane case (1956)[41] resulted in an acquittal for Du Pont, the Court allowing a market definition that included other flexible packaging materials. So the *per se* rule is uncertain in its application. Even if problems of market definition were absent, the case for a 60-64 per cent threshold is weak. The problem identified in Chapter 5 is more one of oligopoly than of the dominant firm. This has led to various suggestions for reform. Kaysen and Turner[42] proposed an alternative structural test for market power, 'where, for five years or more, one company has accounted for 50 per cent of more of annual sales in the market, or four or fewer companies have accounted for 80 per cent of sales'. A White House Task Force on Antitrust Policy in 1968 suggested even more stringent conditions, with an objective to bring the four firm concentration ratio in all markets below 50 per cent, and individual firm shares below 12 per cent. The implementation of the policy is also in some doubt. Clearly the statement of clear market share rules might deter some firms from growing in a particular market. But if concentration already exceeds the limit, or if it increases owing to factors beyond the control of the firms (e.g. failure of rivals), then dissolution of the large firms into smaller units is the logical step. Given the evidence of Chapter 2 that large firms in many sectors exceed the size necessary to obtain full scale economies, there are no economic objections to such a proposal. But the basis for the policy is still weak. There is no strong evidence

[38] P. Asch, J. J. Seneca, 'Is Collusion Profitable?', *R. Econ. Stats.* 58 (1976), 1–12.

[39] *U.S.* v. *Aluminium Company of America et al.*, 148 F. 2d 416 (1945).

[40] Prior to the aluminium case, the position was somewhat different. In the steel case, *U.S.* v. *United States Steel Corporation et al.*, 251 U.S. 417 (1920), the Supreme Court ruled '. . . the law does not make mere size an offense, or the existence of unexerted power an offense. It . . . requires overt acts . . .'

[41] *U.S.* v. *E.I. du Pont de Nemours and Co.*, 351 U.S. 377 (1956).

[42] Kaysen and Turner, op. cit. 106 ff.

to support the contention that concentration on its own is undesirable. The balance of the discussion of evidence on market structure and price–cost margins in Chapter 7 was that concentration only permits firms to exploit an opportunity provided by barriers to entry. But it is not easy to see how *per se* rules could be extended to cover barriers to entry as well.

7   PIECEMEAL INTERVENTION IN MARKET STRUCTURE

We must now turn to the piecemeal policy approach which was first suggested by Markham,[43] but only recently has taken formal shape, in articles by Williamson.[44] The basic ingredients of the problem are as before. But this time the approach consists in taking cases one at a time and making piecemeal improvements, taking the second-best into account where necessary. Thus the policy relies on a 'rule of reason' as distinct from the *'per se'* approach of 'workable competition'.

The difference from 'workable competition' policy is that a very large elements of discretion is introduced into the administrative or legal arrangements for anti-trust policy. No form of market structure, conduct, or performance can be declared against the public interest *a priori*.

The mechanics of the approach are illustrated by Williamson for the case of a large monopolistic firm where the adverse effects of increased market power are thought to be offset by efficiency gains from economies of scale. The very simplest case is shown in Figure 16.8. Initially the industry is supposed to be competitive, with $P = AC_1$. Over time it is predicted that costs will fall (due to scale economies) to AC_2, but the sector will be monopolized by a large firm with price rising to P_2.[45] The trade-off involved is the cost saving A_2 against the deadweight loss of consumers' surplus A_1. It should be noted that we ignore the distributional effect represented by the rectangle A_3. Nor do we take account of the fact that the cost saving accrues as profit to the entrepreneur and the deadweight loss to the consumers.

The net economic effect of large scale is said to be positive if

$$A_2 - A_1 > 0$$

---

[43] Markham, op. cit.

[44] O. E. Williamson, 'Economies as an Anti-trust Defense: The Welfare Trade-offs', *A.E.R.* 58 (1968), 18–36.

[45] In Williamson's example the monopoly is to be brought about by a merger. However, the same analysis applies to any case where the market comes to be dominated by a large firm. We note that $P_2 > P_1$, in the analysis must imply a substantial barrier to new entry.

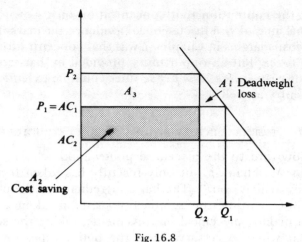

Fig. 16.8

i.e. if

$$\Delta AC \cdot Q_2 - \tfrac{1}{2}\Delta P \cdot \Delta Q > 0.$$

Dividing through by $P_1 Q_1$ and putting $\epsilon = (\Delta Q/Q_1)/(\Delta P/P_1)$ for the elasticity of demand in the region of the competitive price and remembering that $P_1 = AC_1$ we have

$$\frac{\Delta AC}{AC_1} - \tfrac{1}{2}\epsilon \frac{Q_1}{Q_2}\left(\frac{\Delta P}{P}\right)^2 > 0$$

Williamson presents a tabulation of values at which this expression is zero. The main result of his analysis is that fairly sizeable price increases are acceptable if there is even a small decrease in costs. For example with a demand elasticity of unity a 2 per cent reduction in costs is sufficient to offset a 20 per cent price increase.

Williamson and subsequent writers have complicated this expression in various ways. For example, Williamson[46] included the possibility that the initial price might be greater than average cost; Rowley[47] has emphasized that the costs of monopoly will include X-inefficiency and that this should be taken into the reckoning. Ross[48] argued that Williamson's formulation should be amended to

[46] O. E. Williamson, 'Economies as an Anti-trust Defense: Correction and Reply', *A.E.R.* 58 (1968), 1372–6.
    [47] C. K. Rowley, *Anti-trust and Economic Efficiency* (London, 1973).
    [48] P. Ross, 'Economies as an Anti-trust Defense: Comment', *A.E.R.* 58 (1968), 1371–2.

include the stream of costs and benefits over time, suitably discounted. An important element of this argument is that internal
growth of firms in a growing competitive market will enable economies of scale to be realized eventually. Thus the gain from scale
economies by creating an immediate monopoly could be shortlived,
while the loss from increased market power would be for all time.
Williamson[49] subsequently amended his criteria to include this possibility. The analysis presented so far has ignored the possibility of
secondary welfare consequences in related markets. However these
clearly exist and should be incorporated in the analysis, along the
lines suggested in section 3 above. Finally it would be possible to
investigate, within this framework, some of the distributional effects
of the merger.

In theory the piecemeal approach has much to commend it. It
can take care of second-best difficulties, and it makes any trade-off
explicit. This is much better than hiding the difficulties behind the
mysterious veil of competition. In practice the whole matter is much
more difficult. To estimate the trade-off one would need hard
empirical evidence on the degree to which the change in market
structure would (i) lower costs, (ii) raise prices, (iii) reduce output
(i.e. knowledge of demand elasticities), (iv) cause X-inefficiency, not
to mention all the cross-effects in related markets. Once again, our
knowledge lags way behind our needs in anti-trust matters. And we
should note that a qualitative inquiry into gains and losses
completely misses the point that it is the *quantitative* trade-off that
matters.

The 'piecemeal' approach is exemplified by the approach to anti-
trust in the U.K.[50] The relevant institutions are the Restrictive
Practices Court, set up in 1956 to implement an Act designed to
regulate restrictive agreements between firms, and the Monopolies
Commission, which is designed to investigate cases of market power
(currently any firm with market share exceeding 25 per cent). The
Restrictive Practices Act (and subsequent legislation up to the Fair
Trading legislation of 1973) requires all agreements between firms
to be registered, including information agreements. The Registrar
can then refer the agreements to the Court, where they are presumed

[49] O. E. Williamson, 'Economics as an Anti-trust Defense: Reply', *A.E.R.* 59 (1969),
954-9.
[50] The best single source for U.K. policy on restrictive agreements is D. Swann *et al.*,
Competition in British Industry (London, 1974). The work of the Monopolies Commission is described in A. Sutherland, *The Monopolies Commission in Action*, D.A.E. Occasional Paper 21 (Cambridge, 1969); C. K. Rowley, *The British Monopolies Commission*
(London, 1966). In the text we confine our attention to the principles on which these
operate.

to be against the public interest until the parties demonstrate otherwise. It can only be proved beneficial if it satisfies at least one of six
conditions or gateways, which are:

(*a*) the agreement is necessary to protect the public from injury
in connection with the use of goods;

(*b*) the restriction enables the public to receive specific and substantial benefits;

(*c*) the restriction is reasonably necessary to counteract measures
taken by any one person not party to the agreement with an interest
to prevent or restrict competition in relation to the trade in which
persons party to the agreement are engaged;

(*d*) the restriction is reasonably necessary to enable the persons
party to the agreement to negotiate fair terms for the supply of
goods to, or the acquisition of goods from, any one person not party
thereto who controls a preponderant part of the trade or business of
acquiring or supplying such goods;

(*e*) the agreement is necessary to prevent a serious and persistent
adverse effect on the general level of unemployment;

(*f*) removal of the restriction would be likely to cause a reduction
in the volume or earnings of the export business which is substantial
in relation either to the whole export business of the U.K. or to the
whole business of the trade.

To these are added the 'tailpiece': the benefits must outweight the
detriments arising from the agreement.

Swann *et al.*[51] report that 2,660 agreements had been registered
by 1969. 1,240 of these were abandoned, 960 were varied to render
them innocuous, and another 90 had lapsed by effluxion of time. The
key decision was that in the Yarn Spinners case (1959),[52] when the
Court found for the agreement under gateway (*e*), but struck it down
on the 'tailpiece'. At this point many agreements were terminated, as
the parties felt that the Court was going to take a hard line. But the
Court has not done so uniformly. For example, the cement manufacturers were allowed to keep their agreement on the grounds that
they were charging 'reasonable prices'. Part of their argument was
that the agreement permitted 'orderly marketing' in a cyclical
industry, thus reducing risk, lowering the cost of capital, and hence
resulting in lower prices. Despite this and other examples,[53] the main
impact of the legislation has been nearer to that of the Sherman Act,
section 1 than might have been anticipated, since the vast majority
of restrictive agreements have disappeared. As reported in Chapter 5,

[51] Swann *et al.*, op. cit.   [52] *In re* Yarn Spinners Agreement, LR 1RP 118 (1959).
[53] For examples, Black Bolt and Nut Association's Agreement, LR 2RP 50 (1960),
Permanent Magnet Association's Agreement, LR 3RP 119 and 392 (1962).

price competition has followed in a number of these markets, judging from the evidence of Swann *et al.* The Monopolies Commission has a mandate to investigate cases of 'monopoly'. Cases are referred to it (under the 1973 Fair Trading Act) by the Director General of Fair Trading. The criterion for a reference is a market share exceeding 25 per cent. The task of the Commission is to weigh each case on its merits to determine the public interest. Its conclusions are then published for the government to act upon if they wish to do so. The Commission could recommend dissolution, but the government would have to seek the approval of Parliament to put such a recommendation into effect. Not surprisingly the Commission has not found it easy to weight the costs and benefits of each case. So it has come to rely heavily on the rate of return on capital earned by the firm as an indicator of abuse of monopoly power. Rowley[54] has pointed to a number of difficulties in this procedure. First, the valuation of the assets of the firm is in doubt. Should historic cost or replacement cost be used? Second, what should be the correct standard of comparison, particularly where a high profit rate represents the returns to a successful, but risky, innovation? Furthermore, the lack of any specific method of investigating each case has led to inconsistencies in reports on different cases, as Sutherland[55] has noted.

We conclude that the difficulties of piecemeal assessment are so great that policy institutions either incline to a *per se* approach for safety (the Restrictive Practices Court), or become inconclusive in their effect (the Monopolies Commission).

8   DIRECT CONTROLS ON PRICES AND PROFITS

The basis of 'workable competition' and 'piecemeal' approaches to public policy towards the private sector is the hope that by judicious intervention in market structure, and/or by the banning of some forms of market behaviour, it will be possible to improve performance. The difficulty is that we simply do not know enough about the structure–behaviour–performance link to be certain that performance will indeed improve. So the alternative is to intervene directly on performance, and particularly on prices and profits. We should note that we are not concerned here with the general imposition of price controls as part of a price–wage freeze to combat inflation or in time of war. That has an impact (hopefully) on the general price level, and only very subordinately on relative prices. Of course the

[54] C. K. Rowley, 'Monopolies Commission and the Rate of Return on Capital', *E.J.* 79 (1969), 42–65.
[55] Sutherland, op. cit.

consequences of prolonged price control may be very serious for the firms if they are unable to raise prices to cover increased costs, including the cost of depreciating capital at current values (rather than historic cost). The result may be a sharp decline in real profits, and a subsequent fall in investment. It all depends on how the price control is administered. However our purpose here is to discuss price and profit control as an alternative method of dealing with market failure in situations where anti-trust of the traditional kind is thought to be ineffective. It would not be a *general* intervention in private sector pricing, which would in the long run represent the demise of the private capitalist system.

The use of price control as an anti-monopoly device has been explored systematically by Scherer.[56] We illustrate the case of a collusive oligopoly in Figure 16.9. Industry demand is given by DD.

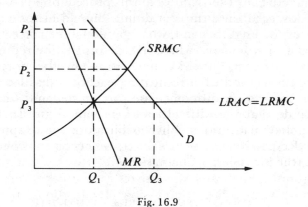

Fig. 16.9

The oligopoly sets a price P_1 to maximize their monopoly profit (where marginal revenue equals the sum of their marginal cost curves: we ignore the problem of market shares arising where different firms have different costs). In this situation the price controllers can achieve some immediate improvement (ignoring second-best problems) by fixing a price P_2. Output is increased and the price is lower. However they may be tempted to remove excess profits altogether by setting the competitive price P_3: the result would be that firms would produce Q_1 as before, but there would be excess demand of Q_1Q_3. The answer seems to be that a gradual reduction of the controlled price is called for, to give time for the firms to expand output to Q_3, along their long-run average cost curves. We should note here that price control (and profit control) is compatible with either

[56] Scherer, op. cit. 413–16.

idealist or piecemeal approaches to policy. The difference will be that in the former case the objective will be to bring prices down to long-run marginal cost in all cases, while in the latter the basis for action will be more *ad hoc*. Price control does, of course, improve on piecemeal anti-trust. For example, in the merger case discussed in the previous section it was a matter of trading off the welfare loss of a higher price against the gains in efficiency. With price control the trade-off disappears, since it is possible to have the gains from scale from the merger *and* bring prices down to the new cost level (assuming the absence of second-best considerations). The analogy is with pricing policy for nationalized industries in a second-best world.[57] The objection to price control is that the controllers are unlikely to know the true costs of the operations of the firms. Reported costs may be inflated by X-inefficiency or even by falsification of the books, and without the aid of expert staff the price controllers will not be able to challenge the cost estimates of firms. As a result, there is no incentive to keep costs down.

An alternative to price fixing is the determination of an acceptable profit rate on capital, leaving the firm to operate within the constraint. Superficially this is an attractive alternative as it does not require the policy maker to know the precise cost and demand conditions of each sector in which he wishes to intervene. This method of regulating potentially monopolistic utilities in the private sector has been widely adopted in the United States. It has not been formally adopted by U.K. policy makers. However Rowley[58] has shown that consideration of the rate of return on capital has formed an important part of Monopolies Commission investigations. If this became widely known, firms liable to investigation might begin to work to such a profit figure in self-defence. We are therefore very interested to know how a firm might react to a profit constraint of this kind.

Let us suppose that the firm in question is a monopolist with monopoly price and output. The profit constraint is intended to bring profits down to a competitive level, as incorporated in the true long-run average cost curve. As in the case of price control the hope would be that gradual reduction in profit rate permitted would induce expansion of output to the competitive level.

However this is not at all certain. One response of the firm could be to increase their fixed costs by unnecessary expenditures. This would absorb the excess profits and leave the situation as before. In a managerial firm this is not at all unlikely.[59] A second possibility is that the firm might cheat by padding the capital base of the firm

---

[57] Turvey, op. cit.   [58] Rowley, op. cit. (1969).
[59] M. Z. Kafoglis, 'Output of the Restrained Firm', *A.E.R.* 59 (1969), 583–9.

with capital that is in reality obsolete. However a profit controller could presumably keep a check on activities like this, and prevent them. Third, the firm may cross-subsidize between different lines of business, offsetting losses in one area with monopoly gains on other sales. Ideally the 'fair rate of return' should apply to each market in which the firm operates. The fourth possibility was discovered by Averch and Johnson,[60] and has attracted a series of subsequent articles.[61] This is the theoretical point that control of profit rates may lead to inefficient use of factors even where the firm is operating on the production frontier. The debate has been summarized in the form of textbook cost curve analysis by Borts and Stein.[62] The basic point of their analysis is that if a firm is allowed a return of S on each unit of capital, it maximizes its profits by having as large a capital stock K as is compatible with earning the permitted return S. The effect of this is illustrated in Figure 16.10. The monopoly output is q_0. With optimal capital stock K_0, and cost of capital i, the average costs of the firm are $AC(K_0, i)$. The capital stock is optimal in the sense that marginal revenue is equal to marginal cost in the long run (LMC). No expansion or contraction of the enterprise could increase profits. Now a profit rate constraint of S is imposed. So average 'cost', including the allowable return on capital, is $AC(K_0, S)$. But the firm is then making excess profits. It must expand its scale of operations, by adding to capital until the increase in output produces exactly the permitted return on capital at the market clearing price. Such a point is at output q_1 where $AC(K_1, S)$ is tangential to the demand curve. This is a profit maximizing position, since $MC = MR$ subject to the constraint that the over-all return on capital is no more than S.

From this new position for the firm we may draw certain conclusions. The first arises from the fact that at q_1 short-run marginal cost is less than long-run marginal cost. So short-run average cost at that point must be more than long-run average cost, and the optimal

[60] H. Averch, L. Johnson, 'Behaviour of the Firm under Regulatory Constraint', *A.E.R.* 52 (1962), 1052–69.

[61] E. E. Zajac, 'A Geometric Treatment of Averch-Johnson's Regulated Firm Model', *A.E.R.* 60 (1970), 117–25; W. J. Baumol, A. Klevorick, 'Input Choices and Rate of Return Regulations: An Overview of the Discussion', *Bell Journal*, 1 (Autumn 1970), 162–90; E. E. Bailey, J. C. Malone, 'Resource Allocation and the Regulated Firm', *Bell Journal*, 1 (Spring 1970), 129–42; A. B. Atkinson, L. Waverman, 'Resource Allocation and the Regulated Firm: Comment', *Bell Journal*, 4 (Spring 1973), 283–7. See also the reply by E. E. Bailey, 288–92. E. Sheshinki, 'Welfare Aspects of a Regulatory Constraint: A Note', *A.E.R.* 51 (1961), 175–8; J. Callen, G. F. Mathewson, H. Mohring, 'The Benefits and Costs of Rate of Return Regulations', *A.E.R.* 66 (1976), 290–7.

[62] J. L. Stein, G. H. Borts, 'Behaviour of the Firm under Regulatory Constraint', *A.E.R.* 62 (1972), 964–70.

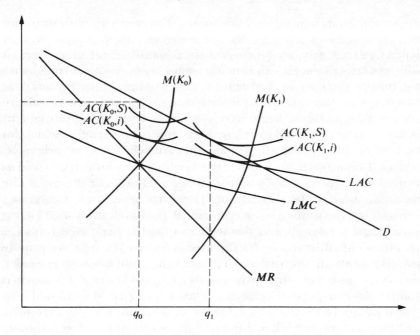

Fig. 16.10

factor proportions for that output (given by the point on the long-run average cost curve) are not being used. Second, since long-run marginal cost is greater than short-run marginal cost it must follow that

$$\frac{i}{MPK} > \frac{W}{MPL}$$

i.e. that the ratio of cost of capital to the marginal product of capital (long-run marginal cost) exceeds the ratio of the wage (W) to the marginal product of labour (short-run marginal cost).

From this it follows that

$$\frac{MPL}{MPK} > \frac{W}{i}$$

which with a normal production function implies that the production technique is too capital intensive.

There has been some debate in the literature as to how serious the Averch–Johnson effect is. But there is very little empirical evidence. A rare study, by Spann,[63] tested for the effect in an investigation of factor use in electricity generating. Using a production function approach, he derived expressions for factor shares which included the 'fair rate of return' as an explanatory variable. Regression analysis led him to the conclusion that the coefficient of this variable was significantly different from zero, especially when plant data were used, indicating that the Averch–Johnson effect was present. Some work by Emery on the electricity industry as a whole in the U.S. (reported by Johnson[74]) suggests that the degree of over-capitalization may be substantial. There has been some discussion of welfare implications. In a piecemeal welfare analysis, ignoring second-best for simplicity, the welfare losses of the distortion in factor use are small compared to the gains from expanding output and reducing price. Some orders of magnitude have been computed by Sheshinki, and by Callen, Mathewson, and Mohring,[65] and suggest that the Averch–Johnson effect is relatively unimportant.

Discussion of 'fair rate of return' regulation as a general policy measure is hampered by the fact that experience of regulation is confined to a small range of natural monopolies. It is difficult to know whether the observed deficiencies of the system reflect regulation in general, or the rather specific circumstances of those industries. Several of the distortions listed by Kahn[66] refer directly to public utilities. For example, the resistance to peak load pricing, the acquisition of excess standby capacity, the resistance to inter-regional co-operation in the planning of investment, and the excessively high standards of service supplied will relate primarily to the 'service' expected by the public (and by the regulatory agencies) from utilities such as electricity supply and public transport systems. Shepherd[67] blames poor results in the regulated industries on the mediocrity of the regulatory agencies, and on the inflexible nature of the contracts between firms and the regulators. In particular the contracts grant to the firms absolute monopoly rights in designated markets, so they are protected against new entry however inefficient they may become, and however much they fail to adjust to market

[63] R. M. Spann, 'Rate of Return Regulation and Efficiency in Production', *Bell Journal*, 5 (Spring 1974), 38–51.

[64] L. L. Johnson, 'Behaviour of the Firm under Regulatory Constraints: A Reassessment', *A.E.R. Papers and Proceedings*, 63 (1973), 90–7.

[65] Callen *et al.*, op. cit.

[66] A. E. Kahn, *The Economics of Regulation*, Vol. II (New York, 1971).

[67] W. G. Shepherd, 'Entry as a Substitute for Regulation', *A.E.R. Papers and Proceedings*, 63 (1973), 98–105.

requirements. This would not matter if the regulatory agencies were highly efficient in checking abuses, but Shepherd suggests that they lack the necessary expertise. He suggests that 'entry' should be made easier, not by means of new production units, but rather changes in control via takeover. A further practical difficulty is the identification of a 'fair rate of return' in each industry, making allowance for risk, especially where innovation is involved. Presumably this should reflect shareholder evaluations of the cost of capital. Leland[68] defines a fair rate of return as that pattern of profits which is just sufficient to attract capital to its present use. Profit rates will vary according to the success of the innovation, the demand conditions in the market, and so on: a given rate is not a useful tool for regulation. Regulators instead should fix *prices* such that the market value of the firm is equal to the value of the capital employed in the firm, with no ceiling on realized rates of return.

[68] H. E. Leland, 'Regulation of Natural Monopolies and the Fair Rate of Return', *Bell Journal*, 5 (Spring 1974), 3–15.

17

PUBLIC POLICY AND THE DEVELOPMENT OF FIRMS

In contrast to the development of public policy towards market structure and monopoly there has been little coherent thinking about the policy implications of the more dynamic aspects of firm behaviour that were discussed in Part III. The tools for analysing market structure problems are simply inadequate to cope with questions about conglomerate mergers, or the optimal life of a patent, or the desirability or otherwise of an investment cartel. Obviously market structure considerations will still be important. In Part III we saw that the expenditures of the firm were strongly influenced by market structure, and that the expenditures affected market structure in the long term. But there are two further ingredients. The first is that firms' expenditures on investment, R and D, advertising, and so on are the means by which the economy allocates resources intertemporally. The second is that these expenditures involve uncertainty as to their outcomes. So we need to ask how far the pattern of expenditures accords with the requirement of social optimality in respect of allocation over time under uncertainty. Policy must then be framed so as to satisfy these requirements, in addition to the static optimality considered in the previous chapter. Some of the policy problems may not admit of solutions that satisfy both sets of requirements. If, for example, it is true that monopoly leads to misallocation of resources in the short run, but creates the best conditions for investment in R and D in the long term, then we must accept a trade-off between short-run welfare losses and long-term gains. This aspect is emphasized in what follows.

The chapter proceeds by examining the conditions for social optimality when time and uncertainty are introduced, and how a competitive capital market could meet these requirements. The actual deficiencies of the capital market in this respect are then outlined before a more detailed discussion of the policy issues raised by investment, research and development expenditures, advertising, and mergers.

1   THE DYNAMIC PARETO CONDITIONS

Superficially at least there is no problem in extending the static Pareto analysis to a dynamic economy. The trick is to date all commodities

and factor inputs by the time period in which they are to be produced or provided. So a good produced at period 1 is distinguished
from the same commodity produced in period 2. And the same for
factors. Then the same analysis of Pareto conditions holds for all
goods and factor inputs, however they may be dated. For example
the marginal relative utility of good I at time t_1 and good II at time
t_2 must be equal to the marginal rate of transformation between the
two goods in the two time periods. The marginal rate of transformation must be the same for all firms with the option of making good I
at period t_1 and good II at period t_2. And the marginal relative utility
must be the same for all consumers on the exchange side.

These abstractions can be made a little more manageable. The
relative marginal utility is simply the rate at which consumers are
willing to forgo present consumption in the expectation of greater
consumption in the next period. The usual assumption in consumption theory is that, *ceteris paribus*, consumers prefer present goods
to future goods, so that the rate of time preference is positive, i.e.
consumers require greater consumption in the next period to
compensate for the loss of a given consumption in the current
period. Denote these by y_1 and y_0, and let the marginal utility of
consumption be given by $U'(y_0)$ and $U'(y_1)$. Then the requirement is
that

$$\frac{U'(y_0)}{U'(y_1)} = -\frac{\Delta y_1}{\Delta y_0}$$

We may define the rate at which consumers are prepared to defer
consumption in return for greater future consumption as

$$q = \frac{\Delta y_1 - \Delta y_0}{\Delta y_0}$$

which is called the consumers' time preference rate. So

$$\frac{U'(y_0)}{U'(y_1)} = -(1 + q)$$

The marginal rate of transformation can be similarly interpreted.
The method by which society transforms current goods into future
goods is, of course, by the accumulation of capital goods. As for

consumption, the return can be expressed in incremental form, with q now representing the rate of return on real capital goods. This must then be equal to the consumers' time preference rate for the situation to be Pareto-optimal.

We remind ourselves that fulfilment of the marginal conditions leads to *a* Pareto optimum, i.e. a point on the welfare frontier. But there is no reason to believe that the distribution of utilities implied in such a point is optimal for society. All the previous reservations apply and there is an important new one. It is that the point reached incorporates only the preferences of current consumers. Presumably (at least at the present level of abstraction) the utility functions of persons living now should incorporate their preferences for the rest of their lives, and it is these that are taken into account in reaching the optimal exchange conditions. What are not taken into account are the preferences of consumers not yet born, who will be entering the economy within the time horizon of the current set of consumers. Somehow their interests have to be taken into account. Otherwise the current consumers may plan to use up all resources in maximizing their own lifetime consumption and leave no consumption possibilities for their descendants. One escape is to argue that current consumers have sufficient altruism to take the preferences of their children into account. However there is no way of saying whether they do so adequately: only the children can decide that.

2   ENVIRONMENTAL UNCERTAINTY

The further complication that arises particularly in the context of dynamic models is the existence of environmental uncertainties. These are states of the world about which *nobody* can have certain knowledge, for example the weather, or technological advance, which greatly affect the conditions under which resources are transformed into goods between time periods. Arrow[1] has shown that in abstract this problem can be dealt with as in the case of time. Every commodity is labelled not only with the time period in which it is produced but also the state of nature under which it is produced. Thus, to take an obvious agricultural example, we might describe a commodity as 'next year's wheat, if there is more sunshine than average in July and August'. Or in the case of a factor, 'my labour, ten years hence, if my health remains as good as it is now', is a possible factor input in a possible state of the world. Then, argues Arrow,

---

[1] K. Arrow, 'The Role of Securities' Markets in the Optimal Allocation of Risk Bearing', *R. Econ. Studs.* 31 (1964), 91–6.

with all commodities appropriately labelled, the same marginal conditions hold, not only with respect to time periods, but also with respect to states of the world. This abstract picture is not very easy to understand intuitively, since as consumers we are not used to making choices about possible states of the world (unless we are inveterate gamblers). Meade[2] has provided an example involving two states of the world—wet weather and fine weather—and two goods, umbrellas and parasols. Thus there are four commodity-states altogether. It may help if we consider briefly the meaning of the marginal relative utility between a pair of these commodity-states to see what they mean. We may think of each consumer trading in pieces of paper on which are written promises to deliver the good in question under the given state of nature. Then at the margin his willingness to trade 'wet–umbrellas' for 'fine–parasols' will depend on two things: the marginal utility of goods under the given weather conditions, and the consumer's expectation that the two states of nature will occur. Suppose then that there are two consumers, one of whom attaches a high probability to wet weather and the other of whom attaches a high probability to dry weather. How can it be that their marginal relative utilities for the two commodity options are the same? The answer is that the pessimist will wish to hold more 'wet–umbrella' options, the lower marginal utility of the umbrellas themselves being offset by the high probability of the occurrence of wet weather for that consumer. The optimist will do the same for parasols. So long as the marginal rates at which they are prepared to exchange the pieces of paper are the same, no improvement in their welfare can take place.

On the production side, we may take an agricultural example, again tracing the uncertainty to the weather. We look at 'grass (for cattle) if wet', and 'wheat if dry'. Assume that a farmer has a given area of land. Then the marginal rate of transformation between the two commodities is the rate at which, decreasing the land given to grass and transferring it to wheat, the yield of 'grass–wet' decreases and the yield of 'wheat–dry' increases. This marginal rate of transformation, we should note, is a purely technical relationship. It involves no judgement on the part of the farmer about the probability of the two states occurring. For Pareto efficiency the marginal rates of transformation must be equalized on all farms where grass and wheat are competing crops. If they were not it would be possible to increase potential output in both states of the world.

The general optimum requires that the marginal relative utilities between commodity-states, which *do* reflect consumer assessments

[2] J. E. Meade, *The Theory of Indicative Planning* (Manchester, 1970).

of the probabilities of the states, should equal the technical marginal rate of transformation just described. Similar conditions should hold for factors of production and goods, and for pairs of factors. Finally we recall that satisfaction of the conditions only leads to the welfare frontier.

In the Appendix we provide a formal analysis of the Pareto conditions under environmental uncertainty. This may satisfy those who find our intuitive arguments too vague.

3   TIME AND ENVIRONMENTAL UNCERTAINTY IN THE CONTEXT OF A PRICE SYSTEM

In principle the problem of time and environmental uncertainty appears to be soluble by the creation of as many markets as there are time periods and states of nature. The time point is covered by the creation of futures markets, and the states of nature by contingency markets. The number of such markets required defies imagination and, as Radner[3] has pointed out, no economic actor would be able to carry out the necessary computations across all markets to maximize profits or utility. So we are still at a very high level of abstraction. However it is easy to see that if such markets did exist, and if everyone could do the required computations, acting as price-takers, all the Pareto conditions would be fulfilled. All consumers would maximize their utility by setting their marginal relative utilities equal to the ratio of the prices of the commodity-states. Producers maximize profits by setting their marginal rates of transformation equal to the same prices ratio. We note that in so doing they are simply equating a *technical* rate of transformation to a *given* price ratio: uncertainty does not enter the picture (except that producers may, in an imperfect world, be ignorant of the full set of production possibilities). Since the price ratios are common to all producers and consumers, all the marginal conditions must be fulfilled. (For a formal demonstration of these, see the Appendix.) A precisely analogous argument holds for commodities distinguished by time periods (dates) rather than states of the world. Again we remind ourselves of the arguments of the previous chapter that this can only be regarded as *the* optimum for society if we make the 'capitalist assumption' that the ownership of factors is of itself just, together with the rewards that accrue when equilibrium is established in every market. If we want to take the distribution of welfare into account then satisfaction of the Pareto conditions is not sufficient.

[3] R. Radner, 'Competitive Equilibrium under Uncertainty', *Econometrica* 36 (1968), 31–58.

Of course, the required futures and contingency markets do not exist in the real world. But it is frequently asserted that money markets, insurance markets, and the stock market are substitutes for them, and that they provide an important service by reducing the number of separate markets that are needed. The point can be made first in the context of a two-period model without environmental uncertainty. The link between the two periods is that consumption forgone in the first period provides for the creation of capital goods which will lead to increased production in the second period. Suppose all the futures markets exist. Then firms receive in the first period payments for goods to be provided immediately and payments for second-period deliveries. The latter payments they use to acquire capital goods to enable them to meet second-period requirements. The proposed alternative is a money capital market. Individuals forgo consumption in the first period, and use their savings to buy interest-bearing bonds, which they redeem in the second period to provide cash for their second-period purchases. Firms supply bonds in the first period, use the cash to acquire capital goods, and then repay the bonds in the second period from the proceeds of sales of goods. In general, we assume that consumers have positive time preference—i.e. they value deferred goods less highly— so the interest rate in the bond market will be positive. This is their incentive to defer consumption. To make the matter absolutely clear we give an example. We consider a two-period case involving a single good: so outputs in two periods are y_0 and y_1. Further, output of y_1 depends on y_0 forgone in the first period. Suppose that markets exist in the first period for both first- and second-period production, i.e. P_0 and $\hat{P}_1$. Then the price ratio $\hat{P}_1/P_0$ indicates consumer preferences between deliveries in the two periods. Firms maximize profits by setting $\hat{P}_1/P_0 = \Delta y_0/\Delta y_1$.

The alternative is the existence of a money market with interest rate i. Let us assume that the price will be P_1 in the second period. Then firms borrow money and convert y_0 into capital to produce y_1 up to the point where the money return is equal to the interest rate, i.e.

$$\frac{P_1 \Delta y_1 - P_0 \Delta y_0}{P_0 \Delta y_0} = i$$

$$\frac{P_1}{P_0(1 + i)} = \frac{\Delta y_0}{\Delta y_1}$$

This condition is identical to that of the futures market when $P_1 = \hat{P}_1(1 + i)$. So, given the money market, the consumer lends $\hat{P}_1$ to the firms: in the second period he receives $P_1 = \hat{P}(1 + i)$ which is sufficient to buy the good in question. The firm, investing with an expectation of a second-period price of P_1, and with cost of capital i, is led to the required marginal rate of transformation.

Now precisely the same type of argument can be applied to contingency markets. Let us assume away the problem of time and focus solely on states of the world. If contingency markets exist there will be a price for a particular good for all possible states of the world. Let us consider two states, Θ and z, and assume that the contingency prices are $\hat{P}(\Theta)$ and $\hat{P}(z)$. Then consumers set their marginal relative utility equal to this price ratio, and firms their marginal rates of transformation equal to it too. The alternative system is to have a set of contingency securities (referred to in the literature as Arrow–Debreu[4] securities). These would be like insurance policies, in that they would involve premia Π_Θ and Π_z, with the promise to pay one monetary unit should Θ or z occur. Suppose further that the actual prices of the good under states Θ or z are $P(\Theta)$ and $P(z)$. Then these prices must be linked to contingency market prices by the relations,

$$\hat{P}(\Theta) = \Pi_\Theta P(\Theta) \quad \text{and} \quad \hat{P}(z) = \Pi_z P(z)$$

Then the consumer is indifferent as between contingency markets, or the use of insurance markets and then conventional markets once the state of the world is known. If we assume that the insurance contracts are sold by the relevant firms they also will be indifferent as between the two systems. The money they collect in premia $\sum_\Theta P(\Theta)\Pi(\Theta)$ will be identical to their receipts from contingency markets. Once again the advantage of this method of doing things is the reduction in the number of markets required. If there are z states of the world, and n goods, the number of contingency markets required would be $z \times n$. With contingency securities all that are required are z security markets, and then n commodity markets once the state of the world has been determined—a total of $z + n$. In the same way the existence of money capital markets precludes the necessity for futures markets in all goods, and replaces them with one money market for each time period.

Now it is argued, especially by Diamond,[5] that a stock market in a

---

[4] Arrow, op. cit., and G. Debreu, *Theory of Value* (New Haven, 1959), Ch. 7.
[5] P. A. Diamond, 'The Role of a Stock Market in a General Equilibrium Model with Technological Uncertainty', *A.E.R.* 57 (1967), 759-76.

capitalist economy does much to provide the necessary markets. In purchasing a share in a company, the consumer is acquiring the right to a portion of the profits of the company, where those profits depend on the state of the world which occurs. This can be illustrated by a very simple case. Assume that there is one security for each and every state of the world, and that these securities are sold by firms, each firm issuing a mixture of securities relevant to the states of the world affecting its own productive processes. Each security is of the form that it entitles the shareholder to a unit payment, if the specified state occurs. The price of the securities—i.e. the premia Π_Θ —are determined in a perfect market for each security. The demand for securities will depend on each individual's consumption plan under given states of nature, and the probability which he attaches to that state of nature occurring. The supply of securities by the firms can be deduced from the contingency prices implicit in the security prices. If the firm knows the prices that will prevail under particular states of the world, $P_i(\Theta)$, the security prices enable it to calculate contingency prices $\hat{P}_i(\Theta) = \Pi(\Theta)P_i(\Theta)$. These contingency prices then determine its (riskless) profit maximizing output across products and states of nature. Denote the outputs by $Q_i(\Theta)$, and assume that $P_i(\Theta)$ is also the per unit profit (no other inputs required). Then the firm will supply securities, which will pay $\sum_i P_i(\Theta)Q_i(\Theta)$ if Θ occurs. The total raised by the sale of the securities will be $\sum_i \Pi(\Theta)P_i(\Theta)Q_i(\Theta)$, which is the revenue $\sum_i \hat{P}_i(\Theta)Q_i(\Theta)$ which the firm would receive in a contingency market. When Θ does occur all firms will supply goods to the value $\sum_i P_i(\Theta) \cdot Q_i(\Theta)$ and pay this out to shareholders. Shareholders, of course, are holding precisely that number of the relevant securities to enable them to fulfil expenditure plans if Θ occurs. So they are expecting to spend $\sum_i P_i(\Theta) \cdot Q_i(\Theta)$, and do so. All markets clear. Now it may be objected

that firms do not issue different securities for each state of the world that affects them. Instead they issue shares, which may be thought of as composites of the securities which we have just described. This means that the shareholder has to hold the underlying securities in the proportions determined by the firm, given its production possibilities. However this will not invalidate the argument if there are at least as many shares as there are underlying securities/states of the world. By appropriate juggling of his shareholdings the individual can obtain any desired mix. If the problem of environmental uncertainty can be dealt with by this device, there is no difficulty in extending the argument to include intertemporal analysis. In addition to the contingency security markets described above there will have to be bond markets for intertemporal allocation of consumption and production. There is no reason why these should not be amalgamated with contingency securities in the shares that firms issue, so long as there are more shares than time periods. Indeed we usually think of a share yield as reflecting both a pure 'time' return on money, and a 'risk' premium. We may doubt whether there are sufficient shares to perform all these tasks, but at least a capitalist economy can cope. The task for public policy follows the 'idealist' pattern, set out for the problems of market structure in the previous chapter. The correction of market failure is now extended to capital markets as well. Again it is an 'all-or-nothing' solution, which ignores the problem of second-best. And it can only be regarded as best for society if the 'capitalist assumptions' are acceptable.

However we simply cannot ignore the problem of second-best. In the static analysis of the previous chapter we referred to the problems raised by taxation, which demand a second-best approach. So too the dynamic competitive model has difficulties that cannot be solved by the existence of the appropriate capital markets.

The first of these difficulties is the existence of 'moral hazard', which can be best illustrated by example.[6] Let us suppose that two relevant states of the world for a firm are the success or failure of some particular research and development project which it is undertaking. Success will imply a much cheaper production method: failure involves continuing with current production methods. Under the Pareto-efficient model sketched above the risk in this case would be covered by the firm issuing appropriate quantities of securities relevant to the two states of the world. All risk would be absorbed by the holders of the securities. But immediately that happens it is a matter of indifference to the manager of the firm whether the project fails or succeeds. The 'moral hazard' is that he will not put as much effort into the project as he might otherwise. There is no accurate way of distinguishing the slacker from the honest failure (though a succession of failures might attract attention). The conclusion is that a perfect capital market (as outlined above) is *too* perfect to be operational.

The second of these difficulties arises in the transition from a full set of contingency and futures markets to their surrogate bond and contingency security markets, or share market. It is true that bond markets and contingency-security markets can make the equivalent

[6] K. Arrow, 'Economic Welfare and the Allocation of Resources for Invention', in *The Rate and Direction of Inventive Activity*, N.B.E.R. (Princeton, 1962).

money transfers to contingency and futures markets. But one can only be sure they will make the *right* transfers, if all consumers and firms also know the *prices that would prevail* in contingency markets (or alternatively the prices that will hold at all future dates under all states of the world). This point has been emphasized for inter-temporal decisions by Leijonhufvud.[7] By purchasing bonds the consumer only expresses his intention to consume a certain value of goods at a time period in the future. He does not have to specify in which time period he proposes to consume. And he certainly does not specify which goods he will be consuming. In fact, he will not be able to do so unless he has accurate information as to future prices. Entrepreneurs, for their part, are given only one price—the rate of interest. Their investment programme can only be based on their *estimates* of the prices in various markets at different points in time. In the absence of futures markets they do not have precise information as to the required pattern of capital formation. In aggregate the uncertainty caused by lack of information may lead to a shortfall of investment, and to a wrong allocation of investment as between sectors and time periods. The same argument holds *a fortiori* for contingency markets. Again the purchase of contingency securities by consumers only indicates to the firms the aggregate level of demand if a particular state of the world occurs. But the information about the structure of demand is lacking (and consumers themselves will not be able to make these consumption decisions without knowledge of the missing prices).

These difficulties are enormously destructive of any naive faith in the efficiency of perfect capital markets in coping with the dynamic allocation of resources in an economy. If we remain at a very high level of abstraction, we might pursue the Paretian ideal by a number of policy measures. We might for example take steps to create the relevant contingency and futures markets. And we could set up a corps of highly trained 'moral hazard' inspectors to determine whether unfavourable states of the world were due to negligence or to chance. However this approach has been justly criticized by Demsetz[8] as the 'nirvana' approach to policy. He identifies three flaws in the argument. The first is the 'grass is always greener' fallacy. This is the belief that failures in the perfect markets may be remedied by creating some new governmental institution to put things right. A good example is state ownership and control of

---

[7] A. Leijonhufvud, *On Keynesian Economics and the Economics of Keynes* (New York, 1968).

[8] H. Demsetz, 'Information and Efficiency: Another Viewpoint', *J. Law Econ.* 11 (1969), 1–22.

industries with increasing returns to scale. It is easy to formulate rules by which such enterprises should operate. It is another to ensure that they will in fact do so. They become institutions with their own managerial goals and aspirations. The second flaw is that the perfect competition analysis never considers the cost of creating markets. The capital and insurance markets in any advanced country are major employers of highly skilled manpower and other resources. The absence of markets for specific risks may be due to the high costs of creating such markets. Exactly the same point must apply to non-market institutions that are proposed to solve market failure problems. Is the absorption of resources to this end justifiable? The third flaw, argues Demsetz, applies particularly to 'moral hazard'. It is the fallacy that 'people could be different', that 'moral hazard' is a regrettable feature of the real world that upsets an otherwise delightful picture. Demsetz would prefer a theory of optimal allocation that takes moral hazard explicitly into account. Thus instead of the depressing task of comparing the institutions of a second-best world with the perfect world where all the necessary information exists and moral hazard can be wished away, we can get down to a more fruitful task of examining alternative institutional arrangements for dealing with the world as it really is. This could be interpreted in two ways. Either as a plea for the restatement of Pareto conditions in a world where information is imperfect, and where risks cannot be fully insured, to form the ideal for a dynamic 'workable competition' approach. Or as a proposal for a second-best approach. We discuss these two possibilities in the next two sections.[9]

4   A CONSTRAINED PARETO OPTIMUM

The first possibility has been explored by Stiglitz.[10] He starts from the premise that the full set of Arrow–Debreu markets does not exist and could not be created. A constrained Pareto Optimum is then described as the best that could be achieved by a central planner, who lacks the information that a full set of Arrow–Debreu markets would give, i.e. he is not able to simulate the course of the economy

---

[9] The analysis of this section has been, of necessity, somewhat abstract. However, we may note that the two key problems emerging from the abstract analysis are imperfect information and uncertainty. These problems are precisely those that enter the calculations of the growing firm in a capitalist economy. They are central to capital investment, finance, merger, investment in R and D, and investment in markets. The abstract and the 'real-world' problems are identical. This is our excuse for pursuing this theme through two more sections.

[10] J. E. Stiglitz, 'On the Optimality of the Stock Market Allocation of Investment', *Q.J.E.* 86 (1972), 31–60.

over all possible states of the world. Instead we assume that the mean and variance of returns to investment in each sector can be estimated, and that consumer preferences for mean and variance are known. The production possibility frontier for society can be derived by choosing bundles of projects which maximize return for a given aggregate variance, as demonstrated by Markowitz[11] for risky assets. An important feature of this derivation is that in arriving at the frontier the contribution of an individual project to aggregate variance is determined by the covariance of returns with all other projects. Any unsystematic variance (i.e. that not correlated with returns on other projects) is diversified out in aggregate (unsystematic elements on one project are set against unsystematic deviations in the returns to other projects). Having derived the frontier, the optimal point is chosen when the trade-off between risk and return is equal to the consumers' marginal rate of substitution for them. A common marginal rate of substitution for all consumers is required by Pareto optimality.

This model goes some way towards relaxing the information requirements that are assumed. Knowledge of mean and variance of returns of different sets of investment possibilities is certainly less than knowledge of production possibilities under all conceivable states of the world. Even so we admit that this limited level of knowledge is still too optimistic to be the basis for a standard to which one might reasonably expect real world economies to conform. And once again we must enter our usual caveat that satisfaction of the Pareto conditions only takes us to the welfare frontier. The distribution of income still has to be determined.

Next we must consider whether the Pareto optimal result will be attained by consumers and firms acting independently in the context of a competitive price system. The obvious real-world analogue is the stock market. We assume that all projects are undertaken by firms which issue shares (Stiglitz[12] has shown that the financial policy of the firm is irrelevant unless there is a possibility of bankruptcy, so we ignore the possibility of bond financing or internal financing of projects). We also assume that there is a risk free asset. Our discussion in Chapter 14 showed that in equilibrium there is a unique price of risk (variance of returns). Each consumer has the same portfolio of shares in combination with different amounts of the riskless asset. And each consumer reaches his asset position by setting his marginal rate of substitution of mean return for risk equal

[11] H. Markowitz, 'Portfolio Selection', Cowles Commission Papers, New Series, 60 (1952).
[12] J. E. Stiglitz, 'On the Irrelevance of Corporate Financial Policy', *A.E.R.* 64 (1974), 851–66.

to the given market price of risk in terms of return. There is however some doubt as to whether a similar result will obtain on the productive side of the economy. The firm must evaluate production plans by considering the covariance of returns with all other projects in the economy, and investing to the point where the marginal contribution to aggregate variance is equal to the market price of risk in terms of return. The alternative criterion is that the firm should seek to maximize its market value, since the capital asset pricing model explicitly incorporates the market price of risk and the assets contribution to aggregate variance in the valuation formula. We recall (Chapter 14) that the valuation of the firm is given by

$$V_j = \frac{\bar{D}_j}{r} - \frac{\Theta}{r} \operatorname{cov}(\tilde{D}_j, \tilde{D}_m)$$

where V_j is market valuation. $\bar{D}_j$ is mean return, r is the riskless discount rate, Θ is the price of risk, and the covariance term gives the covariance of the firm's returns with returns on the market portfolio. We differentiate this expression with respect to I_j, investment in the firm, and set this equal to zero for a maximum:

$$\frac{dV_j}{dI_j} = \frac{1}{r} \cdot \frac{d\bar{D}_j}{dI_j} - \frac{\Theta}{r} \cdot \frac{d \operatorname{cov}(\tilde{D}_j, \tilde{D}_m)}{dI_j} = 0.$$

This gives the condition:

$$\frac{\partial \bar{D}_j}{\partial I_j} \Big/ \frac{\partial \operatorname{cov}}{\partial I_j} = \Theta$$

i.e. the return–risk trade-off should be set equal to the market price of risk.

However a series of articles has suggested that matters may not be so simple. One difficulty, suggested by Stiglitz,[13] and Jensen and Long,[14] is that a firm cannot assess its covariance with other returns unless the investment plans of all firms are somehow given. But if a firm explicitly takes the other firms' plans as fixed, and then maximizes its valuation, it is no longer acting as a price taker in the

[13] Stiglitz, op. cit. (1972).
[14] M. C. Jensen, J. Long, 'Corporate Investment Under Uncertainty and Pareto Optimality in Capital Markets', *Bell Journal*, 3 (1972), 151–74.

market for risk and the result is not Pareto optimal. A more subtle difficulty has been suggested by Fama.[15] As a firm increases its output, it increases its output of both systematic and non-systematic risk. The systematic (or covariance) risk will be properly priced. But the non-systematic risk will create new opportunities for aggregate risk reduction via diversification, which will not be properly taken into account. These theoretical issues are still not fully resolved.[16] However it is arguable that these technical matters are insignificant compared to two other requirements of the model. The first is the amount of information required by firms. Very few will be able to estimate the covariance of returns on a project with returns on projects taken elsewhere in the economy. This is in addition to the problem of forecasting returns on its own projects in the absence of futures markets. Second, as will be explained in the next section, the capital market has fundamental imperfections that prevent it from performing the role that the analysis requires.

5 IMPERFECTIONS OF THE CAPITAL MARKET

The capital market has already been discussed in two previous chapters. In Chapter 10 we examined the supply of new finance to the firm via the capital market. The major defect is simply that the market is imperfect for a wide range of borrowers, particularly small firms and new firms that have no previous experience. Thus a risky new venture is quite unlikely to obtain finance by selling shares. The usual policy response is the creation of new lending institutions that can provide funds for special categories of borrowers. Governments have made a particular point of supplying alternative sources of funds for R and D projects. The difficulty with such lending is the familiar one of 'moral hazard'. If the institution providing the funds takes an effective shareholding in the firm undertaking the R and D project, then funds may be less conscientiously applied than if the firm had to carry some of the risks itself.

Quite apart from these special categories of finance, most existing firms rely on retained profits to finance investments, thus avoiding the transactions costs and the disciplines of applying to the market. This would not matter if the capital market was effective in its alternative role as an asset pricing market. Efficiency in this case requires that the valuation of the asset should immediately and

---

[15] E. F. Fama, 'Perfect Competition and Optimal Production Under Conditions of Uncertainty', *Bell Journal*, 3 (1972), 509–30.

[16] J. Mossin, *Economic Efficiency of Financial Markets* (Lexington, 1977), provides a summary of the literature.

accurately reflect any changes in the mean or variance of returns to the firm, as the capital asset pricing model requires. The risk of the firm's operations would then be effectively transferred to the shareholders. The managers would have to pursue policies which were in the interests of shareholders, the discipline being either dismissal or the threat of takeover by another firm. However the analysis of Chapter 14 suggested that these rigorous conditions do not hold, even in a weak form. The market does reflect published information about the firm, but market discipline is insufficient to bring the managers into line with shareholders preferences.

The conclusion from this brief analysis is that the market bears some of the risks of enterprise but by no means all of them. The practical import of the situation can best be understood by examining the position of the manager. Assume first, for comparison, that capital markets are perfect. The manager has a particular project in mind, and he publishes information to shareholders concerning it. If he is asking for new funds they can support the project by purchasing new shares, thus taking the risks on themselves in so far as the returns are covariant with the returns of other shares. Alternatively if he proposes to use retentions, they can indicate their approval by marking up the value of the shares appropriately. If the project then *fails* to meet expectations, the manager cannot be blamed (unless he has been negligent: we assume that shareholders keep a sufficient watch on the operations of the firm to obviate the possibility of moral hazard). In this situation, the risks are shifted to the shareholders, without any loss being suffered by the manager, unless the project is so disastrous that bankruptcy occurs, and he loses his job. Next we make the alternative assumption that the manager finances the project out of retained earnings without recourse to the capital market, and without seeking the specific approval of shareholders. In this case failure can bring an accusation from the shareholders that the manager has made an incompetent choice of investments, and in principle at least the manager could be replaced, or the firm could be taken over. In practice, the discipline is weak, even for very poor managements. But the transfer of risk from the shareholders to the manager is evident. The manager has the task of selecting projects which will yield satisfactory returns to the shareholders, and to that extent he takes the responsibility. If he is at all risk averse, we will expect him to avoid risky projects since he is looking solely at the aggregate variance of his own projects, and not at their covariance with all other projects in the economy as Pareto optimality would require. There is no obvious set of policies that could mitigate this effect of real-world capital markets, since it is rational for the shareholders to act in the way described. They simply do not have the kind of perfect informtion that would enable them to assess the potential returns from a project. We therefore abandon the attempt to prescribe a competitive norm for the capital market, which could be the complement to the workable competition approach to monopoly described in the previous chapter.

Instead we use an extension of piecemeal welfare analysis to evaluate investment, advertising, R and D, and mergers in the subsequent sections of this chapter. In each case we assume that the actual level of expenditure is determined by the management of the firm, acting in their own interests. To a large extent these will coincide with the interests of shareholders. For example, both may agree that a particular advertising campaign is a profitable use of funds for a firm in given circumstances. But owners and managers are likely to diverge in their attitudes to risk for reasons fully described above. However society may take a very different view of the benefits to be derived from actions that are in the narrow interests of both the managers and the shareholders of a particular firm.

6   INVESTMENT

The two big issues have already been identified. The first is that a capital market of the kind described, however perfect its operations may be, gives only an aggregate pattern of society's willingness to defer consumption. So the pattern of investment occurring may not be optimal, for two reasons. The first is that all firms may be uncertain as to the right size of the market at some future date, so they may be conservative about investment totals. The second is that without a futures market in which all contracts may be secured now, individual firms have no idea as to what will be the size of their share in the total market. This has been advanced persuasively by Richardson[17] as a reason for believing that perfect competition in a dynamic setting will be quite imperfect. Firms may refuse to invest in a sector for fear of overinvestment, if all firms act independently.

The second issue is that the capital market can only shift uncertainty partially, because of moral hazard, and the impossibility of creating sufficient securities to cover all contingencies. We conclude that real-world firms will have to carry considerable risk themselves. The effect of risk bearing by firms is a reduction in investment in risky sectors, below that which might be regarded as socially optimal. This point may be illustrated from the mean-variance analysis discussed previously. That analysis reduces the problem of uncertainty

[17] G. B. Richardson, *Information and Investment* (Oxford, 1960).

to one of risk by assuming that each firm (and shareholders) does have complete information concerning the outcomes of its investment decisions in terms of the mean, variance, and covariance of returns. We have already determined an optimal point for society under these conditions. Clearly if managers evaluate their firms by exactly the same criteria as shareholders, applying the shareholders' portfolio equilibrium price to covariance risk, the investment of firms in risky sectors should match the willingness of shareholders to trade mean return for covariance of return with their portfolio. However, if firms weight variances of returns alone, then investment in risky industries will be less than optimal. If this conclusion holds for risk, it will also hold, *a fortiori*, in the case of uncertainty, where the information problem is that much greater.

Two features of the actual operations of firms modify these results. The first is the existence of managerial objectives in the growth of firms. Figure 17.1 shows the familiar growth–valuation

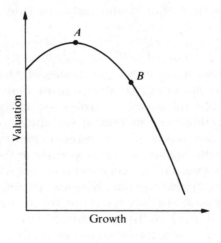

Fig. 17.1

trade-off derived from the Marris model. That analysis suggests that a stockholder utility maximizing firm will operate at *A*. The managerial firm is not subject to strong market disciplines and can therefore operate at *B*, investing more. The effect of risk on this analysis is never made explicit. If we assume that the curve represents a market valuation along the lines of a capital asset pricing model, then presumably the downward sloping part of the curve represents not only a lower mean return but also increased covariance risk (a faster-growing firm may be less stable). The manager cannot shift risks to the shareholder, so he will make his own risk evaluation of returns. But the weakness of market discipline acts to reduce the effective risk to him, since only a disaster will lose him his job. The resultant effect on investment plans may be quite small. One could argue therefore that the weakness of market discipline is good since it reduces managerial risk, and permits managerial firms to invest more.

The difficulties arising from lack of information about future market shares are also mitigated by the existence of inter-firm agreements of various kinds. Market sharing cartels were discussed in Chatper 5 where we saw that these inevitably led to agreements on investment. They have been defended by Richardson[18] on the grounds that they reduce market uncertainty and thus permit a stable expansion of industry output in line with demand. The prior requirement is that the firms in the industry should agree concerning the likely trend in industry demand. In so far as these arrangements do reduce uncertainty they are to be welcomed. But the danger is that they may become monopolistic in intent as well. Exactly the same objection applies to information agreements.

Richardson[19] has also pointed to a wide range of phenomena which effectively regulate the relations between firms, but do not go as far as a full cartel. He gives various examples. One is the establishment of trading relationships between firms that seek to stabilize flows of goods between them. These relationships are often cemented by shareholdings in each other's firms. A second is the existence of sub-contracting on a permanent basis. A third is the way in which large retail chains effectively control and co-ordinate their suppliers to the extent of detailed product specification and production scheduling. These trading relationships are an alternative to full vertical integration. That is ruled out by the basic dissimilarities in the activities of pairs of firms, which could cause management problems in a single firm. The social gains arising are similar to those listed by Williamson for vertical integration, the most important of which is the reduction of uncertainty. All these agreements between firms present a trade-off between static misallocation of resources, and possible benefits in terms of intertemporal allocation. As we saw in the last chapter, the U.S. anti-trust policy approach to agreements denies the possibility of net benefits. The U.K. Restrictive Practices Court rejected a defence of the kind advanced by Richardson in the Water-Tube Boilermakers case, but accepted it

---

[18] G. B. Richardson, 'The Theory of Restrictive Practices', *O.E.P.* N.S. 17 (1965), 432–49.

[19] G. B. Richardson, 'The Organisation of Industry', *E.J.* 82 (1972), 883–96.

in the Cement case.[20] Both industries were subject to sharp fluctuations in demand, with the possibility of price cutting in recessions, and uneven growth in capacity,

Policy on investment has concentrated on subsidies, and on provision of information.

Investment subsidies and their effects were discussed in Chapter 11. Their justification proceeds directly from the arguments of this chapter. If firms cannot shift risk entirely to shareholders, then this is an example of private cost exceeding social cost, and the textbook solution is a subsidy to bring the cost down. Hence various forms of investment grant, specifically tied to investment outlays. They have the effect of raising the mean of the returns on the firms' own contribution of money capital, and thus reducing the possibility of a negative return. But they also have the disadvantage associated with moral hazard: managers may become inefficient.

Indicative planning is an attempt to provide firms with some of the information that is lacking to them due to the absence of futures markets for commodities. We recall that the problem is that without this information firms cannot translate consumers' generalized demand for commodities at the future date into a specific pattern of investment. So the structure of investment may be wrong, and firms may not invest enough because of lack of information. The problem is however made much worse by the introduction of environmental uncertainty. Then firms need to know not only the pattern of demand over time, but also in each state of nature, *and* the consumers' evaluation of the probability of each state occurring. Now in *principle*, as Meade[21] has shown, these problems could be solved by a set of indicative plans. The method he suggests is a meeting in the Albert Hall for all the citizens. This would then have the task of reconciling all supplies and demands for goods and factors over time and over states of nature by conducting a Walrasian auction with civil servants as the auctioneers. This meeting could then set prices for all states and time periods which would guide all economic decisions up to the horizon. This is equivalent to providing a full set of Arrow–Debreu contingency commodity markets.

In practice, indicative planning is a much more lowly tool. The French case has been studied by Lutz,[22] who provides a good summary of what is practicable. A plan has a micro and macro aspect. All firms in a sector are asked to submit investment plans for

---

[20] *In re* Water-Tube Boilermakers' Agreement, LR 1 RP 285 (1959); *In re* Cement Makers Federation Agreement, LR 2 RP 241 (1961).

[21] Meade, op. cit.

[22] V. Lutz, *Central Planning for the Market Economy*, I.E.A. (London, 1969).

a number of years in advance. Total investment and output plans are then examined for intersectoral inconsistencies. Where a bottleneck is observed, the planners go back to the sector and try to persuade firms to raise their targets. The final plan is published with sectoral targets. The intention is that successful matching of growth plans in each sector will make firms more confident, and inspire them to fulfil their production plans. However we may doubt the efficacy of this operation. First, it does nothing to remove market uncertainty, since it does not go down to the level of determining market shares for individual firms. Suppose the plan shows a need for more investment in a particular sector. Then a firm may still be reluctant to increase its investment for fear of increased investment by others leading to overcapacity. Second, the plan cannot do anything to deal with the problem of uncertainty about states of nature. It is open to different firms to interpret the future differently. Then the publiation of a single figure based on the views of all firms does not in any way represent a consensus as to the future of the sector. So there is no reason for a sectoral total to be accepted by the individual firm.

The alternative type of plan is that which starts from a given national growth target which is broken down into sectoral forecasts. It then takes on the nature of a virtuous confidence trick.[23] So long as the resources are in fact available, setting high targets *which are believed* will induce more investment in all sectors, which in turn will create the necessary aggregate demand to justify higher sectoral targets. The key elements here are that the targets should be believed, and that the resources are forthcoming. But it could be effective in a situation where firms are not investing sufficiently due to uncertainty about the development of their markets. Again a substantial reduction in uncertainty will only be possible where the plan also deals with the problem of firm market shares.

This suggests that indicative planning might most usefully develop as a series of investment cartels with a number of members representing the public interest. Their task would be to prevent monopolistic restriction of output, and to provide a national information base on which the industry could make forecasts. But there could still be the problem of a recalcitrant firm that refused to accept the view of industry prospects suggested by the cartel. It might be necessary to compel it to accommodate its investment to sectoral plans. The investment cartel might wish to extend its activities to data collection and dissemination, and to the pooling of information from R and D. A particular form that these arrangements might take are 'planning agreements' between major firms in each sector and the

---

[23] S. Brittan, 'Inquest on Planning in Britain', *Planning*, 33, no. 499 (1967).

government. The rationale is that not only do these firms account for a substantial part of sectoral investment, but also for much investment in the private sector as a whole. Unless their plans can be co-ordinated, there is a danger of a shortfall in aggregate investment, and also of particular sectoral shortages.[24]

7   ADVERTISING

The normal defence of advertising is that a market economy cannot work effectively unless consumers are informed about all goods that are available and at what prices. In a stationary economy there would be a very limited need for such information. But in a growing economy, with new products and constant changes in relative prices, the need for information is very considerable. This is frequently forgotten by those who describe all advertising as waste. However, as Kaldor[25] pointed out, we may doubt whether the market mechanism will generate the correct level of information. His argument is that advertising is supplied at zero price to the consumer, when the cost to society is positive, and so too much is demanded. If a price were charged, then less information would be absorbed than is in the interests of a profit maximizing firm. Instead advertising is sold as a joint product with the goods, the price of which is therefore higher. Some consumers are unwilling 'purchasers' (in the sense that they cover the costs) of more advertising than they really want.

Telser[26] has defended advertising, arguing that Kaldor's points are misconceived. The fact of joint supply does not indicate market failure *per se*. Many products are in joint supply because it reduces costs, and that is true of information. The point is illustrated in Figure 17.2. Let DD be the social demand curve for advertising messages as information. The cost of advertising messages is constant at OA_1 when these are sold separately. This cost is made up of two elements: OA_2 is the cost of producing the information, A_2A_1 is the transactions costs involved in collecting payment from consumers

[24] The U.K. has a recent history of attempts by policy makers to improve informational efficiency at the sectoral level. The 'Little Neddies' were set up in the 1960s as committees of businessmen and trade unionists from a particular industry, with civil servants from the National Economic Development Office. Their role was to improve the available information, to identify particular problems of the sector, and to suggest remedies. Recent U.K. developments have included the extension of these committees to more narrowly defined markets or sectors, and the attempt to initiate planning agreements. These moves are described in D. L. Hodgson, 'Government Industrial Policy', *National Westminster Bank Quarterly Review* (Aug. 1977), 6–18.

[25] N. Kaldor, 'Economic Aspects of Advertising', *R. Econ. Studs.* 18 (1940–1), 1–27.

[26] L. G. Telser, 'Supply and Demand for Advertising Messages', *A.E.R. Papers and Proceedings*, 56 (1966), 457–66.

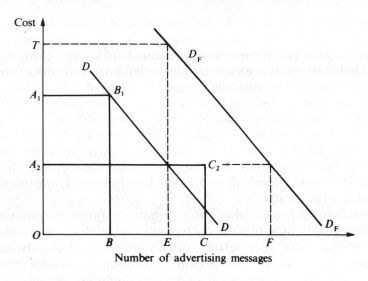

Fig. 17.2

(e.g. in selling *Which* magazine). The alternative, Telser argues, is joint supply, with a cost per message of OA_2. We construct the area OA_2C_2C so that it represents the same resource cost as separate supply OA_1B_1B. So long as the amount of information put out by the firm is less than OC then joint supply is preferable, despite the fact that EC represents messages with a social value less than their social cost.

There is a further powerful argument against Kaldor's position, which is that in practice it will be difficult, if not impossible, to create a market in information. This is the problem of appropriability. Consumers will not be willing to purchase information unless they can verify its value to them: but it is hard to see how they can do this without first having the information. But having done that, they are hardly likely to be willing to pay for it! So some other market arrangement is essential. Leaving supply of information to firms may be the only practicable method of doing this, though the public good situation is the theoretical prescription. This argument does not do justice to Kaldor in one respect. He argued that the effective demand curve for advertising under joint supply was determined by the firm, and would not necessarily coincide with the consumers' demand curve, e.g. the curve $D_F D_F$ in the diagram. Hence misallocation was more likely. There are two reasons for thinking that the firm's demand curve is to the right of DD. The first is that advertisers cannot direct information *solely* to potential customers, so some resources will be used to convey information to those who are not customers. Second, advertising is not only informative, it is also persuasive. (It is, incidentally, difficult to accept Telser's argument that customers *wish* to be persuaded.) We saw in Chapter 12 that advertising could increase the profitability of firms in two complementary ways. The first is that it may create barriers to entry, and the second is that it may enable a firm to gain a larger market share. Both of these represent monopoly gains to the firm, which are a powerful incentive. They also lead to static welfare losses, as Posner[27] has emphasized. On these grounds there is every reason to believe that the firm's demand schedule for advertising lies to the right of that of society.

A further defence of advertising is that it reduces uncertainty for the firm.[28] If it is effective in changing demand for a product, it could also be used to insulate a firm's market and prevent undue fluctuations in demand. The role of advertising is to maintain brand loyalty, and prevent random switching. It could also remove the uncertainty attached to investments, especially in new products, by ensuring a demand for the product. The ability of firms to control and plan their markets in this way has been the theme of Galbraith's work.[29] However at least one empirical study, by Telser,[30] suggests that advertising leads to a *less* stable market share situation, though changes in market shares may not be a good indicator of their ability to stabilize sales of a single product. There is a danger that in an oligopoly situation the desire to stabilize market shares will lead to a build-up of competitive advertising expenditures, without an increase in stability for the constituent firms. Disarmament will only be possible by agreement. This is a clear case where there is a trade-off between short-run and long-run welfare objectives. Reduction in risk, which encourages the firm to undertake a greater number of risky projects, must be set against the short-run welfare losses that are likely to arise from advertising. Unfortunately we cannot begin to quantify the magnitudes involved in this trade-off.

Advertising has never been made a systematic target for public policy in either the U.K. or the U.S., and the advertising firms have gone to considerable lengths to ward off attack.[31] It is virtually

[27] R. A. Posner, 'The Social Costs of Monopoly and Regulation', *J.P.E.* 88 (1975), 807–27.
[28] I. Horowitz, 'A Note on Advertising and Uncertainty', *J.I.E.* 18 (1970), 151–60.
[29] J. K. Galbraith, *The New Industrial State*, 2nd edn. (London, 1972).
[30] L. G. Telser, 'Advertising and Competition', *J.P.E.* 72 (1964), 537–62.
[31] Advertising firms in both the U.S. and the U.K. have promoted academic studies in attempts to defend their activities. See J. Backman, *Advertising and Competition* (New York, 1967), for the U.S. and Advertising Association, *The Economics of Advertising: A Study by the Economists Advisory Group* (London, 1967), for the U.K., for examples.

impossible to decide how much advertising would be socially beneficial. We may only guess that the demand for advertising by firms
exceeds socially desirable levels. If we could assess this more accurately we would be in a position to employ a tax on advertising to
arrive at the optimal level. In Figure 17.2, the firm's demand curve
for advertising is $D_F D_F$, so OF messages are supplied at average cost
OA_2. But the social demand curve is DD, giving OE as the optimal
level of messages. Imposition of a tax of $A_2 T$ on the cost of advertising would lead to optimal supply. However the unrealistic nature
of this proposal is apparent when one considers that the deviations
of private and social demand curves for advertising are likely to be
quite different across industries and even between firms in the same
industry. An alternative solution is to provide consumers with information from a public agency, coupled with severe restrictions on
private advertising. The agency would however find it difficult to
assess the socially desirable level of information in different industries, particularly in cases of promotion of innovations.

8   NEW PRODUCTS AND NEW PROCESSES

(a) The welfare economics of R and D

Arrow[32] has identified three problems in the welfare analysis of R
and D. The first is simply risk aversion on the part of firms. Risk
cannot be shifted to shareholders, partly because they cannot be persuaded to buy shares, but also because of the problem of 'moral
hazard'. If all risks were transferred to the shareholders, then all
incentives for the firm would be removed. As we have already noted,
the ability to finance R and D from retentions, and the relatively
weak discipline of the stock market mitigates the effect of risk in
reducing investment in R and D. Precisely how much the adverse
effect is offset is hard to say. The second is that much R and D produces information that is not appropriable as a good, and cannot
normally be traded in markets. Possible users of information cannot
express their demand for it until they actually possess the information to evaluate it. But once they have the information there is no
reason to pay for it. This may be partly overcome by the existence of
a patent system, which we will discuss below. But where the patent
system is less than fully effective in protecting rights in information
(which is highly likely), the inability to recoup the full reward from
creating new information by R and D is certain to reduce the allocation of funds to that purpose. The third point raised by Arrow is

[32] Arrow, op. cit. (1962).

that once information is created by R and D, it is socially optimal that it should be transferred at zero cost. It is a typical example of an indivisibility, and raises the usual market failure considerations. We note that this requirement runs directly contrary to the solution to the problem of inappropriability via a patent system. Arrow concludes that taking all these three elements of market failure into account, the total resources devoted to R and D will be less than optimal, and there will be a tendency to avoid projects which carry particular uncertainty. One might add that, in the absence of a patent system, one will expect the shortfall of investment in R and D to be greater for product innovation than for new processes. It may be easier to safeguard the latter by industrial security measures.

The analysis of Arrow has received an extension in articles by Hirshleifer[33] and Marshall.[34] Hirshleifer points out that an invention has two effects. The first is technological—it gives society a new way of using resources. It therefore has very considerable social utility, and one would wish the information to be available for all producers. This is Arrow's point. The second effect is pecuniary. A change in technology will lead to changes in relative prices in the economy. So, argues Hirshleifer, the first possessor of new information has considerable opportunities of profit. Perceiving the changes in productive methods that will be brought about by the invention, he may buy (at current prices) shares or commodities whose price is about to rise, and sell (at current prices) commodities etc. whose price will fall. Then he releases his information and collects his profits. This is an ingenious argument, and it tends to counter the argument of Arrow that returns to R and D are too low. Indeed Hirshleifer argues that it may lead to too much R and D investment in cases where a number of individuals are all hoping to speculate on their own particular information. For each may believe that the others are wrong in their estimation of their own information, and thus pursue their own R and D programme. However the argument is weakened by two further points. The first is that individuals may not have the resources to speculate effectively on their superior information. The second is that firms may not be able to collect the full speculative reward in situations where they are known as innovating firms. 'Outsiders' may watch the actions of such firms and copy them, hoping to share the speculative gains. Marshall points the parallel with 'insiders' and 'outsiders' in the stock market.

That social and private returns to innovation diverge has been

[33] J. Hirshleifer, 'The Private and Social Value of Information and the Reward to Inventive Activity', *A.E.R.* 61 (1971), 561–74.
[34] J. M. Marshall, 'Private Incentives and Public Information', *A.E.R.* 64 (1974), 373–90.

established in a study by Mansfield *et al.*[35] of a sample of 17 innovations, 13 products and 4 processes. A typical product was one that was sold to another firm as an input, thus enabling that firm to cut its price from P_1 to P_2 (see Figure 17.3). Assuming no change in the profits earned by the firm, the gains to consumers are shown by the area P_1P_2AB (and these are real gains, not just transfers of surplus

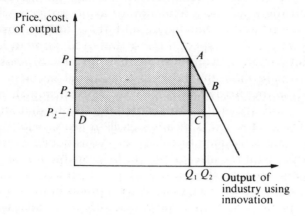

Fig. 17.3

because of the reduction in costs). However part of the price P_2 is monopoly gains to the innovator equal to $(P_2 - i)$ per unit. So there is an additional social gain equal to P_2BCD, which is not passed on to consumers, but is the private gain of the innovator. Inevitably then the private return is less than the total social return (shown by the hatched area in the diagram). What was startling about the results of Mansfield *et al.* is the size of the discrepancy. In 13 cases the private return was less than the social return, and in 11 cases it was half or less than half of the social return. A stain-remover, for example, had a social return of 116 per cent on R and D expenditures, but a private return of 4 per cent. We should note that the private returns are not adjusted for risk, and are measured before tax. Mansfield *et al.* comment that in many cases the private return was so low that with hindsight the firms would not have undertaken the R and D expenditure. We may also note their finding that the size of the discrepancy between social and private returns was correlated positively with the social returns on the project and negatively with the capital cost of producing an imitation. The first represents the incentive to imitate: major innovations are more likely to attract

[35] E. Mansfield, J. Rapoport, A. Romeo, S. Wagner, G. Beardsley, 'Social and Private Rates of Return from Industrial Innovations', *Q.J.E.* 91 (1971), 221–40.

the efforts of rival firms. The second represents the difficulties that rivals will face in so doing. The ease with which patents can be circumvented in each case was not a significant variable.

(b) Technical change

Chapter 12 examined the hypothesis that process innovation is to be associated with particular types of market structure. The Schumpeter hypothesis that 'monopoly' is good for innovation was found to be satisfied in four respects. First, a high profit level provides the funds, via retentions, for R and D activity. Second, large firms are more likely to have the large R and D departments and thus realize economies of scale in research: however they may not make such good use of the research as medium-sized firms. Third, successful process innovation in oligopoly gives the firm a more flexible and thus more profitable strategy in product markets. Fourth, oligopolitic rivalry may stimulate greater allocations to R and D within an industry than would otherwise be the case. Unfortunately then we are faced with a trade-off between welfare in the short run and long run. The conditions which lead to static market failure happen to be those that do most to stimulate long-run increases in efficiency. If we seek to make markets less 'monopolistic' we are then faced with the problem of giving adequate incentives to R and D. A partial answer to this is the patent system.

The patent system is a non-market institution with the purpose of overcoming the difficulties of creating a market in knowledge. It operates by assigning the discoverer of a new good or process a property right on that information for a limited number of years. At the end of the period the information becomes freely available to all. It thus involves a compromise between the need to create incentives for the production of new information, and the social requirement that information should be freely available to all for no more than the costs of transmitting it. There is therefore a social trade-off, which can best be analysed in the context of piecemeal welfare economics. Such an analysis has been provided by Nordhaus.[36] We follow here the geometric reinterpretation given by Scherer.[37]

We look only at a cost reducing invention, and confine our attention to small 'run of the mill' improvements. The returns to such an invention are illustrated in Figure 17.4. The industry is initially in competitive equilibrium at output X_0 with costs C_0. The invention

[36] W. D. Nordhaus, *Invention, Growth and Welfare* (Cambridge, Mass., 1969).

[37] F. M. Scherer, 'Nordhaus' Theory of Optimal Patent Life: A Geometric Reinterpretation', *A.E.R.* 62 (1972), 422–7.

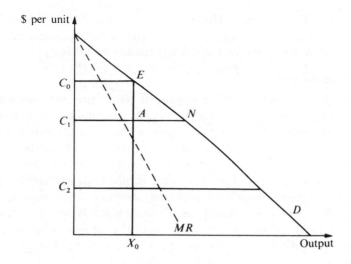

Fig. 17.4

reduces costs to C_1. The firm which holds the patent can either obtain royalties $C_0 E A C_1$ itself, or drive others out of business and take the same in monopoly rents. We define the change as a small change, since price and output are not affected. For a major cost reduction—i.e. to C_2—profit maximizing would dictate a lower price and higher output. Ignoring this possibility, and assuming a linear demand curve, we see that the returns to the patent holder are a linear function of the cost reduction. However these returns are only available over the patent life: so the present value to the firm is the annual returns appropriately discounted over the patent life. This is shown in Figure 17.5 by the rays $Q(BT)$ where the subscripts 1, 2, 3 indicate increasing patent life. The ray moves in a clockwise direction with increasing patent life—but because of the discounting procedure, extensions of the life bring decreasing increments to present value.

The expression for returns must be confronted by the relation between investment in R and D and the consequent cost reduction B which is expected. This is shown in the diagram by the function $B(RD)$. There are assumed to be at first increasing returns (in terms of cost reduction) and then later diminishing returns to expenditure on research. Given the patent life, the firm maximizes profits at the point where the marginal investment in R and D brings an equal marginal return to present value. Such a position for T_2 is at B^*,

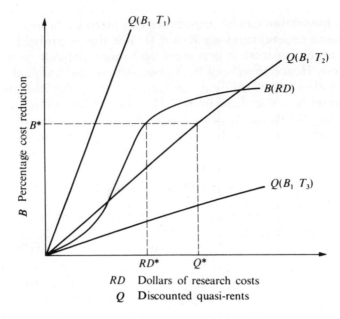

RD   Dollars of research costs
Q   Discounted quasi-rents

Fig. 17.5

where the slope of the two functions is equal (or the horizontal distance between the curves, which represents Q^*-RD^*, the expected profit, is a maximum). It is also necessary that a positive profit be earned: a patent life of T_1 would not induce this firm to invest in R and D at all. Clearly a longer patent life—e.g. T_3—would increase research expenditure somewhat, but not much if there are sharply decreasing returns.

The socially optimal patent is determined by finding that life for which social returns are highest, given the above profit maximizing behaviour by firms. The social returns to invention are C_0EAC_1 during the patent life (reduction in costs of producing the same output X_0 of the good), and C_0ENC_1 thereafter, again appropriately discounted (at a social discount rate). The social cost is the outlay on R and D. The solution depends on the elasticity of the demand function, and on the precise shape of the R and D function $B(RD)$. This analysis does not deal with the uncertainty aspect of R and D at all: it considers only the question of providing returns to invention.

Kamien and Schwartz[38] have extended the analysis to incorporate other important features of innovation. The first, as pointed out by Barzel,[39] is that the timing of innovation is important. The point at

[38] M. Kamien, N. Schwartz, 'Patent Life and R. and D. Rivalry', *A.E.R.* 64 (1974), 183–7.
[39] Y. Barzel, 'Optimal Timing of Innovations', *R. Econ. Stats.* 50 (1968), 348–55.

which an innovation can be introduced can often by brought forward by increased expenditures on R and D. But this is probably subject to diminishing returns: it gets more and more difficult to speed up the process. Hence there will be a point where the marginal benefits from an earlier innovation date are just offset by the marginal cost. This represents a social optimum. The second feature is rivalry between firms. Rivals will tend to accelerate their R and D programmes in order to win the race to the patent office. This may lead to an innovation date *before* the social optimum date. The private incentive to firms to accelerate the R and D programme is determined by the degree of exclusion provided by the patent, and by the patent life.

These complications make it extremely difficult to make any generalizations about optimal patents.

We should realize that a patent system is only a partial answer to the need to provide conditions for R and D without incurring short-run losses in welfare due to 'monopoly'. While it does provide market incentives, it does not cover the point that large R and D efforts are more efficient, nor does it ensure an adequate supply of funds for R and D, except in the sense that innovative success will breed larger profits. Finally it is evident that a patent system is probably *not* required to protect an innovating firm that has a degree of market power.

Various alternative institutional arrangements to overcome the problems of uncertainty in R and D have been experimented with. One method is the cost-plus contract, which is used particularly by governments in R and D contracts. The firm is able to shift all of the uncertainty as to the outcome to the government. Unfortunately this raises all the problems of moral hazard, though the government as a major promoter of R and D may have sufficient specialized staff to evaluate the reasons for failure. Such agreements are less common between firms for this reason. Another pattern is the sharing of R and D. This may operate in a number of ways. One is an agreement to share information between firms. But this may have an adverse effect on the incentives to do R and D. An alternative is the formation of industrial research centres, financed by firm contributions, with the results being available to all members. This may suffer from remoteness from market considerations, and from moral hazard.

(c) Product differentiation and new products

The beneficial effect on welfare resulting from a process invention which reduces the use of resources in making a good has never been in doubt. But the welfare consequences of product innovation, in particular the extension of product differentiation, has often been a subject of dispute. That some product heterogeneity is acceptable was strongly urged by Chamberlin.[40] He argued that standardization of products (to ensure perfect competition) ignored the advantages of consumers in being able to choose between a range of product qualities. Recently this proposition has been rigorously explored in the 'characteristics' framework of the 'new' demand theory (see Chapter 3). Results in this area are not fully established, so we rather tentatively follow the analysis of Lancaster.[41]

His main tool of analysis is the product differentiation curve (*PDC*) shown in Figure 17.6 for goods that can be described solely in terms of amounts of characteristics Z_1 and Z_2. (The curve would become a surface for more than two characteristics.) The curve

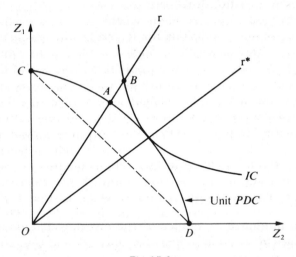

Fig. 17.6

shows the differing combinations of characteristics (Z_1, Z_2) that can be produced with a unit input of resources. The *PDC*s for different resource levels are assumed homothetic with the unit *PDC*. The preferences of one consumer in characteristics space are represented by an indifference curve with the usual shape. In the diagram, the consumer would prefer the characteristics combination represented by r^*. Now suppose that the combination r is the only one available. Then the consumer will require extra resources represented by the ratio *OB/OA* incorporated in the good with characteristics r to compensate for the non-availability of the combination r^*. This

[40] E. H. Chamberlin, *Towards a More General Theory of Value* (New York, 1957).
[41] K. Lancaster, 'Socially Optimal Product Differentiation', *A.E.R.* 65 (1975), 567–85.

compensation ratio is a measure of welfare loss.

Lancaster uses this framework to explore the conditions for socially optimal product differentiation. If all goods are produced under conditions of constant returns to scale then there is no reason why as many goods as there are consumer preferences should not be available. (However if the goods can be 'unscrambled' to their underlying characteristics for purposes of consumption, then this degree of diversity is unnecessary. Resources can be saved by producing only the single characteristics goods C and D, which can then be combined linearly in consumption along the line CD. However, the assumption that goods can be so 'unscrambled' can be challenged (see Chapter 3).) The more interesting case is that of increasing returns to scale. Intuitively it is evident that great scale economies in production could make it socially optimal to produce a single good, the greater efficiency of resource use being sufficient to compensate all consumers, according to their compensating ratios. Between these two extreme cases the general case will have a number of goods with different characteristics, each supplying consumers in a segment of the *PDC*. We can characterize the nature of the optimal solution as follows. Let the market be divided into N segments, with N goods each with characteristics r_i, and each segment divided by characteristics ratios R_i and R_{i-1}. Then the output required to bring all consumers in a segment up to a specified welfare level is given by $Q_i = Q_i(r_i, R_i, R_{i-1})$. The optimal characteristics, r_i, are given by $\partial Q_i / \partial r_i = 0$ (minimizing required output) for given R_i, R_{i-1} with solution Q_i^*. The total resource use is given by $V = \sum\limits_i F_i(Q_i^*)$ which

we wish to minimize by choice of the dividing characteristics ratios, R_i. Any given R_i is an argument for only Q_i^* and Q_{i+1}^* so minimizing resource use requires

$$\frac{\partial V}{\partial R_i} = \frac{\partial Q_{i+1}}{\partial R_i} F'_{i+1} + \frac{\partial Q_i}{\partial R_i} F'_i = 0$$

i.e.

$$-\frac{\partial Q_{i+1}}{\partial R_i} \bigg/ \frac{\partial Q_i}{\partial R_i} = \frac{F'_i}{F'_{i+1}}$$

where F'_{i+1} and F'_i represent the marginal resource costs of additional outputs of goods with characteristics r_i and r_{i+1}. The interpretation of $\partial Q_{i+1} / \partial R_i$ is the amount of extra output Q_{i+1} that will be required to compensate the marginal consumer when the dividing ratio shifts marginally. This is simply the compensating ratio for the consumer at the dividing ratio. Of course, a shift in R_i involves an *increase* in one compensating ratio, but a *decrease* in the other, since the dividing consumer is getting further away from one good, but nearer to the other. So $\partial Q_{i+1}/\partial R_i$ and $\partial Q_i/\partial R_i$ will have different signs. Now we introduce prices, and consider the consumer on the dividing ratio. He must find that the expenditures on the goods i and $i+1$, which are equivalent in satisfaction to a unit of his (unavailable) preferred good, are the same (otherwise he would no longer be the consumer on the dividing ratio). In other words, the inverse of the price ratio must be equal to the ratio of the two compensating ratios. So we have

$$\frac{P_i}{P_{i+1}} = - \frac{\partial Q_{i+1}}{\partial R_i} \bigg/ \frac{\partial Q_i}{\partial R_i} = \frac{F_i'}{F_{i+1}'}$$

i.e. the ratio of the prices must be equal to the ratio of the marginal costs.

Since there is a continuum of consumers and goods, the same relation holds for any neighbouring pairs of goods. So the same relation of price to marginal cost (if not equality) must hold for all goods.

In principle then we can determine the optimal conditions of product differentiation, and hence the optimal number of products and the necessary pricing arrangements.[42] The more difficult task is to determine how far different market structures will lead to the desired result, and here the literature is far from unanimous. The interesting case is that of returns to scale. Lancaster suggests that free entry until excess profits have been eliminated leads to more differentiation than is socially optimal.[43]

The discussion so far has concentrated solely on the issue of differentiation. This raises the question whether we need another analysis to deal with new products. But the definition of new products raises conceptual difficulties. It is hard to think of a product that contains a completely *new characteristic*. But in so far as a product falls within the characteristics space of existing products, it cannot be

[42] A more general analysis is that of H. E. Leland, 'Quality Choice and Competition', *A.E.R.* 67 (1977), 127–37.

[43] An alternative framework of analysis, not pursued here, makes specific the analogy with location theory (L. G. Telser, 'On the Regulation of Industry: A Note', *J.P.E.* 77 (1969), 937–52). The equivalent of Lancaster's compensating ratio is the cost of 'transport' (in psychic terms), which is assumed constant for all consumers. An optimal location pattern can be derived (to maximize net social benefit), and this is then compared with the results of free entry spatial competition models. Unfortunately, the conclusions of the analysis are no more generally established than those analyses which deal directly with 'characteristics' space.

qualitatively different from a differentiated product. So the previous analysis applies: if there are fewer products than are socially optimal then the introduction of a new one will be a welfare gain.

The role of the patent system in respect of product innovation is unclear. The main defect of the previous analysis has been the assumption that the technology of new characteristics combinations is freely available, and that the choice of characteristics is costless. That is not of course the case. The creation of a new differentiated product may well involve a great deal of expenditure on R and D. Yet once it has been produced and sold, a competitor could purchase an example and set about copying it, presumably at a lower cost, since he would not have to bear the expense of all the 'false starts' encountered by the innovator. Without some degree of patent protection, nobody would be prepared to undertake the risks of new product R and D. At the same time, the dangers of monopoly in the short run are all too evident; the firm may simply exploit a monopoly position. Further, the development of differentiated products with different characteristics to the first will probably be socially desirable. So too 'wide' a patent, in terms of characteristics specifications, could be bad. Again, we have a case of trade-off between short-run and long-run welfare objectives with no easy method of assessing the correct weights.

(d) Patent systems in practice

The actual working of patent systems has been subjected to thorough scrutiny by Taylor and Silberston,[44] and by Scherer.[45] The two issues have been whether the patent system has worked effectively as an incentive to R and D, and whether the monopolies which patents create should be mitigated by a compulsory system of licensing. Taylor and Silberston obtained questionnaire evidence from 44 U.K. companies in research-intensive sectors: chemicals (including pharmaceuticals), petroleum refining, electrical equipment, mechanical engineering, and synthetic fibres. Scherer's evidence came mainly from 22 large U.S. corporations (and related to the year 1956), supplemented by information obtained by a postal questionnaire from 69 other firms. Again research-intensive firms were emphasized in the sample. One line of inquiry in both studies was the extent to which R and D expenditure depended on the incentive provided by patents. In Scherer's sample most firms gave no importance to

---

[44] C. T. Taylor, Z. A. Silberston, *The Economic Impact of the Patent System* (Cambridge, 1973).

[45] F. M. Scherer, *The Economic Effect of Compulsory Patent Licensing*, New York University, Monograph Series in Finance and Economics (1977).

patents. They were more interested in innovation as a means to main-taining their competitive position. In Taylor and Silberston's study, the firms were asked what proportion of their R and D expenditure was dependent on patent protection. Out of 32 firms answering the question, 17 thought the proportion was negligible and only 6 thought that more than 20 per cent of their expenditure was so dependent. Patent royalties accounted for only 12 per cent of the royalties accruing to R and D in these companies in 1968. Interest-ingly, few of the firms had actually refused requests for patent licences in 1966–8. But more than half admitted that they would only license certain key patents in return for exceptionally valuable patents of a competitor, which suggests that patents are an important protection for at least some areas of the firm's R and D.

Wilson[46] presents a study of the determinants of licensing of patents between firms, as measured by the royalty payments that they make. His sample was 350 firms from the Fortune 1000 list, which reported data for royalty spending and R and D in 1971. He argued that firms were likely to seek licences from rivals in cases of major technical innovations, but would simply 'design around' a new product which was simply a combination of known character-istics in a different characteristics mix. He found evidence to support both these contentions in that royalty payments by firms were positively correlated with 'technological opportunity' in the sector, but negatively related to the 'complexity' of the products. Taylor and Silberston also reported that firms in pharmaceuticals and chemi-cals, sectors of high technological opportunity, adopted a policy of sharing patents with rivals, though not with prospective entrants.

The second issue concerns the effect on R and D activity of patent rules which required an innovator to license his innovation to rivals at a 'reasonable fee', fixed by arbitration if the parties could not agree. In Taylor and Silberston's study, this was only a serious issue in pharmaceuticals, where firms foresaw losses of important markets. It was the same firms who had most feared the loss of patent protec-tion. In other sectors, firms believed that other barriers would deter new entry, and that 'know-how', which cannot be protected by patent, is just as important as the technical description of the product or process. Their evidence also suggested that firms believed it was reasonably easy to 'design around' a patent for a product, or to imitate a process. Scherer[47] presents a study of R and D intensity in 679 U.S. companies in 1975. Of these, 44 had previously been

[46] R. W. Wilson, 'The Effect of Technological Environment and Product Rivalry on R. and D. Effort and Licensing of Innovations', *R. Econ. Stats.* 59 (1977), 171–8.
   [47] Scherer, op. cit. (1977), 68–75.

required by the anti-trust authorities to license one or more of their key patents; these were identified by dummy variables depending on the qualitatively assessed importance of the patent ('appreciable', 'substantial', and the number of such decrees), and the elapsed time since the decree. The argument is that the granting of such decrees may have a substantial effect on the behaviour of firms, especially soon after the decree. Allowing for inter-industry differences by means of dummy variables, Scherer found no evidence that compulsory licensing was a disincentive. Indeed the evidence suggested that high R and D/sales ratios were positively correlated with compulsory licensing in previous years. However the direction of causation is not clear. It could be that R and D intensive firms are the ones that make important discoveries, and thus attract the attention of anti-trust authorities. Scherer's other source of information, the 1956 questionnaire, suggested that firms involved in major compulsory licensing decrees had reduced their registration of new patents in subsequent years. So the explanation may be that the firms did not reduce their R and D expenditure, but relied on secrecy rather than patents to protect the results.

The theoretical case for public policy intervention in the field of R and D is based on two propositions. The first is that, without patents, markets provide insufficient return to the innovator. The *prima facie* case is supported by the evidence of Mansfield *et al.*[48] Our exploration of patents has shown that it would be singularly difficult to assess the right degree of patent protection. Moreover the empirical evidence is that firms get little help from the patent system, and rely on other barriers to protect their markets. Pharmaceuticals and chemicals are exceptions to this rule. The second proposition is that uncertainty will induce risk averse managers to do less R and D than the social optimum. Something may be achieved by loss offsets against tax liability to reduce the risk. But it seems likely that expenditures on R and D are insensitive to the cost of funds. The alternative is to allow firms to get larger, so that they can have larger R and D efforts and diversify their risks, as explained in Chapter 13. The use of retentions is also important. We return therefore to the basically Schumpeterian proposition that short-run losses in welfare due to the existence of large firms may be justified by the long-run gains due to their progressiveness.

---

[48] Mansfield *et al.*, op. cit.

9   MERGERS

In Chapter 18[49] we identified three forms of merger, horizontal, vertical, and conglomerate. We will consider these in turn.

The horizontal merger involves two sorts of issues. The first is the trade-off between scale economies and market power. This case was the example chosen by Williamson[50] to illustrate his piecemeal approach to market structure problems, discussed in section 7 of Chapter 16. The welfare gains from efficiency are offset by X-inefficiency losses and by consumer surplus losses. The second set of issues reflects other advantages of scale, especially in expenditure on R and D, discussed in the previous section.

The effect of vertical integration on costs was discussed in Chapter 2. Williamson's analysis[51] details how substitution of internal organization for market exchange can lead to a reduction in transactions costs. The essential point is that internal orgnization may be better than bargaining at co-ordinating the activities of the two firms. This arises partly from the difficulties of constructing a complete contract between two firms, due to dynamic uncertainties. One possibility is a once-for-all contract that specifies all future contingencies, by negotiating separate contracts for all states of the world. The alternative is a series of short-term contracts, so it can respond more flexibly to different states of the world. A second difficulty about contracts is the possibility of 'strategic misrepresentation'. A particular case is 'moral hazard'. Suppose the contract specifies supply of a component input under uncertain conditions as to final cost and performance. Who then bears the risk? Specification of a cost-plus arrangement may simply lead to carelessness on the part of the supplier. With vertical integration the risks are borne by the unified firm, *and* moral hazard is avoided since all operations are subject to a single managerial control. The advantages of vertical integration are therefore very relevant to the problems posed in the initial sections of this chapter—the lack of information and technological uncertainty. In so far as vertical integration reduces these difficulties, for the supplying firm at least, it will lead to a better allocation of resources in the long run. Unfortunately there will also be losses in the short run, in the sense that the supplier may refuse to provide the

---

[49] The evidence presented in Chapter 14 suggests that the efficiency gains from mergers are likely to be small, in so far as current profitability is an adequate indicator of efficiency. See p. 486.

[50] O. E. Williamson, 'Economies as an Anti-trust Defence: the Welfare Trade-offs', *A.E.R.* 58 (1968), 18–36.

[51] O. E. Williamson, 'The Vertical Integration of Production: Market Failure Considerations', *A.E.R. Papers and Proceedings*, 51 (1971), 112–23.

services or inputs to other firms once vertical integration has taken place. Unless other sources of supply can be found, the integrated firm may be able to take a monopoly position in the product market, and prevent entry by other firms.

Conglomerate mergers were discussed in Chapter 13. Our conclusion was that, although in a world of perfect capital markets such mergers do not contribute to shareholders' wealth, they do enable the *managers* of a firm to reduce the risk to themselves by diversifying the activities of the companies. The force of this argument is mitigated by the weakness of the capital market discipline. But as we have suggested previously, the managers will none the less wish to avoid disasters, especially bankruptcy. Hence the effect of a diversifying or conglomerate merger should be to encourage the firm to take more risky projects of all kinds. The objections to conglomerates relate to the misallocation that may result from cross-subsidization between sectors of the conglomerate.[52] It is unlikely that this would continue indefinitely, but there is the danger that a firm may deliberately accept losses in one market in order to create a monopoly, or maintain it against new entry. This need not involve price cutting, but could be achieved by expenditures on advertising out of proportion to the sales in that part of the firm. Once again the long-run welfare gain involves short-run losses (due to market failure), and a quantitative assessment of gains and losses is essential.

Anti-trust policy towards mergers in Britain and the United States has reflected the same dichotomy as monopoly policy, discussed in the previous chapter. In the United States, since the Celler–Kefauver Act of 1950, the amended section 7 of the Clayton Act can be interpreted as a *per se* rule against horizontal mergers between firms with substantial market shares. The two big questions are the definition of the market, and the definition of a substantial share. Scherer[53] shows that the courts have tended to define markets quite broadly, taking the wider definition in cases of doubt. They have also shown a disposition to overrule any merger that would give the combined firm a market share of 20–30 per cent. More importantly, in 1968, the U.S. Department of Justice published merger guidelines[54] setting out precisely the conditions under which they would challenge a merger. For example, where the four firm concentration ratio was

---

[52] J. F. Weston, 'The Nature and Significance of Conglomerate Firms', *St. John's Law Review*, 44 (1970), 66–80. Reprinted in B. S. Yamey (ed.), *The Economics of Industrial Structure* (Harmondsworth, 1973).

[53] F. M. Scherer, *Industrial Market Structure and Economic Performance* (Chicago, 1970), 476–82.

[54] A. D. Neale, *The Anti-trust Laws of the USA: A Study of Competition enforced by Law*, 2nd edn. (Cambridge, 1970), Appendix.

greater than 75 per cent, no firm with more than 15 per cent of the market would be permitted to merge with any firm with 1 per cent or more. For concentration ratios less than 75 per cent, the limit of 1 per cent in acquisition applied to any firm with more than 25 per cent of the market. Similar rules were promulgated for smaller firms involved in mergers. By contrast, the U.K. policy stance on mergers has been generally permissive. There is no *per se* prohibition of mergers. However, mergers can be referred to the Monopolies Commission for an inquiry into the gains and losses, if the market share of the merging firms exceeds 25 per cent or if the gross assets to be acquired exceed £5 million. Between 1965 and 1973, according to Gribbin,[55] about 800 mergers fell into this category. Yet only 20 were referred to the Commission. Seven were voluntarily abandoned, and another six were found to be contrary to the public interest. Subsequently the number of references to the Commission has increased, but the proportion attracting an adverse report has fallen. The difficulty with a piecemeal 'rule of reason' approach to mergers is that each investigation requires a major research effort by the Commission. Even then, the gains and losses can only be expressed in the most general and qualitative terms. Meeks[56] has argued that the present neutral attitude to mergers in the U.K. should be replaced by a presumption against, unless the firm can *prove* substantial efficiency gains, without substantial detriments. This would be much closer to the procedure of the Restrictive Practices Court, where the onus is on the firm to show that the agreement serves the public interest. Meeks is primarily motivated by his discovery that the profitability of firms tends to fall after merger. Hannah and Kay[57] argue that the rise in concentration due to merger cannot be shown to have many substantial social benefits, and may have serious detriments. So they too would prefer to see a stronger anti-merger policy.

10   NO CONCLUSIONS—YET

The structure–conduct–performance model has dominated the discussion of public policy in industrial economics. Policy itself has become entangled in the minutiae of market conduct. Reading the literature one quickly becomes involved in a fascinating *mélange* of laws, cases, and disputed profits, and the economics disappears from

[55] J. D. Gribbin, 'The Operation of the Mergers Panel since 1965', *Trade and Industry* (17 Jan. 1974).

[56] G. Meeks, *Disappointing Marriage: A Study of the Gains from Merger* (Cambridge, 1977), p. 13.

[57] L. Hannah, J. Kay, *Concentration in Modern Industry* (London, 1977), Ch. 8.

view. In the last chapter and this we have tried to stand back from the details and ask the fundamental question once again, which is simply this: how effective is the capitalist system at allocating the scarce resources of the economy to the ends desired by society? Every part of these two chapters has to be read in the context of the companion sections in the appropriate chapters in Parts II and III. Having done that we must evaluate as best we can. The analysis will not permit us to come down unequivocally, but ambiguously, in favour of 'competition' as a norm (unless we make competition an end in itself). The case for competition, even as a means of achieving static optimality in resource allocation, is defective. More seriously, that analysis has deflected attention from the important issues discussed in this chapter. The tendency to view R and D, advertising, investment, and mergers as *ad hoc* extensions to the static allocation problem is thoroughly misleading. The firm is the place where current resources are transformed, via investment and R and D, into future consumption for society. One is tempted to say that this is a much more important function than serving current needs. But that would be to exaggerate the case. Rather policy needs to discover the reality, in a capitalist system, of the trade-off between short term and long term. And it needs to realize the essential complementarity between the many activities of the firm—some beneficial, others harmful—in furthering its own objective. In making the assessment, the proper tool will be piecemeal welfare analysis. This is not necessarily a prescription for inaction. The analysis, coupled with our empirical knowledge, may enable us to define areas of market structure or business conduct where there is a strong presumption of detriments. Cartels are an obvious case in point, and horizontal mergers may be. Firms would then be permitted to present cases for exception before some investigative body. The most seious deficiency of our understanding is the effect of risk and uncertainty on the behaviour and decisions of the firm. We have had to place a possible benefit to the credit of advertising and mergers, simply because large size and captive markets may be joint with more beneficial activities such as R and D and investment. We are not in a position to make a judgement on these matters yet.

APPENDIX. A FORMAL ANALYSIS OF PARETO OPTIMALITY

The main complication in a formal analysis is notation. So we will set this out with some care to begin with.

Firms	$1 \ldots k \ldots n$
Consumers	$1 \ldots j \ldots m$
Goods (including factors)	$1 \ldots i \ldots l$
States of the World	$1 \ldots \Theta \ldots z$

The total output of good i in all firms given the state of the world Θ is denoted by

$$Y_i(\Theta)$$

The production of good i in firm k, given state of the world Θ, is $y_i^k(\Theta)$.

The consumption of good i by consumer j, given state of the world Θ, is $y_i^j(\Theta)$.

We now derive the conditions for production, exchange, and the general optimum.

Production

The production function of firm k is given by,

$$f_k[y_i^k(\Theta)] = 0 \quad \text{for all } i \text{ and for all } \Theta.$$

i.e. the pattern of inputs and outputs differs between states of the world.

To obtain the relevant condition we set society the objective of maximizing output of good 1 under the state of the world 1, $Y_1(1)$ (or minimizing, if it is an input), subject to fixed levels of output for other goods, $Y_i^*(\Theta)$, and subject to the production possibilities of every firm in the economy.

By the usual Lagrange multiplier technique we maximize the expression,

$$L = Y_1(1) - \sum_i \sum_\Theta \phi_{i,\Theta} \left(\sum_k y_i^k(\Theta) - Y_i^*(\Theta) \right) - \sum_k \sum_\Theta \lambda_k f_k[y_i^k(\Theta)]$$

when the first constraint excludes the pair $i = 1$, $\Theta = 1$, since it is that output that is being maximized. $\phi_{i,\Theta}$ are Lagrange multipliers for each good in each state of the world, and λ_k are Lagrange multipliers for each firm. The variables are the output of each good in each firm under each state of the world.

The first order conditions are

(1) $$\frac{\delta L}{\delta y_i^k(\Theta)} = -\phi_{i,\Theta} - \lambda_k \frac{\delta f_k}{\delta y_i^k(\Theta)} = 0 \quad \begin{array}{l} \text{for all } i, k, \text{ and } \Theta \text{ excluding} \\ \text{the pair } i = 1, \Theta = 1 \end{array}$$

(2) $$\frac{\delta L}{\delta y_i^k(1)} = 1 - \lambda_k \frac{\delta f_k}{\delta y_i^k(1)} = 0$$

Solving gives:

$$-\phi_{i,\Theta} = \frac{\delta f_k/\delta y_i^k(\Theta)}{\delta f_k/\delta y_i^k(1)}$$

So

$$\frac{\phi_{i,\Theta}}{\phi_{l,z}} = \frac{\delta f_k/\delta y_i^k(\Theta)}{\delta f_k/\delta y_l^k(z)}$$

where l, z is a different good under a different state of the world.

The left-hand side of this expression is a ratio common to all firms in the economy (since the multipliers refer only to goods and states of the world). The right-hand side can only be interpreted as the marginal rate of transformation between good $i(\Theta)$ and good $l(z)$. So we have the standard requirement that the marginal rate of transformation should be the same for all firms.

Exchange

The main point of interest is the specification of the utility function. We could simply provide a general utility function including all goods under all possible states of the world.[58] But it is helpful to make the probability aspect explicit by using the expected utility hypothesis. That is, the consumer maximizes utility by weighting the utility of various outcomes by his subjective probability of their occurrence. So the individual utility function is given by

$$V_j = \sum_i \sum_\Theta U_j(y_i^j(\Theta))h_j(\Theta)$$

where U_j is his measure of utility, and $h_j(\Theta)$ is his expectation that state of the world Θ will occur.

To obtain the conditions for an optimum, we maximize the utility of individual, 1, V_1, subject to the requirement that total consumption of goods does not exceed the fixed supplies, $Y_i^*(\Theta)$, and that all other consumers reach a given level of utility. We note that the Lagrange multipliers we use here have no relation to those in the previous section (although the same symbols are used).

$$L = \sum_i \sum_\Theta U_1(y_i^1(\Theta))h_1(\Theta) - \sum_i \sum_\Theta \phi_{i,\Theta}\left[\sum_j y_i^j(\Theta) - Y_i^*(\Theta)\right]$$

$$- \sum_{j=2}^m \lambda_j\left[\sum_i \sum_\Theta U_j(y_i^j(\Theta))h_j(\Theta) - V_j^*\right]$$

The conditions are:

---

[58] K. Arrow, 'The Role of Securities' Markets in the Optimal Allocation of Risk Bearing', *R. Econ. Studs.* 31 (1964), 91–6.

(1) $\dfrac{\delta L}{\delta y_i^1(\Theta)} = \dfrac{\delta U_1}{\delta y_i^1(\Theta)} \cdot h_1(\Theta) - \phi_{i,\Theta} = 0$

(2) $\dfrac{\delta L}{\delta y_i^j(\Theta)} = -\phi_{i,\Theta} - \lambda_j \dfrac{\delta U_j}{\delta y_i^j(\Theta)} h_j(\Theta) = 0$ for all $j \neq 1$ and all i and Θ

Writing $\dfrac{\delta U_j}{\delta y_i^j(\Theta)} \cdot h_j(\Theta) = U_i^j(\Theta)$, we derive the conditions

$$\frac{U_i^1(\Theta)}{U_l^1(z)} = \frac{U_i^j(\Theta)}{U_l^j(z)} = \frac{U_i^m(\Theta)}{U_l^m(z)}$$

where i and l are pairs of goods, j and m are pairs of consumers, and Θ and z are two states of the world. This condition is the familiar one that marginal relative utilities should be the same for all consumers. The explicit roles of utility and subjective probabilities can be seen by writing out the conditions in full.

$$\frac{\dfrac{\delta U_j}{\delta y_i^j(\Theta)} \cdot h_j(\Theta)}{\dfrac{\delta U_j}{\delta y_l^j(z)} \cdot h_j(z)} = \frac{\dfrac{\delta U_m}{\delta y_i^m(\Theta)} \cdot h_m(\Theta)}{\dfrac{\delta U_m}{\delta y_l^m(z)} \cdot h_m(z)}$$

The $\partial U/\partial y$ expressions give the marginal utility of the goods to each consumer and the h expressions are their evaluations of the probability of differing states of the world.

The General Optimum

Satisfaction of the production conditions takes society on to the production frontier, which we may describe by

$$F[Y_i(\Theta)] = 0$$

We then proceed as before to maximize the utility of one individual in society subject to the constraint of the production frontier, and the constraint of keeping all other individuals at a given utility level. The Lagrangean is:

$$L = \sum_i \sum_\Theta U_1(y_i^1(\Theta))h_1(\Theta)$$

$$-\phi F[Y_i(\Theta)] - \sum_{j=2}^{m} \lambda_j \left[\sum_i \sum_\Theta U_j(y_i^j(\Theta)) \cdot h_j(\Theta) - V_j^* \right]$$

The first order conditions are:

$$(1) \quad \frac{\delta L}{\delta y_i^1(\Theta)} = \frac{\delta u_1}{\delta y_i^1(\Theta)} \cdot h_1(\Theta) - \phi \frac{\delta F}{\delta Y_i(\Theta)} = 0$$

$$(2) \quad \frac{\delta L}{\delta y_i^j(\Theta)} = \phi \frac{\delta F}{\delta Y_i(\Theta)} - \lambda_j \frac{\delta U_j}{\delta y_i^j(\Theta)} \cdot h_j(\Theta) = 0$$

Writing F_i for $\dfrac{\delta F}{\delta Y_i(\Theta)}$, we have

$$\frac{F_i}{F_l} = \frac{U_i^j(\Theta)}{U_l^j(z)}$$

i.e. the marginal rate of transformation in production must be equal to the marginal relative utility (which is in turn common to all consumers).

Finally we recall that satisfaction of the three sets of conditions leads only to the welfare frontier.

The Price System and Pareto Optimality

We assume that there are as many 'markets' for each good as there are time periods and states of the world associated with the production and consumption of the good. All the markets are perfect, with consumers and producers acting as price takers.

Let the futures/contingency markets give prices $P_i(\Theta)$. All firms and all consumers are price takers.

The consumer maximizes his utility subject to his budget constraint. His utility is given by

$$V_j = \sum_i \sum_\Theta U_j[y_i^j(\Theta)] \cdot h_j(\Theta)$$

and his budget constraint is, recalling that y represents goods and factors

$$\sum_i \sum_\Theta y_i^j(\Theta) \cdot P_i(\Theta) = 0.$$

The relevant Lagrangean is

$$L_j = \sum_i \sum_\Theta U_j(y_i^j(\Theta) \cdot h_j(\Theta) - \lambda \sum_i \sum_\Theta y_i^j(\Theta) \cdot P_i(\Theta)$$

The conditions are of the form:

$$\frac{\delta L_j}{\delta y_i^j(\Theta)} = \frac{\delta U_j}{\delta y_i^j(\Theta)} \cdot h_j(\Theta) - \lambda P_i(\Theta) = 0$$

i.e.

$$\frac{\dfrac{\delta U_j}{\delta y_i^j(\Theta)} \cdot h_j(\Theta)}{\dfrac{\delta U_j}{\delta y_i^j(z)} \cdot h_j(z)} = \frac{P_i(\Theta)}{P_i(z)}$$

i.e. the consumer sets his marginal relative utility equal to the ratio of the two contingency prices. (Alternatively Θ and z may be thought of as different time periods.)

The firm seeks to maximize profits as usual, subject to its production function. Profits are given by,

$$\Pi_k = \sum_i P_i(\Theta) y_i^k(\Theta)$$

So the appropriate Lagrangean is,

$$L = \sum_i \sum_\Theta P_i(\Theta) y_i^k(\Theta) - \lambda f_k(y_k^i(\Theta)).$$

The first order conditions are of the form:

$$\frac{\delta L}{\delta y_i^k(\Theta)} = P_i(\Theta) - \lambda \frac{\delta f_k}{\delta y_k^i(\Theta)} = 0.$$

So we derive

$$\frac{\delta f_k / \delta y_i^k(\Theta)}{\delta f_k / \delta y_l^k(z)} = \frac{P_i(\Theta)}{P_l(z)}$$

i.e. the firm sets the marginal rate of transformation equal to the ratio of the prices. We note that this condition does not in any way involve the firm's assessment of the probability of z or Θ occurring (as it did in the relevant consumer condition). It relates solely to the physical possibilities of transformation between one state of the world and another.

The conditions for the firm and for the consumer imply that both equate their MRU and MRT to the relevant price ratio. So the condition for a general optimum $MRU = MRT$ is satisfied automatically.

AUTHOR INDEX

SUBJECT INDEX